REGNUM STUDIES IN MISSION

Christians Meeting Hindus

An Analysis and Theological Critique of the Hindu-Christian Encounter in India

REGNUM STUDIES IN MISSION

A full listing of all titles in this series appears at the close of this book

REGNUM STUDIES IN MISSION

Christians Meeting Hindus

An Analysis and Theological Critique of the Hindu-Christian Encounter in India

Bob Robinson

regnum

First published 2004 by Regnum Books International
in association with

Paternoster is an imprint of Authentic Media
9 Holdom Avenue, Bletchley, Milton Keynes, Bucks, MK1 1QR
1820 Jet Stream Drive, Colorado Springs, CO 80921, USA
OM Authentic Media, Medchal Road, Jeedimetla Village,
Secunderabad 500 055, A.P., India
www.authenticmedia.co.uk
Authentic Media is a division of IBS-STL UK, a company limited by guarantee
(registered charity no. 270162)

Regnum Books International is a Two-Thirds World publishing company for the International Fellowship of Evangelical Mission Theologians (INFEMIT), formed of the African Theological Fellowship, the Latin American Theological Fraternity and Partnership in Mission Asia.
PO Box 70, Oxford OX2 6HB, UK
PO Box 76, Akropong-Akuapem, Ghana
Jose Marmol 1734, 1602 Florida, Buenos Aires, Argentina
Post Bag No 21, Vasant Kunj, New Delhi 110057, India
c/o Glad Sound SDN, BHD, PO Box 1019, Jalan Semangat, 46970 Petaling Jaya, Malaysia
55 Fair Drive, Costa Mesa, CA 92626, USA

10 09 08 07 06 05 04 7 6 5 4 3 2 1

British Library Cataloguing in Publication Data
A catalogue record for this book is available from the British Library.

ISBN 978-1-506475-26-4

Typset by Profile, Culmdale, Rewe, Exeter and

Distributed by 1517 Media in the US and Canada

To my dearest Heather

with gratitude for thirty plus years in the dialogues of life, love, marriage, parenting and other ministries.

Contents

Preface

It is a commonplace observation to note that in a world of growing interdependence, lack of interest in or respect for the religions of others is at least insensitive and at worst harmful. Nonetheless, with rare exceptions, serious, intentional and sustained inter-faith dialogue is a relatively novel and recent enterprise. This book looks in detail at one such encounter - recent intentional Christian-Hindu dialogue in India - and asks why and how the practice of dialogue has come to displace, for some, previous attitudes of confrontation and monologue.

The displacement is well illustrated by the authoritative Catholic Encyclopedia. In 1910 the author of its article on 'Hinduism' could write that, apart from "the abortive theosophic movement... one finds no trace of Hindu influence on Western civilization. We have nothing to learn from India that makes for higher culture. On the other hand, India has much of value to learn from Christian civilization."[1] Yet, less than sixty years later, the same entry in the revised edition of the same Encyclopedia asserted that "to a Christian, Hinduism presents on the whole the most profound praeparatio Evangelica that the world has seen"[2] and some twenty years further on William Cenker regards the Hindu-Christian encounter in India as perhaps "the most vibrant example of interreligious dialogue existing today."[3] In his conclusion to an extensive survey of interreligious dialogue in India, Kuttianimattathil takes it as well established that Catholics "accept the different religious traditions as God's gift to humankind.... The sincere adherents of these religions are members of God's Kingdom."[4] The change over the course of less than a century well illustrates the shift towards Christian-Hindu dialogue and it is a movement found among Protestants as well as Catholics. The shift is, of course, by no means complete. In the nicely reworked aphorism of a Hindu observer of

1 Charles F Aiken, 'Hinduism' in *The Catholic Encyclopedia* (New York: Robert Appleton Company, 1910), volume VII, 359.

2 Bede Griffiths, 'Hinduism', in *New Catholic Encyclopedia* (New York: McGraw Hill, 1967), volume 6, 1136.

3 'Hinduism', in *The New Dictionary of Theology*, edited by Joseph A Komochak and others (Wilmington: Michael Glazier, 1987), 469.

4 Jose Kuttianimattathil, *Practice and Theology of Interreligious Dialogue: a Critical Study of the Indian Christian Attempts since Vatican II* (Bangalore: Kristu Jyoti Publications, 1995), 635.

Christianity: "Reformers have so far tried to change India; the point, however, is to understand India"[5] - and the advocates of dialogue expect that dialogue will contribute greatly towards that understanding.

The opening chapter sets the encounter in its Indian context and traces the history and development of the dialogue from the 1960s through to the 1990s and looks especially at the contributory factors that led to the advocacy and practice of Hindu-Christian dialogue in India.

Chapters 2-4 offer a comprehensive and critical analysis of the actual encounter. A typology for the definition of dialogue emerges and there is discussion of the means of dialogue (especially informal means), conditions for its fruitful practice, and its reported results. There is a comprehensive analysis of the justification of dialogue by both Christians and Hindus. A substantial critique of the dialogue follows, with attention given to the many factors that impede its progress.

Chapters 5 and 6 then draw on aspects of the Christian tradition as attention moves to a critical examination of the ways in which the dialogue has been justified in Christological categories and then outlines distinctly Indian categories that can and do enhance understanding and dialogue between the two faiths. A final chapter discusses the future of the encounter.

Scope

The book is restricted in scope in that it considers the Hindu-Christian encounter, especially the intentional meeting called dialogue, mainly during the last four decades of the twentieth century, and mainly in India itself. It is acknowledged that there are at least 10 million Hindus living in the West and some 20 million living elsewhere outside India, but the meeting of Hindus and Christians in those places - perhaps even more complex than in India itself - is not considered (although a small amount of relevant literature from Sri Lanka and Bali is noted at several places). Considerations of space have also precluded discussion of the somewhat distinctive approach to dialogue of the Orthodox Christian community in India. The study takes some account of wider global discussions of dialogue. These do have an impact upon thinking in India and are

5 Chaturvedi Badrinath, *Finding Jesus in Dharma. Christianity in India* (Delhi: ISPCK, 2000), 1.

influenced, in turn, by that context. For example, two of the first three Directors of the WCC's Sub-unit on Dialogue have been from India and Sri Lanka, and in Vatican circles the Consilium Pro Dialogo Inter Religiones has made considerable use of the presence in Rome of Indian theologians.

Acknowledgements

The work grows out of a doctoral dissertation in theology successfully defended at the University of London in 1992 with Professor Geoffrey Parrinder as appointed Advisor. The research and consultation undergirding both the thesis and the book was undertaken in the 1980s and 1990s especially in India but also with help from other individuals, institutions and libraries too numerous to mention in Singapore, Australia, New Zealand, Britain, France and the USA. My indebtedness to the help of many is enormous and one reason for this is because of the point made by the New Zealand poet James K Baxter that all writing is a form of robbery - from family, children, employer and God.

Exclusive Language and Indian and American English

In quotations, changes have not been made to the regrettable use of exclusive language regarding gender and religious community, nor to the grammar and syntax found in some Indian English, nor to American spelling; neither has the disapproving or condescending "[sic]" been used to draw attention to them.

Sanskrit Diacritical Marks

The use of diacritical marks (employed in different ways in the academic community) is omitted. However, those who are familiar with them will recognise the words used and those who are not familiar will note that standard English translations are given. Sanskrit words used in quotations are left as they are found except for the omission of diacritical marks.

Abbreviations

AAS	The Addis Ababa Statement: 'The World Council of Churches and Dialogue with Men of Other Faiths and Ideologies. (An Interim Policy Statement and Guide-Lines)', in *LFEM*, 47-54. [Cited according to numbered paragraphs]
ABR	*American Benedictine Review*
ACFOR	Secretariatus Pro Non Christianis, 'The Attitude of the Church towards the Followers of Other Religions: Reflections and Orientations on Dialogue and Mission', *BSPNC*, 19 (1984), 126-41. [Cited according to sections; often referred to as 'Dialogue and Mission']
AF	*Asia Focus*
AJT	*Asia Journal of Theology*
AM	The Ajaltoun Memorandum: 'Dialogue between Men of Living Faiths - the Ajaltoun Memorandum', in *DBM*, 107-17
AP	*Aryan Path*
ATA	MAC Warren, *A Theology of Attention* (Madras and Delhi, 1971)
ATR	*Anglican Thelogical Review*
BPCD	*Bulletin Pontificium Consilium Pro Dialogo Inter Religiones*
BSIMS	*Bulletin of the Scottish Institute of Missionary Studies*
BSPNC	*Bulletin Secretariatus Pro Non Christianis*
BTF	*Bangalore Theological Forum*
CBCI	Catholic Bishops' Conference of India
CC	*Cross Currents*
CCAN	*Christian Conference of Asia News*
CD	*Current Dialogue*
CF	*Ching Feng*
CGR	*Conrad Groebel Review*
CISRS	Christian Institute for the Study of Religion in Society
CM	*Clergy Monthly*
CMS	*Clergy Monthly Supplement*
CO	*Christian Orient*
CR	*Clergy Review*
CTM	*Currents in Theology and Mission*
DA	*Dialogue and Alliance*
DBM	*Dialogue Between Men of Living Faiths*, edited by Stanley J Samartha (Geneva, 1971)

DD	*Dharma Deepika*
DkM	*Die katholischen Missionen*
DM	*Documenta Missionalia*
DR	*Downside Review*
EAPR	*East Asian Pastoral Review*
ER	*The Ecumenical Review*
ERT	*Evangelical Review of Theology*
Et	English translation
FABC	Federation of Asian Bishops' Conferences
FTF	*Face to Face: Essays on Inter-Faith Dialogue (London, 1971)*
GIRD(1)	Dialogue Commission of the Catholic Bishops' Conference of India, *Guidelines for Inter-Religious Dialogue (Revised edition)* (Varanasi, 1977) [Cited according to numbered sections]
GIRD(2)	Dialogue Commission of the Catholic Bishops' Conference of India, *Guidelines for Inter-Religious Dialogue,* second revised edition (Delhi, 1989) [Cited according to numbered sections]
GOD	*Guidelines on Dialogue with People of Living Faiths and Ideologies* (Geneva, 1979)
H-CD	*Hindu-Christian Dialogue. Perspectives and Encounters,* edited by Harold Coward (Maryknoll, NY, 1989)
HCSB	*Hindu-Christian Studies Bulletin*
HTR	*Harvard Theological Review*
IBMR	*International Bulletin of Missionary Research*
ICHR	*Indian Church History Review*
IES	*Indian Ecclesiastical Studies*
IJS	*Indian Journal of Spirituality*
IJT	*Indian Journal of Theology*
IMA	*Islam in the Modern Age*
IMC	International Missionary Council
IMR	*Indian Missiological Review*
I-RD	*Inter-Religious Dialogue,* Devanandan Memorial Volume 3, edited by Herbert Jai Singh (Bangalore, 1967)
IRM	*International Review of Mission*
ITD	Klaus Klostermaier, *Indian Theology in Dialogue* (Madras, 1986)
ITQ	*Irish Theological Quarterly*
ITS	*Indian Theological Studies*
JAAR	*Journal of the American Academy of Religion*
JAM	*Journal of Asian Mission*
JD	*Journal of Dharma*
JES	*Journal of Ecumenical Studies*
JJRS	*Japanese Journal of Religious Studies*

JMB	*The Japan Missionary Bulletin*
JSR	*Journal for the Study of Religion*
JTS	*Journal of Theological Studies*
KJ	*Kristu Jyoti*
KS	The Kandy Statement. 'Christians in Dialogue with Men of Other Faiths', *SE*, 3 (1967), 52-56
LFEM	*Living Faiths and the Ecumenical Movement*, edited by Stanley J Samartha (Geneva, 1971)
LV	*Lumen Vitae*
LW	*Living Word*
MB	*Modern Believing*
MS	*Mission Studies*
MT	*Mission Today*
NCCR	*National Christian Council Review*
NIC	*North India Churchman*
NRT	*Nouvelle Revue Théologique*
NZM	*Neue Zeitschrift für Missionswissenschaft*
OBMR	*Occasional Bulletin of Missionary Research*
OT	*Omnis Terra*
PD	*Pro Dialogo*
PE	*Pro Ecclesia*
PEW	*Philosophy East & West*
PMVB	*Pro Mundi Vita Bulletin*
PSB	*Princeton Seminary Bulletin*
RR	*Review for Religious*
RS	*Religion and Society*
RSt	*Religious Studies*
RTL	*Revue Théologique de Louvain*
SB	*SEDOS Bulletin*
SBET	*Scottish Bulletin of Evangelical Theology*
SBRS	*Scottish Journal of Religious Studies*
SdZ	*Stimmen der Zeit*
SE	*Study Encounter*
SIC	*South India Churchman*
SJT	*Scottish Journal of Theology*
SM	*Studia Missionalia*
SR/SR	*Studies in Religion/Sciences Religieuses*
SWC	*Studies in World Christianity*
TAN	*Teaching All Nations*
TM	*Third Millennium*
TS	*Theological Studies*
TT	*Theology Today*
TUCH(1)	Raimundo Panikkar, *The Unknown Christ of Hinduism* (London, 1964)

TUCH(2)	Raimundo Panikkar, *The Unknown Christ of Hinduism. Towards an Ecumenical Christophany* (London, 1981)
TZ	*Theologische Zeitschrift*
USQR	*Union Seminary Quarterly Review*
VJTR	*Vidyajyoti Journal of Theological Reflection*
WCC	World Council of Churches
WFE	*World Faiths Encounter*
WTJ	*Wesleyan Theological Journal*
WW	*Word and Worship*
ZAM	Zurich Aide-Mémoire. 'Christians in Dialogue with Men of Other Faiths', *IRM*, 59 (1970), 382-91 [Cited according to numbered paragraphs]
ZM	*Zeitschrift für Mission*
ZMR	*Zeitschrift für Missionswissenschaft und Religionswissenschaft*

CHAPTER ONE

The Path to Dialogue in India*

A. The Historical Context

The history of the Christian-Hindu encounter has yet to be written,[1] but an account of some of its features will facilitate an understanding of the currents out of which recent interest in dialogue has flowed.

A church of the Syrian tradition has existed in South India from at least the third century.[2] In the socio-cultural realm it assimilated or, more likely, never abandoned a number of customs often designated 'Hindu'. In terms of church architecture and liturgy a certain degree of Hindu influence is apparent although this did not extend to the use of distinctly Indian terminology in its theology – hence Menon's description of a church that was "Hindu in culture,

---

* The focus of this chapter is historical and descriptive; the Table of Contents indicates those many topics relevant to an analysis of the Hindu-Christian encounter to which discussion will return in the chapters that follow.

1 One lengthy and widely read account from a strongly expressed Hindu viewpoint – and very critical of what it sees as the excessively accommodating attitudes of the Ramakrishna Mission and Gandhi towards Christianity – is Sita Ram Goel, *History of Hindu-Christian Encounters AD 304 to 1996*, second edition (New Delhi: Voice of India, 1996). However, Goel's ability to write objectively is called into question when his own reading of Christian origins concludes that: "the gospels are now regarded as the First Nazi Manifesto by knowledgeable historians, sociologists, and psychologists, and Christianity itself as a Big Lie" (438f).

2 On the history of the ancient Orthodox Syrian Church see Leslie Brown, *The Indian Christians of St Thomas*, second edition (Cambridge: Cambridge University Press, 1982); SN Rao, 'Encounter of Hindus with the Ancient Thomas Christians in Kerala,' *JD*, 19 (1994), 138-59. See also the comments in the relevant sections of Stephen C Neill, *A History of Christianity in India: The Beginnings to AD 1707* (London, 1984); A Mathias Mundadan, *History of Christianity in India. Volume 1: From the Beginning up to the Middle of the Sixteenth Century (1542)* (Bangalore, 1984) and Samuel H Moffett, *A History of Christianity in Asia. Volume I: Beginnings to 1500* (New York, NY: Harper Collins, 1992.

Christian in religion, and oriental in worship."[3] Nor did the arrival of Catholic missionaries in the 16th century and Protestant in the 18th century contribute much to the Hindu-Christian encounter upon which the proponents of dialogue might build. Even the most sympathetic of the European missionary appraisers of Hinduism – for example, Roberto Nobili (1577-1656)[4] and Bartolomaeus

---

3 KP Kesava Menon in his foreword to *Christianity in India,* edited by AC Perumalil and ER Hambye (Alleppey: Prakam, 1972), 7. MM Thomas concludes that it was a church that "acquiesced in a plurality which meant the co-existence of several religious communities professing and practising their religions in spiritual isolation from each other" ('A Christ-centered Approach to Other Religions in the Indian Pluralistic Context' in *Christian Uniqueness Reconsidered. The Myth of a Pluralistic Theology of Religions,* edited by Gavin D'Costa (Maryknoll, NY: Orbis Books, 1990), 51. According to Anand Amaladass, it was a church that tolerated belief in fatalism, transmigration of souls and witchcraft ('Dialogue between Hindus and the St Thomas Christians,' in *H-CD,* 16); he regards it as "striking" that there was no dialogue between the traditions (23). But it must also be noted that there is no documentary evidence for these conclusions; they are inferred from custom and traditions. See also Placidus, 'Hindu in Culture, Christian in Religion, Oriental in Worship', *Östkirkliche Studien,* 5 (1960), 89-104; SN Rao, 'Encounter of Hindus with the Ancient Thomas Christians in Kerala', *JD,* 19 (1994), 138-59; A Mathias Mundadan, 'Cultural Communication Encounter of the St Thomas Christians with the Hindus in Kerala,' *JD,* 24 (1999), 244-54.

4 Of many studies, the most relevant for our purposes are: Vincent Cronin, *A Pearl to India: The Life of Roberto de Nobili* (London: Rupert Hart-Davis, 1959); S Rajamanickam, 'Roberto de Nobili and Adaptation,' *ICHR,* 1 (1967), 83-91; Andre Rocaries, *Robert de Nobili SJ ou le Sannyasi Chrétien* (Toulouse, France: Editions Priére & Vie, 1967); S Rajamanickam, *The First Oriental Scholar* (Madras: Diocesan Press, 1972); Edward R Hambye, 'Robert De Nobili and Hinduism,' in *God's Word among Men: Papers in Honour of Fr Joseph Putz SJ,* edited by George Gispert-Sauch (Delhi: Vidajyoti Institute of Religious Studies, 1973), 325-333; D Jeyaraj, 'Contribution of the Catholic Church in Tamilnadu in the 17th -19th Centuries to an Understanding of Christ,' *IJT,* 23 (1974), 181-90; Frank De Graeve, 'Roberto de Nobili: a Bold Attempt at Inculturation?,' in *Religion in the Pacific Era,* edited by Frank K Flinn and Tyler Hendricks, (New York, NY: Paragon House Publishers, 1985), 31-42; Soosai Arokiasamy, *Dharma, Hindu and Christian according to Roberto de Nobili: Analysis of its Meaning and its Use in Hinduism and Christianity,* Documenta *Missionalia,* 19 (Rome: Gregorian University Press, 1986); S Rajamanickam, 'Robert de Nobili: Christianity in the Indian Version,' *Jeevadhara,* 17 (1987), 304-21; Francis X Clooney, 'Christ as the Divine Guru in the Theology of Roberto de Nobili,' in *One Faith, Many Cultures: Inculturation, Indigenization, and*

Ziegenbalg (1682-1719)[5] – were convinced, both before and after their encounter, of the doctrinal and moral superiority of Christianity.

B. Some Hindu Reactions

1. Classical Orthodoxy

What are not so clear, however, are Hindu attitudes to religious and other pluralism in the same classical era.[6] KS Murty draws attention to the near unanimous acceptance in classical Hinduism of the view taken by the *Mimamsa* (the authoritative text on the exegesis of the Vedas) that, because of the eternal nature of the Vedas, all other scrip-

---

Contextualization, The Boston Theological Institute Annual Volume 2, edited by Ruy O Costa (Maryknoll, NY: Orbis Books, 1988), 25-40; Francis X Clooney, 'Roberto de Nobili, Adaptation and the Reasonable Interpretation of Religion,' *Missiology*, 18 (1990), 25-36; Richard V DeSmet, 'R de Nobili as Forerunner of Hindu-Christian Dialogue,' *HCSB*, 4 (1991), 1-9 [reply, Francis X Clooney, 21-22]; Sita Ram Goel, *Catholic Ashramas: Sannyasins or Swindlers?* (New Delhi: Voice of India, 1994), 14-21; Utz Podzeit, 'Begegnung im "sich-öffnend-dasein-für": Die Sammlung De Nobili als Ort des dialogischen Gesprächs,' in *Hermeneutics of Encounter: Essays in Honour of Gerhard Oberhammer on the Occasion of His 65th Birthday*, Publications of the De Nobili Research Library 20, edited by Francis X D'Sa and Roque Mesquita (Vienna: Sammlung De Nobili, 1994), 291-303; Augustin Saulière, *His Star in the East*, revised and re-edited by S Rajamanickam (Madras: De Nobili Research Institute, 1995); Thomas Anchukandam, *Robert De Nobili's Responsio (1610). A Vindication of Inculturation and Adaptation* (Bangalore: Kristu Jyoti Publications, 1996); FX Clooney, 'Robert De Nobili's Response to India and Hinduism, in Practice and Theory,' *TM*, 1 (1998), 72-80.

5 See D Hans Werner Gensichen, 'Daring in Order to Know: the Contribution of Christian Missionaries to the Understanding of Hinduism, 1550-1850,' *ICHR*, 20 (1986), 83-103, and his 'Abominable Heathenism: a Rediscovered Tract by Bartholomaeus Ziegenbalg,' *ICHR*, 1 (1967), 29-40; Brijraj Singh, 'Ziegenbalg, Hindus and Hinduism,' *ICHR*, 31 (1997), 24-60; and his *The First Protestant Missionary to India: Bartholomaeus Ziegenbalg (1683-1719)* (New Delhi: Oxford University Press, 1999).

6 The issue is complex. See, for example, KM Panikkar, *India's Contact with the World in the Pre-British Period* (Nagpur, 1964), and part II of Wilhelm Halbfass, *India and Europe. An Essay in Understanding* (Albany, NY, 1988), especially chapter 11, 'Traditional Indian Xenology.' Discussion will return later to the claim that there was, in fact, a missionary dimension in classical Hinduism; see below, chapter 4.C.1.

tures are unacceptable to orthodox opinion.[7] To this were added the social prohibitions of the *Dharmasastras* against any contact with foreigners (*mlecchas*). It may have been these sanctions that led to premodern Hindu authors declining to discuss non-Indian religions.[8] Or there may have been some kind of caste-based lack of communication with the surrounding brahminical culture – although the reticence does seem to have been more than ethnocentrism.[9]

However, beginning in the 18th and 19th centuries, matters began to change and the resultant polarisation has had continuing consequences for the more recent encounter. On the one hand Hindu pandits wrote a number of anti-Christian treatises[10] and, in both Buddhist and Hindu folklore – in other words at the important and widespread level of oral tradition – there also emerged a number of highly negative appraisals. Young's summary is that the "otherness of Jesus ... in the adversarial myths and folktales of resistance to Christianity ... is symptomatically demonic, dangerous and disordering." And he adds: "It is an otherness that is hardly congenial to the more benign images of him that are prevalent among

---

7 His conclusion is that those who claim belief in the truthfulness of all religions as the received Hindu position claim this "only on their own authority and do not represent the orthodox Hindu tradition" (*Revelation and Reason in Advaita Vedanta* (New York, 1959), 219). Nonetheless, there are difficulties – at least from a western viewpoint – in defining the precise meaning of the traditional Hindu view(s) of 'orthodoxy.'

8 Richard Fox Young, '"Extra Vedos Nulla Salus",' *ZMR*, 66 (1982), 84. Anand Amaladass calls it "a stance of incuriosity and self- satisfaction" ('The Scope of Dialogue,' *HCSB*, 2 (1989), 3). "It has always puzzled me that no reference to Christianity seems to emerge in the enormously long Sanskrit literature of so many centuries" (George Gispert-Sauch, letter to writer, 23 March 1983).

9 It was, according to Halbfass, "a sophisticated theoretical structure of self-universalization and self-isolation. Seen from within this complex, highly differentiated structure, the mlecchas are nothing but a faint and distant phenomenon at the horizon of the indigenous tradition." (*India and Europe*, 187).

10 See, for example, the works discussed by Richard Fox Young, in his *Resistant Hinduism. Sanskrit Sources on Anti-Christian Apologetics in Early Nineteenth-Century India* (Vienna, 1981). Also useful is Hugald Grafe, 'Hindu Apologetics at the Beginning of the Protestant Mission Era in India,' *ICHR*, 6 (1972), 43-69; and there is interesting material in Richard Fox Young and Subrammanium Jebanesan, *The Bible Trembled: the Hindu-Christian Controversies of Nineteenth-Century Ceylon*, Publications of the De Nobili Research Library, 22 (Vienna: Indological Institute of the University of Vienna, 1995).

Hindus ... nowadays."[11] However, alongside these negative appraisals, a more positive aspect of the Hindu-Christian encounter is found in the reactions of others. Of these there is space to consider only a representative few and even then only to consider their immediate relevance to the continuing Hindu-Christian encounter.[12]

2. *Rammohun Roy*

Rammohun Roy (1772-1833) was a Bengali literary figure, social reformer and the founder of the Brahmo Samaj reform movement.[13]

---

11 Richard Fox Young, 'Adversarial Images of Jesus Christ in 18th- and 19th-Century Buddhist-Hindu Folklore,' *DD*, 2.2 (December 1996), 67.

12 It could be argued that Dayananda Sarasvati (1824-83) whose followers formed the Arya Samaj (perhaps more influential than the Brahmo Samaj) and Keshub Chunder Sen (1838-84) ought to be included – but the choice has been made to offer a representative view of examples of the Hindu-Christian encounter. Useful surveys are found in: DS Sarma, *Studies in the Renaissance of Hinduism in the Nineteenth and Twentieth Centuries* (Benares, 1944); MM Thomas, *The Acknowledged Christ of the Indian Renaissance*, second edition (Madras, 1976); Eric Sharpe, 'Neo-Hindu Images of Christianity' in *Neo-Hindu Views of Christianity*, edited by Arvind Sharma (Leiden: EJ Brill, 1988), 1-15; Samuel Rayan, 'Hindu Perceptions of Christ in the Nineteenth Century,' in *Concilium*, 1993/2, 13-23; Choong Chee Pang, 'Issues in the Hindu-Christian Debate during the Nineteenth Century Bengal Renaissance,' *ERT*, 10 (1995), 367-92. Neo-Hinduism and the terms 'reform' and 'renaissance' (each with notions of cultural partiality) are discussed by Paul Hacker, 'Aspects of Neo-Hinduism as Contrasted with Surviving Traditional Hinduism,' in *Kleine Schriften*, edited by Lambert Schmithausen (Franz Steiner Verlag, 1978), 580-608. Some wider background issues are also helpfully discussed in Antony Copley, *Religions in Conflict. Ideology, Cultural Contact and Conversion in Late Colonial India* (Delhi: Oxford University Press, 1997).

13 His writings have been the object of discussion; see, for example, AK Ray, *The Religious Ideas of Rammohun Roy. A Survey of His Writings on Religion Particularly in Persian, Sanskrit and Bengali* (New Delhi, 1976); Helbfass, *India and Europe*, chapter 12; JN Pankratz, 'The Response of the Brahmo Samaj,' in *Modern Indian Responses to Religious Pluralism*, edited by Harold G Coward (Albany, NY: State University of New York Press, 1987), 19-38; S Cromwell Crawford, 'Raja Ram Mohun Roy's Attitude towards Christians and Christianity,' in *Neo-Hindu Views of Christianity*, 16-65, and *Ram Mohan Roy: Social, Political and Religious Reform in 19th Century India* (New York: Paragon House, 1987); Dermot Killingley, *Rammohun Roy in Hindu and Christian Tradition. The Teape Lectures, 1990* (Newcastle upon Tyne: Grevatt and Grevatt, 1993); Bruce Carlisle Robertson, *Raja Rammohan Ray: The Father of Modern India* (New Delhi: Oxford University Press, 1995).

He raised a number of the issues subsequently considered to be important in the encounter.

Firstly, he is significant as an example of a not uncommon Hindu reaction to Christianity: the acceptance of certain moral elements but the rejection of much of its doctrinal content. The attempt to reduce Christianity to its supposed moral essence and then to compare this (in Rammohun's case, favourably) with a somewhat reduced Hinduism drew criticism from both orthodox Hindus and most of the missionary community as well. Rammohun was, in fact, raising several complex hermeneutical questions about both faiths. These are seen, for example, in his preference for the synoptic Gospels over the rest of the Christian scriptures, his preference for the moral content of those Gospels (at the expense of the historical, miraculous, eschatological and doctrinal elements)[14] and his preference for the Vedas and Upanisads among the Hindu scriptures.

Secondly, Rammohun Roy may be viewed as representative of the Hindu renaissance which may itself be seen, in part, as one result of the Hindu-Christian encounter of the 18th and 19th centuries.[15] He is representative, as Margaret Chatterjee points out, in that he shared two key beliefs of the renaissance: "a conviction that a transcendent mystery lay behind all religious traditions, and that religious praxis ... must serve the betterment of the everyday life of humankind."[16]

Thirdly, he may well be an example of conscious multiple religious allegiance. Whether this was the result of the intentional cultivation of various *personae* in dealing with a number of differing constituencies or whether, as Killingley asserts, the careful reading of his works forbids a designation of him "simply as a Hindu, a Christian, a Muslim or a rationalist"[17] remains uncertain – and in this regard he is not alone in the Hindu-Christian encounter.

---

14 So the question of Kaj Baagø: 'Ram Mohan Roy's Christology – an Early Attempt at Demythologization?,' *BTF*, 1.1 (January 1967), 30-42. See also: Antony Kolencherry, 'Hindu-Christian Encounter in the 19th Century India. Rammohun Roy's Interpretation of the Christian Scriptures,' *Review of Ethnology*, 7 (1981), 145-57.

15 Of many studies see, for example, on the period 1875-1914, *Neo-Hindu Views of Christianity*; and David Kopf, *The Brahmo Samaj and the Shaping of the Modern Indian Mind* (Princeton, NJ: Princeton University Press, 1979).

16 'Reflections on Religious Pluralism in the Indian Context,' *HCSB*, 7 (1994), 8.

17 *Rammohun Roy in Hindu and Christian Tradition*, 160.

3. Ramakrishna and Vivekananda

From the very extensive literature by or about two other Bengalis, Ramakrishna Paramahamsa (1836-1886) and Swami Vivekananda (1863-1902), the following points may be noted.[18] Their influence has been greatly magnified by the work of the Ramakrishna Mission (founded by Vivekananda in 1897). Unlike more militant Hindu organisations, it has consistently advocated and itself displayed a tolerant, friendly attitude towards minority religious tra-

18 See for example: Arvind Sharma, 'Hinduism and Christian Missionary Activity: A Case Study for the 19th Century. The Ramakrishna Mission,' *ICHR*, (1973), 151-58; Hal W French, 'Swami Vivekananda's Experiences and Interpretations of Christianity,' in *Neo-Hindu Views of Christianity*, 82-105; Anantanand Rambachan, 'Swami Vivekananda: a Hindu Model for Interreligious Dialogue,' in *Interreligious Dialogue: Voices from a New Frontier*, edited by M Darrol Bryant and Frank K Flinn (New York: Paragon House, 1989), 9-19; John Prentice, 'Swami Vivekananda and Universal Religion,' *SJRS*, 12 (1991), 46-55; BP Siddhashrama and K Ramachandra Nair, 'Swamy Vivekananda's Perspective of Religion: Its Implication for War and Peace', *JD*, 17 (1992), 363-75; Narasingha Prosad Sil, 'Vivekananda's Ramakrsna: An Untold Story of Mythmaking and Propaganda,' *Numen*, 40 (1993), 38-62; Anil Sooklal, 'The Neo-Vedanta Philosophy of Swami Vivekananda,' *Nidan*, 5 (1993), 33-50; Ronald W Neufeldt, 'Reflections on Swami Vivekananda's Speeches at the World Parliament of Religions, 1893,' *HCSB*, 6 (1993), 1-3; Sunrit Mullick, 'Protap Chandra Majumdar and Swami Vivekananda at the Parliament of Religions: Two Interpretations of Hinduism and Universal Religion,' in *A Museum of Faiths: Histories and Legacies of the 1893 World's Parliament of Religions*, Classics in Religious Studies 9, edited by Eric J Ziolkowski (Atlanta: Scholars Press, 1993), 219-33; Anantanand Rambachan, 'Interpreting Another Tradition: Vivekananda on Christ and Christianity,' *Anima*, 20 (1994), 127-33, and *The Limits of Scripture: Vivekananda's Reinterpretation of the Vedas* (Honolulu: University of Hawaii Press, 1994); Nair Kiran Ramachandran, 'Religious Communication of Swami Vivekananda: An Exposition of Hinduism to the World,' *JD*, 19 (1994), 175-86; CV Mathew, 'Ramakrishna Movement: its Legacy to Hindu Spirituality and India,' *DD*, 1 (1995), 33-48; Thillayvel Naidoo, 'A Century Along the Road of Truth, Non-Violence and Religious Dialogue,' *Journal for the Study of Religion*, 8 (1995), 71-84; Michael Stroeber, 'Sri Ramakrishna, Swami Vivekananda, and Hindu-Christian Dialogue,' *HCSB*, 8 (1995), 28-35; Anantanand Rambachan, 'The Spirituality of Swami Vivekananda' in *Hindu Spirituality, vol 2: Postclassical and Modern*, World Spirituality series, edited by KR Sundararajan and Bithika Mukerji (New York, NY: Crossroad, 1997), 299-318; Narasingha P Sil, *Ramakrishna Revisited. A New Biography* (Lanham, MD: University Press of America, 1998).

ditions and a sympathetic acquaintance with at least parts of the scriptures of those faiths.

A second reason for the continuing influence of the Mission has been the successful undergirding of its views and practices by the philosophy of Vedanta, especially its *advaitic* view of religion. So, (a) the world's religions are said to be but different paths to the same end: realisation of the Absolute. Ramakrishna claimed to have entered deeply into the *sadhanas* (means of spiritual attainment) of Hinduism, Islam and Christianity, and to have found them to lead to the same depth despite differences in name and practice.[19] (b) Because of the essential unity of religions, attempts to proselytise or any spirit of competition between religions are said to be wrong. (c) Despite an emphasis upon the equality of religions there is a belief that they are but imperfect expressions of that *sanatana dharma* (the eternal religion) whose clearest expression and fulfilment is found in the comprehensive and universally valid *advaita* Vedanta.[20] One result of this belief is a tendency to interpret Christianity from an *advaitic* viewpoint. Thus Vivekananda sees Christ as one of the great avatars but as essentially an *advaitin* (and a teacher of *advaita*) and attaches little importance either to the historicity of the Gospels or their emphasis upon the cross and resurrection. One Christian response within India has been that, despite Vivekananda's spirit of informed friendliness, he "regards Christianity from the lofty eminence of *advaita*"[21] and does not seem to have made serious attempts to understand the implications of what Christians understand about Christ.[22]

---

19 See the discussion by Hal W French, 'Reverence to Christ through Mystical Experience and Incarnational Identity: Sri Ramakrishna,' in *Neo-Hindu Views of Christianity*, 66-81. Wider discussion is found in Claude Stark, *God of All. Sri Ramakrishna's Approach to Religious Plurality* (Cape Cod, MA: Claude Stark Inc, nd [1974].

20 The international dimensions of the Mission's work underline the claim that Hinduism has a universal message: a not unimportant claim in India where Islam and Christianity make the same claim. See also the issues raised by Ronald W Neufeldt, 'The Response of the Ramakrishna Mission,' in *Modern Indian Responses to Religious Pluralism*, 65-84.

21 Robin HS Boyd, *An Introduction to Indian Christian Theology* (Madras, 1969), 60. A more positive Indian Christian response is: KP Aleaz, *Harmony of Religions: the Relevance of Swami Vivekananda* (Calcutta: Punthi-Pustak, 1993) and 'Ramakrisna Mission's Contribution to Christian Thought,' *WFE*, no 18 (Nov 1997), 21-32.

22 Stanley J Samartha, *The Hindu Response to the Unbound Christ*, Inter-Religious Dialogue Series, 6 (Madras, 1974), 59. See also: VC Samuel, *The Ramakrishna Movement. The World Mission of Hinduism* (Bangalore: CISRS,

4. *MK Gandhi*

Mahatma Gandhi (1869-1948) repeatedly stressed his belief in the equality of the major religions on the grounds both of their common origins in the unknowable God and also of their revelations, although imperfect, of the Truth that is God.[23] Gandhi persistently asserted this equality in the face of very considerable communal tensions. Alongside this belief in equality must be set Gandhi's distinctive application of *swadeshi* (loyalty to one's immediate environment) to religion as justification for his view that individuals should hold to the religion of their birth. One consequence was a rejection of any exclusive claims to possession of religious truth. His criticisms of proselytism in general and most missionary work in particular seem to have sprung from this dislike – though the principle also led to his acknowledging the virtue of valuing and affirming what others valued in the religious sphere.[24]

Several other features of Gandhi's thought are relevant for our discussion. (a) His consistent appeal to the common ethical values

---

1959); MM Thomas on 'Some Christian Critiques' of Vivekananda's thought in his *The Acknowledged Christ of the Indian Renaissance*, 126-48; CV Mathew, *The Saffron Mission. A Historical Analysis of Modern Hindu Missionary Ideologies and Practices* (Delhi: ISPCK, 1999), chapter IV.

23 Further material on Gandhi's views of religion includes: Margaret Chatterjee, *Gandhi's Religious Thought* (Notre Dame and London, 1983); William W Emilsen, *Violence and Atonement: The Missionary Experiences of Mohandas Gandhi, Samuel Stokes, and Verrier Elwin in India before 1935* (Frankfurt am Main: Peter Lang, 1994); Daryl M Balia, '"Flowers from the Same Garden": Gandhi's challenge to Christianity,' *Missionalia*, 23 (1995), 355-65; Thillayvel Naidoo, 'A Century Along the Road of Truth, Non-Violence and Religious Dialogue,' *JSR*, 8 (1995), 71-84; Christine Arber, 'Gandhi's Concept of God,' *SJRS*, 17 (1996), 20-46; Rudolf C Heredia, 'Tolerance and Dialogue as Responses to Pluralism and Ethnicity: The Relevance of a Gandhian Discourse,' *Social Action* (India), 47 (1997), 346-64; Judson B Trapnell, 'Indian Sources on the Possibility of a Pluralist View of Religions,' *JES*, 35 (1998), 210-34; JTF Jordens, *Gandhi's Religion: a Homespun Shawl* (New York, NY: St Martin's Press, 1998).

24 See his *Christian Missions*, edited by Bharatan Kumarappa, second edition (Ahmedabad, 1960). See also: A. Pushparajan, 'Gandhi's Views on Conversion,' *IMR*, 3 (1981), 103-18; Shiv Kumar Gupta, 'Relevance of Mahatma Gandhi's Views on Proselyism,' *JRS*, 28.1 (Spring 1997), 85-90. But the potentially stultifying effects of swadeshi have also been noted; see, for example, MM Thomas, 'Towards a Redefinition of Gandhianism,' in his *Ideological Quest within Christian Commitment: 1939-1954* (Bangalore, 1983), 236-52.

that seemed to him to be found within the diversity of religions. (b) What Margaret Chatterjee calls "an uncanny awareness of the barriers to interreligious understanding" (whether these were doctrines, rituals or other practices seen as provocative or offensive – and the need for practical solutions).[25] (c) The way in which actual work on specific projects brings together people of differing faiths. A second relevant strand is the sympathetic attention Gandhi gave to the person and teachings of Christ – especially the Sermon on the Mount, which he contrasted sharply with westernised Christianity.[26] His eventual decision to remain a (not uncritical) Hindu followed prolonged enquiry into and even struggle with Christianity – such that Minz calls him "a genuine participant in the on-going Hindu-Christian dialogue in the most comprehensive as well as the most intimate sense."[27]

Indian Christians often react critically to what they see as his selective use of their scriptures, his ambiguous attitude to the historicity of Christ and the insufficient attention he gives to the cross and resurrection. Nonetheless, most do concede that in Gandhi (if nowhere else) they recognise the moral and spiritual resources of Hinduism – which is why Klostermaier calls him "the most important and the most influential figure in actual Hindu-Christian dialogue so far"[28] and of a tolerant quest for inter-religious harmony. The encounter between Hinduism and Christianity in the person of Gandhi is a fruitful example of the meeting of the two religions that continues to inspire and challenge.[29]

---

25 'Reflections on Religious Pluralism,' 9.

26 A summary is found in the first part of *Gandhi on Christianity*, edited by Robert Ellsberg (Maryknoll, NY: Orbis, 1991) with some helpful analysis in the second part of the volume and in KL Seshagiri Rao, 'Mahatma Gandhi on Christianity,' in *Neo-Hindu Views of Christianity*, 143-55.

27 Nirmal Minz, *Mahatma Gandhi and Hindu-Christian Dialogue* (Madras, 1970), 157. In fact Minz devotes a chapter to 'Gandhi: A Case of the Internal Hindu-Christian Dialogue' (157-75).

28 'Hindu-Christian Dialogue,' in *ITD*, 248; see also Devadatta Dabholkar, 'Mahatma Gandhi: a Living Embodiment of Hindu-Christian Dialogue,' *HCSB*, 5 (1992), 23-28.

29 For example: Julius Lipner, 'Mahatma Gandhi: a Voice in the Wilderness,' *Theology*, 86 (1983), 324-28; Ignatius Jesudasan, *A Gandhian Theology of Liberation* (Maryknoll, NY: Orbis, 1984); A Pushparajan, *From Conversion to Fellowship: the Hindu-Christian Encounter in the Gandhian Perspective* (Allahabad: St Paul Publications, 1990); Caridade Drago, 'Swaraj: a Paradigm of Liberation,' *IJS*, 7 (1994), 76-104; Joseph Francis, 'Secular and Religious Pluralism in the Gandhian Perspective,' *ITS*, 31 (1994), 117-39;

5. *Sarvepalli Radhakrishnan*

Probably the foremost apologist in the twentieth century for *advaita* Vedanta in particular and for Hinduism in general has been Sarvepalli Radhakrishnan (1888-1975). He argues that Hinduism (at least in its developed form) has the characteristics of *sanatana dharma*, the eternal religion that the world needs but is provided only in part by the religions. More precisely, Radhakrishnan means Vedanta, for "the Vedanta is not a religion, but religion itself in its most universal and deepest significance"[30] – and he clearly regards Vedanta as superior to Christianity's "servitude to one historic fact."[31] In explaining the link between Hinduism and Vedanta he emphasises the non-historical nature of Hinduism whose validity derives from *anubhava* (experience) which serves both as the ground of knowledge and as the central criterion for confirming and validating religious truth. This experience is "of a self-certifying character. ... It carries its own credentials."[32]

One theme of considerable importance to Radhakrishnan is the apparent unity of all religions that he uses as the basis of a discussion of 'The Meeting of Religions.'[33] The actual meeting place he has in mind is the common experience of the Absolute that he believes to be the basis of all the religions. This experience in its purest form constitutes the universal religion behind all religions, the *sanatana dharma*.[34]

Radhakrishnan accepts Christ as a divine incarnation or, more precisely, sees Christ as an *avatara* both in the sense of a descent of God and also as an example of the human realisation of divinity.[35]

Subhash Anand, 'Gandhian Satyagraha: a Theological Model for India,' *VJTR*, 59 (1995), 561-80; Balia, '"Flowers from the Same Garden": Gandhi's Challenge to Christianity'; George Pattery, *Gandhi – the Believer: an Indian Christian Perspective* (Delhi: ISPCK, 1996); J Patmury, *Gandhiji and Sister Maria: a Unique Friendship without Frontiers* (Bangalore: ATC, 1998); Judson B Trapnell, 'Indian Sources on the Possibility of a Pluralist View of Religion,' *JES*, 35 (1998), 224-30.

30 *The Hindu View of Life* (London, 1927), 23.

31 *The Bhagavadgita*, sixth edition (London, 1960), 157.

32 *The Hindu View of Life*, 15. See also the section 'The Religion of the Spirit,' in his 'Fragments of a Confession' in *The Philosophy of Sarvepalli Radhakrishnan*, edited by Paul A Schilpp (New York, 1952), 60-72.

33 A chapter title in *Eastern Religion and Western Thought* (London, 1939) (306-48).

34 'Fragments of a Confession,' 80.

35 See, for example, his *The Heart of Hindusthan*, second edition (Madras, 1932), 101.

The cross and resurrection receive little emphasis, and mainly in *advaitin* terms,[36] and he dismisses Christianity's claim to uniqueness as untenable and the worst form of prejudice against other faiths.[37] Not unexpectedly, Radhakrishnan's views have provoked considerable discussion within the Indian Church (much of it critical) and beyond.[38] But his writings remain an influential advocacy of one substantial Hindu viewpoint that, for all its tendencies towards monistic absolutism (and hence the desired goal of a "featureless unity"[39]) still sees the "different religions not as incompatibles but as complementaries, and so indispensable to each other for the realisation of the common end."[40]

---

36 See his *Eastern Religion and Western Thought*, 97, 175f; and *The Bhagavadgita* 36.

37 *Eastern Religion and Western Thought*, 326-37.

38 For example: JE Lesslie Newbigin, *A Faith for This One World?* (London: SCM Press, 1961), 30-41; Stanley J Samartha, 'S Radhakrishnan: Jesus Christ – One among the Many,' *RS*, 11 (1964), 38-52; JG Arapura, 'India's Philosophical Response to Religious Pluralism,' in *Modern Indian Responses to Religious Pluralism*, 171-91; Ishwar Harris, 'S Radhakrishnan's View of Christianity,' in *Neo-Hindu Views of Christianity*, 156-81; Thomas, *The Acknowledged Christ of the Indian Renaissance*, 161-90; Daniel Acharuparambil, 'The Hindu View of the Divine as Interpreted by Dr S Radhakrishnan,' *IMR*, 1 (1979), 198-218; Robert N Minor, *Radhakrishnan: A Religious Biography* (Albany, NY: State Univ of New York Press, 1987); AL Herman, 'Religion, Relativism and Radhakrishnan,' *SJRS*, 10 (1989), 116-22; Julius J Lipner, 'Radhakrishnan on Religion and Religions,' *SJRS*, 10 (1989), 123-37; J Feys, 'Dr S Radhakrishnan on Religion: a Few Questions,' *Sevartham*, 15 (1990), 85-95; Boyd H Wilson, 'Sarvepalli Radhakrishnan's Use of Christian Scripture: An Introduction,' *Arasaradi Journal of Theological Reflection*, 4 (1991), 31-52; Bina Gupta, 'Radhakrishnan and His Universal Synthesis: A Critical Analysis,' *Dialogue and Alliance*, 6 (1992-1993), 76-103; Robert Neil Minor, 'Sarvepalli Radhakrishnan and Religious Pluralism,' *Studia Missionalia*, 42 (1993), 307-27; Margaret Chatterjee, 'Reflections on Religious Pluralism in the Indian Context,' *HCSB*, 7 (1994), 2-12; *S Radhakrishnan: A World Philosopher*, edited by GSS Sreenivasa Rao (Madras:, CLS, 1994); JG Desai, 'The Spiritual Idealism of Radhakrishnan with Special Reference to Vedanta,' *Nidan*, 8 (1996), 1-33; Lawrence P Dorairaj, 'Radhakrishnan's Approach to Religion: Reflections Based on "An Idealist View of Life",' *JD*, 23 (1998), 209; chapter 2 of Gavin D'Costa, *The Meeting of the Religions and the Trinity*, Faith Meets Faith Series (Maryknoll, NY: Orbis Books, 2000). For a vigorous challenge to the philosophical position represented by Radhakrishnan see Daya Krishna, *Indian Philosophy – a Counter Perspective* (Delhi: Oxford University Press, 1996).

39 *Religion in a Changing World* (London, 1967), 134.

40 *The Hindu View of Life*, 43. Chatterjee points out that such realisation is "not

C. Continuing Christian Reflection

1. Some Protestant Missionary Reflections

During the first half of this century missionaries continued to provide a fruitful meeting point for Christian and Hindu worldviews; as Halbfass points out, at least some of them embodied "a desire to understand whose singular power and problematical nature arise from their deep and uncompromising desire to be understood."[41]. For example, although the Scottish educationalist JN Farquhar (1861-1929)[42] is associated with a view of "the religion of Jesus" (as the liberal theology of his age put it) as the fulfilment of the religious desires of humankind, his advocacy of such a view was based upon firsthand scholarly knowledge of and sympathy with the Hindu tradition. His best known work, *The Crown of Hinduism*, is a mainly factual survey of some nine issues in Hinduism; it was in this context that he sought to demonstrate "how Christ provides the fulfilment of each of the highest aspirations and aims of Hinduism."[43] The notion of fulfilment became, during the first few decades of this century, "almost the accepted orthodoxy for large numbers of thoughtful Christians, both Asian and Western",[44] even though Farquhar's

---

so much a path as something to be transcended" – which leaves little by way of incentive for exploring the paths of others ('Reflections on Religious Pluralism,' 11; see too the comments of Lipner, 'Radhakrishnan on Religion and Religions').

41 *India and Europe*, 53 (original emphasis). It is interesting to note the opinion of Nirad Chaudhuri that missionaries were at times more perceptive observers of Hinduism than many other categories of viewer (*Hinduism* (London: Chatto and Windus, 1979), 104-18. See also Eric J Sharpe, *Faith Meets Faith*; Kenneth Cracknell, *Justice, Courtesy and Love: Theologians and Missionaries Encountering World Religions, 1846-1914* (London: Epworth Press, 1995).

42 For a discussion of Farquhar's thought see Eric J Sharpe, *Not to Destroy but to Fulfil: The Contribution of JN Farquhar to Protestant Missionary Thought in India before 1914* (Lund, 1965), and 'The Legacy of JN Farquhar,' *OBMR*, 3 (1979), 61-64.

43 *The Crown of Hinduism* (London, 1913), 457. It was a view that had already been gaining acceptance in those Christian circles influenced by liberal and evolutionary ideas; see Sharpe, *Faith Meets Faith*, 35f. For another study of the notion applied to an Indian setting see: Robin Boyd, 'The Gospel as Fulfilment in 19th and Early 20th Century Gujarat,' *ICHR*, 7 (1973), 83-90.

44 AJ Boyd, *Christian Encounter* (Glasgow, 1961), 74; see also Sharpe, *Faith Meets Faith*, 20; and Boyd, *An Introduction to Indian Christian Theology*, 90.

careful account of the theory was often imprecisely repeated. (For Farquhar, fulfilment meant the voluntary replacement of one faith by another within an individual and not merely the development of one religion from a lower to a higher state.)

There were, however, other opinions about the Hindu-Christian encounter. It was another Scot, the educationalist AG Hogg (1875 – 1954), who provided the most searching criticism of Farquhar's fulfilment hypothesis from within India itself[45] and who also offered his own carefully formulated exposition of a Christian worldview in a Hindu milieu.[46] Mention should also be made of two others. Firstly, CF Andrews (1871-1940) of the Cambridge Brotherhood in Delhi whose deep admiration for the poet Rabindranath Tagore and for Gandhi were indicative of his own commitment to Indian independence and cultural renewal such that MM Thomas writes of him that "no other representative of Western Christianity had been so completely accepted by Indian political and religious leaders."[47]

---

45 For example, in his review of *The Crown of Hinduism* in *IRM*, 3 (1914), 171-73. See also Sharpe, *Not to Destroy*, 350-52.

46 An introduction to Hogg's thought is found in Eric J Sharpe, *Alfred George Hogg, 1875 – 1954: An Intellectual Biography* (Chennai: Christian Literature Society, 1999); see also the discussion, together with some of his writings, in Eric J Sharpe, *The Theology of AG Hogg* (Madras, 1971). See also Sharpe, *Faith Meets Faith*, 37-44; James L Cox, 'Faith and Faiths: the Significance of AG Hogg's Missionary Thought for a Theology of Dialogue,' *SJT*, 32 (1979), 241-56, and 'AG Hogg and the Theology of Non-Christian Faith,' *BSIMS*, ns, 1 (1982), 17-24.

47 'A Christ-centered Approach to Other Religions,' 51. Of Andrews' own works, *The Renaissance in India. Its Missionary Aspect* (London, 1912) is a fine example of his approach in the area most relevant to this present study. For further analysis see, for example: MM Thomas, 'Basic Approaches to Power: Gandhiji, Andrews and King,' *RS*, 16.3 (Sept 1969), 15-25; Mathew P John, 'The Religion of CF Andrews,' *ICHR*, 4 (1970), 147-50; Daniel O'Connor, 'Dialogue as Communion: C F Andrews and Munshi Ram,' in *God's Word among Men*, 73-83; Eric J Sharpe, 'The Legacy of CF Andrews,' *IBMR*, 9 (1985), 117-21; Daniel O'Connor, *Gospel, Raj and Swaraj: The Missionary Years of C F Andrews, 1904-1914*, Studies in the Intercultural History of Christianity, 62 (Frankfurt am Main: Peter Lang, 1990); Ashish K Mondal, 'Charles Freer Andrews: a Disciple Extraordinary,' *ICHR*, 25 (June 1991), 49-62; Jeffrey Cox, 'C F Andrews and the Failure of the Modern Missionary Movement,' in *Modern Religious Rebels*, edited by Stuart Mews, (London: Epworth Press, 1993), 226-244; Eric J Sharpe, 'C F Andrews 1871-1940: the Most Trusted Englishman in India,' in *Mission Legacies: Biographical Studies of Leaders of the Modern Missionary Movement*, American Society of Missiology Series 19, edited by Gerald H Anderson, Robert T Coote, and Norman A Horner (Maryknoll, NY: Orbis, 1994), 316-23.

Secondly, the American, E Stanley Jones (1884 – 1973) whose emphases on 'The Indian Christ',[48] on the potential of Christian ashrams, and on the Kingdom of God (rather than the Church) were intended to help the Indian Christian community towards a distinctly Indian identity. Particular note should be taken of the 'Round Table' conferences he organised, which enabled an unprecedented series of meetings of people of different faiths[49]- even if their worth has been assessed in a number of ways.[50]

2. *Some Indian Christian Responses*

A majority of Indian Christians may think it unnecessary or unwise to engage in dialogue with Hindus. One reason for this has been the generally closed, communal spirit of the Indian Church; another has been a theological conservatism derived from the "simple, inward-looking, individualistic pietism" which was brought from the West.[51] There were, however, some notable exceptions. For example, Sadhu Sundar Singh (1889-1929; "perhaps the most famous Indian Christian who has yet lived, and whose influence has been widespread and prolonged")[52] combined a deeply christocentric faith with a quite positive attitude towards Hinduism

48 In, for example, his *The Christ of the Indian Road* (London, 1926; second Indian edition: Lucknow, 1977).

49 See his *Christ at the Round Table* (London, 1928). For secondary studies see Richard W Taylor, *The Contribution of Stanley Jones*, Confessing the Faith in India Series, 9 (Madras: CLS, 1973); and 'The Legacy of E Stanley Jones,' *IBMR*, 6 (1982), 102-07; Paul AJ Martin, *Missionary of the Indian Road: the Theology of Stanley Jones* (Bangalore: Theological Book Trust, 1996) and the literature cited there.

50 Richard W Taylor could write in the early 1970s that "even now I know of nothing like this experience-based dialogue." (*The Contribution of Stanley Jones*, 11.) But Stephen C Neill, an actual participant in some of the 'Round Tables' could write that Christian participants found that the meetings only revealed "the extreme poverty of the non-Christian religions"; despite much talking, "of a direct experience of God there was little trace" ('Dialogue as a Method of Encounter' in *Concise Dictionary of the Christian World Mission*, edited by Stephen Neill and others (London: USCL, 1971), 165f.

51 Richard W Taylor, 'Christ Acting in Our Society,' in *Indian Voices in Today's Theological Debate*, edited by Horst Bürkle and Wolfgang MW Roth (English edition, Lucknow, 1972), 163.

52 Boyd, *An Introduction to Indian Christian Theology*, 92.

including an extensive use of Hindu terminology.[53]

Exceptions of a different kind are to be found in the works of the three South Indian theologians: AJ Appasamy (1891-1976), Vengal Chakkarai (1880-1958) and Pandipeddi Chenchiah (1886-1959).[54] Appasamy worked out his theology in terms of the *bhakti* tradition and its personalist philosophical justification as found in Ramanuja. Perhaps his most influential work is that in which he elaborates *Christianity as Bhakti Marga*,[55] drawing upon both the Fourth Gospel and the rich tradition of Tamil *bhakti* literature, both Hindu and Christian.[56]

---

53 A collection of all of his Urdu writings between 1922-28 is found in *The Christian Witness of Sadhu Sundar Singh*, edited by T Dayanandan Francis (Madras: CLS, 1989). For secondary studies see: Burnett H Street and AJ Appasamy, *The Message of Sadhu Sundar Singh* (New York, NY: Macmillan, 1921; London: 1922 as *The Sadhu: a Study in Mysticism and Practical Religion*); Arthur Bruce Moss, 'The Religious Teaching of Sadhu Sundar Singh,' *Methodist Review*, 114 (1931), 122-25; CF Andrews, *Sadhu Sundar Singh* (London, 1934); G Francis S Gray, 'Sadhu Sundar Singh and the Non-Christian Religions,' *IRM*, 48 (1959), 421-26; Boyd, *An Introduction to Indian Christian Theology*, 92-109; Friedrich Heiler, *The Gospel of Sadhu Sundar Singh* (Et: Lucknow, 1970 and Delhi, 1989); Janet Lynch-Watson, *Saffron Robe: a Life of Sadhu Sundar Singh* (London: Hodder, 1975); Eric J Sharpe, 'Sadhu Sundar Singh and His Critics: an Episode in the Meeting of East and West,' *Religion*, 6 (1976), 48-66; Eric J Sharpe, 'Christian Mysticism in Theory and Practice: Nathan Soderblom and Sadhu Sundar Singh,' *Religious Traditions*, 4 (1981), 19-37; TE Riddle, *The Vision and the Call: a Life of Sadhu Sundar Singh* (Delhi: ISPCK, 1987); Michael Biehl, *Der Fall Sadhu Sundar Singh / Theologie zwischen den Kulturen*, Studien zur interkulturellen Geschichte des Christentums, 66 (Frankfurt am Main: Peter Lang, 1990); T Dayanandan Francis, 'Sadhu Sundar Singh: the Lover of the Cross,' *AJT*, 4 (1990), 24-35; Eric J Sharpe, 'The Legacy of Sadhu Sundar Singh,' *IBMR*, 14 (1990), 161-67; Chandrashekar Soans, 'The Water of Life in an Indian Cup: Towards a Contextual Theology', *Koinonia*, 5 (1993), 218-39; P Surya Prakash, 'The Contribution of Sadhu Sundar Singh: Preacher and Theologian,' *BTF*, 3.2 (July 1999), 101-16.

54 Useful studies of these three theologians are found in: Gurukul Theological Research Group of the Tamilnad Christian Council, *A Christian Theological Approach to Hinduism: Being Studies in the Theology of A.J. Appasamy, V. Chakkarai and Chenchiah* (Madras, 1956); Herwig Wagner, *Erstgestalten einer einheimischen Theologie in Südindien* (Munich, 1963) (although Wagner's critical remarks are perhaps excessively culturally conditioned: see Kaj Baagø, 'Indian Indigenous Theology,' *IRM*, 55 (1966), 221-25); Vengal Chakkarai Rajasekaran, 'The Rethinking Group of Madras: The Champion of Inter-Religious Co-operation,' *ICHR*, 27 (1993), 97-106.

55 Second edition: Madras, 1930.

Of the three, Chakkarai appears to have been the most sensitive to the Indian milieu in which an Indian theology is to be formulated. In fact, of all Indian theologians, he makes the most extensive use of Hindu terminology, drawing from many streams of Hindu thought.[57] His *Jesus the Avatar*[58] is a substantial attempt at an Indian christology and views Christ as "the permanent Avatar." And in a discussion of 'The Relations between Christianity and Non-Christian Faiths', Chakkarai indicates that his own experience as a Hindu and his knowledge of the religion leaves him in no doubt that "the Hindu can be saved and is saved by the grace of God, apart from the historical Jesus."[59] Chenchiah acknowledges a debt to *yoga* as taught by Aurobindo and others in his attempt to construct a theology based upon direct experience (*anubhava*) of Christ and to be lived as "the *yoga* of the Spirit." He did not accept the description of Christ as an *avatara*. His attitude towards Hinduism was very positive.[60]

3. *Some Roman Catholic Discussions and Initiatives*

Catholic discussion of the encounter was, by comparison with Protestant reflection during the first six decades of this century, less extensive and more conservative in tone. In India, specific instruc-

---

56 For a critical appraisal of Appasamy's thought see Boyd, *An Introduction to Indian Christian Theology*, 118-43 and T Dayanandan Francis, 'A J Appasamy: a Christian Forerunner of Inter-religious Dialogue in India,' in *Keeping Hope Alive: Theological Insights from the Past – for Today*, edited by Jesudas Athyal (Madras: Academy of Ecumenical Indian Theology and Church Administration, 1993), 119-32. See also T Dayanandan Francis, *AJ Appasamy: a Christian Forerunner of Inter-Religious Dialogue in India* (Madras: CLS, 1991).

57 Boyd, *An Introduction to Indian Christian Theology*, 166.

58 Second edition, Madras, 1930. For critical studies of Chakkarai's theology and methodology see: Boyd, *An Introduction to Indian Christian Theology*, 165-85; T Thomas, *The Theology of Chakkarai* (Bangalore, 1968); TV Philip, 'Chakkarai and the Indian Church,' in *Society and Religion: Essays in Honour of MM Thomas*, edited by RW Taylor (Madras, 1976), 153-65.

59 In *Rethinking Christianity*, edited by DM Devasahayam and AN Sudarisanam (Madras, c 1938), 63-77 (quotation from 75).

60 See, for example, 'Jesus and Non-Christian Faiths,' in *Rethinking Christianity*, 47-62. Two useful studies are DA Thangasamy, *The Theology of Chenchiah with Selections from his Writings* (Bangalore, 1966) and OV Jathanna, *The Decisiveness of the Christ-Event and the Universality of Christianity in a World of Religious Plurality* (Berne, 1981), 352-435. See also Boyd, *Introduction to Indian Christian Theology*, 144-64.

tions (prohibiting, for example, entry into Hindu temples, shared prayer, the reading of Hindu scriptures and the active or passive or even mere material assistance at the religious functions of non-Catholics) severely restricted the range and depth of permitted contacts between converts from Hinduism and the society from which they came. It seems not unfair to say with Emprayil that, in the years before the second Vatican Council, the spirit of most (Catholic) missionaries was that of "active hostility or grudging tolerance towards the practices and beliefs of non-Christians."[61] However, there were occasional exceptions, including an original and sustained attempt to establish an identity as a 'Hindu-Catholic' by Brahmabandhab Upadhyaya (1861-1907),[62] the Bengali national-

---

61 Thomas Emprayil, *The Emerging Theology of Religions. The Contribution of the Catholic Church in India* (Rewa, 1980), 1. Note too the remarks of a missionary that the Church came to 'conquer,' deeply convinced that her mission was to replace and absorb all that did not conform to her teachings and structures (R Antoine, 'Dialogue,' in *All India Seminar: Church in India Today, Bangalore 1969* (New Delhi, nd [1969]), 106).

62 Sometimes known by his original name Bhavani Charan Banerji. For a critical study (more sympathetic than the title implies) see Alfons Väth, *Im Kampfe mit der Zauberwelt des Hinduismus. Upadhyaya Brahmabandhav und des Problem der Uberwindung des Hoheren Hinduismus Durch des Christentum* (Berlin and Bonn, 1928). Also useful are B Animananda, *The Blade: Life and Work of Brahmabandhab Upadhyaya* (Calcutta, nd [c1947]); Boyd, *An Introduction to Indian Christian Theology*, 63-85 and passim; George Gispert-Sauch, 'The Sanskrit Hymns of Brahmabandhav Upadhyaya,' *RS*, 19.4 (December 1972), 60-79; Antony Mookenthottam, *Indian Theological Tendencies* (Berne, 1978), 34-43; K.Aleaz, 'The Theological Writings of Brahmabandhav Upadyaya Re-examined,' *IJT*, 28 (1979), 55-77; Antonia Fonseca, 'A Prophet Disowned. Swami Upadhyaya Brahmabandhav,' *Vidyajyoti*, 44 (1980), 177-94; Maurice Maupilier, *Les Mystiques Hindous Chrétiens (1830-1967)* (Paris, 1985), 159-65; Jose Vetticatil, 'Brahmabandhav Upadhyaya,' *Jeevadhara*, 17 (1987), 322-43; Julius J Lipner, 'A Case Study in "Hindu Catholicism": Brahmabandhab Upadhyay (1861-1907),' *ZMR*, 72 (1988), 33-54; KP Aleaz, *The Gospel of Indian Culture* (Calcutta: Punthi Pustak, 1994), 214-56 and *Christian Thought through Advaita Vedanta* (Delhi: ISPCK, 1996), 9-38; Sathianathan Clarke, 'The Jesus of Nineteenth Century Indian Christian Theology: an Indian Inculturation with Continuing Problems and Prospects,' *SWC*, 5 (1999), 32-46; Julius J Lipner, *Brahmabandhab Upadhyay. The Life and Thought of a Revolutionary* (Delhi: Oxford University Press, 1999); John Vattanky, 'A Patriot, Pioneer of Inculturation,' *VJTR*, 63 (1999), 657-66; Timothy C Tennent, *Building Christianity on Indian Foundations: The Legacy of Brahmabandhav Upadhyay* (Delhi: ISPCK, 2000).

ist and Christian *samnyasi* who sought to follow Hinduism as his *samaj dharma* (set of social obligations) but Christianity as his *sadhana dharma* (way of salvation and religious life). His extensive use of Hindu categories, especially those of Shankara, and the strongly anti-ecclesiastical sentiments of his later years, brought him into sharp and even bitter conflict with the hierarchy of the Indian Catholic Church – an unfortunate situation if, as Julius Lipner asserts, his theological conclusions "are largely neo-Thomism in Sanskritic disguise"[63]. His works do not seem to have been widely read by Hindus, but among Indian Christian theologians his creative attempt to develop the *advaitin* description of *Brahma* as *Saccidananda* – and hence a description of the Trinity – has had some influence (see chapter 6.G below) and the notion of 'Hindu-Catholic' has evoked discussion.[64]

The only noteworthy attempt to follow the example of Brahmabandhab was the work of a group of Jesuit Indologists, mainly Belgian, led by Georges Dandoy (1882-1962)[65] and Pierre Johanns (1882-1955)[66] who for some twenty years from 1922 edited a monthly journal *The Light of the East*. The journal was meant to be a vehicle for working out a reconstructed Catholic theology (in Thomist categories) based on aspects of the exposition of Vedanta – an attempt made in considerable detail in a series of 137 articles by Johanns, 'To Christ through the Vedanta.'[67] Two further examples of

---

63 Lipner, *Brahmabandhab Upadhyay*, 387 – though this appraisal is disputed by KP Aleaz who writes that Brahmabandhab's contribution to Indian theology is "totally distorted" by Lipner (review in *AJT*, 13 (1999), 474).

64 See, for example: Thomas Ohm, '"Hindu-Katholizimus",' *ZMR*, 40 (1956), 53f; Turmes, 'Samaj Dharm and Sadhan Dharm,' *CMS*, 6 (1962-63), 330-34; Richard V De Smet, 'Comments on Samaj- dharma and Sadhana-dharma,' *CMS*, 6 (1962-63), 335-37; Michael Amaladoss, 'Qui Suis-je? Un Catholique-Hindou,' *Christus*, 22 (1975), 159-71.

65 See J Bayart, 'In Memoriam Georges Dandoy s.j.,' *CMS*, 6 (1962-63), 104-15.

66 These two, with Brahmabandhab and the missionary Indologists J Bayart, R Antoine, Fallon and R De Smet, are known as 'The Calcutta School'; see Joseph Mattam, 'Interpreting Christ to India Today: the Calcutta School,' *IJT*, 23 (1974), 191-205, and on Johanns see Mattam, *Land of the Trinity. A Study of Modern Christian Approaches to Hinduism* (Bangalore, nd [c 1975]), 17-43.

67 *Light of the East*, 1 (1922) – 12.7 (July 1934). These were also published as four booklets (*To Christ Through the Vedanta*, 3rd edition; Ranchi, 1944) and more recently as two volumes, compiled by Theo de Greef (Bangalore: United Theological College, 1996). Klostermaier states that Johanns later retracted "as a dead track" the supposed approach to Christ 'through the Vedanta' ('Hindu-Christian Dialogue,' in *ITD*, 251).

Jesuit scholarly interest have been *The Clergy Monthly*[68] (begun in 1937) which has contained many articles on the relationship between Christianity and Hinduism; and the symposium *Religious Hinduism,* first published as a series of letters between 1957 and 1959 before being published in twice revised book form.[69]

Within the Indian Catholic Church official interest in the inter-religious encounter grew slowly. After the establishment of the Catholic Bishops' Conference of India (to be abbreviated as CBCI) in 1944, the First Plenary Council of India was convened in 1950. Although the decrees of the Council have been called the "first official church document offering a clearly positive approach to the spiritual values of the world religions",[70] their appraisal is cautious in tone. Claims made by Hindus about the equality of religions and the acceptability of some form of syncretism are rejected; there is an acknowledgement of "truth and goodness outside the Christian religion, for God has not left the nations without a witness to Himself, and the human soul is naturally drawn towards the one true God" but not without mention of "the inadequacy of all non-Christian religions" when judged in the light of Christ's unique mediation of divine salvation.[71] However, one modest set of initiatives was allowed (or tolerated): the setting up of a few ashrams and some small interreligious study centres.[72]

In December 1956 there was held in Madras a 'Study-Week on Indian Culture and the Fullness of Christ' whose conclusions stressed the need to recognise the positive values found in Indian thought and to use Indian philosophical categories to express them – albeit in a form "crowned with Christian wisdom."[73] In 1958 a 'Seminar of Seminary Professors on Indian Religions and Philosophies' was held in Bangalore at which there was a detailed comparative study of Christianity and Hinduism, especially in the light of Panikkar's thesis about the unknown presence of Christ in

---

68 Now called *Vidyajyoti Journal of Theological Reflection* and published in Delhi.

69 Edited by Richard De Smet and Josef Neuner (2nd edition, 1964; 3rd edition, Allahabad, 1968).

70 Thomas Emprayil, *The Emerging Theology of Religions,* 18.

71 Decree no. 11; see *The Christian Faith: In the Doctrinal Documents of the Catholic Church,* edited by Josef Neuner and James Dupuis (Philadelphia, 1972), 272. Decrees 24 and 25 are also relevant – and equally cautious.

72 To the role of these discussion will return; see below, chapter 2.B.

73 *Indian Culture and the Fullness of Christ: All India Study Week, 6th-13th December 1956* (Madras: The Madras Cultural Academy, 1957), 30.

Hinduism.[74] In these decrees and seminars the initiatives in formulating an increasingly positive attitude to Hinduism most often seemed to come from non-Indian sources (i.e. from foreign-born theologians and missionaries and non-Indian theologies).[75]

D. PD Devanandan and Recent Protestant Initiatives

The Christian-Hindu dialogue now advocated in India is not a direct development of the relationships that existed during the first six decades of this century, and earlier. There were, of course, many friendly and fruitful meetings but there was nothing inevitable about the way in which concern for intentional dialogue grew from them. Of greater importance was a series of events near the beginning of the 1960s. Because Protestant initiatives appear to have been more significant at that time than Catholic, discussion begins with them.

One organisation closely involved in dialogue at both theoretical and practical levels has been the Christian Institute for the Study of Religion and Society (to be abbreviated CISRS) founded in Bangalore in October 1957 by the National Christian Council of India and the Christian Institute for the Study of Society in order to facilitate Christian participation in nation-building and to promote inter-religious dialogue.[76]

1. Devanandan's Thought

The first director of CISRS was Paul David Devanandan (1901-1962). He attempted a careful analysis of Hinduism and gave considerable impetus to Protestant concerns for dialogue; for these

---

74 For a brief summary of the Seminar see D Simon Lourdusamy, 'Meeting of Religions I – Indian Orientations,' in *Meeting of Religions*, edited by Thomas A Aykara (Bangalore, 1978), 14.

75 George Gispert-Sauch thinks that the few Indians teaching in seminaries in the 1950s and 1960s held "very cautious attitudes [about Hinduism], perhaps because they felt quite insecure in a foreign-dominated set up" (letter to author).

76 See Kaj Baagø, *A History of the National Christian Council of India: 1914-1964* (Nagpur, nd [1965]), 82f. A more detailed account and analysis of the Institute (especially its publications), is found in A Frank Thompson, *The Christian Institute for the Study of Religion and Society, a Research Arm of Christian Churches in India* (Lewiston, NY: Edwin Mellen Press, 1992); AM Abraham Ayrookuzhiel, 'Indian Religious Heritage and Social Transformation: Change of Perspective within the CISRS,' *RS*, 40.1-2 (1993), 75-92; Saral K Chatterji, 'Emerging Perspectives of the Network,' *RS*, 40.1-2 (1993), 3-56.

reasons his views, and those of the publications and discussions he encouraged, merit careful analysis.[77] In his writings there is a constant stress upon one theme: God's new creation in Jesus Christ.[78] This new creation has a cosmic, christological foundation;[79] it also has an eschatological aspect: the new age is already in our midst and yet it awaits a future fulfilment.[80] One result of the new creation is the formation of a new humanity in Christ.[81] Although "the Church is even now the sphere of the new creation",[82] it is not the exclusive sphere. At times Devanandan seems to imply a universalism that considers all people to be actual sharers in the new humanity;[83] but in other places he seems to mean only that the scope or

---

77 The only substantial study of Devanandan's thought is: Joachim Wietzke, *Theologie im Modernen Indien – Paul David Devanandan* (Bern, 1975) – but not available to this writer. See also RA Robinson, 'Preparation for Dialogue' (unpublished MA dissertation, University of Canterbury, New Zealand, 1976); 120-61; Beat Hänni, 'Ansätze für einen Dialog mit Menschen anderen Glaubens: zur Religionstheologie von Paul David Devanandan,' *Reformatio*, 32 (1983), 421-28; Erik Breye, 'Devanandan and Neo-Hinduism,' *Sevartham*, 10 (1985), 59-74; Friedrich Huber, 'The Relevance of the Bhagavad Gita according to Paul David Devanandan,' *RS*, 34.1 (March 1987), 53-65; MM Thomas, *Risking Christ for Christ's Sake* (Geneva, 1987), 85-104; J Jayakiran Sebastian, 'Prepared to be Courageous: Some Issues in Dialogue in India Today,' *BTF*, 20 (1988), 24-43; Mark Heim, 'Choosing Roots: the Contexts for Christian Theology in India,' *This World*, no 21 (Spring 1988), 88-101; Siga Arles, 'Mission in The Indian Culture Context: The Significance of Paul David Devanandan,' *IJT*, 35 (1993), 55-63; Creighton Lacy, 'Paul David Devanandan 1901-1962: the Church in Society and Nation Building,' in *Mission Legacies*, 355-61.

78 See his *Preparation for Dialogue*, edited by Nalini Devanandan and MM Thomas (Bangalore, 1964), iv; (to be cited as *Preparation*); *I Will Lift Up Mine Eyes Unto The Hills*, edited by Stanley J Samartha and Nalini Devanandan (Bangalore, 1963), 64. (This work to be cited as *I Will Lift*. See also his *Christian Concern in Hinduism* (Bangalore, 1961), 119f and his, *The Gospel and Renascent Hinduism* (London, 1959), 47f. These last two volumes will be referred to as *Christian Concern* and *Gospel* respectively. When a passage cited occurs in both works it will be cited in the form: *Christian Concern*, 119f/*Gospel*, 47f.

79 See *Christian Concern*, 118f/*Gospel*, 47; compare *Preparation*, 181f.

80 See *Christian Concern*, 92, 108, 135/*Gospel* 29, 42, 61; *I Will Lift*, 136f; *Preparation* 179-81.

81 See *I Will Lift*, 128.

82 *I Will Lift*, 159; compare *Preparation*, 136, 182.

83 *Christian Concern*, 108, 113/*Gospel* 42; *The Gospel and the Hindu Intellectual* (Bangalore, 1959), 23.

intention of the Christian message is universal.[84]

One noteworthy contribution of Devanandan has been his analysis of the renascence and reformation of Hinduism during the past 150 years. Although he gives a detailed consideration to the course and variations within this renascence,[85] our concern is to note his attempt at a Christian analysis of the phenomenon. Devanandan concedes there may be sociological and psychological reasons for this religious renascence; but he also believes that the observer cannot resist the impulse of the faith that believes in a God who is also the Lord of history, and in a creative spirit who is ever at work in the world, redeeming it even in its present involvements and directing its course to the ultimate fulfilment of His purpose, and that in all religious revival God is somehow at work.[86]

However, it must also be noted that Devanandan discerns this divine activity not in the 'classical theology' of Hinduism, but only in its renascent phase, especially its new anthropology.[87] It is a weakness in his analysis of Hinduism that he fails to acknowledge the continuing (even growing) influence of the conservative strands of Hinduism.[88]

There are also many areas of common social concern in which Devanandan calls for collaboration between Christians and others in India. For example, he urges the common building of a secular society in India "based on consideration of social justice, personal values and human rights."[89] Christian service might also involve

---

84 'Christian and non-Christian Faith,' *IJT*, 3 (1957), 76.

85 *Christian Concern*, 59-77/*Gospel*, 7-21; 'The Resurgence of Non-Christian Religions,' in *The Theology of the Christian Mission*, 148-57; 'Resurgent Hinduism,' in *Christianity and the Asian Revolution*, edited by Rajah B Manikam (Madras, 1954), 123-37; 'The Renaissance of Hinduism, *Theology Today*, 12 (1955), 189-205; 'The Renascence of Hinduism in India,' *ER*, 10 (1958), 52-65; also: Erik Breye, 'Devanandan and Neo-Hinduism,' *Sevartham*, 10 (1985), 59-74.

86 *Christian Concern*, 82; see also *Preparation*, 188 (and compare 177); 'Resurgent Hinduism,' 137; 'The Renaissance of Hinduism,' 205; 'The Emphases and Impact of Hinduism,' *NCCR*, 82 (1962), 367; 'Religions in Modern India - Present Significance,' *Church and Society*, 5 (September 1962), 20f.

87 See *Christian Concern*, 112.

88 As noted by: Marcus Braybrooke, *The Undiscovered Christ. A Review of Recent Developments in the Christian Approach to the Hindu* (Madras, 1973), 16; Young, '"Extra Vedos Nulla Salus",' 85.

89 *Christian Concern*, v. This theme is discussed at considerable length in *Christian Participation in Nation-Building*, edited by PD Devanandan and MM Thomas (Bangalore, 1960).

collaboration with the Gandhian inspired *Sarvodaya* (welfare of all) movement that Devanandan appraises at some length.[90]

2. *Beyond Dialectical Theology*

A further aspect of Devanandan's thought is his creative reaction to Kraemer's assertion of discontinuity between Christianity and the religions, a reaction that is especially significant when set alongside his indebtedness to and agreement with most other aspects of Kraemer's theology.[91] Devanandan sees a close relationship between religion and culture such that endorsement of discontinuity would lead to the cultural isolation of Christians in pluralistic India. He was willing and able to use issues raised by contemporary Hindus and post- Independence secular thinkers as points of contact in a way that dialectical theologians would not. His attitude to culture was more positive than that of Kraemer and even of many of his fellow Indian Christians although it might be argued that he does not always consistently explore links which he himself thought to exist between culture and the religious worldview undergirding it.

Devanandan was, then, able to offer substantial reasons both practical and theological for a Christian commitment to Christian-Hindu dialogue and to do so in a way that fully recognised a new theological context after Kraemer and a new national context after Independence.

3. *CISRS*

Devanandan began a joint editorship of the CISRS quarterly journal *Religion and Society* in 1957.[92] Of the nineteen issues published before his death in August 1962, nine had themes directly related to inter-religious relationships, including articles by Hindu writers; other issues contained reports, individual articles and book reviews on the Hindu-Christian encounter. CISRS also published or sponsored a number of pamphlets and monographs including the

---

90 *Preparation*, 15-21; *Christian Concern*, 66-68/*Gospel*, 18-20.

91 See MMThomas, *The Christian Response to the Asian Revolution* (Lucknow, 1967), 99f; Hallencreutz, *New Approaches to Men of Other Faiths*, 32f. Joachim Wietzke considers that, to Devanandan, Kraemer 'was the revelation of what it means to be a theologian' (letter to author, 11 November 1983).

92 Volume 4, numbers 1 and 2 were still called the *Bulletin of the Christian Institute for the Study of Society*.

'Inter-religious Dialogue Series.'[93] Devanandan encouraged other Indian Christians to help formulate a theology that acknowledges the challenge of Kraemer's thought but passes beyond it. One example was the Seminar organised by CISRS on Kraemer's *Religion and the Christian Faith.* It produced a critical response to Kraemer both in the light of the Indian context and as part of an ongoing international 'study process' of the IMC.[94] Another seminar sponsored was by CISRS in October 1958, at Nagpur, on the topic 'The Christian Approach to Renascent Hinduism.' Most of the 25 participants were from Indian (Protestant) theological colleges. The papers prepared for the Seminar and its conclusions contain a sympathetic acknowledgement of a genuine divine presence and activity in all religions, including contemporary Hinduism, and the Report on 'The Basis and Content of a Christian-Hindu Dialogue' moves well beyond what the neo-orthodox position might be thought to imply.[95] One major figure in this movement was the lay theologian MM Thomas (1916-1996) who was director of CISRS from 1962-75.[96]

It is at about this time that the word 'dialogue' began to be applied to Christian-Hindu discussion. An article by John Piet published in 1958 contains what is probably the first significant use of the word in Indian Protestant circles in the more intentional and formal senses elaborated in this book.[97]

In global Protestant circles in the early 1960s there was discussion about whether the meeting place between believers is to be sought

---

93 Published by the Christian Literature Society, Madras, for CISRS.

94 The Seminar, held in Bangalore in March 1958 and attended by 13 participants and 3 visitors, is reported in *RS*, 5.2 (June 1958), 59-78.

95 See *RS*, 6.1 (February 1959); the Report is found in 78-81.

96 See his *My Ecumenical Journey* (Trivandrum: Ecumenical Publishing Centre, 1990).

97 'Basis of an Inter-Religious Dialogue,' *RS*, 5.2 (June 1958), 30-39. Before this, the word was occasionally used, but with the meaning of 'conversation.' A good example is found in the Report mentioned above ('The Basis and Content of a Christian-Hindu Dialogue') where, despite the title, the word 'dialogue' does not once occur. Instead, the verb 'to converse' is used once and the noun 'conversation' is found eighteen times. A further early use of the word 'dialogue,' with meanings beyond that of the discursive, is found in Murray Rogers, 'The Content of a Christian-Hindu Dialogue,' *RS*, 6.1 (February 1959), 68-71.

in their common humanity rather than in shared religious faith.[98] Discussions initiated by CISRS also raised this question; at a Biennial Council meeting of the Institute there was "debate as to whether the inter-faith meeting should be related primarily to 'religious' striving or 'human' aspirations."[99] But by the middle of the decade it was agreed that the Indian Christian attitude to people of other faiths had, as a conference report put it in 1966, "taken a new form", especially in the Protestant churches.[100] During the 1960s not only did CISRS continue to sponsor meetings to discuss inter-religious relationships,[101] but other Protestant bodies were also willing to take or to be associated with such initiatives.[102] Meetings also began to be held on an ecumenical basis[103] and with participation by

---

98 During 1960-1961 the WCC, as part of its continuing study of 'The Word of God and the Living Faiths of Men,' held consultations in various parts of the world and these were evaluated at Nagpur in March 1961 and an 'Interim Statement' attempted to summarise the findings of the entire study-process. Two important bases for the inter-religious encounter were emphasized: the recognition that the religions are in fact 'living faiths,' and an awareness of 'common humanity.' The Statement was published as 'Christian Encounter with Men of Other Faiths,' *Bulletin of the WCC Division of Studies*, 7.1 (1961), 3-10.

99 Editorial, *RS*, 12.1 (March 1965), 6; see also 82.

100 The report gave four reasons for the new and positive assessment: an extension of the spirit of the ecumenical movement; a growing appreciation of the Indian cultural heritage; the impact of the renewal of other Indian religions; the impact of secularisation ('Christian Faith in the Contemporary Indian Context,' *RS*, 13.3 (September 1966), 56).

101 For example, the Biennial Council of CISRS held in Nagpur, February 1965, included a consultation on 'The Christian Basis, Meaning and Scope of Inter-Faith Dialogue.' Some papers appear in *RS*, 12.1 (March 1965) and a Report (74-76, 82f).

102 The Kerala Christian Council, for example, was a co-sponsor with CISRS of a Seminar held at an ashram near Kottayam, 14-16 June 1962, on the subject 'Hindu and Christian Concepts of Ultimate Truth' – the title given to *RS*, 11.3 (September 1962) in which some of the papers presented to the Seminar were published.

103 Samartha notes that one of the earliest occasions on which Roman Catholics joined with Orthodox and Protestant Christians to participate in dialogue with Hindus was at the Kottayam Seminar mentioned in note 76 above; see his 'Dialogue as a Continuing Christian Concern,' 145. CISRS and the (Catholic) Institute of Indian Culture, Bombay, jointly sponsored a 'Consultation on the Theology of Hindu-Christian Dialogue' in Bombay, 4-8 January 1969; see the Report in *RS*, 16.2 (June 1969), 69-88.

members of other faiths as well.[104] Much of the subject matter and conclusions of these and other meetings are incorporated into the chapters that follow, as are the contributions of a number of theologians active during the period. Note must also be taken of some other publishing ventures besides that of CISRS. The *Indian Journal of Theology*, which first appeared in 1952, has carried material on themes closely related to the Hindu-Christian encounter. Several publishers have encouraged the discussion of such themes and a number of Protestant theological colleges and other institutions have also occasionally produced material in their own publications.[105] And, of course, a number of individuals have contributed greatly to the continuing discussion.

E. Further Catholic Initiatives in Dialogue

1. *The 'Circle'*

Although no individual in the Indian Catholic Church assumed a role as influential as that taken by Devanandan among Protestants, mention must be made of a small ecumenical group committed to dialogue. The 'Circle', as it became known, met in the early 1960s under the leadership of Jacques-Albert Cuttat (then Swiss

---

104 The first occasion on which CISRS brought together Christians (about a dozen) and Hindus (seven in number) was for a 'Colloquium on the Hindu and Christian Views of Man' held in Nagpur, 10-13 October, 1960. Some of the papers presented are found in *RS*, 7.3 & 4 (Oct. & Dec. 1960) together with JB Carman, 'The Nagpur Colloquium at Work' (129-36). Another fairly early example of a structured meeting of Hindus and Christians was that organised by Douglas Steere in Ootacamund in April 1967: see Klostermaier, 'Hindu-Christian Dialogue,' in *DBM*, 17-20.

105 For example, the Christian Literature Society, Madras; the Indian Society for the Promotion of Christian Knowledge, New Delhi; the Lucknow Publishing House, Lucknow. From among institutions note *BTF* published by the United Theological College, Bangalore; *Indian Cultures*, Jabalpur; *NCCR*, Nagpur; and occasional publications by the Tamil Nadu Theological Seminary, Madurai; Gurukul Lutheran Theological College and Research Institute, Madras.

Ambassador to India),[106] Murray Rogers (the Anglican founder of the Jyotiniketan Ashram, Uttar Pradesh) and Swami Abhishiktananda (Henri Le Saux, 1910-1973), in order to discuss Christian and Hindu spirituality. Although a number of non-Catholics were members[107], its theological emphasis was Catholic. For a number of years it met annually for about a week to give attention to 'inner dialogue', that intense Christian reflection on Hindu experience that it believed must precede actual meetings with Hindus.[108] The group's approach to dialogue was in terms of inner spirituality – a significant change of emphasis from the earlier attempts of, for example, the Calcutta School to find a meeting point in a Christian reinterpretation of one or more Hindu philosophical systems.

It must be added, however, that the Circle consisted mainly of non-Indians. Although the ecumenical nature of the group may have enabled the recognition of a wider range of potential approaches to dialogue, its contribution appears not (or not yet) to have been widely acknowledged within the Indian Church. It has been criticised for failing to get beyond internal dialogue,[109] and its fairly close relationship with the Christian ashram movement may not have helped.

The contribution of Abhishiktananda to the Hindu-Christian encounter is considerable – particularly what he called "a Christian approach to advaitic experience"[110] – and discussion will return to

---

106 Cuttat's major literary contribution to the discussion, *Expérience Chrétienne et Spiritualité Orientale* (Paris, 1967) comes from the meetings. See also the comments of Mattam, *Land of the Trinity*, 74-104, Klaus Klostermaier, 'Jacques-Albert Cuttat, a Pioneer of Hindu-Christian Dialogue,' *HCSB*, 2 (1989), 4; Judson B Trapnell, 'Two Models of Christian Dialogue with Hindus: Bede Griffiths and Abhishiktananda,' *VJTR*, 60 (1996), 101-10, 183-91, 243-54; George Gispert-Sauch, 'Christ and the Indian Mystical Tradition – Swami Abhishiktananda,' *Jeevadhara*, 27 (1997), 193-206; Joseph Molleur, 'The Transformation of Dom Le Saux – Swami Abhishiktananda,' *IJT*, 39 (1997), 35-42.

107 As well as Murray Rogers, they included John Cole (Presbyterian) and Herbert Jai Singh (Methodist).

108 The meetings are listed in the Appendix at the end of the chapter.

109 Richard W Taylor, 'Current Hindu-Christian Dialogue in India,' in *H-CD*, 122f.

110 The subtitle of his Saccidananda (Revised edition in English (Delhi, 1974)). An excellent account of his life and thought is found in Marie- Madeleine Davy, *Henri Le Saux: Swami Abhishiktananda* (Paris, 1981); see also Emmanuel Vattakuzhy, *Indian Christian Sannyasa and Swami*

him in a later chapter. Mention should also be made of two other foreign-born Catholic priests. Jules Monchanin (1895-1957), cofounder of the Saccidananda Ashram in Tamilnadu with Abhishiktananda in 1950. His thought is similar to that of Abhishiktananda though more intellectualist in approach, with a less positive appraisal of *advaita* and with an emphasis upon the conversion or Christianisation of India.[111] And Bede Griffiths (1906-1993), an English Benedictine who was closely involved with two ashrams – in Kerala and then at Shantivanam in Tamil Nadu where his deep interest in interreligious and intercultural dialogue devel-

---

Abhishiktananda (Bangalore, 1981); Sara Grant, 'Time-bomb or Tomb-stone? Reflections on the Private Journal of Swami Abhishiktananda,' *Vidyajyoti*, 52 (1988), 83-97.

111 On Monchanin see: Abhishiktananda, 'Le Père Monchanin,' *La Vie Spirituelle*, 98 (1958), 71-95; *Swami Parama Arubi Anandan (Fr J Monchanin) 1895-1957. A Memorial* (Shantivanam, nd [1959]); L Raymond, 'Abbé Jules Monchanin,' *CMS*, 6 (1962-63), 286-91; H de Lubac, *Images de l'abbé Monchanin* (Paris, 1967); JG Weber, 'Jules Monchanin: An Introduction and Two Essays,' CC, 19 (1969), 81-90, and *In Quest of the Absolute: the Life and Works of Jules Monchanin* (London, 1977); Joseph Mattam, 'Modern Catholic Attempts at Presenting Christ to India,' *IJT*, 23 (1974), 207-11; the chapter on Monchanin in Mattam, *Land of the Trinity* (144-79); Raymond Rossignol, 'La rencontre de l'hindouisme et du christianisme. Un pionnier: le Père Monchanin,' *Chrétiens Ensemble*, Mai 1983, 37-40; Francoise Jacquin, 'La mission par la Trinité: Jules Monchanin,' *Communio*, 8 (1983), 89-95. 'Abbé Jules Monchanin and India, "the land of the Trinity",' in *God's Word among Men*, 195-229; Andre Couture, 'Jules Monchanin et Henri Le Saux, pionniers de la rencontre avec l'hindouisme,' in *Le Christ et les cultures dans le monde et l'histoire*, edited by Gilles Langevin and Raphael Pirro (Montreal: Bellarmin, 1991), 168-78; Sten Rodhe, *Jules Monchanin: Pioneer in Christian-Hindu Dialogue* (New Delhi: ISPCK, 1993); Sten Rodhe, 'Christianity and Hinduism: a Comparison of Views Held by Jules Monchanin and Bede Griffiths,' *VJTR*, 59 (1995), 663-77; Thomas Matus, 'Yoga, Multi-Culturalism, and Evangelization,' *Studia Missionalia*, 44 (1995), 251-74. A fairly complete anthology of Monchanin's writings is found in his *Mystique de L'Inde, Mystère Chrétien. Ecrits et Inédits*, edited by Suzanne Siauve (Paris, 1974). Together Monchanin and Le Saux wrote *An Indian Benedictine Ashram* in 1951 (revised edition: *A Benedictine Ashram*, Douglas, Isle of Man, 1964).

oped,[112] – has enjoyed considerable popularity in the West even if contribution to an understanding of Hindu-Christian relations has been assessed in various ways, not all of them positive.[113]

While these individuals may not be typical of the missionary community as a whole there is other research that suggests a steady shift during the 1960s and 1970s towards a more liberal attitude towards the religions[114]though not without misgivings in some quarters.[115]

2. *Influences from Outside India*

We have already noted the influence of a number of foreign-born missionaries on the movement towards dialogue. Mention might also be made of Hans Küng's contribution to the Conference on 'Christian Revelation and Non-Christian Religions' held in Bombay,

---

112 See, for example, his *The Marriage of East and West* (London: Collins, 1982); *The Cosmic Revelation: The Hindu Way to God* (Springfield, IL: Templegate, 1983); and *River of Compassion: a Christian Commentary on the Bhagavad Gita* (New York, NY: Continuum, 1995). For secondary references see: Wayne Teasdale, 'Bede Griffiths and the Uniqueness of Christianity,' *Communio*, 11 (1984), 177-86; Kathryn Spink, *A Sense of the Sacred: A Biography of Bede Griffiths* (London: SPCK, 1988); David M Brookman, 'Bede Griffiths: Prophet of Cultural Transformation,' *Anima*, 16 (1989), 61-69; Raimundo Panikkar, 'A New Vision or Reality (A Tribute To Bede Griffiths),' *JD*, 18 (1993), 285-93; Judson B Trapnell, 'Bede Griffiths, Mystical Knowing, and the Unity of Religions,' *Philosophy and Theology*, 7 (1993), 355-79; Sten Rodhe, 'Christianity and Hinduism: a Comparison of Views Held by Jules Monchanin and Bede Griffiths,' *VJTR*, 59 (1995), 663-77; Beatrice Bruteau, compiler, *The Other Half of My Soul: Bede Griffiths and the Hindu-Christian Dialogue* (Wheaton, IL and Madras: Quest Books, 1996); Judson B Trapnell, 'Two Models of Christian Dialogue with Hindus: Bede Griffiths and Abhishiktananda,' *VJTR*, 60 (1996), 101-10, 183-91, 243-54, and 'Bede Griffiths as a Culture Bearer,' *ABR*, 47 (1996), 260-83; Jesu Rajan, *Bede's Journey to the Beyond* (Bangalore: ATC, 1997); Lourdu Anandam, *The Western Lover of the East: A Theological Enquiry into Bede Griffith's Contribution to Christology* (Kodaikanal: La Salette Publications, 1998); Shirley Du Boulay, *Beyond the Darkness: a Biography of Bede Griffiths* (New York, NY: Doubleday, 1998); Kuruvilla Pandikattu, 'Human Life as Dialogical. Bede Griffiths' Theology of Religions', *TM*, 3 (2000), 84-101.

113 See, for example, Ursula King who calls his *The Marriage of East and West* "simplistic, if not to say myopic", based on unexamined assumptions best called "spiritual romanticism" and a work that "must be judged an example of 'soft thinking'" (review in *CR*, 67 (1982), 338.

114 See Anton Karokaran, *Evangelization and Diakonia* (Bangalore, 1978), 223-50.

115 See, for example, J Britto Chethimattam, 'The Scope and Conditions of a Hindu-Christian Dialogue,' *IES*, 3 (1964), 294-96.

November 1964.[116] In his paper 'The World Religions in God's Plan of Salvation' Küng took what he described as a "somewhat negatively critical look at the ecclesiocentric view" represented in the axiom "No salvation outside the Church" (37), and contrasted it with the "theocentric view" of the destiny of non-Christian humanity in which "the starting point is not the Church but God's will and plan of salvation" (37). In a reversal of the traditional view he argued that, "as against the "extraordinary" way of salvation which is the Church, the world religions can be called ... the "ordinary" way of salvation for non-Christian humanity" (51f). Despite the controversy (both within and beyond India) caused by some of the papers read to the Conference, and the statements adopted by it, within a few years similar conclusions were being accepted within the Indian Catholic Church – with Papal and Conciliar statements and the views of European theologians cited in support.[117] The 'Historical Note' that introduces the official Indian Catholic *Guidelines for Inter-Religious Dialogue*[118] acknowledges the considerable influence on the development of interest in dialogue within India of: (a) the teaching of Pope Paul VI on dialogue in his encyclical *Ecclesiam Suam* in 1964 (*GIRD(2)*, 6); (b) his visit to India in 1964 during which his addresses made frequent and complimentary references to Indian religious aspirations (*GIRD(2)*, 6); and (c) the positive assessment of the world's religions found in the documents of the Second Vatican Council.[119] The formation of the Secretariat for

---

116 The papers read to the Conference were first published in an issue of *IES*, 4. 3-4 (July-October, 1965) and later, edited by Josef Neuner, as *Christian Revelation and World Religion* (London, 1967); Küng's essay is found at 25-66; further references are given after quotations in the text. Küng did, of course, continue to develop his theology of the religions. See, for example, *On Being a Christian* (Et: London, 1977), 89-116 and *Christianity and the World Religions* (New York, 1986).

117 The somewhat shifting currents of Catholic opinion about the religions is a topic to which discussion will return in chapter 4.C below.

118 Revised draft (Varanasi, 1977) to be referred to as *GIRD(1)*; second revised edition (New Delhi: CBCI Centre, 1989) to be referred to as *GIRD(2)*. Further references to both editions of the *Guidelines* are to the numbered sections of its texts.

119 See the lengthy discussion in *GIRD(2)*, 7; Joseph Masson, 'Vatican II and Post-Conciliar Theology of Evangelization,' in *Service and Salvation*, edited by Joseph Pathrapankal (Bangalore, 1973), 41-51; Kurien Kunnumpuram, *Ways of Salvation. The Salvific Meaning of Non-Christian Religions According to the Teaching of Vatican II*, (Poona, 1971) especially chapter 3. For an important dissenting voice – arguing that Vatican II and post-Conciliar documents do not legitimate pluralism or inclusivism – see D'Costa, *The Meeting of Religions and the Trinity*, chapter 4.

Non-Christian Religions at the Vatican in May 1964 was also to be of considerable importance in consolidating the new approaches initiated by the Second Vatican Council.[120]

3. *The Dialogue Commission of the CBCI*

Official encouragement to Catholics to journey along the path to dialogue has come from the deliberations and statements of the CBCI and the Federation of Asian Bishops' Conferences (FABC).[121] The meeting of the CBCI in 1960 made a number of practical recommendations about contact with other religions, especially as a means of developing the Indian character of the Church.[122] By 1966 the word 'dialogue' was firmly established in its deliberations and statements[123] and in the title of the CBCI Dialogue Commission which began in 1966 as a 'Commission for Ecumenism and Dialogue';[124] it later became the separate 'Commission for Dialogue and Relations with non-Christian Religions and Others' in 1970.[125] The Commission "promotes the spirit and practice of dialogue in the Church in India; it offers inspiration, direction and help where necessary, and is a centre for co-ordination and information about the practice of dialogue by the Church" (*GIRD(1)*, 80).

However, despite wide-ranging statements of its Commission on Dialogue,[126] a search of the Minutes of its meetings reveals that the CBCI itself gave little and often no attention to inter- faith relationships at its General Meetings. In 1970 the Commission's Chairman expressed anxiety about the imprecise definition and other difficulties of his task[127] and in 1971 the Bishops spoke not of dialogue but with concern about those theological trends (including emphases

---

120 See the large number of references to the documents of Vatican II in *GIRD(2)*, especially the lengthy section 7.

121 A helpful summary of the relevant CBCI and FABC documents is found in Jacob Parappally, 'Church's Dialogue with Cultures and Religions', *TM*, 3 (2000), 24-41.

122 *Report of the Quinquennial Meeting of the Catholic Bishops' Conference of India, 1960* (Bombay, nd), 67.

123 *Report of the General Meeting of the Catholic Bishops' Conference of India, Delhi, October 13-20, 1966* (New Delhi, 1966), 56, 59, 125-28.

124 *Report of the General Meeting ... Delhi*, 7f, 56.

125 *Report of the General Meeting of the Catholic Bishops' Conference of India, Ernakulam, January 7-16, 1970* (New Delhi, 1970), 39f.

126 Beginning with its Report in 1970; see *Report of the General Meeting ... Ernakulam*, 240-46.

127 *Report of the General Meeting ... Ernakulam*, 240.

upon personal faith and freedom of conscience and speculation about 'anonymous Christianity') which had led to diminished missionary zeal in India.[128] The 1974 meeting, as we shall see, gave considerable attention to the themes of evangelization (mainly) and also dialogue. However, a careful survey of other CBCI meetings during the 1970s indicates little consideration of inter-faith relations – which would seem to reveal as somewhat optimistic Kuttianimattathil's conclusion that the "inspiration, enthusiasm and power" of Vatican II did, in fact, "shake the Indian Church out of her inertia and come to grips with her existence in a land of religious pluralism in a realistic and meaningful way."[129]

Nonetheless, the Dialogue Commission remained active, notably because of the ability and energy of its first Secretary, Albert Nambiaparambil, but its future role seems less clear with the absorption of the Commission into the larger 'Commission for Proclamation, Ecumenism and Dialogue' (from January 1982),[130] although from April 1986 it became the 'Commission for Ecumenism and Dialogue.'[131] Mention needs also to be made of the National Biblical Catechetical and Liturgical Centre in Bangalore instituted in 1966 by the CBCI with DS Amalorpavadass (1932-1990) as its Founder-Director until 1982.[132] The Centre has pioneered inculturation and – not without controversy – has carefully drawn on some Hindu resources in doing so.[133]

4. *Four Conference Statements (1969-1974)*

A second and richer source of information about attitudes to dialogue is found in statements from four meetings held during a six year period of considerable reflection on dialogue and related themes.

---

128 *Report of the General Meeting of the Catholic Bishops' Conference of India, Bombay, April 15-16, 1971* (New Delhi, 1971), 18.

129 Kuttianimattathil, *Practice and Theology of Interreligious Dialogue*, 75.

130 'The New Commissions of the CBCI,' *WW*, 15 (1982), 140-42.

131 Details of the history, activities and publications of the Commission are found in Kuttianimattathil, *Practice and Theology of Interreligious Dialogue*, 143-61.

132 For an evaluation of Amalorpavadass see John E England, 'Watershed Figures in Asian Theology 8: DS Amalorpavadass (1932-1990),' *PTCA Bulletin*, 6.1 (April 1993), 6-9.

133 Some analysis is found in Gerwin van Leeuwen, *Fully Indian, Authentically Christian: a Study of the First Fifteen Years of the NBCLC (1967-1983)* (Bangalore: NBCLC and Kampen: JH Koch, 1990).

(a) The Declaration of the 'All-India Seminar on the Church in India Today' held in Bangalore, 15-25 May, 1969.[134] The Seminar had been preceded by a number of regional studies and was attended by a much higher proportion of lay delegates than the other three meetings to be considered; for that reason the Bangalore Declaration may be the most representative of the attitude of the Indian church as a whole.[135]

(b) The Declaration of the 'International Theological Conference on Evangelization and Dialogue in India', Nagpur, 6-12 October, 1971.[136] About 100 delegates attended, mostly theologians, and there is greater theological precision than in the Bangalore Declaration.[137]

(c) The Declaration of the 'All-India Consultation on Evangelization', Patna, 3-8 October, 1973.[138] This Consultation was attended by 332 delegates involved in missionary and pastoral work.

(d) The Communication of the CBCI to the Roman Synod in 1974.[139]

---

134 The Declaration, to be referred to as the Bangalore Declaration, is found in *All India Seminar*, 239-47. See also *Ever Ancient, Ever New: A Report on the All India Seminar on the Church in India, May 15-25, 1969* (New Delhi, 1969); and *Orientation Papers, All India Seminar on the Church in India Today* (New Delhi, 1969).

135 See 'General Impressions of the Seminar,' *All India Seminar*, 544f, and Tarcy Mascarenhas, 'The All-India Seminar on the Church in India – An Analysis,' *IES*, 8 (1969), 152-70.

136 The Declaration, to be referred to as the Nagpur Declaration, is found in *Service and Salvation*, 1-16; references are to the section numbers of the Declaration. Another anthology and analysis is found in *Evangelisation, Dialogue and Development: Papers Presented to the International Theological Conference at Nagpur in 1971*, edited by Mariasusai Dhavamony (Rome, 1972).

137 See Pathrapankal in *Service and Salvation*, v; James Dupuis, 'Nagpur International Theological Conference,' *CM*, 35 (1971), 458-73; Clement Godwin, 'The First International Theological Conference on Evangelization and Dialogue in Asia, with Special Reference to the Indian Context,' *Verbum SVD*, 13 (1972), 276-89; Walbert Bühlmann, *The Search for God* (Maryknoll, NY, 1979), 86-97; Emprayil, *The Emerging Theology of Religions*, 33-36.

138 The Declaration, to be referred to as the Patna Declaration, is found in *Light and Life We Seek to Share* (Bangalore, 1973), 368-85; references are to the section numbers of the Declaration.

139 The CBCI Communication, as we shall call it, is found in *Report of the General Meeting of the Catholic Bishops' Conference of India, Calcutta, January*

Of the many subjects discussed in these statements one seems to have contributed significantly to interest in dialogue: the perceived need for the Church in India to become more deeply Indian in its whole life.[140] The Nagpur Declaration attributes the widening vision to the growing confidence of a church with a clearer understanding of its own identity (11).[141] The Patna Declaration also sees "the greater appreciation of the religions and cultures of our country" as a sign of growth within the Church (3). In the CBCI Communication there are a number of forceful statements about the way in which "the Church in India must realise her genuine Indian identity" (12; see also 14, 15). The quest for such identity was facilitated by the presence of a growing number of Indian teachers in Catholic theological faculties and seminaries;[142] and by the greater leadership role assumed by Indian Catholics.

The influence of the more open attitude to other faiths encouraged by Vatican II was often mentioned at the Nagpur Conference[143] and the Patna Consultation,[144] but only briefly in the statements issued.[145]

Although the pragmatic considerations of increased inter-religious understanding and inter-communal harmony are briefly mentioned,[146] greater emphasis is given to the belief that "dialogue between Christians and Hindus will bring about a mutual spiritual enrichment and make possible a real collaboration in tasks of com-

---

6-14, 1974 (New Delhi, 1974), 124-40. References are to the section numbers of the Communication.

140 Karokaran, *Evangelization and Diakonia*, 138; see also Bangalore Declaration, 241 and 244.

141 This growing confidence is reflected in the extensive publicity given to the Nagpur Seminar and its findings by comparison with the conditions of considerable secrecy in which the Bombay Conference had been held seven years earlier. Because it is located in a country notable for its religious pluralism, the "Church in India is called upon to be an earnest pioneer of inter-religious dialogue" (52) – but the document makes no comment about the centuries of inactivity in terms of dialogue.

142 According to Gispert-Sauch, "from the late 60s to the present ... very often the most radical thinking in favour of positive appreciation of Hinduism has come from the young Indian teachers and professors – people like Amaladoss, Pathiadan, Panikkar, D'Souza, Pearl Drego, Amalorpavadass, T.K. John etc." (personal communication, 23 March 1983).

143 See *Service and Salvation, passim; Evangelization, Dialogue and Development, passim*

144 See *Light and Life, passim.*

145 For example, Nagpur Declaration, 12.

146 Patna Declaration, 40; see also *GIRD(2)*, 34.

mon concern."[147] Because of her location in a country notable for its religious pluralism, "the Church in India is called upon to be an earnest pioneer of inter-religious dialogue."[148] To the extent that the *Guidelines* and the four statements accurately reflect the collective thinking of the Indian Church they do document the growing concern for dialogue with Hindus.

5. *Two Decades of Consolidation*

The decades of the 1980s and 1990s saw the consolidation of the commitment to dialogue. A number of examples from within India (and a few from beyond) might be used to illustrate this continuing concern. In 1984, the Bishops recommend that educational institutions have a staff member responsible for organising dialogue; and, "as the laity are most in contact with people of other faiths, they should be specially trained to become the main agents for dialogue."[149] The same emphasis upon lay initiatives and responsibility in dialogue is repeated two years later.[150] The Papal visit to India in 1986 also saw the requirement of humble loving dialogue underlined.[151] The 'Charter of Priestly Formation for India', approved in 1988, and a related document the following year, both affirm that experience of dialogue and christological reflection on it should form part of the theological formation.[152] A revised edition of the *Guidelines for Inter-Religious Dialogue*[153]was published in 1989 and further illustrates the movement towards dialogue in official Indian Catholic circles. (Both this document and the Apostolic Exhortation *Ecclesia in Asia* (1999) will be discussed in chapter 4 below.)

Two further documents well illustrate a degree of interest in dialogue by the Indian Catholic Church into the 1990s. The Statement of the 'National Consultation on Mission in India Today'[154] reported

---

147 Patna Declaration, 38; see also Bangalore Declaration, 243f.

148 CBCI Communication, 52.

149 *Report of the General Meeting of the Catholic Bishops' Conference of India, Nagpur, February, 1984* (New Delhi, [nd]), 135.

150 *Report of the General Meeting of the Catholic Bishops' Conference of India (Goa, April 1986)* (New Delhi, [nd]), 71f.

151 The text of the pertinent remarks is found in *BSPNC*, 21 (1986), 123-42.

152 See *Report of the General Meeting of the Catholic Bishops' Conference of India (Shillong, November 1989)* (New Delhi, [nd]), 24-39.

153 Second revised edition (New Delhi: CBCI Centre, 1989).

154 See 'Statement of the CBCI Consultation on Mission, Ishvani Kendra, Pune, 4-9 January, 1994', *ITS*, 31 (1994), 74-98; reference in the text to the numbered paragraphs of the Statement.

the results of a survey of some 1500 priests and 3800 sisters that found that about twenty percent of them "either organised or participated in interreligious dialogue and prayer during the past year" (12). Proclamation and dialogue are both seen as an integral part of mission (51). Dialogue is not a matter of the mere exchange of views "but a specific mode of being and way of life" (56). However, it should also be noted that annual meeting of the (mainly Catholic) Indian Theological Association in 1999 saw interreligious relations as both problematical and hopeful. Only one of the meeting Statement's 33 paragraphs mentions dialogue and then only to speak of the church's "genuine contribution" in "India's experiment with multi-religiosity and multi-culturalism." But it also added that "many joint ventures with other religious bodies could be planned and undertaken." Reconsideration of previous positions and attitudes would help and "the maintaining of institutions and service-centres with multi-religious co-responsibility would help."[155]

F. Comment

On the Christian side of the encounter some of the changes have been traced that, especially since the end of the nineteenth century among some Protestants and more recently in Roman Catholic circles, have led to interest in dialogue. In both cases there has been not only a growing reluctance to claim what previous generations had regarded as the doctrinal and ethical superiority of Christianity – and at times asserted with impatience or contempt – but also an increasing readiness to consider Hinduism in positive terms and to talk of increased understanding and co-operation and even of mutual spiritual enrichment (and discussion will return to this issue in chapter 3 below). Within 'mainstream' Christian circles there has been a declining confidence in (or, perhaps, a redefinition of) the uniqueness of the Christian message and the urgency (or even desirability) of evangelism. By the early 1990s the 'progressive' wing of Indian Protestantism was sure that even the notions of fulfilment and inclusivism were outmoded and in need of replacement by a theocentric non-normative pluralism[156] and there have been

155 'Hope at the Dawn of the 21st Century. Statement of the Indian Theological Association, Twenty-second Annual Meeting, April 24-29, 1999, Ishvani Kendram Pune,' *ITS*, 36 (1999), 354-65; quotes from paragraph 31.

156 See, for example, KC Abraham, 'Paradigm Shift in Contemporary Theological Thinking,' *BTF*, 24.3-4 (Sept – Dec 1992), 53-61.

related shifts within Indian Catholicism.[157] These shift have, in part, been caused by a growing awareness of the profound cultural and nationalist implications of an increasingly self-confident Hinduism. There had, of course, been discussion (and controversy) between Christians and Hindus in the period before the mid-twentieth century. However, since this coincided with the period of colonial rule and virtually unfettered missionary enterprise, "conversations ... were seldom between equal partners."[158]

Also noteworthy has been the attention given in Christian circles to neo-Hinduism; this seems to have been the result of its apparently better informed and more sympathetic response to Christianity and perhaps also because its literature has been considerable, and in English, and consequently more accessible than the smaller volume of relevant works from more conservative Hindu circles. In fact, during the past 150 years the level of mutually sympathetic Hindu-Christian contact has been much higher in the large cosmopolitan centres, especially Calcutta, Bombay and Madras, than in the rest of India. It was been in the cities that nationalism, western values and reformed and reforming neo-Hinduism made the greatest impression and facilitated contact between Hindus and sympathetic missionaries engaged in urban or higher educational work and their educated Indian Christian colleagues. But a decidedly narrow view of the Hindu-Christian encounter would be gained if attention were restricted to these predominantly urban contacts.

On the Hindu side too there have been changing attitudes. Within what is called the Hindu renascence (perhaps best understood as a continuing reality, and including those Hindus discussed in section B above) three major streams are discernible – each with potentially positive implications for dialogue with Christianity: theistic (for example, Ram Mohun Roy), non-dualistic (including Vivekananda and Radhakrishnan), and social-reformist (including Gandhi and many in the first two categories). The theists could – and do – speak confidently about God (often described in personal terms) as the object of rational belief and socially- responsible worship, sometimes in *bhakti* categories, and with a highly sympathetic response to Jesus. The advaitins could – and do – emphasise the virtues of tolerance and acceptance of the essential unity of the religions, but often in such a way as to place non-dualism at a higher level than other approaches to the Absolute, including the personal

157 As a survey of, say, *Vidyajyoti* during the 1960s – 1990s will make clear.

158 EJ Sharpe, 'Dialogue of Religions,' in *Encyclopedia of Religions*, Mircea Eliade, Editor in Chief (New York, 1987), volume 4, 345.

theism of Christianity. And the social reformers could – and do – acknowledge that, in part at least, the example or criticism of Christian institutions and missionaries has motivated their activities. But, with some exceptions (for example, the approach of Ram Mohun Roy), the responses were often either defensive or aggressive in the face of critical Christian comment. As Neufeldt concludes from his survey, "dialogue is a less frequent factor than are polemics and apologetics in Hindu Renaissance responses to Christianity."[159] Undoubtedly the dynamics of an imperial and colonial context affected the encounter in an inevitably negative way. Perhaps, as an Indian Christian rather poignantly asks:

> Had the Christ of the Gospels been introduced to India in a context of equality and freedom, and had the meaning of the cross and the dimensions of love been presented in a different manner, more positively and respectfully, would there not have been a wider, deeper, more beautiful response?[160]

Hindu misgivings about the more recent but somewhat novel Christian approach in terms of dialogue are not surprising. These (and other) Hindu responses, including the militantly aggressive response of nationalistic Hinduism, are discussed in some detail in the chapters that follow. But before they are considered, a critical analysis of the meaning, means and supposed justification of such dialogue will be undertaken.

Appendix. Meetings of the 'Circle'.

Details of and reflections upon its meetings are found as follows:

(i) At Almora, April 1961: see Abhishiktananda, *Hindu-Christian Meeting Point*, revised edition (Delhi, 1976), 12-18.

(ii) At Rajpur, April 1962: Bede Griffiths, 'Meeting at Rajpur', *CMS*, 6 (1962-1963), 137-55; Abhishiktananda, *Hindu-Christian Meeting Point*, 18-25.

(iii) At Delhi, April 1963: Abhishiktananda, *Hindu-Christian Meeting Point*, 26-32. (This was a small group preparing for the following meeting.)

(iv) At Nagpur, December 1963 – January 1964: Abhishiktananda, *Hindu-Christian Meeting Point*, 32-45 and, *passim*, in the remaining chapters, 5-8.

---

159 Ronald Neufeldt, 'The Response of the Hindu Renaissance to Christianity,' in *H-CD*, 42.

160 Samuel Rayan, 'Hindu Perceptions of Christ in the Nineteenth Century,' 22.

(v) At Jyotiniketan Ashram, Uttar Pradesh, April 1964: Mary Kalapesi, 'Some Reflections on the Fourth Meeting on Hindu and Christian Spirituality at Jyotiniketan Ashram, April 1964', *RS*, 11.4 (December 1964), 71-76; Klaus Klostermaier, 'Einübung des Inneren Zwiegesprächs', *Kairos*, 7 (1965), 54-61; and *ITD*, 2-5.

Further comments on the meetings are found in C Murray Rogers, 'Hindu and Christian – A Moment Breaks', *RS*, 12.1 (March 1965), 37-39.

CHAPTER 2

The Meaning and Practice of Christian-Hindu Dialogue

A. The Informal Encounter

Although this study gives particular attention to the formal Hindu-Christian dialogue, much of the actual encounter between Hindus and Christians is, of course, necessarily informal in character. Many of the Hindu and Christian writers cited in the last chapter are examples of a kind of informal dialogue: there was rather little by way of formal meeting but considerable interaction of the two worldviews – and sometimes with the person of Jesus as the catalyst.[1] There are many situations in India where informal dialogue has long been an established reality made possible and often inevitable by the proximity of neighbours of differing faiths.

1. The Realities of Informal Dialogue

The scholarly discussion of dialogue has not given as much attention to informal and incidental aspects of the encounter as to the formal. Such informal dialogue often amounts to an implicit though unstructured meeting of aspects of the Hindu and Christian worldviews but too often discussion of the Hindu-Christian encounter is confined to the meeting of what has been called the elite traditions of the two faiths. In a study of what he calls the "popular religious consciousness" of Hinduism in Kerala, Ayrookuzhiel notes the large number of ways in which this consciousness diverges from classical understandings of the Hindu tradition and he goes on to comment that the Christian approach to dialogue with Hinduism has relied too heavily on the written and historical aspects of each faith, "forgetting that dialogue has to take place between people

1 Thomas, *The Acknowledged Christ of the Indian Renaissance*, Samartha, *The Hindu Response to the Unbound Christ* and Jacques Dupuis, *Jesus Christ at the Encounter of World Religions*, (Et: Maryknoll, NY: Orbis Books, 1991), 15-45.

based on their living experience in these traditions".[2] Another experienced observer confesses to being "astounded by the extent to which attempts to document and understand the encounter ... have concentrated almost exclusively on the interaction of the classical theological and philosophical elements [of the two faiths]." But, as he also points out, these elite traditions do not reflect the reality of the religious faith and practice of the great majority who see themselves as Hindus and Christians in India.[3] Theirs is a complex cultural intermingling and the continuity of traditional (Hindu) culture into the lives of the usually minority Christians is one that has received a certain amount of attention.[4] For Christians, this dual world (as it might be called) includes simultaneous participation in two religious traditions, especially in the necessities of village society. It constitutes a constant, unintended but unavoidable double belonging. In particular, it is at what Hiebert calls the "middle level"[5]of the Indian worldview – the level of daily pragmatic decision making, the level of relating to spirits, ancestors and fateful events – that the continuities with Hinduism are likely to be greatest, and hence replete with the realities of informal dialogue. For this reason, academics and others who limit themselves to what fellow academics and a literate elite say in formal exchanges – or say about such formal encounters – miss the vast contribution of what non-academic Hindus and Christians, speaking simply "from faith

---

2 AM Abraham Ayrookuzhiel, 'The Living Hindu Popular Religious Consciousness and Some Reflections on it in the Context of Hindu-Christian Dialogue,' *RS*, 26.1 (March 1979), 23f. He goes on to argue for dialogue at those points of growth that centre upon certain people and movements in popular Hinduism.

3 David C Scott, 'Forest and Village: Popular Hindu-Christian Encounter,' *HCSB*, 9 (1996), 36.

4 Carl Gustav Diehl, *Church and Shrine. Intermingling Patterns of Culture in the Life of Some Christian Groups in South India* (Uppsala, 1965); PY Luke and JB Carman, *Village Christians and Hindu Culture* (London, 1968); S Estborn, *Our Village Christians. A Study of the Life and Faith of Village Christians in Tamil Nadu* (Madras: Christian Literature Society, 1969); P Solomon Raj, *A Christian Folk Religion in India* (Frankfurt am Main: Peter Lang, 1986). There are also some useful comments in John B Carman, 'Continuing Tasks in Inter-Religious Dialogue,' *ER*, 22 (1970), 207f. For some studies from the perspective of the social sciences see the bibliography provided in Scott, 'Forest and Village,' 40, n 12.

5 Paul G Hiebert, 'The Flaw of the Excluded Middle,' *Missiology*, 10 (1982), 35-47; Hiebert's study centres on India and Indian worldviews.

to faith," have learnt in their informal dialogue.[6] The most common forms of the Hindu-Christian encounter are, then, the most prosaic: the everyday meetings and the unavoidable cultural immersions of life of which conversation itself is perhaps the most basic. The "very use of the word dialogue [in its formal sense] often indicates that ... ordinary conversation has broken down or not even started."[7]

One example of informal dialogue is ordinary friendship. Sustained friendship is both a means of and one of many conditions for fruitful dialogue: "nothing less than a setting of intimate friendship, the growth of many years contact, is necessary for serious personal dialogue," and by comparison with which the value of meetings on inter-faith dialogue can be said to be strictly marginal.[8] Friendship can, in fact, be seen as a hermeneutical key for interreligious understanding.[9]

2. Double Belonging

As well as simultaneous participation in the two religious traditions, marriage between Christians and Hindus offers another example of informal even if somewhat 'enforced' dialogue – often with its own tensions.[10] The lives of the children of such partnerships can contain elements of the 'double-belonging' that in itself constitutes a form of implicit dialogue between the two faiths. The revised second edition of the official Catholic *Guidelines for Inter-Religious Dialogue* points out that "inter-faith marriages offer a unique situation for an inter-religious dialogue in depth" (*GIRD(2)*, 108. Such marriage is not as frequent in India as it is in other parts of Asia (Sri Lanka, for example) and it is discouraged in protestant

---

6 Robert D Baird, 'Academic Study and the Phenomena of Dialogue,' *HCSB*, 3 (1996), 7-11.

7 JE Lesslie Newbigin, 'Confessing Christ in a Multi-Religion Society,' *SBET*, 12 (1994), 132.

8 C Murray Rogers, 'Inter-Faith Dialogue,' 240; see also DG Moses, 'Some Reflections on Personal Dialogue,' *AF*, 5 (1970), 249-51; Warren, *ATA*, 54f; James L Fredericks, 'Interreligious Friendship: a New Theological Virtue,' *JES*, 35 (1998), 159-74.

9 The first of the three lectures by Daniel O'Connor, *Relations in Religion* (New Delhi: Allied Publishers, 1994) on what can be done to heal the "deep crisis in relations between religions" (xi) is on such friendship.

10 See, for example, Astrid Lobo Gajiwala on her Christian-Hindu marriage: 'My Marriage is Not a Sacrament,' in *Frontiers in Asian Christian Theology*, edited by R Sugirtharajah (Maryknoll, NY: Orbis Books, 1994), 161-78 and 'The Spirit of Dialogue,' *VJTR*, 58 (1994), 485-95.

circles (vigorously among conservative protestants) but in those situations where it does occur the mere fact of the occurrence may itself indicate a diminished consciousness of communal and religious consciousness.[11] Double belonging is a phenomenon whose study might yield interesting conclusions about the nature of and issues raised in dialogue at an everyday level.[12] Another complex phenomenon is 'churchless Christianity' (perhaps better called 'indigenous Christ-centred movements')[13] and, at least in India, it can imply a measure of dual religious identity and can be regarded as another example of informal Hindu-Christian dialogue. As Felix Wilfred points out, there may well be millions of such implicit admirers and even followers of Jesus Christ in Asia who do not belong to the visible church:

> Thousands of such people frequent our churches, assist at our religious services, and visit our shrines and pilgrimage centres. Many of them claim to have experienced Jesus Christ in their lives, and others have tried to interpret him.[14]

11 It is disappointing that the lengthy study by Joseph A Fonseca, *Marriage in India in a Christian Perspective: a Historical Social Theological Investigation* (Bangalore: Redemptorist Publications India, 1988) has only a brief section on 'Mixed Marriages' (242-44) and that deals with both interchurch and interreligious marriages – and with virtually no analysis or discussion of an issue that affects many Christians.

12 Such a study could usefully be modelled on a parallel study: Peter Gottschalk, *Beyond Hindu and Muslim. Multiple Identities from Village India* (Oxford: Oxford University Press, 2000). (Gottschalk's study does contain a few interesting references to Christians.)

13 See Herbert E Hoefer, *Churchless Christianity* (Madras: APATS and Gurukul Lutheran Theological College and Research Institute, 1991; a new and expanded edition (Pasadena, CA: William Carey Library) is scheduled for 2001). Hoefer believes that from the dual participation by unbaptised Christian believers a "'Christ-ized' Hinduism is emerging in India (207-09). Two shorter studies are by MM Thomas, 'The Church – the Fellowship of the Baptised and the Unbaptised?' in *Liberating Witness: Dr K Rajaratnam's Platinum Birth Anniversary Commemoration*, volume 1, edited by Prasanna Kumar (Madras: Gurukul Lutheran Theological College and Research Institute, 1995), 8-15, and Julian Saldanha, 'Unbaptised Disciples of Christ?', *TM*, 1 (1998), 20-27, who links the phenomenon to the work of the *Logos*.

14 Felix Wilfred, 'Images of Jesus Christ in the Asian Pastoral Context: an Interpretation of Documents from the Federation of Asian Bishops' Conferences', *Concilium*, 1993, no. 2, 58. See also the observations of Kathleen Healy, 'Christ beyond Christianity: Jesus Christ, the Hindu and the Church!', chapter 2 of her *Christ as Common Ground: A Study of*

3. *Literature and Art*

Certain forms of communication may also contribute, both positively and negatively, to informal and implicit dialogue. Films cannot help but touch on religious themes at times[15]- though debate will continue about the role of cinema as a moulder rather than a reflection of community values and religious opinions, especially opinions about religious and other minorities. Indian newspapers, magazines and novels do the same as does the rich Indian traditions of poetry[16] and other literature.[17] Some have suggested that this form of implicit discursive dialogue be harnessed for good. Devanandan, for example, considered that inter-communal and other misrepresentation would be less frequent or less damaging were there to be a better informed public opinion; to this end he called for "a determined effort through helpful literature to create in the minds of people informed respect for other faiths".[18]

The visual arts constitute another rich example of potential reli-

---

Christianity and Hinduism (Pittsburgh, PA: Duquesne University Press, 1990). The issue of *intentional* double belonging is one to which discussion will return below; see chapter 4.C.3.

15 See, for example, the surveys by Prabhu Guptara, 'Religion Has Shaped Indian Film,' *NCCR*, 102 (1982), 358-68; and TK Thomas, 'The Christian Image in Hindi Films,' *NCCR*, 93 (1973), 381-83; see also Christopher Coelho, 'How Hindus Filmed the Life of Christ,' *Vidyajyoti*, 48 (1984), 383-87.

16 For a discussion of nationalist poets writing about Christ, see Prema Nandakumar, 'Two Nationalist Poets in Jesus Christ', *HCSB*, 8 (1995), 38-41.

17 See, for example, Varkey, 'The Image of Christianity in the Newspapers,' *IMR*, 9 (1987), 241-59, and the many examples (especially from Hindi novels and newspapers) in Roger H Hooker, *Themes in Hinduism and Christianity: a Comparative Study* (Frankfurt am Main, 1989). Hooker has also written *The Quest of Ajneya. A Christian Theological Appraisal of the Search for Meaning in His Three Hindi Novels* (Delhi: Motilal Banarsidass, 1998).

18 *Preparation for Dialogue* (Bangalore, 1964), 129; see also 131. See also: Lederle, 'Discovery of Dialogue,' 1979, 70; John B Chethimattam, 'The Scope and Conditions of a Hindu-Christian Dialogue,' *Concilium* 3.1 (March 1965), 87.

gious and cultural dialogue, albeit in an informal manner.[19] For example, Hindu and not Indian Christian artists initiated Indian Christian art in the sense of paintings of Christ.[20] In fact, as Samartha notes,

> India might be the only place where persons of other faiths, without crossing over the visible boundaries that separate them from Christians, have related themselves to Jesus Christ through art. ... [Through art] Jesus Christ seems to move beyond the structures of the church ... in order to establish new relationships with adherents of other faiths. There seems to be an "unbaptized *koinonia* [fellowship]" outside the gates, which the church is most reluctant to recognise or even talk about.[21]

Jyoti Sahi provides an example of the intentional promotion of creative inculturation by means of paintings, buildings, books and articles.[22] Lederle sees the publishing enterprise that he helped to

---

19 See Mathew Lederle, 'Interpreting Christ through Indian Art,' *IJT*, 23 (1974), 232-41; 'Christian Themes in Indian Painting,' *Vidyajyoti*, 47 (1983), 390-97; and *Christian Painting in India through the Centuries* (Anand, 1986). See also Klostermaier, 'Hindu-Christian Dialogue – its Religious and Cultural Implications,' *SR/SR*, 1 (1967), 96); Richard W Taylor, *Interpretations of Jesus in Indian Painting* (Madras, 1975); 'Communication Through Art Forms,' *NCCR*, 100 (1980), 631-39; Herbert E Hoefer, editor, *Christian Art in India* (Madras: Gurukul Publications, 1981); Kathleen Nicholls, 'Christ in Indian Painting,' *TRACI Journal*, no. 21 (1981), 9-18; Gottfried Rothermundt, 'Umstrittene indische christliche Kunst,' *ZMR*, 66 (1982), 8-16; John F Butler, *Christian Art in India* (Madras, 1986) – though Butler's study is disappointingly thin in terms of interaction with or the influence of the Hindu context; Caroline MacKenzie, 'Art and Architectecture as Locus for Dialogue: Inter-Religious Dialogue through Art.' *HCSB*, 4 (1991), 31-34.

20 See Samartha, *One Christ – Many Religions*, 89-91.

21 Stanley J Samartha, 'The Cross and the Rainbow: Christ in a Multireligious Culture,' in *Asian Faces of Jesus*, edited by RS Sugirtharajah (Maryknoll, NY: Orbis, 1993), 117f. Samartha gives a number of further examples of this inter-religious 'border-crossing' on pp 356-62 of his 'Religion, Language and Reality. Towards a Relational Hermeneutics', *Biblical Interpretation*, 2 (1994).

22 Some of his more recent writings include *The Child and the Serpent: Reflections on Popular Indian Symbols* (London: Routledge and Kegan Paul, 1980); 'Trends of Indigenisation and Social Justice in Indian Christian Art,' *IJT*, 31 (1982), 89-95; 'Jesus Christ in Indian Art,' *KJ*, 1 (1984), 4-10; *Stepping Stones: Reflections on the Theology of Indian Christian Culture* (Bangalore: ATC, 1986); 'Myth, Story and Symbol as Revelation', in *Emerging India and the Word of God*, edited by Paul Pathanangady (Bangalore: National

form, 'Art India', as a means by which Indian Christian artists, may "be in dialogue with their cultural traditions".[23] Architecture and the notion of 'holy ground' also have implications for dialogue. Jyoti Sahi calls for the architecture of churches and ashrams to express the spiritual implications of the church's mission in multi-cultural India; and this can have a critical edge to it: "the church building must not only ground a community in its past but should also act as a sign of liberation from former systems of oppression."[24]

4. The Study of Religion

It is sometimes suggested that study of or research into one religion by a member of another is an implicit form of dialogue. Dialogue can also be seen as a method for the study of religion.[25] But usually such study is seen as a desirable precondition for dialogue or an accompaniment of it. A Hindu academic, for example, writes of the necessity of ensuring that dialogue is conducted in a spirit of trust, sympathy and appreciation and, for this, "one principal condition is the promotion of the academic study of religions".[26] As an accompaniment of dialogue the academic study of religion is said to be necessary in order to avoid superficiality and to realise the com-

---

Biblical, Catechetical and Liturgical Centre, 1991), 299-315; 'Search for the Spiritual in Art in the Context of Inter-Faith Harmony', in *Shabda, Shakti, Sangam*, edited by Vandana Mataji (Rishikesh: Vandana Mataji, 1995), [Christian section], 409-12; 'Cosmaos and Primal Permanence', in *Re-visioning India's Religious Traditions: Essays in Honour of Eric Lott*, edited by David C Scott and Israel Selvanayagam (Delhi: ISPCK, 1996), 155-71; 'Some Reflections on the Relation of Art to the Mission of the Church from an Indian Perspective', in *Culture, Religion and Society: Essays in Honour of Richard W Taylor*, edited by Saral K Chatterji and Hunter P Mabry (Delhi: ISPCK, 1996), 41-55; *Holy Ground. A New Approach to the Mission of the Church in India* (Auckland: Pace Publishing, 1998); and with P Middleton, *Adisthan: Sacred Space, Indian Christian Ventures* (Bangalore: NBCLC, 1993). See also Sebastian Elavathingal, 'The Theology of the Unfolding Image in Jyoti Sahi's Art,' *TM*, 1 (1998), 26-36.

23 'Discovery of Dialogue,' 71.

24 *Holy Ground*, 176.

25 See Klaus K Klostermaier, 'Interreligious Dialogue as a Method for the Study of Religion,' *JES*, 21 (1984), 755-59.

26 Santosh Sengupta, 'On the Understanding of Other Religions,' in *DBM*, 91f (quotation from 92).

plexity and depth of the issues raised.[27] The academic study of religion is one means by which the circle of those engaging in Hindu-Christian dialogue could be expanded.[28] The formation of the Society for Hindu-Christian Studies in November 1994 (following the appearance of the *Hindu-Christian Studies Bulletin* in 1988) may also make a modest contribution to informal dialogue. Its 'Statement of Purpose' declares that one of its aims is "the fostering of dialogue and interreligious conversation, carried forward in a spirit of openness, respect and true inquiry."[29] This might not greatly widen the circle of those involved in dialogue but could still be considered a "necessary luxury" in the context of religious pluralism.[30] An interesting and not unrelated possibility is that Protestant Bible translation in India has been an unrecognised but implicit form of dialogue.[31] Nonetheless even the study of religion is not necessarily a value-free exercise; Samartha raises the possibility of a link between what he calls the "Northern research industry" and neo-colonialist enterprises in the South.[32]

Actual centres for this study of and reflection on other faiths are said to be essential for dialogue[33] and existing institutions for religious education are among the obvious places for such study and

---

27 Lederle, 'Discovery of Dialogue,' 70f. See also *GIRD(2)*, 80f; Aloysius Pieris, 'The Legitimacy and the Limitations of the Academic Approach to Inter-faith Dialogue,' *Dialogue*, ns,1 (1974), 39-43; Mariasusai Dhavamony, 'Scientific Study of Religions and Dialogue,' *BSPNC*, 10 (1975), 319-27; Stanley J Samartha, '*More* than an Encounter of Commitments,' *IRM*, 59 (1970), 392.

28 Carman, 'Continuing Tasks,' 205. But for a somewhat dissenting voice (arguing that engaged "dialogue in depth" and the detached academic study of religion are methodologically incompatible and cannot be engaged in simultaneously) see Baird, 'Hindu-Christian Dialogue and the Academic Study of Religion,' 221-23.

29 As found at the internet site the Society maintains at: <http//www.acusd.edu/theo/hcs-1>

30 So argues Francis X Clooney, 'Hindu-Christian Studies as a Necessary Luxury in the Context of Today's Pluralism,' *HCSB*, 7 (1994), 39-44.

31 See John B Carman, 'Protestant Bible Translations in India: An Unrecognized Dialogue?,' *HCSB*, 4 (1991), 11-20 (with comment: 21-25).

32 Stanley J Samartha, *One Christ – Many Religions*, 40. He also raises the question of "why the North feels so compelled to study Southern religions when the people being studied feel so little interest in studying the religions of the North" (41). This seems to suggest that Christianity is a religion of the 'North' – a difficult conclusion to sustain given that more Christians live in the 'South' than in the 'North'.

33 Lederle, 'Discovery of Dialogue,' 71.

research.[34] One seminary – Dharmaram College, Bangalore – established The Centre for the Study of World Religions in August 1971 "as a forum for dialogue and encounter" between individuals from different world religions. It invites Hindu scholars to participate in its teaching, research and consultation. The Centre also publishes the *Journal of Dharma*.[35] The hope has also been expressed that Indian universities might also expand their limited number of courses in Religious Studies and thereby contribute to inter-religious understanding.[36]

5. *Co-operative Endeavour*

The form of dialogue sometimes called 'secular dialogue'[37] has clear implications about the means by which it might occur. Sharing in the common task of community-building has immediate and daily consequences "in neighbourhood, market place, office, workshop, clubs and centres of learning" – places where the Christian partner in dialogue is to show openness and friendliness and to have "a keen sense of the religious values that inspire the lives" of fellow Indians.[38] For Christian organisations dialogue should extend to cooperation with religious and other groups in order to foster open and fraternal community relations.[39] Nambiaparambil reports a favourable response to multi-religious panels organised in 12 centres on the topic of 'Values in a Fast-changing World', adding that discussion on religion itself is avoided.[40] For Christian institutions

34 See J Russell Chandran, 'Christian Contribution to Religious Dialogue,' *IMA*, 3.2 (May 1972), 74; The *Commissio Technica* for Seminaries, *Programme of Priestly Formation for India* (Delhi, 1970), 48-50; and *GIRD(2)*, 80f. The *Guidelines* mentions 'Faculties and Departments of Philosophy and Theology along with the wish that these institutions "could offer scholarships and guidance to members of other religions so that they can do research on Christian topics" (81).

35 See 'Chronicle,' *JD*, 1 (1975), 160. In 1977 a 'Centre for Indian and Interreligious Studies' was established in Rome as an extension of the Bangalore Centre.

36 For example, Chandran, 'Christian Contribution to Religious Dialogue,' 74.

37 For a definition and discussion of 'secular dialogue' see sections C.2 and E.2 below.

38 *GIRD(2)*, 70. See also Abhishiktananda, *The Church in India Today*, 270f.

39 *GIRD(2)*, 72. De Souza also discusses "the activities best suited to practical dialogue"; see his 'Dialogue Between Religions in India,' 87f.

40 Albert Nambiaparambil, 'India,' in *Mission in Dialogue*, edited by Mary Motte and Joseph R Lang (Maryknoll, NY, 1982), 414.

this dialogue in action will include cooperation with Government and other agencies (*GIRD(2)*, 69, 71). The possibility is raised that, in the name of dialogue, medical, educational and social work projects that have hitherto been established separately might be re-established as joint Hindu-Christian enterprises.[41] And there is even the suggestion that in the supposed commonality of healing sessions at a village level as led both by traditional Hindu healers and Christian charismatics there might be a foundation for Hindu-Christian dialogue.[42]

6. *Gatherings and Organisations*

As well as the meeting of individuals, larger organised gatherings can also enable informal dialogue and a number of groups, action groups and associations have been established with this in mind.[43] The Catholic *Guidelines* notes occasions when members of different religions will meet simply to discuss human problems in the light of religious values and experiences; for such occasions scholarly knowledge is said to be less important than simply seeking to learn how others live out their faith (*GIRD(2)*, 76f).

Official ecclesiastical endorsement has also been given to participation in existing religious, semi-religious and inter-religious associations (*GIRD(2)*, 72, 96). In 1981 the Dialogue Commission of the CBCI sponsored a 'World Conference of Religions', in Kerala, to which some 223 delegates (some from outside India) were invited.[44] Co-operation with organisations such as the Gandhian ashrams is encouraged (*GIRD(2)*, 72) and Christians are reported as closely linked with the founding of a number of inter-religious associations.[45]

---

41 'Religious Resources for a Just Society,' 17.

42 See Joseph Velamkunnel, 'The Healing Mission and Interreligious Dialogue,' *VJTR*, 63 (1999), 351-60; however, it must be said that the author seems to underestimate the problems and resistance such an enterprise might face (especially from more conservative Christians) – though the issue of healing might form a fruitful topic for discussion.

43 See Kuttianimattathil, *Practice and Theology of Interreligious Dialogue*, 96-100. For one specific example see: T Amaldass, 'Fellowship for the Promotion of Inter-Community Living in a Pluralistic Society,' *RS*, 26.1 (March 1979), 73-77.

44 See 'A Meeting of Religions,' *NCCR*, 102 (1982), 12-16.

45 See, for example, the report in *NCCR*, 99 (1979), 51f. (Reports of such gatherings also appear regularly in *BPCD* and *HCSB*.)

7. Participation in Festivals and Worship

The realities of joint participation by Hindus and Christians in the worship and festivals of the other is well known and interesting (or confused) religious accommodations seem to be made as a result. Dempsey, for example, draws attention not only to mutual participation (including a Hindu medium transmitting for a deceased Catholic nun) but provides examples of considerable dependence (for example Hindu festivals supposedly dependent upon Catholic or Orthodox blessing for success).[46] Lederle lists feasts, requests for blessings at ceremonies, natural calamities, weddings between Hindu and Christian partners and para-liturgical events, as occasions for "inter-religious prayer meetings … where a dialogue situation exists".[47]

8. Some Results of this Informal Dialogue

Some of the results are obvious – for example an enhanced understanding of the other, despite the misunderstanding and stereotypes that remain. But other consequences of the implicit meeting of the two worldviews are and were far less assured. For example, at least some aspects of the Hindu renascence and Indian nationalism derive from the encounter of some Hindus with Christian missionaries. The notion of disinterested social service might well derive from the encounter and it might even be argued, with Richard Fox Young, that

> until Protestant Christianity arrived in South Asia the organisational infrastructure for expressing disinterested benevolence was almost entirely lacking. … It might be said that the wheel of social change in South Asia has a Christian hub and a Buddhist-Hindu rim.[48]

---

46 Corinne G Dempsey, 'Rivalry, Reliance, and Resemblance: Siblings as Metaphor for Hindu Christian Relations in Kerala State,' *Asian Folklore Studies*, 57 (1998), 51-70. A parallel example is provided by David Mosse, 'Catholic Saints and the Hindu Village Pantheon in Rural Tamil Nadu,' *Man*, ns, 29 (1994), 301-32, and 'The Politics of Religious Synthesis: Roman Catholicism and Hindu Village Society in Tamil Nadu,' in *Syncretism/Anti-Syncretism: the Politics of Religious Synthesis*, edited by Charles Steward and Rosalind Shaw (London: Routledge, 1994), 85 – 107. See also Paul Younger, 'Hindu-Christian Worship Settings in South India', in *H-CD*, 191-97.

47 'Discovery of Dialogue,' 70.

48 Unpublished paper cited by Vinoth Ramachandra, *Faiths in Conflict? Christian Identity in a Multicultural World* (Leicester: IVP, 1999), 78.

If Fox is correct then the results that he discerns certainly derive from dialogue as informal and implicit rather than formal. Fox also holds that the same encounter was responsible for a number of other changes in Hindu beliefs (for example the understanding of *murti* (idol / image / icon)) and practices (for example *sati*). These are all examples of what we shall call 'interior dialogue' occasioned by informal dialogue. The provision of Christian ashrams as open non-evangelising meeting places has, according to Sara Grant, enabled the person of Jesus to make sense to Hindus and others.[49] Given that, as we have argued, academic study is an implicit means of dialogue it might also be argued that such study has added (or ought to add) to the range of what constitutes the formal academic study of religion.[50]

9. Comments

Informal dialogue can be called "a process of osmosis" that it seems true to say, "has not been theologically evaluated and articulated creatively".[51] Nonetheless, as Klostermaier notes, this informal dialogue differs from what he calls "the ordinary prearranged dialogue" in a number of ways:

> It is less systematised, less theological and much more complex. It is also much more challenging. In daily life, the rules of courtesy which determine the reactions in a formal discussion among intellectuals are sometimes forgotten, and convictions clash rather hard and sharp.[52]

At least from a Christian perspective, attention is well drawn to the potential value of the "simple but important casual encounters" of everyday life (*GIRD(2)*, 78)[53] and the importance of preparing members of congregations to make sensitive use of them in fostering understanding and co-operation.[54]

---

49 Sara Grant, 'Jesus Christ as Locus for the Meeting of World Religions?,' *JD*, 19 (1994), 300-13.

50 So argues Scott Daniel Dunbar, 'The Place of Interreligious Dialogue in the Academic Study of Religion,' *JES*, 35 (1998), 455-69.

51 [Indian Theological Association], 'Towards a Theology of Religions: An Indian Christian Perspective,' *ITS*, 26 (1989), 78, 80. Panikkar can speak of a "constant symbiosis" between the two faiths ('The Ongoing Dialogue,' xii).

52 'Hindu-Christian Dialogue,' 15.

53 See also: 'The Basis and Content of a Christian-Hindu Dialogue,' *RS*, 6.1 (February 1959), 79f.

54 For example, 'Consultation on Theology,' 79; 'India: Seminar on Dialogue

Informal dialogue is not without its confusing and even negative aspects. The confused understanding of the phenomenon of double naming among Christians (in which they will at times use a given 'Christian' name while continuing to be known by a traditional/Hindu name) is a minor illustration of difficulties in forming a coherent view of the relationship between the two traditions.[55] A Western observer helpfully advocates the metaphor of the simultaneous rivalry and reliance of siblings to describe "the flawed yet ultimately peaceful associations" between Hindus and Christians (in Kerala).[56]

B. Formal Dialogue

Almost all the means of dialogue mentioned above may be called informal in another sense: they are not dependent upon the approval of or initiatives by religious institutions or leaders, and attention now turns to that more explicit and formal dialogue implemented and maintained with institutional sanction.[57] Among Catholics we have noted the important role played by the 'Commission for Dialogue for Relations with non-Christian Religions and Others' during the 1970s. None of the Protestant churches has, however, had a comparable body responsible for initiating and co-ordinating dialogue; most initiatives have come from CISRS and similar study centres and theological institutions. Among those Christians who advocate dialogue there is agreement about the desirability that it be "done in an ecumenical spirit and in consultation and cooperation" with other churches.[58] As noted, a

---

with Non-Christians,' *OT*, no. 57 (January 1974), 98; 'Preparation of Congregations for Dialogue with People of Other Faiths and Ideologies,' *Church of South India, Minutes of the Sixteenth Synod, 1978* (Madras, nd), 43f.

55 See Luke and Carman, *Village Christians and Hindu Culture*, 190f – though this could simply be ascribed to lack of teaching and appropriate pastoral care.

56 Dempsey, 'Rivalry, Reliance, and Resemblance,' 51; but it betrays a less than empathetic understanding then to add that this ambiguous motif is "regularly challenged ... in the totalizing claims of official religious rhetoric prescribed by some Hindu and Christian religious professionals" (52). If it is the case that pressing and ubiquitous problems force the blurring of traditional religious boundaries there will be those, both Christian and Hindu, who (on the grounds of received religious authority)- cannot acquiesce.

57 The historical context is outlined in chapter 1 above.

58 *GIRD(2)*, 38; see also De Souza, 'Dialogue Between Religions in India,' 82.

number of meetings for formal Hindu-Christian dialogue have been initiated not only within India but also beyond, for example at the dialogue arranged by the WCC[59] and meetings organised by the World Conference on Religion for Peace and similar groups and attended by both Indian Christians and Hindus. The advantage that occasions of formal dialogue have over informal is their intentionality: the careful structuring that enables a meeting at greater depth than the occasional contacts of everyday living.

1. Ashrams and Interreligious Centres

One important opportunity for more formal Hindu-Christian dialogue has been provided by the intentional use or establishment of interreligious centres and communities to promote dialogue at a variety of levels. Some of this is clearly informal but many examples date from the 1960s and are better considered as part of a new dimension to interreligious relations.

One option has been to use existing (usually long-standing) monastic institutions, both Hindu and Christian, as meeting places; in fact the phenomenon of monasticism itself constitutes common ground for the meeting of at least some from each tradition.[60] The official Guidelines endorses an earlier call for "small ashramas, houses, centres of dialogue, closely integrated in their respective milieus" and notes the special value of centres in university cities.[61]

Christian ashrams have also been important examples of the

---

59 See the remarks by Eck on "institutional dialogue" in 'What Do We Mean by "Dialogue"?', 9f.

60 See, for example, Jules Monchanin and Henri Le Saux, *Ermites du Saccidananda* (Paris, 1956); A. Elinjimittam, *Monasticism, Christian and Hindu-Buddhist* (Bombay, 1969); Thomas Merton, 'Monastic Experience and the East-West Dialogue,' *BSPNC*, 4 (1969), 39-45; M Francis Acharya, 'Towards a Loka Sannyasa Samaj? For a World Monastic Order?' *IES*, 13 (1974), 186-202; Mariasusai Dhavamony, 'Monasticism: Hindu and Christian,' *BSPNC*, 13 (1978), 40-53; Joseph Parecattil, 'Monasticism in Dialogue,' *BSPNC*, 14 (1979), 176-82; 'Monasticism in Christianity and World Religions,' *SM*, 28 (1979) [whole issue]; *Monastic Life in the Christian and Hindu Traditions: A Comparative Study*, edited by Austin B Creel and Vasudha Narayanan (Lewiston, NY: Edwin Mellen Press, 1990; chapter 5 (on meditational asceticism) in John Brockington, *Hinduism and Christianity* (London: Macmillan, 1992).

61 *GIRD(2)*, 79; see also 'The Basis and Content,' 81. For a similar plea from a mainly Protestant Consultation see 'Consultation Working Group Reports,' 111.

adaptation of an Indian institution[62] and as centres from which initiatives in dialogue have sprung.[63] There are some who still consider them to be important in the Hindu-Christian encounter[64] they are seen as attempts to provide "a new form of Christianity that is not alien to Indian culture and spiritual traditions,"[65]a congenial and sympathetic context in which to meet some of the many Hindus for whom the institutional church is a barrier to interest in Christianity.[66]

---

62 See, for example, the classic study by P Chenchiah, V Chakkarai and AN Sudarisanam, *Ashrams and Sadhus: Ashramas Past and Present* (1941; reprint: Madras: Christian Literature Society, 1996). Also useful are: C Murray Rogers, 'Hindu Ashram Heritage: God's Gift to the Church,' *Concilium*, 9.1 (November 1965), 73-78; Vandana, *Gurus, Ashrams and Christians* (Bombay: St Paul Publications and Delhi: ISPCK, 1978); Michael O'Toole, *Christian Ashram Communities in India* (Pune: Ishvani and Indore: Satprakashan, 1983); Paul Pattathu, *Ashram Spirituality. A Search into the Christian Ashram Movement against its Hindu Background* (Indore: Satprakashan Sanchar Kendra, 1997). For a detailed study of the cultural (including Brahmanical and socioeconomic) background of the ashram system see Patrick Olivelle, *The Asrama System: History and Hermeneutics of a Religious Institution* (New York: Oxford University Press, 1993).

63 See the comprehensive discussion in Kuttianimattathil, *Practice and Theology of Interreligious Dialogue*, 59f, 78-90 and the literature cited there.

64 For example, 'The Basis and Content,' 81; 'Statement of the All India Consultation on Ashrams,' *Vidyajyoti*, 42 (1978), 383-85; Emmanuel Vattakuzhy, *Indian Christian Sannyasa and Swami Abhishiktananda* (Bangalore, 1981), 191-203; Mathew Lederle, 'Ashrams and Dialogue,' *WW*, 17 (1984), 108-13; Francis Audiau, 'Les Ashrams Chrétiens en Inde,' *SB*, 26 (1994), 35-39; a number of the essays in Sara Grant, *Lord of the Dance and Other Papers* (Bangalore: Asia Trading Corporation, 1987) are about ashrams; see also her 'Jesus Christ as Locus for the Meeting of World Religions?,' *JD*, 19 (1994), 300-13, 'The Contemporary Relevance of Christian Ashrams: Reflections in the Light of an Ecumenical Experience', in *Culture, Religion and Society*, 111-30, and 'Ashrams and Inter-religious Spirituality,' *TM*, 1 (1998), 90-96; *RC Das. Evangelical Prophet or Contextual Christianity*, edited by HL Richard (Delhi: ISPCK for CISRS, 1999), 106-16. There is a good summary of the contribution of the ashram movement to dialogue in Kuttianimattathil, *Practice and Theology of Interreligious Dialogue*, 84-89.

65 Sebastian Elavathingal, 'Saccidananda Ashram – Narsinghpur: a New Paradigm for Inter-Religious Dialogue,' *TM*, 3 (2000), 67.

66 See, for example, Herbert Jai Singh, 'Rethinking Church in India,' *RS*, 10.4 (December 1963), 10; Philipos Thomas, 'Christian Ashrams and the Evangelization of India,' *ICHR*, 11 (1977), 204-21; Sarah Grant, 'Reflections on Hindu-Christian Dialogue in an Ashram Context,' *RS*, 26.1 (March 1979), 42-58; Jacob Kavunkal, 'Christian Ashrams,' *Verbum SVD*, 20 (1979), 68-78; Brenda Lealman, 'Siva Dances for the Christians,' *Theology*, 82 (1979), 344-49.

A number of Catholic presbyteries, convents, and other centres are now called ashrams;[67]some seminarians have spent time in Hindu ashrams during their training.[68] The willingness of some Catholic priests and sisters to live in radical poverty and simplicity is another form of an implied and visible and fruitful dialogue with the majority culture in India.

However, the continuing role of Christian ashrams is unclear. Those that started under Protestant leadership have often faltered under their second generation leaders.[69] Stanley Samartha, in an article published in 1980, comments that the ashram movement "has almost dried up."[70] The first edition of the official *Guidelines* on dialogue contains a list of ashrams (mostly Catholic: *GIRD(1)*, 81) with only one minor reference to the role of ashrams in promoting dialogue though there are more extensive references in the second edition (*GIRD(2)*, 5, 77, 79). In conservative and some official Catholic circles the involvement has been regarded with suspicion (for example, because of its adaptations from Hinduism, the status of its *gurus* and *samnyasis*, and its relationship to church structures); the response from proponents of the ashram movement is that the institution is neither essentially Hindu (or Christian) but part of a shared Indian cultural heritage.[71] But an opinion often heard among Indians, Christian and Hindu, is that Christian ashrams are mainly "for foreigners"[72] and some recent conservative Hindu comment has been extremely negative.[73] Nonetheless, one observer thinks the

---

67 Patrick D'Souza, 'India,' in *Mission in Dialogue*, 25f.

68 Nambiaparambil, 'India,' in *Mission in Dialogue*, 416. Nambiaparambil gives other examples of new kinds of ashrams (415f). See also, Augustine Thottakara, 'Religious Education in Hinduism Ancient and Modern,' *Jeevadhara*, 14 (1984), 316f.

69 See the comments of Richard W Taylor, 'Christian Ashrams as a Style of Mission in India,' *IRM*, 68 (1979), 281-93.

70 Samartha, 'Partners in Community: Some Reflections on Hindu-Christian Relations Today,' *OBMR*, 4 (1980), 80. The story of the Christa Prema Seva ashram in Pune illustrates the changing fortunes of the ashram movement; see Barbara Noreen, *Crossroads of the Spirit* (Delhi: ISPCK, 1994).

71 For comments see Vandana, *Social Justice and Ashrams* (Bangalore, 1982) and 'Ashrams – Some Illusions and Fears,' *WW*, 17 (1984), 33-40, 13; *Christian Ashrams: a Movement with a Future?*, edited by Vandana Mataji (Delhi: ISPCK, 1993).

72 See, for example, Nambiaparambil, 'Dialogue in India,' 268.

73 See, for example, Sita Ram Goel, *Catholic Ashrams: Sannyasins or Swindlers?* (New Delhi: Voice of India, 1995) in which he opts for the second of his two suggested answers.

Catholic ashram movement will remain small in size and influence, but will continue to provide "an important point of contact for dialogue with Hinduism."[74]

As well as ashrams, there have been other centres have been established under Catholic sponsorship to facilitate interreligious meeting. The best known of the earliest of these have been Shanti Bhavan in Calcutta and Snehasadan in Pune.[75] After some twenty years at Snehasadan, Matthew Lederle believes that such centres will have "an affinity to the spirituality of the Bhagavad Gita and to what Christians call 'contemplation in action'".[76] Since the late 1960s, a number of other centres have been established with dialogue particularly in mind; Aikiya Alayam in Madras (founded in 1969) is one of the better known examples.[77] A workshop at the All-India Consultation in Patna in 1973 called for the formation of small communities that would be thoroughly Indian in ethos, closely identified with the cultural surroundings, open to people of all faiths and with a prayer room furnished in simple Indian style.[78] The potential usefulness of these centres for exposing seminarians and others to inter-faith dialogue has also been noted.[79]

2. *'Live-together' Sessions*

One distinctive means of dialogue organised by the CBCI Commission on Dialogue has been 'live-together' sessions in which members of different religions have spent several days together for fraternal friendship, prayer, meditation and shared reflections, while sharing the costs of the occasion.[80] The sessions are said to have been "very fruitful for the growth of mutual understanding and of the right attitudes to other religions, and for the deepening

---

74 George Soares-Prabhu, 'The Indian Church Challenged by Pluralism and Dialogue,' *SB*, 26 (1994), 190-92 (quotation from 192).

75 Some details are given in Kuttianimattathil, *Practice and Theology of Interreligious Dialogue*, 61.

76 'Discovery of Dialogue,' 68 (for further details about the centre see 69-71). On other urban centres see Hirudayam, 'Dialogue in Tamilnadu,' 427.

77 See the comprehensive discussion in Kuttianimattathil, *Practice and Theology of Interreligious Dialogue*, 91-102 and the literature cited there.

78 *Light and Life and Life We Seek to Share* (Bangalore, 1973) 326f; see also the Patna Declaration, 39.

79 Patna Declaration 39; 'Consultation Working Group Reports,' 111.

80 See Nambiaparambil, 'Dialogue in India: An Analysis,' 270 – the article goes on to give details of the first nine of these live-together sessions in 1973, 1974 and 1975 (272f). See too the discussion in *GIRD(2)*, 92-95.

of the personal religious awareness of the participants" (*GIRD(2)*, 92) and to give opportunities to "come to know one another at a level of religious sharing that is almost non-existent in daily life."[81] Most of the gathering have a pre-announced theme but considerable opportunity is given for prayer, music and *bhajans*, scriptural readings and discussion.[82] Some Hindu participants understandably anxious about possible Christian intentions to use the occasions as a means to proselytise. However, on some such occasions Hindus have accepted an invitation to share fully in the eucharist, said to be more readily understood and accepted by them than baptism. (This has led to the creative and courageous suggestion that the eucharist might, at least in India, become a welcoming and initiating symbol for such individuals, with any talk of baptism deferred until a later time.[83])

3. *Shared Worship*

Although shared worship has been mentioned above as a means of informal dialogue, it can also be seen as contributing to intentional dialogue as well. The intentional celebrating together the festivals of each, or at least visiting temples, churches, ashrams and homes has also been suggested as a means of dialogue,[84] as has sharing in pilgrimage.[85] More controversial is the possibility that joint worship, usually of a fairly informal kind, might function as a kind of formal dialogue. Manickam calls for the starting and encouraging of "dialogical circles of actual religious experience", and inter-religious prayer meetings.[86] And the official *Guidelines for Inter-Religious Dialogue* anticipates such occasions with its discussion and suggestions about their careful preparation.[87] The analysis of such activity

81 Anand Nayak and Anne-Marie Abrard, 'Hindu-Christian Dialogue in India,' *PMVB*, 88 (1982), 10.

82 See the suggestions in *GIRD(2)*, 82-85.

83 Sara Grant, 'Towards a Practical Indian Ecclesiology,' *Vidyajyoti*, 49 (1985), 29-35.

84 '*Religious Resources for a Just Society*,' 18.

85 See P Arockiadoss, 'The Hindu and Christian Pilgrimage Traditions and the Practice of Common Worship,' in *Sharing Worship: Communicatio in Sacris*, edited by Paul Puthanangady (Bangalore: NBCLC, 1988), 647-58.

86 TM Manickam, 'Anubhava as Pramana of an Indian Christology,' *Jeevadhara*, 1 (1971), 243. See also '*Religious Resources for a Just Society*,' 18f and Chethimattam, 'The Scope and Conditions of a Hindu-Christian Dialogue,' 93.

87 *GIRD(2)*, 82-91.

is much less well developed and is usually offered in a tentative manner. The acceptability of such worship might depend upon whether it is seen as joint worship in the sense of a joint approach along the *same path*, as it were, to the divine (presupposing a common religious experience), or as worship together, with each continuing along a trajectory from their own tradition, but *in the presence* of the other.[88] For Catholics the perspectives of the Second Vatican Council have enabled a new theological evaluation of the possibility of shared worship. One analysis, for example, explains that in the past "concern for one's own orthodoxy" precluded sharing in the worship of others but that now "the fulfilment of our mission in a spirit of dialogue" enables a limited but real and sincere participation on the grounds of mutual openness of the parties to one another provided individual religious identities are respected. It is *as Christians* and *as Hindus* that the joint participation occurs.[89] The problematical dimension seems much less pronounced among Hindu participants in such shared worship one remedy for which might be the practice of silent prayer. After an analysis of some of the problems involved, Nayak suggests that "the awakening of the heart through silence and silent awareness can be a solid ground where Hinduism and Christianity can meet".[90]

4. *Conferences, Seminars, Consultations and Literature*

The most detailed sources of reflection on formal Hindu-Christian dialogue are conferences, seminars, consultations and other occasional gatherings and the literature generated by reflection on the Hindu-Christian encounter. Some of the meetings have brought together Christians and Hindus for periods of intentional discussion; others have been intramural discussions called by, for example the National Biblical, Catechetical and Liturgical Centre or the Indian Theological Association or CISRS (though less frequently in recent decades). The meetings have employed a variety of formats and have taken place in a variety of settings – regional, national and

88 See, for example, the discussion in a joint edition of *PD/CD* 1998 on 'Interreligious Prayer.'

89 Paul Puthanangady, 'Participating in the Worship of Other Faiths,' *TM*, 2 (1999), 46-56 (quotations from 47). See too the discussion by Albert Nambiaparambil, 'Inter-Faith Worship of Inter-Religious Fellowship,' in *Sharing Worship: Communicatio in Sacris*, 597-604.

90 Anand Nayak, 'Christian-Hindu Prayer in Interreligious Dialogue', *HCSB*, 13 (2000), 34 (article: 32-34).

international. They are too many to list here[91] but the analysis that follows draws heavily upon them and upon the writings of those who in a variety of publications have discussed the encounter.

C. The Definition of Dialogue

Having looked in some detail at the actual encounter, both informal and formal, it is now possible to attempt to clarify more precisely the meaning of dialogue. In general terms, Hindu-Christian dialogue means the conversation or exchange that results from the meeting of Hindu and Christian. The actual encouragement of dialogue is sometimes said to be more important than either its definition or its justification in theological or sociological or other categories. Moreover, the variety of cultural and religious backgrounds from which participants come, the variety of reasons for which they meet and the variety of presuppositions they hold – about, for example, the nature of religion and religious faith – seem to preclude any precise or universally agreed definitions of dialogue. Nonetheless, a typology of definitions has begun to emerge during the four decades of our survey[92]- but what follows is this writer's own conclusions about what constitutes the Hindu-Christian encounter.

1. Discursive Dialogue

The least complex mode of the formal encounter might be called

---

91 The attempt made by Kuttianimattathil in his *Practice and Theology of Interreligious Dialogue*, 173-228, indicates the range of such meetings.

92 For some examples of different typologies of dialogue see Richard W Taylor, 'The Meaning of Dialogue,' in *I-RD*, 55-64; Johannes Aagaard in *Oecumenica. Annales de Recherche Oecuménique 1969*, edited by FW Kantzenback and V Vajta (Paris, 1969), 132-47; Samartha, '*More* than an Encounter of Commitments,' 392f; EJ Sharpe, 'Dialogue and Faith,' *Religion*, 3 (1973), 92-94; 'The Goals of Inter-Religious Dialogue,' in *Truth and Dialogue: the Relationship Between World Religions*, edited by John Hick (London, 1974), 81-89; and 'Dialogue of Religions,' in *The Encyclopedia of Religions*, (Mircea Eliade, editor in chief; New York, 1987), volume 4, 347; AM Mundadan, 'Hindu-Christian Dialogue: Past Twenty-Five Years,' *Jeevadhara*, 11 (1981), 375-94; Arvind Sharma, 'The Meaning and Goals of Interreligious Dialogue,' *JD*, 8 (1983), 225-47; 'Dialogue and Mission,' 28-35; Jacques Dupuis, 'Forms of Interreligious Dialogue,' *BSPNC*, 20 (1985), 164-71; *ACFOR*, 28-35; S Wesley Ariarajah, 'Pluralism and Harmony', *CD*, no. 25, 17-19.

"discursive dialogue,"[93] or the "dialogue of discourse,"[94] that is, conversation that seeks clarity of understanding, sometimes as a shared quest. Because discursive dialogue intends to clarify, it includes the effort to understand or even to search for truth.[95] Eric Sharpe believes discursive dialogue might equally well be called dialectic or debate.[96] It approximates what has been called the "theological" type of dialogue,[97] or the "intellectual-theological approach" to the encounter.[98] Such meeting is not without precedents before the 1960s, but rarely in the intentional and even formally sanctioned communal sense now used by Christians. There is also a sense in which "parliamentary dialogue" (large assemblies for inter-religious discussion)[99] and even the academic study by Hindus and Christians of the others' faith constitute forms of discursive dialogue,[100] although usually person to person discussion is meant. Discursive dialogue can at least clarify the intellectual content of religious beliefs and thereby contribute to understanding.

2. *Secular Dialogue*

This second kind of dialogue intends principally to facilitate a joint approach to social and other problems in the 'secular' realm. It has also been called "practical dialogue,"[101] the "dialogue of action,"[102] the "social approach" to dialogue[103]and "dialogue through collaborative action"[104]. The Indian Catholic *Guidelines* speaks of this form of dialogue as "sharing in common enterprises" (*GIRD(2)*, 68-75)

---

93 By Sharpe, 'Dialogue and Faith,' 92f; 'The Goals of Inter- Religious Dialogue,' 82f; 'Dialogue of Religions,' 347.

94 Ariarajah, 'Pluralism and Harmony', 17-19.

95 So Samartha, '*More* than an Encounter of Commitments,' 392.

96 'Dialogue and Faith,' 92.

97 Alfred De Souza, 'Dialogue Between Religions in India,' *IMA*, 3.3 (August 1972), 81f; Diana L Eck, 'What Do We Mean by "Dialogue"?,' *CD*, no. 11 (December 1986), 10f.

98 AM Mundadan, 'Hindu-Christian Dialogue,' 384-88.

99 See Eck, 'What Do We Mean by "Dialogue"?,' 5-8.

100 See Robert D Baird, 'Hindu-Christian Dialogue and the Academic Study of Religion,' in *H-CD*, 223f; Carman, 'Continuing Tasks in Inter-Religious Dialogue,' 204f; Samartha, '*More* than an Encounter of Commitments,' 393.

101 De Souza, 'Dialogue Between Religions in India,' 81f, 87.

102 Ariarajah, 'Pluralism and Harmony,' 17-18.

103 Mundadan, 'Hindu-Christian Dialogue,' 389-93.

104 A Poruthur, 'A Decade of Dialoguing: a Non-Elitist Approach,' *MT*, 2 (2000), 489.

and "dialogue in action";[105]it is what Hans Staffner calls "dialogue with people promoting social welfare".[106] Newbigin, in defining "types of dialogue," includes the possibility of joining with others "in common tasks, civic responsibilities, actions for political or social change ... where we can share together in common objectives."[107] Secular dialogue is also described as a "common search for human liberation and community"[108] and an international meeting of Hindus and Christians defined "one of the most profitable and powerful forms of dialogue" as "working together with our neighbours in concrete projects of social action".[109] Kuttianimattathil summarises a wide range of discussion of this topic under the heading 'Action for justice leads to and is served by interreligious dialogue.'[110] It is also called the "dialogue of life" in the sense that dialogue assists "the construction of the true human community".[111] Kalliath uses what he calls a "bridge-paradigm" in describing the servant role of the church in the co-operative building up of communities."[112] The basis of this kind of dialogue is usually said to be the shared recognition of common concerns[113] though its practice is not, of course, dependent upon prior agreement about definition or precise goals. In fact, there is a sense in which an implicit form of secular dialogue is a common occurrence since "members of all reli-

---

105 *GIRD(2)*, 70. Angelo Fernandes also speaks of "the dialogue of action" ('Summons to Dialogue,' in *The Summons to Dialogue* (Hong Kong, 1983), 37 and *ACFOR* of the "dialogue of deeds" (31). See too Hirata Satoshi, 'Towards an Action-Oriented Dialogue with People of Other Faiths in Asia,' *AJT*, 1 (1987), 515-22.

106 Section heading in his *Dialogue, Stimulating Contact with Hindus* (Anand: Gujurat Sahitya Prakash, 1993), 13-62.

107 JE Lesslie Newbigin, 'Confessing Christ in a Multi-Religion Society,' *SBET*, 12 (1994), 132.

108'Consultation Working Group Reports,' RS, 26.1 (March 1979), 108-10.

109'*Religious Resources for a Just Society.' A Hindu-Christian Dialogue* (Geneva, 1981), 17.

110 Section heading for his *Practice and Theology of Interreligious Dialogue*, 526-31.

111 Angelo Fernandes, 'The Call to Full Ecumenism,' *VJTR*, 53 (1989), 72f. SJ Emmanuel also speaks of a "dialogue (dialectic) of life that encompasses religion, culture and socio-economic conditions" ('Inter-Religious Dialogue in Asia at a Turning Point,' *ZMR*, 73 (1989), 240).

112 Antony Kalliath, 'Indian Secularism: a Theological and Spiritual Spectrum of Hindu-Christian Meeting,' *JD*, 19 (1994), 314-31; this is also what Subhash Anand has in mind when he writes of 'Consecrated Secularity: Theological Basis and Practical Implications,' *VJTR*, 59 (1995), 145-60.

113 See further below in chapter 3.C.

gions are already deeply involved in this form of dialogue," as they share in the common tasks of community and nation building.[114] More specific tasks range from ecological concern[115] to hunger, health and population issues.[116]

Most discussions of 'secular dialogue' use the adjective to refer to the discussion of the 'secular' realm – admittedly implying a distinction that is artificial to many Indians. But it can also mean the *kind* of dialogue described or contemplated – that is, one that makes no assumptions about the religious commitment of the participants or even assumes the possibility of some kind of 'neutral' or religionless ground on which to meet. Some discussions of secular dialogue link it with the discursive form. Samartha describes discursive dialogue as "an investigatory discussion among people who face common needs and common problems. It leads to a progressive accumulation of knowledge which can be useful to the community".[117] Those who do link the two forms of dialogue often add that secular dialogue is not merely a possible extension of other forms of meeting but should be seen as a necessary corollary. Anto Karokaran believes that in India dialogue has no meaning and is "an unpardonable luxury" if it is restricted to religious and intellectual questions and remains unrelated to the nation's problems.[118] But it must also be said that it is difficult to conceive Christian-Hindu dialogue of any depth that was wholly restricted to discussion of the 'secular' realm without in some way touching upon the religious faith of the participants.

The origins of this 'secular' approach to Hindu-Christian dialogue are to be found, in part at least, beyond India. In Catholic circles the notion of the Church in dialogue with the contemporary

---

114 *GIRD(2)*, 68. See also 'Consultation Working Group Reports,' 109.

115 See, for example, the series of articles on 'The New Master-Paradigm: Ecology' that constitute the bulk of *HCSB*, 6 (1993).

116 See, for example, Mark R Sills, 'Social Ethics and a Conversational Model: a Christian-Hindu Encounter,' dissertation, Wesley Theological Seminary, 1974.

117 '*More* than an Encounter of Commitments,' 392 (emphasis added). Eric Sharpe describes secular dialogue as "one type of discursive dialogu" ('Dialogue and Faith,' 95), although in another paper he places secular dialogue in a category of its own ('The Goals of Inter-Religious Dialogue,' 85-87).

118 *Evangelization and Diakonia* (Bangalore, 1978), 185. See also: 'Consultation Working Group Reports,' 108; Pierre Fallon, 'The Demands of Dialogue in the Indian Situation,' in *Service and Salvation*, edited by Joseph Pathrapankal (Bangalore, 1973), 309.

world was an important emphasis in the encyclical *Ecclesiam Suam* which influenced the discussion of mission and dialogue both at the Second Vatican Council and also in India itself (for example, *GIRD(2)*, 6, 30). "Dialogue belongs to the very being of the Church in the world" and finds its expression in ministries of love and service (*GIRD(2)*, 30). In Protestant circles one particular neo-orthodox emphasis was widely discussed both in India and beyond: the supposed transcendence of the Gospel over all religions, cultures and ideologies.[119] The discussions of 'secular theology' and, more recently, 'liberation theology' have also been read by Indian Protestants and have contributed to the development of secular dialogue.[120] And Kurt Dockhorn, writing in an Indian context, considered that "fundamental mutual affirmation" was no longer the basic concern of dialogue (at least for the liberal Protestants known to him) but that the central issue had become "the cause of the suppressed".[121] MM Thomas had long emphasised that God was also at work in the 'secular' sphere of life where Christians are to cooperate with all who work for the common good.[122]

One feature of secular dialogue is its ambivalent attitude towards the religious faith – or absence of faith – of the partners in dialogue. Sometimes this form of dialogue is said to be about social need that "concerns all believers".[123] But other definitions of secular dialogue seem to minimise the 'religious' dimension; people are said to enter dialogue not so much as Hindus and Christians but as people "engaged in the common struggle of humanity".[124] In such dialogue "religion will be a small and comparatively unimportant part of the

---

119 One example of this discussion was the interest in Indian circles in a volume written by a former student of Kraemer, Arend van Leeuwen, *Christianity in World History* (London, 1964). An example of Protestant interest is that almost the whole issue of *RS*, 14.1 (March 1967) (1-56) is given to an analysis of *Christianity in World History* and a discussion of its relevance to India.

120 See Mundadan, 'Hindu-Christian Dialogue,' 389. The influence of liberation theology is discussed in chapter 6.H below.

121 'Identity, Dialogue and Involvement,' in *For the Sake of the Gospel*, edited by Gnana Robinson (Madurai, 1980), 148. See also chapter 6.H below with its discussion of Jesus as *Satyagrahi*.

122 See, for example, 'Editorial,' *RS*, 16.2 (June 1969), 1-5, and his *Salvation and Humanisation* (Madras, 1971).

123 Nagpur Declaration, 28 (emphasis added). (For publication and other details of the Nagpur, Bangalore and Patna Declarations, see above, chapter 1.) See also *GIRD(2)*, 68.

124 Herbert Jai Singh in *I-RD*, 48.

whole".[125] An emphasis upon the human rather than the religious dimension of shared concern may in fact make a common approach to social problems easier. The question then arises whether such 'secular' dialogue should continue to be called 'inter-religious' dialogue. One answer is that dialogue is "co-terminous with life" because the Christian faith is "religionless" and not concerned simply with some spiritual dimension of life.[126] Or it might be argued that any dialogue about "the structures and values and the foundations of a genuine human community can truly become an inter-faith dialogue at spiritual depth"[127] – presumably because these issues are ultimately religious in character. Perhaps this is what Ariarajah means in writing that where Hindus and Christians work together for liberation and reconciliation, "there has been a growing together that bears the mark of genuine dialogue".[128] On the other hand Panikkar considers that true dialogue occurs at the "religious" rather than the "profane level of a merely cultural relationship" where "pragmatic criteria" are decisive. [129] Another advocate of dialogue argues that Hindus would more sympathetically understand the Christian Dharma "if it had nothing to speak for it on the temporal plane".[130] The appeal of Christianity "would then be on a spiritual level" only – a prospect of which he approves.[131]

The admissibility and significance of secular dialogue as a distinct form of Christian-Hindu dialogue depends upon presuppositions about the validity of the secular-spiritual dichotomy and, in turn, upon judgements about the importance to be attached to the secular over against the spiritual realm in India in general and

---

125 C Murray Rogers, 'The Content of a Christian-Hindu Dialogue,' *RS*, 6.1 (February 1959), 69. De Souza objects to the adjective 'secular' because it implies a form of dialogue inferior to theological discussion ('Dialogue between Religions in India,' 82).

126 Rogers, 'The Content of a Christian-Hindu Dialogue,' 69.

127 'Editorial,' *RS*, 12.1 (March 1965), 8.

128 S Wesley Ariarajah, 'A World Council of Churches' Perspective on the Future of Hindu-Christian Dialogue,' in *H-CD*, 259f.

129 Panikkar, *TUCH(2)*, 40f. It is noteworthy that Panikkar omits from this second edition his previous relegation of striving for cultural progress to a merely pragmatic level devoid of religious significance (*TUCH(1)*, 9) – a relegation which drew sharply critical remarks in an Editorial in *RS*, 12.1 (March 1965), 7.

130 Abhishiktananda, *The Church in India* (Madras, 1969), 12.

131 *The Church in India*, 54. Karokaran cites a number of others, both Catholic and Protestant, who make the same point (*Evangelization and Diakonia*, 113f).

among advocates of dialogue in particular. Is fruitful common ground for dialogue to be found in a shared religious quest or a shared secular concern, or both? Does the prospect of increasing secularisation provide a motivation towards dialogue? These are questions to which discussion will return (for example in chapters 3.D and 7.C.2 below).

3. *Interior Dialogue*

Its principal advocates call this third form of dialogue 'interior' or 'inner' dialogue because it concerns the 'interior' and prior preparations of Christians and the Christian community for the 'external' encounter of actual dialogue with Hindus. It has also been called the "spiritual-contemplative approach" to dialogue.[132] It has also been called a "passing over" (and "coming back") from one religion to another[133] and has been defined by one notable advocate, Raimundo Panikkar, as "intrareligious" dialogue: "an inner dialogue within my self, an encounter in the depth of my personal religiousness, having met another religious experience on that very intimate level."[134] On the face of it, 'interior dialogue' looks like no dialogue at all given the absence of any tangible partner. However, such reflection can be seen as an individual or mono-communal self-questioning that has the would be or hoped for partner's point of view in mind and for this reason it does seem reasonable to describe it as a form of dialogue.

In India, most proponents of interior dialogue have been Catholic or Anglican and members of the 'Circle' have been closely identified with it. Murray Rogers, a member of the Circle, gives a full account (from a distinctly Christian viewpoint) of interior dialogue.[135] He describes four stages. The first is that of ensuring that the Christian is "unshakeably rooted in Christ" and thereby able to

---

132 Mundadan, 'Hindu-Christian Dialogue,' 380-84.

133 Frank Whaling, *Christian Theology and World Religions* (Basingstoke, 1986), 129f, 140f, 167f, 173f, developing an idea of John Dunne in his *The Way of All the Earth* (Notre Dame, IN, 1978).

134 *The Intrareligious Dialogue*, revised edition (Mahwah, NJ, 1999), 73f.

135 C Murray Rogers, 'Hindu and Christian – A Moment Breaks,' *RS*, 12.1 (March 1965), 35-44; further references to the article are given in the text itself. Also useful is: James D Redington, 'The Hindu-Christian Dialogue and the Interior Dialogue,' *TS*, 44 (1983), 587-603 and as 'Hindu-Christian Dialogue and Interior Dialogue' in *Religions in Dialogue: East and West Meet*, edited by ZP Thundy and others (Lanham, MD: University Press of America, 1985), 239-59.

face the challenge of the encounter – especially since stage two demands openness "in order that the non-Christian religious experience may begin to happen within us". The principal method advocated by the Circle for understanding and experiencing Hindu spirituality, especially the *advaitin* experience of interiority, is meditation upon the Upanishads. This will enable the Church to receive India's message through India's scriptures.[136] Simply put, the aim of inner dialogue is what another writer calls "the assumption of Hindu spirituality into our Christian spirituality".[137] But for this to happen the Christian must temporarily put aside much of the conceptual expression of faith (which would intrude and distort) so that the message and especially the experience of the Upanishads might be fully received.[138]

Stage three is said to be a deeper awareness of the uniqueness and transcendence of Christ and Christian faith. One consequence of this will be that, although differences between Christian and other (or "pre-Christian" as Rogers twice calls it (p 41)) spirituality and experience will persist at a rational level, at a deeper level their "supernatural complementarity" will be perceived (p 41). The fourth and final stage is the deepening together of the Hindu and Christian spiritualities although Rogers does not discuss the means of this deepening. Perhaps it includes the re-reading of the Bible seeking to understand it anew in the light of the reality of the *advaitin* experience of the divine.[139]

Although interior dialogue is valuable in itself, its preparatory quality is often stressed.[140] Only when this preliminary inner dialogue between Christian and Hindu spirituality has been engaged should the Christian attempt 'external' dialogue.[141] It also seems that an interior or silent dialogue inevitably accompanies the actual meeting also as questions and reflection are stirred by the

---

136 For an example of the method (using themes for meditation from the Upanisads and New Testament) see Sara Grant, *Descent to the Source.Texts for Meditation from the Hindu and Christian Scriptures* (Bangalore, 1987).

137 Klaus Klostermaier, 'Hindu-Christian Dialogue,' in *DBM*, 12.

138 This temporary suspension of evaluation (also proposed as a condition for 'existential dialogue') is discussed in C.3 below.

139 Klostermaier, 'Hindu-Christian Dialogue,' 12-14.

140 For example: Mary Kalapesi, 'Some Reflections on the Fourth Meeting on Hindu and Christian Spirituality,' *RS*, 11.4 (December 1964), 72; Rogers, 'Hindu and Christian – A Moment Breaks,' 40; 'Inter-Faith Dialogue,' *AF*, 5 (1970), 242; Panikkar, 'Inter Religious Dialogue: Some Principles,' *JES*, 12 (1975), 408.

141 C Murray Rogers, 'Inter-Faith Dialogue,' *AF*, 5 (1970), 242.

encounter. Struggle and even anguish might mark such interior dialogue; an example seems to be found in Gandhi both before and after his decision to declare himself a Hindu and not a Christian.[142] And any reading by Hindus and Christians of the scriptures and writings of the other's tradition (especially when accompanied by reflection or meditation) might also be called a form of interior dialogue. One Hindu writes of an interior dialogue (centred on interest in the person of Jesus) in which "my interest in Jesus was encouraged and deepened by Hindu writers".[143]

It will become apparent that there is a close link between interior dialogue and the 'existential dialogue' to be described below. A notable proponent of this form of dialogue was another member of the Circle, Swami Abhishiktananda whose *Ascent to the Depth of the Heart*[144] is a fine example of the inner journey. The aim of interior dialogue is to prepare Christians for dialogue of an existential nature with Hindus. One of a number of characteristics shared by the two forms of dialogue is a strong contrast between the 'spiritual' and the intellectual bases of the inter-religious meeting. A "mental and cerebral faith" is said to be quite inadequate;[145] it is a "contemplative disposition of the soul" that is essential.[146] A number of presuppositions about the common ground on which Christians and Hindus meet are clearly held by the advocates of interior dialogue.

4. *Existential Dialogue*

'Existential' dialogue refers to the most comprehensive mode of formal Christian-Hindu encounter. Because it emphasises the inter-

---

142 See the discussion by Nirmal Minz, *Mahatma Gandhi and Hindu-Christian Dialogue* (Madras, 1970), 157-75.

143 Anantanand Rambachan, cited in S Wesley Ariarajah, 'Christology in Asia: Perspectives from Hindu-Christian Dialogue,' *CTC Bulletin*, 7.3 (December 1987), 34.

144 Et: Delhi: ISPCK, 1998; the volume is a selection from his Spiritual Diary, 1948-73. Of the many secondary studies, the work that perhaps best elaborates the intentions of inner dialogue (and not without a critical edge) is Antony Kalliath, *The Word in the Cave. The Experiential Journey of Swami Abhishiktananda to the Point of Hindu-Christian Meeting* (New Delhi: Intercultural Publications, 1996). Discussion will return to Abhishiktanda in chapter 6.F below.

145 Rogers, 'Hindu and Christian – A Moment Breaks,' 40.

146 Abhishiktananda, 'The Way of Dialogue' in *I-RD*, 85. See also Klostermaier, 'Hindu-Christian Dialogue,' 12.

personal nature of the meeting,[147] and because the essential point of contact is sometimes said to be the common humanity of those meeting, it has also been called "Buberian"[148] and "human"[149] dialogue. Although none of the adjectives suggested for this form of dialogue is completely satisfactory, 'existential' is perhaps the most comprehensive and least misleading. "Buberian" is inadequate because Buber's name is even less well known than the ideas he is identified with; and the existentialism that the definition has in mind is more complex than Buber's, though no less religious. "Human" is misleading because a number of advocates of existential dialogue (mainly Catholic) set common spiritual experience over against common humanity – or prefer the former to the latter – as the basis of dialogue. And, although the use of 'existential' is not commonplace among Indian participants in dialogue, it is not unknown and the adjective is a fairly comprehensive summary of what this form of dialogue intends. Gonsalves, for example, links an existential perspective directly with Hindu-Christian dialogue and the three traditional *margas*.[150] Indian writers are able to bring out many existential aspects of a Hindu world and life view that coincide with the kind of relationship that proponents of existential dialogue want for the meeting.[151]

As might be expected, existential dialogue has a number of characteristics that call for individuality, freedom and authenticity in the encounter. Religious experience receives special emphasis, particularly in Catholic reflections upon dialogue and for this reason it has been called "religious"[152] and "spiritual"[153] dialogue. "It is at the

---

147 See, for example, 'Consultation on the Theology of Hindu-Christian Dialogue,' *RS*, 16.2 (June 1969), 72 (cited as 'Consultation on Theology'); see also Anthony Adair, 'Towards a Hindu-Christian Dialogue,' *Contemporary Review*, no. 208 (February 1966), 85.

148 Richard W Taylor, 'The Meaning of Dialogue,' 56.

149 Eric J Sharpe, 'Dialogue and Faith,' 93f; 'The Goals of Inter-Religious Dialogue,' 83-85; 'Dialogue of Religions,' 347.

150 Francis A Gonsalves, 'A Theological Epilogue to Buber's Dialogue', *Vidyajyoti*, 62 (19980, 580-95.

151 See, for example, the three articles on 'Existentialism in Hinduism,' published in *Krisht Vidya* [Rajpur], 2.2 (June 1982), 1-30; K Guru Dutt, *Existentialism and Indian Thought* (Bangalore, 1960); Munduvel V George, 'Existentialism and its Message to Indian Thought Patterns,' *IJT*, 11 (1962), 68-74.

152 Raimundo Panikkar, 'The Ongoing Dialogue,' in *H-CD*, xviif.

153 Eck, 'What Do We Mean by "Dialogue"?,' 13f; it also approximates to what Ariarajah calls the "dialogue of spirituality" ('Pluralism and Harmony', 17-19).

level of experience where we most intimately meet" (*GIRD(2)*, 77). The Bangalore Declaration also defines dialogue in experiential terms.[154] The language of experience is often used in conjunction with the metaphor of the depth of dialogue in which "deep communion with the Absolute and with one another" occurs.[155] A Hindu speaker is found using the metaphor in urging a shift from dialogue at the superficial level of "concepts, formulations and systems of thought to the deeper level of the heart".[156] Panikkar seems to agree: what he proposes in the face of the differing systems of Christian and Hindu thought is "both the traditional Advaitic solution and the equally traditional Christian answer: religious truth is existential and non-objectifiable".[157] Such truth is said to be "Too deep for dogma" – the title of a description of the prayer relationship between a Hindu ashram and a Salesian monastery.[158]

Not all advocates of dialogue draw a strong contrast between its intellectual and existential components. Some definitions link the two and see dialogue as both communication of knowledge and sharing of religious experience,[159] both mutual understanding and mutual acceptance (*GIRD(2)*, 77). Sometimes existential dialogue is seen as an extension of discursive dialogue,[160] or discursive dialogue

---

154 *Bangalore Declaration*, 257. In similar vein: Karokaran, *Evangelization and Diakonia*, 183; Raimundo Panikkar, 'In Christ There is Neither Hindu Nor Christian,' in *Religious Issues and Inter-Religious Dialogues*, edited by C Weihsun Fu and GE Spiegler (New York, 1989), 475. Further on the role of experience in the dialogue, see chapters 3.G and 6.D below.

155 *GIRD(2)*, 86 see also Abhishiktananda, 'The Depth-Dimension of Religious Dialogue,' *Vidyajyoti*, 45 (1981), 202-21; and *Saccidananda: A Christian Approach to Advaitic Experience* (revised edition in English: Delhi, 1974), 11-13, 86; Klaus Klostermaier, *Hindu and Christian in Vrindaban* (Et: London, 1969), 102. Compare Xavier Irudayaraj: "dialogue consists more in silent togetherness than in verbal exchange" ('Dialogue Experience,' *Vidyajyoti*, 40 (1976), 132); on the place of silence in this dialogue, see also *ATA*, 1f. See also Abhishiktananda, *The Church in India*, 63; Christopher Duraisingh, 'Issues in Mission and Dialogue: Some Reflections,' *IRM*, 78 (1988), 409, Margaret Chatterjee, 'The Presuppositions of Inter-Religious Communication,' *RSt*, 3 (1967), 396. In similar vein see Anand Amaladoss, 'The Scope of Dialogue,' *HCSB*, 2 (1989), 3.

156 A Mr Jeyavelu, cited by Ignatius Hirudayam, 'Dialogue in Tamilnadu,' *LV*, 29 (1974), 422.

157 *TUCH(2)*, 21.

158 By George Seif in *RR*, 54 (1995), 681-84.

159 See CBCI Communication, 52.

160 'Consultation on Theology,' 76

is said to derive its meaning from the existential form.[161] But the most frequently found definitions of existential dialogue usually do imply a contrast with the discursive form. Panikkar calls for an "existential encounter"[162] – because "religions meet in the heart rather than the mind".[163] A different aspect of the same contrast is found in the claim that the principal reason why Christian initiatives in dialogue in the past have usually been fruitless is because "the old polemic, or at best, scholarly approach to Hinduism failed to make living contact" with Hindus.[164] Authenticity – a term whose meaning is not always easily grasped – is also said to be an essential quality of dialogue and a means of distinguishing such dialogue from less profound forms. Taylor, for example, claims that, by comparison with discursive dialogue, "real dialogue in its radical or Buberian form involves a venturesome unfolding to each other in authenticity".[165] For Klostermaier, "real" dialogue takes place at "an ultimate personal depth" and need not include the discussion of religious matters at all.[166] The use of the adjective "spiritual" is often another indication that the existential characteristics of dialogue are mainly in mind.[167]

There is widespread agreement among the proponents of existential dialogue that their preferred form of dialogue is, at least potentially, more profound and more significant than the discursive form in which both intellect and theology may unhelpfully intrude.[168] The attempt fully to understand should always be fuelled by the 'heart' rather than the 'head'.[169] 'Intellectualising' is a barrier

---

161 C Murray Rogers, 'Dialogue Postponed,' *AF*, 5 (1970), 216.

162 *TUCH(2)*, 43-45.

163 *TUCH(2)*, 43; see also 35f. So also, Jacques-Albert Cuttat, *Spiritual Dialogue Between East and West* (Delhi, 1961), 10. See also Abhishiktananda, 'The Way of Dialogue,' in *I-RD*, 85; he does, however, allow a role for the mind, "provided it puts itself at the disposal of the Spirit" (85).

164 Mary Kalapesi, 'Some Reflections on the Fourth Meeting on Hindu and Christian Spirituality,' *RS*, 11.4 (December 1964), 72.

165 'The Meaning of Dialogue,' 58 (emphasis in original).

166 'Dialogue – the Word of God,' in *I-RD*, 119. Panikkar also uses the adjectives "authentic" and "real" ('Rules of the Game in the Religious Encounter,' *AF*, 5 (1970), 225f).

167 For example, Mathew Lederle, 'Discovery of Dialogue,' *RS*, 26.1 (March 1979), 59.

168 See, for example, Roger Hooker, 'Evangelism, Dialogue and Worship,' *Vidyajyoti*, 40 (1976), 128.

169 To use the language of Wendy Doniger O'Flaherty, *Other Peoples' Myths* (New York, NY: Macmillan, 1988), 7-24.

between people; existential dialogue, on the other hand, is said to foster relationships of love, openness and genuine understanding.[170] For this reason the language of poetry and song, and the use of symbols rather than abstract concepts is much more likely to catch the nuances of searching that constitute key elements in the popular piety of both traditions – as an evangelical commentator rather poignantly shows from the Indian context.[171]

However, it is difficult fully to endorse all of the critical contrasts drawn between discursive and existential dialogue. The aims and results of the former (including the academic study of religion)[172] in facilitating understanding between Christians and Hindus are not unimportant given the known effects of misinformation at both the inter-personal and inter-communal levels. Moreover, there is the danger of an incomplete or distorted appreciation of partners in dialogue if the intellectual component of their faith is not given appropriate weight. Much more than love and openness are required if the faith of another, and the intellectual and cultural context from which it derives and which has helped to shape it, is to be understood. Neither the Christian nor the Hindu in dialogue can be fully understood simply and wholly as a solitary 'person'; each is the end product of a long and continuing process of religious, cultural and intellectual moulding, and discursive dialogue can enable an appropriately critical understanding of this process.[173]

Perhaps there is an analogy between types of dialogue and two of the traditional Christian 'approaches' to God in which there is a distinction between theology (thinking about God) and contemplation or encounter (the open, vulnerable meeting of God). Theological reflection is necessary if theology is not to abandon its role of always seeking to understand the whole of Christian experience; so discursive dialogue seeks to understand the partner in dialogue and to set the encounter in a social, historical and religious context that is wider than the actual face to face meeting of Christian and Hindu. But theological reflection, necessary as it is, can intrude upon the contemplative process and introduce an ele-

---

170 Hooker, 'The Meaning of Dialogue,' 57f.

171 Kathleen Nicholls, 'Indian Spirituality: in Search of Truth and Reality,' *ERT*, 22 (1998), 362-74 (reprinted from *Doing Theology in Context*, edited by Sunand Sumithra (Bangalore, 1994).

172 See Carman, 'Inter-Faith Dialogue and Academic Study of Religion,' in *DBM*, 1-86 and his remarks about Klostermaier's criticism of 'comparative religion' in 'Continuing Tasks,' 203f.

173 See also Sharpe, 'The Goals of Inter-Religious Dialogue,' 84f.

ment of pragmatic analysis into the encounter, whether with God or with a person of another faith.

D. The Conditions for Dialogue

Between the means of dialogue and its intended results stand a number of conditions and inhibiting factors. These are now described, beginning with those most closely linked with discursive dialogue, but noting that many of the conditions for successful discursive dialogue apply, as well, to other forms of the Hindu-Christian meeting.

1. An Acceptance of Religious Pluralism

In India it is not at all difficult to acknowledge the fact of religious pluralism – but somewhat differing conclusions concerning dialogue are drawn from it. If this pluralism is seen to reveal the "authentic and precious spiritual values in all religious traditions,"[174] then its acceptance will certainly encourage dialogue. On the other hand, if religious pluralism is simply the acknowledgement of what Painadath see as the incomprehensibility of the mystery of the Divine, the fragmentary and necessarily limited character of all human perception, and the inevitable cultural conditioning of all expressions of religion, then the humility induced by such acknowledgement might also encourage dialogue.[175]

For one partner in dialogue to accept the presence of genuine spiritual values in the life of the other is not to deny how different these values might be. In fact one danger to the authenticity of dialogue is said to be an unwillingness to accept the other as different (*GIRD(2)*, 52). Such unwillingness may derive from the *a priori* assumption that all religious experience is essentially the same despite differences in language. Among some Hindus there is a tendency to assimilate partial truths found elsewhere to a Vedantic worldview, though the more common Hindu view is to justify religious pluralism on the grounds of differing spiritual insight and ability (*adhikara*) and the consequent choice of differing forms of the

---

174 G Gispert-Sauch, 'Reflections for a Theology of Evangelization and Dialogue,' in *Service and Salvation*, 323. A similar point is made by Cyril Veliath, 'Christianity and Religious Pluralism,' *JMB*, 42 (1988), 15-20.

175 Sebastian Painadath, 'The Meaning and Scope of Religious Pluralism,' *Jeevadhara*, 27 (1997), 353-61.

divine (*Istadevata*).[176] Nonetheless, the well-known Swami Chidananda, speaking to an interreligious gathering, could state that an atmosphere for dialogue would only come when the church in India publicly declared that all religions worship the same and only God[177] – the kind of viewpoint that can draw critical comment, even within India, about a refusal really to accept religious diversity and its positive contribution "to the multicoloured fabric of human experience".[178] Some Hindu advocates of dialogue express a concern that the vedantic view does not allow the distinctiveness of the different religious faiths fully to be appreciated. Rambachan, for example, argues that there is a Hindu assessment of pluralism that is "complex, challenging and not as uncritically accepting of all paths as it is sometimes made out to be".[179] Sivaraman writes that "the Hindu in dialogue with religions like Islam and Christianity stands in special need of acknowledging them as worlds in themselves with their own centres, axis and structure, that they represent ways of thinking and feeling that he simply cannot assimilate into his own".[180] These faiths are to be recognised not merely as equally valid alternative paths to the same Goal, but as "alternative absolutes" that exclude one another in any but a transcendental sense.[181] And some Christians are, of course, also found advocating a thoroughgoing acceptance of religious pluralism – not merely in

---

176 For a discussion of the latter view of religious pluralism and its implications for dialogue see Seshagiri Rao, 'Human Community and Religious Pluralism: A Hindu Perspective,' in *Dialogue in Community*, edited by CD Jathanna (Balmatta, 1982), 163-66. Also helpful is KR Sundararajan, 'The Hindu Models of Interreligious Dialogue,' *JES*, 23 (1986), 239-50.

177 Cited in 'Introduction' to *Lead Me to the Real: The Hindu-Christian Dialogue* (Hong Kong, 1984), 5.

178 Chatterjee, 'The Presuppositions of Inter-Religious Communication,' 395.

179 Anantanand Rambachan, 'Religious Pluralism: a Hindu Perspective,' *CD*, no. 17 (December 1989), 25 (in which he is critical of Vivekananda's advaitin framework); in similar vein is his 'What Difference Does Religious Plurality Make?,' *CD*, no. 34 (2/ 1999), 24f.

180 K Sivaraman, 'Resources in Hindu Morality and Religion,' in *Towards World Community*, edited by Stanley J Samartha (Geneva, 1975), 27.

181 'Resources in Hindu Morality and Religion,' 29. His discussion of 'alternative absolutes' questions the views of those Hindus who espouse religious relativism (26); he argues that 'the claim to final truth is an integral part of religion and must be experienced existentially' (27). See further, chapter 4.C.1 below, and: Michael Amaladoss, 'Tolerance and Religious Faith,' *ITS*, 20 (1983), 199-215; and *Modern Indian Responses to Religious Pluralism*, edited by Harold Coward (Albany, NY, 1987).

descriptive but in prescriptive terms as well.[182]

The acceptance of religious pluralism also implies an acceptance of religious liberty. "Without the prior condition of liberty dialogue as a genuine encounter of commitments would be impossible".[183] In personal terms, dialogue requires "the freedom to be committed to one's own faith and to be open to that of another to witness, to change and to be changed".[184] Religious liberty also implies that both the Hindu and Christian traditions might wish to accept the prospect of present and future religious pluralism but without renouncing centrally important beliefs. All who insist upon freedom of self-definition and the maintenance of doctrinal distinctiveness must surely extend that liberty to others if dialogue is to flourish. Dialogue is inhibited when partners insist on defining others in their own categories[185] which is one reason for the inter-communal suspicion and hostility in contemporary India that greatly inhibits dialogue – a matter to which discussion will return.

Among Christians a further inhibition concerns the need for substantial change in the traditional theological appraisal of other faiths if there is to be an acceptance of religious pluralism. Writing in 1976, Ariarajah could speak of an apparent *impasse* to which initiatives in inter-faith dialogue had come: "very little of this new experience can be expressed within the framework of traditional theology".[186] Whether the 'Copernican revolution' in the theology of religions (proposed by John Hick and accepted by Knitter and a number of Indian Christians) will prove compelling to all Christians is uncertain. It does appear that if Hindu-Christian dialogue is to flourish at the deepest level (in terms of what we have called existential dialogue) then one condition will be openness to what Chatterjee calls "the intellectual and emotional welcoming-accept-

---

182 There is a useful summary of the usual reasons in Michael Amaladoss, 'Theological Bases for Religious Pluralism', in *Communalism in India*, edited by S Arulsamy (Bangalore: Claretian Publications, 1988), 115-38; and, in considerable detail, Jacques Dupuis, *Toward a Christian Theology of Religious Pluralism* (Maryknoll, NY: Orbis, 1997).

183 Samartha, '*More* than an Encounter of Commitments,' 393. A similar point is made by Panikkar, 'Inter-Religious Dialogue: Some Principles,' 408.

184 Samartha, 'Dialogue as a Continuing Christian Concern,' *ER*, 23 (1971), 136. Further on openness, see chapter 4B2 below.

185 Stanley Samartha 'The Other Side of the River,' unpublished paper, 1983, 10. He goes on to agree with a statement that "self- serving descriptions" of other peoples' faiths are some of the roots of "prejudice, stereotyping, and condescension" (*GOD*, 18).

186 'Towards a Theology of Dialogue,' 4.

ance of diversity,"[187] and acceptance of a substantial measure of equality in the meeting. As Felix Wilfred reminds western Christians: "Asia is not a *tabula rasa* [blank sheet]. It has its own spiritual landscape ...." This provides a distinctive context for proclamation of the Christian message that should not be understood in Asia "in terms of an ahistorical universal missiology." And neither do the western categories of 'inclusivism' and 'pluralism' fit well either. Wilfred concludes from an analysis of Asian Catholic Bishops' statements that their acceptance of the religious plurality does not mean that they

> subscribe to a multiplicity of theophanies and divine mediations, each one independent in its own religious universe and equally valid. So we could say that the position of the Asian bishops is neither inclusivism nor pluralism.[188]

At the same time, the cause of dialogue is not helped by an uncritical endorsement of all that might be accommodated in the name of an eclectic pluralism; as Samartha observes, "a critical principle has to be developed lest people flounder in a sea of relativism".[189] Moreover, D'Costa has cogently argued for the logical impossibility of sustaining a pluralist view of the religions given that tradition-specific criteria are always applied to distinguish acceptable from unacceptable religious options[190]- which would not imply the abandonment of dialogue but would require greater emphasis upon its discursive and secular aspects and less emphasis upon the existential. It might also be expected that other conserva-

187 'The Presuppositions of Inter-Religious Communication,' 395.

188 'Images of Jesus Christ in the Asian Pastoral Context', 55.

189 Stanley Samartha, 'Religious Identity in a Multi-Faith Society,' *CD*, no. 13 (December 1987), 6. Elsewhere he writes about "the risk of ... uncritical friendliness" ('Interreligious Relationships in the Secular State,' *CD*, no. 11 (December 1986), 27). Margaret Chatterjee also offers some critical comments in her 'Reflections on Religious Pluralism in the Indian Context,' *HCSB*, 7 (1994), 2-12 as does Diana Eck in chapter 5 of her *Encountering God: a Spiritual Journey from Bozeman to Banaras* (Boston, MA: Beacon Press, 1993).

190 Gavin D'Costa, 'The Impossibility of a Pluralist View of Religion,' *RSt*, 32 (1996), 223-32; and *The Meeting of Religions and the Trinity*, chapter 1. In chapter 4 of *The Meeting of Religions* he argues that Vatican II and post-Conciliar documents legitimate neither pluralism nor inclusivism. There is further discussion of this issue in chapter 5.I below where a restatement and refinement of D'Costa's views is noted from his *The Meeting of Religions and the Trinity*, Faith Meets Faith Series (Maryknoll, NY: Orbis Books), chapter 1.

tive Christians might be willing to accept pluralism in descriptive but not prescriptive categories.

2. *Sympathetic Understanding*

One part of informed understanding is accurate and reasonably comprehensive knowledge of the beliefs and practices (and perhaps history) of the others' religious tradition,[191] including their own particular understanding(s) of those beliefs and practices – even if it is difficult fully to enter into the plausibility structure of another religious tradition. The *Guidelines* states the importance of accurate information about other religions being taught at all levels of the Christian community and not merely in the classrooms of schools, colleges and seminaries (*GIRD(2)*, 58-63). Problems arise in dialogue when this accurate knowledge is not present,[192] or when participants use terminology from their own tradition that is not intelligible to others. Without informed understanding, differences may not be noted, or may be attributed to wrong causes because of hasty categorisation (*GIRD(2)*, 49, 52) and inadequate interpretation (*GIRD(2)*, 52). Both of these may, in turn, be caused or made worse by the misunderstanding that is liable to occur when one partner is not using their mother tongue. In fact, it is sometimes suggested that while, "in India dialogue through the medium of English may still have its place", there are distinct benefits if it takes place in the mother tongue of the participants.[193]

The choice of an appropriate and agreed philosophical or religious framework may also be important. This need not necessarily mean agreement on "a common rational philosophy" such as the enlargement and use of "a sufficiently comprehensive system such as that of Thomas Aquinas or Sankara" (as Chethimattam once proposed).[194] But without discussion of the kind of language and terminology that might allow one person in dialogue to apprehend the meaning of another there is always the danger that the encounter may take the form of parallel monologues. Appropriate method is

---

191 See, for example, *GIRD(2)*, 51; Chethimattam, 'The Scope and Conditions of a Hindu-Christian Dialogue.'

192 See an example cited by Joseph Masson, 'The Opinion of Various Hindus on Dialogue,' *BSPNC*, 7 (1972), 39.

193 *GIRD(2)*, 50; also 'India: Seminar on Dialogue with Non Christians,' 98; Lederle, 'Discovery of Dialogue,' 71; Carman, 'Continuing Tasks,' 204; Abhishiktananda, *The Church in India*, 60.

194 Chethimattam, 'The Scope and Conditions of a Hindu-Christian Dialogue,' 87.

another concern; for example, Christian participants might learn from one aspect of traditional Hindu procedure in debate: the determining and restating of the opposing viewpoint.[195]

What we have called 'interior dialogue' has, within its own definition and aims, a clear understanding of the means and conditions of its implementation. A key verb is 'to listen' – for example, "to listen to what the Hindu Scriptures mysteriously foreshadowed of Christ with the same openness to the Spirit" as that with which the Bible is also read.[196] And perhaps even 'listening' fails adequately to convey the intention of such dialogue since the aim is "to penetrate as deeply as possible into the secret of the experience enshrined in the Upanishads, leaving aside all reference to anything else".[197] Nonetheless, such a process at least begins with careful, 'open' listening.

3. *Suspension of Evaluative Judgement?*

For what we have called interior dialogue, some additional (though not alternative) conditions are suggested. One is the call to *epochè*: the provisional placing in parenthesis (meaning the phenomenological 'suspension') of all those evaluative processes (psychological, religious, cultural) that might impede a profound hearing of the other. It is an attitude of silencing oneself so as to hear the other's self-understanding.[198] Its character is *provisional.*[199] To fail to reopen the bracket would be to fail to respond honestly and fully; or, as Knitter understands it, the reopening occurs by the rediscovery of the truth of one's faith through the dialogue itself.[200] But if the condition of *epochè* is not met Cuttat believes that the encounter may become merely another form of monologue – an exercise in apologetics in which there is a refusal ever to place convictions in paren-

---

195 Kana Mitra, 'A Hindu Self-Reflection,' *JES*, 17 (1980), 121f.

196 Abhishiktananda, *Hindu-Christian Meeting Point*, revised edition (Delhi, 1976), 27; see also his *Saccidananda*.

197 *Hindu-Christian Meeting Point*, 95.

198 See Cuttat, *The Encounter of Religions* (New York, 1960), 30f, and *Spiritual Dialogue Between East and West* (Delhi, 1961) 13; Taylor, 'The Meaning of Dialogue,' 60; Rogers, 'Hindu and Christian – a Moment Breaks,' 39; Kalapesi, 'Some Reflections,' 73f; Joseph Mattam, *Land of the Trinity* (Bangalore, [1975]), 77-79, and, from other perspectives, De Souza, 'Dialogue Between Religions in India,' 84f; and AJ Toynbee, *A Humanist's Approach to Religion* (London, 1956), 295f.

199 See, for example, Kalapesi, 'Some Reflections,' 72; Abhishiktananda, 'The Way of Dialogue,' in *I-RD*, 86f.

200 *No Other Name?* 205-31.

thesis at all – or a form of implicit syncretism in which the parenthesis becomes a permanent bracketing out of of conviction and evaluation.[201] The quest for an empathetic but non-evaluative dialogue seems futile.

This *epochè* is most appropriate for internal dialogue and often unavoidable or assumed for secular dialogue. But its appropriateness for the existential mode of the encounter can be challenged.[202] It can be argued that authenticity in this form of dialogue *requires* the honesty of conviction and the acknowledgement of the reality of the differences of discrete religious particularities that the *epochè* seeks to bracket off.[203] Perhaps "some degree of disinterestedness" is a more appropriate condition;[204] or, in the words of a Hindu academic: "If I want to understand the Christian religion, I must put away Hindu preconceptions".[205]

4. Dialogue as Personal

Of all the conditions suggested for dialogue, none receives greater emphasis than a cluster of qualities that emphasises the inter-*personal* dimension of the encounter. "Dialogue is not a matter of discussions but of relationships. It has more to do with people than with ideas".[206] This means a readiness to respond to the partner in dialogue not merely as an adherent or representative of a different religious tradition, but as a person (although it is, of course, an unhelpful and misleading abstraction – and near impossible in India – to isolate a person from their religio-cultural tradition). Dhavamony writes, "when I meet a Hindu ... I will approach him as a person, one of the wonderful works of God and of his grace. ... With this perspective the approach becomes sacred".[207] The condi-

---

201 This raises the question of the tension between openness and commitment – an issue that will be discussed in chapter 4.B below.

202 There is an excellent summary of the issues for and against the notion of *epochè* in Kuttianimattathil, *Practice and Theology of Interreligious Dialogue*, 477-83.

203 See, for example, Panikkar, *The Intrareligious Dialogue*, 40-52.

204 'Hindu-Christian Dialogue: Its Religious and Cultural Implications,' in *ITD*, 236f.

205 Sankaranarayan, cited in Report on Nagpur Conference, *RS*, 7.3 & 4 (October and December 1960), 136.

206 Stanley J Samartha, 'Christian Concern for Dialogue in India,' *CD*, no. 9 (December 1985), 3. See also Taylor, 'The Meaning of Dialogue,' 64.

207 Mariasusai Dhavamony, 'Evangelization and Dialogue with Hindus,' in *Light and Life We Seek to Share*, 147.

tions suggested by Taylor for 'authentic' dialogue include: mutuality, directness, presentness, intensity, ineffability and "a kind of believing-in-love".[208] To this list a number of other proposed qualities are added: honesty,[209] truthfulness (*GIRD(2)*, 43), sympathy,[210] generosity,[211] goodwill,[212] deep friendship,[213] patience,[214] curiosity,[215] respect,[216] freedom,[217] reverence,[218] worship,[219] prayer,[220] holiness[221] and a quiet and relaxed spirit.[222]

Hope is sometimes given particular emphasis; in one statement it is called "the most fundamental attitude" necessary for those who enter dialogue.[223] Also important are mutual trust[224] and belief that the partner in dialogue is speaking sincerely.[225] Such trust might only flow from the "reconciliation and forgiveness for injuries inflicted through ignorance, prejudice or even ill will" that are also

---

208 'The Meaning of Dialogue,' 56.

209 'Consultation on Theology,' 77; *GIRD(2)*, 43; Vandana Mataji, '*Living with Hindus.' Hindu-Christian Dialogues: My Experiences and Reflections* (Bangalore and Delhi: ITA and ISPCK, 1999).

210 'Consultation on Theology,' 76.

211 'Hindu-Christian Dialogue: Its Religious and Cultural Implications,' 236.

212 L Sundaram, 'The Value of Inter-Faith Dialogue,' *HCSB*, 2 (1989), 8.

213 Moses, 'Some Reflections on Personal Dialogue,' 249.

214 In a vivid expression, Jules Monchanin once spoke of the witness of his ashram to Christian-Hindu dialogue as born "in an atmosphere of geological patience" (*Mystère de l'Inde, Mystère Chrétien* (Paris, 1977), 92). See also Abhishiktananda, *The Church in India*, 60-62; Dhavamony, 'Evangelization and Dialogue with Hindus,' 148; CBCI Communication, 52.

215 *FTF*, 8. Taylor writes: "We enter dialogue with the best and humblest kind of curiosity, in which expectancy and reverence and dread all have their place." (8)

216 'Conclusions of the National Seminar on Crisis of Faith,' 332.

217 Michael Amaladoss, 'Dialogue and Mission: Conflict or Convergence?,' *Vidyajyoti*, 50 (1986), 85.

218 Kalapesi, 'Some Reflections,' 173; C Murray Rogers, 'Hindu Influence on Christian Spiritual Practice,' in *H-CD*, 200.

219 Hooker, 'Evangelism, Dialogue and Worship,' 127f.

220 *GIRD(2)*, 40 where it receives a strong emphasis as a necessary condition for fruitful dialogue.

221 Mattam, *Land of the Trinity*, 185.

22 'Basis and Content,' 79.

223 'Consultation on Theology,' 72; see also *GIRD(2)*, 45, 112. "Spiritual expectancy" is also mentioned in 'The Basis and Content,' 78; and "fearlessness" (*Lead Me to the Real: the Hindu-Christian Dialogue*, 43).

224 Panikkar, 'Inter-Religious Dialogue: Some Principles,' 408.

225 Chethimattam, 'The Scope and Conditions of a Hindu-Christian Dialogue,' 86.

seen as "an essential dimension of dialogue".[226] Humility is also important: the humility to acknowledge "the difficulties that others feel with regard both to us and to our faith,"[227] and the humility to acknowledge that in the presence of the mystery of God, both Hindu and Christian admit their ignorance.[228]

Empathy – "the ability to enter into the spirit and mind of another" and to receive the "full impact" of that person's spirituality[229] – is also emphasised. The "informed understanding" noted above is said to require an apprehension of the "inner experience" which words, concepts and symbols attempt to express (*GIRD(2)*, 51). Chatterjee examines in some detail the conditions for the desirable possibility of being able to say, "I know what it means to you" in inter-religious conversation.[230] Both an "imaginative orientation" and a "willingness not to be put off by [the] unfamiliarity of … the style of expression of a particular faith"[231] seem to be part of this empathy.

Also related to empathy is love that is widely regarded as another essential prerequisite. Love of God is sometimes meant (for example, *GIRD(2)*, 44); but usually the meaning is what Panikkar calls "that urge and force which impels us toward our fellow-beings," even in the face of their discouragements.[232] Dialogue is both the expression of love and yet is also dependent upon the presence of love.[233] This love expresses itself in the kind of listening that draws the other to speak, and the kind of speaking that draws the other to listen.

These, then, are the principal conditions proposed for fruitful

226 *Theses on Interreligious Dialogue* (Hong Kong, 1987), 15.

227 KS, 55. See also: 'Consultation on Theology,' 76; *GIRD(2)*, 43, 45; *ATA*, 7-23, 50; Abhishiktananda, *The Church in India*, 60; *Lead Me to the Real: the Hindu-Christian Dialogue*, 43.

228 Samartha, 'Indian Realities,' 315.

229 *GIRD(2)*, 49. A similar point is made by Rogers, 'The Content of a Christian-Hindu Dialogue,' 71.

230 'The Presuppositions of Inter-Religious Communication,' 395-99.

231 Chatterjee, 'The Presuppositions of Inter-Religious Communication,' 396. See also Carman, 'Inter-Faith Dialogue and Academic Study of Religion,' 84; and Knitter on "the role of imagination" in *No Other Name?*, 213-16.

232 Panikkar, 'Rules of the Game in the Religious Encounter,' *AF*, 5 (1970), 227. In similar vein see Chatterjee, 'The Presuppositions of Inter-Religious Communication,' 396.

233 Concerning love as a condition for dialogue see also Sadiq, 'Inter-Faith Dialogue and Communication of the Gospel,' *RS*, 12.1(March 1965), 14; Frank Whaling, *An Approach to Dialogue with Hinduism* (Lucknow, 1966), 73.

Hindu-Christian dialogue;[234] that many of them can be met, or met in part, is suggested by the reported results of such dialogue.

E. The Results of Dialogue

The reported results of Hindu-Christian dialogue may be summarised in terms of the typology proposed in section C above – noting again the tendency for categories to overlap.

1. Discursive Dialogue

Increased understanding is not often mentioned as a specific result of the encounter; perhaps this result is self-evident. When enhanced understanding is mentioned it is sometimes in terms of a diminishing of ignorance; perhaps, in Indian terms, 'the removal of *avidya*' would be a better expression. Roger Hooker, for example, in listening to Hindu friends found that he was

> failing to pick up the stories, the allusions, and the assumptions which lay behind what was being said, but were left unsaid because everyone present – except me – knew what they were. And so I formulated what for me remains the cardinal first principle of all communication – and therefore of all inter-religious dialogue: I can only understand what another person says if I have first understood what they have left unsaid.[235]

And this understanding requires considerable knowledge of the content of the beliefs and practices of the other.

A Hindu Swami of the Order of Ramakrishna, after a long study of Catholic mystical theology concludes that, as well as a number of parallels with Hinduism, there are real and not imagined differences as well: "In the two traditions spiritual life has neither the same perspective nor the same foundation."[236] Such an admission of significant different can facilitate dialogue. However, discursive dialogue is more often linked with other commendable results: for example, the Catholic *Guidelines* links "deeper knowledge" and

234 Two other frequently suggested conditions for dialogue – profound commitment to one's own religion and openness to the faith of others, and the apparent tension between these two conditions – are discussed at some length in chapter 4 below.

235 In his *Narrating Our Nations*, cited in *Ambassador*, no. 17 (Spring 1999), 10.

236 Siddheswarananda, *Hindu Thought and Carmelite Mysticism* (Et: Delhi: Motilal Banarsidass, 1998), 32. Howeever, it should also be noted that he also embraces the usual neo-Hindu notion of an essentialist religious pluralism in which there is a common core metaphysical or "extrareligious truth" (85).

"mutual understanding" with, among other things, "an opportunity to preserve and promote the spiritual and religious patrimony of mankind" and "a greater common dedication to the Lord of all" (*GIRD(2)*, 34). The curricula of seminaries and houses of formation now include courses on Indian religions. However, one observer warns that the result is limited to "a theoretical and superficial book knowledge, without much acquaintance with the lived reality of the religions" – although he does concede that this is better than "the absolute prejudiced blankness with which priests and religious of a generation ago entered Indian society." The same writer believes that the dialogue centres started in various parts of India may have led to a degree of enhanced understanding "in certain very limited circles of western educated Hindus, but not dialogue at any depth."[237] A volume on *Major Hindu Festivals: a Christian Appreciation*[238] has been produced.

The reports of increased understanding derive not only from greater self-understanding of the content of the faith of the other but also to self-discovery and self-understanding as well. In this way the mirror, as it were, of another faith enables an enhanced self-understanding. Dupuis, who lived in India for many years, writes that the "shock of the encounter will often ... force Christians to revise gratuitous assumptions, and destroy deep-rooted prejudices or overthrow certain overly narrow conceptions or outlooks."[239] This is "the salutary 'discovery' of the extent of ... ignorance of the beliefs and practices of other religions."[240] And this enhanced self-understanding includes increased "knowledge of ourselves as seen, understood and accepted by others".[241]

Within the Christian community the increased self-understanding includes greater ecumenical openness as well.[242] The possibility is also

---

237 Soares-Prabhu, 'The Indian Church Challenged by Pluralism and Dialogue,' 190.

238 Subhash Anand (Bombay: St Paul Publications, 1991).

239 Jacques Dupuis, *Toward a Christian Theology of Religious Pluralism*, 382.

240 De Souza, 'Dialogue Between Religions in India,' 82.

241 *GIRD(2)*, 34; see also 'Religious Resources for a Just Society,' 16.

242 *GIRD(2)*, [39] – this section is, mistakenly it seems, left unnumbered; Nambiaparambil, 'Dialogue in India: An Analysis,' 274; Samartha, 'Partners in Community,' 81; Samartha goes on to give one actual and several potential areas of such cooperation. See also S Wesley Ariarajah, 'The Impact of Interfaith Dialogue on the Ecumenical Movement,' in *Pluralism and the Religions: The Theological and Political Dimensions*, edited by John D'Arcy May (London: Cassell, 1998), 7-21; and 'Wider Ecumenism: A Threat or a Promise?', *ER*, 50 (1998), 321-29.

noted that increased contact with other faiths may lead to a greater appreciation of the pluralism within the Church itself in India.[243]

2. *Secular Dialogue*

Sometimes the results of 'secular' dialogue are simply reported as the common recognition of shared goals and the discovery of "how much can be done together".[244] More specific accomplishments include the establishment of various co-operative groups and enterprises.[245] There are also reports of secular dialogue acting as "an encouragement to greater solidarity" (*GIRD(2)*, 34) and leading to the mutual enrichment of an awareness of common humanity and a sense of the unity of all people[246] – a unity that the religions cannot obscure.[247] Nation building is also said to give "a common language of discourse at spiritual depth".[248] Samartha goes further and argues that there is evidence that secular dialogue contributes to "the process of critical transformation" that has been taking place in a number of (religious) communities in India[249] (though he undoubtedly knows of the considerable resistance to such 'transformation' – resistance generated both by inertia and by ideological opposition and suspicion).

3. *Interior Dialogue*

The intramural self-understanding said to result from this form of dialogue is described in various ways. A realisation of ignorance of the faith of others is reported.[250] The spirit of self-criticism that pervades some Indian Christian writing seems also to be a result. In India there is some evidence of what Küng reports in global terms: the religions, once seen as an external quantitative challenge to Christianity, now pose what might be called an internal qualitative challenge[251] and the preparation of the Christian community for actual dialogue is one consequence of such a challenge.

---

243 CBCI Communication, 35.
244 *'Religious Resources for a Just Society,'* 3.
245 See, for example, Nambiaparambil, 'Dialogue in India: An Analysis,' 277f.
246 'Consultation on Theology,' 85.
247 'Consultation Working Group Reports,' 108.
248 MM Thomas, 'Christology and Pluralistic Consciousness,' *IBMR*, 10 (1986), 106.
249 'Indian Realities,' 14.
250 Nambiaparambil, 'Dialogue in India: An Analysis,' 277.
251 Hans Küng, *On Being a Christian* (Et: London, 1976), 99f.

In general terms there is also said to be a renewed and deepened respect for the teaching of other faiths. More specifically, Eck and Klostermaier write of an enhanced understanding of the mystery of the incarnation of Christ because of their encounter with Hinduism.[252] Ravi Ravindra discovers *the Yoga of the Christ in the Gospel according to Saint John*[253] and Bede Griffiths is enabled to write *River of Compassion: a Christian Commentary on the Bhagavad Gita*[254] because of his reflections on Hinduism. Whaling draws attention to hermeneutical insights for understanding the Biblical world-view(s),[255] and Klostermaier writes of the re-examination of theological method.[256] Painadath reports on the possibility of "inter-religious hermeneutics"[257](which draws attention to the way in which, as Clooney puts it, "the pluralist's focus on Mystery serves as an oddly effective protection' against rigorous attention to the claims of the religious texts of others).[258] From a prolonged and close study of the Upanishads, Coward reports several 'rediscoveries': the Bible as oral tradition, the study of the Bible as a devotional exercise, the power of chanted prayer and other neglected features of Christian spirituality.[259] Manickam reports on what might be learnt from Hindu practices of fasting and abstinence.[260] And the ancient ideal of worldview expressed as a commentary (*bhashya*) on scripture has found Christian expression in Vandana's commentary on the Gospel of John (*Waters of Fire*)[261] and Boyd's attempt at a systematic Christian theology based on the Epistle to the Romans (*Khristadvaita*).[262]

---

252 Diana Eck, 'The Religions and Tambaram: 1938 and 1988,' *IRM*, 78 (1988), 384; Klostermaier, *Hindu and Christian in Vrindaban*, 75-87.

253 Shaftesbury: Element Books, 1990.

254 Warwick, NY: Amity House, 1987.

255 *An Approach to Dialogue with Hinduism*, 79-82.

256 Klostermaier, 'Hindu-Christian Dialogue: Its Religious and Cultural Implications,' 239f.

257 Sebastian Painadath, 'Towards an Inter-Religious Hermeneutics,' *WW*, 20 (1987), 83-90.

258 See Francis X Clooney, 'Reading the World in Christ: from Comparison to Inclusivism,' in *Christian Uniqueness Reconsidered: the Myth of a Pluralistic Theology of Religions*, edited by Gavin D'Costa (Maryknoll, NY: Orbis, 1990), 63-80 (quotation from 78).

259 Harold G Coward, 'Hinduism's Sensitizing of Christianity to Its Own Sources,' *Dialogue and Alliance*, 7 (1993), 77-85.

260 Thomas M. Manickam, 'What Christians Can Learn from the Hindu Practice of Fasting and Abstinence,' *WW*, 15 (1982), 58-62.

261 Madras, 1981.

262 Subtitled: *a Theology for India* (Madras, 1977).

4. Existential Dialogue

This widest of categories brings a correspondingly wide range of reported results. There is said to be increased sensitivity,[263] mutual acceptance and love.[264] Mutual spiritual enrichment is also mentioned – most often in the sense of a deepening of personal faith as a result of the Christian Hindu encounter.[265] For some Christians the enrichment is quite unexpected.[266] Even scholars report transformation.[267] Dialogue is also said to lead to the realisation that the divine saving will makes God present to everyone.[268]

The effect of growth as a result of dialogue is elaborated in a number of ways. The Nagpur Declaration states that the growth may, in fact, be "a kind of deeper *metanoia* or conversion to God".[269] The faith of Christians is said to be "deepened" by the incorporation of the resources of others.[270] Another proponent of dialogue writes of faith being "released" as a result of the Christian-Hindu encounter.[271] Dialogue is also said to offer a number of reminders of truths and experiences already known; for example, a reminder of personal relationship with God observed in Hindu friends.[272] One participant concludes that dialogue is an inadequate word to describe the depth of the encounter; he suggests "communion" as a more accurate term.[273]

The suspension of evaluative judgement suggested by some advocates of interior and existential dialogue is said to result in a clearer understanding of some aspects of Hinduism. For example, there is the claim that the issue of caste looks less unacceptable when viewed from the standpoint of dialogue.[274] Equally problem-

---

263 'Consultation on Theology,' 86.

264 *GIRD(2)*, 34; see also the consequences of a 'Live-Together' cited by Nambiaparambil, 'Church in India – Dialogue in Progress,' 265f.

265 For example, 'Consultation on Theology,' 85; *GIRD(2)*, 34.

266 'Dialogue in India: An Analysis,' 282; so also Rogers, 'Hindu and Christian – A Moment Breaks,' 39.

267 For example, Francis X Clooney, 'The Transformation of the Scholar as a Factor in Hindu-Christian Studies,' *HCSB*, 3 (1990), 1-6.

268 Amaladoss, 'Dialogue and Mission: Conflict or Convergence?,' 63.

269 Nagpur Declaration, 27.

270 'Consultation Working Group Reports,' 106.

271 Nambiaparambil, 'Dialogue in India: An Analysis,' 275. On religious growth as a goal of dialogue, see chapter 3.F below.

272 DG Moses, 'Some Reflections on Personal Dialogue,' 250f.

273 Rogers, 'Inter-Religious Dialogue,' 241.

274 Ishanand Vempeny, 'Dialogical Standpoint Illustrated by the Caste-System,' *Jeevadhara*, 3 (1973), 428-44.

atical is the claim that the understanding of *advaita* in a "supra-mental" sense (meaning "the primacy of the inner realisation over metaphysical theory") enables a Christian apprehension at a deeper level than traditional Christian insistence upon the ultimate distinction between God and the world.[275] It is also claimed that those exposed to "dialogue in depth ... become aware of the relativity and insufficiency of all formulations and symbols".[276] However, there are, of course, difficulties with this appeal to religious experience (see below chapter 3.L).

Other reported results include the admission that dialogue exposed personal prayer and meditation as very superficial by comparison with the devotion of Hindus.[277] The employment of "possessive religious language" with its pretensions to the exclusive apprehension of truth is seen as needing to be abandoned or modified.[278] And dialogue also leads to the experience of self-examination and the "confession of one's own hypocrisy".[279] Given these results, it is not surprising to read that dialogue leads to the shedding of prejudices.[280] Probably only encounters as profound as those described or advocated by what we have called existential dialogue could have such far-reaching consequences. Moreover, these consequences can be described in communal terms as well. Nambiaparambil claims that "slowly but steadily" the public worship of the Catholic community is changing. The singing of *bhajans*, once "limited to the Hindu temples, has become a common feature in the Christian institutions" and Catholic seminarians may spend time in Hindu ashrams.[281] The use of *yoga* is encouraged in some places.[282]

Among Hindu participants in dialogue the range of reported results is almost as wide as that noted by Christians. Feelings of complacency and self-sufficiency are exposed and "a felt sense of incompleteness" is said to have arisen in dialogue. There is also the recovery of a sense of "self-assurance or adequacy and completeness," and the "recognition of a new source of strength, hitherto

275 Mary Kalapesi, 'Some Reflections,' 75.

276 Klostermaier, 'Hindu-Christian Dialogue: Its Religious and Cultural Implications,' 237.

277 Moses, 'Some Reflections on Personal Dialogue,' 250; Rogers, 'Inter-Faith Dialogue,' 241.

278 Nambiaparambil, 'Dialogue in India: An Analysis,' 283.

279 Nambiaparambil, 'Church in India – Dialogue in Progress,' 267.

280 Nambiaparambil, 'Dialogue in India: An Analysis,' 276; *GIRD(2)*, 34.

281 Nambiaparambil, 'India,' in *Mission in Dialogue*, 416.

282 See, for example, Nambiaparambil, 'India,' 416.

undetected".[283] Other reports speak of renewed and critical self-examination of Hinduism,[284] and of participants in formal dialogue finding their own faith not only challenged but also renewed and re-experienced.[285] Spiritual enrichment[286] and a transformed "spiritual perspective"[287] are also claimed. Such dialogue is also said to raise the question of whether the encounter, when it leads to critical self-enquiry and even transformation, might be described as "making Hindus better Hindus" – a result, it could be argued, of the Hindu-Christian encounter in the (perhaps ongoing) Hindu renaissance – but a consequence that would undoubtedly disturb some Christians even as it encourages others.[288]

The definition of dialogue in existential categories emphasises the importance of the inter-personal dimension of the Hindu-Christian meeting. Perhaps at this personal level most has been achieved; perhaps at the inter-communal level most remains to be done in terms of the hopes of the proponents of dialogue.

F. Comment

A wide range of meanings is, then, given to the word 'dialogue'; its usage has become "extremely elastic" in the view of one commentator who prefers a narrow definition that would exclude most informal dialogue and much of what has been called existential dialogue above.[289]

Concerning each of the various categories of formal or intentional dialogue, critical comment might be made. Discursive dialogue can readily display a degree of intellectual detachment more typical of western views of religion than Indian. Such dialogue requires little engagement beyond the stimulus of the exchange of facts and opinions and may imply that commitment and faith are optional components of what it means to be religious. Such an implication may actually impede the fruitful meeting of Hindu and Christian

---

283 K Sivaraman in 'Dialogue Between Men of Living Faiths – The Ajaltoun Memorandum,' in *LFEM*, 18.

284 Rambachan in Ariarajah, 'Christology in Asia,' 25.

285 For example, '*Religious Resources*,' 3.

286 For example, Hirudayam, 'Dialogue in Tamilnadu,' 423.

287 S Maharajan cited by Hirudayam, 'Dialogue in Tamilnadu,' 424.

288 See, for example, Klostermaier, 'Hindu-Christian Dialogue: Its Religious and Cultural Implications,' 238; Mariasusai Dhavamony, 'Tension between Evangelization and Dialogue,' in *Light and Life We Seek To Share*, 96.

289 Baird, 'Hindu-Christian Dialogue and the Academic Study of Religion,' 229.

(as noted in the discussion of interior and existential dialogue) or obscure the reason why the meeting often remains fruitless. It might also be argued that discursive dialogue could be conducted through the medium of literature and observation – that is, without actual meeting face to face. Nor does discursive dialogue require the spirit of goodwill, growth and positive change that most advocates of its interior and existential (and even secular) forms intend. In fact, it can be used for purposes of apologetic and even polemic – as, for example, with the informed dialogue conducted by many of the writers for the *New Religious Movements Update* journal (formerly published in Aarhus, Denmark, and then in Hong Kong). Nonetheless, discursive dialogue is usually characterised by interest and curiosity and also by a measure of reaction and response to the beliefs and practices of the other. The reported responses to and results of the discursive form of dialogue do seem to justify its employment in fostering good inter-religious relations.

'Interior dialogue' requires no actual contact between Hindu and Christian and so, as already noted, could be seen as no dialogue with the phrase able to be dismissed as oxymoronic given the absence of any actual partner. Taylor comments that its advocates "seem to engage in dialogue with *Hinduism*. ... But they all too often spend very little time in dialogue with Hindus".[290] This may sometimes or often be true but it is the explicitly *preparatory* nature of this form of dialogue that is its major justification. According to Eck, without the preparation of inner dialogue, "all dialogue is mere posturing and position taking. It is inner dialogue that makes dialogue genuine."[291]

Questions might also be raised about 'secular dialogue': (a) concerning the appropriateness of the adjective 'secular' in an Indian context; and (b) because it can seem to skirt the issue of religious faith or belief. Its continued use will depend upon a pragmatic understanding of the adjectives 'secular' and 'religious', and on an emphasis upon the 'diapraxis' that both religious traditions believe ought to be seen alongside the verbal elaboration of faith.[292] As will be seen below (chapter 3.B), there are substantial reasons for advocating a 'dialogue of action'.

Not unexpectedly, it is 'existential dialogue' that has attracted most discussion. One criticism of such dialogue centres upon its

---

290 'Current Hindu-Christian Dialogue in India,' 122f (original emphasis).

291 'What Do We Mean by "Dialogue"?', 15.

292 The fact that this balance is not always found has been "a hindrance to inter-faith dialogue" ('Consultation Working Group Reports,' 108).

apparent individualism that seems to take too little account of the community that inevitably shapes the individual. On the other hand this form of encounter can actually act as a reminder that the Hindu and Christian traditions are, in fact, *living* faiths; Hindus and Christians are not merely religious persons in a general religious sense. In view of the considerable catalogue of results and responses reported by those who have embraced this form of dialogue it is difficult to sustain the criticism that "though this approach rests on high ideals, it may prove to be little more than a theoretical stance".[293] Much more problematical is the claim that is central to a number of elaborations of existential dialogue (for example, those of Panikkar and Klostermaier) that it does, or should, take place at an experiential level that it is beyond verbal description or logical comprehension. Such an implication attracts criticism (see below, chapter 3.L); however, the criticisms need not invalidate the use of the phrase, provided its presuppositions about the place of religious experience are acknowledged and not declared to be beyond scrutiny. If such dialogue is seen as more than conversation and even regarded as an important form of religious activity, this may well render analysis and comment more difficult – but not impossible. And, while it is certainly good to see dialogue leading to a reassessment of each tradition by some of its adherents, there may well be a point where revision and reconception end. To give one example: Clooney's question about extending the canon of Christian scripture as a result of the encounter with other sacred texts[294] would be a massive shift, especially in less liberal streams of Christianity – but even there it might force a re-examination and restatement of a long-cherished position not usually stated with reference to other faiths.

Much of the problem with the definition(s) of dialogue centres on the starting points and understanding of religion that are assumed and used. To employ a phrase from christology, dialogue can be seen as beginning 'from below', or 'from above'. To begin 'from below' is to initiate dialogue from, for example, shared social concern or common humanity or life itself or the faith and practice of the religious other. To start 'from above' is to start from Scripture or theology, or to assume a unity of religious experience. In turn, these different (but not necessarily mutually exclusive) starting points relate directly to the motivation and goals of dialogue. And the

293 Sharpe, 'Dialogue of Religions,' 347.

294 Francis X Clooney, 'Extending the Canon. Some Implications of a Hindu Argument about Scripture,' *HTR*, 85 (1992), 197-215.

understanding of religion is also of consequence. If religion has various levels or components then dialogue will relate differently to each of them. Dialogue with the 'core experience' will at least include a discursive component and will move on to inner and existential dialogue depending on how that experience is seen to relate to one's own faith. Dialogue with the collective tradition and its symbols and practices will certainly require a discursive interaction and perhaps more if that tradition challenges one's own. On the other hand, dialogue with the tradition's theological / philosophical interpretation may not need to go beyond an encounter in a thorough-going discursive sense. Kitagawa distinguishes between the 'inner' and 'outer' meaning of religion and religions.[295] Each religion has an inner meaning that provides its affirmation of truth – "autobiography" as he calls it that enables an adherent to enter a specific community of meaning and truth. But religions also have a "biography" insofar as they recognise their participation in a larger human community. It is this double orientation that requires differentiation in understanding the exercise of dialogue.

The advocacy and practice of dialogue has had an affect upon Hindu-Christian relations. Despite indifference, impediments and even opposition (see below, chapter 4.A) there is evidence of some changing attitudes, at least among some Christians and Hindus. An experienced observer of Christian-Hindu dialogue in India considers that the participants in dialogue have been "witnesses to the joy of getting out of the ghettos of isolation and of entering into religious communion".[296] That 'joy' is not, however, widely evident. One reason is that a number of difficulties, both practical and theoretical, have been encountered as Hindus and Christians have met in dialogue; these difficulties will be considered in detail below (chapter 4). Some of the problems relate to the wide range of reasons given for engaging in dialogue, and it is to these reasons that discussion now turns.

---

295 See Joseph M Kitagawa, *The Quest for Human Unity: A Religious History* (Minneapolis: Fortress Press, 1990).

296 Nambiaparambil, 'Church in India,' 266.

CHAPTER 3

The Justification of Christian-Hindu Dialogue

Dialogue by Christians with people of other faiths – or, at least, most forms of dialogue – is a somewhat novel enterprise within the Christian tradition. Although there are certainly are pragmatic reasons for dialogue, there seem to be few biblical and other precedents for such dialogue. In fact, it may be the case that, as Eric Sharpe puts it,

> the historian of religions is forced to point out all the same that the Bible offers only limited support, by way of the theology of natural revelation, to the kind of position some of the more advanced dialogicians seem to want to accept as normative. One does not have to be a conservative evangelical to recognise that the phrase "interreligious dialogue" is in biblical terms practically meaningless. The biblical record does not speak of "religion" and "the religions" in our sense. It speaks unequivocally of God and the gods (and goddesses), and of the folly of [idolatry].[1]

On the other hand, it must also be noted that a panel of Indian theologians can offer what it sees as ample biblical evidence for the enterprise.[2] There is a Greek verb, *dialogizomai*, that is used in the New Testament and means to ponder, to consider, or to converse, discuss or argue.[3] This, at most, parallels dialogue in its discursive sense of sustained conversation. Apart from this verb it might be possible to justify from the teaching and example of the New Testament a willingness to enter "sustained, informed, respectful conversation" with the beliefs of others even if those beliefs are regarded as mistaken.[4] But it certainly seems difficult to sustain

---

1 Eric J Sharpe, 'Mission between Dialogue and Proclamation,' in *Redemption and Dialogue: Reading* Redemptoris Missio *and* Dialogue and Proclamation, edited by William R Burrows (Maryknoll, NY: Orbis, 1994), 169.

2 See *Biblical Insights on Inter-faith Dialogue: Some Material for Study and Reflection*, edited by Israel Selvanayagam (Bangalore: The Board for Theological Text-Books Programme of South Asia, 1995).

3 See I Howard Marshall, 'Interfaith Dialogue in the New Testament,' *ERT*, 13 (1989), 196-215; and 'Dialogue with Non-Christians in the New Testament,' *ERT*, 16 (1992), 28-47.

4 See Terry C Muck, 'The New Testament Case for Interreligious Dialogue,' *Insight*, 110 (1995), 7-21 (quote from 16).

much of what contemporary discussion means by dialogue; there is nothing, for example, in the New Testament to correspond with a dialectical quest for new truth. At most, the goal is to correct misunderstandings of the Christian message, not to reformulate it, and it does not seem that such dialogue would have been considered a meeting between equal partners in search of truth. The history of both the Christian and Hindu traditions offers little by way of sustained reflection on this or any other reason for dialogue with others[5] and so the justification of Hindu-Christian dialogue has little by way of precedent. For this reason its justification is especially important and not immediately self-evident from either tradition.

Nonetheless, the proponents of dialogue do offer reasons for the intentional encounter and the suggested reasons, or clusters of reasons, can be arranged in an order that approximately corresponds with the definitions of dialogue suggested in the preceding chapter. The reasons fall into some eleven categories that, like the definitions already offered, can be arranged in order of increasing complexity according to the presuppositions upon which they are based.

A. Understanding and the Reduction of Tension

The simplest reason for entering into dialogue is the perceived need to understand why others believe and act in the ways they do, and to offer explanations in turn.[6] This enables misunderstandings to be removed and positive understanding to be deepened[7] – and so it is not the same either as defensive apologetic, or polemic.[8] Religiously plural societies such as India experience interreligious conflict – or, at least, an exacerbation of politically, economically and caste – generated tensions by religious differences and misunderstanding. Division and opposition between religious communities often seems to be an unnecessary burden to add to a nation (or world) already and painfully divided by other issues.[9]

---

5 See further, briefly, in chapters 1.B above 4.B below.

6 See, for example, 'The Basis and Content of a Christian-Hindu Dialogue,' *RS*, 12.1 (February 1965), 80.

7 See, for example, John B Chethimattam, 'The Scope and Conditions of a Hindu-Christian Dialogue,' *Concilium*, 3.1 (March 1965), 93. A good example of an attempt to understand and correct misunderstanding and misrepresentation is found in Deepak Sarma, 'Is Jesus an Hindu? SC Vasu and Multiple Madhva Misrepresentations', *HCSB*, 13 (2000), 19-25.

8 Cf Peter Berger's notion of reciprocal antidefamation (*The Heretical Imperative*, 166).

9 See, for example, Chethimattam, 'The Scope and Conditions,' 83; KL

Interreligious understanding is especially important in situations of inter-communal tension, actual or potential, where ignorance, social isolation and prejudice can and do breed misunderstanding, fear and alienation. Devanandan could complain of "the prevailing ignorance among Christians of the content and claims of contemporary Hinduism"[10] as well as a misunderstanding of the nature of Christianity among Hindus.[11] And a Hindu scholar considers that communal hatred and tension are "precisely due to the lack of understanding of each other."[12] For this reason there is certainly a continuing role for 'Dialogue as Conflict Resolution'.[13]

The origins and characteristics of inter-communal tension in India are complex and certainly include economic, sociological and political components. One constituent of the religious component of inter-communal misunderstanding may be the relatively 'closed' conditions under which the different religious traditions developed and became perceived at times as alien or threatening to others. The effects of modernisation may have weakened some of these relatively closed conditions but other dynamics may have exacerbated their negative consequences.

Nonetheless, considerable concern has been expressed about the isolation of much of the Indian Church from Indian society. In 1958 MM Thomas considered that the isolation had been "so total" that Christians and Hindus simply did not understand each others' religious motivations.[14] A study of the Church in Delhi at about the same time described it as "an ingrown community, distinct from, and set over against, other communities. ... It is characterized by apprehension and suspicion of those outside."[15] The degree of isola-

---

Seshagiri Rao, 'Human Community and Religious Pluralism: A Hindu Perspective,' in *Dialogue in Community*, edited by CD Jathanna (Balmatta, Mangalore, 1982), 161-63.

10 *Christian Concern* 128/*Gospel* 55; see also *Christian Issues in Southern Asia*, 61f, 142f. (Details of these publications and their abbreviations, and of that found in the footnote 11 below, are given in chapter 1 above.)

11 Preparation, 189.

12 KR Sundararajan, 'Contact with Practicalities,' in *Towards World Community*, edited by Stanley J Samartha (Geneva, 1975), 136 (the context suggests he had Hindu-Muslim tensions in mind). See also PR Rajgopal, *Communal Violence in India* (New Delhi, 1987), who gives considerable statistical information as well.

13 The title of an article by Michael Amaladoss (*VJTR*, 63 (1999), 21-36).

14 MM Thomas, 'A Seminar on Kraemer's Book *Religion and the Christian Faith*,' *RS*, 5.2 (June 1958), 65.

15 James Alter and Herbert Jai Singh, *The Church in Delhi* (Lucknow, 1961), 159.

tion varies, of course, and is usually thought of as greater in the north than in the south of India. In part it accounts for (or, perhaps more accurately, it has done nothing to help modify) the image of Indian Christians as an unIndian or even alien community. A survey of the portrayal of Indian Christians in Hindi films concluded that they are usually shown as no more than "flotsam drifting on the surface of Indian life."[16]

Among some Hindus, there is concern about intercommunal tensions and questions are raised about the appropriate attitude to be held by Hindus, as the majority religion in India, towards minority faiths. It has also been suggested that popular estimates of the alienation felt by minorities are much greater than that actually perceived by the minorities themselves.[17] It may also be the case that minorities are perceived as a threat in proportion to their relative size.[18] The precise nature of and reasons for intercommunal prejudice and violence, and the sociological conditions under which they develop are undoubtedly complex and it seems fairly clear that religion is not the primary cause of such violence but is exploited for potential political and economic advantage; religion is often the instrumental but not the causative factor. But it seems not unreasonable to suggest that dialogue in its discursive sense can help overcome alienation, misunderstanding and the isolation of communities.[19] At the very least, the way of dialogue seems to offer a means towards a more positive cohabitation in place of the self-con-

16 TK Thomas, 'The Christian Image in Hindi Films,' *NCCR*, 93 (1973), 381. The same volume of the *Review* also contains the following related articles: RD Singh, 'Image of Christian Community in India' (58-65); 'Correct Image of Christians' (416), and 'Indian Christian Character Must Change' (468).

17 'Alienation of Minorities,' in *NCCR*, 101 (1981), 365f.

18 For example: Singer, When a Great Tradition Modernizes: An Anthropological Approach to Indian Civilization (Chicago, 1980), 339.

19 See, for example, Alfred De Souza, 'Dialogue Between Religions in India,' *IMA*, 3.3 (August 1972), 89; *GIRD*, 34; 'Reconciliation in India. Statement of the Annual Meeting of the Indian Theological Association,' *ITS*, 20 (1983), 71-80; Augustine Kanjamala, 'The Church's Mission in Reconciling Various Conflicts in India,' *IMR*, 5 (1983), 120-33; Godwin R Singh, *In Search of Communal Harmony* (Delhi, 1985); Stanley Samartha, 'Interreligious Relationships in the Secular State,' *CD*, no. 11 (December 1986), 25; Bosco Puthur, 'Our Mission Today in the Context of Communalism vs. Religious Indifference,' *LW*, 93 (1987), 408-26; KN Thakur Das, 'Communal Tension. Is Inter-faith Dialogue the Solution?' *CCAN*, 22.9 (15 September, 1987), 10-12; and see below, chapter 7.C.1 on the future of dialogue.

tented passivity, insecure suspicion and aggressive chauvinism found at present in both communities.

B. Common Social Concern

Commitment to common social concern is acknowledged by Christian and Hindu advocates of dialogue as both a reason for and a basis of dialogue[20]- as the discussion of 'secular dialogue' (see above, chapter 2.C.2 and 2.E.2) makes clear. Such dialogue will mean that urgent human needs can be tackled together rather than separately – even to the extent of the future joint establishment of medical, educational and other institutions hitherto established separately.[21] Joint reflection and action in the face of ecological degradation is another issue.[22] Seshagiri Rao considers that one purpose of dialogue is the co-operative effort of Hindus, Christians and others to overcome all injustice,[23] and Samuel Rayan maintains that "action for justice and liberation is the basis for dialogue."[24] An Asian Franciscan Seminar saw *Dialogue with Asian Religions as* [a] *Condition for Total Human Development.*[25]

The importance of 'nation-building' as one of the concerns common to both Hindu and Christian in independent India has often

---

20 See, for example, *GIRD(2)*, 68-75; Stanley Samartha, 'Partners in Community: Some Reflections on Hindu-Christian Relations Today,' *OBMR*, 4 (1980), 81; MM Thomas, 'Role of Religion in the Struggle against Poverty in India,' in *Religion, Ideology and Counter-Culture*, edited by Philip Mathew and Ajit Muricken (Bangalore, 1987), 103-11; Michael Amaladoss, 'Befreiung: ein interreligiöses Projekt,' in *Verlass den Tempel*, edited by Felix Wilfred (Freiburg, 1988), 146-78; Walter Fernandes, 'Social Action and Inter-Religious Dialogue,' *Vidyajyoti*, 53 (1989), 589-600.

21 S Wesley Ariarajah, 'A World Council of Churches' Perspective on the Future of Hindu-Christian Dialogue,' in *H-CD*, 254. He goes on to suggest a joint commitment that "we should not do separately what we can do together" (255).

22 For example, the bulk of *HCSB*, vol 6 (1993) is given over to papers that elaborate Christian and Hindu concerns for the environment.

23 'Human Community and Religious Pluralism,' 162; see also Anand Amaladass, 'The Scope of Dialogue,' *HCSB*, 2 (1989), 3f.

24 'Spirituality for Inter-Faith Social Action,' in *Liberation and Dialogue*, edited by Xavier Irudayaraj (Bangalore: Claretian Publications, 1989), 73.

25 Published Colombo, 1978; see also 'International Seminar on "Dialogue with Asian Religions as Condition for Total Human Development",' *Verbum SVD*, 20 (1979), 189-96; and Yohan Devanandan and Sarah Fernando, 'Dialogue in the Context of Development,' *ER*, 37 (1985), 445-51.

been noted.[26] And in contemporary Hindu exegesis of the Bhagavad Gita it has not been uncommon to hear the ideal of *niskamakarma* (disinterested action) applied to nation building. Several consequences have followed from an emphasis upon dialogue in the context of nation building. Those who meet in this way do so as citizens of India and not simply as members of different religious groups. In fact, argues Samartha, it is because of this new incentive to meet together that, in India, "the relationship between religions is slowly changing from conflict to co-existence, from acquaintance to understanding and from mere confrontation to more active co-operation."[27] In more recent discussion in this area – as in wider discussion – the notion of nation-building has been dropped (because of its postcolonial reminders) and the related appeal is for national integration which itself has become a reason for dialogue.[28]

Another writer endorses secular dialogue in order to break through the "isolated Christian sub-culture" by means of participation in the total environment.[29] If religion is to be mentioned at all in secular dialogue it should be regarded as part of the "ideological superstructure" that contributes to those forces that frustrate the realisation of human community – discussion about which is "the most worthwhile subject of dialogue" between Christians and Hindus.[30] And Pieris argues for a distinctly Asian model of liberation theology with liberation as the primary task of dialogue.[31]

---

26 See, for example, 'Editorial,' *RS*, 5.2 (June 1958), 1f; 'Basis and Content,' 78; 'Consultation on the Theology of Hindu-Christian Dialogue,' *RS*, 16.2 (June 1969), 84; Anto Karokaran, *Evangelization and Diakonia* (Bangalore, 1978), 115; Bangalore Declaration, 240f, 245; Nagpur Declaration, 28f. (For details of these Declarations, see chapter 1above.)

27 Stanley Samartha, 'Major Issues in the Hindu-Christian Dialogue Today,' in *I-RD*, 146.

28 See, for example, DeJohn Romus, 'Interreligious Dialogue Concern for National Integration,' *IJT*, 40 (1998), 71-83.

29 Kurt Dockhorn, 'Identity, Dialogue and Involvement,' in *For the Sake of the Gospel*, edited by Gnana Robinson (Madurai, 1980), 147f. On the bases of dialogue as reconciliation and humanisation see: GD Kaufman, 'Christian Theology and the Modernization of the Religions,' *BTF*, 7.2 (July-Dec. 1976), 81-118.

30 Dockhorn, 'Identity, Dialogue and Involvement,' 149.

31 Aloysius Pieris, 'Non-Christian Religions and Cultures in Third World Theology,' *Vidyajyoti*, 46 (1982), 158-70, and 227-45; see also Cyril Desbruslais, 'A Liberative Vision for a Pluralistic Society,' *VJTR*, 59 (1995), 711-17. Discussion returns to the theme of Jesus as *Satyagrahi* in chapter 6 below.

Even among those who do not speak in such radical terms there seems to be widespread agreement that pressing social concerns offer an urgent incentive to a dialogue which may otherwise become both empty and unrewarding if attempts are made to confine it to discussion of religious matters alone. Moreover, "communal piety separates; social justice unites" – which is one reason why a joint engagement in social justice is said to be central to dialogue.[32] Put simply: in a pluralist setting, justice is an inter-faith task.[33] There may also be a common women's or feminist perspective that engages the concerns of women of all faiths and women of no faith.[34] The energies of young people, often alienated from formal Hindu and Christian religious participation, might also be re-engaged by common social action.

However, it must also be added that during the past two decades there seems to have been a shift away from the explicit description of common social action as a form of interreligious dialogue. This writer's impression is that 'dialogue' is a word that is now much less often used by advocates of a common interreligious response to social needs. And, even among those who do continue to use the word in a secular context, a religious dimension is not always absent – though perhaps because of fear that such an emphasis might be divisive, or because of sensitivity to the aggressive and exploitative potential of religion, it receives relatively little attention.

C. Common Humanity and the Ideal of Community

A further significant basis and starting point for dialogue has been the common humanity said to be shared by people of different faiths. The positive contribution of religious faith to the ideal of community has also been acknowledged.[35] As early as 1959 dialogue in India is said to arise "from the common humanity the

---

32 M Thomas Thangaraj, 'Teaching Theology in a Multifaith Context,' in *Ministerial Formation in a Multifaith Milieu*, edited by Sam Amirtham and S Wesley Ariarajah (Geneva, nd [c 1986]), 34.

33 See George Pattery, 'Justice: an Inter-Faith Task,' *JD*, 19 (1994), 260-74.

34 See Aruna Gnanadason, 'Living in Harmony with Each Other: a Feminist Perspective,' *CGR*, 14 (1996), 91-98.

35 See, for example, C Winckelmans, 'Modern Hinduism and the Nation-building Endeavour,' *IJT*, 21 (1972), 9-17; J Russell Chandran, 'Plurality of Religious Faith and Living in Community,' *RS*, 33.3 (September 1986), 73-80; S Wesley Ariarajah, 'The Role of Religion in the Unity and Harmony of the Nation,' *JD*, 12 (1987), 57-62.

Christian shares with ... Hindu fellow-citizens."[36] Another Report, some ten years later, states that dialogue "arises from [the] recognition of our common humanness."[37] Writers associated with CISRS, especially MM Thomas, have placed particular emphasis upon the cultural and sociological context of interreligious dialogue and co-operation in arguing that common humanity, not common religion or religious experience, is the common denominator in the meeting of people of different faiths.[38] Thomas' words (when Director of CISRS) about the Institute's relationships with others in India make it clear that he was unhappy with the prospect of taking "any kind of common religiosity" as the basis of discussion and joint action; rather, it was always common humanity that was asserted as the basis.[39]

The Christian appeal to a common humanity is not merely because of a pragmatic desire to justify interreligious dialogue and co-operation in non-controversial categories; theological reasons are advanced as well. Perhaps the most common are the implications of the Biblical statements about humanity made in the image of God (Genesis 1.26a, 27a) and about the unity of humankind (Acts 17.26a).[40] Devanandan's emphasis upon a new humanity in Christ has already been noted and this emphasis is related to his concerns for dialogue and nation building.[41] And, in the Indian context, it is difficult to consider the ideal of common humanity without considering the example of Gandhi; as David Scott observes, "one is hard pressed to think of others who represented the common humanity

---

36 'Basis and Content,' 78. The notion of common humanity was one of the most frequently suggested bases for interreligious dialogue in the 1960s; see, for example, KS, 53.

37 'Consultation on Theology,' 85.

38 See, for example, TV Philip, 'Issues in Evangelism among the Educated Secularized Indians,' *RS*, 15.4 (December 1968), 40; 'Editorial' (by Herbert Jai Singh) in *RS*, 12.1 (March 1965), 2.

39 In Christian Institute for the Study of Religion and Society. Report for 1968 and 1969 (Bangalore, 1969), 38. See also Thomas' Salvation and Humanisation (Madras, 1971). It is significant that his response to John Hick's God and the Universe of Faiths is entitled Man and the Universe of Faiths (Madras, 1975). For a further comment on MM Thomas at this point see Karokaran, Evangelization and Diakonia, 110-12.

40 See further: David C Scott, 'A Christian Basis for Inter-Faith Dialogue,' *RS*, 12.1 (March 1965), 21-27; *ATA*, 55.

41 See the comments of Nirmal Minz, 'Theologies of Dialogue – A Critique,' *RS*, 14.2 (June 1967), 9; and S Andrew Morton, 'The Humanism of Paul Devanandan,' *IJT*, 30 (1981), 16.

of both Hindus and Christians to a greater degree than Gandhiji"[42]- which is why he commanded such a degree of respect across barriers of religion and class and continues to exemplify a dialogical ideal.

Related to the idea of common humanity is that of the unity of humanity which is also sometimes suggested as a basis of dialogue.[43] As Kitagawa points out,

> humankind, divided into diverse linguistic, ethnic, religious, cultural, geographical and other groupings, has never ceased its attempts to integrate human communities – very often inspired by religious visions of unity.[44]

But it must also be added that a certain balance is required between the motivation provided by the ideals of common humanity and the realisation of unity, and the acceptance of religious pluralism that is usually suggested as one of the conditions for fruitful dialogue in India. Sundararajan, who believes that "unity and difference ... constitute the dynamics of dialogue", notes this need for balance.[45] According to Rambachan, Hinduism's emphasis upon the spiritual unity of all existence remains largely a spiritual ideal whose realisation "can only be [achieved] through dialogue and action with others."[46]

However, notions such as human unity and common humanity are open to the same criticism as the concept of the unity of religion, namely, that they impose an idealised abstraction upon a dynamic and complex reality. At the same time increased awareness of the unity of humankind, actual or potential, has made more visible and more poignant the incongruity of religious divisions.[47] A Catholic Statement in the 1990s (as the communal tensions became more pronounced) saw one aim of dialogue as the hope "to relate to [other

---

42 David C Scott, 'Response to Devadatta Dabholkar,' *HCSB*, 5 (1992), 25f.

43 CBCI Communication, 52; see also 'Consultation on Theology,' 77 and Paul Knitter, 'Interreligious Dialogue and the Unity of Humanity,' *JD*, 17 (1992), 282-87.

44 Joseph M Kitagawa, *The Quest for Human Unity, A Religious History* (Minneapolis: Fortress Press, 1990), xiii.

45 'Contact with Practicalities,' 134.

46 Anantanand Rambachan, 'Religious Pluralism: A Hindu Perspective,' *CD*, no. 17 (December 1989), 27. See also TP Urumpackal, 'Dr S Radhakrishnan's Vision of an Emerging World Community,' *BSPNC*, 23 (1988), 131-41.

47 Chethimattam, 'The Scope and Conditions of a Hindu-Christian Dialogue,' 90 – a more plausible viewpoint than that with which he continues: "and has emphasized the need for a single religion for humanity."

religions] in view of forming one communion of communities, especially in this time of communal strife."[48] Perhaps the notion of *harmony* – which is less static and abstract and implies the continuing recognition of religious particularities (in other words a highly differentiated unity) – is a better basis (as a consultation in 1996 argued).[49] And *solidarity* is another concept that recognises plurality – with examples available from the Hindu-Christian encounter.[50]

The idea of a shared humanity also points to the distinctly personal basis of dialogue in which meetings are not meetings of Hinduism and Christianity but the encounter of human beings, of individual Hindus and Christians.[51] It has also been suggested that dialogue not only presupposes the recognition of a shared humanity but also constitutes a prerequisite for its full expression since "we cannot be fully human ... unless we live in deep communion and, therefore, in true interreligious dialogue" with others.[52] Dialogue is "a natural development of ... common inter-personal experience. The *inter-personal character* of human existence is the metaphysical basis for all forms of dialogue."[53] It is, in fact, the movement from thinking and talking about 'them' to thinking and talking in some way about 'us'.

The notion of common humanity as a basis for dialogue is not of

48 'Statement of the CBCI Consultation on Mission, Ishvani Kendra, Pune, 4-9 January, 1994', paragraph 56.

49 See 'Working for Harmony in the Contemporary World: a Hindu-Christian Dialogue,' *CD*, 29 (1996), 16-20.

50 The life of Verrier Elwin offers such an example in the Indian context; this is the topic of the second lecture in Daniel O'Connor, *Relations in Religion* (New Delhi: Allied Publishers, 1994) with implications drawn out for contemporary interreligious relations in India (31).

51 'Consultation on Theology,' 84; and see above, chapter 2.C.4. Another Consultation concluded that "The inter-personal character of human existence is the metaphysical basis for all ... dialogue" ('Consultation Working Group Reports,' 106 (original emphasis)). See also: Xavier Alphonse, 'The Human Being as the Meeting Point of Religions and Cultures – a Christian Perspective,' *VJTR*, 61 (1997), 509-14.

52 George Gispert-Sauch, 'Reflections for a Theology of Evangelization and Dialogue,' in *Service and Salvation*, edited by Joseph Pathrapankal (Bangalore, 1973), 323. See also: Michael Amaladoss, 'Towards a Culture of Wholeness,' *Vidyajyoti*, 47 (1983), 67f; 'Evangelization in Asia: A New Focus?' *Vidyajyoti*, 51 (1987), 18-20. However, there are relatively few Catholic examples of the appeal to common humanity.

53 'Consultation Working Group Reports,' 106 (original emphasis).

Indian origin; it originated in global Protestant discussions[54]. But the same factors that appear to have contributed to its acceptance elsewhere also seem to have influenced Indian Christian reflection on the theology of dialogue. Among these factors were:

(a) The neo-orthodox suspicion of religion and 'religiosity', and the related emphasis upon the transcendence of the Gospel over all life;

(b) An increasing hesitation, especially in religiously pluralistic contexts, for the church to make potentially divisive assertions about the particularity of the Christian community and an increasing readiness by some to move discussion with members of other communities away from such controversial and sensitive areas and towards subject matter which underlines common ground between Christians and others;

(c) A decreasing confidence in traditional Christian theological claims about the uniqueness of Christ and the Christian scriptures and the urgency of mission;

(d) The positive influence of secularisation on religious thought and action together with an emphasis upon the world as the most appropriate and necessary meeting place of Christian and neighbour.

These are some of the factors that led to the search for a more widely acceptable cultural or sociological basis for dialogue and the employment, at least by Protestants, of 'common humanity' as such a basis. In other words, the notion of common humanity seems mainly to derive, inductively, from changes within Protestantism and the Protestant perception of the world, and only in small measure from such theological propositions as the divine image in the human person, the unity of humankind and a new humanity in Christ.

However, in Protestant circles during the 1970s, the notion of common humanity – or even more distinctly theological reasons for engagement in dialogue – was supplemented and for a number of writers replaced by the more concrete ideal of 'community', in either a world or regional sense, as the basis for inter-faith dialogue. (The change is even more clearly discernible in global ecumenical

54 It was especially prominent in ecumenical Protestant circles in the early 1960s.

statements about dialogue.[55])

A number of individuals also discuss what one of them calls "the quest for community through dialogue."[56] One of Samartha's concerns has been the divisive role that religions often play in multi-faith communities – a role that dialogue might help change.[57] More recently, he has argued that (in India) "human solidarity at depth is even more important than separate religious labels",[58] and that new communities should be formed that cut across the religious boundaries that at present separate people.[59] For Duraisingh, "the ultimate goal of dialogue is the coming into being of a common human community willed by God."[60] The ideal of community, then, has become an important motivation for dialogue both globally and in the Hindu-Christian meeting.

---

55 The change can be traced through the following documents and volumes published between 1967 and 1979: KS, 53f; ZAM, 21f; *Towards World Community*, edited by Stanley J Samartha (Geneva, 1975), 5-8, 115-29, 133-36; *Faith in the Midst of Faiths*, edited by Stanley J Samartha (Geneva, 1977), 12-15, 38-47, 136-40, 187; see also: Ariarajah, 'A World Council of Churches' Perspective,' 253-60. By the time of the publication of *GOD* in 1979 the number of distinctly theological reasons suggested as a basis for dialogue are few and their elaboration, in terms of community, meagre (see the first part of *GOD*, especially 9-11) – at least by comparison with the discussion in Protestant circles during the previous twenty years of the reasons for dialogue.

56 Stanley J Samartha, 'Dialogue as a Continuing Christian Concern,' in *LFEM*, 155.

57 'Dialogue as a Continuing Christian Concern,' 155.

58 'Interreligious Relationships in the Secular State,' 26. Thangaraj argues for a shift in emphasis "from ecclesial community to human community" ('Teaching Theology in a Multifaith Context,' 34). Compare Diana L Eck (writing of Indian communalism): "in accenting and circumscribing one's own identity, one destroys the common ground of shared culture" ('Moderator's Report. Working Group on Dialogue,' *CD*, no. 14 (June 1988), 10).

59 'Mission in a Religiously Plural World,' 323; see also his 'Dialogue as a Continuing Christian Concern,' 140f.

60 Christopher Duraisingh, 'Issues in Mission and Dialogue: Some Reflections,' *IRM*, 78 (1989), 411. See also: S Wesley Ariarajah, 'Towards a Theology of Dialogue,' *ER*, 29 (1977), 3f.

D. The Challenges of Modernity and Postmodernity

If common social concern and the quest for community are reasons for dialogue in contemporary Indian life, then it must also be added that India is a pluralistic society in which the forces called modernisation and secularisation (and secularism, its ideological expression) have directly or indirectly challenged traditional Indian religious loyalties of every kind.[61] Modernisation, and the increased communication, information and education it facilitates, offers the knowledge that it is possible to live by other religious worldviews – or none at all.[62]

One response has, of course, been a reactive quest for a new sense of religious identity. There has been a religious rediscovery, renewal and even renaissance as, for example, "modern means of communication, facilitating travel and assembly, have democratised and popularised festivals ... and pilgrimages."[63] There has also been reaction in the more negative fundamentalist, communalistic and stridently nationalistic senses.[64] But modernisation has also facilitated the interaction of religious communities. A Hindu advocate of dialogue believes that the growth of communication has largely contributed to a climate of dialogue.[65] Increased knowledge of other communities seems inevitably to raise questions about communal distinctiveness. As in other parts of Asia, modernisation and urbanisation in India seems to have begun to challenge the traditional integration of culture with religion in a way that may help to remove some of the cultural-communal constituent of barriers

---

61 For some summative comments see, for example: Rob van der Zwan, 'Searching for Indian Secularization: an Unassuming Quest for Secularization in the Indian Christian Context Since 1947,' *Exchange*, 19 (1990), 91-151; Michael Amaladoss, 'Secularization and India: Modernization and Religion in an Eastern Country,' *Exchange*, 21 (1992), 34-48; Thomas Kochuthara, 'Secularism and Secularisation: Theological Reflections,' *VJTR*, 62 (1998), 239-50.

62 In sociological terms, "modernity pluralizes both the institutions and plausibility structures" of traditional societies (Peter Berger, *The Heretical Imperative* (London, 1980), 17); but, for some warnings about the non-homogenous nature of the effects of modernity in India, see, for example, Sudipta Kaviraj, 'Modernity and Politics in India,' *Daedulus*, 129 (2000), 137-62.

63 Amaladoss, 'Secularization and India,' 40.

64 This is a topic to which discussion will return in chapter 7 below.

65 Santosh Sengupta, 'On the Understanding of Other Religions,' in *DBM*, 87.

between religions, or at least show it to be a less than decisive component.[66]

Secularism is sometimes seen as a threat to religion. The Patna Declaration for example, defines dialogue as a response "to the fact of religious pluralism and secularism in our modern society."[67] But a number of individual writers have also drawn attention to the way in which, as one of them puts it, "the rising tide of secularism indirectly brings the religions together by challenging some of their basic convictions."[68] As MM Thomas observes, "bringing religions and ideologies to dialogue on their traditional spiritual terms unaffected by the pressure of modernity is now impossible."[69] And a Hindu advocate of dialogue draws attention to the way in which "today, unquestioning surrender to the assumptions of a materialistic world view" is part of the "bondage to those things which blind us to the reality of God." He suggests that "mutual dialogue can reinvigorate" both Christians and Hindus in the task of responding to consumerism and its self-centred value system.[70] Others, however, reject the related notion of a common religious 'front' against secular forces.[71]

Nonetheless, it is over against a number of the issues raised by modernisation that the call is sometimes heard for interreligious

---

66 A similar point is made by Chethimattam, 'The Scope and Conditions of a Hindu-Christian Dialogue,' 89. In India there is a very considerable variation in the effects of modernization; see, for example, *Tradition and Modernity* in India, edited by AB Shah and CMM Rao (Bombay, 1965); Part I (chapters 1-3) of MM Thomas, *Man and the Universe of Faiths* (Madras, 1975); William H Newell, 'Secularisation and Hinduism,' in *Explorations in the Family and Other Essays*, edited by Dhirendra Narain (Bombay, 1975), 533- 43; Austin B Creel, 'Secularisation and Hindu Tradition,' *RS*, 22.4 (December 1975), 77-92; Rudolf Heredia, 'Religion and Modernization in India,' *Indica*, 18 (1981), 27-50; Ninian Smart, 'The Dynamics of Religious and Political Change: Illustrations from South Asia,' *BTF*, 16 (1984), 79-96.

67 No. 28. See also EV Mathew, 'Dialogue in the Context of Secular Events,' *RS*, 12.1 (March 1965), 51-56.

68 Samartha, 'Major Issues,' 145. A similar point is made, for example, by Chethimattam, 'The Scope and Conditions of a Hindu-Christian Dialogue,' 89; and *ATA*, 59f (citing Fallon).

69 'A Christ-centered Humanist Approach to Other Religions in the Indian Pluralistic Context,' in *Christian Uniqueness Reconsidered*, 57.

70 Anatanand Rambachan, 'Keynote Address, Hindu Christian Consultation, Varanasi, India, October 23-27, 1997,' *CD*, no. 31 (December 1997), 37f.

71 For example, Raimundo Panikkar, 'Rules of the Game in the Religious Encounter,' *AF*, 5 (1970), 224.

dialogue and co-operation. Stanley Samartha urges inter-faith partnership in order to meet the need for "spiritual resources to undergird the struggle for justice."[72] Catholic statements often speak in similar ways about dialogue so that "moral values may be strengthened",[73] or the "forces of religion" be promoted and co-ordinated.[74] Both Hindus and Christians might well be found, perhaps even together, raising the possibility of a transcendent reference point for the concerns of secularised or uncertain neighbours.

However, another response to secularism has been what Samartha calls a process of "critical transformation" in all India's religious communities because of criticism directed at any spirituality that appears to be indifferent to or only selectively concerned about pressing social needs.[75] This 'secular' challenge has added weight when placed in the context of the increased acceptance in modern India of values derived from the Hindu renaissance and from liberal western and other modern or fairly modern sources: values such as the assertion of human dignity and individuality, a sense of national solidarity and an acceptance of science, technology and social planning. (In fact science may have played a modest but real role in the Hindu-Christian encounter.[76]) It is even claimed that "moral responsibility" to the common historical destiny accomplished by modernisation is "the *only* theme that challenges different religions ... toward inner intra-faith reform, around which they can enter into any kind of meaningful interfaith dialogue."[77]

A further level of complexity is provided by the advent of postmodernity whose contours in India are, of course, highly specific to the subcontinent.[78] Commentators have often noted the uneven

---

72 Samartha, 'Partners in Community,' 81.

73 'Message of Pope John Paul II to the People of Asia,' *Vidyajyoti*, 45 (1981), 295.

74 JBM Shirieda, *BSPNC*, 13 (1978), 163.

75 Stanley J Samartha, 'Indian Realities and the Wholeness of Christ,' *Missiology*, 10 (1982), 309f. See also Kaufman, 'Christian Theology and the Modernization of the Religions.'

76 See Lynette EL Thistlethwayte, 'The Role of Science in the Hindu-Christian Encounter,' in *Religious Traditions in South Asia: Interaction and Change*, edited by Geoffrey A Oddie (Curzon Press, 1998), 81-90. The 'Hindu-Christian-Science Trialogue' is the subject of a thematic issue of *HCSB*, 10 (1997).

77 MM Thomas, 'Christology and Pluralistic Consciousness,' *IBMR*, 10 (1986), 106 (emphasis added).

78 Avijit Pathak, *Indian Modernity: Contradictions, Paradoxes and Possibilities* (New Delhi: Gyan, 1998); Richard M Eaton, '(Re)imag(in)ing Other²ness: A Postmortem for the Postmodern in India,' *Journal of World History*, 11 (2000), 57-78

effects of the acids of modernity upon the Indian fabric and the same is true of postmodernity. Perhaps because the notion of postmodernity is a western construct its usefulness in the Indian context is somewhat limited. Nonetheless, postmodernity coheres well with the traditional Indian emphases on experiential and epistemological decenteredness, pluralism and inclusiveness.[79] But the difficulties in a postmodern analysis of communal violence, for example, illustrate some of its limitations.[80] And the way in which Indian postmodernist (and postcolonial) historiography has also "challenged the linear and teleological structures that underlay all the metanarratives of modern Indian history"[81] presents an equal challenge to most Christian understanding of history and to some of the totalising visions of recent Hindu fundamentalism as well.

E. Understanding and the Quest for Truth

Yet another reason for dialogue is to explore the relationship of enhanced understanding to a shared quest for truth. One definition describes Hindu-Christian dialogue as "the service of truth and concern for truth."[82] But it must be noted that the quest for truth in the context of dialogue starts in quite different ways. One starting point is the assumption that neither party may have the truth. Sharma, for example, contrasts the "missionary situation [where] truth is indivisible – I have it, you don't" with the "dialogical situation ... [where] truth is indivisible – I have it, but you may have it too" with the further conclusion that "the truth is not so much with me or with you but in-between us."[83] Another starting point is the acknowledgement and clarification of the differences in belief and practice between Hinduism and Christianity; "an important aim of

---

79 Sara Grant provides one of a number of possible illustrations when she writes of a new (postmodern) generation of younger ashram visitors whose "somewhat 'supermarket' attitude to the different religions ... and openness to input from others often stimulates free and unselfconscious sharing across religious boundaries." ('Ashrams and Inter religious Spirituality,' *TM*, 1 (1998), 91.

80 Ashutosh Varshney, 'Postmodernism, Civic Engagement, and Ethnic Conflict: a Passage to India,' *Comparative Politics*, 30 (1997), 1-20 who points out that the validity of postmodern arguments about ethnic conflict depends upon the absence of interethnic networks of civic engagement.

81 Eaton, '(Re)imag(in)ing Other^{2}ness,' 59.

82 'Consultation on the Theology of Hindu-Christian Dialogue,' 77.

83 Arvind Sharma, 'Towards a Theory of Dialogue,' *CD*, no. 32 (December 1998), 36.

the dialogue is to find out where the parties do really differ."[84] One variation upon the theme of understanding as a motivation for dialogue is that of self-understanding. Usually increased self-understanding is seen as a result of, rather than as a reason for, dialogue (see above chapter 2.E.3); but it has already been noted that one important component of 'interior dialogue' is the attempt to enhance Christian self-understanding prior to actual conversation with Hindus.

Sometimes 'the truth' that is sought in dialogue appears to mean an accumulation of knowledge and wisdom by people seeking solutions for common needs and common problems.[85] There is even what Sharpe calls "reformist dialogue": the conviction that parts of one's own tradition need reform and that a partner in dialogue might provide help.[86] Or one goal of dialogue might be defined as the creative transforming of "illuminating aspects and questings in other viewpoints" and their integration into one's own changing perspective.[87] But usually the common search for truth is described in more conventional religious language, with Christians sometimes appealing to the promise that the Spirit will lead believers into all the truth.[88] This promise is said to give no advantage to the Christian community; rather, Christians are to abandon the promotion of one particular formulation of truth because "the Mystery of God or Truth or *Dharma* is too profound to be exhausted by any particular apprehensions of it."[89] The quest for truth is to be a shared venture with each partner conscious of grasping a truth that neither

---

84 Chethimattam, 'The Scope and Conditions of a Hindu-Christian Dialogue,' 92; see also *GIRD(2)*, 31 and Devanandan *Christian Concern*, 127/*Gospel*, 54.

85 Samartha, 'More than an Encounter of Commitments,' 96.

86 Eric J Sharpe, 'Hindu-Christian Dialogue in Europe,' in *H-CD*, 102.

87 Julius J Lipner, 'Through a Prism Brightly. The Christian Message in the Hindu World,' *Vidyajyoti*, 44 (1980), 162.

88 For example, Samartha, 'Dialogue as a Continuing Christian Concern,' 154. More recent statements tend to avoid such language, preferring to speak of, for example, "the progressive awareness of truth" in dialogue ([Indian Theological Association], 'Towards a Theology of Religions,' *ITS*, 26 (1989), 78).

89 Samartha, 'Religion in a Religiously Plural World,' 319. See also his 'More than an Encounter of Commitments,' 402 and his 'Christian Concern for Dialogue in India,' *CD*, no. 9 (December 1985), 5; Panikkar, *TUCH(2)*, 35; Arvind Nirmal, 'Some Theological Issues Connected with Inter-Faith Dialogue,' *BTF*, 12 (1980), 113-15; Klaus K Klostermaier, 'The Future of Hindu-Christian Dialogue,' in *H-CD*, 268; Thomas Emprayil, *The Emerging Theology of Religions* (Rewa, 1980); 70; and many others.

fully possesses.[90] Christians who embrace this pluralist assessment of religious truth find a sympathetic response from many Hindus especially if, as with most Hindus, they underline an experiential basis for the knowledge and authentication of truth. Because of the way in which Gandhi so embodies the quest for truth his example may continue to enable a fruitful dialogue. If it is true of Gandhi that, as Lipner asserts the,

> Single distinguishing mark of his life and thought was a whole-hearted and passionate quest for truth, wherever it may be. He looked for truth to any recognised source, Hindu or non-Hindu,[91]

then there is potential for fruitful dialogue.[92]

F. The Promotion of Religious Growth

A further reason given for dialogue is the suggestion that it can assist the spiritual development of individuals, communities and even whole religious traditions. This is what Staffner calls 'Dialogue with people striving towards closer union [with] God.'[93] Although one tradition learning from another is sometimes meant,[94] usually mutual growth is expected. The theme of mutual spiritual enrichment is especially prominent in Catholic discussions of Hindu-Christian dialogue. The Catholic *Guidelines* states that the aim of a Christian in dialogue is not to convert, "but to share in a spirit of sincerely and truly disinterested brotherly love the treasures of his faith, while seeking at the same time to be enriched by the religious values to be found in the others."[95] Moreover, the

---

90 Compare the comments of Chethimattam, 'The Scope and Conditions,' 86. See also Klaus K Klostermaier, 'A Hindu-Christian Dialogue on Truth,' *JES*, 12 (1975), 157-71.

91 Julius J Lipner, 'Mahatma Gandhi: a Voice in the Wilderness?,' *Theology*, 86 (1983), 325; Lipner is not unaware of problems in grasping Gandhi's meaning and conclusions. (See also the comments and bibliography in chapter 1.B.4 above.)

92 See further in section G and chapter 5.E below; however, it is only one of several approaches to the issue: see below, chapter 4.B and 4.C.

93 Section heading in Hans Staffner, *Dialogue, Stimulating Contact with Hindus* (Anand: Gujurat Sahitya Prakash, 1993), 63-100.

94 See the many examples cited in chapter 2.C.4 and 2.E.4 above.

95 *GIRD(1)*, 20; the text has 'seeing,' corrected above to 'seeking.' The second edition of the Guidelines softens these sentiments when it states that "the intention of the participants in a dialogue activity is not to convince the others of their own beliefs or to bring them over to their religious communities, but rather in sincerity and disinterested love to give witness to their

growth can be seen as more than enlarged understanding or even spiritual perception: "Dialogue ... is ... a means to lead to a realisation and to an encounter with Reality as such."[96] In christological terms, dialogue is essential in order to seek "the fulness of Christ."[97] And a not untypical Hindu reason for dialogue is that it enables the participants to "seek the total spiritual nourishment which God has furnished us through various religions."[98] This last reason is echoed by Ariarajah when he implies his agreement with the perspective that comes to the Hindu-Christian dialogue seeing "only relative value" in the historical expressions of religion and preferring "the emergence of an authentic religious life for contemporary society that has the imprint and input of the spiritual resources of the different traditions."[99]

One variation on the theme of mutual spiritual help is the idea that dialogue intends not so much to enrich – that is to contribute to the faith of others by the addition of knowledge or the inspiration of example – but to deepen, that is, to act as a catalyst or even as a 'provocation' in order to enable others to understand more profoundly the meaning or potential meaning of their own religious tradition. Thus the *Guidelines* reports examples of members of different religions living together for short periods not only to share religious experience but also "in order to help each other to a deeper and more authentic commitment to God within our own religion."[100] Chethimattam considers that the Christian in dialogue does not need to bring into Hinduism elements which are foreign to it, but should try to "make explicit what is implicit in its authentic elements", and so will deepen Hindu experience.[101] In fact, the Gospel itself will acquire a new depth "under the impact of Asian religiosity and in particular of Hinduism."[102]

---

own faith and to be enriched by the religious values found in others." *GIRD(2)*, 35.See also *GIRD(2)*, 31 and the Patna Declaration, 38.

96 Klaus K Klostermaier, 'Hindu-Christian Dialogue: Its Religious and Cultural Implications,' in *ITD*, 238. (He also describes dialogue as "this compelling search for the Truth" (244).)

97 'Conclusions of the National Seminar on Crisis of Faith,' *Vidyajyoti*, 41 (1977), 332.

98 Nityabodhananda, 'Dialogue and Devotion,' in *DBM*, 94.

99 S Wesley Ariarajah in *H-CD*, 252.

100 *GIRD(2)*, 93; see also 'Conclusions of the National Seminar on Crisis of Faith,' 332.

101 'The Scope and Conditions of a Hindu-Christian Dialogue,' 91.

102 Michael Amaladoss, 'Towards a Culture of Wholeness,' *Vidyajyoti*, 47 (1983), 71f.

The goal of deepening the faith of another is often qualified, at least by Christian writers, by the use of the adjective 'authentic' (as in the passages cited above). This is, it may be presumed, to avoid the endorsement of every belief and practice of the partner in dialogue, although the distinction between 'authentic' and other forms of faith is, in turn, liable to be a matter of some conjecture.

The motivation for dialogue provided by the prospect of spiritual growth is said to apply to religious traditions as a whole. It has been suggested that Christians should encourage a certain degree of syncretism within Hinduism, at least as a transitional stage, on the grounds that "it is much more important for Hinduism to become more Christian than for us to convert a few Hindus."[103] Bühlmann's appeal might, at least, be reworded as a suggestion that, in India, dialogue with Hinduism be seen and encouraged as a means of the reformulation of Christian faith so that it 'become more Indian'. Even if Hocking's notion of reconception is difficult to accept, there are a number of Indian examples of change and growth within one religious tradition because of stimulus or challenge from another. Mention has already been made of the way in which the Hindu renaissance of the nineteenth century was stimulated, at least in part, by the encounter with Christianity. Although it hardly corresponds with what is now meant by 'dialogue' the encounter may be viewed as an example of one faith contributing to the growth of another, and even, in Christian terms, of one faith, serving another.[104]

Growth can also mean the rediscovery of elements that have been neglected or even abandoned. In some Indian Protestant circles, and

---

103 Walter Bühlmann, *The Coming of the Third Church* (Maryknoll, NY, 1967), 241. Bühlmann's language is somewhat tendentious; it is not uncommon to find Hindus reporting that their experience of dialogue has left them more convinced of the truth of Hinduism. Bühlmann's suggestion is not unlike WE Hocking's proposal for the 'reconception' of religions; that is, the deliberate reformulation and deepening of the 'essence' of a religious tradition by means of the stimulus or even criticism offered by another tradition (*Living Religions and a World Faith* (New York, 1940), 190-208). However, despite the occasional claim to the contrary, the kind of radical development implied by reconception has not actually occurred in the Hindu-Christian encounter.

104 See, for example, DS Amalorpavadass, *Purpose and Motivation of Missionary Activity* (Bangalore, 1970), 17f. The Gospel has "not only saved Hindus by converting them to Christianity, it has also somewhat saved Hinduism to the extent of making it a little more prophetic and thereby a little more salvific" (19). another tradition (*Living Religions and a World Faith* (New York, 1940), 190-208).

among a smaller number of Catholics, the 'secular' dimension of ministry and mission has been emphasised in a way that has led to uneasiness with almost any appeal to transcendence. It is this minority that Samartha has in mind when writing that the 'religious' aspect of Indian life must again be acknowledged.[105] Samartha's discussion also raises a related possibility: that dialogue might help some aspects of religious traditions to be set free from certain of the philosophical, cultural or 'imported' religious forms with which they have become identified. Hindu-Christian dialogue might help some Hindus to move away from a dependence upon wholly *advaitin* categories of thought and might help some Indian Christians to be less dependent upon Western theological and philosophical categories. Dialogue then seems to have considerable hermeneutical significance, including the reminder it might bring about the conditioned nature of all religious language.

G. Common or Complementary Religious Experience

In the section above, the intention to provide mutual spiritual enrichment and the deepening of faith clearly presupposes common or, at least, compatible religious experience. In this section the supposed ground on which the participants in dialogue meet is said to be the common experience of the divine, especially the spiritual or mystical experience which supposedly constitutes the core of every religion and which, as already noted (chapter 2.B.3), can lead to the advocacy of joint meditation and worship.

Among Christian advocates of dialogue, Roman Catholic writers often suggest this basis though it is not confined to them.[106] Mariasusai Dhavamony, for example, writes of the shared religious ground between Hindus and Christians provided by the common experiences of awe, religious wonder, guilt and hope, and by common respect for human life and humane values.[107] Sara Grant assumes "the common awareness of roots going down into the

105 'Indian Realities,' 303; he appears to mean those who "seem to know more about Western theology than Indian religions" (304).

106 An ecumenical Consultation, for example, offered the simple definition that "Dialogue is sharing in religious experience" ('Consultation on Theology,' 79).

107 Dhavamony, 'Evangelization and Dialogue with Hindus and Followers of Other Religions in India,' in *Light and Life We Seek to Share* (Bangalore, 1973), 147. A similar point is made by Anthony Adair, 'Towards a Hindu-Christian Dialogue,' *Contemporary Review*, No. 208 (February 1966), 84f.

same unseen waters."[108] Not untypical of Indian Catholic opinion during the past three decades is the call to recognise in people of other religions, "the striking resonance of the same ineffable mystery which their religious experience embodies."[109] One writer calls for a "Hindu-Christian spirituality."[110] One obviously controversial appeal is to the notion of *dharma* as the shared universal norm by which both Christians and Hindus are said to live[111] – but it remains controversial because of the way that *dharma* has been used to support the oppressions of the caste system. Nonetheless, the concept of *dharma* is the basis of much of the report that attempts to summarise a formal Hindu-Christian dialogue held in New Delhi in 1995.[112]

Sometimes the common ground is said simply to be belief in the divine,[113] but it is usually described in more experiential terms. The imagery of depth within the human spirit recurs (as in section F above), sometimes as the locus of the 'ultimate awakening' about which both Hindus and Christians are said to be concerned – a concern that lies beneath their culturally conditioned *dharmas*. To cite an Indian Seminar report: "Dialogue at its highest level is spiritual and religious communion, the experiencing in common of the religious reality."[114] For this reason worship[115] and prayer[116] may become a meeting point. In Panikkar's view, "fellowship arises because we

---

108 'Ashrams and Inter-religious Spirituality,' 90.

109 'Statement,' in *Research Seminar on Non-Biblical Scriptures*, edited by DS Amalorpavadass (Bangalore, 1974), 682. See also the (rather uncritical) comments of Leela D'Souza, 'Religious Experience – Its Relevance in Mission Today,' *MT*, 2 (2000), 503-12.

110 Subhash Anand, 'Yesu-Darsana: toward a Hindu-Christian Spirituality,' *VJTR*, 58 (1994), 716-37.

111 See, for example, the attempt by Somen Das in his *Dharma of the Twenty-First Century: Theological-Ethical Paradigm Shift* (Calcutta: Punthi Pustak, 1996).

112 'Working for Harmony in the Contemporary World: A Hindu-Christian Dialogue,' *CD*, no. 29 (January 1996), 16-20.

113 For example, Chethimattam, 'The Scope and Conditions of a Hindu-Christian Dialogue,' 83; Devanandan, 'Christian and Non-Christian Faith,' *IJT*, 3 (1957), 75.

114 *All India Seminar: Church in India Today* (New Delhi, nd [1969]), 341. See also Klaus K Klostermaier, 'Dialogue – the Work of God,' in *I-RD*, 119.

115 Antony Pulickamandapam, 'Worship as a Hindu-Christian Meeting Point,' *CO*, 18 (1997), 62-76.

116 See, for example, Vandana Mataji, *Nama Japa. The Prayer of the Name in the Hindu and Christian Traditions* (Delhi: Motilal Banarsidass, 1995) assumes the commonality of prayer in the two traditions.

all live by faith in spite of the diversity of our beliefs;"[117] a liberal Protestant argues that because all the religions are an expression of a singular dynamic faith – they are no longer mutually exclusive systems but "reciprocally interacting processes within a singular continuum."[118]

The appeal to shared religious experience is frequently made by Hindus as well. One particular aspect of religious experience to which a number of Hindus appeal is its complementary nature. Sivaraman, a *Saiva Siddhanta* theist, speaks of "a felt sense of incompleteness" and "a sense of the need for the truly other."[119] Others argue that the perceived complementarity is between whole religious traditions or aspects of the different traditions.[120] Sengupta, for example, believes both in "the singularity of religious faith" and that "the distinctive emphases of different religions are complementary to one another."[121] Such complementarity can even act as a corrective for each tradition.[122] The promotion of the essential unity of the religions is an urgent necessity in a climate of inter-religious suspicion.[123]

Some Christian writers also appeal to the complementary nature of the Hindu witness to God,[124] sometimes explained in terms of the complementarity of the unavoidably historically and culturally con-

---

117 'Inter-Religious Dialogue: Some Principles,' *JES*, 12 (1975), 407.

118 Christopher Duraisingh, 'Issues in Mission and Dialogue,' *IRM*, 78 (1988), 401.

119 Cited by Samartha, 'More than an Encounter of Commitments,' 395.

120 For one such study see: Bandhu Ishanand, 'Individualistic Hinduism versus Altruistic Christianity,' *ITS*, 25 (1988), 134-70.

121 'On the Understanding of Other Religions,' 91. See also Ignatius Hirudayam, 'Dialogue in Tamilnadu,' *LV*, 29 (1974), 422.

122 See, for example, Rambachan, 'Religious Pluralism: A Hindu Perspective,' 27.

123 So argues BP Siddhashrama, 'The Necessity for Unity of Religions,' *IJS*, 7 (1994), 118-29.

124 For example, Klostermaier, 'An Essay on the Complementarity of Hinduism and Christianity,' in *ITD*, 266-70; Adair, 'Towards a Hindu-Christian Dialogue,' 84 and the examples he cites; Abhishiktananda, *Saccidananda, passim*; 'Consultation on Theology,' 85; Justin Panakal, 'The Relationship between Christian and Non-Christian Spirituality,' *LW*, 78 (1972), 20-41; S Wesley Ariarajah, 'Hindu Spirituality: An Invitation to Dialogue?,' *ER*, 38 (1986), 75-81; J Kattackal, 'Meditation in the Religious Philosophies of India,' *ITS*, 26 (1989), 284-304; VF Vineeth, 'Interreligious Dialogue Past and Present: a Critical Appraisal,' *JD*, 19 (1994), 36-58.

ditioned nature of all talk of the Absolute,[125] and an "admission of the fragmentary and 'incomplete' nature of each tradition."[126] John Robinson could speak of the mutual complementarity of Hindu and Christian reality and truth as "two-eyed."[127] The hope of "a greater common dedication to the Lord of all, each being helped and inspired by the others" (*GIRD(2)*, 34) is also given as a reason for dialogue. Love, essential for dialogue, hears the "variegated tones and tunes of the one and only, yet polyphonic symphony."[128] 'Interior dialogue' makes considerable use of assumptions about shared religious experience (for example, longing for union with God)[129] as the basis for dialogue. Other Christian reflections also suggest that the search for the absolute, or "passion for the Truth",[130] constitutes a significant basis for Hindu-Christian dialogue. Several Catholic statements are even more explicit and precise. The official Indian Catholic *Guidelines*, for example, argues that Indian Christians "share in our own specific way, and from within our faith perspective in the Indian quest for God. ... The Christian therefore shares in his way in that search for God which is the soul of all authentic religion" (*GIRD(2)*, 16).[131]

---

125 Theses on Interreligious Dialogue (Hong Kong, 1987), 14.

126 Klostermaier, 'An Essay on the Complementarity of Hinduism and Christianity,' 269. For a careful analysis see Klostermaier's 'All Religions Are Incomplete – Complementarity as Theoretical Mode to Guide the Praxis of Interreligious Dialogue,' *DA*, 7 (1993), 60-76.

127 John AT Robinson, *Truth is Two-Eyed* (London, 1979). A closely similar point is made by Bede Griffiths, *The Marriage of East and West* (London: Collins, 1982).

128 Panikkar, 'The Rules of the Game in the Interreligious Encounter,' 227. For further Christian appeals to complementarity see: Rogers, 'Dialogue Postponed,' AF, 5 (1970), 221, and his 'Hindu Influence on Christian Spiritual Practice,' *H-CD*, 198-206; Panikkar, *TUCH(2)*, 55; Bede Griffiths, *Return to the Centre* (London, 1976), 82-87, and 70 (for him Truth is ultimately one and discovered in both faiths (70, 112, 120)); *Theses on Interreligious Dialogue*, 11.

129 Abhishiktananda, *The Church in India* (Madras, 1964), 61. Cuttat writes in similar vein about "every pure yearning after the Sacred" and his conviction that each elicits some kind of divine response (*The Encounter of Religions* (New York, 1960), 31). Sharpe concludes that the basis of interior dialogue is "intuitive recognition of a shared experience of the Transcendent Reality" ('Dialogue and Faith,' *Religion*, 3 (1973), 95).

130 'Consultation Working Group Reports,' 107.

131 See all of *GIRD(2)*, 13-16 where the notion of a search for God is greatly elaborated from *GIRD(1)*, 11.

The advantages of the language of 'quest' (or 'pilgrimage') are twofold: (i) it makes decidedly fewer claims to knowledge or experience of the divine or Absolute. (ii) it seems to point to actual areas of shared experience; for example, Ayrookuzhiel, on the basis of a survey of popular religion in Kerala, concludes that the quest is similar for Hindus and Christians.[132] As well as a common search for God, dialogue could also be founded upon what might be called the idea of a "common presence" before God.[133] In fact dialogue will help both partners "to realise more fully that divine Presence within, and to live more and more truly according to it."[134] The comparative study of the monastic life in the two traditions also provides material that suggests to some commentators a certain complementarity.[135]

There is, of course, a considerable Christian mystical tradition whose intentions and experiences may not be unrelated to *bhakti* and some aspects of the *advaitin* and other traditions within Hinduism.[136] Hindus are often surprised to learn of Christian mystical spirituality; it has the potential to become a fruitful topic for discussion if not the actual common ground on which Christians and Hindus meet. Some Christian advocates of interior dialogue have approached their meditation on the Bible and the Upanishads in the belief that the truth of both scriptures "is verified by personal experience and existential relevance."[137] This is not unlike the Hindu

---

132 AM Abraham Ayrookuzhiel, 'The Living Hindu Popular Religious Consciousness and Some Reflections on it in the Context of Hindu-Christian Dialogue,' *RS*, 26.1 (March 1979), 22.

133 See, for example, Samartha, '*More* Than an Encounter of Commitments,' 105, and 'Indian Realities,' 315. Compare Panikkar: "Religions meet at their common source, not simply on the plane of ideas or ideals, but in the very depth or ground of religion." "Hinduism and Christianity, as two religions believing in God, undoubtedly meet in God..., the Absolute, the Ultimate" (*TUCH(2)*, 42, 48).

134 Abhishiktananda, *The Church in India*, 63; see also: Gispert-Sauch, 'Reflections for a Theology of Evangelization and Dialogue,' 323; see also Patrick D'Souza, 'India,' in *Mission in Dialogue*, edited by Mary Motte and Joseph R Lang (Maryknoll, NY, 1982), 25.

135 See *Monastic Life in the Christian and Hindu Traditions: a Comparative Study*, edited by Austin B Creel and Vasudha Narayanan (Lewiston, NY: Edwin Mellen Press, 1990).

136 See, for example, Moti Lal Pandit, 'Seeking Community with Indian Mysticism,' *NCCR*, 105 (1985), 184-90, and 'Some Common Mystical Themes in Trika Shaivism and Christianity,' *ITS*, 26 (1989), 48-70; compare Johann Figl, 'Mystik und Dialog der Weltreligionen,' *ZMR*, 73 (1988), 14-25.

137 Mary Kalapesi, 'Some Reflections on the Fourth Meeting on Hindu and Christian Spirituality,' *RS*, 11.4 (December, 1964), 72.

view that regards *anubhava* as being of primary importance both as a means of divine revelation and as a criterion for testing its validity (see also chapter 6.E below).

Related to the appeal to a common spirituality is the advocacy of dialogue as a means of fostering or strengthening "spiritual and moral values" with the clear presumption that these values are shared (or at least compatible). A Catholic seminar, for example, argued that by means of the exercise of such virtues as kindness, humility and sacrifice there will be fostered "an 'osmosis of values' that will prove a most valuable form of dialogue."[138] And a Hindu scholar argues that dialogue should lead to a "co-operative endeavour in ... promoting morality and spirituality."[139] The survey of popular Hindu religious experience referred to above is used to explore the possibility of "Hindu-Christian dialogue to evolve a common value system."[140]

Even with an appeal to spirituality there is at times an employment of quasi-military terminology. The Catholic *Guidelines* speaks of dialogue among those who are interested in "strengthening the forces of religion" (*GIRD (2)*, 9). The usual meaning of such language is that the 'forces of religion' are under attack from the 'forces of secularism' and that a 'common front' should be formed by the religions. Both Catholic and Hindu leaders have made such calls; those Protestants who have used military analogies have tended to use them not about a common front of religious believers against secularism but because, as one of them writes, a co-operative "*dharmayuddha* (a just or righteous war) must be declared and fought against all kinds of injustice and oppression."[141] Again, assumptions about common or complementary spirituality appear to be present; and the specific origin or actual content of the spiritual values or resources is not made clear. The mere fact that they are 'religious', 'spiritual' or even 'moral' seems to be regarded as sufficient justification for their use.

H. Towards an Indian Theology and Inculturated Church

Attention now turns to a cluster of reasons that offer more distinctly (Christian) theological bases for engagement in dialogue. This is

138 'India: Seminar on Dialogue with non-Christians,' *OT*, no. 57 (January 1974), 98; see also: CBCI Communication, 52.

139 Seshagiri Rao, 'Human Community and Religious Pluralism,' 163 and 166.

140 Ayrookuzhiel, 'The Living Hindu Popular Religious Consciousness,' 22-25.

141 Samartha, 'Partners in Community,' 81f.

not to ignore the theological justification that could be offered for the appeals to common humanity, community and even common religious experience as bases for dialogue, but the bases already considered are those that could be and are held by a number of Hindus as well. Despite potential misunderstanding of its apparently exclusive claims, the making clear of a distinctly theological basis for the Christian approach to dialogue is centrally important for a number of proponents of dialogue; Protestant advocates are often especially emphatic at this point. It can be argued that "the common human concerns of contemporary history" are not themselves sufficient reason for a Christian commitment to dialogue because the commitment is not to be seen as an occasional response to pressure from the world, nor is it a matter merely of pragmatic expediency for the sake of inter-communal harmony.[142] If it is true that dialogue "is an approach integrally rooted in the foundations of the Christian faith",[143] then there is the risk of misunderstanding if these foundations are not explicitly acknowledged. Perhaps there is no sustainable independent starting point apart from personal (and communal) religious conviction.

To emphasise this particular Protestant starting point is not to imply that Catholic reflections do not make clear the importance of theological perspectives,[144] nor is it to overlook the discussion above about community in which attention was drawn to recent Protestant attempts to define the basis of dialogue in sociological rather than theological categories. Nonetheless, there has been a tendency during recent decades for most Protestant discussions of dialogue to argue that Christian theology not only justifies commitment to dialogue but actually requires it as well. There is, of course, a degree of tension between all such statements about belief in a clearly defined theological starting point and the openness to the views of others that also appears to be required for fruitful dialogue; it is a tension to which discussion will return (chapter 4.B).

To acknowledge the importance of a theological basis for dialogue is to raise the question of what might be the most appropriate form to be taken by Christian theology in India today. Mention has been made of the Christian mystical tradition as providing a basis

142 Samartha, 'Dialogue as a Continuing Christian Concern,' 153.

143 J Russell Chandran, 'A Christian Approach to Other Religions,' *BTF*, 7.2 (July-December 1975), 12.

144 The CBCI *Guidelines*, for example, begins with 'Historical Note' (*GIRD(2)*,5-12) and then turns to 'Theological Perspectives' (*GIRD(2)*,13-39).

for dialogue. Similar suggestions have been made about the accumulated experience incorporated in the contemplative spirituality practised within global Christianity,[145] and about the Christian tradition of 'negative theology'.[146] However, these forms of theology are all derived from non-Indian sources. They may indicate potentially fruitful points of contact with Hinduism but both Catholics and Protestants have also been anxious that the whole Church in India assumes a more distinctly Indian character in its theology, liturgy and general ethos. [147] For this reason Hindu-Christian dialogue has been seen as one means of assisting the process described successively since the 1950s as 'adaptation', 'Indianisation', 'indigenisation', 'inculturation',[148] 'contextualisation' or even [the] 'incar-

---

145 See Samartha, 'Partners in Community,' 82, and Matthew Lederle, 'Discovery of Dialogue,' *RS*, 26.1 (March 1979), 65f. Also relevant is Catholic discussion of the link between contemplation and evangelisation; for example: Nagpur Declaration, 43; DS Amalorpavadass, *Approach, Meaning and Horizon of Evangelisation* (Bangalore, 1973), 74f; Clement Godwin, 'The First International Theological Conference on Evangelization and Dialogue in Asia,' *Verbum SVD*, 13 (1972), 286-88.

146 'Consultation on Theology,' 80; negative theology "agrees with the unique character of advaitic experience and is apt to bring us into deepening dialogical communion with the advaitic spiritual tradition of India" (80).

147 Evangelical Protestants seem to be the least concerned but even they display some interesting examples of indigenisation; see for example, the research reported (with a valuable bibliography), by Roger E Hedlund, 'Indian Instituted Churches: Indigenous Christianity, India-Style,' *MS*, 16 (1999), 26-42, and his 'Previews of Christian Indigeneity in India', *JAM*, 3 (2001), 213-29. If RC Das is fairly called 'evangelical' then he is another (earlier) example of concern among evangelicals for indigenisation; see section E (101-46) of his *RC Das. Evangelical Prophet or Contextual Christianity*.

148 It is helpful to note that Catholic discussion is mainly in terms of 'inculturation' and Protestant in terms of 'indigenisation.' Usually Catholic discussions pay little attention to Protestant works, and vice versa; an exception which also discusses Orthodox contributions (but is decidedly flawed in other ways) is KP Aleaz, *The Gospel of Indian Culture* (Calcutta: Punti Pustak, 1994). For a discussion of the changing terms see: Pearl Drego, 'The Mission of the Local Church and the Inculturation of the Gospel,' *Vidyajyoti*, 45 (1981), 260f. For partial historical surveys see: Ulrich Meyer, 'Indigenisation – A Critical Review of the Discussion in India 1942-65,' *ICHR*, 7 (1973), 91-120; S Immanuel David, 'The Development of the Concept of Indigenisation among Protestant Christians in India from the Time of Henry Venn,' *ICHR*, 11 (1977), 100-13; A Pushparajan, 'The

nation'[149] [of the Gospel], and of identifying those elements within Hinduism that might be critically adapted for use by the Christian community.[150]

A related issue is the perceived need for Indian Christianity to rid itself of what are considered to be essentially Western forms of the expression of the Christian faith – forms that are inappropriate and even alien when used in India.[151] Dialogue, it is said, has already enabled the Church in India to begin to enter into this new phase of

---

Christian Encounter with Indian Culture,' *IMR*, 9 (1987), 8-23. The first use of the term 'inculturation' is usually attributed to Joseph Masson in 1962; see the comments of David J Bosch, *Transforming Mission: Paradigm Shifts in Theology of Mission* 4th edition (Maryknoll, NY: Orbis Books, 1992), 455, and Gavin D'Costa, 'Inculturation, India and Other Religions', *SM*, 44 (1995), 121-47. Later it was criticised as implying 'one-way traffic' and 'interculturation' was suggested as an improvement that suggested mutuality and partnership.

149 See, for example, Joseph Mattam, *Land of the Trinity. A Study of Modern Christian Approaches to Hinduism* (Bangalore, nd [1975]), 185f; Samuel Rayan, 'Flesh of India's Flesh,' *Jeevadhara*, 6 (1976), 259-67.

150 The literature is extensive; see, for example: KN Sahay, 'Indigenization of Christianity in India,' *Man in India*, 61 (1981), 17-36; Joseph Thekedathu, 'Inculturation in the Context of Asian Social Realities,' in *Inculturazione e formazione Salesiana* (Rome, 1984), 247-51; Arul M Varaprasadam, 'Inculturation: the Crucial Challenges in the Indian Situation,' in *Building the Church in Pluricultural Asia*, edited by Arij A Roest Crollins (Rome, 1986), 39-62; Mathew Paikada, 'Kirche in Indien und Inkulturation,' *ZMR*, 71 (1987), 200-18; Chacko Valiaveetil, 'Inculturation: the Need and the Scope,' *IMR*, 9 (1987), 24-31; Felix Wilfred, 'Some Heuristic Propositions on the Relationship of Christianity to non-Christian Religions and Cultures,' *ITS*, 24 (1987), 220-29; 'Inculturation as a Hermeneutical Question,' *Vidyajyoti*, 52 (1988), 422-36; 'World Religions and Christian Inculturation,' *ITS*, 25 (1988), 5-26; Michael Amaladoss, *Becoming Indian: the Process of Inculturation* (Rome and Bangalore: Dharmaram Publications, 1992). On the relationship with dialogue see: Xavier Irudayaraj, 'Inculturation and Inter-Faith Dialogue,' *WW*, 19 (1986), 123-29.

151 Robin HS Boyd, *India and the Latin Captivity of the Church: The Cultural Context of the Gospel* (London, 1974). The size of the problem is made clear in George Mathew, 'Content Analysis of Theological Journals in India,' *RS*, 28.4 (December 1981), 67-92, which concluded that most journals were heavily dependent on contributions from Western Protestant males. See also: Chethimattam, 'The Scope and Conditions of a Hindu-Christian Dialogue,' 90; Pierre Fallon, 'The Demands of Dialogue,' in *Service and Salvation*, 312; Panikkar, 'The Rules of the Game,' 225f; Aloysius Pieris, 'Western Models of Inculturation: How Far Are They Applicable in Non-Semitic Asia?,' *EAPR*, 22 (1985), 116-24.

its life by learning "to approach in a more positive manner the religious soil of Hindu India",[152] to embrace the religio-cultural experiences of the people of India,[153] to be baptised in "The Jordan of Asian Religiosity."[154] It seems to be important in the context of national independence that the Church eschews any 'colonial' dependence upon Western ways of expressing its faith and practice.[155] One theologian believes that all Asian theology "ought to be a *dialogical theology*, a theology that is informed and shaped by interfaith dialogue." This will not only be a theology for dialogue or a theology of dialogue, but a theology *in* dialogue.[156]

There seems widespread (if not unanimous) agreement that Indian Christian theology and practice ought to be recognisably Indian in character. But this agreement leads to the question of how much of the understanding and wisdom of the Hindu world and lifeview(s) can be incorporated into that theology and practice to enable a more Indian *darsana*? It is one thing to call for a deep and radical understanding of the Hindu heart and mind in order communicate the Christian message.[157] But how much further should the Indian church go? Should, for example, the epistemology of its theology be distinctly Indian in texture?[158] Should its understanding of God be extended by the Hindu understanding of God as feminine?[159]

---

152 Fallon, 'The Demands of Dialogue,' 310, 312.

153 See Abraham, 'Paradigm Shift in Contemporary Theological Thinking.'

154 Aloysius Pieris, 'Mission in the Local Church in Relation to the Non-Semitic Religions of Asia,' in *Mission in Dialogue*, 436-39.

155 See, for example, RS Sugirtharajah, 'Postcolonialism and Indian Christian Theology,' *SWC*, 5 (1999), 229-39.

156 J Paul Rajashekar, 'Theological Education in a Pluralistic Context,' in *Ministerial Formation in a Multifaith Milieu*, 112 (original emphasis). On the quest for an Indian theology, see also: VP Thomas, 'The Indian Christian Theology and its Identity,' *RS*, 25.3 (September 1978), 26-33; George Gispert- Sauch, 'Shankaracharya and Our Theological Task,' *Vidyajyoti*, 42 (1978), 348-55; Thomas Manickam, 'Indian Culture as a Theological Base,' *Jeevadhara*, 14 (1984), 368-77; OV Jathanna, 'Indian Christian Theology: Methodological Reflections,' *BTF*, 18 (1986), 59-74.

157 As argued by Dayanand Bharati, *Living Water and Indian Bowl. (An Analysis of Christian Failings in Communicating Christ to Hindus, with Suggestions toward Improvements)* (Delhi: ISPCK, 1997).

158 As advocated by KP Aleaz, *The Role of Pramanas in Hindu-Christian Epistemology* (Calcutta: Punthi Pustak, 1991) – though it should also be noted that both the (contributed) foreword to the book and some reviews of it (for example, by Anand Amaladass in *HCSB*, 5 (1992), 39f) have voiced critical concerns about Aleaz's methodology.

159 See Joseph Sebastian, *God as Feminine. Hindu and Christian Visions: a Dialogue* (Frankfurt: Peter Lang, 1995).

If it is believed that Christianity is capable of incarnating itself in any culture and that Hinduism is, on the whole, amenable to this possibility,[160] then the incarnation will be extensive – even if there is not or cannot be an affirmative answer to Arvind Sharma's question about what could be called the *ultimate* inculturation: "Can Christian Theology Be *Astika?"*[161] (that is, become 'orthodox' Hinduism).

However, it should also be noted that attempts at inculturation have drawn criticism – especially from those who see it as the 'Hinduisation' of the Christian faith. Liturgical adaptation in particular – for example the use of '*om*'[162] and use of Hindu scriptures – has generated opposition in Indian Catholic circles[163] and even Vatican disapproval,[164] as have other aspects of inculturation.[165] At the very least the controversy may have acted as a reminder that the Gospel can never be fully identified with any one culture though debate will continue over the limits of the identification that is necessary and possible. Nonetheless, there can be no doubt of official

---

160 This thesis is forcefully and competently argued in Hans Staffner, *Jesus Christ and the Hindu Community. Is a Synthesis of Hinduism and Christianity Possible?* (Anand, 1988). For a study of an earlier presentation of Staffner's position see: A Pushparajan, 'Sociological Aspects of Inculturation,' *ITS*, 18 (1981), 271-88.

161 The title of an article by Sharma in *IJT*, 37 (1994), 10-13.

162 See Ignatius Hirudayam, 'OM-AMEN,' *WW*, 10 (1987), 267-72; George Gispert-Sauch, 'A Controversial Syllable,' *Vidyajyoti*, 45 (1981), 232-38, including a bibliography (232 n 1) to which add: George Sebastian, 'The Mystery of OM,' *Vidyajyoti*, 45 (1981), 447f. For a (perhaps unexpected) defence of the use of *om*, by a Baptist missionary, see George Gillespie, '*Om* as Christian Symbol,' *Foundations*, 17 (1974), 336-45.

163 See, for example, Nambiaparambil, 'India,' 421; Pearl Drego, 'India,' in *Mission in Dialogue*, 534; *Light and Life We Seek to Share*, 324; and periodic series of indignant letters in the correspondence columns of *The Examiner* (Bombay). For a survey of the process and its criticism see: Julian Saldanha, 'Liturgical Adaptation in India: 1963-1974,' *Vidyajyoti*, 40 (1976), 20-31; Paul Hacker, 'Das katholische Christentum im Gegenuber zum Hinduismus,' in *Weltmission in der Weltkrise*, edited by Johannes Dormann (St Augustin, nd [1978]), 31-46; George Gispert-Sauch, 'Liturgical Inculturation Questioned,' *Vidyajyoti*, 46 (1982), 546-52; Ajit Lokhande, 'Hinduisierung christlicher Liturgie?,' in *Wirklichkeit und Theologie*, edited by Werner Prawdzik (Nettetal, 1988), 73-102.

164 Despite a ban, the 'New Orders for the Mass in India' was widely used; see: Arnulf Camps, *Partners in Dialogue: Christianity and Other World Religions* (Et: Maryknoll, NY, 1983), 193-99.

165 See, for example, Part One of van Leeuwen, *Fully Indian, Authentically Christian: a Study of the First Fifteen Years of the NBCLC* (1967-1983).

Catholic commitment to an appropriate level of inculturation[166]- a commitment reinforced in the recent Apostolic Exhortation *Ecclesia in Asia* (20-23). In the Indian Catholic Church a close link has been seen between 'Hindu-Christian Dialogue and the Formation of an Indian Christian Theology.'[167] The need for a radical catholicity has also been given as a reason for Hindu-Christian dialogue.[168] And, of course, the Second Vatican Council gave particular impetus to the hope for a widened and more profound catholicity within the Church. One asset possessed by the Catholic church is its ability to direct liturgical and other reform 'from above' – though, as we have noted, there is still an audible current of dissent at times.

In Protestant circles one reason for interest in inculturation and the quest for an Indian theology, especially during the 1960s, was the diminishing influence of the theology associated with Hendrik Kraemer whose vigorous criticism of syncretism seems to have discouraged actual personal and prolonged interreligious contact. As MM Thomas complains, "in the post-Tambaram period any effort at indigenisation of Christianity was dubbed syncretistic without examining it",[169] and in Protestant circles it required the efforts of individuals such as Devanandan, Thomas himself, Chandran and others to realise some of the positive potential of interreligious dialogue and co-operation.[170] In other words, the need for an Indian theology (and the Hindu-Christian dialogue derived from that need) must be seen in the context of the Indian Church's situation in a post-colonial, post-Kraemerian and post-Conciliar setting.

But there is yet another questioned to be posed alongside the issue of the *extent* of inculturation: the question of *which* aspects of an undoubtedly rich and diverse Indian culture will be used in the quest for an 'authentically Indian' church. As a western observer comments, It is entirely possible to achieve shallow contextual 'success': "the creation of a theology wonderfully adapted to fossilized elements of traditional culture, while the real contemporary life of people passes by on another path."[171] And even if the 'classical' tra-

166 See the balanced summary of progress in Jacob Kavunkal, 'Mission as Inculturation,' *VJTR*, 63 (1999), 860-69.

167 The title of the concluding chapter of Mattam, *Land of the Trinity*.

168 See for example, Chethimattam, 'The Scope and Conditions of a Hindu-Christian Dialogue,' 87; and Panikkar, *TUCH(2)*, 4, 16f.

169 'Christ-Centred Syncretism,' 29.

170 The related issue of syncretism and 'double-belonging' will be discussed in chapter 4.C below.

171 S Mark Heim, 'Choosing Roots: The Contexts for Christian Theology in India', *This World*, no. 21 (Spring 1988), 89.

ditions of Hinduism remain significant worldviews for many Indians, their dominant Sanskritic culture and brahmanical religion have been experienced as oppressive and alienating for most Indian Christians – and cannot realistically provide the cultural framework that contextualisation seeks.

One further aspect of Indian church life that has acted as an incentive for Christian-Hindu dialogue is the ecumenical movement. Within the Protestant churches there was considerable interest during the 1950s and 1960s in the movement and the widening of religious horizons seems not unrelated to interest in dialogue. The Nasrapur Consultation in 1966 specifically linked the growth of ecumenical activity with a new concept of mission which sees mission as not simply extending denominational boundaries but in realising the Lordship of Christ over the whole realm of human activities both Christian and other.[172] A similar implication is drawn by Abhishiktananda who, having described the fruitfulness of ecumenical dialogue, goes on to add: "We wonder whether the same could not happen in the dialogue with Hindus."[173] In other words, a renewed and broadened ecclesiology might be seen as both a result of the ecumenical movement and as an incentive to a greater openness towards other faiths and to dialogue.[174]

I. Dialogue as a Means of Mission

Some have seen dialogue as a means of implementing the Christian mission in general, and even evangelisation in particular. But others – including most Hindu commentators – have found the relationship between, and even compatibility of, dialogue and mission to be highly problematical. For this reason the issue of dialogue and mission is discussed in some detail in the next chapter (4..D).

---

172 *Findings of the National Consultation*, 23.

173 *The Church in India*, 62f. It is also interesting to notice the way in which words and phrases such as 'ecumenicity' and 'an ecumenical spirit' occur in the writings of some Hindu advocates of dialogue; for example: K Sivaraman, 'Resources in Hindu Morality and Religion,' in *Towards World Community*, 29; and Seshagiri Rao, 'Human Community and Religious Pluralism,' 163.

174 For example Chandran, 'Christian Contribution to Religious Dialogue,' 67; Chethimattam, 'The Scope and Conditions of a Hindu-Christian Dialogue,' 92.

J. The Activity of God in Dialogue

Another substantial basis for dialogue seen from a predominantly Christian perspective is provided by what might be called the activity of God. At times this action is located in the world – in which case dialogue is derived from an understanding of how God works providentially among people.[175] Indian Protestant thought has tended to this point of view. Sometimes the divine activity is located primarily in the Church for, although the "Word of God" is said to be the ultimate basis of dialogue (and present in the hearts of all people), "this dialogue finds its first expression within the Church herself" (*GIRD*, 15). But in the revised edition of the Guidelines this ecclesiocentric perspective is transformed; it now reads that "the Word of God...constitutes...the ultimate basis of dialogue, for we believe that He is present by His grace in the hearts of all people of goodwill" (*GIRD(2)*, 29).

The same (usually Catholic) emphasis upon the Church as the focus of God's dialogue with the world usually also acknowledges the presence and activity of God in the world's religions. God's self-communication is found in all faiths; in personal terms this means that "God speaks to me" through the beliefs, practices and loyalties of a neighbour of another faith.[176] The Christian in dialogue is said to know that "when I go to meet a Hindu, I find that God is there to meet me."[177] A key CBCI statement defines dialogue as "the response of Christian faith in God's *saving presence in other religious traditions and the expression of the firm hope of their fulfilment in Christ*."[178] Another Catholic document defines the basis of dialogue as "faith in the universal salvific will of God."[179] Moreover, the point is often made that such positive statements are not derived from abstract principles but from "the compelling presence of God which Christians in India encounter in their daily experience with the adherents of other religions."[180] The claims made about the presence and activity of God are considerably more positive and explicit than

---

175 For example, 'Consultation Working Group Reports,' 111.

176 'Consultation on Theology,' 79.

177 Dhavamony, 'Evangelization and Dialogue,' 148. See also Nagpur Declaration, 27: "in dialogue each partner listens to God speaking in the self-communication and questioning of ... fellow-believers."

178 CBCI Communication, 52, original emphasis (quoted and endorsed in *Gird(2)*, 5); and the Nagpur Declaration, 14 and 16.

179 *Theses on Interreligious Dialogue*, 8. See also Vempeny, *Krsna and Christ*, 418.

180 Karokaran, *Evangelization and Diakonia*, 179.

those found in the documents of Vatican II and it is not surprising that the conclusions about Hindu-Christian dialogue drawn from them are more positive and explicit than the Conciliar statements about dialogue. Given belief in the active and discernible presence of God in other faiths, it follows that the Indian Church should take up the task of "seeking and discovering, meeting and worshipping God, where He is present and active"[181]- a calling that is clearly conducive to dialogue.

Indian Protestant assessments of the degree and kind of divine activity in dialogue have tended to be less explicit and less positive than Catholic appraisals. This has been partly because of a perceived lack of Biblical warrant for belief in such activity, partly because of the continuing influence of neo-orthodox attitudes which have seen the Biblical revelation as standing sharply over against the basically monistic axes about which the Asian religions are said to revolve, and partly because of a preference for describing the inter-religious interface in terms of common humanity. Nonetheless, many Protestants have, of course, spoken of God's activity in dialogue. John Sadiq, for example, sees divine revelation as a model for dialogue: "Dialogue as an art of spiritual communication has its roots in God's own action" and no further grounds for its practice are needed than the fact that God has spoken to humanity.[182] And "in dialogue we allow ourselves to be led by God" – which is why neither the practice nor outcome of dialogue can be predetermined or prejudged.[183]

The self-communication of God is described in ways that further amplify belief in divine activity as a reason for dialogue. Firstly, there is the incarnation, viewed as God's dialogue with humankind. According to the Vatican II document *Dei Verbum*, 3, this dialogue began at the beginning of human history and has become tangible in the incarnation. In Jesus "the divine-human dialogue is fully revealed. He is dialogue in flesh." (*GIRD(2)*, 28). A protestant commentator writes that "God in Jesus Christ has himself entered into relationship with men of all faiths and all ages. ... To be in dialogue

181 'Workshop Report,' *All India Seminar*, 340. See also Karokaran, *Evangelization and Diakonia*, 182; and John Kurichianil, 'The Holy Spirit the Main Agent in the Mission of the Church,' *ITS*, 31 (1994), 348-67.

182 'Inter-Faith Dialogue and Communication of the Gospel,' *RS*, 12.1 (March 1965), 10; so also Whaling, *An Approach to Dialogue with Hinduism*, 96.

183 'Consultation on the Theology of Hindu-Christian Dialogue,' 86.

is therefore, to be part of God's continuing work."[184] The second locus of God's revelation as an incentive for dialogue is the human community. Since the whole of humanity is made by God it stands in an ongoing relationship with God and such a relationship "makes dialogue not another option but an imperative for the Church."[185] Duraisingh argues for a development of one Protestant emphasis during the 1960s, that of *missio Dei*: dialogue is essential because people of other faiths may also be agents of the *missio Dei*, and "dialogue without an awareness that it participates in the *missio Dei* will become mere conversation."[186] And the third place in which God's revelation may be seen is in the world's religions; one reason for entering into dialogue is because of "God's purposeful activity in and through other faiths."[187] When Diana Eck shares what she calls "the sense of delight and revelation ... and perhaps some sense of both the majesty and mystery of the Divine" with Hindu worshippers in a temple, she goes on to explain that for her, as a Christian, "it is Christ who enables Christians ... to recognize God especially where we don't expect to do so, and where it is not easy to do so."[188] This is a perspective that, as already noted, is quite strongly affirmed by a number of Catholic proponents of dialogue.

Some discussions of the activity of God are also concerned to make clear its trinitarian dimension. The definition of Sadiq cited above, that sees the basis of dialogue residing in God's communication with humanity, goes on to add that God does this "through His Word, in fullness of time made flesh, and continues to do so through His Holy Spirit."[189] Catholic discussions often make the same point.[190]

Mention has already been made of the incarnation and now draw attention to the claim that the activity of the Spirit constitutes a reason or basis for dialogue. Occasionally the locus of this activity is

---

184 Stanley Samartha, 'Dialogue as a Continuing Christian Concern,' 153. See also: Swearer, *A Theology of Dialogue*, 10f. (Chapters 5 and 6 below consider in some detail various attempts to use Christology as a basis and reason for dialogue.)

185 Ariarajah, 'Towards a Theology of Dialogue,' 10.

186 'Issues in Mission and Dialogue: Some Reflections,' 404f (quotation 405). A useful summary and analysis of the discussion of the *missio Dei* concept is found in Rodger C Bassham, *Mission Theology* (Pasadena, 1979), 67-71.

187 Ariarajah, 'Towards a Theology of Dialogue,' 11. See further discussion of this point in chapter 4.C.2 below.

188 Encountering God: a Spiritual Journey from Bozeman to Banaras, 79.

189 'Inter-Faith Dialogue and Communication of the Gospel,' 10.

190 For example, Theses on Interreligious Dialogue, 9.

said to be the church, in which the Holy Spirit encourages dialogue.[191] More frequently the activity of the Spirit is located in other religions. The Indian Catholic *Guidelines* cites with approval a statement that, "confident in the Holy Spirit's action which overflows the bounds of the Christian community, we wish to further dialogue with other religions."[192] The theme of discerning the Spirit's voice through people of other faiths is also found. The Christian in dialogue is said to realise the constant possibility of learning from others because the Spirit of God can speak through "brothers or sisters" of other faiths (*GIRD(2)*, 45). There is also a suggestion that the Spirit prepares the Hindu partner for dialogue for, "if one thing is certain it is that such deep dialogue between two believers, Hindu and Christian, cannot be arranged or 'set up'."[193] Christ and his Spirit are active in the world, "illuminating hearts, leading to God, calling to repentance and inspiring all things",[194] and making real the love that motivates dialogue.[195]

Sometimes the Spirit is said to be discernible in the actual encounter itself.[196] Dupuis believes that "the principal agent of interreligious dialogue is the Spirit of God who animates the partners."[197] Accordingly, in such a situation what is required is "listening in prayer and meditation to the voice of the Holy Spirit as He speaks to us in the existential meeting with Hindu Spirituality."[198] According to Duraisingh, "The primary purpose of dialogue is ... to stand under the Spirit of truth and love that manifests itself, piercing through the logos of both the witnesses."[199] Discussion of the

---

191 For example, Abhishiktananda, *The Church in India*, 64; 'Basis and Content,' 80.

192 The statement is from the 1974 Synod of Bishops as cited in *GIRD(2)*, 32. As evidence for this overflowing work of the Spirit the *Guidelines* cites 1 Corinthians 2.11, John 3.8, Psalm 104.30; not every advocate of dialogue would be persuaded that these verses can sustain belief in the activity implied. On the Spirit and the religions, see also: Jacob Kavunkal, 'Cosmic Economy of the Spirit and the Non-Christian Religions,' *IMR*, 3 (1981), 19-28; Angelo Fernandes, 'Summons to Dialogue,' in *The Summons to Dialogue* (Hong Kong, 1983), 23.

193 Rogers, 'Hindu and Christian – a Moment Breaks,' 41f.

194 'Consultation on the Theology of Hindu-Christian Dialogue,' 78.

195 Lead Me to the Real: the Hindu-Christian Dialogue (Hong Kong, 1983), 42.

196 For example, Rogers, 'The Content of a Christian-Hindu Dialogue,' 69f; 'Basis and Content,' 79.

197 Jacques Dupuis, Toward a Christian Theology of Religious Pluralism, 382.

198 Kalapesi, 'Some Reflections,' 72. Similarly, *GIRD(2)*, 35.

199 'Issues in Mission and Dialogue,' 409; he also refers to "the Subject matter of the dialogue, the Spirit" (409).

Spirit's activity beyond the boundaries of the Christian community is a prominent feature in Catholic discussion of dialogue, but it is also found elsewhere. The Anglican Murray Rogers, for example, believes that interior dialogue includes "listening to the Spirit from within the Hindu experience of the Mystery."[200] This is because, in his view, "the Spirit has been drawing Hindus into the orbit of Christ" for millennia.[201]

One justification of dialogue is, then, the activity of God – and it is interesting to note a Hindu assessment of this claim. Sharma traces "the changing theistic pattern" in the Christian missionary assessment of the religions over the centuries so that now "in a dialogue situation God is not so much with us as *amongst* us, or with us with a very different sense than at the beginning – he is now with us all."[202] As always, however, references to the activity of God do raise the question of the possibly arbitrary nature of such appeals.

K. Dialogue as a Fruit of the Gospel

There is a cluster of reasons which proposes commitment to dialogue because of certain qualities or attitudes implied by the Christian understanding of the Gospel. The first and probably most widely suggested of these is love. An ecumenical consultation, for example, agreed that "the *motivation* for inter-faith dialogue will be, for the Christian, the experience of *love*, God's love for man providing the paradigm."[203] Even as "God's action in Christ through the Spirit ... is a dialogue of love" so is the Christian to be motivated by love as he meets a person of another faith.[204] Dialogue is a witness to the love of Christ,[205] and "an expression of Christian neighbourliness."[206] Abhishiktananda believes that for Christians the "inner demand" of love will make dialogue "something spontaneous."[207] A number of statements about the theology of inter-faith dialogue do,

200 Dialogue Postponed,' 222; he is alluding to an opinion of JA Cuttat, with which he clearly agrees.

201 'Hindu and Christian – a Moment Breaks,' 40.

202 Sharma, 'Towards a Theory of Dialogue,' 37.

203 'Consultation Working Group Reports, 106 (original emphasis). A similar statement came from the 'Consultation on Theology': "Living out our Christian life is in itself a dialogue; it takes us to the other in love and service" (79).

204 Sadiq, 'Inter-Faith Dialogue and Communication of the Gospel,' 14.

205 Taylor, 'Christian Motivation in Dialogue,' in *FTF*, 10f.

206 Samartha, 'The Other Side of the River' (unpublished paper, 1983), 10.

207 The Church In India, 64.

in fact, commence at this very point. For example, the Indian Catholic *Guidelines* begins its lengthy discussion of 'Theological Perspectives' with a definition of Christians in dialogue as people who know themselves to be the outcome of God's love, "a sign of God's own gift to this world." Because of this they are to live in constant dialogue with the community; "Dialogue is the law of our being" and Christians fail in their vocation if they fail to love every single individual (*GIRD(2)*, 13).

Love and community are related in another way. The Church itself is meant to be a sign and a symbol of a true community of forgiveness, reconciliation, love and freedom, the offer of which "inevitably leads to dialogue."[208] The experience of Christian freedom itself is often seen as a major incentive to dialogue. Perhaps the ideal of the Zurich Aide-Mémoire has not yet been realised in the Indian church; nonetheless, it does point to important theological principles for dialogue when it states that, for Christians, "Christ releases us to be free to enter into loving, respectful relation with all human beings. It is the grace of God that draws us out of our isolation into genuine dialogue" with others.[209] So Ariarajah urges the church "to break away from bondage to dogmatism into the freedom of the Spirit."[210]

These appeals to love and freedom can, however, lead advocates of dialogue in many directions. As *conditions* for dialogue the presence and practice of both virtues are certainly desirable. But their utility as principles, especially theological principles, in establishing bases for what, in historical perspective, is the somewhat novel endeavour of Christian-Hindu dialogue, is less certain. On the one hand the appeals to love and freedom, especially when supposedly approved by the Spirit, can be used to endorse a widely varying number of opinions, and with an added degree of plausibility once it is implied that these new conclusions replace older untenable positions of reactionary resistance to necessary change and growth in interreligious relations. And on the other hand the appeals to love, freedom and a number of equally desirable ideals that have been seen in this chapter to be possible bases for Hindu-Christian dialogue can, in fact, conceal a number of unacknowledged presuppositions and problems.

208 Samartha, 'Dialogue as a Continuing Christian Concern,' 153.
209 ZAM, 2.
210 Ariarajah, 'Towards a Theology of Dialogue,' 5; the 'dogmatism' he has in mind is fear of syncretism.

L. Comment

A number of reasons are, then, able to be given for the justification of Hindu-Christian dialogue and they can be arranged in order of complexity according to the kind of dialogue being considered and the presuppositions on which they are based. Some of the reasons are shared by both Hindu and Christian participants in dialogue; others offer more distinctly Christian theological reasons for engagement in dialogue. Each of the proffered sets of reasons for dialogue has been found to have points of validity. However, they often contain unacknowledged presuppositions as well, and raise questions to which attention must be given if the reasons offered are to commend themselves within India (and beyond).

The first two sets of reasons (increased understanding and common social concern) contain much that is acceptable and commendable. Nonetheless, three comments might be made. (a) From a wider religious/theological standpoint, these reasons often reveal a rather static view of humanity by comparison with the bases of human need, mutual growth and even common pilgrimage suggested by most elaborations of the Hindu and Christian tradition. (b) Some Christians find it unacceptable that "an abstract noun like justice can be given this ultimate status [of universal basis for human unity and co-operation] whereas the person of Jesus Christ cannot";[211] and some Hindus might wish to raise a parallel objection. The same comments might also be made concerning the role of the somewhat idealised and abstract notion of the unity of humanity and a shared quest for community, especially when little attention is given to the ground or reality on which such unity might be based. (c) Even if one or more forms of dialogue are required by the necessities of understanding and good community relations, it is difficult to formulate a theory and theology of interreligious dialogue on such pragmatic considerations.[212] What people think ought to be done in a given situation depends at time quite acutely upon what they

---

211 Lesslie Newbigin, cited in Jean Stromberg, 'Christian Witness in a Pluralistic World,' *IRM*, 78 (1988), 431. Elsewhere he is critical of the appeal to a common pool of human values: "the 'values' of justice and compassion cannot be permanently sustained apart from some belief about the facts which correspond to these values. ... Questions of ultimate truth are involved." (*The Gospel in a Pluralist Society*, 159).

212 Christopher Lamb (who has worked as a consultant in interreligious relations in Britain for many years) complains about "the theology of other faiths being hijacked by the need for good community relations" (verbal communication to this writer).

believe; how or even why one ought to act is not always self-evident. Given the multidimensional nature of religion, the ideal of dialogue is not a single ideal; there are ethical, social and conceptual dimensions that will vary among the religions.

The suggestion of a joint search for truth may also constitute an appropriate basis for dialogue. But when the wide diversity of understandings of truth in Hinduism and Christianity is acknowledged,[213] then certain questions must be raised; for example: the considerable problem of the determination of validating epistemological criteria (if any) – how they are to be found and whether they are to be elaborated in conjunction or interplay with those of the other faith. Both among Christian and other proponents of dialogue there is often the assumption that mutual criticism or simply the clash of opinions inevitably leads (perhaps in Hegelian fashion) to the disclosure of some fuller truth – to which it must be said that dialogue does not offer some privileged mode of access to the truth.[214] There is also the question of the *intended limits* of dialogue as the joint quest for truth. In a somewhat forcefully written critique of liberal Christian approaches to dialogue – what he calls "an underlying scholarly orthodoxy on the goals and functions of interreligious dialogue" – Griffiths argues against those who maintain that understanding is the only legitimate goal of dialogue. Theirs, he asserts, is the evaluation and critical judgement (other than that directed against one's own faith) is inappropriate, and that the active defence of the truth and practices of one's own position is to be avoided. Such an approach according to Griffiths, produces a discourse that is "pallid, platitudinous and degutted."[215]

The notion of religious growth as a basis for dialogue often makes assumptions about the desirability of change and its facilitation by dialogue. These assumptions imply that without dialogue such change might not or perhaps even could not take place and either or both traditions would remain incomplete in some way. Questions about the means of such growth might also be raised,

---

213 See Hendrik M Vroom, *Religions and the Truth. Philosophical Reflections and Perspectives* (Et: Grand Rapids and Amsterdam, 1989), chapters III and VI.

214 Cf John Milbank's remarks in his 'The End of Dialogue,' in *Christian Uniqueness Reconsidered*, 182.

215 Paul J Griffiths, *An Apology for Apologetics. A Study of the Logic of Interreligious Dialogue*. Faith Meets Faith series (Maryknoll, NY: Orbis, 1991); quotation from xif. The sharp rejection of the work by Hans Ucko, the director of the WCC's Office of Inter-religious Relations (see his somewhat belated review in *IRM*, 84 (1995), 315) seems only to confirm the validity of Griffiths' basic position.

especially if the view is accepted that the instrumental function of scripture, institutions and practices is markedly different in the two religious traditions: in Hinduism they are instrumental for the realisation of *moksa* and then, in most Hindu traditions, transcended in a way not usually advocated in Christianity.[216]

Perhaps the most problematical reason advanced for dialogue is that of the complementary character of religious experience. As with the notion of religious growth there is an implication of imperfection or incompleteness without such complementary experience – an implication that would be rejected by at least some Hindus and some Christians. Acknowledgement needs also to be given to the quite different axes around which the Hindu and Christian traditions revolve. Without an understanding of this difference apparent similarities and complementarities may well be misleading.[217] The notion of common faith – contrasted with divergent beliefs articulated from that faith (a distinction that is "essential for a world in dialogue" according to one advocate of Hindu-Christian dialogue)[218] – also raises problems, especially if this faith is seen as inaccessible to logical scrutiny (as maintained by some advocates of dialogue). As Baird asks, "if we have no access to the thing itself, how do we verify if the experience itself is the same (though *variously* described) *or* different (*as* described)?"[219] But it must also be added that the appeal to complementary experience does at least acknowledge some real differences between the two traditions – reflection on which might enable further understanding.

An appropriately critical evaluation of the appeal to religious experience as a basis for Hindu-Christian dialogue is difficult to elaborate. For one scholar, the academic study of religion "accepts this witness to a self-authenticating experience as an object of study, and it does not censure it any more than it approves it or participates in it."[220] The usual objections to any appeal to religious expe-

216 See the elaboration of 'Religion as Instrumental,' in Coward, *Pluralism. Challenge to World Religions*, 96f.

217 For example, Sabapathy Kulandran, Grace: a Comparative Study of the Doctrine in Christianity and Hinduism (London, 1964), 255.

218 James D Redington, 'The Hindu-Christian Dialogue and the Interior Dialogue,' *TS*, 44 (1983), 602.

219 Robert D Baird, 'Hindu-Christian Dialogue and the Academic Study of Religion,' in *H-CD*, 227 (original emphasis).

220 Baird, 'Hindu-Christian Dialogue and the Academic Study of Religion,' 220. He also warns against any reductionism that would imply that, when academic enquiry is no longer applicable, what is said to remain does not exist (225f).

rience remain: all experience is made available by means of a complex epistemology; it is necessarily interpreted experience and may not function so much a pointer to a common centre for the religions as a covert (even if unwitting) endorsement of any number of parochial claims and viewpoints.

The appeal to common religious values or experience is equally problematical. Too often the claim by Hindus or Christians that certain values are 'moral' or 'spiritual' is regarded as self-evident justification for assumptions about a common source for both traditions that thereby justifies dialogue. The appeal to religious experience, especially if it claims that all the religions are variations on one common experience of the central single reality shared by them all, is also open to question given that it elevates one aspect of the religious traditions above others. No religious experience is 'raw'; both Hindus and Christians stand within cultural and verbal traditions which influence both the experience itself and any description of it. Experience is never experience of experience, but supposedly of some Other whose description will be conditioned by each tradition (and a multitude of cultural and linguistic factors). However, there has yet to emerge a definition of this Other that is recognisably the shared centre of both traditions.

Dialogue is an obvious and even necessary means to assist the process of indigenisation or inculturation. But even here questions need to be asked. Although the Gospel can never be fully identified with any one culture, debate will continue over the limits of the identification that is necessary and possible. In the case of India there is the further question of whether there is a common *Indian* (as opposed to Hindu) culture that Christians can claim in their quest for contextualisation.[221] If, as Justin Charles believes, "India cannot claim to have a particular culture of its own [because] India is a multi-linguistic, multi-racial, and multi-religious nation, hence a multi-cultural nation"[222] then it might be asked *which* of India's cultures the Gospel ought to employ in the process of inculturation. A further question relates to *which* strands of Hinduism can or should be appropriated; there is, for example, the issue of whether use can or should be made of the Sanskritic theological tradition given its long association with Brahminical dominance.[223] (Moreover, considerably more energy and continuing creativity is needed than that implied by Sugirtharajah's comments – presumably written from a

---

221 As assumed by Michael Amaladoss, 'Difficult Dialogue,' *VJTR*, 62 (1998), 575f.

222 'Inculturation of the Gospel in India,' *SIC*, February 1993, 4.

223 This is an issue that will be discussed in chapter 6.H below.

Western desk – about "the exhausted indigenisation / contextualisation model. All around there is a hermeneutical fatigue, and a feeling that we have heard these things before."[224] By way of a response it might be observed that the place and shape of Christianity in India is surely too fragile and urgent for such a mood.) A further issue, alongside those raised in section H above, is to ask whether such a pragmatic intention might not diminish attention given to the other person as person and not simply as a source of material to assist the process of inculturation. And one final observation might be to draw attention to the growing influence – especially upon the young – of those globalising tendencies that almost everywhere flatten or distort the contours of cultural identity. In its own way what has come to be called postcolonial discourse has pointed out that the influences of globalisation on Indian society have made difficult the quest for a supposedly authentic Indian cultural identity. As the realities of postcolonial pluralism lead to complex and hyphenated or multiple identities, so the defining of an appropriate contextualistion becomes more problematical.

References to the present, and prevenient, activity of God as the initiator and sustainer of dialogue, often as the Spirit, raise the question of the possibly arbitrary nature of such an appeal. The activity of God in the world is not in question; but the criteria by which this activity might be known – especially when it is used to justify the relatively novel endeavour of Hindu-Christian dialogue – need carefully to be delineated. The same criticism might be offered of the notion that the fundamental Gospel principles of love and freedom lead necessarily to dialogue. The utility of such principles, able to be used to endorse a wide variety of viewpoints about the Hindu-Christian meeting, is limited unless also carefully delineated.

In most of the discussion it is possible to discern the differing weight given by Protestant and Catholic to the various attempts to justify dialogue. Some of the reasons given (for example the appeal to common humanity) appear to derive substantially from theological reflection outside India. However, despite the problems, there are substantial reasons why Christians and Hindus might enter into dialogue with one another. The reasons offered are numerous – which, given the diversity within the two traditions, may enable at least some of the reasons to be taken up by most Hindus and most Christians. Nonetheless, some practical impediments and questions about the compatibility of dialogue with other aspects of Christian and Hindu beliefs and practices remain. These are addressed in the next chapter.

---

224 'Postcolonialism and Indian Christian Theology,' 237.

CHAPTER 4

A Critique of Christian-Hindu Dialogue

The preceding two chapters have offered a critical analysis of the meaning, practice and justification of Christian-Hindu dialogue – and further criticism is now suggested. On the one hand, a number of shortcomings within the Christian and Hindu communities seem to impede the practice of dialogue. There are also unresolved problems at a theoretical level and three of these issues will be discussed.

A. Impediments to Dialogue

1. *Within Both Communities*

Dialogue is rarely, if ever, between equals and a variety of factors can impede its progress. Mention has already been made of the conditions that seem to encourage fruitful dialogue, especially an acceptance of religious pluralism, informed understanding, and existential openness (see above, chapter 2.D): the absence of any of these qualities will hinder dialogue. There are other factors found, or liable to be found, in both the Christian and Hindu communities that also appear to act as impediments. The identification and removal of hindrances to dialogue is of considerable importance if, as Athyal asserts, "actual dialogue in an atmosphere of mutual respect, frankness and earnestness is very rare"[1] or even if, as Karokaran writes, Hindu-Christian dialogue has simply lost the vitality and enthusiasm it once displayed.[2] Leaving to one side the

1 Saphir Athyal, 'A Theology of Mission in Relation to Hinduism,' in *The Good News of the Kingdom*, edited by Van Engen, Gilliland and Pierson (Maryknoll, NY: Orbis, 1993), 247.

2 Anto Karokaran, 'Dialogue and Interculturation,' *MT*, 1 (1999), 37-48.

more naïve of the analyses,[3] discussion now turns to the major hindrances identified.[4]

(a) Minimising Differences

There are those in each community who minimise the differences between the two traditions. Some Christians, anxious to repudiate exclusivist claims to uniqueness, speak in this way. Panikkar argues that dialogue is to be based on faith – an attitude that transcends differences "because it pierces through them, as it were, and goes deep down to that real which is the religious real par excellence."[5] We have already noted that some Hindus assert the unity of religions in a way that assigns differences to the accidents of geographical and ethnic separation. However, to believe that the minimising of differences might hinder dialogue is not to endorse a sectarian spirit; rather, it is to argue that

> there is no conceivable reason to limit, on *a priori* grounds, Hindu-Christian dialogue only to that form of verbal (or other) communication that results in agreement or eliminates witness and affirmation, in either direction, on principle.[6]

Moreover, honesty and integrity require partners to recognise difference and disagreement. And, as Milbank points out, there are situations where "sympathy turns out to be a mode of betrayal. One should be beware of sympathy, because too often we sympathize with what we can make to be like ourselves."[7]

---

3 For example, one dialogue statement observed that "in spite of several Hindu Christian dialogues we regret to note that many people in India continue to live in religious isolation from one another" ('Statement of Hindu-Christian Dialogue, Varanasi, February 1992,' *HCSB*, 5 (1992), 45).

4 For some general analyses see: Michael L Fitzgerald, 'Interreligious Dialogue Today: Obstacles and Opportunities,' *JD*, 19 (1994), 70-73; Alphonsus Mathias, 'The Future of Interreligious Dialogue: Threats and Promises,' *JD*, 19 (1994), 10-19; Michael von Brück, 'Interreligious Communication and the Future of Religion,' *JD*, 19 (1994), 224-34; Felix Machado, 'Hindu-Christian Encounter: General Problematic,' *VJTR*, 60 (1996), 825-42; Michael Amaladoss, 'Difficult Dialogue,' *VJTR*, 62 (1998), 567-79; Karokaran, 'Dialogue and Interculturation.'

5 Raimundo Panikkar, 'Rules of the Game in the Religious Encounter,' *AF*, 5 (1970), 226 (original emphasis).

6 Eric Sharpe, 'Hindu-Christian Dialogue in Europe,' in *H-CD*, 113.

7 'The End of Dialogue,' 178; in fact, Milbank concludes that for critical understanding "it will be better to replace 'dialogue' with 'mutual suspicion.'" (190)

(b) Emphasis on Fundamental Differences

Another impediment is an overemphasis on the differences between the two faiths, noting that one condition for dialogue is said, not unnaturally, to be freedom from communal or polemical spirit (*GIRD(2)*, 68 and 54). Certainly there should be what Chatterjee calls "the intellectual and emotional welcoming-acceptance of diversity",[8] but not in such a way as to inhibit discourse with those of different opinions.

(c) Difficulties in Mutual Comprehension

One consequence of the fact that Hindus and Christians comprehend reality in somewhat different ways is the realisation that the practice of dialogue is no easy matter. The reality of this fundamental difference is one explanation why dialogue can be difficult and mutual comprehension can become profoundly difficult – for example, when attempting to elaborate the nature of the divine. The problem is compounded by the question of language, given that English is often the medium of organised dialogue.[9] And, underlying the issue, are more profound hermeneutical issues concerning the ontology of language, the status of ('inner') religious experience and the sociology of knowledge and communication – which can also impede mutual comprehension.[10]

(d) Diversity of Internal Opinion

Both Hindu and Christian opinion is divided over the issue of dialogue. Some of these differences will be elaborated in the sections on mission and the evaluation of other faiths that follow in this chapter. Diversity of opinion within the Christian church is no new phenomenon. Pluralism may even be prized as a proof of true catholicity; others see it as a sign of weakness.[11] It seems clear that widely diverging opinions about dialogue do, however, hinder the Indian church's commitment to it. One consequence of such divid-

---

8 Margaret Chatterjee, 'The Presuppositions of Inter-Religious Communication – A Philosophical Approach,' *RSt*, 3 (1967), 395.

9 According to Sivendra Prakash (a pseudonym for Abhishiktananda), there are capable and willing sadhus ready to meet Christians, but "they know only Hindi whereas all your learned discussions are in the foreign English" (in 'Dialogue Postponed,' *AF*, 5 (1970) 215).

10 See the remarks of Stanley J Samartha and the literature cited by him in 'Mission in a Religiously Plural World,' *IRM*, 78 (1988), 317; and Hans-Jürgen Findeis, 'Languages of Religions and Intercultural Communication,' *ZMR*, 73 (1989), 257-83.

11 See, for example, Anthony Adair, 'Towards a Hindu-Christian Dialogue,' *Contemporary Review*, no. 208 (February 1966), 85.

ed opinion is the report that at times there appears to be more agreement in dialogue between some Hindus and some Christians than between Christian participants themselves.[12] The diversity of opinion about dialogue within the Indian church is, however, not always reflected in the opinion of Christian delegates to formally arranged dialogue.

The labels 'Hinduism' and 'Christianity' are umbrella or generic terms for a wide spread of beliefs and practices; in fact, Hinduism may well be best understood as an open-ended and polycentric construct referring to a group of traditions.[13] This need not necessarily constitute an impediment to dialogue (if the diversity is understood – and accepted – by the other) but in practice it sometimes does seem to be an irritant. Protestant participants in dialogue need to acknowledge Catholic (and Orthodox) points of view, and Hindus that popular beliefs and practices are as valid an expression of Hinduism as the classical philosophical systems.[14] Each of the 'great traditions' of Hinduism and Christianity comprises numerous 'little traditions'[15] and, of course, no one individual or group can presume to speak for either tradition as a whole.

---

12 Klaus Klostermaier, 'Hindu-Christian Dialogue,' *DBM*, 19. In similar vein: John B Carman, 'Continuing Tasks in Inter-Religious Dialogue,' *ER*, 22 (1970), 200; Wilfred C Smith, 'Mission, Dialogue, and God's Will for Us,' *IRM*, 78 (1988), 369f.

13 Or, to use a well-known image, Hinduism may be likened to an ancient Banyan tree under whose generous spaciousness there shelters a variety of more or less related beliefs, traditions and practices. For a helpful discussion of various descriptions of Hinduism see Julius Lipner, *Hindus: Their Religious Beliefs and Practices* (London and New York: Routledge, 1994), chapter 1. Also useful is the discussion by Brian K. Smith, 'Questioning Authority: Constructions and Deconstructions of Hinduism', *International Journal of Hindu Studies*, 2 (1998), 313-39.

14 This latter point is well made by AM Abraham Ayrookuzhiel, 'The Living Hindu Popular Religious Consciousness,' *RS*, 26.1 (March 1979), 5-25. Too often Hindu participants in dialogue appear to mean by Hinduism that portion of neo-Hinduism that derives from the syntheses of Ramakrishna and Vivekananda.

15 To use the expressions made popular by Milton B Singer, *When a Great Tradition Modernizes: An Anthropological Approach to Indian Civilization* (Chicago, 1980). For a recent discussion of aspects of this pluralism in contemporary Hinduism see: 'Hindus and their Isms: A Symposium on some of the Complexities of a Dominant Religion,' *Seminar* [New Delhi], no. 313 (September 1985). See also the comprehensive review in *Orthodoxy, Heterodoxy and Dissent in India*, edited by SN Eisenstadt and others (Berlin, 1984).

In turn, the diversity raises the question of the representative status (if any) of those who do participate in dialogue. Not even Catholic participants in and proponents of dialogue can assume the understanding and support of the whole Indian Catholic community. And the diversity among Hindus poses problems for Christian organisations issuing invitations to participate in formal dialogue.[16] Should an invitation go to one whose very willingness to speak would show, as Milbank puts it, "an alienation from the seamless narrative of a tradition which never felt the need for dialogical self-justification?"[17] Dialogue is not simply a meeting of individuals – for individuals cannot be severed from their religious traditions. Perhaps meetings are consultative rather than representative: a meeting between Hindus and Christians rather than between Hinduism and Christianity. In one sense the issue of diversity need only be seen as making dialogue more complex (or interesting or challenging), and by no means impossible. After all, dialogue is between people.

(e) Women and Other Marginalised Groups

One substantial way in which diversity of internal opinion remains unheard is a failure to acknowledge the opinion and contribution of women and other marginalised groups in dialogue. The actual role of women in all but informal dialogue has been very slight – as a survey of the names of participants in Hindu-Christian gatherings, and the literature as a whole, would undoubtedly reveal. (The first edition of the official Catholic *Guidelines for Inter-Religious Dialogue* of the CBCI, for example, has no mention of the place of women in dialogue. In the revised edition women are specifically mentioned when it is said that they have a role in educating children to live in a religiously plural country.[18]) Perhaps the major reason for the very limited participation of women in formal dialogue is the male dominance of those positions of leadership and power from which par-

16 See, for example, Allan R Brockway, 'With Whom Do we Dialogue?,' *CD*, no. 12 (June 1987), 3f, and S Wesley Ariarajah, 'Ecumenical Issues in Dialogue,' *CD*, no. 9 (December 1985), 12. Discussion returns to this issue in section 3(a) below.

17 'The End of Dialogue,' 178.

18 *GIRD(2)*, 58.

ticipants in organised dialogue are usually drawn.[19]

Many of the informal means of dialogue are, of course, open to women; in fact, some of the meeting places, precisely because they are away from the centres of organised religion and formal dialogue (so dominated by men), are particularly congenial to the meeting of women. That Christian and Hindu women so often meet on the margins of power, from which they feel varying degrees of exclusion, may actually be an additional cause of common concern, even unity, between them. The women's movement in India has often expressed concern about the negative impact of communalism on women (and children) as the result of male-dominated politicking.[20]

Moreover, it seems certain that women can and do bring a substantial contribution to the dialogue in which they do participate. Eck writes of the "many ways in which women's participation in interfaith dialogue changes the nature of the dialogue significantly ... [and] holds immense potential for education and attitudinal change."[21] The usually peripheral position of women, and their experience of diversity within their own traditions (again, often more substantial than that known by male leaders), may also make them more open to the changes that are usually a condition of fruitful dialogue. Women do not share greatly in the 'centre' and are constantly "adjusting the 'public tradition' to their own experience of the tradition"[22]- which means that their knowledge and appreciation of internal diversity can enable an appreciation of the diversity of the partner tradition in dialogue.

Another of the beneficial contributions brought by women to dialogue is said to be their critique of "narrow or exclusivist ways of theological thinking."[23] It may also be that women will help

19 Examples of this are found in the papers presented to a conference on 'The Authority of the Religions and the Status of Women,' most of which are published in *RS*, 32.2 (June 1985). For further comment on the position of women see: Kana Mitra, 'Women in Hinduism,' *JES*, 20 (1983), 585-601; KV Thampuran, 'Hinduism and its Impact on Women,' *RS*, 32.3 (April 1985), 11-19; Ursula King, 'Women and Spirituality. Critical Reflections on Christianity and Hinduism,' *Vidyajyoti*, 52 (1988) 225-33, 258-69, 327- 39; *We Dare to Dream. Doing Theology as Asian Women*, edited by Virginia Fabella and Sun Ai Lee Park (Maryknoll, NY, 1989).

20 See, for example, Aruna Gnanadason, 'Living in Harmony with Each Other: A Feminist Perspective', *CGR*, 14 (1996), 91-98.

21 Diana Eck, 'Moderator's Report,' *CD*, no. 16 (August 1989), 11.

22 Eck, 'Moderator's Report,' 21; see also 12.

23 Eck, 'Moderator's Report,' 11 – for example, concern about the presence of God, or truth or salvation in other religions (21).

Christian theology give attention to the feminine in its understanding of the divine, perhaps helping, for example, the advent of Bishop Appasamy's hope that "as Christianity becomes naturalized in India the idea of God as Mother will find a rapid entrance into Christian thought."[24] Vandana and Ishpriya also suggest intuition and contemplation among the skills and gifts women bring to the Hindu-Christian encounter.[25]

Related to the contribution of women to dialogue is the wider question of how the viewpoint and needs of other marginalised groups in Indian society might be addressed in dialogue. In Vinay Samuel's judgement, Christian witness and dialogue must not be restricted to "literate and sophisticated Hindus"; rather, it should begin with the questions and judgements of the marginalised, especially women and the poor.[26] If attention is to be given to the plight of the oppressed untouchables, then a dialogue between Hindu and Christian *dalits* would be far more appropriate than the usual meetings between upper caste Hindus and westernised, often urban, Christians.[27]

(f) Caution and Suspicion

One reason for resistance to dialogue is an understandable concern faithfully to conserve the truth – perhaps seen as unique and eternal and even necessary for the world's healing – that each tradition holds. There are also fears of changes to old patterns of life and resistance to the diminishing or loss of power, influence and identity. Some of this opposition is not surprising; the wounds inflicted by

---

24 AJ Appasamy, *The Gospel and India's Heritage* (London and Madras, 1942), 73. See also Frank Whaling, *An Approach to Dialogue with Hinduism* (Lucknow, 1966), 82f.

25 See their 'Women's Role in Inter-Religious Dialogue,' *WW*, 15 (1982), 287-91.

26 'Selected Readers' Responses to Wesley Ariarajah's Letter,' *IRM*, 72 (1983), 97. He adds, rather pointedly: "The aim of Christian witness is not to enable the literate sophisticated Hindu to have a religious encounter with a mystical figure from another religious tradition" (97). See also Herbert Hoefer, 'Local Village Theology,' *NCCR*, 101 (1981), 13-23; Xavier Irudayaraj, 'Inculturation and Inter-Faith Dialogue,' *WW*, 19 (1986), 129; Felix Wilfred, 'Dialogue Gasping for Breath?, *Vidyajyoti*, 51 (1987), 464; Walter Fernandes, 'Social Action and Inter-Religious Dialogue,' *Vidyajyoti*, 53 (1989), 589-600.

27 Dalit interests are not well served by most present dialogue; see Richard W Taylor, 'Current Hindu-Christian Dialogue in India,' in *H-CD*, 126. Discussion returns to Dalit concerns in chapter 6.II below.

centuries of communal rivalry and social isolation cannot quickly be healed. As Panikkar observes, "the history of this encounter has a loaded karma."[28] Critical remarks are also directed at the institutions of Christianity and Hinduism whose conservative and impersonal dynamics seem to hinder dialogue,[29] and whose shortcomings an individual participant in dialogue can never completely disown. One consequence of long-standing inter-communal suspicion is the deliberate choice of avoidance of contact with the other. Even in the absence of reasonable grounds for suspicion it seems true that lack of trust or the "unjustified imputation of wrong motives" to partners in dialogue also act as hindrances to a fruitful meeting together (*GIRD(2)*, 53). And, as Chatterjee points out, most religions have a word to describe the religious outsider, "and the word is never a flattering one."[30] Christian proponents of dialogue might also draw attention to the theological reasons they perceive to undergird the ambiguous nature of religion – including its capacity to function as a vehicle of self-centredness and self-assertiveness.

There is one positive reason for lack of interest in dialogue: the suspicion that it can be an unnecessary distraction from the more urgent call to confront oppression and injustice; not all Hindus and Christians know of or have opportunity to participate in what we have called secular dialogue. However, it might also be argued with Samartha that, "without touching the deepest core of people, that is, the religious and cultural roots, social justice is likely to remain only a matter of power relationships in the community rather than a consequence of profound change in human values."[31] (On the other hand, there is the temptation to avoid the difficult issue of communalism. But, as Amaladoss points out, any dialogue that does not attend to such problems "will probably limit itself to the ethereal spiritual level and attract a particular class of people ... [who] are not really affected by such problems. Such dialogue ... will be irrelevant."[32])

(g) Minority Interest

The fact that interest in dialogue is, as we have noted, confined to a minority of Christians and Hindus is of concern to advocates of dialogue. In situations where it is mainly the negotiators who are per-

---

28 'The Ongoing Dialogue,' in *H-CD*, ix.

29 For example, by Klaus Klostermaier, 'The Future of Hindu-Christian Dialogue,' in *H-CD*, 266.

30 'The Presuppositions of Inter-Religious Communication,' 391.

31 Stanley J Samartha, 'Christian Concern for Dialogue in India,' *CD*, no. 9 (December 1985) 3.

32 'Difficult Dialogue,' 575.

suaded of the need for openness and respect there is clearly a problem. The fact that the Indian Catholic *Guidelines* urges that "ways should be found to see to it that this kind of dialogue does not remain introverted and the privilege of a small elite" indicates the danger,[33] as does Samartha's admission that "under the present circumstances it has to be dialogue *of the few* on behalf of the many."[34] But this also points to the danger of taking the particular for the universal – assuming that Christians (or one kind or denomination of Christians) or Hindus interested in dialogue in some way do, or can, or should, speak for others.

2. *Among Christians*

(a) The Poor Image of the Church

One further impediment to dialogue is the low regard with which many Hindus hold the church in India. Some Hindus regard it as unworthy or unnecessary as a means of mediating Christ and his teachings. Others regard it as a hindrance because of its compromised association with un-Indian culture,[35] especially when nationalistic aspirations imply a search for religious national self-sufficiency (which in turn raises questions about the extra-territorial loyalty of Indian Christians, especially Catholics).[36] As an Indian Christian acknowledges, traditional Indian tolerance is willing "to accept the influence of Christ and his Gospel. But this acceptance is

33 *GIRD (2)*, 80. A charge of elitism might also be raised when a conference of theologians calls for "the *enlightened* members of various religions" to take up the task of dialogue; ([Indian Theological Association], 'Toward a Theology of Religions. An Indian Christian Perspective,' *ITS*, 26 (1989), 78 (emphasis added)).

34 'Christian Concern for Dialogue in India,' 5 (original emphasis). See also Alfred De Souza, 'Dialogue Between Religions in India,' *IMA*, 3.3 (August 1972), 88f; Clement Godwin, 'The First International Theological Conference on Evangelization and Dialogue in Asia,' *Verbum SVD*, 13 (1972), 284; A Poruthur, 'A Decade of Dialoguing: a Non-Elitist Approach,' *MT*, 2 (2000), 485.

35 The westernised ethos of at least the urban expression of Protestant Christianity in India is well brought out in Lionel Caplan, *Class and Culture in Urban India: Fundamentalism in a Christian Community* (Oxford, 1987), *passim*.

36 Patrick D'Souza considers that, "In India because of certain historical facts, Christianity is still considered an alien reality and a threat to India's, chiefly the Hindus' aspirations and ideals" ('Mission and Dialogue,' *BSPNC*, 20 (1985), 154).

not extended to the institution of the Church which is seen as foreign and is identified … with colonial power."[37] As the phenomenon of 'unbaptised believers' seems to show, the church becomes an obstacle to Christian mission.[38]

A related perception of Christians as lacking spiritual depth provides another difficulty: what Prakash calls the "lack of real interiority in the lives of most Christians" that he regards as a great "stumbling-block" to Hindus.[39] Moreover, these apparent weaknesses must be set over against Christian claims or perceived claims to supposed spiritual or moral or intellectual superiority; these also inhibit the flow of dialogue.[40]

(b) Suspicion of Dialogue

If Hindus have reason to feel mistrust towards Christian initiatives in dialogue, those very initiatives are often under attack from other Christians who regard them as disturbing and even threatening.[41] Such suspicion often springs from a negative appraisal of Hinduism – an appraisal that derives in part from theological opinion, but it is also linked with the minority status of Christians in India – matters to which discussion will return. Major changes (both psychological and theological) in Christian attitudes appear to be necessary before the Indian church could even be said to be open to the prospect of dialogue. (See too the comments on pluralism in chapter 2.D.1.) A CBCI discussion of the role of Christian families in India spoke of

---

37 Michael Amaladoss, 'L'Eglise en Inde: vingt ans après Vatican II,' in *Le retour des certitudes*, edited by Paul Ladrière and René Luneau (Paris, 1987), 21 (my translation).

38 See Leelamma Athyal, 'Church: An Obstacle to God's Mission?', in *Mission Today: Challenges and Concerns*, edited by Abraham P Athyal and Dorothy Yoder Nyce (Chennai: Gurukul Lutheran Theological College and Research Institute, 1998), 41-56.

39 In 'Dialogue Postponed,' 218. See also: Abhedananda, *Why a Hindu Accepts Christ and Rejects Christianity* (Calcutta, 1965); TMP Mahadevan, 'The Christian Image in India,' in *Debate on Mission*, edited by Herbert Hoefer (Madras, 1979), 299-305.

40 See, for example, Abhishiktananda, *The Church in India* (Madras, 1969), 60; *GIRD(2)*, 45; 'Consultation on the Theology of Hindu-Christian Dialogue,' 77, 85; 'The Basis and Content of a Christian-Hindu Dialogue,' *RS*, 6.1 (February 1959), 79.

41 In Catholic circles, a good example is found in Victor J Kulanday, *The Paganized Catholic Church in India* (Madras: The Laity, 1985). A Protestant example of a critical reaction to an initiative in dialogue is found in 'Dialogue with the RSS,' *NCCR*, 100 (1980), 309-15.

"complete isolation" and of "closed groups" within much of the Indian Catholic community. By way of contrast, "openness would mean ... to shed all sorts of fears, suspicions and prejudices towards non-Christians."[42] In the early 1980s a Catholic analysis (of Asia generally) described one reaction to dialogue as "hostility" – an attitude that "is opposed to dialogue even with followers of other Christian Churches, and more so, with members of other religions."[43] Nambiaparambil notes the depth of lay suspicion towards dialogue.[44] Even if there is an acceptance of dialogue, it can amount to what Amaladoss calls "half-hearted" dialogue: dialogue seen as near-proclamation, or an interim measure before the more important task of proclamation is begun. And he notes that one solution is to shift the focus of contact with others to an emphasis on social or economic development – which generates much less suspicion.[45] Kuttianimattathil suggests that, even after the Papal visit in 1986, with its encouragement of dialogue, "many individual bishops" did not really support and promote the official CBCI endorsement of it.[46]

(c) Non-Indian Initiatives

It has also been noted that even when there has been interest in Hindu-Christian dialogue, it has been mainly non-Indians who have encouraged it. Chethimattam could write in 1965 that "the main source ... of inspiration for the dialogue is the missionary zeal of the Western missionaries"; during the previous ten years the "great majority of participants" in meetings to foster Christian-Hindu relations had been Europeans.[47] More than twenty years later Richard Taylor writes that, "from the Christian side, at the intellectual level at least, it is overwhelmingly outsiders" who

---

42 Report of the General Meeting of the CBCI ... 1979, 68f.

43 'The Federation of Asian Bishops' Conferences and Dialogue,' *SB*, no. 17/83 (1983), 334f.

44 'India – Kerala: Dialogue in India: an Examination and Evaluation,' *BSPNC*, 7 (1972), 69. See also Prudent De Letter, 'Dialogue within the Church in India,' *Vidyajyoti*, 40 (1976), 60-72; Mariasusai Dhavamony, 'Lay People and Interreligious Dialogue,' *OT*, 22 (1988), 434-44.

45 'Difficult Dialogue,' 568f.

46 Jose Kuttianimattathil, Practice and Theology of Interreligious Dialogue: a Critical Study of the Indian Christian Attempts since Vatican II (Bangalore: Kristu Jyoti Publications, 1995), 142f.

47 John Chethimattam, 'The Scope and Conditions of a Hindu-Christian Dialogue,' 90f.

engage in dialogue.[48] However, it must also be added that this dependency upon non-Indian energies had considerably diminished by the 1990s, especially in the Catholic church.

(d) Lack of Protestant Interest in Dialogue

As already noted, there has been considerable discussion within the Indian Protestant community about dialogue. However, the interest seems to be confined to a relatively small number of advocates, and this small degree of interest is reflected in the information and publicity organs of the Indian Protestant church. An indication of this is to be found in a partial review of the number of articles on or related to Christian-Hindu dialogue to be found in the official monthly journals of the Churches of North India and South India.[49] As far as this writer knows, none of the major Protestant churches has a staff member to initiate or sustain interest in dialogue. Interviews with knowledgeable observers of the Churches of North India and South India confirm a lack of interest in Christian-Hindu dialogue among Bishops and pastors.[50] There does seem to have been a degree of change during the 1980s. Taylor reports that surveys during that decade of groups of theologically trained respondents (some 1600 in total) indicated that between 70% and 90% of them agreed that "A strong emphasis should be given to training persons to engage in dialogue with other faiths." But it must be added that there is a degree of ambiguity about the results and one of the directors of the

---

48 He means 'Westerners, recent converts from high-caste origins, and Syrian Christians who rank with or near Brahmins in their home state of Kerala' (Richard W Taylor, 'Current Hindu-Christian Dialogue in India,' in *H-CD*, 125).

49 For example, between 1970 and 1985 the *South India Churchman* (Madras) published only two articles directly related to dialogue with Hinduism and three others indirectly related. During the period 1977 to 1985, the *North India Churchman* (New Delhi) published no articles directly related to the subject and only two indirectly related.

50 Roger Hooker speaks of 'a theology of non-theology' concerning dialogue (interview, 16 November 1982). Daniel O'Connor reports the same lack of interest (interview, 17 November 1982). Bishop Lesslie Newbigin indicates a similar lack of interest in the Church of South India with a tendency to "leave it to CISRS." He feels that one reason for lack of interest among CSI pastors is that they are often in contact with Hindu villagers who know little about 'Hinduism'; or they deal with knowledgeable Hindus with whom they are ill-equipped to enter into dialogue (interview, 19 November 1982). A 'Consultation on the Praxis of Inter-religious Dialogue' also noted that "many pastors do not encourage dialogue" ('Consultation Working Group Reports,' 110).

survey comments that "not all those who are positive about Hindu-Christian dialogue actually give it much priority in practice."[51] Stanley Samartha's summary of the situation (in 1985, was that, "by and large, *officially* during the past twenty years the contribution of the Protestant churches in India to the discussion of the serious issues in dialogue has been minimal."[52] A previous Secretary of the National Council of Churches of India is even more critical; writing in 1987 he summarised the response of the Protestant churches to religious pluralism as "rather hesitant, negative and rather reactionary as that of a threatened minority."[53]

In more theologically conservative or evangelical circles the same lack of enthusiasm is found. Athyal considers that many evangelicals are "not convinced that the exercise [of dialogue] is worth the demands it makes of them."[54] This derives from a rather negative appraisal of Hinduism as a worldview and value system[55] and, as Athyal also concedes, the "negative reaction to the notion of dialogue is to a large degree conditioned by the fact that it is promoted primarily by more liberally oriented Christians."[56] (But having said that, Athyal then goes on to state "evangelical Christians would have no problems relating to Hindus on matters of community life and social issues, and would be willing to participate with them in neighbourhood functions and events."[57] And they may be happy with "the sort of dialogue that will further mutual understanding" and that will clear up misunderstandings and prejudices.[58])

(e) The Impediment of Religion

There has also been, especially in Protestant circles, a somewhat critical assessment of the importance of religion itself. One practical consequence of this assessment is that, as Samartha notes, during the 1970s, "by and large Indian Protestant Christian leaders seem to have rejected the very notion of "religion" as a significant category

---

51 Details are given in Taylor, 'Current Hindu-Christian Dialogue in India,' 120-22 (second quotation from 122).

52 'Christian Concern for Dialogue in India,' 3 (original emphasis).

53 GR Singh, 'Interfaith Dialogue at Local Congregational Level,' *NCCR*, 107 (1987), 527.

54 'The Gospel and Hinduism,' 152.

55 This negative appraisal is elaborated in section C.2(a) below.

56 'The Gospel and Hinduism,' 153.

57 'The Gospel and Hinduism,' 152.

58 'The Gospel and Hinduism,' 153.

in ongoing life in India."[59] (And, as we shall see, there seems to be a similarly negative appraisal in evangelical circles.) Although there is not the same suspicion of religion in Catholic circles, there are those who point out that dialogue has been the concern of those very elites that are socially dominant and whose class and caste oppression of the poor impedes liberation. As Samuel Ryan asks, "Could dialogue with dominant classes ever be humanly authentic, spiritual and liberative unless it takes the form of an honest socio-religious critique of and challenge to their faith-practices?"[60]

(f) Narrow Definition of Dialogue

Another difficulty has sometimes been a truncated understanding of dialogue that usually limits it to the discursive form. This is the mode of dialogue that TK Thomas calls "largely cerebral, and disembodied, activity. Its preoccupations are in the main conceptual."[61] Samartha notes the way in which formal dialogue usually employs a western conceptual framework in its formulation of themes and their treatment, and the use of time limits and the English language. There is, he complains, an "almost total emphasis on religious *ideas* to the exclusion, at least in earlier meetings, of religious *life*, symbols, spirituality ...."[62] Chatterjee makes a similar point in arguing that one condition for understanding what the faith of others means to them is "the rejection of the concept of propositional truth in religion."[63] And Prakash also finds a Christian emphasis on discursive dialogue to be an impediment to a true meeting.[64]

(g) Fear of the Consequences of Dialogue

The official Catholic *Guidelines for Inter-Religious Dialogue* considers the possibility of dialogue becoming "a threat to real faith" leading "less instructed fellow Christians to bewilderment and doubt about the value of their faith" – though it attributes these consequences to

59 Stanley J Samartha, 'Partners in Community: Some Reflections on Hindu-Christian Relations Today,' *OBMR*, 4 (1980), 80f.

60 'Spirituality for Inter-Faith Social Action,' 69.

61 'Dialogue at a Dead-end?,' *CCAN*, 13.7 (15 July 1978), 1.

62 Stanley J Samartha, *One Christ – Many Religions*, 14 (original emphasis); he is suggesting that that the format and content of many formal dialogues have changed in recent years.

63 'The Presuppositions of Inter-Religious Communication – A Philosophical Approach,' *RSt*, 3 (1967), 396.

64 'Dialogue Postponed,' 214. David C Scott expresses a concern about dialogue as an exercise in comparative religion ('A Christian Basis for Inter-Faith Dialogue,' *RS*, 12.1 (March 1965), 15).

ambiguity of both language and attitudes by advocates of dialogue (*GIRD(2)*, 56. However, for most Indian Christians in local congregations there are other more immediate and perhaps more persuasive reasons for lack of interest in dialogue. There is, in many congregations, reluctance or even fear of anything that might influence or diminish membership. One consultation noted the "fear that the dialogue approach may be a first step to return to Hinduism, that Christians lose their identity, that it may lead to compromise"; a congregation or denomination touched by such fear is likely to act more as a barrier than a bridge in the Hindu-Christian encounter. There are good reasons, therefore, why the consultation concluded that "it is important to promote ... dialogue in the Church itself", although even in the face of such promotion, it is possible that "a minority can obstruct a project for dialogue."[65]

(h) Reticence to Go beyond the Discursive

Attention has already been drawn to the apparent reticence of ecumenical Protestant initiatives in dialogue to move beyond the discursive to evaluation and even critical judgement.[66] A not unrelated point is made by a Hindu academic who expressed frustration with the reticence of many Western Christians to speak wholeheartedly of their convictions about the truth or value of Hinduism and to go beyond "a mere exchange of courtesies."[67]

3. *Among Hindus*

Christian advocates of dialogue have often seen a difficulty in the perceived lack of interest or response by potential Hindu partners in dialogue; "the interest in Christianity showed by some of the nineteenth and early twentieth century [Hindu] reformers has not continued into the twentieth century."[68] Almost all initiatives in dia-

---

65 'Consultation Working Group Reports,' 111, 110.

66 See the analysis of Paul Griffiths and his *An Apology for Apologetics. A Study of the Logic of Interreligious Dialogue* discussed in chapter 3.L above.

67 See JL Mehta, *Philosophy and Religion: Essays in Interpretation* (New Delhi: Munshiram Manoharlal, 1990), 68; he expresses his own preference for an atmosphere of "liebende Kampf" (loving struggle – a phrase from Karl Jaspers).

68 Margaret Chatterjee, 'The Prospect for Hindu-Christian Interaction,' *HCSB*, 2 (1989), 2. See also Abhishiktananda, *The Church in India*, 60; Taylor, 'Current Hindu-Christian Dialogue in India,' 123f; Klostermaier, 'The Future of Hindu-Christian Dialogue,' in *H-CD*, 265

logue seem to come from the Christian side.[69] There seem to be a number of reasons for this lack of symmetry.

(a) Structure

One imbalance on the Hindu side is the absence of the structural organisation found among Christians. As Rambachand points out, Hinduism is a decentralised tradition which means, among other things, that it is "often slow to identify, analyze and respond to contemporary challenges."[70] Hindu leaders do not *ex officio,* possess the authority or representative status that Christian leaders may have – and this can raise the question "Who speaks for Hinduism?"[71] And, as a Hindu participant commented on a meeting for dialogue arranged by a department of the WCC, the "great organisational power and resources" of the Christians were among the "reminders that the dialogue [was] organised under Christian auspices."[72] Some Christian advocates sympathetically acknowledge this fact.[73]

(b) Majority Status

Because Hinduism is the majority religion in India (Hindus make up some 82% of the population; Christians less than 3%), most Hindus have had less opportunity or need to understand Christianity than Christians have had to understand the Hindu tradition. The generally conservative nature of Hinduism, with its emphasis upon the preservation of orthopraxis and *dharma,* undoubtedly acts as a disincentive to dialogue as well, although what we have called "the challenges of modernity" (see chapter 3.D) may cause some changes. The emergence of 'neo-Hinduism' with strong communalistic and nationalistic convictions has not helped – an issue to which discussion will return.

(c) Understanding of Religion

Perhaps the most substantial reason for lack of Hindu interest in dialogue derives from one or other of the various Hindu understandings of religion itself – especially what Rambachand calls "the

---

69 Harold Coward, 'Hindu-Christian Dialogue: a Review,' *HCSB,* 25-27.

70 'Keynote Address, Hindu Christian Consultation,' 29.

71 See the detailed discussion of this question in the ten articles, the introduction and the response on 'Who Speaks for Hinduism?' in *JAAR,* 68 (2000), 705-835.

72 Unnamed Hindu participant cited in *AM,* 18.

73 See, for example, Samartha, 'The World Council of Churches and Men of Other Faiths and Ideologies,' 196; De Souza, 'Dialogue Between Religions in India,' 88.

tendency to overlook the significance of doctrinal differences."[74] This is discussed in section C below but it is connected with a question that Rambachand (and others) have asked: "If a sincere desire to engage and understand the other is a pre-requisite for meaningful dialogue, why is it that Hindu scholars and intellectuals have not exemplified any serious interest in the Judeo-Christian tradition?"[75] This not only "constitutes an impediment to Hindu-Christian dialogue" but may also reflect "the unfortunate belief that Hindus may not have much, if anything, to learn from Christianity" – and that because of the all-embracing nature of Hinduism.[76]

(d) Suspicion of Christian Motives

There is also the suspicion that, given traditional Christian views of mission and conversion, dialogue is but a new means of proselytising or otherwise promoting Christian interests and a concealed Christian agenda.[77] Memories of colonialism and its association with "aggressive Christian missionary enterprise" also linger and hinder interest in dialogue.[78] Even attempts at inculturation are

---

74 'Keynote Address, Hindu Christian Consultation,' 33.

75 'Keynote Address, Hindu Christian Consultation,' 35; he contrasts this with the disinterested study of Hinduism by some Christians (35).

76 'Keynote Address, Hindu Christian Consultation,' 35. This reflects the experience of Bede Griffiths who complains that in some 25 years in India "I have hardly ever found an educated Hindu who is really open to dialogue, who really wanted to understand Christian faith as something 'other.'" This is because they feel that "they have the absolute and final truth." (*The Cosmic Revelation: the Hindu Way to God* (London: Collins, 1983), 113.)

77 See, for example, Sankaranarayanan, 'Hinduism and its Attitude to Christianity,' *RS*, 6.1 (February 1959), 13-19; RK Guru Dutt, 'Is Inter-Religious Dialogue Possible?,' *RS*, 23.3 (September 1976), 45-58; 'Dialogue Postponed,' 211-13; Nambiaparambil, 'Dialogue in India,' 276f; the opinions cited by Taylor, 'Current Hindu-Christian Dialogue in India,' 123. The suspicion is especially forcefully expressed in recent nationalistic Hindu writings such as: Sita Ram Goel, *History of Hindu-Christian Encounters AD 304 to 1996*, second edition (New Delhi: Voice of India, 1996) and *Pseudo-Secularism. Christian Missions and Hindu Resistance* (New Delhi: Voice of India, 1998); and more moderately by Arun Shourie, *Missionaries in India: Continuities, Changes, Dilemmas* (New Delhi: ASA Publications, 1994); and note the response by Vishal Mangalwadi, *Missionary Conspiracy: Letters Written to Arun Shourie on the Role of Christian Missions in India*, second edition (New Delhi: Nivedit, 1996 and Carlisle: OM Publications, 1998).

78 Anantanand Rambachan, 'Religious Pluralism: a Hindu Perspective,' *CD*, no. 17 (December 1989), 25. The same point is made by Anand Amaladass, 'The Scope of Dialogue,' *HCSB*, 2 (1989), 3.

regarded with suspicion.[79] The result is that "there is still an ocean of distrust to be navigated."[80] Moreover, discussion with Hindus often reveals the presumption that Christians do, in fact, begin conversations with people of other faiths from a position of supposed superiority. Christian claims about the uniqueness of Christianity, or the role of the Church in mediating such uniqueness (especially when expressed in possessive or triumphalistic language) undoubtedly impede dialogue as well.

4. *Comment*

There are, then, many hindrances to dialogue. Often their causes lie well beyond the control of its advocates and practitioners. The meeting of two great religious traditions is inevitably complex: the meeting of individuals who, while not representing a given faith, bring their own understanding, experiences and even prejudices (known and unknown) to the meeting. Perhaps these impediments are an unavoidable part of the journey of dialogue – and should be seen as such.

Some of the impediments discussed appear to warrant further analysis, including analysis from a sociological perspective. On the one hand there is the minority consciousness of Christians with what appears to be the consequential fear of assimilation and erosion or loss of identity. One study concludes that, in an effort to keep its own rights as a minority, "the church in India seems to be losing its own integrity and self-hood. ... The minority consciousness makes the church a self-defensive rather than a positive and creative minority."[81] The minority status is not simply a matter of numerical size alone; one survey in 1984 estimated that some 65 percent of Christians belonged to scheduled castes and some 10-15 percent to scheduled tribes[82] – thus reinforcing the sense of disadvantage. But for some Christians it might be found that one aspect of minority consciousness is an enhanced sense of identity and even

---

79 See, for example, *Catholic Ashrams: Adopting and Adapting Hindu Dharma*, with a preface by Sita Ram Goel (New Delhi: Voice of India, 1988). The Ashram movement is used by Christians to "hoodwink Hindus" (x); "the Christian mission is not only a destroyer of living religions but also of living cultures" (xv).

80 Rambachand, 'Keynote Address, Hindu-Christian Consultation,' 29.

81 George Oommen, 'Minority Consciousness of Christians in Post-Independent India,' *BTF*, 17.2 (April-June 1985), 34.

82 M Azariah, 'Church's Response to Issues and Concerns of Christians of Scheduled Castes' Origin,' *SIC*, September 1984, 13-15.

freedom that has actually enabled, and not hindered, entry into dialogue, especially informal dialogue. And greater understanding of the impediments to dialogue might also come from analysis of the 'majority consciousness' of Hindus, with its indifference to or even inordinate fear of minorities. Communalism has ambiguous implications for dialogue – as does the role of religion in Indian life, and for the same reasons.

Despite general Hindu reluctance to initiate dialogue, there are some exceptions. One Hindu academic writes of "an urgent need for Hinduism also to formulate ... a rationale for initiating and entering into dialogue with other traditions", because it is convinced "that it embodies authentic insights about the nature of God and the way of truth."[83] Even if Hindus might be reluctant to organise or even promote dialogue this does not mean that some are not willing participants. Moreover, it might also be argued that, if there are compelling reasons for commitment to dialogue, then this obligation is not reduced because other religious believers do not show an equal interest in dialogue. At the same time, Christians must not underestimate the negative impact of traditional Christian language. In a helpful reflection on his years as Secretary to the Inter-Religious Dialogue Commission of the CBCI, Nambiaparambil urges Christians to understand and anticipate the impact of language they might consider to be descriptive (for example, Jesus as 'Lord', 'Saviour', 'the Son of God'). The problems are liable to be acute when Christians use language of uniqueness with a dialogue partner whose worldview makes difficult the grasping of notions of uniqueness. As Nambiaparambil asks, "am I as a Christian disposed to grasp the offence that our Hindu ... friends may take who hear my faith-assertion as totalitarian, monopolistic, exclusive, possessive and isolationist?"[84] The solution is not Christian silence but

---

83 Rambachan, 'Religious Pluralism: A Hindu Perspective,' 26f.

84 Albert Nambiaparambil, 'Evangelization and Inter-Religious Dialogue,' *IMR*, 17.2 (June 1995), 76f. (He goes on to urge the avoidance of comparative language that implies the superiority of the Christian position; let Christ remain absolute while Christians use the language of witness to explain what Christ and the church mean to them.) In similar vein Christoph Schwöbel writes that 'The question that arises when God is presented as being exclusively at work in Christianity is whether this does not reduce the universality of God to such an extent that God is made to appear as the tribal deity of a rather imperialistic form of Western Christianity." ('Particularity, Universality, and the Religions', in *Christian Uniqueness Reconsidered*, 31.)

more thoughtful consideration of *how* the Christian position is best and least offensively communicated.

B. Commitment and Dialogue

Both commitment to one's own faith and a genuine openness to the faith of others are often said to be conditions for fruitful dialogue. However, does this mean that dialogue becomes, as John Taylor puts it, "an encounter of representatives in a contest of comparisons or, worse still, a contest of courtesies"?[85] What is the relationship between commitment and openness? Does one necessarily or possibly exclude the other?

1. Commitment to One's Own Faith

Most of those who enter dialogue do so because they are committed and wish to remain loyal to their own religious tradition.[86] This commitment may be linked with mission – and not Christian mission only, as is seen in the mission of Buddhists into South, East and South East Asia, and the missionary activity of Islam and some Hindus.[87]

(a) Interior Dialogue and Conversion

Advocacy of interior dialogue includes one reason offered for the necessity of commitment in dialogue. It is found in what Cuttat calls his 'Golden Rule': "the more deeply I go into my own religion, the more I become capable of penetrating and assimilating the core, the really positive content, of other religious perspectives."[88] This he believes to be a precondition for an individual successfully to enter dialogue. Advocates of interior dialogue often use the terminology

85 John V Taylor, 'Introduction' to Klostermaier, *Hindu and Christian in Vrindaban*, viii.

86 J Russell Chandran, 'A Christian Approach to Other Religions,' *BTF*, 7.2 (July-December 1975), 13. In similar vein, see: JE Lesslie Newbigin, *The Open Secret: An Introduction to the Theology of Mission*, revised edition (Grand Rapids, MI: Eerdmans, 1995), chapter 10, *passim*; Panikkar, *TUCH(2)*, 35; C Murray Rogers, 'Hindu and Christian – A Moment Breaks,' *RS*, 12.1 (March 1965), 40; Knitter, *No Other Name?*, 207.

87 Discussion returns to the issue of mission in section D below.

88 Jacques-Albert Cuttat, *The Encounter of Religions* (New York, 1960), 31. He continues: "this attitude seems to us the only one capable of providing a 'sacred ground' for the inter-religious meeting." Nambiaparambil makes a similar point in 'Dialogue in India: An Analysis,' 277.

of conversion in this context; they do not mean conversion to Christianity or Hinduism but "a conversion to deeper levels of thought and of spiritual experience of the Absolute."[89] One means of achieving this interiority is sometimes said to be the practice of contemplation.[90] Hindu participants in formal and informal dialogue not infrequently make the related point that they discern what one of them calls a "lack of real interiority in the lives of most Christians" (section A.2(a) above).

(b) All Are Committed

Other commentators extend the need for commitment to include all participants in dialogue. Stephen Neill, for example, maintained that "real dialogue is possible only if all the interlocutors are committed, resolute and uncompromising; only so are we able to uncover to one another the riches of the religious inheritance into which we have ourselves entered."[91] The Indian Catholic *Guidelines* states that participants in dialogue "do not meet in a superficial manner… Rather they reach out for each other from the very core of their respective faiths." (*GIRD(2)*, 31 also 41).

(c) Commitment and Dialogue

That such commitment does not impede dialogue is a point made by a number of participants. Mary Kalapesi eschews the surrender of convictions but nonetheless underlines the need "to silence all voices that could impede our listening to the other and letting that other as other … speak."[92] The fact that some recent Christian dialogue with the highly conservative Hindu nationalist Rashtriya Swayamsevak Sangh (RSS) has been initiated by evangelical leaders (while attracting criticism from non-evangelical Christians) may illustrate the principle that the highly committed can and do at times appreciate dialogue with those who also strongly embrace

---

89 Rogers, 'Dialogue Postponed,' 219. Abhishiktananda, *Hindu-Christian Meeting Point*, revised edition (Delhi, 1976), 116 (also 28); *GIRD(2)*, 30; and Mary Kalapesi, 'Some Reflections on the Fourth Meeting on Hindu and Christian Spirituality,' *RS*, 11.4 (December 1964), 74.

90 See, for example, Nagpur Declaration, 38-47, 51. The Declaration also concedes that "recent contemplative life in India has not had the appeal that one would expect" (51).

91 *Christian Faith and Other Faiths*, second edition (London 1970), v (which is not to imply that other Christian advocates do not also regard commitment by other than Christian participants as a necessary basis for dialogue). In similar vein see: Newbigin, *The Open Secret*, chapter 10, *passim*.

92 'Some Reflections,' 73f (original emphasis).

their convictions.[93] A number of other advocates of dialogue, while endorsing openness, suggest that this desirable requirement does not mean that Christians (or any others) must suspend their faith.

(d) Commitment and Passing Judgement

However, there are unavoidable consequences of the commitment of those who participate in dialogue. It may lead, for example, to the passing of evaluative judgements about the beliefs and practices of the partner(s) in dialogue. As Sharpe points out,

> open, courteous discussion between Christians and non-Christians on matters having to do with faith or beliefs ... has frequently led to the passing of Christian theological judgements on the non-Christian material – a procedure that is at least defensible, and may be inevitable[94]

and, of course, such judgements might be expected from a Hindu partner in dialogue in turn. Both partners might well agree that, as religious believers, neither has a viewpoint that transcends commitment and allows an impartial judgement of other commitments. This is, in effect, D'Costa's point about "the doomed quest for a neutral vantage point" when a person from one religious tradition engages with another.[95] It is the reality of religious commitment that makes problematical Panikkar's call for intercultural dialogue and the abandonment of *all absolutisms* as a means of the 'cultural disarmament' that he sees as a condition for world peace.[96] If this means

93 See the news report, 'Critics Assail Dialogue with Hindu Radicals', posted by S David, Bangalore, 14 May 2002, http://www.christianitytoday.com/ct/2002/006/20.33.html.

94 Eric J Sharpe, 'The Goals of Inter-Religious Dialogue,' in *Truth and Dialogue*, edited by John Hick (London, 1974), 82f. Sharpe has used the example of both Indian Christians and missionaries to India to illustrate the related point that lack of sympathy and respect do not necessarily flow from being persuaded of the theological inadequacy of some or many aspects of another faith; see also *Faith Meets Faith, passim*, and his 'Mission Between Dialogue and Proclamation,' in *Redemption and Dialogue*, edited by William Burrows (Maryknoll, NY: Orbis Books, 1994), 161-72. See also Griffiths, *An Apology for Apologetics, passim*.

95 See Gavin D'Costa, 'Whose Objectivity? Which Neutrality? The Doomed Quest for a Neutral Vantage Point from Which to Judge Religions,' *RSt*, 29 (1993), 79-95. The same point is a repeated and valuable theme in the writings of Lesslie Newbigin.

96 Raimon Panikkar, *Cultural Disarmament: the Way to Peace* (Et: Louisville: WJK Press, 1995); much does, of course, depend on the link between commitment and the 'absolutisms' against which Panikkar writes. A number of related points are made by Paul F Knitter, *One Earth Many Religions. Multifaith Dialogue and Global Responsibilities* (Maryknoll, NY: Orbis Books, 1995).

the abandonment of fanaticism it might well be justifiable – but certainly in everyday dialogue the requirements of sincerity, honesty and integrity just as certainly rule out compromise or reductionism or the abandonment of wholehearted commitment.

2. *The Necessity of Openness*

As well as commitment, openness to others (and their beliefs) is also seen by most proponents of dialogue as a condition for its fruitful exercise. After all, if dialogue is only or primarily a meeting of unshakeable *commitments* there is the possibility that no question can really be heard and no changes or growth enabled. The alternative is "openness eliciting openness".[97] The grounds for this openness are many but the realities of religious pluralism (both the fact of such pluralism and a positive theological assessment of it) are usually meant.[98] For Vineeth, the theologically-based embrace of pluralism has a christological component because in it, "my faith in Christ and my vision of all religions embrace one another in such a way that my commitment remains totally unshaken and my openness to all religions gets a Christ dimension."[99]

(a) Varieties of Openness

There are references in the Hindu-Christian dialogue to "concerned openness"[100], "loving openness"[101], "openness and readiness to learn and be enriched"[102], "total openness"[103], and "openness of heart and spirit"[104] as conditions for dialogue. Both the "openness of truth"[105]

---

97 To use a section heading in Albert Nambiaparambil, 'Interreligious Dialogue: Dimensions and Challenges', *TM*, 3 (2000), 107-09.

98 On the acceptance of pluralism, see chapter 2.D.1 above; on the acceptance of religious pluralism as 'theological act' slowly evolving from the realities of Indian life, see VF Vineeth, 'Committed to Christ and Open to All Religions,' *TM*, 4 (2001), 22-32.

99 'Committed to Christ and Open to All Religions,' 32.

100 RW Taylor, 'The Meaning of Dialogue,' in *I-RD*, 56.

101 Taylor, 'The Meaning of Dialogue,' 58.

102 Anto Karokaran, Evangelization and Diakonia (Bangalore, 1978), 184; see also Mariasusai Dhavamony, 'Evangelization and Dialogue with Hindus,' in *Light and Life We Seek to Share* (Bangalore, 1973), 146; *GIRD(2)*, 17, 49.

103 Roger H Hooker, 'Evangelism, Dialogue and Worship,' *Vidyajyoti*, 40 (1976), 128-30.

104 KS, 55.

105 J Russell Chandran, 'Christian Contribution to Religious Dialogue,' *IMA*, 3.2 (May 1972), 74.

and "openness to truth"[106] are advocated, as is a "certain porosity."[107]

The abandonment of exclusive claims to truth is also said to be a requirement for the necessary openness and empathy needed for understanding another faith "from within."[108] Openness implies a readiness to accept from the other[109] or to be corrected by the other;[110] it may even require a spirit of repentance and forgiveness (*GIRD(2)*, 47). It is a "double openness in Christ to God and the world";[111] it certainly implies a commitment to pluralism and tolerance.[112]

However, a warning might also be sounded: there are examples of 'openness' that might be described as sentimentally facile or destructively self-critical. These attitudes are more likely to harden the position of the closed or suspicious or doubtful mind than to help it to open.

(b) Vulnerability and Risk

Vulnerability and risk are also said to be preconditions of dialogue. Newbigin endorses the notion of vulnerability because "We do not possess the truth in an unassailable form. ... When in true dialogue the true disciple will be exposed without defense in ... dialogue."[113] The Indian Catholic *Guidelines* speaks of the risk and cost of dialogue so that "dialogue demands a growth in courage"(*GIRD(2)*, 46). Clooney acknowledges that the encounter at a scholarly level can and does lead to conflict with one's own religious tradition.[114] Raimundo Panikkar even speaks in terms of a kind of conversion; he believes that neither Christian nor Hindu will fully understand

---

106 Samartha, '*More* than an Encounter of Commitments,' 96. Panikkar writes of the need for "a great intellectual openness" (*TUCH(2)*, 35).

107 Chatterjee, 'The Presuppositions of Inter-Religious Communication,' 400.

108 See, for example, Chethimattam, 'The Scope and Conditions of a Hindu-Christian Dialogue,' 86, 91. Dhavamony sees this understanding as a condition for discerning the "active principle" that motivates the partner in dialogue ('Evangelization and Dialogue with Hindus,' 148).

109 'Conclusions of the National Seminar on Crisis of Faith,' *Vidyajyoti*, 41 (1977), 333.

110 'Consultation on the Theology of Hindu-Christian Dialogue,' 76f.

111 MM Thomas, 'The Open Church,' *NCCR*, 95 (1975), 415.

112 See *Religious Pluralism: an Indian Christian Perspective*, edited by Kuncheria Pathil (Delhi: ISPCK, 1991); Rudolf C Heredia, 'Pluralism, Tolerance and Dialogue,' *VJTR*, 60 (1996), 255-64.

113 *The Open Secret*, 184. See also Henri Teissier on 'Une conversion réciproque par le dialogue,' in *La Mission de l'Église* (Paris, 1985), 178-80.

114 Francis X Clooney, 'The Transformation of the Scholar as a Factor in Hindu-Christian Studies,' *HCSB*, 3 (1990), 1-6.

the other's faith until each is converted "in one way or another" to the other's faith.[115] And a Hindu participant in dialogue is wary of any dialogue that excludes the most critical questions. He adds: "If it is impossible to lose one's faith as a result of an encounter with another faith, then I feel that the dialogue has been made safe from all possible risks."[116]

(c) Relationship between Commitment and Openness

This relationship is described in different ways. For example, a consultation of Christian proponents of dialogue spoke of loyalty and commitment to Christ, adding that "at the same time we have to be open to the leading of his Spirit."[117] The Catholic *Guidelines* balances the Christian belief that in Jesus Christ "God has given a final and definitive Word of Salvation" and they "see in Christ the unique and full revelation of God" with a call for an awareness of the imperfect living out of that knowledge so that the Christian will be open to "any help" to be derived from the response of others to the "all-pervading grace of God." In other words, the Christian is to be a pilgrim alongside many pilgrims of other faiths (*GIRD(2)*, 76). Perhaps it requires a deep *commitment* in order to be prepared for the *openness* of dialogue.

3. Comment on Commitment and Openness

There is, then, a tension between these two conditions for fruitful dialogue. Not all advocates of dialogue acknowledge the tension; some emphasise only one of these suggested conditions and so do not seem conscious of possible conflict. However, the tension must be acknowledged, not least because of its inhibiting effects on dialogue.

(a) Inhibiting Effects

The very fact that those who enter dialogue are usually committed to their own faith can inhibit openness and dialogue but this com-

---

115 *TUCH(2)*, 43, though he does not seem to regard this as a necessity or possibility for all (43). See also by Panikkar: 'Rules of the Game in the Inter-Religious Encounter,' 224; 'Faith and Belief: on the Multireligious Experience,' *ATR*, 53 (1971), 228f; 'The Internal Dialogue,' 55.

116 R. Sundara Rajan, 'Negations: An Article on Dialogue among Religions,' *RS*, 21.4 (December 1974), 74.

117 'Consultation on the Theology of Hindu-Christian Dialogue,' 77; in similar vein: Hirudayam, 'Dialogue in Tamilnadu,' 421.

mitment seems to be an unavoidable corollary of religious belief itself.[118] Religious people *are* located in a specific tradition.[119] There seems to be something about the very nature of religious commitment that gives it an absolute or near-absolute importance for the believer – and the requirements of dialogue cannot alter this.[120] If the commitment of the believer includes a sense of insecurity and fear of losing identity, then that may also lead to a fear of openness that inhibits dialogue.[121] Moreover, some Hindus point out that this fear is not unexpected among Christians whom they perceive to be intolerant and narrow-minded by comparison with tolerant and open Hindus – the very contrast Radhakrishnan once drew between "a fanatic faith in an inflexible creed" and "an attitude of comprehensive charity"[122].

The question, therefore, is whether commitment renders dialogue impossible (because of the perhaps inevitable consequences of the necessary claims to truth made by the committed believer and the possible sense of betrayal if this is not maintained) or makes dialogue pointless or difficult (because the objects and objectives of faith are liable to be conceived so differently by Christian and Hindu). At the same time, the cause of dialogue is not helped by an indifference to or an ignoring of the real differences that exist

---

118 For a discussion of religions as 'systems of belief' (that render dialogue difficult), see John Bowker, *Licensed Insanities: Religions and Belief in God in the Contemporary World* (London, 1987). See also the comments of Chethimattam, 'The Scope and Conditions of a Hindu-Christian Dialogue,' 86.

119 Cf Paul J Griffiths: "to be confessional is simply to be open about one's historical and religious locatedness, ones specificity, an openness that is essential for serious theological work and indeed for any serious intellectual work that is not in thrall to the myth of the disembodied and unlocated scholarly intellect." ('The Uniqueness of Christian Doctrine Defended,' in *Christian Uniqueness Reconsidered*, 169.)

120 Cf Jürgen Moltmann: "A religion which has given up claiming uniqueness … is of no special interest. As a Marxist or as a Muslim, I believe I would have little interest in a Christianity that makes vital concessions before entering into conversation with me." ('Is "Pluralistic Theology" Useful for the Dialogue of World Religions?,' in *Christian Uniqueness Reconsidered*, 155.)

121 The link between exclusive claims and self-identity as a minority is well brought out in a section entitled 'Psychological Dimension' by Thomas Thangaraj in his 'Jesus Christ: the ONLY Way to God and to Human Flourishing', *CD*, no. 37 (June 2001), 8.

122 *The Hindu View of Life* (London, 1927), 28.

between Christian and Hindu – even when the motivation is openness and love. One opinion is that, "In dialogue ... love and truth are inseparable. The ruthless fanatic for truth is just as incapable of dialogue ... as the Christian who, out of a spurious love, keeps silent."[123]

(b) A Widened View of Truth

One attempt to resolve the tension between commitment and openness is to concede that the committed participant in dialogue is making a sincere and informed truth-claim, but to qualify the concession by arguing that dialogue can, for the open-minded, result in a *widened* view of that claim as elements of the truth are found elsewhere (perhaps in dialogue itself). Avoiding talk of absolute certainty may better make the same point. In a discussion of 'The Question of Truth-Claims in Inter-Religious Dialogue', Nirmal points out that all language about 'Reality' is necessarily analogical, symbolic, metaphorical and orientated towards a variety of models. He argues that religious truth claims are 'faith-affirmations' (with an experiential derivation) and are therefore open to revision. In dialogue, there is, of course, a meeting of other truth claims and other 'faith-affirmations'[124] – and thus, at the very least, the prospect of a more modest sense of truth that renders dialogue a little more open.

The same point is made in the statement that each individual's "conception [of truth] is imperfect and calls for completion"[125] or should allow a willingness for reformulation,[126] or "a more open, generous and inclusive understanding of God and his ways."[127] Even if the mystery of Christ and the Gospel is considered to be "total and definitive, the understanding and living of this mystery can grow until the end of time, and this through dialogue."[128] The Indian Catholic *Guidelines* speaks of the requirement for dialogue of

---

123 W Morgenstern, 'Selected Readers' Responses to Wesley Ariarajah's Letter,' 92. In similar vein is Samartha's call that "commitment ... not lead to fanaticism nor openness to shallow friendliness" ('Mission in a Religiously Plural World,' 320).

124 Arvind Nirmal, 'Some Theological Issues Connected with Inter- Faith Dialogue,' *BTF*, 12 (1980), 113-15 and, in similar vein, Michael Amaladoss, 'Dialogue and Mission: Conflict or Convergence?' *Vidyajyoti*, 50 (1986), 67.

125 'Consultation on the Theology of Hindu-Christian Dialogue,' 77.

126 Chandran, 'A Christian Approach to Other Religions,' 13.

127 S Wesley Ariarajah, 'Towards a Theology of Dialogue,' *ER*, 29 (1977), 11.

128 Mariasusai Dhavamony, 'Tension between Evangelization and Dialogue,' in *Light and Life We Seek to Share*, 95.

"a deep commitment to faith" but adds that it remains open to new insights and new means of expressing them (*GIRD(2)*, 41). In other words, dialogue may lead to new insights into religious truth so that a prior understanding is revised or even rejected. The same point about the imperfect apprehension of truth is implied when the image of pilgrimage is used. The committed person is said to be *en route* – journeying, certainly, but not yet arrived.[129] Among Christian proponents of dialogue, the notion of fulfilment (especially christological fulfilment) also affirms a sense of both commitment and openness.[130]

(c) A Modified View of Commitment

Another means of easing the tension between commitment and openness is to lessen or otherwise modify the degree of commitment usually expected from participants in dialogue. Nirmal believes that theological statements are always exploratory and tentative; there is "no *permanent* commitment to them."[131] Lipner draws attention to what he calls the layers of non-integral ideas and symbols that have been attached to the cores of the different religions and whose removal, he argues, allows a more profound encounter.[132] As Dupuis puts it, "openness demands that what is relative be not absolutized, whether by incomprehension or intransigence."[133] And Samartha argues that "the forces of history" are blurring the boundaries of the once distinctive and fixed systems of thought of the religions.[134] This would constitute a further reason for a lessened emphasis upon the received beliefs of a given religion. Even Christians from a more conservative theological position seem to be open to a modified view of commitment. Newbigin, for example, argues that, alongside a firm commitment to Christ, Christians must also be "penitently aware" that their grasp of Christian truth

---

129 See, for example, Nambiaparambil, 'Dialogue in India. An Analysis of the Situation,' 279; and his 'Church in India – Dialogue in Progress,' in *Evangelizzazione E Culture* (Rome, 1976), 267-69; Chandran, 'A Christian Approach to Other Religions,' 13; *GIRD(2)*, 76; Copeland, 'Christian Dialogue with Major World Religions,' 60; *ACFOR*, 21.

130 See chapter 5.D below.

131 'Some Theological Issues Connected with Inter-Faith Dialogue,' 112 (emphasis in original). See also, Samartha, '*More* than an Encounter of Commitments,' 393.

132 Julius J Lipner, 'Dialogue and Encounter,' *DR*, 93 (1975), 58-63.

133 Toward a Christian Theology of Religious Pluralism, 379.

134 '*More* than an Encounter of Commitments,' 401f.

is weak and confused, and may have to be corrected by an encounter with the living experience of people of other faiths.[135] Moreover, there are novel situations in what we have called 'secular dialogue' where there are "no prepared positions."[136]

Such openness may even evoke language about the necessity of conversion from claims to the possession of final truth to a realisation of common possession by God or the Absolute[137] – in other words, conversion to what might be seen as the wider truth of God as revealed through dialogue. Or, the tension between commitment and openness might be seen as an example of the ubiquitous tension between the particular and universal aspects of (claims concerning) revelation. *Commitment* to a particular revelation can lead to the recognition of what might remain *un*revealed and unknown – with a consequential openness to what and where that further revelation might perhaps be sought and found.

It is not surprising that Hindu participants in dialogue also endorse a view that would avoid any overemphasis upon or attachment to a particular *dharma* or to any given formulation of belief. Commitment to *dharma* "can never be more than expressions, approximations. Absolutising them ... may be the most common temptation of believers."[138]

(d) An Inescapably Paradoxical Tension?

Despite the attempts to resolve the tension between commitment and openness the tension nonetheless remains. Perhaps there is an inescapable paradox in simultaneous commitments to religious truth and genuine openness. The notion of paradox is familiar to Hindus and Christians and both traditions are familiar with the notions of ambiguity and insecurity in the struggle to know the divine. If "the dialectics of either/or do not apply so easily to an Asian mentality,"[139] the Indian context might be allowed to help encourage an attempt to live with both commitment and openness. Klostermaier argues that

---

135 *The Finality of Christ*, 21. There may well be value in exploring what the evangelical Miroslav Volf proposes: "provisional certitude as an authentic Christian way." See his 'A Study in Provisional Certitude' in *The Unique Christ in Our Pluralist World*, edited by Bruce J Nicholls (Carlisle: Paternoster Press, 1994), 103f.

136 Newbigin, 'Confessing Christ in a Multi-Religion Society,' 133.

137 See, for example, Nambiaparambil, 'Church in India,' 268.

138 Abhishiktananda attempting to express a Hindu viewpoint writing as Sivendra Prakash in 'Dialogue Postponed,' 218.

139 Panikkar, 'The Ongoing Dialogue,' xi.

> only a paradox prepares the mind for a new experience. Only a paradox induces an existential knowledge ... beyond the conceptual level in which the paradox constitutes a contradiction. The paradox is well known to the teachers of *Brahmavidya* also.[140]

It seems that dialogue sometimes leads to an enforced honesty and encounter with new kinds of questioning and scrutiny that uncover both depth and shallowness in the faith even of the committed. The metaphor of growth might also be recalled (see chapter 3.F) as participants in dialogue reinterpret and perhaps appropriate more deeply (see chapter 2.E.4) their own faith tradition in the meeting. And perhaps the metaphor of pilgrimage is also helpful; after all, a pilgrim is both committed (or, at least, has sufficient conviction and resources to have begun the journey) and open in the sense of not entirely knowing the destination (or perhaps the precise route) that the journey will entail.[141]

The qualities of love and faith might also help resolve the tension between commitment and openness. Love has always been esteemed in the Christian community and among Hindus too – especially those influenced by the *bhakti* tradition. It is central to the Christian notions of commitment to God and others and it has implications for openness. Love certainly implies respect for the 'otherness' of others; it will not want to impose. Faith also plays a part. Vineeth, in discussing the question of why Christians "limit God's power of self-communication and universal salvific will to a particular event in history," writes that the question is "answered by the believing Christian not by reason but by faith."[142] In the final analysis, perhaps a more precise description of the tension (born of the actual experience of the Hindu-Christian interface) is not between commitment and openness, but between an inescapable

---

140 *ITD*, 96, citing Isa Upanishad 12; Bhagavadgita 7.4-13; 9.4-24; 10. (The problems of discourse supposedly 'beyond the conceptual level' have already been noted.) A Statement by Indian theologians declares that "Like all realities, dialogue too is a paradox: a paradox of rootedness and mobility, conviction and openness, commitment to one's own ideas and open appreciation of others" ('Towards a Theology of Religions,' 77f). Note, however, the cautionary remarks concerning paradox by Robin HS Boyd, *An Introduction to Indian Christian Theology*, revised edition (Madras, 1975), 231.

141 Cf the comments of D Jeyaraj in discussing the notion of pilgrimage in dialogue: "A Pilgrim is a free person, the only controlling factor being the holy place or holy water beckoning the pilgrim. It is not a triumphal march but a humble walking" (review of *Pilgrims in Dialogue* in *HCSB*, 5 (1992), 41).

142 'Committed to Christ and Open to All Religions,' 29.

faith-commitment, however qualified, and a combination of (mutual) respect, tolerance and loving, non-coercive, coexistence.

Finally, it must also be noted that traditional christology allows this same combination of commitment and openness: commitment to the divine revelation said to be found in Christ together with an openness to true divine revelation found elsewhere – and there are parallel claims in at least some parts of the Hindu tradition.

C. The Evaluation of Other Faiths

A third problem area concerns the relationship between dialogue and the evaluation within Hinduism and Christianity of other faiths. Much has been written about such evaluations; it need not be repeated except to consider its relevance to the issue of dialogue.[143]

1. Hindus

(a) 'Neo-Hinduism' and the Equality and Harmony of Religions

Although there is a considerable diversity within Hinduism, it is the accommodating understanding of what has been called 'neo-Hinduism' that is often heard from Hindu participants in formal Christian-Hindu dialogue. This is the somewhat liberal stream within contemporary Hindu thought into which currents from the nineteenth century Hindu renaissance and western liberal values, often transmitted through the medium of English and even Christian missionary education, have flowed. The quest for truth, and certain assumptions about complementary religious experience, have been noted as incentives for Hindu-Christian dialogue (see chapter 3.E-G above). For neo-Hinduism these derive from the seemingly obvious equality and essential 'inner' unity and harmony of religions. Vivekananda (and others) employed and extended the classical concept of "many paths, one goal", originally used of the Vedic traditions, to include a place for other religious traditions.[144] Rambachan is especially critical of the influence of Vivekananda's concessions to the Enlightenment critique of the authority of scripture that led him to subordinate such authority to *anubhava* (personal experience). This amounts to a radical divergence from the advaitin system of Sankara of which Vivekananda

143 Some historical background to what follows has been given in chapter 1.

144 See the elaboration by Halbfass, *India and Europe*, chapters 18 and 22 and the comments on Vivekananda in chapter 1.B.3 above.

claimed to be the heir and, according to Rambachan, it has been uncritically accepted within neo-Hinduism.[145] One immediate consequence is that differences of belief and practice are seen as unimportant – both within Hinduism itself and between Hinduism and other religions; it leads to the uncritical assertion that all religions lead to the same goal.[146] This failure to take difference seriously, together with the belief that individuals and ethnic groups have their own peculiar *dharmas* which are the paths or levels best suited to their understanding and birth,[147] does at least have the potential to minimise interreligious tension and conflict. But there are other consequences of these notions of *swadharma* and the equality of religions.

(i) Margaret Chatterjee believes that the "the *swadharma* idea ... operates to discourage basic curiosity about what Christians believe."[148] And, as Rambachan observes: "If all paths are self-sufficiently capable of leading to liberation and if all differences can be explained away as semantic ones, there is not much to be learnt" from inter-religious conversation[149] – one reaction to which is

---

145 See chapters 1-3 of Rambachan, *The Limits of Scripture: Vivekananda's Reinterpretation of the Vedas;* in chapters 4-6 he elaborates the means and extent of the divergence from traditional advaitin orthodoxy.

146 The Limits of Scripture, 135.

147 See, for example, Nikhilananda, *Hinduism. Its Meaning for the Liberation of the Spirit* (Madras, 1968), chapter XI; Sarvepalli Radhakrishnan, *Eastern Religions and Western Thought,* second edition (London, 1940), chapter VIII; and, for a restatement of Vivekananda's position: Anantanand Rambachan, 'A Hindu Model for Interreligious Dialogue,' *CD*, no. 12 (June 1987), 7-12. *On the Essential Unity of All Religions,* see the magnum opus of Bhagvan Das bearing that title (sixth edition; Bombay, 1960). Also useful is the survey by Ram Narayan Vyas, *The Universalistic Thought of India* (Bombay, 1970); Arvind Sharma, 'All Religions Are – Equal? One? True? Same?: a Critical Examination of Some Formulations of the Neo-Hindu Position,' *PEW*, 29 (1979), 59-72.

148 'The Prospect for Hindu-Christian Interaction,' 2; she writes further (she states) about this link in her *The Religious Spectrum* (New Delhi, 1984). Halbfass also draws attention to what he sees as the neo-Hindu inclusivism that makes no real effort to understand the West – whose "very openness is a form of self-assertion" that precludes the need for genuine dialogue (*India and Europe*, 227) – but Halbfass's analysis is subjected to a strong critique by Copley, *Religions in Conflict*, 56-58 and parts II and III.

149 Anantanand Rambachan, 'Religious Pluralism: A Hindu Perspective,' *CD*, no. 17 (December 1989), 25; (this is not Rambachan's view).

Christian disappointment.[150] In fact, Rambachan – in illustrating his contention that Hinduism has not "satisfactorily resolved all of the problems of religious pluralism" – sees Vivekananda's as an inclusivist position that amounts to an assertion that "all truths are partial and find their culmination in *advaita*."[151] However, it must also be added that the general Hindu endorsement of religious pluralism is by no means always uncritical. Rambachan draws attention to both explicit and implicit scriptural criticism of false religious paths and adds that Hinduism "has never legitimatized everything that transpires in the name of religion"; nor have leaders such as Ramakrishna.[152] Nonetheless, at least some aspects of the Hindu appeal to the unity and harmony of the religions have met with a critical Christian response.[153]

(ii) There is also the problem than many Hindus not unnaturally suppose that the somewhat novel Christian commitment to dialogue implies agreement with the notion of the equality and even unity of religions.[154] Disappointment – sometimes acute – can result from such an assumption.

(iii) A third consequence of the Hindu view of religion concerns its

---

150 See, for example, Charles Ryerson, 'A Theological Approach to the Renascence,' *RS*, 12.2 (June 1965), 75; *Christian Institute for the Study of Religion and Society. Report for 1968/69* (Bangalore, 1969), 39; and 'Consultation on the Theology of Hindu-Christian Dialogue,' 76; Bede Griffiths, 'Mission in Dialogue,' 51 where he complains about Hindu proponents of the vedanta for whom "all questions have been answered. Christianity is included in their scheme: there is nothing to learn. We do find in dialogue that even the more serious ones like that are convinced they have the whole truth and they don't care to listen."

151 'Keynote Address Hindu Christian Consultation,' 30; he argues that the 'Hare Krishna' position is similar (30f). Dupuis also summarises this often-heard Hindu position as 'inclusive universality' (*Toward a Christian Theology of Religious Pluralism*, 290).

152 'Religious Pluralism: A Hindu Perspective,' 26. On Ramakrishna's attitude see also Ronald W Neufeldt, 'The Response of the Ramakrishna Mission,' in *Modern Indian Responses to Religious Pluralism*, edited by Harold Coward (New York, 1987), 65-84 and the comments on Ramakrishna in chapter 1.B.3 above.

153 For example, the review article by Balwant Paradkar, 'Dr Bhagvan Das: "Essential Unity of All Religions",' [see note 143 above] *RS*, 10.3 (September 1963), 95-102; Joseph Veliyathil, 'Religious Unity,' *LW*, 83 (1977), 283-90. On a related issue, see Paul Hacker, *Inklusivismus, Eine indische Denkform* (Vienna, 1983).

154 See, for example, Nambiaparambil, 'India – Kerala: Dialogue in India,' *BSPNC*, 7 (1972), 69f.

Christian participants. One reason for Hindu reluctance to enter dialogue seems to be that its context and content continue to be determined by the Western pioneers of dialogue.[155] For many Hindus, this means an overly cerebral and talkative style with insufficient emphasis upon the inner dimension (an impediment already noted in section A.2(a) above). This is why, as Wesley Ariarajah notes, Christian "doctrinal claims about Christ, or belief statements on what God has done in Christ leave the Hindus unimpressed."[156] For many Hindus religious truth is, rather, experientially self-authenticating; "Scriptures should emphasize experience and not fact. Fact bound religion ... is doomed."[157]

(iv) A further consequence is the obstacle posed by what Hindus see as the exclusive and untenable claims of what Nikhilananda calls "those for whom the Personal God is the ultimate reality." Although Nikhilananda does not use the word 'dialogue' he elaborates an appealing and non-exclusivist vedantin view of it in terms of a circle whose centre is God and whose radii are the different religions: "the nearer we are to God, the closer we shall feel toward other religions. In God we all meet."[158] But it must also be noted that the vedantin advocacy of tolerance has also proved problematical for non-Hindus.[159]

(b) Conservative Hinduism

It must also be observed that there are other Hindu attitudes to the religions besides those of neo-Hinduism. As noted in chapter 1 above, classical Hinduism maintained an attitude of indifference and at times hostility towards Christianity. As one Hindu scholar acknowledges, there appears to be a longstanding Hindu aversion "to *comprehend* from within" the faith and traditions of others, for "such an approach to what is other is somewhat alien to the genius of our entire tradition and the task therefore correspondingly difficult and against the grain for us."[160]

---

155 Taylor, 'Current Hindu-Christian Dialogue in India,' 126.

156 'Witness to Hindu Neighbours,' *IRM*, 72 (1983), 86.

157 S Ramasamy, [book review], *HCSB*, 2 (1989), 5.

158 Nikhilananda, *Hinduism*, 174, 187.

159 See, for example, Joseph Vithayathil, 'Religious Tolerance in India,' *LW*, 78 (1972), 351-62; Robert N Minor, 'Sarvepalli Radhakrishnan on the Nature of "Hindu" Tolerance,' *JAAR*, 50 (1982), 275-90; Harold Coward, 'Intolerance in the World's Religions,' *SR/SR*, 15 (1986), 428f.

160 JL Mehta, 'Problems of Inter-Cultural Understanding in University Studies of Religion,' in *Study of Religion in Indian Universities*, 35 (original emphasis). He adds that even within India's own indigenous religious and philo-

There are other Hindu attitudes towards Christianity. For example, there is the employment of selective appropriation – and the corresponding disappointment or even confusion because of Christian resistance to it.[161] Sundararajan also draws attention to a "border-crossing" tradition within Hinduism: the crossing of borders only to co-opt and then erase the boundary (for example with Gautama the Buddha and, to some extent, with the person of Jesus). But he also concedes that this is a somewhat imperialistic model that is not suited to Hindu-Christian dialogue.[162] Moreover, there is a considerable variety of opinion among Hindus concerning Hinduism itself; the most significant figures in the Hindu renaissance differed markedly in their understanding of the essential elements of Hinduism.[163] (Some have followed the absolutist *advaita* and others the theistic vedanta; often Sankara's position was assumed to be normative for vedanta – but this too was disputed by some.) Some of this variety flows from the fact that there is no single authoritative tradition of Hinduism,[164] although that need not constitute an impediment to dialogue. In fact, it may simply act as a reminder (or incentive) to the Christian participant not to presume the faith of a Hindu partner in dialogue can be known in advance.

However, there is also the continuation of what Young calls 'resistant Hinduism' which has found good reason from within the

---

sophical traditions, "the other was allowed to live, ... but without any effort at mutual dialogue and understanding." Nor was there any "explicit intellectual attempt within our tradition, in the long history of its encounter with Christianity and Islam, to understand them in their difference or to let them address us in their truth" (36); the same attitude has not been absent from Christianity or Islam.

161 See the comments of John B Carman, 'Inter-faith Dialogue and Academic Study of Religion,' in *DBM*, 83.

162 KR Sundararajan, 'The Hindu Models of Inter-religious Dialogue,' *JES*, 23 (1986), 239-50.

163 See Ronald Neufeldt, 'Religion and Irreligion,' in *Religion and Irreligion*, edited by Hugo Meynell (Calgary, 1985), 25-44.

164 See Singer, *When a Great Tradition Modernizes*, 34-38; Wendy D O'Flaherty, 'The Origin of Heresy in Hindu Mythology,' *History of Religions*, 10 (1971), 271-333. See also GC Nayak, 'Approach of Hinduism to its Scriptures,' *JD*, 21 (1996), 307-19 who argues that the most widespread and representative position in Hinduism is that acceptance of the authority of the Vedas constitutes orthodoxy. On the other hand, Samartha seems anxious to deny the notion of heresy in Hinduism and to affirm even conservative Hindu apologists as expressing a tolerant pluralism (*One Christ – Many Religions*, 168 n 13 and 81f).

Hindu tradition for resistance to the claims of other *dharmas*.[165] A militant expression of the same attitude is found in the Vedic 'fundamentalism' of Dayananda Sarasvati (1824-83)[166] and the Arya Samaj founded by him, and in the more recent, and rapidly growing, Visva Hindu Parisad and other groups linked with the Rastriya Swayamsevak Sangh which in turn has provided ideological dynamic to the Bharatiya Janata Party, a dominant political force in the 1990s.[167] It is possible that such examples of Hindu militancy may be imitative of parallel attitudes in Islam and Christianity, and even provoked by them – as Radhakrishnan suggested.[168] Samartha calls the phenomenon a hardening of the core of Hinduism as it reacts to the question of conversions to Islam and Christianity.[169] It could also be argued that the images of resistance and hardening might more accurately (and more sympathetically) be described in terms of defence and protection.[170] This strand of Hinduism has, of

---

165 Richard Fox Young, *Resistant Hinduism. Sanskrit Sources on Anti-Christian Apologetics in Early Nineteenth-Century India* (Leiden and Vienna, 1981) – a resistance that he calls "incorrigibly obdurate" (19); cf Halbfass, *India and Europe*, 430 where he claims that Hindu pluralism has little to do with toleration. It must also be acknowledged that, from a Hindu point of view, the phenomenon of 'resistant Christianity' is hardly unknown either.

166 However there is an opinion that considers Dayananda not to have been as parochial as the views soon associated with the Arya Samaj; see Arvind Sharma, 'Dayananda Sarasvati: an Ecumenist?,' *SJRS*, 11 (1990), 24-36.

167 Two useful analyses are: *Contesting the Nation: Religion, Community, and the Politics of Democracy in India*, edited by David Ludden (Philadelphia, PA: University of Pennsylvania Press, 1996) and Christopher Jaffrelot, *The Hindu Nationalist Movement in India* (New Delhi: Viking, 1996); for some helpful comments on what he calls "politicized Hinduism" from an anthropologist, see Paul G Hiebert, 'Missiological Issues in the Encounter with Emerging Hinduism,' *Missiology*, 28 (2000), 52-55.

168 *Eastern Religions and Western Thought*, 312. Veena Das calls the phenomenon "the semiticization of Hinduism": the assertion that Hinduism must have a creed, unity and worldwide organisation as Islam and Christianity (cited by Eck, 'Moderator's Report,' 6) – though others have doubted the appropriateness of the phrase.

169 Stanley J Samartha, [Book Review], *RS*, 28.4 (December 1981), 94; on the inevitable political consequences see his 'Dialogue and Politicization of Religions in India,' *IBMR*, 8 (1984), 104-07. Something of this spirit has been revealed in the negative reaction of some Hindu leaders to the visits to India of Pope John Paul 2.

170 See, Neufeldt, 'The Response of the Hindu Renaissance to Christianity,' 42f; but even the conciliatory Samartha calls neo-nationalistic Hinduism "a majority with a minority complex" (*One Christ – Many Religions*, 23).

course, assumed a highly visible politicised form in recent years and has included energetic appeals to the notion of *Hindutva* ('Hindudom'),[171] the strength of *dharma* and the power and sufficiency of distinctly Hindu resources.

Conservative Hinduism, and its indifference to or rejection of dialogue, is also a reminder that Hindu attitudes to pluralism are varied and complex.[172] This is illustrated by yet another aspect of the Hindu understanding of religious plurality: the phenomenon of *ishtadeva* ('chosen deity') by which an individual chooses which of a number of deities to worship. This notion of chosen commitment has, at least potentially, both positive and negative implications for an understanding of religious plurality and for dialogue.[173] Western proponents of dialogue tend to overstate the degree of acceptance of pluralism within Hinduism.[174] There also appears to have been a shift away from such acceptance within a large segment of Hindu opinion (even if the pluralism is rather naively characterised by Eck as an ethos that was heterogeneous, co-operative and appreciative of diversity) to a "mere plurality" – meaning an ethos with a heightened awareness of social divisions and with a weakened tolerance for diversity and ambiguity.[175] An enquiry into the reasons for such a shift is probably the domain of the sociologist and social anthropologist, but the impact of secularisation may well have helped accentuate in a negative way the diversity of Indian pluralism.

These two currents in Hinduism (neo-Hinduism and conservative Hinduism) can and surely will take Hindu-Christian dialogue in quite different directions.

---

171 This is a notion widely popularised by VD Savarkar, *Hindutva: Who Is a Hindu?* (Bombay: SS Savarkar, 1969).

172 As the relevant chapters in Modern Indian Responses to Religious Pluralism illustrate.

173 These are well elaborated by Anantanand Rambachan, in his 'Significance of the Hindu Doctrine of Ishtadeva for Understanding Religious Pluralism,' *CD*, no. 37 (June 2001), 26-29.

174 For example, Eck, 'Moderator's Report,' 5f; Coward, *Pluralism. Challenge to World Religions*, chapter 4. The actual position seems better stated by MM Thomas: "Physical nearness [of religious communities] existed in ... India without producing what we now call a pluralistic consciousness. [They] ... were largely isolated from each other without a common language of discourse at spiritual depth" ('Christology and Pluralistic Consciousness,' *IBMR*, 10 (1986), 106). See also Stanley Samartha, 'Interreligious Relationships in the Secular State,' *CD*, no. 11 (December 1986), 22, 27.

175 Eck, 'Moderator's Report,' 5f.

2. Christians

There has been considerable discussion within the Christian tradition, especially in recent decades, of the significance of other faiths. The intention of this section is not to describe at length the various positions but to point out some implications for dialogue of the most significant Christian attitudes.

(a) Protestant Evangelicals

The most conservative of Protestants (perhaps deserving the label 'fundamentalist') display little interest in dialogue with Hindus except in the limited sense of talking with Hindus in order to evangelise. 'Dialogue' is not a word or concept that finds favour among them (nor is it a practice favoured by the most conservative of Indian Catholics); there is nothing in Hinduism from which Christians might learn or be edified or encouraged into dialogue.

Other evangelicals, while continuing to emphasise the uniqueness and finality of the revelation and salvation found in Christ, are not as negative in their evaluation of Hinduism. The evangelical leader, Saphir Athyal, illustrates this ambivalence. On the one hand he acknowledges that "the typical evangelical is totally negative when it comes to appreciating Hinduism as a philosophical system" because of its supposed association, he says, with idolatry, superstition, fear of spirits and demons and so on.[176] But he also acknowledges some blind spots in the usual evangelical appraisals and continues: "there is much of value and usefulness to inter-religious dialogue, and its positive benefits should be noted" – which he elaborates in terms of increased understanding, acceptance, respect and the possibility of common social action. However, he also questions the ultimate goal of dialogue if it minimises the offence of the Gospel or impedes the call to faith in Christ.[177] A younger evangelical, Vinay Samuel, is perhaps more conciliatory in tone. He writes, for example, that "in dialogue with Hindus, we are in dialogue with members of a religious tradition that includes great spiritual giants. Only ignorance mixed with arrogance would dismiss all such as not of God." Nonetheless, he goes on to question Hindu views about truth and religious pluralism, and the ethical and social implica-

176 'The Gospel and Hinduism,' 152.

177 'The Gospel and Hinduism,' 153-56. See also by Athyal: 'Asian Views of Dialogue,' *Christianity Today*, 17 June 1977, 44, 46; 'The Uniqueness and Universality of Christ,' in *The New Face of Evangelicalism*, edited by C Rene Padilla (London, 1976), 49-66; and 'A Theology of Mission in Relation to Hinduism.'

tions, especially for the marginalised,[178] of these Hindu views. In other writings Samuel balances commitment to Jesus as the unique but universal Lord and saviour with an attitude of respect for religious experience in general and for Hinduism and its place in Indian culture.[179] In general terms, Indian evangelical opinion does not differ significantly from that of global evangelical discussions.[180]

But it should also be noted that, in the writings of evangelicals, an attitude of indifference (or resistance) to dialogue usually appears as a consequence of convictions about the universality of alienation

---

178 'Selected Readers' Responses to Wesley Ariarajah's Letter,' 96. See also Vinay Samuel and Chris Sugden, 'Dialogue With Other Religions – an Evangelical View,' in *Sharing Jesus in the TwoThirds World,* edited by Vinay Samuel and Chris Sugden (Bangalore, 1983), 177-204. For other qualified evangelical endorsements of dialogue see: Paul Sudhakar, 'How to Prepare the Churches for Dialogue,' *RS,* 26.1 (March 1979), 36-41; Samuel T Kamaleson, 'The Use of Dialogue in Evangelism,' unpublished paper, nd [c. 1973]; *Kristiya Drishtana: a Christian Viewpoint,* edited by V Thampu, K Nicholls and C Raj (New Delhi: TRACI, 1989). Other evangelical reflections are found in part 4 of George David, *Communicating Christ among Hindu Peoples* (Chennai: CBMTM Publications, 1998) and Kathleen Nicholls, 'Indian Spirituality: in Search of Truth and Reality.' Although he is based in Sri Lanka, Vinoth Ramachandra is another evangelical who has given considerable attention to issues of religious pluralism; see, for example, his *The Recovery of Mission: Beyond the Pluralist Paradigm* (Grand Rapids, MI and Carlisle: Eerdmans and Paternoster, 1996) and his *Faiths in Conflict. Christian Integrity in a Multicultural World* (Leicester: Inter-Varsity Press, 1999).

179 There is a summary and analysis of Samuel's thinking in Chris Sugden, *Gospel, Culture and Transformation.* A Reprint with a New Introduction of Part Two of *Seeking the Asian Face of Jesus,* Regnum Studies in Mission (Oxford: Regnum, 2000), 80-88.

180 There is not space to trace the evolving evangelical theology of religions but four conference statements are indicative. The Lausanne Covenant, issued by the influential and representative International Congress on World Evangelization in 1974 – a gathering of some 2500 evangelicals, half of them from the Third World. It denied the possibility of salvation outside of Christ and rejected as "derogatory to Christ and the Gospel every kind of ... dialogue which implies that Christ speaks equally through all religions." The Covenant did endorse "that kind of dialogue whose purpose is to listen sensitively in order to understand", but only as an activity that is "indispensable to evangelism." (The Lausanne Covenant, paragraphs 3 and 4, found, for example, in *Let the Earth Hear His Voice,* edited by JD Douglas (Minneapolis, 1975), 3-9). The only mention of dialogue with Hindus in the papers presented to the first Lausanne Congress took an unsympathetic position (KN Nambudripad, 'Evangelism of the Hindus,'

from God and the uniqueness of revelation and redemption in Christ, rather than any explicitly negative or critical assessment of the religions themselves.[181] Evangelicals are sometimes cited as examples of those who deny the knowledge of God outside the Christian community. The Lausanne Covenant, however, does recognise that "all ... have some knowledge of God through his general revelation in nature."[182] But this revelation is rarely linked by evangelicals to the presence or activity of God (still less that of

---

in *Let the Earth Hear His Voice*, 797). The seven page Report of the more than 200 Indian delegates to that Congress did not mention dialogue at all in its discussion of Christian witness to Hindus. (See 'India National Strategy Group Report,' in *Let the Earth Hear His Voice*, 1375-81.) The second Lausanne Congress (in Manila in 1989) issued a Manifesto which acknowledged attitudes of "ignorance, arrogance, disrespect, and even hostility" towards adherents of other faiths on the part of some evangelicals, but also spoke of a determination "to bear a positive and uncompromising witness to the uniqueness of Christ" including during dialogue. (*Proclaim Christ Until He Comes. Lausanne II in Manila. International Congress on World Evangelization, 1989*, edited by JD Douglas (Minneapolis, 1990), 30). The two plenary addresses on 'The Challenge of Other Religions' spoke quite positively about dialogue (see 179-190), but group discussion on 'Reaching Hindus' made no mention of dialogue (443f). The 'Iguassu Affirmation' issued by the World Evangelical Fellowship Missions Commission in October 1999 has a section on religious pluralism which is said to "challenge us to hold firmly to the uniqueness of Jesus Christ as Saviour even as we work for increased tolerance and understanding among religious communities" in the face of increased interreligious and ethnic violence and hostility. Commitment to proclamation "in faithfulness and loving humility" is affirmed – but there is no mention of dialogue (see section 5 of 'The Iguassu Affirmation', *IRM*, 89 (2000) 242-247). The Amsterdam Declaration (July 2000) assumes both that "there may well be traces of truth, beauty and goodness in many non-Christian belief systems." It also speaks of sharing the Gospel "with love and humility shunning all arrogance, hostility and disrespect. As we enter into dialogue with adherents of other religions, we must be courteous and kind. But such dialogue must not be a substitute for proclamation." ('Charter of Commitments', no. 6; the declaration is found in *ERT*, 25 (2001), 5-14. Some useful material is also found in Bong Rin Bo, 'Evangelical Responses to Religious Pluralism in Asia', *ERT*, 17 (1993), 70-81.

181 See also Esther Williams, *Sacrifice or Investment? Indian Evangelical Mission 1965-1985* (Bangalore, 1985) where, apart from two very brief references to the study of 'non-Christian religions' as part of a training curriculum (111, 113), there is no mention of the religions, nor of dialogue with them.

182 Lausanne Covenant, paragraph 3.

Christ or the Spirit) in a way that would, in itself, justify and sustain dialogue with Hindus or others.

To the Indian and other names mentioned above there should also be added those of the missionary scholars Stephen Neill and Lesslie Newbigin whose theology is generally more conservative than that of the 'mainstream' Protestants to be discussed below. Concerning Hinduism, Neill writes that "all the categories of the Hindu at once reveal themselves as totally inadequate" for the range of human experience. People need "not to be enlightened, but to be saved."[183] And yet Neill also speaks favourably of Christian "willingness to accept new light, ... and to believe that other faiths may enshrine truths to which we ourselves have been blind" (230), and goes on to speak of informal dialogue with "friends of the other faiths" in which "we come to the other faiths ... not as dogmatists or critics, but in the spirit of humble questioning" (232). Newbigin has written more explicitly and positively about dialogue, but also with considerable emphasis upon its Christian basis as found in commitment to Christ (see section B.1 above). Newbigin also acknowledges the work of God and the presence of Christ in the religions, but he pointedly contrasts this with the way in which the religions (including Christianity) can and do also range themselves against God and the knowledge of God to be found in the Gospel.[184] As with the more conservative evangelicals, Newbigin relates dialogue directly to Christ: the purpose of dialogue "can only be obedient witness to Jesus Christ" (182). But, unlike most conservatives, he disavows the employment of dialogue for intentional evangelistic purposes (182).

(b) 'Mainstream' Protestant and Catholic Opinion

The intention of this section is to underline the link already noted between a changing Christian assessment of Hinduism and the movement towards dialogue.[185] Bosch has pointed out a telling and fairly rapid change of terminology in global Protestant discussions during the period 1963 –1977 when the Christian stance moved

---

183 Neill, *Christian Faith and Other Faiths*, 97; further references in the paragraph are to this volume. Further on Neill see: Tim Yates, 'Stephen Neill: Some Aspects of a Theological Legacy,' *Anvil*, 5 (1988), 151-61. It must also be added that personal discussion and correspondence with Bishop Neill revealed that he was not particularly sympathetic towards dialogue as a formal organised process.

184 See 'The Gospel among the Religions,' in *The Open Secret*, 160-89. (Further references in the paragraph are to this volume.)

185 See above, chapter 3, especially E, F, G, J.

from "Christian witness to" to "Christian encounter with" to "Christians in dialogue with" to "dialogue with" to "dialogue between" (in which the mutuality of dialogue is recognised).[186] This Christian reappraisal of the religions was later summarised in a number of models, each representing a different view of the religions.[187] The first of these – a form of particularism or qualified exclusivism[188] with its claims of Christian possession of a final revelation and unique salvation in Christ – is represented by the opinions of the evangelicals discussed in the section above. Several other models, whose points of view overlap to some extent, are represented by such labels as 'pluralism' and 'inclusivism' though the western descriptions do not quite fit the Indian situation. However, it can be said that 'mainstream' Indian Protestant and Catholic reflections on Hinduism contain a call for an interdependent rather than any adversarial relationship with Hinduism and so have led to support for dialogue among those anxious to move away from previous attitudes.[189]

In Protestant circles changes to the more traditional assessment of the religions are well represented by proponents of dialogue such as Stanley Samartha and Wesley Ariarajah who have been linked with the global ecumenical scene through the WCC.[190] In Catholic circles the terminological shift that best parallels the Protestant shift is the move from an ecclesiocentric to a christocentric to a theocentric

186 David J Bosch, *Transforming Mission. Paradigm Shifts in Theology of Mission*, American Society of Missiology Series, 16 (Maryknoll, NY: Orbis Books, 1991), 484.

187 See the discussions (which use somewhat different terminology and divisions between categories) of Knitter, *No Other Name?*; Alan Race, *Christians and Religious Pluralism* (London, 1983); Gavin D'Costa, *Theology and Religious Pluralism* (Oxford, 1986).

188 The often-found label 'exclusivism' is more negative than most of its proponents intend and it is 'qualified' because, as already noted, most evangelicals are can and do speak of God's presence, activity and certain revelation outside of Christ. (This is an issue to which discussion will return in chapter 5.I below.)

189 Recent theological reflection might also be divided into two other categories, 'christocentrism' and 'theocentrism' – a division which conveniently links with the discussion in chapters 5 and 6 below, and which will be elaborated there in some detail; in fact, the pertinent Protestant reflections are discussed in chapter 5.I.

190 A more recent example is found in the many writings of KP Aleaz whose advocacy of what he calls 'Pluralistic Inclusivism' includes the relational convergence of the religions. See, for example, his 'Pluralistic Inclusivism; a Viable Indian Theology of Religions,' *AJT*, 12 (1998), 265-88.

appraisal of the religions. This transition enables the link between the Church as the sacrament of salvation and dialogue to be maintained.[191] Nonetheless, the principal Catholic evaluation of Hinduism (derived, on the whole, from the 'inclusivist' model of the religions – which is not without its Protestant advocates) is positive and generous in its insistence that revelation and salvation (or the possibility of salvation) are to be found within Hinduism.

One useful starting point for understanding the recent Catholic appraisal of Hinduism is the official *Guidelines for Inter-Religious Dialogue* first published in 1977. According to it "religions have a place in God's plan of salvation according to the measure in which they foster … detachment, knowledge, faith, devotion, and adoration."[192] It is hoped that dialogue will lead to "a greater common dedication to the common Lord" (20) and in schools and colleges "we may well, in a genuine spirit of dialogue, help our students [ie students of other than Christian faith] to deepen their understanding of their own religious traditions and Scriptures" (76). Temples are worthy of respect and "a sincere expression of reverence for God's place" (69). The question of joint prayer with Hindus and others is also touched upon and is seen as possible under certain circumstances (58-62), but participation in joint worship is discouraged even though a respectful presence is permitted (72-75).

Since the writing of the first edition of the *Guidelines*, Indian and Asian (and global) Catholic reflection has continued and the second edition of the document illustrates a growing openness to the religions. Instead of a measured and qualified acceptance of religious pluralism, it is now seen as "a consequence of the richness of creation itself and of the manifold grace of God. … Such pluralism … is in no way to be deplored but rather acknowledged as itself a divine Gift." (*GIRD(2)*, 25) – although the *Guidelines* do go on to view the religions neither as rival nor as parallel movements to Christianity but as "stepping stones in the growing revelation of God 'in many and various ways'"(63). Given that all "authentic prayer" is inspired by the Holy Spirit, and since "we are one with the whole of humanity, it is not only our right but our duty to wor-

191 See, for example, the document *ACFOR*, issued in 1984, section 2.

192 *GIRD(2)*, 25. Further references in the paragraph are to *GIRD(2)*. However, it must also be noted that the christocentric character of the evaluation of Hinduism remains central and, on the whole, determinative. The movement of humanity towards God is related to "the definitive intervention … of Jesus the Lord" (15; see also 28).

ship Him together with others." (82)[193] The meetings of the Indian Theological Association of 1988 and 1989 took an even more positive view of religious pluralism than the official *Guidelines* and indicate the rapidly evolving nature of at least some theological reflection.[194] One significant foundational position is clear from the discussions: a "genuine Christian theology of religions" will only emerge from "the inter-religious praxis of dialogue, liberative action and inculturation"[195] – a theological starting point much repeated in Indian Catholic circles in the 1990s.

The single most important feature of both the Catholic and Protestant changes in this area is probably a shift from the christocentrism of almost all earlier positions. The traditional (christocentric) understanding of salvation history gives little or no scope for a positive appreciation of the religions (and their histories) as redemptive; Indian writers are among those who criticise it.[196] Hinduism is seen as accomplishing God's saving will towards all[197] and this requires a corresponding openness on the part of Christians.[198] A

193 "The intention of a prayer or symbol is its ultimate significance, its last aim, beyond its cultural or local wrapping." (*GIRD(2)*, 82. There is even the possibility of Christian participation in prayer addressed to Hindu deities (88); these are "impressive ways of representing the Divine Reality in human ways" (102). But "active participation" in "strictly religious worship" is discouraged in favour of a respectful and sympathetic "religious presence" – but it is not completely ruled out (103). See further: Michael Amaladoss, 'Praying Together,' *ITS*, 29 (1992), 107-24.

194 The papers and statements of the meetings are found in *Religious Pluralism* (see n 112 above).

195 1988 Statement ('Towards a Theology of Religions: an Indian Christian Perspective. Statement of Indian Theological Association Twelfth Annual Meeting, December 28-31, 1988'), paragraphs 36f. (The whole of the 1988 Statement is found in *Religious Pluralism*, 324-37.)

196 For example, Felix Wilfred, 'A Matter of Theological Education: Some Critical Reflections on the Suitability of "Salvation History" as a Theological Model for India,' *Vidyajyoti*, 48 (1984), 538-56; Stanley J Samartha, 'The Holy Spirit and People of Various Faiths, Cultures and Ideologies,' in *Courage for Dialogue* (Geneva, 1981), 67-71. See further on history in chapter 6.C below.

197 See, for example, CM Cherian, 'Anyone Outside the Grace of God?,' *Vidyajyoti*, 44 (1980), 50-63; Antony K Chirappanath, 'God's Plan of Salvation through Cosmic Revelation,' *IMR*, 3 (1981), 305-09. Amaladoss repeatedly stresses the foundational importance of God's universal saving will in his 'Dialogue and Mission: Conflict or Convergence?'

198 See, for example, Zacharias Paranilam, *Christian Openness to the World Religions. Catholic Approach to the World Religions According to 'Nostra Aetate'*

good example is found in an article by George Gispert-Sauch that begins with a confident summary that the traditional 'one mediator' christological formula is no longer acceptable in Asia – and for two reasons: it renders meaningless the history of religions with their own multiple mediators of the divine and it is an obstacle to authentic dialogue between the religions.[199] The fact of religious pluralism is accepted in a positive spirit, and many examples of this positive attitude are found in discussions about inter-faith dialogue.[200] Towards the end of a very lengthy survey of "the emerging Catholic theology of interreligious dialogue", Kuttianimattathil is able to state that "We affirm that the Spirit is ever at work in the hearts and traditions of peoples drawing all to God. We accept the different religious traditions as God's gift to humankind. ... The sincere adherents of these religions are members of God's Kingdom."[201]

These discussions are generally much more appreciative and positive than official Vatican positions; for example, Amaladoss is quite critical of the document 'Christianity and the World Religions' of the International Theological Commission. He considers that it adopts an *a priori* 'from above' analysis that is out of touch with the contextual experience of the religions encountered by the church in

---

of Vatican II with a Special Reference to Hinduism (Alwaye, 1988); Kuttianimattathil, *Practice and Theology of Interreligious Dialogue*; Francis Fernandez, *In Ways Known to God: a Theological Investigation of the Ways of Salvation Spoken of in Vatican II* (Shillong: Vendrame Institute Publications, 1996); Leonard Fernando, *Christian Faith Meets Other Faiths: Origen's Contra Celsum and its Relevance for India Today* (New Delhi: Vidyajyoti and ISPCK, 1998).

199 George Gispert-Sauch, 'Notes for an Indian Christology,' *VJTR*, 61 (1997), 757.

200 See chapters 2.D.1 and 3.G above and elsewhere in this work. A good example of a plea for open-hearted Hindu-Christian dialogue from an experienced practitioner (albeit with some highly debatable theological assertions about the possibility of a plurality of incarnation or reincarnations) is found in Vandana Mataji, *"Living with Hindus." Hindu-Christian Dialogues. My Experiences and Reflections* (Bangalore and Delhi: ITA and ISPCK, 1999). It might also be noted that Asian Catholic statements about religious pluralism are usually more conciliatory in tone than the general Vatican position; see, for example, the analysis of Felix Wilfred, 'Images of Jesus Christ in the Asian Pastoral Context: an Interpretation of Documents from the Federation of Asian Bishops' Conferences,' in *Any Room for Christ in Asia?* [*Concilium*, 1993, no 2], edited by Leonardo Boff and Virgil Elizondo (London and Maryknoll, NY: SCM Press and Orbis Books, 1993), 51-62.

201 Kuttianimattathil, *Practice and Theology of Interreligious Dialogue*, 635.

India.[202] It may be that the official position will continue gradually to evolve; the important Apostolic Exhortation *Ecclesia in Asia*, proclaimed on 6 November 1999 after the four year project of the Asian Synod of Bishops, for example, asserts a traditional christology but its tone towards the people and culture of Asia is generous, respectful and not triumphalistic.[203] Protestant discussion, although somewhat less voluminous, can raise similar questions; for example, Samartha: "Do the histories of people in India ... have no theological significance in the sight of God, the creator and parent of all humanity?"[204] Many other liberal Protestant writers embrace a similar position. One way of summarising the shift from the traditional critical or cautious assessment of the religions to the newer openness is to note that it is based upon a shift from a deductive to an inductive hermeneutic. In the 1960s the theology of religion worked deductively from biblical and christological premises that led inevitably to christocentric or ecclesiocentric conclusions. But by the 1990s most Catholic and mainstream Protestant assessments are dominated by an inductive hermeneutic in which the experience of the religions is said to play a dominant role.[205]

One further and new feature in the appraisal of the religions is an emphasis upon the Kingdom of God (or Reign of God) as an inclusive model for the whole of humankind. Catholic theology has increasingly used the notion of the Kingdom. It is said to be universally at work; it is much wider than the church: "Where God is accepted, where Gospel values are lived, where man is respected, ... there is the Kingdom."[206] The calling of Christians is to establish the Kingdom and not merely extend the boundaries of the church.[207]

---

202 Michael Amaladoss, 'The Mystery of Christ and Other Religions: an Indian Perspective,' *VJTR*, 63 (1999), 327-38. Another analysis is found in Terrence W Tilley, '"Christianity and the World Religions," a Recent Vatican Document,' *TS*, 60 (1999), 318-37.

203 See, for example, the analysis in Sebastian Karotemprel, 'The Christology of Ecclesia in Asia,' *MT*, 2 (2000), 456-66. Also useful is James H Kroeger, 'Introducing Ecclesia in Asia,' *VJTR*, 64 (2000), 11-17.

204 *One Christ – Many Religions*, 11.

205 See, for example, the discussion of this shift in Tord Fornberg, *The Problem of Christianity in Multi-religious Societies of Today*, Toronto Studies in Theology, 70 (Lewiston, NY: Edwin Mellen Press, 1995), 256-58.

206 Statement of the Federation of Asian Bishops' Conferences cited in 'Some Theological Reflections on the Asian Context of Evangelization,' SB, 24 (1992), 51; it is noteworthy that chapter 2 of the encyclical on the validity of mission, Redemptoris Missio (1990) is entitled 'The Kingdom of God.'

207 For two of many examples of this logic see A Pushparajan, 'Christian

This means that the world's religious traditions do contribute to the building of the Kingdom and their followers can be called "- even without being formally conscious of it – active members of the Kingdom."[208] The consequences for dialogue are very considerable. In the words of Dupuis:

> Dialogue takes place between persons who already belong together to the reign of God, inaugurated in history in Jesus Christ. In spite of their different religious allegiance, such persons are already in communion in the reality of the mystery of salvation. ... Communion in the reality is, however, more fundamental and is of more consequence than the differences at the level of the sign. This explains the deep communion in the Spirit which interreligious dialogue, if it is sincere and authentic, can establish between Christians and other believers. ... Christians and others build together the Reign of God each time they commit themselves of common accord in the cause of human rights, each time they work for the integral liberation of each and every human person, but especially of the poor and the oppressed. They also build the Reign of God by promoting religious and spiritual values.[209]

Because the universal presence and action of the Spirit is said to be calling everyone to the realisation of the oneness of the Kingdom, "dialogue itself is a step towards the Kingdom." (*GIRD(2)*, 28). Dialogue becomes "a journeying together ... towards the Kingdom to which God calls all peoples."[210] Because dialogue helps build the

---

Response to Indian Religions,' *JD*, 19 (1994), 275-99; Mary Motte, 'Diversity and Truth: a Missiological Perspective,' *Missiology*, 23 (1995), 85-90.

208 Dupuis, *Toward a Christian Theology of Religious Pluralism*, 345. For further discussion by Dupuis see also his 'The Kingdom of God and World Religions,' *Vidyajyoti*, 51 (1987), 530-44; *Jesus Christ at the Encounter of World Religions* (Maryknoll, NY: Orbis, 1991), 143-51; and 'The Reign of God, the Religions, and the Church,' chapter 13 of his *Toward a Christian Theology of Religious Pluralism*. It is important to note that Dupuis does not set this view over against christocentrism; "the Kingdom-centered model cannot bypass or avoid the Christocentric perspective" (*Toward a Christian Theology of Religious Pluralism*, 345).

209 *Toward a Christian Theology of Religious Pluralism*, 346.

210 *Theses on Interreligious Dialogue*, 8, 10; very similar language is also used by Angelo Fernandes, 'Summons to Dialogue,' in *The Summons to Dialogue* (Hong Kong, 1983), 37. It is interesting to note that Christopher Duraisingh, writing in 1988, states that 'in the discussion on mission, the ecumenical movement has unequivocally affirmed that the horizon of the mission of the church is the kingdom of God' ('Issues in Mission and Dialogue: Some Reflections,' *IRM*, 78 (1988), 405.

Kingdom, "all believers in God's plan for the world can cooperate in this task."[211] There are detailed studies that seek to show parallels between the Kingdom of God and *dharma*.[212] The belief that "the seeds of the Kingdom" are found scattered throughout Asia (as an Asian Catholic Bishops' document puts it[213]) brings out an important difference between this Asian understanding of the Kingdom and the usual emphasis found in Western theological reflection where "it is said ... that the *Kingdom* cannot be separated from the person of Jesus" whereas the Asian Catholic emphasis "is that *Jesus* cannot be separated from his central message of the Kingdom of God."[214] And the positive link between the Kingdom and the religions also has some Protestant support as well.[215]

However, it must also be added that recent official statements from the Vatican directly challenge the more liberal direction taken by the Indian church in recent decades. *Ecclesia in Asia* (November 1999) asserts a traditional Christology that has been carefully avoided (and usually for pragmatic reasons) by proponents of dialogue in India.[216] And the intentionally confrontational Declaration from the

---

211 D'Souza, 'Mission and Dialogue,' 153. Jose Kuttianimattathil makes a similar point at the conclusion of his survey 'Tracing the Development in the Church's Attitude to Other Religions' (*TM*, 3 (2000)): the changed attitude "should lead us to a greater appreciation of each other and greater cooperation in building the Kingdom of God" (18).

212 See Francis X D'Sa, 'Dharma of Jesus?', in *The Dharma of Jesus: Interdisciplinary Essays in Memory of George M Soares-Prabhu*, edited by Francis X D'Sa (Pune: Institute for the Study of Religion, 1997), 418-68; Sudhil, *The Reign of God and the Establishment of Dharma: A Theological Study of the concept of the Kingdom of God in the Synoptic Gospels and of Dharma in the Bhagavad Gita* (Varanasi: IMS Generalate, 1998).

213 See Wilfred, 'Images of Jesus Christ in the Asian Pastoral Context', 53.

214 Wilfred, 'Images of Jesus Christ in the Asian Pastoral Context', 53 (original emphasis).

215 See, for example, Stanley J Samartha, 'The Kingdom of God in a Religiously Plural World,' *ER*, 32 (1980), 152-65. It is interesting to note that by 1988 Christopher Duraisingh could write that "in the discussion on mission, the ecumenical movement has unequivocally affirmed that the horizon of the mission of the church is the kingdom of God" ('Issues in Mission and Dialogue: Some Reflections,' *IRM*, 78 (1988), 405.

216 See the analysis in S Karotemprel, 'The Christology of Ecclesia in Asia', *MT*, 2 (2000), 456-66. From a wider – but still Asian – perspective, Edmund Chia analyses the Synod for Asia (Rome, April 1998) and the Plenary of the Federation of Asian Bishops' Conferences (Bangkok, January 2000) and discerns a clear division between Vatican-based institutions whose "agenda was doctrinal: a re-affirmation of Jesus Christ as the one and only

Congregation for the Doctrine of the Faith, 'Dominus Iesus' (August 2000) could be seen as an attack on a number of elements central to the current theologies of dialogue and the religions in Indian Catholic circles. For example, it attacks a *de iure* justification of religious pluralism (4), denies the inspired value of non-Christian scriptures (8), asserts a highly christocentric view of salvation (10f), denies the activity of the Spirit "outside or parallel to the action of Christ" (12), defends christological terms such as "unicity", "universality", "absoluteness" and "uniqueness" (15), greatly downplays a 'kingdom centred' theology of mission (19), denies that the Church can be considered "as *one way* of salvation alongside those constituted by the other religions" (21) and places the Church's interreligious dialogue "as part of her evangelizing mission" – which includes conversion (22).[217] In other words, both in tone and contents it seems considerably at odds with much of the official *Guidelines for Inter-Religious Dialogue* not to mention the writings of a number of individuals. It remains to be seen how groups such as the CBCI will react and whether the next edition of *GIRD* will become more conservative in tone.

3. *Syncretism and 'Double-belonging'*

(a) Syncretism

One danger of dialogue is sometimes said to be that, as a result of it, some Hindus and Christians will be tempted to syncretism in the sense of the conjoining (deliberately or otherwise) of elements from the two traditions – usually with the intention of seeking common ground or of dealing with contradictory elements and in either case by means of some reduction of the content of the tradition concerned. Warren, for example, writes critically of "the disintegrating effect of religious syncretism which is endemic to Indian thought"

Savior" and the majority of bishops from Asia whose "agenda was pastoral: how to ensure the church in Asia is faithful to Christ while at the same time being in harmonious relationships with the many great and living religions in Asia" ('The "Absence of Jesus" in the VIIth FABC Plenary Assembly', *VJTR*, 63 (1999), 897.

217 It must be added that the Declaration is more nuanced and qualified than this brief summary might imply but the elements of confrontation are present and intentionally so.

as one difficulty associated with Christian-Hindu dialogue.[218] The Indian Catholic *Guidelines* also warns against it[219] and a Korean Protestant theologian is highly critical of its supposed influence on the Indian church.[220]

However, most Indian theologians and many other observers of the Christian-Hindu encounter appear much less concerned. Most appear more anxious about the inhibiting attitudes generated by fears of syncretism. Usually these fears relate to a perceived attempt to inhibit a legitimate contextualisation or inculturation (and so keep the Indian church in some kind of bondage to Western theology and cultural forms).[221] Ariarajah considers that the greatest obstacle to theological thinking about dialogue is an inordinate fear of syncretism.[222] Stanley Samartha believes "it is meaningless to talk about the danger of syncretism" in contemporary India; "let not the Indian Church waste its time on this topic."[223] It was the goal of inculturation that prompted Hans Staffner to defend the notion of 'Hindu-Christian' in various writings and even to enquire about the possibility of a synthesis of Hinduism and Christianity.[224] It is clear from an examination of Staffner's work that one of his major concerns is the cultural identity of Indian Christians.[225] Another concern

---

218 *ATA*, 59. Saphir Athyal makes a similar point in 'Asian Views of Dialogue,' 44, as does Adair when writing about 'eclecticism' ('Towards a Hindu-Christian Dialogue,' 84). Eclecticism might be defined as the attempt that, "in the search for a common denominator among the various traditions, chooses scattered elements among them and combines these in to a shapeless, inconsistent amalgam" (Dupuis, *Towards a Christian Theology of Religious Pluralism*, 378) – but the same critique can be applied.

219 *GIRD(2)*, 55 – but the warning is very brief and not elaborated.

220 Lee Dong-Joo, 'Study of Modern Indian Indigenization Theory and Hinduistic Syncretism,' in *Kein anderer Name. Die Einzigartigkeit Jesu Christi und das Gespräch mit nichtchristlichen Religionen*, edited by Thomas Schirrmacher (Nürnberg: VTR, 1999), 429-51.

221 On the link between contextualisation and a legitimate 'syncretism' see *Dialogue and Syncretism*, edited by Jerald D Gort and others (Grand Rapids and Amsterdam: Eerdmans and Rodopi, 1989)).

222 'Towards a Theology of Dialogue,' 5.

223 [Book Review], *RS*, 28.4 (December 1981), 94.

224 See his *The Open Door. A Christian Approach to the World Religions* (Bangalore, 1978); 'Von Christlichen Hindus und Hindu-Christen,' *Die katholischen Missionen*, 104 (1985), 51-55; *Jesus Christ and the Hindu Community. Is a Synthesis of Hinduism and Christianity Possible?* (Anand, 1988).

225 See his 'May a Convert Retain His Spiritual Identity?,' *Vidyajyoti*, 40 (1976), 356-62.

is to commend the two traditions to each other's followers which he does by asserting that Hinduism and Christianity are not mutually exclusive because "Hinduism is a culture which has room for many religions"[226] and "Christianity is a religion which can become incarnate in any culture".[227] The key to understanding this thesis is the notion that Hinduism is a culture; this means that a person might remain a Hindu (that is, culturally) while embracing Christianity as their chosen religion – which would require an openness to allow such a person to remain a member of the Hindu community and the removal of certain legal impediments.[228]

One Indian theologian who has explored the issue of syncretism in some detail is MM Thomas.[229] He critically questions the negative appraisals of syncretism by Western theologians such as Kraemer[230] and others. Thomas argues for what he calls a neutral definition of syncretism, taken from the History of Religion, to denote any interpenetration between religions and between cultures. Instead of a simply negative description he proposes a redefinition to cover the reality of "legitimate, relatively legitimate, and illegitimate mingling of different religious systems."[231] The Christian goal would then be a "Christ-centred syncretism" that would enable Christianity to be open to "interpenetration ... but with Jesus Christ as the principle of discrimination and coherence."[232] Failure to encourage, or even to allow, this kind of syncretism, is theologically illegitimate, and prevents the processes of growth, adaptation and experimentation within Christianity.[233] One virtue of Thomas' position

226 Section heading in his *Jesus Christ and the Hindu Community*, 83-99.

227 Section heading in his *Jesus Christ and the Hindu Community*, 101-18.

228 *Jesus Christ and the Hindu Community*, 235-45.

229 See his *Some Theological Dialogues* (Madras, 1977), 156f; *Man and the Universe of Faiths* (Madras, 1975), 155-57; 'Moderator's Report,' in *Breaking Barriers, Nairobi 1975*, edited by David M Paton (London, 1976), 236; 'Christ-Centred Syncretism,' *RS*, 26.1 (March 1979), 26-35; 'The Absoluteness of Jesus Christ and Christ-centred Syncretism,' *ER*, 37 (1985), 387-97.

230 Kraemer's opinions at this point 'remain even today basic theological criteria ... after forty years' (Thomas, 'Christ-Centred Syncretism,' 29).

231 'The Absoluteness of Jesus Christ and Christ-centred Syncretism,' 393.

232 *Some Theological Dialogues*, 156.

233 For a Catholic discussion of some of the same issues, see: AK Saran and Bede Griffiths, 'Further Towards a Hindu-Christian Dialogue,' *CM*, 32 (1968), 213-20. From a more global perspective, see ZAM, 18 and *Faith in the Midst of Faiths*, edited by Stanley J Samartha (Geneva, 1977), 147-49; a number of the chapters in *Dialogue and Syncretism* are also relevant.

might be its theological base, and its careful distinction between critical synthesis and uncritical syncretism. His approach offers some reassurance to those fearful of syncretism since their position usually presupposes a normative form of Christianity from which any departure would be regarded with suspicion. On the other hand, the recent Indian Catholic evaluation of the symbols and ritual of other faiths has (because of the supposed activity of the Spirit) been generally positive in tone and seen as usually as compatible with Christianity. For this reason, "taking them into one's religion with proper discernment or adapting them would not, normally, constitute a case of indiscriminate mixing of religions."[234] It might also be added that most Hindu understandings of religion would not find the prospect of syncretism to be troublesome.

'Double-belonging'

A related phenomenon is 'double-belonging' – the participation of some Indians in both Christianity and Hinduism, or in aspects of both traditions. Examples of syncretism, or something like it, are said to be seen in those Indian Christians who participate in two religious traditions. This double belonging is not an attempt to combine elements of the two traditions, but derives from the necessity or choice to live and participate in both traditions.[235] Carman, for example, argues that it is only in situations where 'syncretism' is potentially or actually present that dialogue takes place for village dwellers.[236] He also draws attention favourably to a further 'higher' syncretism beyond the phenomenon of double participation in which the faith and practice of Indian Christians draws upon the

234 Kuttianimattathil, *Practice and Theology of Interreligious Dialogue*, 465. In similar vein is Michael Amaladoss who, in describing syncretism as the "indiscriminate mixing up of two different religious meaning systems" does male allowance for a legitimate inculturation. ('Praying Together,' *ITS*, 29 (1992), 120, emphasis added.)

235 But it should also be noted that in the most often cited study of double participation – that of Luke and Carman in Andhra Pradesh – the participation was in Christianity and in a village religion standing in an ambiguous relationship with the great or Sanskritic tradition of Hinduism; see Luke and Carman, *Village Christians and Hindu Culture*, especially 146-207. See also the discussion by Ayrookuzhiel, 'The Living Hindu Popular Religious Consciousness'; and the comments on 'Syncretism and Dual Religious Systems,' in Robert J Schreiter, *Constructing Local Theologies* (London 1985), 144-58. See also Margaret Chatterjee, 'The Concept of Multiple Allegiance', chapter VI of her *The Religious Spectrum* (Delhi: Allied Publishers, 1984)

236 Carman, 'Continuing Tasks in Inter-Religious Dialogue,' 207.

language and intention of Hinduism in a way that seems to create what he calls a "Hindu Christianity."[237] Syncretism, or some kind of synthesis, has long been present in Hinduism – from the meeting of the Aryan world view with that of the Indus Valley civilisation in the second millennium BC, to the 'orthodox synthesis' of the six great systems of Hindu philosophy of the first millennium AD, to the emergence of Jainism and Sikhism; in all these India provides examples of a propensity for synthesis. In the nineteenth century, Brahmabandhab Upadhay saw himself as a Hindu Catholic; he wrote in 1898, "We are Hindu so far as our physical and mental constitution is concerned, but in regard to our immortal souls we are Catholic. We are Hindu Catholic."[238]

In the twentieth century attention might be drawn to Gandhi as one possessing something of the same spirit. He has been called "the holy man of our time ... who passes over by sympathetic understanding from his own religion to other religions and comes back again with new insight into his own."[239] It may well be that, in social anthropological terms the Indian perception of the self is sociocentric rather than centred on the individual self. The individual is always conscious of a connectedness with a larger group – which might help explain the phenomenon of double belonging. An anthropological study of Catholicism in Goa highlights the

> intrinsic duality of the Catholic community: its separateness as a group with a specific religious affiliation as well as its embeddedness with Goan Hindus in a common regional culture.[240]

In the contemporary Indian church the notion of double belonging continues to be discussed. This is mainly in Catholic circles where the suggestion of 'Hindu-Catholic' identity has continued to attract comment.[241] Panikkar writes in personal terms of such dual

---

237 'Syncretism,' *Andover-Newton Quarterly*, ns, 4 (1964), 30-43.

238 Cited by Julius Lipner, 'On "Hindutva" and a "Hindu-Catholic" with a Moral for Our Times,' *HCSB*, 5 (1992), 5.

239 John Dunne, *The Way of All the Earth* (London, 1973), vii.

240 Rowena Robinson, *Conversion, Continuity and Change: Lived Christianity in Southern Goa* (London: Sage, 1998), 20.

241 See, for example: Thomas Ohm, '"Hindu-Katholizimus"', *ZMR*, 40 (1956), 53f; Turmes, 'Samaj Dharm and Sadhan Dharm,' *CMS*, 6 (1962-63), 330-34; Richard V De Smet, 'Comments on Samaj-dharma and Sadhana-dharma,' *CMS*, 6 (1962-63), 335-37; Michael Amaladoss, 'Qui Suis-je? Un Catholique-Hindou,' *Christus*, 22 (1975), 159-71. In his *Jesus Christ at the Encounter of World Religions*, 67-90, Dupuis discusses the example of Abhishiktananda. See also Tinu Ruparell, 'On Being Hindu-Christian,' *HCSB*, 11 (1998), 45-48.

participation in both traditions[242] and Abhishiktananda could describe himself as a "Hindu-Christian *sannyasi*."[243] There are some interesting Protestant discussions [244]- and even an evangelical contribution as well[245]- but most Protestant church leaders would not encourage or even allow active participation in Hindu ritual.[246]

Perhaps it is at this point that a Christian advocate of dialogue might reflect upon the challenge of syncretism – even the syncretism that, from a Christian point of view, might be dismissed as unacceptable but reveals, nonetheless, a deep desire for unity and an affirmation of the essential relativity of all structures, creeds and rituals. It is clear that within both Hinduism and Christianity the evaluation of other faiths is of considerable importance in the analysis of dialogue. On the whole, a positive appraisal of the worth of other religions helps to encourage (or, at least, permits) the advocacy and practice of dialogue. A negative appraisal discourages or, at least, restricts the possibility. However, it is also clear that among Hindus and, to a greater extent among Christians, there is a wide divergence of opinion about the religions. If no consensus emerges from the continuing debate then the present wide range of views about the validity and worth of Christian-Hindu dialogue will con-

---

242 'The Ongoing Dialogue,' xf; *The Intrareligious Dialogue*, 40; 'In Christ There Is Neither Hindu Nor Christian: Perspectives on Hindu-Christian Dialogue', in *Religious Issues and Interreligious Dialogues*, 475-90 (and note the reply by Arvind Sharma, 'Perspectives on Hindu-Christian Dialogue: a Reply to R Panikkar', 491-509).

243 James Stuart, *Swami Abhishiktananda: His Life Told Through His Letters* (New Delhi: ISPCK, 1989), 71.

244 Christopher Duraisingh, 'Indian Hyphenated Christians and Theological Reflections. Part II: Alternate Modes of Theologising now Prevalent in India,' *RS*, 27.2 (June 1980), 80-101; J Jayakiran Sebastian, 'Pressure on the Hythen: Aspects of the Search for Identity Today in Indian Christian Theology, (*RS*, 44.4 (December 1997), 27–41); the discussion by Luke and Carman in *Village Christians and Hindu Culture* is from a Protestant perspective as well.

245 Dayanand Bharati, *Living Water and Indian Bowl (An Analysis of Christian Failings in Communicating Christ to Hindus, with Suggestions towards Improvements)* (Delhi: ISPCK, 1997) writes from a generally evangelical perspective and calls himself a "Hindu Christ bhakta."

246 An interesting example is found in the unswerving opposition of VS Azariah, the first Indian Anglican Bishop, to all such participation; see chapter 8 of Susan Billington Harper, *In the Shadow of the Mahatma: Bishop VS Azariah and the Travails of Christianity in British India* (Grand Rapids and Richmond: Eerdmans and Curzon Press, 2000).

tinue to be found – as might be expected from the divergent presuppositions that clearly undergird the contrasting evaluations. If it is assumed that it is possible to separate religion from culture then perhaps an individual might maintain an identity drawn in part from each – but that is a difficult distinction to maintain. On the other hand, if there are aspects of each faith that overlap (and a theory of general revelation might sustain this) then a degree of combination and even integration might be possible and even enriching.

The issues of syncretism and double belonging are also amenable to a fairly straightforward theological analysis. If theology is understood as the ongoing dynamic interpenetration of two horizons – the received *content* of the faith and the cultural *context* in which it is expressed – then the question is not *whether* there will be interpenetration of the two horizons (for that is unavoidable) but one of appropriate *balance*. As Barnes points out:

> To object that such a theory risks descending into the chaos of syncretism raises an obvious problem but rather misses the point. The second horizon only overwhelms the first when a tradition loses touch with its roots. ... We have to be sensitive to the unique character and demands of a tradition and the limits of adaptation to any particular culture.[247]

4. Comment

There is, then, considerable diversity within both the Christian and the Hindu traditions concerning the evaluation of other faiths. But it is within Christianity that the changes have been the greater and it is not surprising that the shifting evaluation at times puzzles observers. One Hindu response has been suspicion and even hostility. Another response verges on the amused; Arvind Sharma characterises what he calls the traditional missionary assumption as "God is with us and the Devil with the others" and summarises the shift from this position (one that "has virtually gone unnoticed") as

> First God is with us and Devil with the others; then God is with us (and Devil more peripatetic!) and you can become one of us and thus be with God; but in a dialogue situation God is not so much with us as *amongst* us, or with us in a very different sense than at the beginning – he is now with us all.[248]

This Christian diversity appears to be deeply entrenched but long-

247 Michael Barnes, *Religions in Conversation: Christian Identity and Religious Pluralism* (London, 1989), 172.

248 'Towards a Theory of Dialogue,' 36f.

standing questions do continue to be asked. For example, there is the issue of whether and what kind of continuity and/or discontinuity might be presumed between the two traditions. The 'mainstream' Protestant and Catholic positions have, as we have seen, suggested many examples of continuity and common ground as bases for dialogue. While not denying that "there may be ... elements ... that formally contradict the Christian faith and are not assimilable" such a cautionary or negative note is rarely heard among proponents of Hindu-Christian dialogue.[249] In fact, it is some evangelicals who argue for what they see as a more balanced position. Athyal, for example, sees sufficient continuity to justify dialogue but also insists on the need to draw attention not only to what he calls "nonnegotiable basics" but also to discontinuity between the Hindu and Christian views of the character of God, the nature and means of salvation and forgiveness, the nature of the world and society (by which he means history, the reality and value of individuals and interpersonal relationships and the issue of sacrificial service to others).[250] There is a measure of diversity in Hinduism but it is small by comparison with the internal Christian diversity and even discord concerning religious pluralism.

D. Dialogue and Mission

During the 1960s, especially in Protestant circles, dialogue was clearly subsumed to mission; for many conservative Christians it still is. Since the early 1970s, especially with a more energetic and structured advocacy of dialogue, some Christians have argued that dialogue is a more appropriate means of approaching Hindus than traditional mission methods. This is partly for pragmatic reasons and partly because of changing theological convictions. Nonetheless, a problem persists.

1. The Problem

The problem is the relationship between dialogue and mission and,

---

249 The quote is from Dupuis, *Toward a Christian Theology of Religious Pluralism*, 381 and he provides a good example of the reticence to elaborate the elements of discontinuity.

250 Athyal, 'A Theology of Mission in Relation to Hinduism,' 248f. And it must also be said that the other principal Indian evangelical theologian, Vinay Samuel, in emphasising the religions as particular and distinctive, does so with little emphasis upon discontinuity and considerable appeal to religious experience as such (see above, nn 174 and 175).

more especially, between dialogue and evangelisation (the specific task of the proclamation of one of the traditions) or mission (which might be seen as the more general promotion or outworking of one of the traditions). The possible relationships between dialogue and mission/evangelisation may be expressed in terms of a series of questions: Is dialogue an activity prior to mission/evangelisation? Is dialogue a means of mission/evangelisation? A dimension of it? An alternative to it? An evasion of it? Or, is mission/evangelisation a hindrance to dialogue? Or the context in which it might or should or must occur? Although these questions are almost only asked by Christians, to the extent that Hinduism has its own sense of mission to Christians and others (see section D.4 below), the same questions might be asked by Hindus – although the usual Hindu elaborations of the religions (especially their supposed unity and/or complementarity) would undoubtedly lessen the tension.

Hooker calls the issue of the relationship a seemingly "insoluble dilemma" given his commitment as a Christian both to dialogue without ulterior motive and to sensitive evangelism, the renunciation of which would be a betrayal of his vocation.[251] Part of the tension is that the good and compelling reasons for dialogue raise the question of why it ought not to be the preferred way of mission, especially when that way would be more congenial to many other Indians.

In the Indian context Dhavamony contrasts the evangelistic task with the practice of dialogue which might appear to "favour syncretism, watering down of the uniqueness and transcendence of the Gospel Message and the claims of Christianity."[252] And Amalorpavadass reports on a period (probably in the late 1960s) during which meetings and seminars revealed tensions and distrust

---

251 Roger Hooker, 'Evangelism, Dialogue and Worship,' *Vidyajyoti*, 40 (1976), 125. And, as Henri Teissier asks, the dilemma is "comment concilier la volonté de respecter l'autre, dans sa culture religieuse ou ses convictions, avec le désir de témoigner du Christ et de son Message?" (*La Mission de l'Église* (Paris, 1985), 175); see the whole chapter, 'Mission et/ou dialogue?' (175-88). See also Dhavamony, 'Tension Between Evangelization and Dialogue,' in *Light and Life We Seek to Share* (Bangalore, 1973), 94; Theodor Ahrens, 'Mission and Dialogue: Contradictory or Complementary?' *ITQ*, 62 (1996-97), 314-30.

252 'Tension between Evangelization and Dialogue,' 95. In Catholic circles, note is taken of the statement in *Ad Gentes* 13: that missionary activity has conversion as its goal – as the authoritative *ACFOR* points out at the beginning of its discussion of the relationship between dialogue and mission (*ACFOR*, 37).

between missionaries (committed to evangelisation) and theologians advocating dialogue. One result was a crisis in the Indian Church regarding missionary motivation, vocation and activity.[253] One reason for convening the Nagpur Conference in 1971 was the perceived need to attempt a resolution of the evangelisation – dialogue tension, but its concluding Declaration merely restated a Christian obligation to both activities.[254] And MM Thomas widens the scope of the question by pointing out that western Christianity, both Catholic and Protestant, reminded Indian Christianity as well as Hinduism of the inherent commitment of the church both to propagation and social transformation (which, at the very least led to what he calls historical dynamism and cultural renaissance). This leads him to pose the question: how might the dynamism and spirit of renaissance be retained "without falling into either the earlier ahistorical stagnant spirituality and caste-structure ... or the aggressive attitudes associated with the period of the colonial mission?"[255]

The questions of conversion and baptism illustrate the complex background to the issue. On the one hand, there are deeply felt Hindu concerns about these matters. But there is also a longstanding Christian concern for the right to witness and to call for conversion and subsequent baptism and entry into the Christian community (a right not to be denied because of examples of proselytism).[256] The question of conversion is not merely a topic to be discussed when Christians and Hindus meet. It has a not insignificant effect upon the way in which the two communities regard one another. As Samartha acknowledges, "from the Hindu point of view [conversion] has disturbing social and political consequences" – which the

253 In *Service and Salvation*, edited by Joseph Pathrapankal (Bangalore, 1973), 24-26.

254 Sometimes in the same sentence (see the Nagpur Declaration, 11, 17); sometimes in adjacent sections (see 18-22 on 'Evangelization' which is followed by 23-29 on 'Dialogue').

255 'A Christ-centered Humanist Approach to Other Religions in the Indian Pluralistic Context,' 51.

256 Devanandan wrote at some length about Christian convictions concerning religious freedom and the rights to evangelise and to call for conversion and baptism. His discussion also included a call for a sympathetic and informed Christian appraisal of the varying Hindu reactions to evangelism; see his *Christian Concern in Hinduism* (Bangalore, 1961), 83-113 – also found as *The Gospel and Renascent Hinduism* (London, 1959), 22-45; *Preparation for Dialogue* (Bangalore, 1964), 120-32; 'The Religious and Spiritual Climate of India Today,' *ER*, 8 (1956), 314f; 'Caste, the Christian and the Nation in India Today,' *ER*, 11 (1959), 278-81.

Indian Church ought to examine.[257] The issue of conversion is only one of the problematical consequences of the traditional view of Christian mission and, as advocates of dialogue realise, many of these negative consequences would be avoided if the model of dialogue determined the approach of Christians to Hindus.[258]

2. *Dialogue and Evangelization*

There is a continuum of possible relationships between the two. The positions at each end of the continuum are useful starting points.

(a) Dialogue as a Means of Evangelization

In 1980 Kurt Dockhorn could report that the viewpoint that sees dialogue as a means of evangelisation "predominates" among pastors and reports the same opinion among participants in a seminar on dialogue at an Indian theological college. He summarises their opinion as: "if dialogue is not a means of mission it leads nowhere."[259] D'Souza notes that the same instrumental view of dialogue is found among Catholics;[260]and even the careful wording of 'Dialogue and Proclamation' concludes that dialogue "remains oriented towards proclamation" (82). The encyclical *Redemptoris Missio* holds that both dialogue and proclamation are authentic, legitimate, necessary and distinct (77) but proclamation has "permanent priority" in the Church's mission (44).

Among Protestant writers it is not unexpected that many evangelicals advocate an explicitly instrumental view of dialogue.[261]

---

257 'Partners in Community,' 79. Also useful are: Abhishiktananda, 'Baptism, Faith and Conversion,' *IJT*, 16 (1967), 189-203; Hans Staffner, 'Conversion to Christianity Seen from the Hindu Point of View, in *Service and Salvation*, 487-501; D Bhatt, 'Theology of Conversion in the Context of Religious Hinduism,' in *Service and Salvation*, 503-13; 'May a Convert Retain His Spiritual Identity?' *Vidyajyoti*, 40 (1976), 356-62; BN Banerjee, 'A Hindu Attitude to Conversions,' *IRM*, 72 (1983), 393-97. For a discussion by a sociologist see: SL Sharma, 'Conversions,' *Seminar* [New Delhi], no. 268 (December 1981), 27-34, and for an antagonistic Hindu reaction see Brahm Datt Bharti, *Christian Conversions and Abuse of Freedom in India* (Vellore, 1980).

258 'Dialogue Postponed,' 220. Discussion will return to the issue of conversion in chapter 7.C.1 below.

259 'Identity, Dialogue and Involvement,' in *For the Sake of the Gospel*, edited by Gnana Robinson (Madurai, 1980), 146f.

260 'Mission and Dialogue,' 152.

261 For example, Samuel T Kamaleson, 'The Use of Dialogue in Evangelisation,' unpublished paper, nd [c. 1973].

Athyal believes that "for a Christian, dialogue is not enough. ... Every person has a right to hear [the Gospel] and true dialogue should lead to one's confrontation of its claims."[262] A mainly Protestant Consultation recommended that the training of evangelists should include the methodology associated with dialogue[263] (although that might simply have meant in addition to evangelistic methods, and it might also be argued that there is a place for discursive dialogue in even the most traditional forms of proclamation). Nonetheless, there are grounds for the suspicion among some Hindus that dialogue may indeed be a means of the attempted conversion of members of the Hindu community.[264]

(b) Dialogue Unrelated to Evangelization

Others are equally certain that dialogue is not and should not be related to evangelization. A Consultation concluded that dialogue "is an activity distinct from evangelisation."[265] The Indian Catholic *Guidelines* states that making converts is not the aim of dialogue.[266] However, there are those who see dialogue as "a betrayal of the duty to evangelize."[267] Panikkar also acknowledges that, were Christianity to abandon its claim upon the world (because of a view of Christ "as a merely partial disclosure of the Divine", as might appear to be advocated by some proponents of dialogue) most Christians would believe they were betraying their mission.[268]

3. *Dialogue as Compatible with Mission*

Nonetheless, there are advocates of dialogue who argue that it is compatible with mission – either with a traditional understanding of evangelization, or with a broader definition of Christian mission.

---

262 Saphir Athyal, 'Asian Views of Dialogue,' 46.

263 'Consultation Working Group Reports,' 110. Whaling, *An Approach to Dialogue With Hinduism*, 18f, 27 expresses a similar view.

264 See, for example, reports by Nambiaparambil, 'Church in India – Dialogue in Progress,' in *Evangelizzazione e Culture*, 265.

265 'Consultation on the Theology of Hindu-Christian Dialogue,' 79.

266 *GIRD(2)*, 39. See also Raimundo Panikkar, 'Rules of the Game in the Religious Encounter,' *AF*, 5 (1970), 223 and the Indian Orthodox Paul Verghese, 'Christ and All Men,' in *LFEM*, 164.

267 'Consultation Working Group Reports,' 110.

268 *TUCH(2)*, 34. J Russell Chandran argues that if the Christian obligation to bear witness to Christ and to make disciples is abandoned in favour of dialogue then dialogue has become 'absolute and truth ... sacrificed for the sake of a misguided openness' ('Discussion: Christianity and Other Faiths,' *USQR*, 20 (1964-65), 183).

(a) Reasons why Dialogue is Compatible with Evangelization

(i) Because they are two different activities.
This point of view argues that dialogue and evangelization are two legitimate but separate activities, each with its own justification. They are separate activities that cannot be undertaken at the same time or with the same people.[269] Chandran is one who is certainly committed to dialogue whose acceptance, he argues, does not imply the compromise of evangelistic commitment.[270] And Christian belief in the activity of the Spirit may include the expectation that as a Christian enters dialogue "the sovereign power of the Spirit can use the occasion for the radical conversion" of both partners in the meeting.[271]

(ii) Because dialogue is a preparation for evangelization.
Dhavamony, for example, defines dialogue in terms of meeting, mutual sharing, listening and receiving and adds that "thus the ground is made ready for evangelization."[272] In another context he raises the possibility that the process of dialogue might create "certain new truths and new light" in the understanding of the partner in dialogue and thus oblige the Christian partner to speak of the Christian message.[273] A Protestant evangelical discussion is also clear that dialogue can serve as a preparation for evangelism[274]and Newbigin writes of the legitimacy of dialogue as "trying ... to achieve mutual understanding as a necessary basis for a true evan-

---

269 Hooker, 'Evangelism, Dialogue and Worship,' 126. In similar vein: *Lead Me to the Real: the Hindu-Christian Dialogue*, 43.

270 But he also rejects 'claims of superiority made by religious groups' ('A Christian Approach,' 11).

271 Newbigin, *The Open Secret*, 187. See also Chethimattam, 'The Scope and Conditions of a Hindu-Christian Dialogue,' 88; *ACFOR*, 39; Israel Selvanahagam, *Evangelism and Interfaith Dialogue*, Selly Oak Occasional Papers (Birmingham: Selly Oak Colleges, 1994) in which he advocates discussion, discernment and mutual correction; Roger Hooker, 'Christian Faith and Other Faiths – the Tension between Dialogue and Evangelism,' *CMS Newsletter*, no. 535 (September/November 1997).

272 Mariasusai Dhavamony, 'Evangelization and Dialogue with Hindus and Followers of Other Religions in India,' in *Light and Life We Seek to Share*, 149; the discussion continues to 151.

273 'Tension between Evangelization and Dialogue,' 95.

274 'The Devlali Letter,' issued at the end of The All India Congress on Mission and Evangelization, January 1976, and cited by Athyal, 'Asian Views of Dialogue,' 46.

gelism."[275] However, such a point of view can lead to a dilemma: "if dialogue *is* a preparation for evangelism then the integrity of the dialogue is destroyed, but if it is *not*, then the great Dominical commission to evangelism is betrayed."[276]

(iii) Because dialogue adds an important dimension to evangelization.

This viewpoint is well expressed in the Patna Declaration which, after pointing out that dialogue fosters respect and understanding, adds that

> far from lessening … zeal, [dialogue] makes … evangelization more inspiring and meaningful. The Christian evangelist, becoming aware, through dialogue, of the omnipresent mystery of God's salvific Love, is urged to share his full Christian faith.[277]

Amaladoss, because of his view that evangelization must be conducted with great respect for the freedom both of God and the listener who responds, believes that "dialogue becomes the context in which even proclamation has to take place."[278] A Protestant opinion expressing the same viewpoint is found in an editorial of *Religion and Society* where the growth of Christianity into fuller universality by a response to the presence of Christ in other faiths, and the evangelising mission of Christianity, are called "two sides of the same coin" that have to be held together in dialogue.[279]

(iv) Evangelization *as* dialogue.

This, according to Karokaran, is the point of view to which the Church in India has come; it is an understanding of evangelization "as a dialogue in which she and the peoples of other faiths … share their experience of the ultimate values of life …."[280] Chethimattam makes a related point in arguing that only by dialogue can the church truly preach the Gospel to the whole world.[281] The Indian Catholic *Guidelines* also discusses the identification of dialogue with

---

275 'Confessing Christ in a Multi-Religion Society,' 133.

276 'Evangelism, Dialogue and Worship,' 126 (original emphasis).

277 Patna Declaration, 29; see also the comments of Nambiaparambil, 'Church in India – Dialogue in Progress,' 262f; his 'Dialogue in India: An Analysis,' 280; the summary of the relevant Workshop discussion in *Light and Life We Seek to Share*, 325f; *Findings of the National Consultation … Held at Nasrapur*, 57.

278 'Dialogue and Mission,' 84.

279 'Editorial,' *RS*, 12.1 (March, 1965), 3.

280 *Evangelization and Diakonia*, 135.

281 'The Scope and Conditions of a Hindu-Christian Dialogue,' 87.

evangelisation in the sense of proclamation but does not endorse this viewpoint since it "does not seem to correspond to the experience of the Church throughout the centuries."[282] Russell Chandran also embraces a radical redefinition of mission. No longer, he argues, is there a polarisation between Christians (who engage in true mission) and non-Christians (who do not). Rather, the divide is between "those who accept the concern of Jesus Christ for the liberation of man from everything which enslaves and distorts human dignity" and those whose religion enslaves and distorts.[283]

(b) Dialogue as Compatible with a Widened Definition of Mission

Probably the most frequent means of attempting to reconcile mission with dialogue is to suggest that dialogue is compatible not with mission in the sense of evangelization but with a broader definition of mission. The Nasrapur Consultation, in discussing mission and dialogue, emphasised that mission is to be understood as "the call to encounter … the living God in Jesus Christ" rather than "a clash between religions."[284] Samartha, in advocating dialogue, implies that the aim of mission is to assist all who are "seeking a fuller and more joyful life here and now." He calls on Christians to be less concerned with their distinctiveness, and particular mission, and "more to be participants in the total life of all multi-religious communities."[285] This leads to a wider and more inclusive understanding of mission as participation in "*God's* continuing mission in the world."[286] And Samartha argues that Christians in mission need not believe that they always have to give – and dialogue is one means of receiving.[287] Samartha also underlines the suitability of witness as the key element of a revised view of mission in the context of dialogue in India: the mood of witness makes it possible for Christians to confess their faith without condemning the faiths of others; "it

282 *GIRD(2)*, 36; so also Nambiaparambil, 'Dialogue in India. An Analysis of the Situation,' 281; 'India,' in *Mission in Dialogue*, edited by Motte and Lang, 414; Murray Rogers, 'Inter-Faith Dialogue,' *AF*, 5, (1970), 244.

283 J Russell Chandran, 'Evangelisation in the Context of Other Religions', in *The St. Thomas Christian Encyclopaedia of India*, edited by George Menachery (Trichur, 1982), 214.

284 *Findings of the National Consultation … Held at Nasrapur*, 57.

285 '*More* than an Encounter of Commitments,' 400f.

286 Samartha, 'Christian Concern for Dialogue in India,' 6 (original emphasis). See also Arvind Nirmal, 'Some Theological Issues Connected with Inter-Faith Dialogue,' *BTF*, 12 (1980), 127.

287 'Indian Realities and the Wholeness of Christ,' *Missiology*, 10 (1982), 310. Similarly: Chandran, 'A Christian Approach,' 12.

removes the threat from mission."[288] And the most recent writings of Samartha virtually preclude mission in even these qualified senses.[289] In other words, many contemporary understandings of dialogue imply a radical revision of the traditional understanding of evangelism and mission.

An important component in the redefinition of mission in order to make it more compatible with dialogue is a revised ecclesiology that diminishes the importance of the church as an institution and eschews any view of mission that aims at the growth of the visible church. This change of emphasis may be traced through the writings of Devanandan and MM Thomas,[290] and others, Catholic as well as Protestant, who see the Kingdom of God (understood as God's active presence in the world) as much wider than the church – a view that coheres with the opinion of some Hindus that the church is unnecessary.[291] Duraisingh is certain that, for those who are committed to the mission of God, "dialogue *is* mission and not just *for* mission."[292] But nowhere have the implications for such a widened view of mission been made clearer than in a recent work by Thomas Thangaraj.[293] He argues that Christian mission must be radically redefined and not begin with narrowly intra-Christian assumptions about the nature of God or the authority of biblical texts. Instead, he proposes that all people be drawn into a conversation about the mission of humanity that is the common task of all people – a mission of "responsibility, solidarity and mutuality" (57). This means there are "no longer 'missioners' and the 'missioned'. All are missionaries in a relationship of mutuality" (57). The church does have its own mission – one of "cruciform responsibility, liberative solidarity, and eschatological mutuality" (64). For a Christian,

---

288 'Christian Concern for Dialogue in India,' 6.

289 Cf *One Christ – Many Religions*, 133 where he is clear that faith affirmations belong within a given faith's life and worship and "as such they should not be extended beyond the faith's boundaries."

290 See the summary in Karokaran, *Evangelization and Diakonia*, 115-19, to which add: Devanandan, *Christian Concern in Hinduism*, 28-32; *Preparation for Dialogue*, 8f, 17f, 24f, 46-51.

291 See the remarks of Samartha, *The Hindu Response to the Unbound Christ* (Madras, 1974), 119.

292 'Issues in Mission and Dialogue: Some Reflections,' 400 (original emphasis). The same point is made by Hans Ucko, 'Dialogue is a Real Mission,' *AJT*, 3 (1989), 15-30.

293 Thomas Thangaraj, *The Common Task: A Theology of Christian Mission* (Nashville, TN: Abingdon Press, 1999); bracketed references in the text are to pages in this volume.

being sent "involves listening to other religious viewpoints, learning from other religious and secular traditions, and mutually enriching one another toward the eschaton" (75) – all of which is clearly compatible with a whole-hearted commitment to dialogue as well. Needless to say, not all Indian Protestants would agree with such a view. For example, the (Methodist) director of the Indian Evangelical Mission discusses mission at some length but with no mention of dialogue. For him mission is evangelism and compassionate service.[294] Among evangelicals in India, as elsewhere, lack of interest in dialogue is usually because of a prior commitment to mission (understood in a conservative sense) that is seen to exclude the practice of dialogue.

In Indian Catholic circles, a similar redefining of mission has occurred. Panikkar rejects as impractical, utopian and a-religious, the idea that any religion might work to replace another; he believes this to be contrary to the fundamental principles of both Christianity and Hinduism.[295] Abhishiktananda also links dialogue with his own understanding of mission as leading not to the growth of the Christian community but to "the assumption of all Hindu spiritual riches into the treasure of the Church."[296] And a Statement on Hinduism by the (Asian) Bishops' Institute for Interreligious Affairs defines mission as activity "to promote in various ways the fulfilment which is God's will"; it then adds that "dialogue is an integral part of this mission."[297]

Moreover, as we have seen, a new emphasis upon the Kingdom or Reign of God has led to a substantial redefining of the nature of mission and evangelization in which it now is given

> a comprehensive meaning, identifying it with the whole mission of the church. In this sense "evangelisation" includes any form of activity undertaken to promote and strengthen the ideal of the Kingdom of God. ...It is clear that dialogue ... is an activity that belongs to the sphere of evangelisation understood in the broad sense. (*GIRD(2)*, 36)

Gispert-Sauch points to the same shift in understanding among Indian theologians, most of whom have come to see evangelization as "transforming society in the light of Gospel values witnessed to

---

294 Theodore Williams, *The Local Church and Mission* (Bangalore, 1984).

295 *TUCH(2)*, 32.

296 *The Church in India* (Madras, 1969), 61; he adds that "once that is done, the so-called conversion of India will be at hand, or rather the recognition by both church and India that they were waiting for each other in the innermost part of themselves." (61)

297 *Lead Me to the Real: the Hindu-Christian Dialogue* (Hong Kong, 1984), 42.

by the Christian community in dialogue with others."[298] The extent of the redefinition is brought out by Hirudayam who not only views "Interfaith dialogue [as] an inseparable part of evangelization", but adds that through the mutual edification of dialogue, people of all faiths "evangelize one another."[299]

Amaladoss also writes of the broadening of the focus of mission. The new Kingdom-centred paradigm sees God's saving will as progressively realised in history with mission and dialogue in a convergent relationship. "Proclamation leading to conversion is seen only as one aspect of evangelisation, the other aspects being dialogue, liberation and inculturation."[300] He interprets this widened view of mission in the multi-religious societies of Asia as "the task of promoting common human and evangelical values [in collaboration] with the members of other religions."[301] Many advocates of dialogue, both Protestant and Catholic, would endorse Samartha's widening of exclusive definitions of mission as he writes that people of all faiths "are called upon to participate in God's continuing mission in the world."[302] And, although limitations of space preclude detailed discussion, the encyclical *Redemptoris Missio* (1990), the document 'Dialogue and Proclamation' (1991) and the apostolic exhortation *Ecclesia in Asia* (1999) have also extended the redefining of mission and interreligious relations begun in the Vatican II

298 Personal communication, 22 March 1983. Two Catholic statements make the same point: 'Second Bishops' Institute for Missionary Apostolate of the Federation of Asia Bishops' Conferences. ... A Letter to the Bishops of Pakistan, Bangladesh, Sri Lanka, Burma and India,' *Vidyajyoti*, 45 (1981), 94; and *For All the Peoples of Asia* (Manila, 1984), 216.

299 Ignatius Hirudayam in *Lead Me to the Real: the Hindu-Christian Dialogue*, 20; see too a similar conjunction of comments by Michael Duraisamy (7). See also K Poovathumkudy, 'Dialogue and Proclamation,' *IMR*, 19 (1997), 149-53.

300 'Dialogue and Mission: Conflict or Convergence?,' 62; see also his: 'Evangelization in Asia: A New Focus?,' *Vidyajyoti*, 51 (1987), 7-28; *Mission Today: Reflection from an Ignatian Perspective* (Rome, 1988); and 'Mission from Vatican II into the Coming Decade,' *SB*, 21 (1989), 353-61. The three-fold definition of mission is now widely in use (at least in official circles) in the Asian Catholic church. It seems to have originated at an early plenary assembly of the Federation of Asian Bishops' Conferences: see *Theses on Interreligious Dialogue*, 4.

301 'Dialogue and Mission,' 81.

302 'Mission in a Religiously Plural World,' 322. Amaladoss also views God's mission as including the activities of other faiths: 'Mission from Vatican II into the Coming Decade,' 355.

decrees *Ad Gentes* and *Nostra Aetate*.[303] The newer material offers a broadened understanding of evangelization that includes dialogue as a legitimate pursuit and not merely as a means of proclamation. And the close link between dialogue and mission is maintained; there is only one mission: the unifying mission of love even if proclamation and dialogue are distinct paths. But the more recent documents remain cautious and at times conservative in tone. *Redemptoris Missio* retains a somewhat narrow ecclesiocentric foundation. 'Dialogue and Proclamation' seems to ignore the considerable and creative response of Asian local churches to religious pluralism. However, *Ecclesia in Asia* does acknowledge that the reality of religious pluralism necessitates a humble spirit of dialogue in which "proclamation is prompted not by sectarian impulse nor the spirit of proselytism nor any sense of superiority" (20). A commitment to interreligious dialogue (29-31) is seen a part of a wider commitment to inculturation (20-33) with dialogue said to be "a part of the church's evangelizing mission, an expression of the mission *ad gentes*" (31).

It seems as if the relationship between mission/evangelization and dialogue depends upon the definition of mission used. If mission is viewed as centred upon the church then dialogue (like inculturation and even the quest for liberation) may well be seen as a means of proclamation that intends to build (up) the church. In other words, the *content* of the Christian proclamation is the key. Dialogue will be much more possible and productive if the message emphasises what *God* is doing in the whole world rather than what God is doing in an individual, or the church or an individual's religion.[304] If mission is seen as centred upon the Kingdom rather than the church then dialogue may assume a more significant role as a means of mutual enrichment and co-operation in a diverse and pluralistic world. Dialogue could, with such an understanding of mission, then become a means of collaboration and not a means of attempted conversion as the church bears witness to the values of the Kingdom wherever they are found. "The proper end of the interreligious dialogue is ... the common conversion of Christians and the members of other religious traditions to the same God." There is a "mutual evangelization [that] builds up, between members of various religious traditions, the universal communion which

303 On the relationship between evangelisation and dialogue see *Redemptoris Missio*, chapter 5 and *Dialogue and Proclamation*, sections 77-82.

304 For a brief discussion of what he calls this post-triumphalist vision of the church see Barnes, *Religions in Conversation*, 116f.

marks the advent of the Reign of God." [305] On this understanding, "Dialogue is the call of the Kingdom, by which the Church can rediscover itself in its fulness as it stretches out towards the universal Kingdom of God beyond its own visible boundaries."[306] Christians are not only to proclaim the Kingdom of God but must also "seek to discern it everywhere, by entering into dialogue."[307] The Kingdom of God has become an important focus in the widened definition of mission that embraces dialogue.

4. *Comment*

There are, then, a number of ways in which the relationship and apparently inevitable tension between the ideal and advocacy of dialogue and the practice of Christian mission have been discussed. Some of the discussions, however, look beyond the tension. They call for or assume a redefinition of mission – sometimes because of the recently advocated theocentric view of the relationship between the religions (see below, chapter 5.I). In general terms it could be said that in liberal Protestant and most Catholic circles in India the discussion has moved from 'dialogue or mission', to 'dialogue for mission', to 'dialogue *and* mission' (in which the two activities are said to coexist rather than compete or be used for the ends of the other activity). So, Amaladoss is found arguing for a dialectical tension between dialogue and mission with them in a "convergent rather than conflictual relationship." He believes that they are converging movements in a common commitment to a new humanity that takes seriously the freedom and creativity of humanity and God.[308] However, it is not clear how this "common commitment", as Amaladoss calls it, might alleviate the tension that most Indian Christians – and Hindus also – discern between dialogue and mission. Most discussions of the issue do assume a continuing tension between the two activities. Some of these discussions regard the tension as an unresolvable paradox that it is necessary to maintain because there are good grounds, from Christian first principles, for commitment to each – in which case, the relationship between the two will be understood in some of the ways described in the sec-

---

305 *Toward a Christian Theology of Religious Pluralism*, 283.

306 *Lead Me to the Real*, 3.

307 Ariarajah, 'Towards a Theology of Dialogue,' 11; see also Duraisingh, 'Issues in Mission and Dialogue,' 405f – where the importance of the Kingdom in ecumenical discussion is noted.

308 'Dialogue and Mission,' 62, 86. We have already noted that concern for a new humanity may justify the practice of dialogue.

tions above. And there are examples where it is not clear whether, from a Christian perspective, a given activity is proclamation or dialogue or both simultaneously.[309]

Other discussions suggest the possibility of commitment to both activities on the grounds that each corresponds with either the 'pilgrim' or (in eschatological terms) the 'realised' dimensions of the church's existence.[310] On these grounds, dialogue might be seen as derived from the church's pilgrim status in which it shares a common human concern and search for fullness and spiritual growth. Because it is imperfect, the church acknowledges its needs for growth in love and openness and therefore engages in dialogue with those who search from within other religious traditions. But, because the church also sees itself as part of a realised eschatological community, it will bear witness to that belief and proclaim the Kingdom of which it sees itself as a sign. This is what makes the Christian commitment to evangelization a continuing necessity. Perhaps there must be a period of transition – greater or shorter in length, as with the wait for the Kingdom – when both activities will be seen as parallel commitments with the degree of overlapping, as it were, dependent upon judgements concerning the extent and nature of God's action in the religions.

Another expression of the same viewpoint speaks of a twofold awareness of God's action in the world: in the church and in the other religions. From this viewpoint, proclamation affirms the action of God in the person bearing witness, whereas "dialogue is the openness and attention to the mystery of God's action in the other believer." The Church is thus located "in a field of forces controlled by these two poles of divine activity" with dialogue and proclamation therefore described as "integral but dialectical and complementary dimensions of the Church's mission of evangelization."[311] Yet another possibility is to see proclamation as especially appropriate in situations of oppression and the presence of "pseudo-religions" whereas "in a context of a country where various

---

309 Some good examples are provided by Albert Nambiaparambil in the opening pages of his 'Evangelization and Inter-Religious Dialogue,' where it is not clear whether his contact with Hindu neighbours might best be called proclamation or dialogue or both.

310 See, for example, *GIRD(2)*,36; Nagpur Declaration, 18; George Gispert-Sauch, 'Reflections for a Theology of Evangelization and Dialogue,' in *Service and Salvation*, 315-30.

311 *Theses on Interreligious Dialogue*, 16, 15. Compare Ans van der Bent, 'Seventeen Promises for Entering into the Dialogue with People of Living Faiths and Practising Religious Pluralism,' *CD*, no. 15 (December 1988), 35.

world religions exist side by side ... dialogue will be the appropriate path."[312] So then, evangelization and dialogue may be held to be aspects of the mission of the church in and to the world. Evangelization corresponds with the church as eschatological; dialogue with the church as pilgrim. If there is a tension between these two it might be seen as necessary and unavoidable. These two aspects of mission will find a somewhat different balance (and even complementarity) both in the individual Christian and within the Christian community. Each is to be respected and encouraged, but without denying the validity and importance of the other (*GIRD(2)*, 38). Perhaps at different times and in different contexts the need for one might be felt to outweigh but not entirely deny the other. Perhaps at all times each might helpfully, even necessarily, be seen as conditioning and safeguarding the other from the inadequacies of one activity with no reference to the other.[313]

In other words, it seems plausible to argue that mission/evangelisation and dialogue are distinct but related to one another because of the way in which each may be derived from a broadly defined understanding of Christian mission. Each may be seen as an attempt to reach out to the Hindu; in some circumstances and contexts one will be more appropriate than the other. But both may be seen as "Christ-oriented"[314] if it is agreed that Christ engaged in both activities; that may be sufficient reason for commitment to each without defining or even anticipating a resolution of the tension between the two.

At the same time, Christian advocates of dialogue may well find themselves also admitting the certain unavoidable bias that their understanding of mission implies. As noted in the discussion about commitment and openness, they may feel compelled to introduce a theological element and bear witness to belief in God's unique and even normative self-revelation in Christ. And, as Gispert-Sauch points out, "This self-understanding cannot be fully expressed by the mere practice of dialogue, however necessary this may be."[315]

---

312 'Statement of the CBCI Consultation on Mission, Ishvani Kendra, Pune, 4-9 January, 1994', paragraph 51.

313 This is the kind of conclusion reached by A Pushparajan, 'Communication of the Gospel in the Context of Interreligious Dialogue,' *ITS*, 22 (1985), 152-71, and J Kottukapally, 'Mission and Dialogue in Conflict?', in *Emerging India and the Word of God*, 536-54 in which he argues that differing situations will require responses from a theocentric or a christocentric or an anthropocentric or an ecclesiocentric perspective.

314 Dhavamony, 'Tension Between Evangelization and Dialogue,' 96.

315 'Reflections for a Theology of Evangelization,' 328.

Although the Christian dialogue will doubtless disclaim any assertion of superiority (perhaps admitting that the process of dialogue acts as a corrective to insensitive evangelism), it is precisely this self-understanding that undergirds the problematical element of tension discussed above. Another Catholic theologian points out that the New Testament as a whole does not appear to offer a foundation for the theology of dialogue as currently advocated. Rather, its use of words such as 'teaching', 'preaching', 'witness', 'conversion' and the compounds of '*angellein*', seem to suggest the primacy of proclamation over dialogue.[316] For this reason conservative Catholic critics have viewed dialogue, and the revised theology of mission that allows for or even necessitates its practice, as a betrayal of traditional mission activity.[317] For rather different reasons Griffiths, as already noted, defends the need for unflinching apologetics in all forms of interreligious dialogue; most conservative Protestants would probably agree. There may be no alternative to the anticipation and honest admission of the problem.

Moreover, it might be noted that some Hindus also feel a not dissimilar tension between mission and dialogue. Rambachan, for example, writes of Hinduism's claim "that it embodies authentic insights about the nature of God and the way of truth", adding that it therefore "has an obligation to share these with enthusiasm and initiative" – with dialogue as "one of the most appropriate ways of offering its gifts."[318] The parallelism of thought and words with Christian discussions is striking. Sharma is persuaded that classical Hinduism was a missionary religion that placed a well-defined segment of its followers under obligation to undertake missionary activity.[319] Perhaps dialogue is necessary in order to preserve the

316 J Lopez-Gay, 'Current Criticisms of the Theology and Practice of "Dialogue",' *BSPNC*, 10 (1975), 330.

317 See, for example, Henry Van Straelen, *The Catholic Encounter with World Religions* (London, 1966), 71-132.

318 'Religious Pluralism: a Hindu Perspective,' 27. Some Christians have no doubt about the missionary intention of some forms of Hinduism; see, for example, Johannes Aagaard, 'Guruism – a Hindu Countermission,' *New Religious Movements Update*, 4.1-2 (May 1980), 5-14; the individuals and groups mentioned by Sharpe, 'Hindu-Christian Dialogue in Europe,' 110f; CV Mathew, 'Hare Krishna Movement and Hindu Mission,' *DD*, 1.2 (1995), 35-49; Mathew, *The Saffron Mission. A Historical Analysis of Modern Hindu Missionary Ideologies and Practices*, chapter 1, especially pp 1-7 and 17-23.

319 Arvind Sharma, 'Hinduism: a Missionary Religion?,' *Journal of the Bihar Research Society*, 62 (1972), 232-37; 'Ancient Hinduism as a Missionary Religion,' *Numen*, 39 (1992), 175-92.

autonomy of each partner – so that the witness of each, and further dialogue, might be made possible. Perhaps the term 'encounter' might, for English speakers at least, be acceptable to cover both the 'mission' of each, and dialogue itself.

This chapter has offered a critical survey of some of the major impediments, both practical and theoretical, to the advocacy and practice of Christian-Hindu dialogue. A degree of reluctance among many Hindus and Christians is one such impediment. And, within Christian discussions of dialogue, difficulties are apparent in understanding the relationship between commitment and openness, dialogue and mission, and between the traditional and more recent evaluation of other faiths. Nonetheless, there may also be no reasonable alternative than to proceed, notwithstanding the ambiguities, lack of clarity and tensions that remain. The impediments, although substantial, do not seem to offer sufficient reason to abandon dialogue given the justification considered in chapter 3 above. Moreover, answers for some of the practical objections and impediments might not be found apart from persistence in dialogue. The actual encounter between Hindus and Christians might help to clarify the theory and theology of the relationship between the two faiths. And the resolution of the tensions between commitment and openness, and dialogue and mission, might only be accomplished, if at all, by continued engagement in both dialogue and mission – provided the affective dimension of dialogue (that is, elements such as respect, goodwill, sincerity and honesty) is present.[320]

Meanwhile, the persistence of the difficulties may well account for the reluctance (or even opposition) of many Indian Christians to accept and practise dialogue. To the extent that this reluctance or opposition is also justified on theological grounds, it might be noted that such theology is usually conservative and would include a conservative view of Christ. Perhaps Christology can offer some grounds for Hindu-Christian dialogue; it is a possibility to which the discussion now turns.

---

320 Cf Terry C Muck, 'Interreligious Dialogue and Evangelism,' *Buddhist-Christian Studies*, 17 (1997), 139-51 in which he draws upon the communication theory of David Krieger.

CHAPTER 5

Christology as the Justification of Christian-Hindu Dialogue

A. The Christological Justification of Dialogue

Because dialogue in many ways constitutes a marked departure from more traditional understandings of Christian mission and the theology of other faiths, the discussion of its theological justification is especially important. Christology has always been central to the self-understanding of the Christian tradition and this has also been true for Indian Christian theology. From a survey of the middle years of the 1970s, Jacques Dupuis concluded that "the centrality and uniqueness of Jesus Christ has become in India the crux of theological debate",[1] including debate about dialogue with Hindus. Moreover, it is sometimes asserted that christology is the distinctive and necessary Christian basis for engagement in dialogue; Stanley Samartha, for example, considers this basis to be the living out of faith in a Christ who has become human on behalf of people of all ages and cultures.[2] So, might dialogue be understood and justified and even enlarged in christological terms?

An examination of attempts to show how this faith might provide a basis or bases for dialogue reveals that three aspects have received particular attention: the example of the Christ of the four Gospels; the analogy of the incarnation; and the implications of what has been called "cosmic christology".

The appeal to the example of Christ as a basis for engagement in dialogue has received surprisingly little attention. Chandran, for example, emphasises the warm acceptance by Jesus of those (relatively few) non-Jews whom he is portrayed as having met. In fact, "the way of recognising others as belonging to the community of faith appears to be his main concern" and can serve as an example

---

1 'Bulletin. Five Years of Theological Reflection in India', *ITS*, 14 (1977), 103.
2 'Dialogue as a Continuing Christian Concern', *ER*, 23 (1971), 139f, employing, it seems, the language of ZAM, 2.

for those who wish to follow his way in dialogue.[3] The Catholic *Guidelines* draw attention to what they describe as the example of a totally open attitude to all that enabled Jesus to receive people of non-Jewish traditions and to recognise in them "a faith greater than that of Israel."[4] Chandran's somewhat idealised view of the encounters of Jesus overlooks the ambivalent and even radically provocative attitude to aspects of his own Jewish community. The example of Jesus is also discussed by Chethimattam who advances the (problematical) argument that Christ's appeal to the 'inner' prophetic meaning of the Old Testament is justification for the attempt in dialogue "to make explicit what is implicit in ... [Hinduism's] authentic elements."[5]

If such qualities as unconditional acceptance are conditions for fruitful dialogue then the example of Jesus does offer some kind of incentive for dialogue. However, the accounts of Christ's meeting with people of faiths other than Judaism are both few and brief, and in them it is the Gentiles who take the initiatives and not Jesus – although he is seen as open to their approaches and commends their faith. But his example offers nothing to justify dialogue as a common search for religious truth or in any of the other senses now usually attached to the enterprise of dialogue.

A second attempt to justify dialogue in christological terms is to view it as an analogy of the incarnation. The way in which the incarnation can be described as God's dialogue with humanity has already been noted (see above, chapter 3.J) and others writing in the Indian context have made the same point. TK Thomas, for example, describes dialogue as "the imperative of the Incarnation" because of the way in which God has already initiated such dialogue in Christ.[6] Felix Wilfred's survey of Asian Catholic missiology reveals, he states, that the Catholic bishops are "seized by the splendour of this

---

3 J Russell Chandran, 'Christian Contribution to Religious Dialogue', *IMA*, 3.2 (May 1972), 73; see also his 'A Christian Approach to Other Religions', *BTF*, 7.2 (July-December, 1975), 15. In similar vein see S Wesley Ariarajah, *The Bible and People of Other Faiths* (Geneva, 1985), 30-33.

4 *GIRD(2)*, 32 – an argument that is absent from the first edition of the document.

5 John Britto Chethimattam, 'The Scope and Conditions of a Hindu-Christian Dialogue', *Concilium*, 3.1 (March 1965), 91.

6 'Inter-Religious Dialogue', *SIC*, February 1971, 10; see also John W Sadiq, 'Inter-Faith Dialogue and Communication of the Gospel', *RS*, 12.1 (March 1965), 10; KS, 53; 'Consultation on the Theology of Hindu-Christian Dialogue', *RS*, 16.2 (June 1969), 79; MM Thomas, *The Acknowledged Christ of the Indian Renaissance* (London, 1970), 308.

mystery of incarnation. ... In the immersion of Jesus and his interaction with the society of his times, the bishops see the paradigm for their own mission."[7]

However, the appeal to the incarnation suffers from several limitations besides those inherent in any use of analogy. By no means all Christians and Hindus understand the incarnation in the factual terms in which the proponents of the analogy appear to use it. If dialogue means the elevation of one supreme and impressive figure – whether that figure be Jesus or Krishna, for example – that elevation might, in fact, hinder dialogue. The model of the incarnation might also seem to stand closer to the monologue of, for example, preaching in which one partner is liable to be seen and heard as decidedly more active and dominant, than to a dialogue between two partners intent on sharing for mutual enrichment. Nonetheless, the analogy of the incarnation does point to such qualities as humility, assimilation and identification, and the self-giving love that evokes a true *commercium* between God and humankind[8] – qualities that also are central to the intended spirit of dialogue. But it does not appear able to sustain the full weight of a continuing commitment to dialogue.

B. The Development of Cosmic Christology

There is one species of christology to which frequent appeal has been made and which does appear to offer a more comprehensive justification of dialogue: that which attempts to elaborate the cosmic significance of the person and place of Christ. This 'cosmic christology' gained a certain prominence during the 1960s and in it Christ is portrayed both as the author or agent of the divine creation and as the sustainer, redeemer and goal of the whole cosmos.[9] The origins of the doctrine do, of course, reside in the New Testament. In a number of New Testament passages Christ is portrayed as the pre-existent one in, through and for (*eis*) whom the universe was created and by whom it is sustained and ruled. Moreover, his death

7 'Images of Jesus Christ in the Asian Pastoral Context,' 56.

8 Compare *Ad Gentes* 22: "... in imitation of the plan of the Incarnation, the young Churches ... take to themselves in a wonderful exchange [*in admirabile commercium assumunt*] all the riches of the nations".

9 There is no fully comprehensive account of the history of cosmic christology. The best study is probably that of Lyons, *The Cosmic Christ* (Oxford, 1982), chapter 1, 'Christ Terminology' (7-73). See also GA Maloney, *The Cosmic Christ from Paul to Teilhard* (London, 1968) and HW Clark, *The Cross and the Eternal Order* (London and Redhill, 1943) 121-39.

and resurrection are seen as a defeat of all evil and a victory that will be acknowledged on a cosmic scale when all things are consummated in Christ in the *eschaton*.[10] The descriptions of Christ as *logos* (Word; eg John 1.1-9, 14-18) and *kurios* (Lord[11]) also have cosmic significance.

In the reappearance of this discussion of a cosmic dimension to christology in theological literature during the middle decades of the twentieth century, the presence and claims of other faiths do not seem to have acted as a stimulus to its elaboration nor was the doctrine applied to the evaluation of these faiths. An examination of the most significant discussions of cosmic christology in Protestant theology during the period 1943-1963 reveals no more than occasional brief passing references to other than Christian religions.[12]

In the early 1960s, with the wider availability of the writings of Teilhard de Chardin[13] and the impact of an address by Joseph Sitter to the third assembly of the WCC in New Delhi in 1961[14], cosmic christology began to attract increasing attention.[15] Although Sittler's address did not itself discuss the relationship between Christ and the extra-Christian faiths, this relationship did receive emphasis in the contributions and interventions in New Delhi of MM Thomas and PD Devanandan of India, and DT Niles of Ceylon.[16] There is

---

10 The principal passages are in the Pauline corpus: Ephesians 1:9f, 20-23; Colossians 1:15-20; see also Romans 1:8; 8:19-22; 1 Corinthians 1:24; 2:6-10; 15:20-28; Philippians 2:9-11; 1 Timothy 3:16. Note also Acts 1:9f; Hebrews 1:2-4; 2:5-9; 1 Peter 3:15 and Revelation 1:17f; 22:13.

11 For example Acts 10:36 and 1 Corinthians 8:6. Philippians 2:10f and 1 Peter 3:15 are also important as examples of the use of Old Testament passages where the title as equivalent to Yahweh is applied to Jesus. See also Revelation 5:9f, 12f.

12 Lyons, *The Cosmic Christ*, suggested most of the literature surveyed.

13 For a discussion of Teilhard's views in the context of religion, see Ursula King, 'Religion and the Future: Teilhard de Chardin's Analysis of Religion as a Contribution to Inter-Religious Dialogue', *RS*, 7 (1971), 307-23; and her *Towards a New Mysticism. Teilhard de Chardin and Eastern Religions* (London, 1980), and *Christ in All Things. Exploring Spirituality with Teilhard de Chardin* (Maryknoll, NY: Orbis Books, 1997).

14 Joseph A Sitter, 'Called to Unity', *ER*, 14 (1962), 177-87.

15 For an analysis of critical responses to the cosmic christology of Teilhard and Sittler, see Lyons, *The Cosmic Christ*, 60-68. For Lyons' discussion of Teilhard see his chapters 7-9 (183-219). On Sittler, see also Horst Bürkle, 'The Debate of the "Cosmic Christ"', in *Indian Voices in Today's Theological Debate*, edited by Bürkle and Wolfgang MW Roth (Lucknow, 1972), 198-205.

16 See the summary in George Johnston, 'Christian Mission and Christ's Prevenience', *TT*, 20 (1963), 32-41.

reason to suggest that the cosmic christology that developed in India should be viewed more as an attempted correction of the christomonism that was thought by some Asian theologians to be central to neo-orthodoxy than a complete rejection of it.[17] But whatever its precise relationship to western theology, Indian Christian thought during the decade 1955-1964 began to appeal to the cosmic dimensions of christology in its growing concern for a re-evaluation of inter-religious relationships.

C. Cosmic Christology and the Re-evaluation of Other Faiths

A convenient starting point is the New Testament basis of the doctrine in the light of some Indian Christian discussion. From Colossians 1, with its assertion of the origin and sustenance of "all things", including spiritual principalities and powers, by and in Christ, it has been argued that such spiritual forces derive their vitality and goodness from Christ.[18] Moreover, since whatever is good is of God (James 1.17) then, according to Hindley, "whatever is good in contemporary movements outside the Christian name comes from Christ".[19] In John 1.9, Jesus is described as "the true light that shines on all" – a statement that has long and widely been used in Christian thought to assert that wherever light is found it owes its origin ultimately to the Logos. Panikkar is only one of a number of writers who appeals to the statement in a context which makes it clear that he sees Christ as the source of the 'light' that is found in Hinduism.[20] Kalapesi describes Christ as the incarnate *Logos* and therefore "our immediate theological principle in the encounter with our Hindu brother".[21] In discussing the most significant trends in christology in Asia during the last decades of the twentieth century, Karotemprel begins with that form of christology

17 Compare the comments of Richard W Taylor, 'Christ Acting in Our Society', *Indian Voices in Today's Theological Debate*, 163-67.

18 JC Hindley, 'The Christ of Creation in New Testament Theology', *IJT*, 15 (1966), 96. Hindley believes, for example, that the doctrine of Christ as cosmic creator enables Christians to speak of "Christ in Hinduism" (95).

19 Hindley, 'The Christ of Creation', 96. Hindley also wonders whether the same point can be concluded from Colossians 2:2f (96).

20 *TUCH(2)*, 49; compare 20; there is further discussion of Panikkar's thought in section F below. See also Hindley, 'The Christ of Creation', 97; *GIRD(2)*, 28; Sebastian Painadath, 'Christology and the Spiritual Heritage of Mankind', *Jeevadhara*, 2 (1972), 238.

21 Mary Kalapesi, 'Some Reflections on the Fourth Meeting on Hindu and Christian Spirituality ....', *RS*, 11.4 (December 1964), 73.

whose "basic assumption is that the Logos, the nameless, the absolute, the transcendent is infinite and the infinite can manifest itself in infinite ways."[22] With the Logos in mind Pieris can write of "the predominantly 'non-Christian' character of Christ" because, although "all of Jesus is Christ, not all of Christ in Jesus".[23] For this reason, Jesus can be described as absolute for Christians but not exhaustive of the Logos. Because the Logos shines everywhere, "so God is manifest in each; each human being becomes a Christophany and theophany."[24]

The influence – especially in Protestant circles – during the 1950s and 1960s of the theme of the lordship of Christ has already been noted. This theme also included reference to the cosmic dimension of christology. Devanandan, for example, speaks of the 'cosmic' dimension of the Christian approach to people of other faiths on the grounds that "Biblical faith repeatedly affirms that the work of Christ is of cosmic significance".[25] Several years later the same theme was emphasised in an Indian Protestant Consultation in 1966 whose Findings argued that, because Christ is the Lord of all history, the whole of humanity is "embraced by God's purpose of salvation"; God is at work in all cultures and religion. Where there is liberation from oppressive religion "Christ is at work there".[26] There is, however, a certain tension or even inconsistency in these Nasrapur 'Findings'. There is not only an assertion of the transcendent Lordship of Christ over history, culture and religion but also an attempt to argue for his cosmic and immanent *presence* within history, culture and religion and about this the Findings are more cautious. For example, while Christ's presence is discerned in liberation from religious oppression, it is his rather more remote "lordship over history" which provides the "context" for an understanding of

22 Sebastian Karotemprel, 'Asian Christological Trends and Christian Mission', *IMR*, 19.3 & 4 (September – December 1997), 57.

23 Aloysius Pieris, 'Does Christ Have a Place in Asia? A Panoramic View', in *Any Room for Christ in Asia?*, 43.

24 Karotemprel, 'Asian Christological Trends and Christian Mission', 58. For further details of the development and role of Logos christology in India, see Jacob Parappally, *Emerging Trends in Indian Christology* (Bangalore: IIS Publications, 1995), 137-60.

25 *Christian Concern* 118f/*Gospel* 47; see also his *Preparation*, 181f.

26 *Findings of the National Consultation on the Mission of the Church* (Nagpur, nd [1966]), 24. The Nagpur Declaration five years later stated that "we believe that the universal spirit of Christ, the Lord of History, is undoubtedly present in the evolution that is taking place today" (2).

renewal within Hinduism itself[27] – presumably because of traditional Protestant reluctance to assert Christ's active presence at the centre, as it were, of other than Christian faiths. This reluctance is often discernible in Protestant discussions during the 1960s and may be contrasted with the more positive attitude of Catholic theologians writing in India during the same period.

The contrast was also apparent during an ecumenical Colloquium on 'The Cosmic Christ', held in 1965. Some of the papers read to the meeting were subsequently published[28] and reveal that the Protestant contributions were decidedly tentative in their application of the doctrine to a theological appraisal of other faiths. One paper argued that cosmic christology not only implies that dualisms between "nature" and "grace", "material" and "spiritual" are misleading (since Christ is Lord of "all things") but also suggests that the traditional distinctions between "Church" and "world", and "Christian" and "non-Christian" may also be misleading.[29] But the relevance to a theology of other faiths of the abolition of these dualisms is not explored.

One paper that did explicitly make the link was that of the Catholic theologian Pierre Fallon on 'The Cosmic Christ and the Asian Revolution'. In it he spoke of the truly cosmic Christ, "already present among those who still ignore Him, … Christ who is at work continuing His work of creation through this momentous process of the renascence of Asia".[30] There had been many previous Christian evaluations of religious renascence in India – for example, that of Devanandan. But what is new in Fallon and a number of other Catholic writers in the early 1960s is the explicit assigning of the renewal in Hinduism to the presence and immanent, saving activity of Christ himself. There has been a long history of a *Logos* and therefore cosmic christology in immanent terms within Catholic theology, but it seems that, with a few exceptions, an ecclesiocentric view of the theology of the religions hindered its development in terms of belief in Christ's activity in the religions. Such activity was usually limited to 'authentic' elements in them. The

27 *Findings of the National Consultation*, 23. Further on this theme see MM Thomas, 'Christ at Work in History', in his *Some Theological Dialogues* (Madras, 1977), 65-72.

28 In *IJT*, 15.3 and 15.4 (July-September and October-December 1966).

29 AF Thompson, 'The Colossian Vision in Theology and Philosophy', *IJT*, 15 (1966), 124. A similar point had been made by JG Bookless, 'The Summing Up of All Things in Christ', *IJT*, 12 (1963), 101, 113f.

30 Published in *IJT*, 15 (1966), 150-153; quotation from 153.

exceptions were the attempts already noted to develop a *Logos* christology and a few other discussions.[31]

Protestants, however, continued to be much more cautious in their use of christological categories in the assessment of other faiths. For example, Devanandan wrote at length about renewal within Hinduism but attributed the renewal either to a general divine influence, or to the ubiquitous creativity of the Holy Spirit. Other Protestants developed the idea of Christ's Lordship but drew quite widely differing conclusions about its implications for a theology of religion. Some felt the secular implications of Christ's rule to be of far greater significance than the merely 'religious'; others continued to see Christ as the critic and judge of all the religions including Christianity. In many ways, some of which overlapped, both Catholic and Protestant theologians in India began to elaborate the consequences of a cosmic christology so that, in 1965, Taylor could write that the belief that Christ acts beyond the Christian community "is at the heart of some of the most stimulating theological thinking being done in India today".[32] As in the Catholic community, there were a number of important antecedents to this belief.[33]

D. Christ and the Fulfilment of the Religions

One view of Christ in cosmic categories that might yield a christological basis for dialogue is the belief that Christ is the fulfilment of the religions. Dialogue might then be seen as a manifestation of an inevitable future unity or even as a partial means of helping to attain it. Another possibility is to see Christ as the present or potentially present fulfilment of the religions – in which case dialogue might again serve as a means of realising the fulfilment. These two possibilities are now considered.

---

31 As well as Panikkar (to whom discussion will return) see Koshy Abraham, *Prajapathi The Cosmic Christ* (Delhi: ISPCK, 1997) who sees Christ as not only historical but in the Vedic categories of Creator, Protector and Redeemer of all; and Saldanha, 'Unbaptised Disciples of Christ?', in which he ascribes a wide range of Indian interest in Christ to the activity of Christ as Logos.

32 Richard W Taylor, 'Christ Acting in Our Society', 158; Taylor and MM Thomas, *Mud Walls and Steel Mills* (New York, 1963), chapter 5, 'What is God Doing in India?', also includes reference to divine activity beyond the Christian community.

33 For example, Taylor himself has on several occasions drawn attention to the use of the notion of the prevenient Christ (who meets Hindus and others 'on the Indian road') in the writings of E Stanley Jones; see above, chapter 1.C.1.

1. *Eschatological Fulfilment*

In some Protestant circles in India in the 1960s one consequence of belief in secularisation as the creative and liberating activity of the Word of God was the advocacy of a realised eschatology in which the unity of all things in Christ is seen as already partly.[34] But the more usual meaning has been that of a unity which, although it has not yet arrived, is contained in the hope of "the final fulfilment of all history, the history of religions included".[35] Devanandan, for example, does not point Hindus to their past (to some unknown Christ), but to the future, the End, when it will be revealed that Brahman is the Father of the Lord Jesus Christ.[36] Nonetheless, the Protestant appeal to the eschatological implications of cosmic christology for dialogue have been rather tentative and few.

Many Catholic writers have been more creative in the elaboration of the link between eschatological fulfilment and the present activity of Christ and it was an important theme for many writers in the 1960s and 1970s. Neuner, for example, argued that every community within humankind is intended by God to be fulfilled in Jesus Christ and "to grow to its final destiny in God through the Incarnate Word". This destiny is the unity of all people and is part of the goal to which God is even now guiding the whole cosmos through Christ.[37] And, concerning Asia as a whole, Fallon saw Christ as "the truly cosmic Christ, already present among those who still ignore Him, preparing them in a thousand manners for this ultimate reunion of all in Him".[38] But there was uncertainty, nonetheless, about whether this fulfilment implied a discontinuity that required a break with the past.[39]

There are several important consequences of the assertion of a final fulfilment in Christ. It reinforces the notion of the Church as a forward-looking and pilgrim community.[40] Moreover, the membership of such a community need not be seen in exclusive terms; the Christian may have a distinctive witness to share with

---

34 Thompson, 'The Colossian Vision in Theology and Philosophy', 124.

35 Bürkle, 'The Debate of the "Cosmic Christ"', 211.

36 *I Will Lift*, 20.

37 Josef Neuner, 'Votum Ecclesiae', in *God's Word Among Men*, edited by G Gispert-Sauch (Delhi, 1973), 162-65 (quotation from 162f). Compare Panikkar, *TUCH(2)*, 2f.

38 Fallon, 'The Cosmic Christ and the Asian Revolution', 153.

39 See, for example, J Britto Chetthimattam, 'Third Christian Colloquy on Hinduism', *IES*, 3 (1964), 139.

40 *GIRD(2)*, 32; see also 45. The Second Vatican Council made the imagery of the pilgrim church popular; see *Lumen Gentium*, 9, 48-50.

non-Christian friends but nonetheless "moves on *with them* toward the consummation of all things in Christ".[41] One reason for present disagreement between the religions is found in the necessarily partial vision enjoyed by each of them. Each may attempt to bear witness to the Absolute but since the Absolute alone is eternal, "all religions including Christianity have an "interim" character" – in which case the recognition of the other as a fellow pilgrim may also serve as an incentive to dialogue *en route*.[42]

Belief in an eschatological fulfilment may also be linked, in a number of ways, with the inter-religious encounter itself. The prospect of this fulfilment is said to explain what are seen as the convergent aspirations of the religions and yet also to sustain dialogue in the face of persistent disagreement (with Catholic writers tending to emphasise the former point and Protestant the latter). The Nagpur Declaration, for example, states that, by its very nature, dialogue "tends towards that ultimate vision of a perfect unification of all ... which can be discerned in the convergent aspirations of the various religious traditions".[43] When another writer considers the inevitable differences that dialogue reveals, he adds the explanation that "genuine dialogue is ... based on the conviction that we differ only to agree eventually, and that this is God's will and purpose for us".[44] Others emphasise the fulfilment and unity that derives from belief in "the saving will of God for the whole world – which does not merely touch individuals in and through their respective religions ... [but] also leads the whole universe to a unity".[45] The Catholic *Guidelines* also maintain a balance between the particularity of the religions and a greater goal when it writes that

> history will culminate in a new form of Existence wherein the meaning and significance of each religion will be revealed and all will find their fulfilment in the ultimate vision of the Divine Mystery when God will be everything to everyone (1 Cor 15:28). (*GIRD(2)*, 112)

Despite the absences of any christological reference in the two

41 Patna Declaration, 29 (emphasis added).

42 Stanley Samartha, 'The Lordship of Jesus Christ and Religious Pluralism', in *Christ's Lordship and Religious Pluralism*, edited by Gerald H Anderson and Thomas F Stransky (Maryknoll, NY, 1981), 36; compare *GIRD(2)*, 36; *ACFOR*, 25 and 26f; *GOD*, 9.

43 Patna Declaration, 26.

44 Thomas, 'Inter-Religious Dialogue', 9. See also 'Consultation Working Group Reports', *RS*, 26.1 (March 1979), 107.

45 Amaladoss, 'Dialogue and Mission', 68.

passages just cited, the link between eschatological hope and dialogue is usually placed in the context of the movement towards the consummation of all things in Christ, and not merely in a theistic context. For example, an ecumenical statement in 1969 declared:

> In dialogue we remain open to the working of the Spirit. It is a quest of faith and obedience, and it springs from the conviction that Christ is Lord of all things. It does not, and indeed cannot, aim at the establishment of a new universal religion. ... God will sum up all things in him, and ... Christ will be the centre of whatever emerges out of our dialogue with men of other faiths.[46]

And Gispert-Sauch argues that the Upanishadic notion of *ekayanam* or 'union point' (of human history and divine reality) is met "in the eschatological convergence point where the risen Lord integrates the whole of creation" including "one element of the Upanishadic search for the One, the search for the unification of the world of multiplicity". The risen Christ is the eschatological horizon of all historical movements – but a horizon that "does not deny the role and function of religions, sacraments, myths, saving figures of history and the historical movements among which history as a religion is included."[47]

2. *Present Fulfilment*

As well as interest in the future dimension of fulfilment in Christ there has also been a continuing interest among Catholic writers in Christ as the present fulfilment of the hopes of humanity. During the period under survey, aspects of this fulfilment theory are often

---

46 'Consultation on Theology', 87. It might be noted, in passing, that the paragraph contains a summary of what were among the main emphases in the theology of Hindu-Christian dialogue during the 1960s, each of which was to receive decreasing attention during the decades that followed, especially in Protestant circles. The paragraph is: (i) explicitly Trinitarian and yet (ii) with a considerable christological emphasis including (iii) a statement about the Lordship of Christ. There is (iv) an acknowledgement of the eschatological context of dialogue, and (v) reference to scripture. The statement (vi) sympathetically notes the concern of those who fear syncretism. See also the Patna Declaration, 29.

47 George Gispert-Sauch, 'Notes for an Indian Christology', *VJTR*, 61 (1997), 763; he also cites 1 Corinthians 15.28 which refers to the risen Christ as the one who integrates the whole of creation and surrenders it "to the One who has subjected everything to him, so that God may be all in all".

mentioned.[48] Christ is described as "the hidden apotheosis of each religion" and so the apotheosis and fulfilment of Hinduism as well.[49] He is "the fulfilment of the best of Hindu aspirations and spiritual longing".[50] Raimundo Panikkar developed a number of analogies to make the same point.[51] The Christian will therefore see, according to this theory, how India's religious writings and stories "have Christ for their deepest meaning; and how he is their Ultimate and Absolute Atman".[52] The *avatara* tradition, for example, represents "the profoundest expression of man's desire and destiny".[53] To believe that Christianity is such a fulfilment is to "adopt a position of deep sympathy to the other religions" – a position that invites dialogue.[54] In other words, this fulfilment implies a definite continuity with the past, and not simply the past of the Jewish and Christian traditions.

Despite the recent appeal to the notion of fulfilment, and the long history of Christian apologetics seeking to employ it or related theories, it has been the subject of critical comment as well.[55] The

---

48 Writing in 1982, Ignatius Hirudayam could state that the theory "is to be found in many clerics even today" ('Maturation of the Asian Church', in *Lead Me to the Real: the Hindu-Christian Dialogue* (Hong Kong, 1983), 10); see also from the documents of Vatican II: Lumen Gentium, 14, 16; Ad Gentes, 9; Nostra Aetate, 2. For a survey of some endorsements of the theory see Frank Ponsi, 'Contemporary Concepts of Mission', *Missiology*, 6 (1978), 149-51.

49 Anthony Adair, 'Towards a Hindu-Christian Dialogue', *Contemporary Review*, no. 208 (February 1966), 86.

50 Abhishiktananda, *The Church in India*, 61. See also: M Blanchard, 'Christianity as Fulfilment and Antithesis', *IJT*, 17 (1968), 5-20; Sradhananda, 'Brahma Vidya Mundir', *CM*, 33 (1969), 346; J Veluthedath, '*Vestigia Christi* in the World Religions', *Verbum SVD*, 23 (1981), 355-62; Thomas Kochumuttom, 'Comparative Theology', *Jeevadhara*, 89 (1985), 395-409. For a Protestant work see Daya Prakash, *Fulfilment of the Vedic Quest in the Lord Jesus Christ* (Bhowali, UP, 1982).

51 *TUCH(1)*, 57-64 – however, in the second edition this section is extensively revised and contains a number of substantial reservations about fulfilment: see *TUCH(2)*, 89-96.

52 Samuel Rayan, 'An Indian Christology: A Discussion of Method', *Jeevadhara*, l (1971), 227.

53 Josef Neuner, cited by Samuel Rayan, 'Interpreting Christ to India', *IJT*, 23 (1974), 224.

54 Ignatius Hirudayam, 'Dialogue in Tamilnadu', *LV*, 29 (1974), 419.

55 For example, see the discussion in Klaus Klostermaier, '"Praeparatio Evangelica" in the Early Fathers', *IES*, 8 (1969), 171-80; he concludes that the notion has limited relevance for dialogue. Another survey, which

essence of the criticism is that the issues of central significance to the religions are not those to which Christ might be said to provide corresponding answers. There appears, in fact, to be a radical discontinuity between Hinduism and Christianity at many points – to use the language of Kraemer (but without thereby implying any sense of superiority). In terms of the metaphor made popular by Rudolf Otto, the major religions revolve around quite different axes – as the phenomenological study of religion has shown.[56] The religions have their own distinctive quests and, even if there are points of comparison and fulfilment, dialogue – it might be argued – has shown that this could be judged a mutual fulfilment with aspects of each tradition complementing the other (see above, chapter 3.G).

Despite the validity of these criticisms, it might be possible to restate the theory of fulfilment in Christ by incorporating the notion of the active presence of Christ within the religions. The principal objection of Dupuis to the fulfilment theory as applied to Hinduism is that it considered the Hindu religion "only as a human quest to be fulfilled by Christianity, not as already containing a divine response however incomplete".[57] But if Christ were to be seen as active (albeit in a hidden way) within Hinduism, then Hinduism would be no merely human quest, but would contain, however imperfectly, a response prompted by God. It is in this latter sense that some advocates of dialogue have used the idea of fulfilment.[58]

Often the notions of present and future fulfilment are linked: "Toutes les religions du monde le cherchent et convergent vers lui,

---

includes a wider range of attitudes by the early Fathers and does see considerable relevance to present dialogue, is found in A Luneau, 'Pour aider au dialogue: Les Pères et les religions non-chrétiennes', *NRT*, 89 (1967), 821-41, 914-39. Klostermaier himself advocates at least a form of the fulfilment theory; see, for example, his 'Pavitrasastram – A Sketch of a Hindu-Christian Sacramentology', in *ITD*, 178-95. For a survey of some 20th century Catholic theologians see Dupuis, *Toward a Christian Theology of Religious Pluralism*, 133-43. For some Protestant comment see: Eric J Sharpe, 'Christ the Fulfiller', *BTF*, 3.1 (January-June 1969), 1-11; JE Lesslie Newbigin, *The Finality of Christ* (London, 1969), 41-44; 'Editorial', *RS*, 5.2 (June 1958), 4; JV Taylor, 'Christian Motivation in Dialogue', in *FTF*, 3, 10.

56 "Admettre ... que les religions, dans leur histoire, se développent en direction du Christ, semble contredire les faits fournis par l'histoire des religions – à l'exception de phénomènes isolés" (HR Schlette, 'Religions', *Encyclopédie de la Foi*, edited by H Fries, (Paris, 1967), Volume IV, 67f); he is commenting on the theory as found in J-A Cuttat, *La Rencontre des Religions*.

57 'The Presence of Christ in Hinduism', *RS*, 18.1 (March 1971), 36.

58 Including Dupuis, 'The Presence of Christ in Hinduism', 36.

l'Alpha et l'Omega".[59] Amaladoss sees God's saving presence everywhere active as God's plan is progressively realised in history before all things are unified and fulfilled in him. The church is certainly not the only form or instrument of this fulfilment.[60] When linked, the two present and future aspects may be said together to relate to dialogue.[61] Assumptions about common spirituality are also reinforced by an eschatological viewpoint; one statement on dialogue links the future unity of humanity with the already discernible "convergent aspirations" of the religions.[62] A more recent Workshop statement verges on a confusion between the factual and mere wish fulfilment in asserting that, in their common "truth-pilgrimage", Christianity and Hinduism "are indeed having the same yearning to reach the ultimate just as two rivers are longing to reach their destination."[63] Another notable definition of dialogue sees it as "the response of Christian faith in God's saving presence in other religious traditions and the expression of the firm hope of their fulfilment in Christ."[64]

3. *Comment*

There are, then a number of ways in which the prospect of eschatological fulfilment and unity in Christ can function as an incentive to Hindu-Christian dialogue. Although the present and future aspects of this fulfilment are sometimes linked, the acceptance of either as a basis for dialogue requires acceptance of a quite different set of christological presuppositions. The present dimension depends in large measure upon the not uncontroversial idea of the active presence of Christ in Hinduism (the subject of section E below). The notion of a future eschatological unity and fulfilment of the religions also raises a number of complex questions. One concerns the theological understanding of history and its fulfilment in Christ. Contemporary theology is cautious about any theory of 'salvation-history' that would impose an evolutionary pattern on

59 "All the religions of the world search for and converge on him, the Alpha and the Omega." Pierre Fallon, 'Lettre de Calcutta', *Christus*, 22 (1975), 247.

60 Michael Amaladoss, 'Dialogue and Mission: Conflict or Convergence', *Vidyajyoti*, 50 (1986), 78f.

61 'Consultation Working Group Reports', 108.

62 Nagpur Declaration, 26.

63 'Statement of a Workshop on "The Issues in Hindu-Christian Relationship" Held in Madurai, 9-11 October 1995,' *CD*, no. 29 (January 1996), paragraph 19.

64 CBCI Communication, 52; cited in *GIRD(2)*, 5; see also 36.

the history to which the Bible bears witness. Nonetheless, that witness does seem to indicate a progressively expanding view of the scope of God's redemption and the mission expected of his covenant people. The view is increasingly universal and inclusive: not only the people of Israel but all people, not only the Christian community but every nation and even the cosmic powers are the intended objects of redemption and fulfilment in Christ.[65]

However, it is not altogether clear what implications this has for an assessment of the religions themselves. The revelation and acts of God to which the Biblical writers bear witness are not restricted to explicitly 'religious' events and persons. The hand of God is seen in some of the history of people and peoples outside the adherents of the old and new covenants, although there is no comprehensive Biblical answer to the questions posed by religious pluralism, and certainly none in terms of the potential unity of the religions. This is one reason why a motive for inter-faith dialogue is not easily provided by the notion of eschatological fulfilment and unity. The official Catholic *Guidelines* seems to embrace both an evolutionary view (the religions are "stepping stones in the growing revelation of God 'in many and various ways'" (*GIRD(1)*, 63; similarly 42)) but in its revised edition the religions are seen in a more self-contained way; they are, in fact, gifts from God (*GIRD(2)*, 25. In other words, the theory of fulfilment may assume and depend upon an older view of the religions that still wants to assess them in a christocentric context; more recent evaluations allow for a far greater autonomy within a pluralistic framework – which is why there are a number of examples of proponents of Hindu-Christian dialogue explicitly rejecting versions of the fulfilment theory that they once held.[66] However, if fulfilment is simply understood in terms of complementarity (whether eschatological or not), then Christianity and Hinduism can be seen as offering mutual insight and understanding. And one final point might also be noted. Although discussion

65 A modest application of this notion is found in a fairly conservative source: JE Lesslie Newbigin who considers that Christianity grows and develops "because in the encounter of the Gospel with new cultures, new aspects of the fullness of God in Christ are brought to light" (*Christian Witness in a Plural Society* (Madras, 1977), 22).

66 For example, Abhishiktananda, *Saccidananda*, xivf, 60, 193-201; the changed subtitle between the first and the revised editions (from *From Vedanta to the Trinity* to *A Christian Approach to Advaitic Experience* indicates the rejection of the notion of fulfilment. See also Griffiths, *Christ in India*, 7 (1984 edition, 'Introduction'). Among Protestants, AG Hogg remains perhaps the most notable critic of the notion; details are found in Sharpe, *Alfred George Hogg*.

above has centred on the notion of Christianity as offering some kind of fulfilment for Hindu aspirations, it is not difficult to imagine the inclusive embrace of Hinduism as the *sanatana Dharma* being understood in a similar way – with Hinduism as the absolute and Christianity as the relative. The way in which neo-Hinduism has understood and included non-Vedic traditions seems to offer a parallel to the Christian notion of fulfilment.[67]

E. Christ as Actively Present in Hinduism

The claim that Christ is actively present in Hinduism is sometimes stated as if it were self-evident. For example, Christ is said to be "the soul and depth of all philosophies and theologies that deserve the name".[68] In India, "poets and prophets ... have abundantly proved their experience of the eternal Christ ... through their lives, teachings and songs".[69] This is the Christ whose presence is said to be found in rather than brought to the Hindu-Christian dialogue.

Contemporary Catholic teaching affirms the possibility of salvation (as understood by the Christian tradition) for those who remain adherents of other faiths. This affirmation has usually been a conclusion drawn from certain christological premises.[70] One Catholic writer who applies this teaching to a Christian evaluation of Hinduism believes it to be established on the *a priori* grounds that, because God wills the salvation of all through Christ, "therefore, it must be recognised as a truth that Christ is at work in Hinduism".[71] The same writer then tries to establish the activity of Christ in Hinduism on *a posteriori* grounds as well: whenever Hinduism enables an individual to understand and to seek such basic human values as life, freedom, love and a sense of community then Hinduism is "a vehicle of the creative, redeeming, transforming

---

67 See, for example, the discussion in Halbfass, *India and Europe*, chapters 18 and 22.

68 Klostermaier, 'A Hindu-Christian Dialogue on Truth', *ITD*, 111.

69 Savarirayan Jesudason, *Unique Christ and Indigenous Christianity* (Bangalore, 1966), 41 (original emphasis). He goes on to cite a Tamil *bhakti* song to Siva as an example.

70 A clear example is found in the Encyclical of John Paul II, *Redemptor Hominis*, 14. As Gregory Baum observes, what is "new and startling" in this Encyclical is the repeated emphasis on the redemptive presence of Jesus "to the entire human family" ('The First Papal Encyclical', *Ecumenist*, May-June 1979, 55).

71 Mel Brady, 'How is Christ at Work in Hinduism?', *TAN*, 9 (1972), 188.

activity of Christ" since God grants such revelation only in Christ.[72]

Other writers also appeal to religious experience within Hinduism. For TM Manickam, "wherever there is an experience of the saving grace of God there is also the *anubhava* [experience]of Christ; for all grace comes from Christ".[73] Some observers claim simply to meet this Christ in the lives of some Hindus and, at times, "even more than in many of my Christian brothers and sisters".[74] But usually belief in the presence of Christ is described more precisely. Dupuis, for example, qualifies the belief when he writes that "Christ is present to Hindus – who presumably are sincere in their adherence to and their practice of Hinduism". And he is more cautious still about the possibility of Christ's presence in what might be called the religious system of Hinduism itself. Nonetheless, Christ is present according to Dupuis (though in a hidden and implicit way) and it is even possible that certain facets of the mystery of Christ "are realised more deeply by some Hindus than they are by many Christians".[75] For Kathleen Healy, the common ground for Hindu-Christian dialogue is "the Christ who existed from the beginning" over whom "Christians have no monopoly".[76] Christ is, therefore, present and active in Hinduism, even if many veils of prejudice, injustice and misunderstandings of the past prevent his being recognised.[77]

If Christ is implicitly present in Hinduism, then Hindus (or, at least, some Hindus) may be regarded as implicit Christians and Hinduism (or aspects of it) as a form of implicit Christianity. CM Cherian considers it to be impossible that an individual of any religion should know God and be committed to him "without being committed to the cosmic Christ whose voice and Spirit fill the universe".[78] Because Christ's Lordship and salvation are truly ubiqui-

---

72 'How is Christ at Work in Hinduism?', 191; he does concede that the signs of Christ's activity in Hinduism are ambiguous (196).

73 TM Manickam, 'Anubhava as Pramana of an Indian Christology', Jeevadhara, 1 (1971), 231 (see also 232, 243).

74 Sradhananda, 'Brahma Vidya Mundir', 344.

75 'The Presence of Christ in Hinduism', 33 (original emphasis), 37, 39. For other claims that christology can be enriched by Hinduism see: 'Conclusions of the National Seminar on Crisis of Faith', *Vidyajyoti*, 41 (1977), 332; and Sebastian Painadath, 'Christology and the Spiritual Heritage of Mankind', *Jeevadhara*, 2 (1972), 230-40.

76 Healy, *Christ as Common Ground: A Study of Christianity and Hinduism*, 8.

77 Chethimattam, 'Third Christian Colloquy on Hinduism', 10.

78 'Jesus Christ Our Wisdom', *Vidyajyoti*, 41 (1977), 440.

tous, there are as many ways of belonging to the Church as there are ways of believing.[79]

There are, then, a number of ways of describing Christ's presence within Hinduism. Although attention has mainly been given to Catholic thought, some Protestant writers are also found affirming such a presence.[80] Many of the statements about Christ's presence are, of course, highly problematical – not least because of problems associated with notions of implicit (or 'anonymous') Christianity – and discussion will return to them. But belief in the presence of Christ in Hinduism does, nonetheless, constitute a major reason why a Christian would be open dialogue; in the words of Amaladoss:

> Since we recognise the mystery of Christ as wider and deeper than its manifestation in the incarnate Christ and as present also in other religions, dialogue with the other religions is also a way of encountering Christ and being enriched.[81]

F. Raimundo Panikkar

Perhaps the most influential advocate of belief in the presence of Christ in Hinduism has been Raimundo Panikkar, whose *The Unknown Christ of Hinduism*,[82]and other writings, have been widely

---

79 C. Winckelmans, 'Reflections on The Church', *IJT*, 20 (1971), 134; see also Mundadan who writes of the "inter-relatedness of the church with other faith-communities on the basis of Christ's presence in them" ('Hindu-Christian Dialogue: Past Twenty-Five Years', *Jeevadhara*, 11 (1981), 390).

80 See, for example: 'Editorial', *RS*, 12.1 (March 1965), 3; 'Editorial', *RS*, 14.2 (June 1967), 4; D Preman Niles, 'Christian Mission and the Peoples of Asia', *Missiology*, 10 (1982), 291; his father, DT Niles, could speak of the "previousness of Jesus" in the lives of people (*Upon the Earth* (Madras, 1969), 46); MA Thomas, *Towards Wider Ecumenism* (Bangalore: Asia Trading Corporation, 1993), has a section on 'Christ active in other religions' (89f). In a more recent example Philip R Meadows argues, on the basis of a Logos christology, that "the Spirit of Christ strives preveniently with humankind to accomplish the eternal *logos* .... Reading salvation Christologically means that, insofar as any way of being religious can represent a species of true religion, then we might say it is the Spirit of Christ who enables Hindus to become Christ-like Hindus ...." ('"Candidates for Heaven": Wesleyan Resources for a Theology of Religions', *Wesleyan Theological Journal*, 35 (2000), 127.

81 Michael Amaladoss, 'The Mystery of Christ and Other Religions', *VJTR*, 63 (1999), 337

82 The work was written by 1957 and published in a first edition in 1964, and

discussed.[83] Christology is a major issue in Panikkar's thought; it

---

in a much-revised edition, with the subtitle *Towards an Ecumenical Christophany*, in 1981. The discussion that follows mainly uses the revised edition whose theology is greatly developed from that of the first edition.

83 See, for example, the various contributions to the 'Symposium in Honor of Raimundo Panikkar', in CC, 29 (1979), 130-230; and also: JB Chethimattam, 'R Panikkar's Approach to Christology', *IJT*, 23 (1974), 219-22; Anton Karokaran, *Evangelization and Diakonia* (Bangalore, 1978), 140-58 and 'Raymond Panikkar's Theology of Religions: a Critique', *VJTR*, 58 (1994), 663-72; Harold G Coward, 'Panikkar's Approach to Inter-religious Dialogue', CC, 29 (1979), 183-89, 192; Thomas Emprayil, *The Emerging Theology of Religions* (Rewa, 1980), 85-93; Newbigin, *The Finality of Christ*, 41-44; Nalini Devdas, 'The Theandrism of Raimundo Panikkar and Trinitarian Parallels in Modern Hindu Thought', *JES*, 17 (1981), 606-20; A Adappur, 'The Theology of Inter-Faith Dialogue', *Vidyajyoti*, 46 (1982), 485-93; Robert Smet, *Essai sur la pensée de Raimundo Panikkar* (Louvain-la-Neuve, 1981); and *Le problème d'une théologie hindoue-chrétienne selon Raymond Panikkar* (Louvain-la-Neuve, 1983); Kana Mitra, *Catholicism-Hinduism: Vedantic Investigation of Raimundo Panikkar's Attempt at Bridge Building* (Lanham, MD, and London, 1987); Dominic Veliath, *Theological Approach and Understanding of Religions. Jean Daniélou and Raimundo Panikkar: A Study in Contrasts* (Bangalore: Kristu Jothi College, 1988) and 'Christ and Religious Pluralism – Raimundo Panikkar', *Jeevadhara*, 27 (1997), 207-20; Arvind Sharma, 'Perspectives on Hindu-Christian Dialogue: a Reply to R Panikkar', in *Religious Issues and Interreligious Dialogues*, 491-509; Paul Knitter, 'Cosmic Confidence or Preferential Option', *BTF*, 23.4 (1991), 1-24; Kenneth Cragg, 'Raimundo Panikkar' in his *Troubled by Faith. Life-Studies in Inter-Faith Concern* (Edinburgh: Pentland Press, 1992), 202-21; Kajsa Ahlstrand, *Fundamental Openness. An Enquiry into Raimundo Panikkar's Theological Vision and its Presuppositions*, Studia Missionalia Upsaliensa 57 (Uppsala: Swedish Institute for Missionary Research, 1993); Parapally, *Emerging Trends in Indian Christology*; C Menacherry, *Christ: The Mystery in History. A Critical Study on the Christology of Raymond Panikkar* (Frankfurt: Peter Lang, 1996); VJ Origen, 'Das Verhältnis von Christentum und Hinduismus im heutigen indisch-christlichen theologischen Denken. Ein Beispiel: Raimundo Panikkar', *TZ*, 52 (1996), 129-49; *The Intercultural Challenge of Raimon Panikkar*, Faith Meets Faith series, edited by Joseph Prabhu (Maryknoll, NY: Orbis Books, 1996); Francis X D'Sa, 'The Interreligious Dialogue of the Future. Exploration into the Cosmotheandric Nature of Dialogue', *VJTR*, 61 (1997), 693-707; AM Mundadan, *Paths of Indian Theology* (Bangalore: Dharmaram Publications, 1998), 90-112; Anthony Savari Raj, *A New Hermeneutic of Reality. Raimon Panikkar's Cosmotheandric Vision* (Bern: Pete Lang, 1998) and 'Overcoming Fragmentation: Discerning the Context of Raimon Panikkar's Cross-cultural Contribution', *MB*, ns, 39 (1998), 4-10; and numerous reviews of *TUCH(1)* and *TUCH(2)*.

includes the quest for "an authentically universal Christology ... which would make room not only for different theologies but also for different religions".[84]

Panikkar's christology certainly has a cosmic dimension. From Hebrews 1:1-3 he concludes both that "the Son" is the inspirer of the sages of Hinduism and that "the Logos himself is speaking" within Hinduism.[85] The first chapter of *TUCH(2)* describes the Christian-Hindu encounter "with the intention of showing that there is in Hinduism a living Presence of ... Christ" (2). Panikkar's cosmic christology includes the traditional assertion that "Christ is the Lord", and is much more than the person Jesus (14, 27). The uniqueness of Christ should be understood as a uniqueness of experience[86] and not in terms of the logical concept of uniqueness (21). Christ may rightly be called Saviour and "the only mediator" but he is, nonetheless, "efficient and present in any authentic religion, regardless of name or form".[87] Although "to see Christ is to reach the Mystery", that Mystery cannot be wholly identified with Christ "even though he is *the* Way when we are on that way. ... Only for the Christians is the Mystery indissolubly connected with Christ" (24f; original emphasis).

As a consequence, Panikkar is reluctant to emphasise the historical particularity of Jesus;[88] Christ may not be particularised by reference to his humanity,[89] nor even by reference to his role as saviour and only mediator,[90] because there are many saviours, each embodying that power to save "which Christians believe to be the spirit of Jesus".[91] For this reason Christ cannot be limited to an historical figure; this would also imply "denying his divinity".[92] The

---

84 Panikkar, 'The Category of Growth in Comparative Religion', *HTR*, 66 (1973), 128.

85 *TUCH(2)*, 1; see also 27 and his *The Trinity and the Religious Experience of Man* (London, 1975), 53f. Page numbers in this and the following four paragraphs are to *TUCH(2)*.

86 In fact, Panikkar defines Christian faith as the personal experience of the uniqueness of Christ: *TUCH(2)*, 21.

87 Panikkar, 'Inter-Religious Dialogue: Some Principles', *JES*, 12 (1975), 409.

88 See, for example, *Salvation in Christ: Concreteness and Universality, the Supername* (Santa Barbara, 1972), 51.

89 Panikkar regards this humanity as a "theophany" of value only to those of the immediate world of Jesus: *Salvation in Christ*, 44.

90 'Inter-Religious Dialogue: Some Principles', 409

91 *Salvation in Christ*, 50. Knitter calls Panikkar's distinction between the universal Christ and the particular Jesus Panikkar's "distinctive contribution to the theocentric model" (*No Other Name?*, 154).

92 'Christians and So-Called "Non-Christians"', *CC*, 22 (1972), 295. Further on

significance of this ahistorical christology[93] becomes more apparent when set in the context of Panikkar's approach to Hinduism. Because Christ is "that reality" that is the origin, sustenance and destiny of all things (49), and because the Hindu scriptures speak of the same reality (49, nn 13-16), therefore "from the point of Christianity, Christ is already present in Hinduism" (40; see also 165, 169). Because this 'Christ' is present in all things, everything is a manifestation of the Logos; "every being is a christophany". Such Christophany redeems Christ from the limitations of time and space and the particularisations of dogmas. This has important implications for dialogue: "It is not a question of 'converting' all the world to Christianity, but of recognizing that the nature itself of reality shows a non dualistic polarity between the transcendent and the immanent in all its manifestations."[94]

Panikkar makes an extended attempt to illustrate this continuity between Christianity and Hinduism by arguing that many Hindus assign some of the functions and 'place' that Christians assign to Christ to Isvara, the personal aspect and self-revelation of Brahman. This he does not only in an attempt to show parallels with christology but also in an attempt to illustrate how his approach might facilitate the resolution of the longstanding problem of understanding Brahman as either *saguna* or *nirguna* (with or without attributes), and to help explain the problematical relationship between the Absolute and the world (152-55). Although Panikkar does not intend a precise identification of Christ and Isvara (see 155, 164), he does suggest that the attributes of Isvara are those which find a true fulfilment in Christ; the *sūtra* he discusses "seems to indicate a way to what the Christian tradition calls God the Father through God the Son" (159).

The notion that Christ might be seen as a bridge between the main Hindu concept of the Absolute and the world is not new to Panikkar. The writings of Upadhyaya had, as already noted, suggested that Christ be seen as *Cit* (consciousness or intelligence) – a concept not unrelated to that intended by use of *Logos* terminology. But there are at least two objections that may be raised. On the one

---

history, see chapter 6.C, below.

93 It is this aspect of Panikkar's christology that seems to have changed significantly between the editions of *TUCH*. In *TUCH(1)* there is a clear continuity between the 'Jesus of history' and the 'Christ of faith' but in *TUCH(2)* the continuity is very difficult to discern; see the discussion in Menacherry, *Christ: The Mystery in History. A Critical Study on the Christology of Raymond Panikkar*.

94 'Christology and Christophany', *TM*, 2.4 (October – December 1999), 20.

hand, Isvara is the word used in many Indian languages by members of the Christian community for God in the full trinitarian sense. On the other hand, many Hindus who are familiar with the concept of Isvara regard it as pointing only to an aspect of the Absolute – one that exists at a level of *maya* and therefore decidedly below the level of the reality inherent in Brahman. Nor would all Hindus agree with the distinction that Panikkar draws between "God" in the later Upanishads (called Isvara by him) and Brahman (137). Panikkar's reply to this objection is unlikely to persuade many Hindus.[95] In brief, he argues that Christian revelation (he means that of Christ as second person of the Trinity) shows how the Isvara need not be seen as belonging to the world of *maya* only. Christ is the example of how the *saguna* Brahman might be understood to possess a supreme value that does not compromise the absolute transcendence of the *nirguna* Brahman (155-162, 164f). Panikkar's argument depends not only upon the logic of analogy, for he believes that Christ is the actual fulfilment and resolution of those desires and tensions which the very concept of Isvara strives to express. But his attempt to facilitate dialogue will require considerable clarification if several important terms (Christ, Isvara, Brahman, and Trinity) are not themselves to add ambiguity and even misunderstanding to discussion between Christians and Hindus. Central to this clarification for Christians may well be his understanding of Christ given his separation of the ontic Christ from the historical Jesus – but opinion is divided over the significance of this separation. Parapally believes that Panikkar does not deny or obscure the historical Jesus but is simply attempting to develop a christology that "is determined by a context of dialogue which considers history as only one dimension of reality". Panikkar's encounter with Hinduism show that an emphasis on the historical Jesus "cannot take us very far in dialogue nor can it explain his real significance to the hearers".[96] On the other hand, as MM Thomas points out, to assert that "'Jesus is Christ' need not mean 'Christ is only Jesus' but Christ anywhere manifested should be like Jesus and continuous with Jesus in some way."[97] And Ramachandra expresses his disappointment at "the almost total absence" of attention to the ministry, teaching, death and resurrection of Jesus – or to any theology of atonement, sin, guilt and the

---

95 Christians also can be critical; see, for example, Hans Küng, *Christianity and the World Religions* (Garden City, NY, 1986), 275.

96 Parapally, *Emerging Trends in Indian Theology*, 174f.

97 'Christology and Pluralistic Consciousness', *IBMR*, 10 (1986), 107.

reality of evil. He is also critical of what he sees as Panikkar's most serious defect: his "preoccupation with the 'hidden' Mystery" while overlooking the way in which Christ has disclosed that Mystery.[98]

Clarification may also be required of his methodology. Despite its title, Panikkar's starting point in *TUCH* when he comes to offer a concrete example of the encounter of Christianity with Hinduism (in Part III of *TUCH*) is an analysis and commentary upon a philosophical text – an example far-removed from his own repeated emphasis upon the centrality of the existential component of a fruitful meeting over against the formulation in philosophical categories of the concepts of God and the Absolute which do differ so widely between and even within both Christianity and Hinduism.[99] Nonetheless, Panikkar believes the "cosmotheandric mystery"[100] is common to all the religions even if beliefs are tradition-specific though he has advocated "cross-fertilization" between these beliefs.[101] More recently, he has stressed dialogue leading beyond static doctrines to deeper self-understanding.[102] As already noted, common ground, actual or potential, is much more likely to be found in shared 'religious' experience. And, as will be suggested below (chapter 6.F), it is possible that the discussion of Christ's own 'realisation', rather than debate about his ontological status, may constitute a potentially significant example of common ground acceptable to both Hindu and Christian.

The discussion generated by the publication of *TUCH* points to a major innovation in attempts to employ christology in the search for a comprehensive theological understanding of dialogue. Of special interest is the fact that Panikkar does not merely employ a cosmic christology but that he also explores some of the possible consequences of acknowledging the immanence of the universal cosmic Christ. Traditionally, christology has laid stress upon the transcendence of Christ, from which transcendence Christ is brought, as it were, by missionary or similar Christian endeavour and offered to those – Hindus, for example – who otherwise do not and would not know him or respond to him. The presuppositions of such an approach have added little to a positive evaluation of what might thereby be called the 'non-*Christ*ian' religions. Panikkar, however,

---

98 *The Recovery of Mission*, 103; he discusses Panikkar in chapter 3 of *The Recovery of Mission* and in parts of chapter 4.

99 For example, *TUCH(1)*, 5.

100 See his *The Cosmotheandric Experience: Emerging Religious Consciousness* (Maryknoll, NY: Orbis Books, 1993).

101 See his *The Intrareligious Dialogue* (New York: Paulist Press, 1978).

102 See his 'Foreword: The Ongoing Dialogue', in *H-CD*, ix-xviii.

explores another approach to christology, one that has certainly stimulated a continuing and sympathetic Christian interest in the meeting of Hindu and Christian. His methodology might well be open to criticism; for example, his longstanding determination to separate form from essence in religion (this requires the removal of the outer covering of historical accidentals from an inner essence). It is also clear that his own thinking has progressed beyond the attempt simply to make Christ more intelligible in a Hindu setting to that of mutual enrichment based on his notion of cosmotheandrism.

G. Cosmic Christology and Dialogue

As might be expected, cosmic christology and Christian-Hindu dialogue are said to relate in a number of differing ways. The Protestant emphasis (towards the beginning of the period under study) upon the Lordship of Christ did not contribute directly to interest in dialogue. But there is an implicit contribution because of the way in which the theme of Christ's Lordship was said to provide an incentive for that increasingly positive and open attitude to other faiths which facilitates commitment to actual dialogue.[103] By the mid-1960s, however, the transition to commitment to dialogue on christological grounds had been made – or, at least, made in progressive circles such as the CISRS in Bangalore. A not untypical example is found in an Editorial in *Religion and Society* in 1965 in which the affirmation of a cosmic christology is immediately related to dialogue: "dialogue is an attempt to know and respond to Jesus Christ who is present and active in other faiths, creating new life in them, judging their worship of the self and the creature, and redeeming their hidden treasures".[104]

However, among those standing within or sympathetic to the Catholic theological tradition, the link between Christian-Hindu dialogue and a number of aspects or consequences of cosmic christology has been made more often, and more explicitly than in Indian Protestant circles. Examples of these different aspects or consequences include the following. (a) *Jesus as the Logos*. The Indian Catholic *Guidelines* argues that the spirit of dialogue is fundamental to the Christian faith because "faith is ... the beginning of salvation

---

103 See, for example, 'The Basis and Content of a Christian-Hindu Dialogue', *RS*, 6.1 (February 1959), 78; see also Murray Rogers, 'The Content of a Christian-Hindu Dialogue', *RS*, 6.1 (February 1959), 71.

104 'Editorial', *RS*, 12.1 (March 1965), 2f; see also 6.

and it is a dialogue between God and the human being. ... Dialogue became incarnate and tangible when God sent his Word (*logos*)".[105] (b) *Common humanity in Christ.* Christology is also linked with the common humanity discussed above (chapter 3.C) as a basis for dialogue. On the basis of Christ's inauguration of the Kingdom of God and his making all things new, the Indian *Guidelines* states that dialogue with others finds its place and meaning, so that "with them we may work for the new Humanity which Christ inaugurated".[106] (c) *Universal presence and activity.* Balasuriya argues that cosmic christology can help make Christians "more docile to the Spirit of God and more open to genuine dialogue" – in place of a former narrow exclusivism.[107] Fallon believes that, since in Asia the cosmic Christ is "already present among those who still ignore Him", and is "slowly building them up into the image of the Son", it follows that the approach to those of other faiths is one in which "we must always contemplate in faith and hope" the image that Christ is shaping in his unknown followers.[108] Some Protestant advocates of dialogue maintain essentially the same basis; for example, that its "frame of reference is the persistently implied affirmation of Christ-centred catholicism – that He is before all things and in Him all things hold together".[109]

Given that the attributes of Christ do include those assigned to him by the proponents of cosmic christology, he could indeed be said to constitute a basis for dialogue.[110] And there are further consequences of the assertion that cosmic christology forms a basis for dialogue.

(i) Christ is said to be at work in the encounter. During dialogue the Christian will have "perceived him [Christ] wonderfully at work in the depth of the experience of our Hindu brother"; dia-

---

105 *GIRD(2)*, 28. (It is interesting to note that *GIRD(1)* at this point stated that *revelation* was the beginning of salvation (14).) See also Kalapesi, 'Some Reflections', 73.

106 *GIRD(2)*, 28; see also Mundadan, 'Hindu-Christian Dialogue', 390.

107 Tissa Balasuriya, *Planetary Theology* (London, 1984), 188.

108 'The Cosmic Christ and the Asian Revolution', 153. *GIRD(2)*, 29 also links Christ's presence in the hearts of all with dialogue. According to Manickam to share "the *anubhava* of any Christ-knowing man, irrespective of his external religious commitment" is to inaugurate a "theology of religious dialogue" ('Anubhava as Pramana of an Indian Christology', 232).

109 Thomas, 'Inter-Religious Dialogue', 10. See also ZAM, 23.

110 See, for example, Rogers, 'The Content of a Christian-Hindu Dialogue', 68. Knitter maintains that a belief in the presence of Christ in the religions is "the only view ... that coherently allows Christians to enter the dialogue with other religions" (*No Other Name?* 141).

logue, once seen as a two-sided event, will be realised to be three-sided.[111]

(ii) Christ is said to speak in the dialogue. Not only will Christians expect to learn from their Hindu partner, "we shall expect Christ to speak to us as to him" in dialogue.[112]

(iii) Christ may even speak through the Hindu partner and can "give us through the other a new insight, and an interpretation of Himself".[113]

(iv) Christ is also liable to be met in the experience of dialogue – even in casual encounters with people of other faiths *(GIRD(2),* 78); Hindus as well as Christians report contemporary experiences of Christ.[114]

In other words, given that he is presumed to be both present and active in Hinduism, it does follow that Christ might be said to be met, to speak and to be at work when Hindu and Christian meet in dialogue.

H. Cosmic Christology: A Critical Comment

Cosmic christology possesses a number of advantages over other possible Christian starting points that might also be claimed to have a universal, cosmic dimension and thereby provide potential common – or more neutral – ground between Hindu and Christian. Two such starting points might be 'God' and 'spirit'.

The word 'God', especially if not qualified in a personal or dualistic sense by the Christian partner, may well be seen as an item of faith common to both traditions. Some Hindus assume the essential unity of all religions in Brahman; some Christians are prepared to assert that all the religions 'revolve around' or in other ways reveal the Absolute. One apparent advantage of such a starting point is that it appears to bypass the scandal of particularity that traditional Christian claims about a unique revelation and salvation in Christ

---

111 C Murray Rogers, in 'Dialogue Postponed', 222.

112 'Basis and Content', 79. Similarly Rogers: The "point of genuine yearning ... is the point at which the Third Person makes Himself known in the dialogue and both Christian and Hindu find themselves being addressed" ('The Content of a Christian-Hindu Dialogue', 71).

113 'Consultation on Theology', 79. In similar vein is Ignatius Hirudayam, 'Dialogue in Tamilnadu', *LV*, 29 (1974), 422.

114 Manickam, 'Anubhava as Pramana of an Indian Christology', 239, 232. Some of Manickam's suggestions are discussed in chapter 6.D below.

appear to make when asserted in India.[115] However, this seeming advantage is purchased at a cost. In the words of the rather forceful appraisal of Richard Taylor:

> Probably all of those who object to the Indian [Christian] propensity for seeing Christ there [in the world] would be willing to see God there. But ... in our Indian culture ... the word "God" may mean so many different things that it is either misleading or truly meaningless.[116]

It might, of course, be possible to reduce some of the ambiguity of the differing meanings of the term 'God' by means of a discussion of the semantic range of the various words for the Absolute in the Sanskritic languages.[117] But, even if Hindu and Christian were to agree on one word, or on a conjunction of words (such as *Brahman* as *saguna-nirguna*) the raising of questions concerning, for example, the relationship between *paramatman* and *atman*, or between God and the world, would almost certainly reveal differences of understanding that no verbal agreement could cover. Neither Hindus nor Christians are usually found claiming the ability to define the Absolute or God exhaustively.

But it is likely that each would defend definitions of the Absolute that would appear to be irreconcilable with those made by the other – and equally probable that belief in 'God' could not, therefore, be considered to be an area of common ground conducive to a far-reaching commitment to dialogue.

The terms 'spirit' (or 'Spirit') and 'spirituality' might also be seen as pointing to that 'spiritual' essence thought by some apologists for Vedanta and some Christian advocates of dialogue to constitute the inner dynamic shared by all religions. Abhishiktananda, for example, places considerable emphasis upon the unity (*ekatvam*) of all things in the Spirit.[118] In fact, he believes that both the *Advaita* and the Christian experience of God share this same mystery of realised oneness in the Spirit.[119] Panikkar argues that the Spirit is God immanent (rather than transcendent) – the Atman that is the Ultimate

---

115 It is the opinion of Thomas Emprayil that, in India, "the problem of God is considered as no theological problem, but Christ is still a stumbling block in the encounter of religions" (*The Emerging Theology of Religions* (Rewa, 1983), 144).

116 'Christ Acting in Our Society', 168 (original emphasis).

117 See, for example, the discussion by Robin Boyd, *An Introduction to Christian Theology* (revised edition, Madras, 1975), 233-37.

118 *Hindu-Christian Meeting Point*, 72.

119 *Hindu-Christian Meeting Point*, 109; see also his *The Church in India*, 130.

Ground and Brahman itself.[120] The terms *sakti* (power),[121] *atman* (spirit) and its cognates *paramatman* and *antaratman* (supreme spirit and inner spirit), are not only known to Hindus but can be, and in fact are, invested with appropriate Christian meaning and are widely used in the Indian Church. Furthermore, Hindus usually identify Brahman with *paramatman* even as Christians identify God as Spirit.[122]

But there are difficulties with the suggestion that a common acknowledgement of 'spirit' or 'Spirit' might function as a basis for dialogue. Within the Christian tradition (including most of the Indian Christian tradition)[123] one major function of the Spirit is seen as that of mediating the presence of Christ – in which case the problem of particularity is hardly avoided.[124] It is also probable that in an Indian context, the word 'spirit' would remain as ambiguous as the term 'God', and for comparable reasons. If used without qualification the word can function as the justification of almost any 'spirituality' that cares to appropriate it. If the word is qualified, it is probable that both Hindu and Christian would draw upon elements in their own traditions that would appear to be irreconcilable with the beliefs of the other. The Christian view of the world, and of definitive revelation in Christ, might, for example, make the definition and nature of the Spirit's activity unacceptably 'concrete' to a Hindu. In other words, the supposed advantages to dialogue of using the words 'God', 'spirit' and their cognates – rather than Christ – are outweighed by their disadvantages. As Panikkar concludes, symbols such as God, Spirit, Truth are liable to truncate reality and limit the centre of life to an abstract principle,[125] which is why

---

120 "At the deepest level of Divinity what there is is the Spirit." (*The Trinity and World Religions* (Madras, 1970), 58; see also 32).

121 And its cognate *mahasakti* (great power) used, for example, by Chenchiah, 'Jesus and Non-Christian Faiths', in *Rethinking Christianity*, 57.

122 For example, Sarvepalli Radhakrishnan, 'The Religion of the Spirit,' in his 'Fragments of a Confession' in *The Philosophy of Sarvepalli Radhakrishnan*, edited by Paul A Schilpp (New York, 1952), 60-72.

123 See, for example, the distinctively Indian categories used by Chakkarai as he explains how the Spirit mediates knowledge of Christ: *Jesus the Avatar*, edited by AJ Appasamy (Madras, 1926), 114-21.

124 Though it must be pointed out that other major functions of the Spirit (according to the Christian tradition) would be more amenable to its utility in dialogue: mediating the presence of God, glorification, divinising the world.

125 See *TUCH(2)*, 27. A similar point is made by Michael Barnes when he argues that Spirit christologies "risk ignoring the historical nature of the

he argues for Christ as the defining point of Christian discourse in dialogue. (Moreover, the Christian understanding of the Spirit is inseparable from Trinitarian belief, a discussion of which – and its relevance to the Hindu-Christian encounter – is doubtless important, but somewhat beyond the scope of this work.)

Cosmic christology does, therefore, appear to provide a more satisfactory starting point for dialogue than the appeal to 'God' or 'Spirit'. Perhaps the principal relevance of cosmic christology is that it enables the prospect of considering christology from a different perspective – one suggested by the recent encounter between Christianity and the religions, including Hinduism. This new perspective need not necessarily imply the repudiation of traditional Christology but perhaps merely the discovery, or rediscovery, of elements long obscured within the Christian tradition. The cosmic dimension of christology – especially of the immanent *Logos* christology suggested by Panikkar and others – may be one such element. In an age of expanding horizons – literally in the realms of scientific discovery, but also in terms of increasing exposure to other religious traditions – faith in Jesus Christ is likely to seem to be merely sectarian unless attempts are made to make clear its universal implications. And, in an Indian Church whose view of Christ is still largely derived from western theology, the successful rehabilitation of such a christology with its implications of Christ as cosmic revealer, redeemer and fulfiller, would have profound implications for the theology and practice of the Christian-Hindu encounter.

Any rehabilitation of cosmic christology will, however, require that attention to be given to several further areas of actual or potential critical comment. These include the following.

(i) The assertion of a cosmic christology also raises the question of the nature of the authority to which the Christian makes appeals as the basis of reasonable belief. One major locus of this authority has usually been the New Testament. But the New Testament embraces a variety of different christologies – of which those making cosmic assertions constitute only one (or perhaps several). If these different christologies are seen as incompatible, then grounds must be established on which some – or none – are to be declared to be centrally important and therefore authoritative for the self-understanding of the Christian tradition, and some to be reject-

Christian revelation, and turning Christ into little more than a cosmic principle which means everything and therefore nothing" (Michael A Barnes, *Religions in Conversation: Christian Identity and Religious Pluralism* (London, 1989), 148).

ed. One reason sometimes given for the rejection of cosmic christology is that it is said to be derived from one or other of the numerous Gnostic or other mythologies of the New Testament period. For these and other reasons the notion of a cosmic dimension to the person of Christ is hardly a live article of faith among most theologians and is even regarded as an impediment to inter-religious relationships and an appropriately modest contemporary Christian view of the world.

(ii) Contemporary usage of the term 'cosmic' tends to refer to the immense size and complexity of the universe, especially as made known by recent astronomical and other scientific discovery; and contemporary theological use of the phrase "cosmic christology" almost never refers to the universe of religion and the religions. In other words, the intended meaning of the term 'cosmic' in the context of a theology of inter-religious relationships will need to be established clearly and not merely presumed.

(iii) If cosmic christology is accepted as a normative christology for Christian self-understanding (or as one of a number of such normative christologies) then questions may be raised about its compatibility with other aspects of the New Testament portrayal of Christ. Among the most critical of these is the relationship between cosmic christology with its post-Easter assessment of Christ as both risen and Lord and the 'Jesus of history'. This is not necessarily difficult if the uniqueness of Christ does not rest simply on later Christian claims but, as Pannenberg puts it, derives from "the eschatological finality claimed by Jesus himself".[126] To establish a plausible continuity between the cosmic Christ and the Jesus of history – and the continuing community that bears his name – would be to enhance the credibility of cosmic christology itself. Although the issue is complex, it does seem clear that for the first Christians the historical Jesus is identical both with the Christ raised by the Father (Acts 2.36 and elsewhere in the apostolic kerygma) and the mystery preached in the earliest church (for example: Romans 16:25; Ephesians 3:4; Colossians 2:2; 4:3; 1 Timothy 3:16).[127] If the link

126 Wolfhart Pannenberg, 'Religious Pluralism and Conflicting Truth Claims: the Problem of a Theology of the World Religions', in *Christian Uniqueness Reconsidered*, 101.

127 For a carefully nuanced discussion of the development of New Testament christology and a defence of the continuity (and discontinuity) between the portrait of Jesus in the Synoptic Gospels and the supposedly 'high' christology of the later New Testament, see Jacques Dupuis, *Who Do You Say I Am? Introduction to Christology* (Maryknoll, NY: Orbis Books, 1994), chapter 3.

is not established there is the probability that the notion of the cosmic Christ will become an abstraction or a symbolic myth.

(iv) If cosmic christology is to retain some sense of continuity with both the Jesus of history and traditional christology (as found, for example in the Patristic creeds) then the humanity of Christ must be asserted in some way. To define and defend a christology that has little or no place for the humanity of Jesus is highly problematical[128] –and traditional christology has always asserted the resurrected humanity of Christ as an article of faith. This is an issue of which Sathianathan Clarke seems to be conscious as he writes of the necessity in the Indian setting of "the composite Jesus" – by which he means "Jesus as the exalted and cosmic one; ... Jesus as the one in solidarity with the lowly and afflicted ... [while affirming] that the 'then-who-is-now' historical Jesus is also the 'now-who-was-then' cosmic One."[129]

(v) Even if cosmic christology were to be considered plausible it would still imply a christocentric view of reality whose problematical implications are discussed in section I below.

(vi) Even if the notion of cosmic christology can be sustained this does not ensure that its utility as a christological basis for dialogue can be established without difficulty. Nor is every claim to the discernment of the presence and activity of Christ able to be endorsed. Such assertions (for example, those noted above about Christ's activity in the revolutions or religions of Asia, or about Christ met in, or speaking through Hindus – or Christians for that matter) are always liable to appear to be arbitrary unless the criteria for their plausibility are clearly established. As Copeland points out, when the notion of a cosmic Logos is divorced from the historic Jesus, "the concept of the Logos can too easily come to mean anything the theologian employing it wishes it to mean. ... The cosmic revelation must be subject to the revelation in the incarnate Logos and not vice versa."[130] If Christ's presence is limited to what are called the 'authentic' elements of Hinduism then, again, the question about criteria must be raised. Nor does the fact of the presence of love, freedom, goodness, various noble aspirations and liberation from

---

128 This point is well made by the Indian evangelical Sunand Sumithra in his 'Conversion: To Cosmic Christ?', *ERT*, 16 (1992), 385-97.

129 'The Jesus of Nineteenth Century Indian Theology: An Indian Inculturation with Continuing Problems and Prospects', *SWC*, 5 (1999), 32-46 (quotation from 45).

130 E Luther Copeland, *A New Meeting of the Religions. Interreligious Relationships and Theological Questioning* (Waco, TX: Baylor University Press, 1999), 56.

oppression necessarily indicate the active presence of Christ. There are simpler and perhaps potentially less offensive explanations in terms of common or divine grace.

With attention given to these areas of actual and potential criticism, it appears that cosmic christology could be said to provide a plausible christological basis for Christian-Hindu dialogue.

One further issue calls for comment. Even if cosmic christology is compatible with other New Testament and post New Testament christologies, the modern encounter between Christianity and Hinduism raises some questions of any christology that are altogether different from those that the classical formulations attempted to answer. As Lyons observes in another context: "The moment comes when the accepted christological categories seem to fail. They are being required to contain more than has gone into their formation".[131] A similar requirement "to contain more" is suggested by the search for an adequate and distinctively Indian christological basis for Christian-Hindu dialogue. Perhaps what is required is a christological category akin to the 'third nature' of Christ proposed by Teilhard[132] – that is, an element within christology that possesses a recognisable continuity with classical christology and yet is able to provide a foundation upon which a commitment to the theory and practice of Hindu-Christian dialogue might be sustained. The next chapter turns to the search for an adequate Indian christology.

I. Christocentrism

The intention of this chapter has been to outline a christology that might sustain or assist Christian-Hindu dialogue. However, one major issue remains: the persistence of what might be called 'christocentrism' in the Christian evaluation of Hinduism and the search for purposeful and fruitful dialogue. The potentially negative implications of this christocentrism might offset even the supposed gains for dialogue of the quest for an authentically Indian christology that is the subject of the next chapter.

By christocentrism is meant those christologies that, however tolerant or positive their evaluation of Hinduism, and however warm their endorsement of dialogue, nonetheless assert that the fullness

131 Lyons, *The Cosmic Christ*, 3.

132 For Teilhard this was the cosmic nature or attribute of Christ which he placed alongside the divine and human natures traditionally assigned to Christ. Teilhard saw this cosmic nature as not incompatible with the two traditional natures; see further: Lyons, *The Cosmic Christ*, chapter 7 (183-98).

of divine revelation and the finality of humanity's redemption centre on Christ. In India this viewpoint has been found among both Protestants and Catholics.

During the 1960s and 1970s such christocentrism was represented among Protestants by, for example, Devanandan, MM Thomas, the earlier writings of Samartha and by many of the discussions of Christian-Hindu dialogue sponsored by CISRS. The principal point of divergence from more conservative Protestant opinion – and a major incentive for dialogue itself – was the positive assessment of Hinduism based upon belief in a universal divine revelation (including revelation through Hinduism) and the universal presence and activity of a cosmic Christ. MM Thomas even argued for a "Christ-centred syncretism".[133]

The Protestant version of christocentrism has been criticised on two counts. The first concerns the possibility of salvation apart from Christ. Although 'mainstream' Protestant opinion in India has, during the period of our survey, contained a number of positive statements about the possibility of salvation beyond the Christian community, they have almost always been made from a christocentric point of view. The second problem concerns the traditional Protestant desire to want to tie Christian faith to the claim the Christ is the world's only saviour and the fullest expression of God's revelation. Even when Christians have formulated a description of Christ as, for example, an *avatara* it has usually been expressed in terms of uniqueness and historical particularity.[134] But this, in turn, is to invite the kind of criticism found in the otherwise sympathetic discussion of Christian claims by the Hindu philosopher KS Murty. He believes that there have been many *avataras* but that these have been discernible only by the faith of those who display loving trust in God.[135] He considers that there is, however, no reason why all should be asked to "believe that the life of a single historical person is the revelation *par excellence* of God". Only an individual's "own predilection" would lead to a declaration that one religious tradition is to be the pattern for others.[136] Especially is this the case when

---

133 'Christ-Centred Syncretism', *RS*, 26.1 (March 1979), 26-35; revised as 'The Absoluteness of Jesus Christ and Christ-centred Syncretism', *ER*, 37 (1985), 387-97.

134 See, for example, AJ Appasamy, *The Gospel and India's Heritage* (London, 1942), 259.

135 *Revelation and Reason in Advaita Vedanta* (New York, 1959), 279-82.

136 *Revelation and Reason in Advaita Vedanta*, 296. For an example of the same issue assuming importance in dialogue see DG Moses, 'Some Reflections on Personal Dialogue', *AF*, 5 (1970), 250f.

Christian concern to lay due stress upon the uniqueness and originality of Jesus leads it to overlook what Hindus see as emphases that Jesus has in common with Hinduism (for example, upon the primacy of the spiritual life, the value of renunciation etc). Of course Protestants – including those sympathetic to Hindu-Christian dialogue – have long been familiar with the problems posed by 'the scandal of particularity' in any claim that in the person of Jesus Christ God has overcome the otherwise relativising actions of history; they have sought to acknowledge and resolve those problems.

During the 1960s and 1970s the generally positive Indian Catholic appraisal of Hinduism was also tempered by qualifications deriving from the christocentric nature of much of that appraisal. Hinduism, despite the grace of God found within it, was seen to fall short in two ways. Either its virtues were attributed to the presence of Christ, or it remained incomplete when measured against the revelation and salvation offered in Christ. However, as we have seen (chapter 4.C.2(b) above), this perspective has changed towards a more pluralistic stance that assigns a greater degree of autonomy to the religions.

Chethimattam offers an example of the first (inclusivist) point of view when writing that those Hindus who are not separated from the grace of God are, "in the Christian view, saved only through the grace of Christ, the one Saviour of the whole of humanity".[137] Also to be found are a number of statements about the essential incompleteness of Hinduism. The Catholic *Guidelines* states that the religions must be placed in the context of the history of salvation so that they do not appear as "rival or parallel movements [to Christianity] but as, in God's providence, stepping-stones to the growing revelation of God" (*GIRD(2)*, 63). Another discussion argued that "the non-Christian religions are orientated towards Christ and his church".[138] Dupuis discussed at some length the way in which Hinduism, through Christ's presence within it, "mediates divine grace". Nonetheless, it is clear to Dupuis that "the visibility of divine grace is lesser in Hinduism than in Christianity" (though he also added that "Christ may be as personally present – or even more – to the Hindu as he is to a Christian").[139]

---

137 Chethimattam, 'The Scope and Conditions of a Hindu-Christian Dialogue', 93. See also above, section F.

138 Title of chapter IV (148-68) of Ishanand Vempeny, *Inspiration in the Non-Biblical Scriptures* (Bangalore, 1973).

139 James Dupuis, 'The Presence of Christ in Hinduism', *RS*, 18.1 (March 1971), 39.

In other words, post-Conciliar Catholic theological opinion in India was usually anxious to move away from ecclesiocentrism and to acknowledge both revelation and redemption outside Christianity. But it also usually continued to assert that Christ is normative for (even if not constitutive of) whatever revelation and salvation are found outside the church. For example, an official Catholic set of theses for discussion could speak of the mystery of the unique and universal mediatorship of Christ, but placed this in the dialectic between the Church and the Kingdom. "Any attempt to appropriate it exclusively to the role of the Church can only relativise it and rob it of its universality". It may well be that Christians "need not reduce it to the limitations of the pilgrim Church which is called to be at the service of the mystery, nor to make it its exclusive possession"[140] but the christocentrism remains apparent. This standpoint, however carefully and charitably qualified and expressed, is unacceptable to Hindus[141] – even if it seems always to endorse dialogue and usually does not call for the conversion of Hindus (except in the sense that all people need to move away from all that dehumanises).

It could therefore be argued that, because of their christocentrism, both the mainline Protestant and principal Catholic positions have shared a fundamental point of agreement that views Hinduism as inadequate in itself or inadequate when measured against what Christ has done and can offer. In other words, there is an essential incompleteness in Hinduism – a point of view not far removed from an assertion of the superiority of Christianity. Clearly, there are potentially negative implications for dialogue if one partner brings to the encounter the claim that, even though Christ might not be the only revelation of God's saving love, he is its fullest and definitive revelation – and that Christians experience the salvation he brings in its fullest measure. It would be difficult to see what such a Christian view of revelation and salvation has to learn from other faiths. Other critics have argued that, from the Christian tradition itself, and from evidence from the encounter with the religions – and from questions that derive from convictions about the historical relativity and fallible finitude of all knowledge and claims to truth – there are good reasons for questioning any

140 *Theses on Interreligious Dialogue. An Essay in Pastoral Theological Reflection* (Hong Kong, 1987), 17.

141 See, for example, the critical comments of Bibhuti Yadav, 'Vaisnavism on Hans Küng: a Hindu Theology of Religious Pluralism', *RS*, 27.2 (June 1980), 32-64.

claim that Christ is necessary for salvation and is the final and decisive revelation of God.[142] From a wider Asian perspective, Pieris urges the development of a truly Asian christology born of dialogue with Asian religions and the abandonment of exclusive Christian claims.[143] Such claims also invite the long-standing Hindu counter-assertion that "the rest of the world is in need of India's vedanta for making its religion more liberal and broadminded".[144]

There are several ways in which this criticism might be answered. There is the assertion (see above: chapter 4.B) that claims to the possession of truth, whether by Christians or Hindus, need not necessarily hinder open dialogue. Cosmic christology might be employed to argue that, although the fullness of divine revelation is found uniquely in Christ (but with knowledge of this fullness tied to the relativities and limitations of particular linguistic and cultural expressions of the Christian community), this same Christ might be discerned and acknowledged elsewhere; in fact, the very act of meeting Hindus might facilitate that discernment and acknowledgement. In the Hindu-Christian dialogue, this latter viewpoint is – as we have seen – well argued by Panikkar.

Although Puthiadam could observe (in 1980) that "at present no Christian seems ready to question the universality and uniqueness of Christianity",[145] in more recent years there has been a growing number of advocates of another viewpoint. This views the religions with reference not to Christ but to a supposed common divine centre such that no one faith can claim to be normative for others. The advocates of this 'theocentrism' eschew the evaluation of the religions in terms of their relationship, actual or potential, to Christ or the Christian church and usually call in question notions of the finality of Christ, or attempts to define truth in terms of Christ; though they do not doubt the distinctiveness of either Christianity or other faiths.[146] This point of view builds upon an extensive vol-

---

142 See, for example, Christopher Duraisingh, 'World Religions and the Christian Claims for the Uniqueness of Jesus Christ', *IJT*, 30 (1981), 168-85 in which he affirms the "decisiveness" of the revelation in Christ – but only for the Christian "paradigm".

143 Aloysius Pieris, 'Speaking of the Son of God in Non-Christian Cultures, eg in Asia', *Concilium*, no. 153 (1982), 65-70.

144 DS Sarma, *The Renaissance of Hinduism* (Benares, 1944), 304.

145 'Christian Faith and Life in a World of Religious Pluralism', 103.

146 See, for example, John Hick, *God and the Universe of Faiths* (London, 1973) and *God Has Many Names: Britain's New Religious Pluralism* (London, 1980); Knitter, *No Other Name?*, chapters 8 and 9.

ume (too extensive to document here) of discussion and affirmation in the more liberal traditions in Christianity about the presence and purposeful activity of God in the religions. Stanley J Samartha (1920 – 2001) is one notable advocate of dialogue with Hindus whose thought has developed from a christocentric to a theocentric view of the religions. He rejects as "patronising" the co-option of those of other faiths by means of the notions of anonymous Christianity or a cosmic christology[147] (although he himself once embraced a form of cosmic christology).[148] Instead, Samartha wants Christians, with those of other faiths, "to draw attention to a transcendent centre, the ultimate mystery".[149] He is critical of the "Christo-monism" of much Christian theology and points to the Gospels where "Jesus Christ himself is theocentric".[150] With this in mind, he calls for an acknowledgement that "no particularity should claim universality" among the world's religions; an alternative possibility may be to "recognise God alone as Absolute and to consider all religions to be relative".[151] Other Indian Protestants argue for a similar shift from traditional christology to theocentrism in the interests of dialogue.[152] For example, they discern an important theocentric dimension to universalistic passages in the Old Testament.[153] And some Indian Catholics also call for a shift from christocentrism to theocentrism.[154] One con-

---

147 See his 'The Lordship of Jesus Christ and Religious Pluralism', in *Christ's Lordship and Religious Pluralism*, edited by Gerald H Anderson and Thomas F Stransky (Maryknoll, NY, 1981), 35. For the evolution of Samartha's thought see Eeuwout Klootwijk, *Commitment and Openness. The Interreligious Dialogue and the Theology of Religions in the Work of Stanley J Samartha* (Zoetermeer: Boekencentrum BV, 1992). Klootwijk has a fairly full bibliography of Samartha's writings; see also 'A Select Bibliography of the Writings of Stanley J Samartha' in *CD*, no. 38 (December 2001), 49-54.

148 See, for example, his *The Hindu Response to the Unbound Christ*, Inter-Religious Dialogue Series, 6 (Madras, 1974), 198-200.

149 Stanley J Samartha, 'Mission in a Religiously Plural World: Looking Beyond Tambaram, 1938', *IRM*, 78 (1988), 323.

150 'The Lordship of Jesus Christ and Religious Pluralism', 27; see also his 'Christian Concern for Dialogue in India', *CD*, no. 9 (December 1985), 6f.

151 'The Lordship of Jesus Christ and Religious Pluralism', 29.

152 For example, V Sharada, 'Truth Requires No Advertisement', *RS*, 27.1 (March 1980), 5-9; M Thomas Thangaraj, 'Teaching Theology in a Multifaith Context', in *Ministerial Formation in a Multifaith Milieu*, edited by Sam Amirtham and S Wesley Ariarajah (Geneva, nd [c 1986]), 34.

153 For example, Chandran, 'Christian Contribution to Religious Dialogue', 72f.

154 See, for example, Emmanuel, 'Inter-Religious Dialogue in Asia at a Turning Point', 235-40.

sequence of a revised (theocentric) christology is that it "provides more theological space for Christians to live together" with others,[155] and, of course, it is conducive to dialogue.[156]

The most recent and perhaps most persuasive of the global theological disavowals of christocentrism are those of John Hick and Paul Knitter – and both link their disavowals with their distaste for what they see as the unacceptable implications of the uniqueness implied by christocentrism. Hick's well known call for a "Copernican revolution"[157] to move the Christian worldview from a christocentric to a theocentric pluralist perspective derives in part from what he repeatedly describes as the unacceptable consequences of belief in the uniqueness of Christ.[158] Knitter assigns the language of uniqueness to the legitimate confidence of the Christian believer in their personal experience of Christ.[159] In *Jesus and the Other Names*,[160] Knitter reaffirms the 'uniqueness of Christ' but within a wider pluralist framework such that Jesus "does bring a universal, decisive, indispensable message" although, probably, "there are *other* universal, decisive, indispensable manifestations of divine reality besides Jesus."[161] A subsequent restatement of Knitter's pluralist christology is to be found in the symposium *The Uniqueness of Jesus*[162] in which he offers 'Five theses on the uniqueness of Jesus'. In

---

155 Samartha, 'Christian Concern for Dialogue in India', 7.

156 Among global discussions see Knitter, *No Other Name?*, chapters 8, 9, 10. Hans Küng also advocates a theocentric understanding of salvation (see, for example, his 'The World Religions in God's Plan of Salvation', in *Christian Revelation and World Religions*, edited by Joseph Neuner (London, 1967) 25-66; and his *On Being a Christian*, 98) though he also writes of other religions as conveying salvation in an imperfect manner by comparison with what is found in Christ; see *On Being a Christian*, 104.

157 In his *God and the Universe of Faiths* (revised edition, London: Fount/Collins, 1977), 131.

158 One of the clearest statements of these supposed consequences found in Hick's 'The Non-Absoluteness of Christianity' in *The Myth of Christian Uniqueness*, 16-36; see also the critique in Marjorie Hewitt Suchocki, 'In Search of Justice', in the same work, 149-61. This is why, as Pannenberg notes, Hick's attempt to displace christocentrism, "hinges on the condition of a prior demolition of the traditional doctrine of the incarnation" ('Religious Pluralism and Conflicting Truth Claims', 100).

159 *No Other Name?* 182-86.

160 Maryknoll, NY: Orbis Books, 1996.

161 *Jesus and the Other Names*, 79.

162 Paul Knitter, 'Five Theses on the Uniqueness of Jesus', in *The Uniqueness of Jesus: a Dialogue with Paul F Knitter*, Faith Meets Faith Series, edited by Leonard Swidler and Paul Mojzes (Maryknoll, NY: Orbis Books, 1997).

thesis 3 he states that "The uniqueness of Jesus' salvific role can be reinterpreted in terms of *truly* but not *only*"[163]and adds that "it is not necessary to proclaim God's revelation in Jesus as *full, definitive,* or *unsurpassable.*"[164] He also writes that while he wants to "clearly affirm that Jesus is normative and universally so," he still questions "whether he is, or can be, the only such norm."[165] In thesis 4 he explains that today, "the uniqueness of Jesus can be found in his insistence that salvation or the Reign of God must be realized *in this world* through *human actions* of love and justice."[166]

From a global ecumenical perspective, a not untypical stance is that of Wesley Ariarajah:

> Whatever useful purpose the terms finality and uniqueness may once have served in interpreting the salvific purpose of God, their usefulness is past. We should abandon these two concepts, along with the theological constructs associated with them.[167]

Ariarajah does not consider that Christians "should give up the centrality of Christ *for the Christian faith,* in both its historical and transcendent dimensions."[168] It is, of course, precisely these latter dimensions that led to the notions of uniqueness and finality but Ariarajah wants to restrict them to the Christian worldview and further qualifies his position when he adds that "it is not the positive affirmation of the centrality of Christ ... that makes these words [uniqueness and finality] obsolete in a religiously plural world, but the negative implications ...."[169] Stanley Samartha is another who, from a pluralistic perspective, is critical of any form of exclusiveness:

> The nature of Mystery is such that any claim on the part of one religious community to have exclusive or unique or final knowledge becomes inadmissible. Exclusiveness puts fences around the Mystery.[170]

---

163 'Five Theses on the Uniqueness of Jesus', 7 (original emphasis).

164 'Five Theses on the Uniqueness of Jesus', 7 (original emphasis).

165 'Five Theses on the Uniqueness of Jesus', 9, n 13.

166 Knitter, 'Five Theses on the Uniqueness of Jesus', 11 (original emphasis).

167 *Hindus and Christians. A Century of Ecumenical Thought* (Amsterdam and Grand Rapids, MI: Rodopi and Eerdmans, 1991), 211 – though he is willing to use the phrase 'the centrality of Christ' (see below).

168 *Hindus and Christians,* 211 (emphasis added).

169 Hindus and Christians, 211.

170 Stanley J Samartha, 'The Cross and the Rainbow: Christ in a Multireligious Culture', in *Asian Faces of Jesus,* edited by RS Sugirtharajah (Maryknoll, NY: Orbis Books, 1993), 113; he also goes on to reject the notion of "the normativeness of Christ" (113).

Samartha also affirms the distinctiveness of Jesus – but only as one of many (and mutually enriching) "different responses to the Mystery of God or *Sat* the Transcendent or Ultimate Reality."[171]

Nonetheless, the theocentric model remains open to criticism. The opposition by theocentrists to christocentrism might be questioned on a number of grounds. (i) At least for the Christian, christocentrism is a species of theocentrism rather than a denial of it. Knowing and following Christ *is* the traditional Christian way of being theocentric;[172] it is a means of achieving a balance between God, church and Kingdom.[173] (ii) An example of this is the assertion of the universal saving love of God – of importance to Christian theocentrists, not least in their critique of what they see as the intolerance of christocentrism. It is difficult to see how a Christian theocentrist can confidently assert knowledge of such love and of such a God without pointing to Christ.[174] Christians may well ask for the location of the alternative epistemological source for such knowledge. It does not seem possible to derive it from an inductive synthesis of religious belief in general. (iii) It can be argued that theocentrism misrepresents the major religions, since a number of them do contain exclusivist elements: they reject, as untrue, incompatible beliefs held by other traditions and to ignore that rejection is to fail to take seriously the otherness of the religions – religions that do claim to speak of what is true in an absolute sense. "Dialogue comes to an end as soon as we cut short the pursuit of the mystery of faith at the heart of the different traditions."[175] (iv) Advocates of theocen-

---

171 'The Cross and the Rainbow', 114; the discussion of distinctiveness continues on to 117. For critical comment on this notion of Mystery see JA DiNoia, 'Pluralist Theology of Religions', in *Christian Uniqueness Reconsidered*, especially 126-28; and Francis X Clooney, 'Reading the World in Christ', in *Christian Uniqueness Reconsidered*, 77.

172 Sebastian Athappilly answers the question of his paper 'Is Christian Revelation Theocentric or Christocentric?': "It is theo-centric in its Christocentrism. Precisely because it is theo-centric, it is Christo-centric. ... The Christo-centrism leads to theo-centrism and is led by it." (in *Emerging India and the Word of God*, 138.)

173 MM Thomas: "I am persuaded that Christocentrism is what relates God, church, and kingdom and keeps that relation inviolate" ('A Christ-Centered Humanist Approach to Other Religions in the Indian Pluralistic Context', 61).

174 As Gavin D'Costa concludes, "normative theocentrism must ... eventually rely on normative Christocentrism" (*Theology and Religious Pluralism. The Challenge of Other Religions* (Oxford, 1986) 36; see 29-36 for the argument).

175 Barnes, *Religions in Conversation*, 81.

trism appear unable to elaborate the actual content of the *theos* that it prefers to Christ for its normative centre: the religions simply do not provide an inclusive portrait of a divine centre or, in fact, of any definable centre at all.[176] And, as Lesslie Newbigin has asked of theocentrism: why should it be believed that an impersonal undefinable abstraction is a worthier and more accessible centre of the religious universe than a known person from recorded history?[177] (In some cases the possibility exists that an inability to specify the centre might, perhaps unwittingly, point to the agenda of the proponents as a covert centre.) (v) Some religious traditions reject the imagery of centrality that is at the heart of the theocentric model. As Athyal asks, presumably with Hinduism in mind, "What is theocentrism when the totality of all is in fact God and there is no question of a center? When God-consciousness is Self-consciousness, the concept of God becomes ... subjective."[178] (vi) It might also be argued that the theocentrists' pluralist view of religious truth-claims as complementary is an *a priori* judgement of them as necessarily partial. However, as D'Costa points out, such a denial of the status of the ultimate claims of a partner in dialogue is damag-

176 For a Zen critique that makes this point see Jung H Lee, 'Problems of Religious Pluralism: A Zen Critique of John Hick's Ontological Monomorphism', *PEW*, 48 (1998), 453-77. For examples from a Christian perspective see: Julius Lipner, 'Does Copernicus Help? Reflections for a Christian Theology of Religions', *RSt*, 13 (1977), 243-58; Duncan B Forrester, 'Professor Hick and the Universe of Faiths', *SJT*, 29 (1976), 65-72; Peter Byrne, 'John Hick's Philosophy of Religion', *SJT*, 35 (1982), 289-301; Newbigin, 'The Gospel Among the Religions', 184-91; Harold A Netland, 'Professor Hick on Religious Pluralism', *RSt*, 22 (1986), 249-61; Mark Heim, 'The Pilgrim Christ: Some Reflections on Theocentric Christology and Enculturation', in *Christian Faith and Multiform Culture in India*, edited by Somen Das (Bangalore, 1987), 102-27; Gavin D'Costa, *John Hick's Theology of Religions: A Critical Evaluation* (London, 1987); GH Carruthers, *The Uniqueness of Jesus Christ in the Theocentric Model of the Christian Theology of Religions: An Elaboration and Evaluation of the Position of John Hick* (Rome, 1988); David Lochhead, *The Dialogical Imperative: A Christian Reflection on Interfaith Encounter* (London and Maryknoll, NY: SCM Press and Orbis Books, 1988), chapter 15.

177 See, for example, his 'Religion for the Marketplace', in *Christian Uniqueness Reconsidered*, 135-48.

178 'A Theology of Mission in Relation to Hinduism', 247. He goes on to add that, "Because there is immense greatness and mystery in the Godhead, humankind needs a concrete and particular expression or self-revelation of him as in Jesus Christ. Otherwise we cannot have even an approximate notion of who he is." (247)

ing to the integrity of the dialogue. "The charges of triumphalism and arrogance may curiously rebound back upon the pluralists who direct these same charges at exclusivists".[179] (vii) Roger Trigg points out how Hick's discussion of pluralism remains at an epistemological level only and ignores ontological reference; "the emphasis is removed from a question about reality to one about our response to that reality."[180] (viii) A final aspect of theocentrism that is open to criticism is that it seems, as MM Thomas puts it, "in general to advocate accepting all religions on their own terms without discriminating between the spirits within them." By contrast, "Christ-centeredness ... provides a principle of spiritual discrimination." As opposed to abstract or universal principles that are "expressions of Western particularism and are less than universal ... Christ is a more transcendent universal ultimate."[181]

Moreover, the advocacy of theocentrism is a subset of a wider pluralist model for interreligious relations. Again, John Hick and Paul Knitter are among the most influential advocates of a prescriptive pluralist paradigm. Hick's understanding of religious pluralism has evolved over the years but a recent definition of what he calls "the pluralist hypothesis" is that religious pluralism is

> the idea that the great world religions are different human responses to the same ultimate transcendent reality. ... [T]he different world religions ... constitute different human responses to the ultimate transcendent reality to which they all, in their different ways, bear witness.[182]

The theocentric model is logically dependent upon such a pluralist model of the religions. A number of telling objections have been made of the pluralist model,[183] including a critique developed by Gavin D'Costa as 'The Impossibility of a Pluralist View of Religions'.[184] He argues that "pluralism must always logically be a form of exclusivism and that nothing called pluralism really exists."[185] This is because

---

179 D'Costa, *Theology and Religious Pluralism*, 38.

180 'Religion and the Threat of Relativism', *RSt*, 19 (1983), 301.

181 'A Christ-Centered Humanist Approach to Other Religions in the Indian Pluralistic Context', 57f.

182 John Hick, *The Fifth Dimension: an Exploration of the Spiritual Realm* (Oxford: Oneworld, 1999), 77. The most comprehensive elaboration by Hick of this understanding is in his *An Interpretation of Religion* (London: Macmillan, 1989).

183 See, for example, Newbigin, *The Gospel in a Pluralist Society*.

184 Gavin D'Costa in *Religious Studies*, 32 (1996), 223-32.

185 'The Impossibility of a Pluralist View of Religions', 225.

> all pluralists are committed to holding some form of truth criteria and by virtue of this, anything that falls foul of such criteria is excluded from counting as truth (in doctrine and in practice). Thus, pluralism operates within the same logical structure of exclusivism and in this respect pluralism can never really affirm the genuine autonomous value of religious pluralism for, like exclusivism, it can only do so by tradition specific criteria for truth.[186]

He then goes on to illustrate his assertion from both Hick and Knitter and arrives at the somewhat provocative conclusion that "usually those called pluralists are exclusivists without knowing it, they are ... anonymous exclusivists!"[187] In a further elaboration of his critique, D'Costa argues that, despite what he calls "its attractive and populist promises of openness, tolerance, and equality in its attitudes to other religions", Christian pluralism actually collapses into what he calls a tradition-specific form of exclusivism. Drawing on the thought of Alasdair MacIntyre, D'Costa defines Christian pluralism as a species of Enlightenment modernity[188]and

> central to the Enlightenment project is a fundamental epistemological and ontological rupture that denies the possibility of God's self-revelation in the historically particular.[189]

So, to return to christology: there are a number of distinctly positive reasons why discourse with Hindus is best framed in christological rather than theocentric or pluralist categories. (a) Christianity in India (and elsewhere) has always drawn attention to the unique and irreplaceable position occupied by Christ in Christian self-understanding. (b) Comment has already been made

---

186 'The Impossibility of a Pluralist View of Religions', 225f.

187 'The Impossibility of a Pluralist View of Religions', 232. D'Costa offers a slightly revised form of the argument against Hick (including a reply to Hick's response to his article in *Religious Studies*) in his *The Meeting of the Religions and the Trinity*, Faith Meets Faith series (Maryknoll, NY: Orbis, 2000), 19-30, 45-47; he also comments further on Knitter, 30-39. Some similar points are made, albeit less clearly, by KP Aleaz, 'Paul F Knitter's Proposal for Relational Uniqueness of Jesus,' *IJT*, 4 (1998), 49f. And, of course, there is considerable evidence – too extensive to document here – of an exclusivist undergirding of many of the strands of Hinduism which makes disappointing the attitude of those many western proponents of dialogue who tend to overstate the degree of acceptance of pluralism within Hinduism.

188 *The Meeting of the Religions and the Trinity*, chapter 1; citation from 'Introduction', 3.

189 *The Meeting of the Religions and the Trinity*, 38.

about the advantages of a concrete christological focus over the more abstract notions of 'God' or 'Spirit'. (c) It might also be argued that it is the person of Jesus that, more effectively than any other aspect of Christianity, enables the Christian 'word' to be enculturated and understood. This is because – to use a helpful metaphor of Mark Heim – "people cross the membranes between different cultures more effectively than ideas or concepts do"[190] and so to focus upon Christ is to help enable the determining measure of Christian belief (Christ) to take an appropriately central place in the discussion. (And, as will be argued in the next chapter, this focus upon Christ can and should be made in distinctly Indian categories.)

As well, a christological focus might be preferred given the importance for the Christian-Hindu encounter of what we have called secular dialogue. This is because the example of Christ seems better to enable a personal and practical focus in the quest for a just society than any basis grounded in the more abstract notion of theocentrism.[191] Even as the example of Gandhi might inspire Hindus (and Christians) and be offered by them as an example for such dialogue, so, as MM Thomas has repeatedly pointed out, the person of Christ inspired and sustained the renascent Hindu discovery of the importance of personhood and history.[192] For this reason, Thomas has insisted upon the continuing potential of a christocentric vision for what he calls "cultural renewal and the humanisation of the corporate structures of life in India".[193]

Further advantages of theocentrism are said to be its openness and tolerance (over against the supposed triumphalism and intolerance of an exclusivist christocentrism) and its epistemological and

---

190 S Mark Heim, 'The Pilgrim Christ: Some Reflections on Theocentric Christology and Enculturation', in *Christian Faith and Multiform Culture in India*, edited by Somen Das (Bangalore, 1987), 119; see also 123.

191 According to Mookenthottam, Christocentrism is "very relevant to the social and secular context of India" (*Indian Theological Tendencies*, 175) – by contrast with a theocentric approach.

192 See *The Acknowledged Christ of the Indian Renaissance* (for example, 56-98) and 'A Christ-centered Humanist Approach to Other Religions in the Indian Pluralistic Context'.

193 'A Christ-centered Humanist Approach to Other Religions in the Indian Pluralistic Context', 54f. A similar point is made in the Apostolic Exhortation *Ecclesia in Asia*, 14: "Contemplating Jesus in his human nature, the peoples of Asia find their deepest questions answered, their hopes fulfilled, their dignity uplifted and their despair conquered. Jesus is the Good News for the men and women of every time and place in their search for the meaning of existence and for the truth of their own humanity."

theological superiority. It is taken for granted by Samartha, for example, that any Christian exclusivism is morally deficient since it entails "condemning other peoples, cultures and religions to an inferior status, to be humiliated, dominated, exploited and conquered".[194] Now it is certainly true that some religious exclusivists have behaved in arrogant and abhorrent ways towards other believers – a phenomenon found not only in Christian history but, among Muslims, Sikhs, Hindus and Buddhists as well (both past, and present).[195] But to concede this point is not to imply that the notion of exclusivism necessarily implies arrogance and intolerance on the part of its advocates. As Harold Coward concludes: "Both Christian and Hindu scriptures are exclusivistic .... Yet in the heart of each scriptural exclusivism there exists a basis for tolerance and dialogue".[196] For a Christian to consider the beliefs or practices of a Hindu (or vice versa) to be wrong is not incompatible with treating that person with tolerant respect as, in fact, most conservative Indian Christians (and Hindus) do.[197] The contingent connections between belief in certain truths and the development of certain attitudes and behaviours is insufficient reason to reject the truths concerned. Sadhu Sundar Singh and AJ Appasamy combined a deeply christocentric faith, and evangelistic zeal, with a quite positive attitude towards Hinduism, including an extensive use of Hindu ter-

---

194 'Mission in a Religiously Plural World', 318.

195 See the examples cited by E Geoffrey Parrinder, *Comparative Religion* (London, 1976), chapter 3; and Harold Coward, 'Intolerance in the World's Religions', *SR/SR*, 15 (1986), 419-31. However, to the charge that claims of the uniqueness of Jesus generate division in pluralist cultures, Vinoth Ramachandra replies that "this is perfectly true, but it seems to be based on the assumption that social conflict must be avoided *at all cost*, an assumption that is itself part of a particular worldview that Jesus and his early disciples call into question" (*Faiths in Conflict? Christian Integrity in a Multicultural World* (Leicester: InterVarsity Press, 1999), 115).

196 'The Experience of Scripture in Hinduism and Christianity', 247.

197 Stanley Samartha appears to be wrong when he writes that "people who make open or hidden claims for exclusiveness find it almost impossible to live together with neighbours of other faiths except on very superficial social terms" ('Interreligious Relationships in the Secular State', *CD*, no. 11 (December 1986), 28). Nonetheless, intolerance and pride certainly can be, and have been, consequences of exclusivism, even as the claim to absolutism has led to an inflated claim to power: see, for example, Norbert Klaes, 'Absolutheitsanspruch und Universalität des christlichen Glaubens – Probleme der Kirche in Indien', *ZM*, 12 (1986), 22f and the comments of Schwöbel on the link between absoluteness and the demonic: 'Particularity, Universality, and the Religions', 40-42.

minology, as have more recent Indian Christian apologists (for example, Paul Sudhakar).

There is also criticism of the view of truth usually embraces by christocentrism (with its acceptance of the principle of noncontradiction) as epistemologically naive, or less plausible than what Knitter calls theocentrism's "new model of truth" as primarily relational, ongoing, complementary and pluralistic.[198] But such a model cannot hide the fact that religious truth-claims may, in fact, contradict rather than complement one another. This cannot be ignored if, as Netland argues, "even in religion, the price one must pay for rejecting the principle of noncontradiction is simply too high".[199] Such a view does assume the epistemological superiority of the principle of noncontradiction over other views of truth[200] – a position challenged by some Hindus and Indian Christians as well. Felix Wilfred, for example, calls for an epistemology that "tries to know, experience and realize reality in its entirety" – "an understanding by intuition" that prefers "wisdom" to the discursive thought and logical analysis received from the West that attempts to resolve contradictions in terms of truth and error; it allows contrary views to be accepted as complementary or as divergent aspects of a greater reality.[201] In India, complementarity and polarity and not opposition or contradiction are said to determine truth; there is no reason to be confused by "too many equally valid possibilities existing side by side. ... The unity of all unities and of all pluralities is

---

198 *No Other Name?*, 217-23. The same argument is advanced (with some reference to the Indian context) by John AT Robinson, *Truth is Two-Eyed* (London, 1979) and, of course, by many others.

199 Harold A Netland, 'Exclusivism, Tolerance and Truth', *Missiology*, 15.2 (April 1987), 84; see also his *Dissonant Voices: Religious Pluralism and the Question of Truth* (Grand Rapids: Eerdmans; Leicester: Apollos, 1991), chapter 4, especially 141-50. Concerning contradictory religious truth-claims, see: William A Christian, *Oppositions of Religious Doctrines: A Study in the Logic of Dialogue among Religions* (London, 1972), and for critical comment on the pluralist view of religious truth-claims (especially the view of Wilfred Cantwell Smith, but pertinent to our discussion) see: W Wainwright, 'Wilfred Cantwell Smith on Faith and Belief', *RSt*, 20 (1984), 357-67; and Hugo Meynell, 'The Idea of a World Theology', *Modern Theology*, 1 (1985), 149-63.

200 For a defence of the universal validity of the principle of noncontradiction see Andrew Kirk, *Loosing the Chains: Religion as Opium and Liberation* (London: Hodder & Stoughton, 1992), 58-62.

201 'Dialogue Gasping for Breath? Towards New Frontiers in Inter- Religious Dialogue', *Vidyajyoti*, 51 (1987), 461f.

metalogical; it stands above the logic of human reason".[202] But quite apart from such a problematical appeal to "metalogic",[203] the traditional Christian notion of truth has been tied to confidence in the truth of Christianity – so that other religious truth claims might be measured against it. For Stanley Samartha, *tarka* (logic) must be subordinated to *anubhava* (experience) because there is a truth greater than all formulations of truth;[204] because Mystery stands above mere reason and language, Hindus and Buddhists participate in the sacred word (scripture), "not through understanding it, but through reciting and hearing it."[205] The Indologist Francis Clooney responds that he is unable to find this attitude in Mimansa, Vedanta or Srivaishnavism, or the Upanishads, and wonders whether "Samartha is not talking about neo-Hindu, nineteenth- and twentieth-century reformulations of Hinduism, which rely on the same experientialist thrust that supports the Christian pluralists."[206] The debate over an appropriate epistemology will undoubtedly continue.

Several other theological issues also merit attention. The first concerns a cluster of words whose meaning(s) must be clarified if they are to continue to be used by the advocates of christocentrism. The words are such adjectives as 'unique', 'decisive' and 'normative' (each with exclusivist implications) and the meaning and appropriateness of their application to Christ. (A parallel consideration would be their application to Krishna.)

Felix Wilfred, for example, considers there to be various 'ways' to the one divine mystery and the way of Jesus is only one path – and it is neither unique nor normative for others. "The central importance of the [notion of] path makes it clear ... why the language of uniqueness is bound to be quite alien in the Indian experience and

202 Swami Vikrant, 'Obstacles to Dialogue', in *Lead Me to the Real: the Hindu-Christian Dialogue*, 38f. For an Indian Christian defence of 'objective truth' over against a pluralistic view, see Shilananda, 'The Objective-Subjective Tension', *IMR*, 8 (1986), 201-10.

203 See the denial by JE Lesslie Newbigin that there is any form of reasoning that is supra-cultural, thereby enabling a scrutiny of all the culturally conditioned forms of rationality from some viewpoint above them: 'Religious Pluralism and the Uniqueness of Jesus Christ', *IBMR*, 13 (1989), 50.

204 See 'Truth and the either/or mind-set' in his *One Christ – Many Religions*, 103-06.

205 'The Cross and the Rainbow', in *The Myth of Christian Uniqueness*, 78.

206 'Reading the Word in Christ', 77.

interpretation of Jesus Christ".[207] Several responses might be made to this *marga* christology. Karotemprel rejects it on the grounds that the uniqueness of Christ is embedded in the earliest witnesses to Christ and beyond that to the self-understanding of Jesus and the understanding of Jesus by his disciples (which can be respectfully contextualised in all cultures). *Marga* christology "is an individual and subjective christology"; it is an example of those recent Asian examples that "tend to dissociate christology from its historical and ontological roots".[208] Moreover, the advocates of christocentrism are not found claiming an exhaustive knowledge of God nor the complete absence of such knowledge in the religions and, fundamentalists excepted, are rarely found advocating the absoluteness of Christ;[209] rather, they argue that, despite historical contingency and the limitations of experience, certain claims about Christ are true. As Surin points out,

> no canons of logic are breached in asserting that God's work to defeat the power of evil reaches its completion in the events surrounding the life of one particular individual. It is entirely compatible with the position ... that God reveals himself to [others], in other times and in other places.[210]

Or, as one theological assessment of Samartha points out, given the biblical evidence for a divine-human encounter in Christ that has universal significance for all people, there are

> difficulties with Samartha's interpretation of Jesus Christ as normative and decisive *only for Christians*. We could ask ...

---

207 'Some Tentative Reflections on the Language of Christian Uniqueness: An Indian Perspective', *VJTR*, 57 (1993), 670. He spells out some implications of this viewpoint in his *Beyond Settled Foundations: the Journey of Indian Theology* (Madras, 1993), 190-97.

208 Karotemprel, 'Asian Christological Trends and Christian Mission', 60, 67.

209 As Samartha points out (when discussing the "transcendent centre" of faith, as he calls it): "Even while its meaning is revealed to us its mystery still remains beyond us" ('Interreligious Relationships in the Secular State', 27). For an attempt to defend the absoluteness of Christianity (meaning the absoluteness of the God revealed by Christ) and to evade the relativising pressures of historical contingency – by claiming absoluteness for the God of the eschatological Kingdom proclaimed by Jesus – see: Carl E Braaten, 'The Problem of the Absoluteness of Christianity', *Interpretation*, 40 (1986), 341-53.

210 Kenneth Surin, 'Revelation, Salvation, the Uniqueness of Christ and Other Religions', *RSt*, 19 (1983), 338. Newbigin argues in similar fashion in his 'Religious Pluralism and the Uniqueness of Jesus Christ'; compare John AT Robinson: "to believe that God is best defined by Christ is not to believe that God is confined to Christ" (*Truth is Two-Eyed*, 129).

> whether openness to plural responses to the Mystery of God cannot go together with the Christian claim that this Mystery is *decisively* disclosed in Jesus Christ. Samartha does not deny the uniqueness of Jesus Christ and his centrality for Christian faith; but why should it be only for Christians?[211]

The notion of the finality of Christ might be understood in such a way as not to exclude progress and growth in understanding both that and other instances of divine revelation.[212] It is probably only a minority of the exclusivists (whether Christian or Hindu) who would argue that the normative (or decisive or definitive) revelation and salvation they claim to experience in Christ or Krishna (say) precludes any other event in history bearing revelatory or salvific significance – even if Christ, or Krishna, is the criterion by which such significance is known and evaluated (thereby limiting the degree of acceptance). Or, more precisely, in the Christian case it would be what D'Costa calls, "a complex and somewhat paradoxical process of discovering, while utilising the Christological criterion [that] takes place in dialogue".[213] A qualified christocentrism also denies the pluralists' claim that God's action can be recognised everywhere without the criterion of a normative event. Moreover, the very logic of such an assertion – whether it has Christ or Krishna in mind – implies the opposite of triumphalism; since it is divine initiative in revelation and salvation there is no room for human pride.

However, the use of adjectives implying uniqueness and normativity becomes especially difficult when they are employed in a universal or prescriptive sense to press their application upon those beyond the community in which they have originated (and for whom few would want to dispute their decisive importance). Christ might well be declared unique and normative for Christians (or Krishna for Hindus); but is that uniqueness and decisiveness to be pressed upon and declared to all – with or without the implication that other revelations are in some way deficient apart from what the new message brings? Is it possible, for example, for Christians plausibly and coherently to assert the uniqueness and universal significance of the Christ-event while at the same time accepting the

---

211 Klootwijk, *Commitment and Openness*, 269 (original emphasis).

212 See DG Moses, *Religious Truth and the Relation between Religions* (Madras, 1950), 116f.

213 *Theology and Religious Pluralism*, 133; D'Costa himself attempts the application of such a christological criterion (123f, 131-36). Arnulf Camps also attempts the exercise at some length; see his *Partners in Dialogue. Christianity and Other World Religions* (Maryknoll, NY, 1983), chapters 6-13.

uniqueness and even universal significance of some or even much (or all) of the Hindu *dharma*? And, if so, what are the critical principles by which such unique and universal claims are to be evaluated? This remains a crucial issue for the christocentrist position, however much qualified.[214]

One solution would be to argue, with Lochhead, that no statement about Jesus, however high its christological content, is a statement about Hindus (or others) *unless* it is tied to additional (ideologically motivated) premises of isolation from, hostility towards or competition with Hindus.[215] The alternative (at least for Christians) may be to formulate a theology of the religions in which the revelation of God in Christ is not the only religious way in which God is revealed;[216] or, in John Robinson's words, to acknowledge that "the light that enlightens" every person, "in no way cancels but on the contrary crowns the revelation in and through the multiplicity of lights. The unique does not absorb or exclude the many".[217] But such an approach, despite its generosity, remains a form of inclusive christocentrism.

A second theological issue is whether the judgement can in fact be sustained that christology should be determinative in the evaluation of inter-religious relationships, including Hindu-Christian dialogue (as christocentrism requires) – or whether that place should be given to more accommodating and inclusive starting points such as the Spirit (noting the hesitations mentioned above) or to the ideal of the Kingdom of God. The notion of the Kingdom might, in fact, offer considerable scope for development as the

---

214 The fact that such supposedly unique or universally decisive actions have an original cultural location – used as an argument against exclusivism since an ethnocultural bias is thereby said to be shown – is inevitable and does not constitute ground upon which, *a priori*, the truth claims of the exclusivist can be dismissed.

215 *The Dialogical Imperative*, 90f; chapters 1-3 (5-22) discuss the ideologies of isolation, hostility and competition. A further noteworthy feature of Lochhead's discussion is his development of a theology of interreligious dialogue on the basis of insights from the (decidedly christocentric) theology of Karl Barth; in particular, he argues that Barth's theology is not closed to dialogue but is, in principle, open to and affirming of any dialogue with the world.

216 See, for example, Michael Amaladoss, 'The Pluralism of Religions and the Significance of Christ', *Vidyajyoti*, 53 (1989), 401-20.

217 *Truth is Two-Eyed*, 99. But Robinson also goes on to make the point that uniqueness can appear to make Christ an anomalous exception "without continuity with or relevance for the rest of history and mankind" (101).

"main focus" of all Christian activity.[218] A focus upon the Kingdom seems to include the central concern of the theocentrists; there is a strong link with the ministry of Jesus; and a clear link with dialogue:

> Nothing, perhaps, can provide ... dialogue with a stronger motive than the sincere realisation that, differences notwithstanding, the followers of the various religious traditions, as co-members of God's Kingdom in history, are fellow-travellers en route towards the fullness of the Kingdom.[219]

In the particular case of christocentrism, not only can its epistemology be defended, it may also embrace a more balanced (even if less congenial) view of the biblical position(s) than the theocentric alternative.[220] It is also important to note that the usual Christian assertion of salvation in Christ as primarily a matter of divine initiative (especially if contrasted with what a Hindu academic describes as the usual Hindu view of redemption as "a matter of attainment through moral actions")[221] has, not unnaturally, acted as an incentive towards Christocentrism.[222]

There are, then, those who continue to argue for belief in the older view of the uniqueness of the person and activity of Christ – the unique *Avatara* because of the resurrection, as Irudayaraj argues

218 See Michael Amaladoss, 'Evangelisation in Asia: a New Focus?', *Vidyajyoti*, 51 (1987), 17f; and see above, chapter 4.C.2.

219 Jacques Dupuis, 'The Kingdom of God and World Religions', *Vidyajyoti*, 51 (1987), 534; the whole article (530-44) is relevant.

220 See Chris Wright, *Thinking Clearly about the Uniqueness of Jesus* (Crowborough, UK: Monarch, 1997), 107-39. For a more inclusive view of the biblical material see: Peggy Starkey, 'Biblical Faith and the Challenge of Religious Pluralism', *IRM*, 71 (1982), 66-77.

221 Santosh Sengupta, 'The Misunderstanding of Hinduism', in *Truth and Dialogue*, edited by John Hick (London, 1974), 106 (though it must be added that there are important theistic strands in Hinduism that also see salvation as a divine initiative).

222 The divergent views of salvation are of note in view of Knitter's revision of theocentrism towards a supposed common centre of 'salvation', by which he means "a shared concern about and effort to remove the sufferings that rack the human family today" ('Theocentric Christology: Defended and Transcended', *JES*, 24 (1987), 47.

with careful reference to the Indian context[223] and in the christocentrism the view implies. From such a viewpoint, the coming of Christ can be viewed as God's means of dealing with the relativising limitations of the historical, with this constituting a universal truth for all religions (alongside universal truths also to be found in them). The christology outlined above implies a rejection of the theocentric model with its apparently diminished christology.[224] In such a model Christ might well seem, at least to Hindu eyes, to be "only an avatar, a manifestation, like which there can be many";[225]or to a Christian to be "reduced to one among many saviours and indicators of the path of salvation."[226] But it is a distinctly qualified christocentrism for a number of reasons.

- If the christocentrism outlined and defended above were to be fitted into a wider trinitarian framework – perhaps along the lines of what D'Costa calls trinitarian christology[227](and including the kind

---

223 See his 'An Attempt at an Indian Christology', 15-19. But it must also be pointed out that the resurrection narratives of the New Testament contain little of the element of proof that a normative christology such as Irudayaraj's wants to make of them. It is also pertinent to note that the resurrection story is treated with scepticism or indifference by many Hindus – as Christians often observe: see, for example, Balwant AM Paradkar, 'Hindu Interpretations of Christ from Vivekananda to Radhakrishnan', *IJT*, 18 (1969), 77.

224 See for example: Surin, 'Revelation, Salvation, the Uniqueness of Christ and Other Religions', 323-43; Julius Lipner, 'Christians and the Uniqueness of Christ', *SJT*, 28 (1975), 359-68; S Mark Heim, *Is Christ the Only Way: Christian Faith in a Pluralistic World* (Valley Forge, PA, 1986), and 'Thinking about Theocentric Christology', *JES*, 24 (1987), 1-16.

225 Amaladoss, 'Dialogue and Mission', 77. In a similar context Newbigin asserts: "The Hindu can speak of many *avatars*, because none of them is part of public history" ('Religious Pluralism and the Uniqueness of Jesus Christ', 52).

226 Karotemprel, 'Asian Christological Trends and Christian Mission', 70.

227 See his 'Christ, the Trinity and Religious Pluralism,' in *Christian Uniqueness Reconsidered*, 16-29. See also his *The Meeting of the Religions and the Trinity*, part II; in the latter volume D'Costa goes so far as to claim that "Trinitarian exclusivism can acknowledge God's actions within other traditions, without domesticating or obliterating their alterity, such that real conversation and engagement might occur" (47). See also, JE Lesslie Newbigin, *The Open Secret*, ch 3, 'The Mission of the Triune God'; and the essays in *The Trinity in a Pluralistic Age: Theological Essays on Culture and Religion*, edited by Kevin J Vanhoozer (Grand Rapids: Eerdmans, 1997). Robert Jenson argues that one of the reason for a Christian elaboration of God in trinitarian terms is to ensure that the identity of this God is not confused with rival claimants to the title 'God' (see his *The Triune Identity* (Philadelphia:

of pneumatological insights generated by Kuttianimattathil[228]) it would help guard against christomonism. A trinitarian perspective has some perhaps unexpected consequences for those who only see uniqueness in terms of exclusivist and christomonistic categories as do the implications of pneumatology[229] for an enhanced theological understanding of the religions.

- There is the question of the *most appropriate* word or set of words to use in defining and defending christocentrism and the traditionally related notion of uniqueness. A consideration might be given to the following terms in order to best describe what Christians mean to assert of Christ: unique as singular; distinctive; original; particular; absolute; unsurpassable; exclusive; superior; decisive; normative; unique; final.[230]
- The adjective 'exclusive' is also often found in the discussion and requires revision. It is an essentially negative term with which even conservative Christians are becoming increasingly dissatisfied. One immediate advantage of the word christocentrism (especially in a pluralist setting) is its positive tone. As with Van Engen's suggestion of 'evangelism' in place of the usual threefold paradigm.[231] The term 'christocentrism' strongly reflects the cen-

---

Fortress Press, 1982), 1-20). For a more inclusivist perspective see Dupuis, *Toward a Christian Theology of Religious Pluralism*, 220-23, 242-44, 262-68.

228 Jose Kuttianimattathil, 'The Holy Spirit and World Religions: the Meaning of God's Revelation', *VJTR*, 63 (1999), 255-66 and 339-50.

229 See, for example, Amos Yong, 'The Turn to Pneumatology in Christian Theology of Religions: Conduit or Detour?', *JES*, 35 (1998), 437-454; '"Not Knowing Where the Wind Blows...": On Envisioning a Pentecostal-Charismatic Theology of Religions', *Journal of Pentecostal Studies*, 14 (1999), 81-112.

230 For a discussion of this issue, see Bob Robinson, 'What Exactly is Meant by the "Uniqueness of Christ"? – An Examination of the Phrase and Other Suggested Alternatives in the Context of Religious Pluralism'; Part one: *Evangelical Review of Theology*, 25 (2001), 362-71; Part two: *Evangelical Review of Theology*, 26 (2002), 76-90.

231 In an attempt to break what he sees as an unsatisfactory impasse between advocates of the usual threefold paradigm (exclusivism, inclusivism and pluralism), Van Engen proposes a fourth perspective, that of 'evangelism'. Van Engen uses this perspective because he wants as a starting point the evangel – by which he means the confession that "Jesus is Lord" – and not any preoccupation with who is 'in' and 'out' of the kingdom. He also believes that this approach incorporates the positive elements of the old paradigm. (Charles Van Engen, 'The Uniqueness of Christ in Mission Theology' in his *Mission on the Way: Issues in Mission Theology* (Grand Rapids: Baker, 1996), especially 176-87.)

tral affirmations of the Christian faith – and for that reason is decidedly more appropriate than the term 'exclusivism'.

- For the Christian partner in dialogue, a qualified christocentrism might well be expressed in terms of four adverbs in order to underline the dynamic nature of dialogue as a relationship, and to emphasise that orthopraxis does (or should) matter to the Christian as much as orthodoxy. If it is claimed, a qualified christocentrism might best be advocated in the following ways.

  (i) *Humbly* – because its advocates do not, and dare not (because of the limited and finite condition of all human knowledge) claim an exhaustive or absolute knowledge of the divine way, even the one they have chosen, or feel has been chosen for them.[232] A problem with absolutist language about Christ is the pretentiousness of any claim framed in human language to have grasped the absolute. In other words, absolutist language suggests what Miroslav Volf, in a paper on 'The Unique Christ in the Challenge of Modernity', calls "modern epistemological absolutism"; in its place he argues for what he calls "provisional certitude as an authentic Christian way".[233] The employment of a kenotic christology might be one way of preserving a non-triumphalistic traditional understanding of incarnation.[234]

  (ii) *Patiently* – because of the vast problem of understanding and communicating between dialogue partners who find common ground between committed positions desperately hard to find at times.[235]

  (iii) *Modestly* – because even the christocentrist should realise that the divine mystery is inexhaustible and that the very certainty of revelation can induce a corresponding clarity, as it were,

232 As Newbigin observes, the fact that the Cross is at the heart of Christian proclamation dramatically relativises every Christian claim to embody the truth of God ('Religion for the Marketplace', in *Christian Uniqueness Reconsidered*, 145f).

233 In *The Unique Christ in Our Pluralist World*, edited by Bruce J Nicholls (Carlisle and Grand Rapids, MI: Paternoster Press and Baker Books for the World Evangelical Fellowship, 1995), 101-04.

234 See the suggestions in David Hadley Jensen, 'The Emptying Christ. A Christological Approach to Interfaith Dialogue', *SID*, 11 (2001), 5-24.

235 It may even be true that "the incommensurability of ultimate systems is unbridgeable" (Ans J Van der Bent, 'Seventeen Promises for Entering in the Dialogue with People of Living Faiths and Practising Religious Pluralism', *CD*, no. 15 (December 1988), 35).

about how much remains unknown; an example is the way in which the task of christological enquiry and understanding is never completed.[236] And, to connect particularity with the traditional Christian claim to universality, the christocentrist will also concede that there are likely to be many ways by which Christ is the only way.

(iv) *Charitably* – for the possibilities of triumphalism and arrogance (because of imagined superiority) remain.

However, christocentrism does remain a *Christian* perspective because of the conviction that, at least for Christians, the Christ-event to some extent stands critically above all religious commitments, whatever their supposed reference or validating point. Further, if the uniqueness and decisiveness of Christ are seen as part of the essential content and distinctiveness of the New Testament and the Christian tradition, then it could be argued that to abandon this christology for the sake of dialogue would violate Christian self-understanding and integrity[237] (and diminish the commitment, mission and service that are offered in the name and spirit of Christ). Moreover, it could also be argued that these claims do not necessarily exclude God's certain revelation, both present and universal, alongside the first century revelation in Christ.

236 Given the obvious constraints of language and culture, there might well be agreement with the statement that there are "inherent limitations to God's self-communication through Jesus Christ" ('Towards an Indian Christian Theology of Religious Pluralism', no. 19).

237 As Monika K Hellwig observes about the traditional Christian claim about Christ, this claim "has become the heart and core of our faith, life, action in the world, and worship. We cannot abandon it without abandoning our faith and tradition" ('Christology in the Wider Ecumenism', in *Christian Uniqueness Reconsidered*, 116).

CHAPTER 6

Towards an Indian Christological Basis for Dialogue

A. Introduction

This chapter asks: is it possible to justify and sustain commitment to Christian-Hindu dialogue on the basis of a christology formulated in distinctly Indian categories? Such inculturation is given as one reason for dialogue (see chapter 3.H above) and is a part of a long-standing and ubiquitous quest among Christians to make the Gospel intelligible in a given religio-cultural context.[1] If it is true, as a Hindu observer of the Hindu-Christian encounter asserts, that "Jesus Christ is an ineradicable part of modern Hinduism. The power of [the] Cross is felt in the lives of many Hindus in different walks of life. Hindus adore Christ"[2] – then it is not unexpected that Christians might attempt to use a christological base as one means of elaborating the encounter. At the same time, a number of aspects of Indian thought might also contribute or commend, both to Hindus and Christians, a view of Christ in distinctly Indian categories – or, at least, a christology or christologies with an enhanced degree of intelligibility to or compatibility with the Hindu world-view(s). Aspects of such a christology have certainly begun to emerge from the Christian-Hindu encounter itself – though there is

1 The Apostolic Exhortation *Ecclesia in Asia* points out that Asian Catholic Bishops in their 1999 Synod "stressed many times the need to evangelize in a way that appeals to the sensibilities of Asian peoples, and they suggested images of Jesus which would be intelligible to Asian minds and cultures and, at the same time, faithful to Sacred Scripture and Tradition. Among them were 'Jesus Christ as the Teacher of Wisdom, the Healer, the Liberator, the Spiritual Guide, the Enlightened One, the Compassionate Friend of the Poor, the Good Samaritan, the Good Shepherd, the Obedient One'." (20; quoting from Proposition 6 of the official list of propositions sent by the Synod to Pope John Paul II.)

2 KL Seshagiri Rao, 'Hindu-Christian Dialogue: A Hindu Perspective', *HCSB*, 14 (2001), 10.

not space to consider every possible image or analogy or parallel.[3]

One pertinent issue in approaching this task is to note the power and place of metaphor in discourse. It is a commonplace observation of recent literary theory that words, images and metaphors are not merely additions to thought they are the actual means of thought and are partly constitutive of understanding.[4] The power of metaphor lies partly in its invitation to the reader or listener to seek meaning in one direction – but not another. However, the force of metaphor is not easily contained. It cannot be constrained into narrow and predictable paths of meaning; there is always, in Paul Ricoeur's phrase, a "surplus of meaning".[5] Once launched into the world of the hearer and reader a metaphor cannot be recalled and tamed. This is one reason why both Christians and Hindus ought to choose carefully from the range of possible metaphors and images for the positions they wish to adopt; once launched – especially into a pluralist setting – they acquire a force and meaning beyond what might have been intended. In India, Christians seem often to underestimate the negative impact of traditional Christian language, not least the traditional metaphors of uniqueness. In a helpful reflection on his many years of enabling Christian dialogue with Hindus, Albert Nambiaparambil urges Christians to understand and anticipate the impact of language they might consider to be descriptive (for example, Jesus as 'Lord', 'Saviour', 'the Son of God').[6] The problems, he writes, are liable to be acute when Christians use the language of uniqueness with a dialogue partner whose worldview makes difficult an understanding or acceptance of notions of uniqueness. And he asks, "am I as a Christian disposed to grasp the offence that our Hindu ... friends may take who hear my faith-assertion as totalitarian, monopolistic, exclusive, possessive and isolationist?" The solution is not Christian silence but more thoughtful consideration of how the Christian position is commu-

3 For example, Christ as eternal *Om* (perhaps equivalent to *Logos*), or *Prajapati* (Lord of all creatures), or *Shakti* (strength or power), or *Yogi* or *Adi Purusha* (the first person), or *Jivanmukta* (one liberated while still living), or the embodiment of *dharma*, or the appeal of the Jesus of the Beatitudes – all of which have been considered either by Christian or Hindu writers.

4 See, for example, George Lakoff and Mark Johnson, *Metaphors We Live By* (Chicago, IL: University of Chicago Press, 1980).

5 See Paul Ricoeur, *Interpretation Theory: Discourse and the Surplus of Meaning* (Fort Worth, TX: Texas Christian University Press, 1976).

6 He is writing of his time as Secretary to the Inter-Religious Dialogue Commission of the Catholic Bishops' Conference of India in 'Evangelization and Inter-Religious Dialogue', *IMR*, 17.2 (June 1995), 76f.

nicated.[7] For this reason the search for less offensive language may well begin with the quest for distinctly Indian alternatives. This may not remove all possibilities of misunderstanding but it may well help remove at least some 'surplus meaning' from the way in which they are received.

In what follows an attempt is made to employ what Lipner calls a "methodologically informed comparative reflection between traditions" with particular attention to context and relative priority. In other words to ask, "In the contextualised comparative process do the elements being compared share a comparable priority-status"; in other words, is the concept "in the Hindu tradition given the same or similar importance thematically as … in Christianity?"[8] For example, does Krishna perform the same kind of function as *guru* (or *avatara*) as Christ does as teacher-master (or incarnation of God) within the Christian tradition? To use the metaphor of religion as language, does the same (or a similar) *grammar* operate despite obvious and even incompatible vocabularies? The answer is that it does appear that a number of dyads are to be found (such as 'teacher-master' and '*guru*', or 'incarnation' and '*avatara*' and that these are amenable to discussion between Christians and Hindus in language that is genuinely analogical and even univocal.

B. Christ as *Guru*

One Hindu concept with potential for providing at least part of a christological basis for dialogue is that of the *guru* ([religious] teacher-guide-master) – in particular the ideals of the *guru* as apprehended in relationship by a *sisya* (disciple), and the *guru* as the

7 'Evangelization and Inter-Religious Dialogue', 77. (He goes on to urge the avoidance of comparative language that implies the superiority of the Christian position; his advice to Christians is let Christ remain absolute while using the less-threatening language of witness to explain what Christ and the church mean to them.)

8 Julius J Lipner, 'Avatara and Incarnation?', in *Re-visioning India's Religious Traditions*, 129.

embodiment of the divine.[9] The notion of the *guru* is part of a long south Asian tradition in which, as Staal puts it, "what counts ... are ancestors and teachers – hence lineages, traditions, affiliations, cults, eligibility, and initiation."[10] Within the Indian Christian community it is not uncommon to find Christian self-identity defined in terms of the Christian as a disciple of Jesus. A number of Indian converts to Christianity speak of the appeal of Jesus (his personality, example and teaching) and their response to his perceived calls to discipleship. From the time of de Nobili it has often been thought both desirable and possible to "sketch a certain pattern of relationship between Jesus and his disciples which India would recognize as that of the *guru*".[11] Another writer, having discussed the terms 'Rabbi', 'Master' and 'Teacher', considers that had the Biblical writers "been writing for [an] ... Indian audience, they would have certainly used the term 'guru'."[12] The commendation of Christ to

9 For a sympathetic Christian account of the Hindu background, see Moti Lal Pandit, 'The Historico-Religious Development of the Concept of Guru', *ITS*, 27 (1990), 273-97; also useful is Vishal Mangalwadi, *The World of Gurus: A Critical Look at the Philosophies of India's Influential Gurus and Mystics*, revised edition (Wheaton, IL: Cornerstone Books, 1992). For a recent discussion of the development of the notion of *guru* in Hinduism, see Suzanne E Stillman, 'Revisioning the Guru: From Vedic Poet-Seer to Bhakti Poet-Saint', paper read to the American Academy of Religion Annual Meeting, Denver, Colorado, 19 November 2001.

10 Fritz Staal, *Rules without Meaning: Ritual Mantra and the Human Sciences* (New York: Peter Lang, 1993), 393.

11 JC Hindley, 'The Jesus of History', in *Indian Voices in Today's Theological Debate*, edited by Horst Bürkle and WMW Roth (Et: Lucknow, 1972), 28. Brahmabandhab makes a similar point in his 'Christ's Claim to Attention', *The Twentieth Century* (1901; reprinted in Kaj Baagø, *Pioneers of Indigenous Christianity* (Madras, 1969), 141-46). For two very sympathetic accounts of contemporary guruism and Christian learning from Hindu *gurus*, see Abhishiktananda, 'A Sage from the East' in *Guru and Disciple* (Et: London, 1974), 1-127; and Vandana, *Gurus, Ashrams and Christians* (Indian edition: Madras, 1980), especially chapter 2; for a reminder that the concept has not met with universal approval, see Catherine Cornille, *The Guru in Indian Catholicism: Ambiguity or Opportunity of Inculturation?* (Louvain: Peters, and Grand Rapids, MI: Eerdmans, 1991). Also interesting is a study from Indonesia – whose culture has been also influenced by Hinduism – is JB Banawiratma, 'Jesus as Guru: a Christology in the Context of Java (Indonesia)', *Exchange*, 8 (1984), 33-57.

12 James Massey, 'The Concept of Guruship in the New Testament', in *The Concept of a Guru in Indian Religions*, edited by Clarence O McMullen (Delhi, 1982) 33; he believes that the New Testament holds the full idea of

Hindus as *Sad-guru* (true teacher or teacher of truth) might be delineated in terms of the necessity of practising spiritual disciplines such as *bhakti*, prayer, service and communal living.[13]

In the Christian tradition Christ is, of course, understood as much more than what is usually implied by the notion of *guru*. For example, it would be difficult for most Christians to set Christ as simply one *guru* alongside many other mediators of realisation. Nonetheless, in some Hindu traditions a saviour figure does appear as a *guru*. In the Saiva Siddhanta tradition, Siva, although immaterial and transcendent, comes as a *guru* in order to instruct and save humanity; this was the reason for de Nobili's presentation of Jesus as the divine, immanent *guru* in which he thus identifies Jesus with "the most important local image of God".[14] Vaisnavism also has a tradition of unshakeable trust in a *guru* whose teaching and initiation lead to enlightenment, not to mention Tantrism in which submission to a *guru* is absolutely necessary. It is not unusual to hear Hindus (from a wide range of traditions) assert that true knowledge is impossible without a *guru*.

Moreover, it is axiomatic in Indian thought that *gurus* teach because of their personal experience; part of their authority derives from the divine origin of their experience. In fact, in India, the *guru* "came to be seen as an embodiment of the divine whose primary purpose was to lead the devotee towards union with a personal God."[15] So Christian *sisyas* might consider themselves to have responded to one whose authority derives from the claim to a filial experience that can mediate a unique knowledge of such a personal God as Father (along the lines of the claims in, for example,

---

Guruship (38). Frank Whaling notes the use of parables and stories by Jesus and Hindu *gurus* (*An Approach to Dialogue with Hinduism* (Lucknow, 1966), 84). A similar conclusion is reached by Xavier Irudayaraj, 'Guru as the Revealer in Indian Religious Tradition', in *Emerging India and the Word of God*, 232-38. See also: David T Abalos, 'The Teacher as Guide', *JD*, 11 (1986), 62-75. For a survey of some New Testament titles of Jesus and the search for Indian equivalents, see: Mathew V Kuzhuvelil, 'Jesus Christ the Sanatana', *Jeevadhara*, 27 (1997), 336-47.

13 See part 2 of George David, *Communicating Christ among Hindus* (Chennai: CBMTM Publications, 1998).

14 Francis X Clooney, 'Christ as the Divine Guru in the Theology of Roberto de Nobili', in *One Faith Many Cultures*, Boston Theological Institute Annual Series, volume 2, edited by Roy O Costa (Maryknoll, NY and Cambridge, MA, 1988), 29. See also (on de Nobili's use of the *guru* concept): Antony Mookenthottam, *Towards a Theology in the Indian Context* (Bangalore, 1980), 27f.

15 Stillman, 'Revisioning the Guru', 12.

Matthew 11.25-30) – to Hindu as well as to Christian.[16] And from the Hindu experience of discipleship the Christian might also learn. From a survey of five contemporary Indian gurus and their *sisyas*, Sham Rao draws attention to certain elements of discipleship which he feels are unnecessarily absent from the Indian Church: for example, a deep personal relationship with and even dependence upon a concrete and tangible object of veneration – the *guru*.[17] The form and intensity of veneration varies; some, for example, like Satya Sai Baba, are addressed and praised (whether or not they are physically present) in *bhajans* in which use is made of an extensive range of divine attributes and names.

The notion of the Christian *guru* is by no means absent from the Indian church. Sadhu Sundar Singh is the most notable example from the past and others have been and are found as *acaryas* ([spiritual] teachers/preceptors)[18] at Christian ashrams. An there is a growing number of Christian *'gurus'* – even if they do not assume the title, at least voluntarily – mostly of pentecostal origins, who function in a way analogous to their Hindu counterparts.[19] There are even calls for catholic priests and protestant pastors to assume the role of *guru*[20]- and some *acarayas* and spiritual directors embrace some aspects of the role.

There remain, however, a number of significant differences between the attributes usually ascribed to the *guru* and those usu-

16 It is such a claim that leads to the Indian Christian designation of Christ as *Jagad-guru* (Universal Guru), or *Sad-guru* (True Guru): on *Jagad-guru* see, for example: Manickam, 'Anubhava as Pramana of an Indian Christology', *Jeevadhara*, 1 (1971), 238; on *Sad-guru* see, for example: Abhishiktananda, *Saccidananda*, revised edition (Delhi, 1974), 202.

17 DP Sham Rao, *Five Contemporary Gurus in the Shirdi (Sai Baba) Tradition* (Madras, 1972), 45f; also: Xavier Irudayaraj, 'Christ – the Guru', *Jeevadhara*, 2 (1972), 241-49; and his 'The Guru in Hinduism and Christianity', *Vidyajyoti*, 39 (1975), 338-51.

18 The literature on the Hindu tradition generally assigns the same meaning to *acarya* as to *guru*.

19 See the study of some twenty popular South Indian Christian *guru* figures of the 1970s as discussed in Werner Hoerschelmann, *"Christian Gurus": A Study of the Life and Work of Christian Charismatic Leaders in South India* (Et: Chennai: Gurukul Lutheran Theological College and Research Institute, 1998). There are also some pertinent comments in Corinne G Dempsey, *Kerala Christian Sainthood: Collisions of Culture and Worldview in South India* (Oxford and New York, NY: Oxford University Press, 2000).

20 Frank Whaling asks: "Can we doubt that the Indian Church would be stronger ... if her pastors had been trained to be Christian *gurus* rather than Christian organisers?" (*An Approach to Dialogue with Hinduism*, 83).

ally assigned to Christ. (i) The cosmic functions assigned to Christ in high christology are not usually ascribed to the Hindu *guru* – though there are some exceptions (for example, Sai Baba[21]) and many *gurus* do assume somewhat regal status.[22] (ii) The *guru* is a living person, present to the five senses, whereas to speak of Christ as alive is usually to speak of him as mediated by other than direct tangible encounter. (iii) Irudayaraj offers as a "christological corrective" to the usual Indian model the fact that, as he puts it, "the pedagogy of Jesus is one of loving invitation and gentle persuasion. It is not based on any extraneous authority but [on] Jesus' own identification with those whom he taught."[23] (iv) Irudayaraj also points out that Jesus offers the model of a crucified *guru*. The notion of a suffering divine *guru* is certainly present in Saivite mythology but absent from Saiva Siddhanta philosophy.[24] He writes "this vision of a crucified guru can clear the concept of guru from its oppressive undertones."[25] Thomas Thangaraj takes up the same theme in his *The Crucified Guru*.[26] He points out that, in the New Testament and the Christian tradition, the dominant place is not given to a picture of a teacher-guru "but the victim-guru, the dying guru, the crucified guru who appears as the guru par excellence."[27] Thangaraj goes on to acknowledge the considerable difficulty of speaking, in an Indian context, of a person with divine power being crucified by ignorant humans and asks whether a Hindu can comprehend a crucified

---

21 Sai Baba is said by his followers to be able to materialise objects and substances, to appear to followers in dreams and visions and even to affect weather patterns.

22 For a rather unsympathetic comment see Nirad C Chaudhuri, *Hinduism: A Religion to Live By* (London: Chatto and Windus, 1979), 303-06.

23 'Guru as the Revealer in Indian Religious Tradition', 236.

24 'Guru as the Revealer in Indian Religious Tradition', 237.

25 'Guru as the Revealer in Indian Religious Tradition', 236. Presumably he has in mind example of coercive and manipulative *gurus* (a phenomenon not without parallels in the Christian tradition). Moti Lal Pandit offers a more explicit warning about such *guru-yogis* in his 'The Spirituality of a Yogi', *DD*, (December 1998), 13f. Julius Lipner makes a related point about the traditional virtue of subservience on the part of the disciple in contrast with "a servility expected and a servility willingly offered" generally in contemporary Hinduism (*Hindus: Their Religious Beliefs and Practices* (London and New York: Routledge, 1994), 94, 191).

26 Subtitle: *An Experiment in Cross-cultural Christology* (Nashville, TN: Abingdon Press, 1994). Thangaraj attempts to use the concept of *guru* from the Saiva Siddhanta tradition.

27 *The Crucified Guru*, 101.

Guru any more than a Jew can comprehend a crucified Messiah.[28] One strength of Thangaraj's study is its functionalist implications: the continuing significance of Jesus is his ability to transform his disciples into a faith community in which Jesus the *guru* will function as God to the disciples.[29] More controversial is his unwillingness to attribute any of the significance of Jesus the *guru* to his person as understood in ontological categories. For Thangaraj,

> Jesus will have to be seen as one of the gurus and not the one and only guru. ... However decisive Jesus may be in the religious quest of his disciples, he is not to be seen as the one and only guru for the whole of humankind. ... The difference between Jesus and other gurus is not in kind or in degree but in pragmatic value.[30]

However, these latter comments do read oddly in the light of an earlier statement by Thangaraj concerning God's "raising Jesus from the dead and appointing him guru for all,"[31] not least because the contextualised specificity of the *guru* (part of the *guru*'s appeal according to Thangaraj) is undermined by the requirement that he be seen as *guru* "for all". And one difficulty with his proposal that christology be understood in pragmatic terms is that he construes functionalist and ontological categories as alternatives. For many Indian Christians, a functionalist christology is not a total christology because function follows substance: Jesus enables transformation because of who he *is* – and this includes his transforming role as *Guru*.[32]

Nonetheless, within the limits acknowledged above, the category of *guru*, especially as perceived by a *sisya*, may add or revive a fruitful dimension to the quest for an Indian christological basis for dialogue. In the face of the usual Hindu perception of Christianity as a cerebral religion, lacking the interiority and direct religious experience into which a *guru* initiates his *sisya*, the Christian affirmation of *gurus* might well act as a partial corrective and facilitate increased trust and dialogue.[33] It is not uncommon to find Hindus attracted by

---

28 He devotes chapter 5 of his work to some of the problematical aspects of the christological employment of the *guru* category – but the chapter is a short one.

29 *The Crucified Guru*, 121.

30 *The Crucified Guru*, 124f.

31 *The Crucified Guru*, 103.

32 Discussion will return to the issue of metaphysics towards the end of this chapter.

33 "[I]t is distinctive of the guru to be able to communicate inner peace and spiritual teaching to the disciple in a way appropriate to the latter's particular circumstances" (Lipner, *Hindus*, 193).

Jesus as an embodiment of the ideal of the wandering *samnyasi,*[34] "fired by the true spirit of renunciation (*vairagya*)" and speaking with authority about the primacy of the spiritual life.[35] The same attraction might also extend to the notion of Jesus as *Sadhu.*[36] Both Hindu and Christian may be able to acknowledge the reality of the discipleship implied by the *guru-sisya* relationship and, from personal experience, something of the demands made by accepting the mantle of discipleship.[37] Even if the person of Christ (especially as understood by Christians as Lord) and the category of *guru* (especially as understood by Hindus) do not wholly cohere, the ideal of the *guru* does appear to point to a shared pedagogical framework acknowledged by both religious traditions. There is also a necessarily communal aspect to disciples gathered around a *guru* (though individualism can also be a feature of both traditions). Moreover, the *guru-sisya* relationship also attaches value to a number of qualities within interpersonal relationships which are often seen as necessary for fruitful dialogue; for example: humility, readiness and openness to learn and to receive, honesty, sympathy, respect and mutual trust.

C. *Avatara* and History

One aspect of Hindu thought with apparent similarities to the traditionally maintained Christian doctrine of divine incarnation in Jesus is belief in *avataras* (divine 'descents' in bodily form) and some Christian theologians have used this Hindu belief to justify dia-

---

34 On the formation and role of the *samnyasi* (monk), and its possible Christian parallels (including the view that "Christians will view it ... as a preparation for Christ") see 'Samnyasa – A Christian Way of Life?', in *ITD*, 122-55 (quotation from 131).

35 See the testimony of Anantanand Rambachan in S Wesley Ariarajah, 'Christology in Asia: Perspectives from Hindu-Christian Dialogue', *CTC Bulletin*, 7.3 (December 1987), 34f (quotation from 34).

36 On the notion of Christ as *sadhu*, see Whaling, *An Approach to Dialogue with Hinduism*, 74f. See also Martin Kämpchen, 'Der Heilige im 1 – Skizzeeiner religions-phänomenologisch vergleichenden Studie', *ZMR*, 67 (1983), 191-205.

37 See Dhirananda Bhatt, 'Authority in the Guru-Sishya Relationship', *Jeevadhara*, 6 (1976), 360-79; Antonio Rodrigues, 'The Guru-Shishya Model of Formation', *ITS*, 20 (1983), 308-26 (especially 321-26); Augustine Thottakara, 'Religious Education in Hinduism Ancient and Modern', *Jeevadhara*, 14 (1984), 315f; Vandana, 'The *Guru-Shishya* Relationship in the Indian Tradition', *TM*, 3.2 (April-June 2000), 60-68.

logue. A not untypical Catholic example is J-A Cuttat who argues that the belief can and should be seen as what he calls "an efficacious symbolic myth"[38]- a view which he elsewhere develops.[39] Christ is the symbol, archetype and fulfilment of all the Hindu and Eastern theophanies[40] or, at least, of the deep desires to which they point. Although there are many *avataras*, that fact in itself is said to point to the consistent presence and active involvement of the divine in the world process and in human history at its various stages of development and need.[41] De Smet calls it "the closest pre-figuration in another religion of the incarnation";[42]Dupuis sees a "striking parallel with the incarnation;[43] and Klostermaier believes it "will have to play an important part" in any Indian christology.[44]

However, an examination of a wider range of opinions concerning the meaning and use of the *avatara* belief reveals a number of problems that introduce difficulties for the suggestion that the belief could be used as an analogy or synonym for the Christian doctrine of the incarnation. For example, there is the issue of comparable significance. Incarnation has been central to the Christian tradition, but the notion of *avatara*, while certainly present in the Saiva and *sakti* traditions, only assumes a comparable significance to incarnation in Vaisnavism (though even there the precise significance varies markedly among the classical scholars).[45] Moreover, both Hindu and Christian opinion is divided over the nature of the reality possessed by the *avatara*.[46] This is one reason why the suitability of the

38 *The Encounter of Religions* (New York, 1960), 57f.

39 'The Religious Encounter of East and West', *Thought*, 33 (1958), 493f; *Spiritual Dialogue Between East and West* (Delhi, 1961), 33f. See also the remarks on *avataras* in Dupuis, 'The Presence of Christ in Hinduism', *RS*, 18.1 (March 1971), 37f.

40 'Christian Experience and Oriental Spirituality', *Concilium*, 9.5 (1969), 63f.

41 Neuner, *Jesus Christ* (Pune, 1974), 172.

42 Richard De Smet, 'Jesus and the Avatara', in *Dialogue and Syncretism*, 161; article: 153-62.

43 *Toward a Christian Theology of Religious Pluralism*, 301.

44 'Kristvidya', in *ITD*, 103. This opinion is found in the revised version of 'Kristvidya' (the original was published as a booklet in 1967) despite Klostermaier's misgivings about the utility of the *avatara* notion in *Hindu and Christian in Vrindaban* (Et: London, 1969), 115.

45 See, for example, Robert W Stevenson, 'The Concept of Avatara in Ancient and Modern Commentaries on the Bhagavadgita', *Journal of Studies in the Bhagavadgita*, 3 (1983), 56-86; Eric J Lott, 'The Mythic Symbol Avatara in Indian Conceptual Formulations', *DA*, 1.2 (Summer 1987), 3-12.

46 See Lott, 'The Relevance of Research in Religions'; De Smet, 'Jesus and the Avatara', 159-61; RC Zaehner, *The Bhagavad-Gita with a Commentary Based*

avatara doctrine as a vehicle for the expression of a distinctively Christian understanding of the incarnation is in dispute.[47] Some Indian theologians (Chakkarai,[48] Appasamy, Dhanjibhai and others sympathetic to the *bhakti* tradition in Hinduism) have accepted and used the *avatara* concept as an appropriate means -given certain safeguards – of expressing belief, in an Indian context, in the incarnation of God in Christ.[49] (For example, the term *Avatara* is used in the Tamil version of the Nicene Creed in which it is stated that "[Christ] came down from heaven"; it is said that no better term is

on the Original Sources (London, 1969), 181-84; E Geoffrey Parrinder, *Avatar and Incarnation* (London, 1970) especially part I, 'Avatars in Hinduism', contains some useful surveys and summaries; Hugo H Culpepper, 'The Incarnation in the Dialogue of the Religions', *RE*, 71 (1974), 75-84; Kurian Mathothu, *The Development of the Concept of Trimurti in Hinduism* (Palai, 1974), 64-72; Eric J Sharpe, 'Avatara and Sakti: Traditional Symbols in the Hindu Renaissance', in *New Religions: Based on Papers Read at the Symposium on New Religions Held at Abo, 1974*, edited by Haralds Biezais (Stockholm: Almquist and Wiksell, 1975), 55-69; Regunta Yesurathnam, 'The Adequacy of the Concept of Avatara for Expounding the Christian Doctrine of Incarnation', *DA*, 1 (1987), 43-52; Mathew Vekathanam, 'Mystery, Myth, History: the Dimensions of Spirituality in the Context of Avatara', *JD*, 13 (1988), 204-216; Eck, *Encountering God*, chapter 4; Jacob Kattackal, *Incarnation and Resurrection in World Religions* (Kottayam: Oriental Institute of Religious Studies, 1999).

47 Useful summaries and appraisals of the arguments for and against may be found in Robin Boyd, *Khristadvaita: A Theology for India* (Madras, 1977), 145-48 and his *An Introduction to Indian Christian Theology* (Madras, 1969), 239f. See also: Samuel Rayan, 'Interpreting Christ in India', *IJT*, 23 (1974), 223-26; Lott, 'The Relevance of Research in Religions', 52f; Ishanand Vempeny, *Krsna and Christ* (Anand, 1988), *passim*; De Smet, 'Jesus and the Avatara', 161f; Piet Schoonenberg, 'Christologie angesichts de Avatara-Lehre', in *Epiphanie des Heils. Zur Heilsgegenwort in Indischer und christlicher religion. Arbeitsdokumentation eines Symposium*, edited by Gerhard Oberhammer (Vienna, 1982), 179-92.

48 See the literature cited in chapter 1.C.2 above.

49 See, for example, S Jesudason, *Unique Christ and Indigenous Christianity* (Bangalore, 1966), 9f, 19; Lott, 'The Relevance of Research in Religions', 53, where he concludes that one particular formulation (Ramanuja's) seems best should Christians wish to use the *avatara* concept; Regunta Yesurathnam, 'The Adequacy of the Concept of Avatara for Expounding the Christian Doctrine of Incarnation', *DA*, 1.2 (Summer 1987), 43-52; Eck, *Encountering God*, chapter 4; NV George, *The Doctrine of Incarnation in Vaishnavism and Christianity: A Critical and Comparative Study* (Delhi: ISPCK, 1997), which emphasises the religions of grace and love that are revealed through Krishna and Christ.

available.) Some Christians have translated *avatara* as 'embodiments'.[50] Although the notion of embodiment is wider than that represented by an *avatara*, it is significant that, in claiming that the two dominant trends of Hinduism are mystical or vedantic, and personal, it is also claimed that "the idea of a personal God is ... just one aspect or a consequence of à more basic religious attitude which may be termed *embodiment*."[51]

In evaluating the *avatara* concept, considerable attention has been given to the kind of reality possessed by the one who descends. From a Hindu viewpoint the law of *karma* cannot but determine the context in which the divine descent is understood. It is inconceivable that the divine should be subject to *karma* and rebirth and this usually leads to the implication that the *avatara* only *seems* to be human (the theory of docetism long rejected in Christian understanding of incarnation) though classical Hindu opinion is divided on the question of the reality and authenticity of the body possessed by Krishna. Nonetheless, as Lipner comments,

> In the Krishna-narratives, the divinity of Krishna is often barely containable, erupting from time to time in explicit theophany. In the Jesus-narratives, Jesus' divinity is latent overall, this hiddenness culminating in the cry of dereliction on the Cross. ... It is the mythopoeic impulse at the heart of *avatara*-theorising that separates the two views of divine descent.[52]

---

50 The translation (rather than literal meaning) suggested by Eric J Lott, 'The Relevance of Research in Religions: Understanding *Avatara* as a Test-Case', *BTF*, 10.1 (January-June 1978), 39. A series of essays (*Gods of Flesh / Gods of Stone: The Embodiment of Divinity in India*, edited by Joanne Punzo Waghorne and others (Chambersburg, PA, 1985)) attempts to "present the embodiment of divinity as the central feature of Hinduism" (Waghorne, 'Introduction', 7). For a more general discussion of the notion of incarnation in a wider (mainly Asian) setting, see George John Hoynacki, '"And the Word was made flesh": Incarnations in Religious Traditions', *AJT*, 7 (1993), 12-34.

51 Norman Cutler, 'Conclusion', in *Gods of Flesh / Gods of Stone*, 169.

52 '*Avatara* and *Incarnation*?', 138. Lipner refers to the passage in the Bhagavata Purana that speaks of Krishna as *apparently* human (1.1.20). The same or related points are also raised by Pierre Johanns, 'L'Avatar et la doctrine du salut ou l'analogue de l'Incarnation dans l'hindouisme', *Rythmes du Monde*, 1.3 (1946), 65-72; AG Hogg, *The Christian Message to the Hindu* (London, 1947), 33-35; Surjit Singh, *Preface to Personality: Christology in Relation to Radhakrishnan's Philosophy* (Madras, 1952), 119 (where he labels the *avatara* belief 'Adoptionism'); PD Devanandan, *The Gospel and Renascent Hinduism*, 42; Whaling, *An Approach to Dialogue with Hinduism*, 57-59; Parrinder, *Avatar and Incarnation*, 209-39, 263-66, 276-79; Stephen

But Lipner also goes on to point out that in Hindu thought the *avatara* remains *real* – or, at least, possesses the kind of conventional reality assigned to this world. However, strong contrasts between the Christian and Hindu constructs remain. For example, there is the Hindu notion of multiple descents (with none definitive), or partial *avataras*. A question might also be raised about the intended scope of the divine descent. In the Christian tradition the intention is universal redemption (with the universality applied by means of a Trinitarian notion of the Divine); in Hinduism the scope remains particular or even simply personal. Moreover, some other Christian theologians, sympathetic to *advaita vedanta* (for example Upadhyaya, Abhishiktananda, Monchanin), argue that the *avatara* concept is inevitably linked with the personalist stream of the Hindu tradition with the consequence that it is the personal *Isvara*, rather than *Brahman*, who becomes incarnate. So, philosophically minded Saivites, for example, reject the concept of *avatara* because they repudiate notions of divine incarnation. This would set Christianity at a lower level than Hinduism – or lower, at least, than *advaita vedanta* – a perception that is perhaps reinforced in Hindu eyes by the common description of Christ as *avatara* in South Indian Christian hymns and poetry about Christ.[53]

Nonetheless, it is not uncommon to find Hindus (including Ramakrishna, Vivekananda and Keshub Chunder Sen) describing Christ as an *avatara*.[54] Sarvepalli Radhakrishnan does not make extensive use of the category but when he uses it he does so in terms of the advaitin notion of identity with God; no notion of uniqueness is implied.[55] Radhakrishnan also appears to endorse belief in a docetist view of the humanity of the *avatara*. He considers it "blasphemous" for a Hindu to say that Krishna could suffer and adds, in

---

Fuchs, 'Hindu Avatars and Christian Incarnation', *The Examiner*, 122 (1971), 543, 559; Camille Bulcke, 'Avatar and Incarnation', *Sevartham*, 6 (1981), 25-50; see also Bulcke, 'Tulsidas and Incarnation', *Sevartham*, 4 (1979), 34-42; Mathothu, *The Development of the tiConcept of Trimurti*, 68-70.

53 See Lott, 'The Relevance of Research in Religions', 36; Boyd, *Khristadvaita*, 145f.

54 See the elaboration in Ronald Neufeldt, 'Hindu Views of Christ', in *H-CD*, 163-69, and Hindley, 'The Jesus of History', 19. For an elaboration of the claim that Jesus was an avatar of Vishnu see Akhilananda, *Hindu View of Christ* (New York, 1949), 15-44. Also interesting is Vinayak Krishna Gokak, *In Defence of Jesus Christ and Other Avatars* (New Delhi, 1979), especially chapter 5.

55 Radhakrishnan, *The Heart of Hindusthan*, second edition (Madras, 1932), 101f.

an apparent reference to Christ: "A suffering God, a deity with a crown of thorns, cannot satisfy the religious soul".[56] A not untypical exegesis, from an advaitin perspective, of the Bhagavadgita 4.6b ("By my creative energy I consort with Nature – which is mine – and come to be") has Krishna commenting: "My embodiment is only apparent and does not touch My true nature".[57] It must be added that, for most Vaisnavites, Krishna is actually a full (*purna*) *avatara*; however, the usual docetism (the *avatara* as a theophany that leaves no footprints on the earth) appears to be incompatible with the traditional Christian understanding of the full humanity of Jesus, including his suffering. Moreover, it is not only Hindus who seem to embrace a form of docetism. Thangaraj draws attention to what he sees as the docetism resident in Tamil Christian portrayals of Christ as *avatara* that leads to an undervaluing of his real humanity and the resulting failure to embrace the comprehensive liberative praxis implied by a revised Hindu-Christian *guru*-christology that is more important to Thangaraj than the traditional categories of Christ as saviour and Lord.[58]

It seems, then, that there are problems in any use of the concepts of *avatara* and incarnation that implies that one can be used as an analogy of the other. In fact, Lipner concludes that

> Substituting *avatara* for Incarnation is conceptually and linguistically inadmissible and religiously highly dubious. Each term carries *substantial* emotional and theological freight that is unique.[59]

But Lipner also feels that the terms may co-exist "through contextual interaction that is theologically both informed and creative."[60] In other words, there do seem to be reasons why the *avatara* concept might, with care, be invested with distinctive Christian meaning and used christologically. The Christian partner in dialogue will certainly comprehend the Hindu premise that in an *avatara* there is to be found an example of personal, visible, particu-

---

56 Sarvepalli Radhakrishnan, *The Philosophy of Rabindranath Tagore* (London, 1918), 15. A central passage is the description of Krishna in the Bhagavadgita "as if laughing" (2.10) – though fully in control of an apparently desperate situation. Lipner's comment is that "Krishna could not be a Man of Sorrows" in the way Jesus was perceived to be, and has never been thus described" ('*Avatara* and *Incarnation*?', 138).

57 Swarupananda, *Srimad-Bhagavad-Gita* (Almora, 1944), 99.

58 See chapter 1 of his *The Crucified Guru*.

59 '*Avatara* and *Incarnation*?', 139 (original emphasis).

60 '*Avatara* and *Incarnation*?', 139.

lar, timely, loving and saving divine intervention to meet urgent needs.[61] The very notion of 'descent' – to draw attention to the literal meaning of *avatara* – is certainly common to both traditions and functions as "a congenial, spatial metaphor for the divine accessibility".[62] But it might be difficult (except through the universality of devotion) to extrapolate from the *avatara* concept to the universal dimensions traditionally assigned by Christian belief to the person of Christ. On the other hand, the *avataras* are to be found in a range of non-human dimensions and times; "as such the divine presence is everywhere, erupting repeatedly and specifically to enhance the point and to sharpen the eyes of devotion"[63]whereas Christianity has maintained not only the singularity of the incarnation in Christ but its finality and unrepeatability as well.[64] In the course of dialogue the similarities and differences between Hindu belief in many *avataras* and Christian belief in a single incarnation may well be significant issues for further discussion – as they have often already been during the history of the Hindu-Christian encounter.[65]

Hindu belief in a multiplicity of *avataras* presupposes a cosmology that includes a cyclical view of history (with different *avataras* entering different ages) and the issue of history and its importance for each tradition adds a further level of complexity to the discussion of *avatara* and incarnation. In India both Christian and Hindu apologists have tended to draw a strong contrast between the supposed dependence or independence of their religious traditions upon history. This, in turn, has implications for the way in which Hindus and Christians assess the person and place of Christ in the context of dialogue. For example, it might not be difficult for a

61 For an emphasis on God's love for humanity as the motivation for the coming of saviours, see: Mariasusai Dhavamony, 'Seers and God-men as "Founders" of Hinduism', *SM*, 33 (1984), 181-225.

62 Lipner, '*Avatara* and *Incarnation*?', 131.

63 Lipner, '*Avatara* and *Incarnation*?', 135; he goes on to add that "The distinctive mythopoeic tendency is a paean to a particular form of divine panimmanence" (135).

64 Nonetheless, Thomas Aquinas acknowledged the possibility of multiple incarnations; see the discussion and analysis in Quentin Quesnell, 'Aquinas on Avatars', *DA*, 1.2 (Summer 1987), 33-42; and Samartha considers that "the theory of multiple *avataras* seems to be theologically the most accommodating attitude in a pluralistic setting" (*One Christ – Many Religions*, 131). For another perspective see Brian Hebblethwaite, 'The Impossibility of Multiple Incarnations', *Theology*, 104 (2001), 323-34.

65 In this regard, see: John Moffitt, 'Incarnation and Avatara: An Imaginary Conversation', *JES*, 14 (1977), 260-87.

Hindu to feel that the tying of Christianity to events in history (especially to the person of Jesus) significantly weakens or even negates its claim to possess universal significance. The reality conveyed by history seems narrow, relative and contingent whereas one "who has seen the real is lifted above all narrowness, relativities, and contingencies".[66] As Aurobindo asks (with the clear implication of an affirmative answer), "is it ... because the historical Christ has been made too much the foundation-stone of the Faith that Christianity is failing?"[67]

In turn, however, Christians have expressed misgivings about Hindu attitudes to history. Most Hindu assessments of Christ are found wanting by Christian commentators and often because of a failure to deal adequately (or at all) with his link to history.[68] An early work by Samartha concluded that "hardly any Hindu thinker has given serious attention to the question of historicity in understanding the life and work of Jesus Christ".[69] The central problem is, he argued, the Hindu apprehension of the status of history itself,[70] and the belief that the absolute not only is not, but cannot be, tied to history. (Samartha goes on to claim that the elaboration of the importance of human historical existence – because of the entry of Christ into history – "will be one of the most significant services which Christology can render to India today".[71])

Such claims might be contrasted with the usual Hindu attitude towards the historicity of incarnation and *avatara*. For Radhakrishnan, the incarnation of Christ "is not an historical event which occurred two thousand years ago. It is an event which is renewed in the life of everyone who is on the way to the fulfilment of his destiny."[72] Vinoba Bhave, in his commentary on the Bhagavad Gita, writes:

Let us not say 'Arjuna had Krishna. Where are we to find our

---

66 Sarvepalli Radhakrishnan, *Eastern Religions and Western Thought*, second edition (London, 1940), 317.

67 Aurobindo, 'The Purpose of Avatarhood', in his *Letters on Yoga* (Pondicherry, 1970), 430

68 For example: Balwant Paradkar, 'Hindu Interpretation of Christ from Vivekananda to Radhakrishnan', *IJT*, 18 (1969), 65-87

69 *The Hindu Response to the Unbound Christ*, 156.

70 *The Hindu Response to the Unbound Christ*, 157; and, in greater detail, his *The Hindu View of History: Classical and Modern* (Bangalore, 1959)

71 *The Hindu Response to the Unbound Christ*, 151. (However, it should also be noted that this apologetic edge to Samartha's discussion of christology is absent from his more recent writings.)

72 *Recovery of Faith* (London, 1956), 126

> Krishna?' Let us not get caught in the fallacy of historicity, that there was an individual called 'Krishna'. Krishna shines in the heart of each one of us, the Inner Ruler.[73]

That is, the writer elevates the person and place of Krishna to a supra-personal level, and for that very reason Krishna is seen to be non- (or perhaps trans-) historical. It is not difficult to imagine some Christians using similar language when speaking of Christ – except for the remark about 'historicity'. But, even here, the Christian commentator will proceed with care when assessing Hindu attitudes to history and will note the close connection with cosmology. The usual Hindu notion of divine pan-immanence, with its embrace of a multiplicity of time-space worlds, means that "the *avatara* is historically *more* contingent than it would be under a more comprehensive, integrated perspective of history as in the Christian."[74] Or it could be argued that, as one sympathetic Christian commentator puts it, the reason for the classical Hindu insistence that "Krishna was *like* a human ... is not to deny that he was a real human being but to highlight the fact that ... historicity implies bondage but ... [Krishna] is never in bondage."[75]

Also important is the role historical investigation plays in the critical retrieval of the past. For example, neo-Vedantic opinion sometimes makes claims about the likelihood that Jesus embraced advaitic categories of thought. Part of a Christian response to such claims is liable to be the statement that it is, at least in part, a matter of historical judgment as to whether Jesus did in fact employ the philosophy of *advaita vedanta* and that scrutiny of the historical context in which Jesus taught is, therefore, both important and necessary. To say this is not to disallow the Hindu partner in dialogue the right to interpret Christ in distinctly Indian categories, advaitin or otherwise. However, the conclusion that Christ was an *avatara* or an *advaitin* would, for a contemporary Christian, depend in part at least upon evidence concerning the purported actions and teaching of Jesus himself as made accessible by the appropriately critical interrogation of history and the earliest Christian records.

The impact of secularisation has already been mentioned. It is possible that a reconsideration by some Hindus of the reality of lin-

---

73 *Talks on the Gita* (London, 1960), 23. In similar vein, S Ramasamy: "*Christ Value* is ineffably more important than Christ- fact" ([book review], *H-CSB*, 2 (1989), 5, original emphasis).

74 Lipner, '*Avatara* and *Incarnation?*', 137 (emphasis added).

75 Francis X D'Sa, 'Christian Incarnation and Hindu Avatara', in *Any Room for Christ in Asia?*, 85, n 8; see also 82.

ear time (over against the more usual consideration of history in cyclical categories)[76] and the status of history itself may be one of the indirect consequences of secularisation and modernisation. It is not uncommon to find some contemporary Hindus sensitive to the charge of an uncritical indifference to the importance of time and history.

However, it is also possible that many or most Western discussions of the Indian view of history may have misunderstood it or, in the case of Christian apologists, have unfairly contrasted it with the supposed western or Biblical linear view of history. Some Christians are concerned about the negative implications for dialogue of the notion of *Heilsgeschichte* ['salvation-history']; as Samartha asks, "Do the histories of people in India [and elsewhere] ... have no theological significance in the sight of God?"[77] One response has been to elaborate 'Indian History as Salvation History'.[78] Another has been to question the alleged absence or unimportance of a sense of history in India's religious traditions. Lipner, for example, points out the way in which the Hindu view of history does allow for the notion of genuine progress.[79] Rayan discusses such a view of history with particular reference to the Bhagavadgita and concludes that the historical dimensions of the Gita are "remarkably profound." He considers that the author of the Gita "shows a keen awareness of holy history" with remarkable parallels to the biblical view of history.[80] Rayan also goes on to elaborate reasons why the Biblical view of history cannot adequately be described as linear; there are cyclical patterns in it and the presence of the *eschaton* within history adds meaning and significance in a way not amenable to the usual forms of Western historical analysis.[81] This view of history is hardly uni-

---

76 See, for example, the comments of Arvind Sharma, 'Notion of Cyclical Time in Hinduism', *Contributions to Asian Studies*, 5 (1974), 26-35. The discussion by KM Panikkar of *The Determining Periods of India's History* is an example of the shift towards a new understanding of history (Bombay, 1962); see also Stanley J Samartha, 'The Significance of the Historical in Contemporary Hinduism', *IJT*, 16 (1967), 95-105.

77 *One Christ – Many Religions*, 11.

78 Title of an article by I Yesudasan, *IES*, 11 (1972), 221-34.

79 See Julius J Lipner, *Hindus: Their Religious Beliefs and Practices* (London: Routledge, 1994), chapter 10, 'Modes of Reckoning Time and 'Progress''

80 Samuel Rayan, 'Indian Theology and the Problem of History', in *Society and Religion, Essays in Honour of MM Thomas*, edited by Richard W Taylor (Madras, 1976), 179f; see also 173-78.

81 'Indian Theology and the Problem of History', 180-91. He further develops the same point in his 'Models of History', *Jeevadhara*, 13 (1983), 5-26. Also useful is A Mathias Mundadan, 'Hindu and Christian Views of History', in

lineal given the way in which the whole of history is taken up and given meaning by the Incarnation.[82] As Amaladoss argues (from the New Testament, but with the Indian context in mind), only as the mystery of Christ is set free from the limitations of its historical particularity (but without severing the link) can its universality be realised.[83] There are, then, important currents in the Hindu tradition that do take history seriously, albeit not in the western critical sense – but then that is not the Biblical writers' understanding of history either.

One further Christian response to those who find the Christian emphasis on history unhelpful in contexts that do not maintain a linear view of history is to affirm the possibility of other means of revelation. As Michael Nazir-Ali points out, these other possibilities often do tend "towards the gnostic" – that is, revelation is accessible only by a privileged few with the requisite insight or 'knowledge'. But he adds that these alternatives "are ... valuable in correcting the historicising bent of much Christian theology by affirming the possibility of divine disclosure in thought, imagery and metaphor as well as in event."[84] Moreover, apart from any changing – or better perceived – view of the Hindu attitude to history, at least some Christians acknowledge the revelatory value of Hindu mythology (with its ability to transcend spatiotemporal barriers and to help symbolise the formless divine) and thereby criticise a certain kind of Christian apologetic since "a great obstacle to inter-faith dialogue in India is the belief that since Christianity is an historical religion, and Hindus have a mythological religion with no known founder, their religion is all false ...".[85]

The implication for dialogue is clear: a revised and less critical approach to India's understanding of history may well enhance Christian appreciation of Hinduism. In other words, Christian partners in dialogue might reconsider their own appeal to history. It is true, as Dupuis points out, that the Christian tradition does "presuppose a density of the historical, not found as such in other tradi-

---

History and Contemporary India, edited by John CB Webster (Bombay: Asia Publishing House, 1971), 67-94 (also found in Mundadan, *History and Beyond* (Aluva: Jeevass Publications, 1997), 49-81).

82 See the comments of Lipner, '*Avatara* and *Incarnation?*', 137.

83 Michael Amaladoss, 'Dialogue and Mission', *Vidyajyoti*, 50 (1986), 74.

84 *From Everywhere to Everywhere. A World View of Christian Witness* (London: Collins, 1990), 130.

85 Vikrant, 'Obstacles to Dialogue', in *Lead Me to the Real: The Hindu-Christian Dialogue* (Hong Kong, 1983), 36, 39-41 (quotation from 39).

tions, without which it cannot be fully understood."[86] But the relationship between the Jesus of history and the traditional christological claims (with their potential for devaluing the reality of history) has proved difficult and problematical for Christian comprehension and elaboration as well. There is good reason for the Christian proponent of dialogue to acknowledge that Christ is called both the revelation and the mystery of the God who remains essentially transhistorical. If it is true that "Jesus Christ ushers us into the presence of God's mystery, before which Hindus and Christians stand together in humility to acknowledge, to affirm, and even to celebrate the ultimate mystery of God, the *Satyasya Satyam* (the truth of the truth)",[87] then there will be an appropriately restrained nuance to Christian discourse about historical particularity. If the implications of a Christian view of history are acknowledged, they could also lead to a positive appraisal of Hinduism on the grounds that, because God has become part of history in the person of Jesus, God in some way thereby affirms and values all human existence with its manifold cultures and traditions – including the Hindu. On the other hand, Christians may well be reminded that, as Dupuis puts it, history and interiority are two equally valid channels for experience of the Divine: "he who acts in history according to the Judeo-Christian tradition is he who is experienced in the 'cave of the heart' according to the Hindu. The God of history is also the 'ground of being'."[88]

D. The Role of *Anubhava*

The epistemological function of *anubhava* in many strands of Hindu thought and its role as a self-authenticating basis of religious authority have already been noted.[89] "The voice of experience is

86 *Toward a Christian Theology of Religious Pluralism*, 384; see also 212-15.

87 Stanley J Samartha, 'Indian Realities and the Wholeness of Christ', *Missiology*, 10 (1982), 315.

88 *Toward a Christian Theology of Religious Pluralism*, 384. And it might be noted that the notion of persuasive 'interior' divine witness is central feature of the (growing) Pentecostal sector of Christianity.

89 See above, chapter 1.B.5. There is a useful survey of the varieties of *anubhava* in Manickam, 'Anubhava as Pramana', 234-38; see also Bede Griffiths, 'Mystical Theology in the Indian Tradition', *Jeevadhara*, 9 (1979), 262-77. A survey covering the period since Ramakrishna is found in KPS Choudhary, *Modern Indian Mysticism* (Delhi, 1981). A good example of the methodological importance of *anubhava* within *advaita* is found in Mark Sunder Rao, *Ananyatva. Realisation of Christian Non-Duality* (Bangalore, 1964), 6, 35-43.

generally regarded by Hindus as indispensable for shaping one's religious orientation";[90] or, as Sankara put it, "the witness of the *atman* is best".[91] There are also important and widespread Indian Christian precedents in the appeal to *anubhava* as the means of the knowledge of God through Christ; Sadhu Sundar Singh, Chenchiah and others might be cited.[92] Indeed, many Indians, both within and beyond the baptised membership of the Christian community, report such experience as the means of encountering the one they name as Christ.[93] The differences between the traditional Christian and Hindu appeals to such *anubhava* are not insignificant. The Christian usually means experience of Christ himself, and usually in terms of the Pauline experience of being 'in Christ' or (among Indian Christians) an encounter with Christ in dreams or visions. Or the experience is said to be mediated by the Holy Spirit; Vengal Chakkarai went so far as to say that "Jesus is the Incarnation or *Avatar* of God; the Holy Spirit in human experience is the Incarnation of Jesus Christ".[94]

Nonetheless, the appeal to *anubhava* is disputed in both traditions. As we have already seen, Rambachan is critical of the influence of Vivekananda's critique of the authority of scripture that led him to subordinate such authority to *anubhava*; this divergence from

---

90 Lipner, *Hindus*, 194.

91 Sankara's commentary on the Brhadaranyaka Upanishad 4.4.8, as cited by Samartha, *The Hindu Response to the Unbound Christ*, 153. (The problematical nature of the appeal to common or complementary religious experience as a basis for Christian-Hindu dialogue has also been acknowledged: chapter 3.G.

92 For a discussion by two Catholics, see: Vandana, 'Indian Theologizing – the Role of Experience', in *Theologizing in India Today*, edited by M Amaladoss and others (Bangalore, 1981), 81-115; and Vikrant, 'Theology as *Anubhava*. An Essay in Comparative Mysticism', in *Unique and Universal. Fundamental Problems of an Indian Theology*, edited by J Britto Chethimattam (Bangalore, 1972), 167-82. It is interesting to note that Mookenthottam regards the role and significance of *anubhava* as the "one common element" of the otherwise somewhat divergent Catholic and Protestant approaches to Indian theology (*Indian Theological Tendencies* (Berne, 1978), 174).

93 See the experiences reported in: 'Consultation Findings. Conference of Converts from Hinduism to the Christian Faith', *RS*, 10.3 (September 1963), 85-94. Also relevant is the phenomenon of unbaptised devotees of Christ; see below, n. 105.

94 *Jesus the Avatar*, Indian Studies 2, edited by AJ Appasamy, second edition (Madras, 1930), 124. On Chakkarai's christology and emphasis upon *anubhava*, see also TV Philip, 'Chakkarai and the Indian Church', in *Society and Religion*, 154-56.

the advaitin system of Sankara of which Vivekananda claimed to be the heir has been uncritically accepted within neo-Hinduism.[95] One consequence is that differences of belief and practice are seen as unimportant – both within Hinduism itself and between Hinduism and other religions – because the direct and supersensuous experience of Brahman is essentially the same irrespective of the language used; it leads to the uncritical assertion that all religions lead to the same goal.[96]

Within Christianity the appeal to experience might also be seen as a corrective of (or a supplement to) those tendencies in Christian thought that centre the knowledge of God primarily upon scripture, salvation history and the historic Jesus – with minimal or even negative weight attached to human experience.[97] For this reason Chakkarai argued that in order to comprehend Christian belief in the person and place of Christ it is the *experience* of Christ, as made known by the Spirit, that is fundamental; "while the historical is the primary element in the Western interpretation, the spiritual is, or will be, the primary element in the Indian conception".[98] It is also important to recall the Biblical precedents for an appeal to religious experience as the basis for Christian belief and mission. There are even some Hindu scriptural parallels to the centrally important New Testament notion of being with or in Christ,[99] and these might be used to qualify the notion of Christ as *guru*: the Christian ideal is not merely to follow Christ but also to be identified with him (compare Galatians 2.20).

More recently, Manickam has also proposed the formulation of an Indian christology in terms of *anubhava*. He defines christology in experiential terms as "the grace-bearing contact with the Christ-event", and describes Christianity as "fundamentally and ultimate-

---

95 See chapters 1-3 of Rambachan, *The Limits of Scripture: Vivekananda's Reinterpretation of the Vedas;* in chapters 4-6 he elaborates the means and extent of the divergence from traditional advaitin orthodoxy.

96 *The Limits of Scripture,* 135. For more general comments on the shortcomings of the appeal to religious truth as ineffable see, for example, the discussion in Netland, *Encountering Religious Pluralism,* 204-11.

97 On the role of Scripture, and its link with experience, in both traditions, see: Harold Coward, 'The Experience of Scripture in Hinduism and Christianity', in *H-CD,* 230-50.

98 *Jesus the Avatar,* 118 (see further 119 and 14). 52; see also Klostermaier, 'Kristvidya', 116, n. 33. But for a liberal Christian critique of Christian claims to *anubhava* of Christ, see RS Sugirtharajah, 'The Bible and Its Asian Readers', *Biblical Interpretation,* 1 (1993), 54-66.

99 Klostermaier, 'Kristvidya', 116, n 33.

ly an anubhava, an experience of the Divine in Christ".[100] Klostermaier deliberately formulates his *Kristvidya* in experiential categories parallel to the Hindu quest for *Brahmavidya*.[101] In his opinion, "India does not require any new dogmas on the nature and person of Christ – India seeks the Christ experience in depth: the experience of reality."[102] Not all Christian advocates of dialogue would agree with Manickam's claim that "wherever there is an experience of the saving grace of God there is also the anubhava of Christ".[103] But if he has in mind "the totality of the anubhava of Indian devotees of Christ"[104]- including the reported experience of other than Christian devotees[105]- then there seems to be some support for his claim. The discussion of reported experiences of Christ raises many epistemological questions, especially for western Christians.[106] Nonetheless, a christology based upon, or giving significant place to, anubhava might also stand as a corrective of cosmic christology – or of those forms of it which, as Lyons notes, seem "to move in speculative regions outside of, and perhaps even at variance with, the Christian's actual experience of Christ".[107] It is significant that

---

100 'Anubhava as Pramana of an Indian Christology', 229, 240. The same point is made by Xavier Irudayaraj, 'An Attempt at an Indian Christology', *IES*, 9 (1970) 15; see also Samuel Rayan, 'An Indian Christology: A Discussion of Method', *Jeevadhara*, 1 (1971), 220. Manickam outlines similar components of a '*Christvanubhava*' in his 'Anubhava as Pramana of an Indian Christology', 241. See also Sebastian Painadath, 'Christology and the Spiritual Heritage of Mankind', *Jeevadhara*, 2 (1972), 237.

101 'Kristvidya', 90f, 10.

102 *Hindu and Christian in Vrindaban*, 108. It must be added, however, that Klostermaier also bemoans the tendency to dismiss the intellectual approach to religion in favour of the emotional and pragmatic; he believes that Hindu-Christian dialogue "must recover the intellectual substance of Hinduism and Christianity." ('The Future of Hindu-Christian Dialogue,' 269.

103 'Anubhava as Pramana', 231. Rayan also writes of "the Christ who is in all and is the Self of all, the Universal Self and the Antaryamin [Dweller within]" ('An Indian Christology', 220).

104 'Anubhava as Pramana', 239.

105 For example, the research on 'double-belonging' mentioned in chapters 2.A.2 and 4.C.3 reported that 38% of the Hindus and Muslims surveyed had prayed to Jesus.

106 For some attempts to answer these questions, see: Thomas F Torrance, 'The Epistemological Relevance of the Holy Spirit', in his *God and Rationality* (London, 1971), 165-92; and Richard Bauckham, *Knowing God Incarnate* (Bramcote, Notts, 1983).

107 *The Cosmic Christ*, 10; see also the discussion on 55f.

Panikkar wants to derive his theology of the Hindu-Christian encounter from an appraisal of Hinduism in existential and experiential categories,[108] and it is difficult to imagine an elaboration of the encounter that does not include reference to an experiential dimension

E. *Bhaktimarga*

The discussion of *anubhava* leads naturally to a consideration of the way of *bhakti* (devotion) and to note its relevance to an Indian christology. For example, in *bhaktimarga* there is usually an understanding of the Absolute as *Isvara;* in fact, in most *bhakti* traditions, *Isvara is Brahman.* That is, *bhaktimarga* presents an understanding of God as personal and yet distinct from the human person. Moreover, the approach to God within *bhaktimarga* is comprehensible to most Christians – especially to those from its more pietistic streams, both Catholic and Protestant. There is an approach to the divine that centres on love, personal devotion and gratitude for salvation alongside a sense of sin and unworthiness. *Bhakti* speaks of the permanent rather than the occasional presence of God – an understanding that probably curtailed the development of the mythology of the *avataras.*[109]

There have been a number of attempts to employ *bhakti* categories in Indian Christian devotion, with the works of Christian *bhakti* poets especially important.[110] One belief (of importance in traditional circles) is salvation through the vicarious suffering of Christ, but this is a difficult concept for Hindus given belief in the impassibility of Brahman and the perceived link between suffering and *karma.* Appasamy attempts to resolve the issue from christological premises in his elaboration of *Christianity as Bhakti Marga.*[111]

---

108 See, for example, the first part of *TUCH(2)*, 'The Encounter' (31-61). In similar vein, Cuttat proposed that the meeting point with Hinduism be 'spiritual experience'; see his *Spiritual Dialogue of East and West,* second edition (New Delhi, 1982), 10f.

109 JL Brockington, *The Sacred Thread* (Edinburgh, 1981), 69. However, it must also be noted that some Hindus understand *bhaktimarga* to be close in meaning to *karmamarga* or *jnanamarga.* But our discussion will confine itself to the more usual meaning in terms of devotion.

110 There is a helpful introduction in Boyd, *Introduction to Indian Christian Theology*, chapter VII.

111 (Madras, 1926), 116-29. See also his *The Theology of Hindu Bhakti* (Madras, 1970) and Martin Alphonse, 'Christianity as Bhakti Religion', *DD*, 1.1 (1995), 5-32.

Parallels between Christian and some Hindu (especially *bhakti*) notions of divine grace and human faith have also been explored in some detail.[112] Moreover, Ramanuja's *visistadvaita* has provided a philosophical framework for the personal theism that undergirds the *bhakti* movement. Its possible utility in elaborating an Indian christology has been suggested by Lott (as noted above in the discussion of Christ as *avatara*) and especially by Appasamy who is drawn to Ramanuja's soul/body analogy to discuss not only the God/world distinction, but also to clarify the relationship of divine to human in Christ and Christ's relationship to his people.[113]

Chakkarai also employs the language and ethos of *bhakti* to elaborate the meaning of Christ's death and, in particular, the way in which the salvation Christ offers is received by his *bhaktas*.[114] Also noteworthy are the writings of the Gujerati convert Dhanjibhai Fakirbhai (1895-1967) whose works have been described as "the theology of love".[115] Panikkar is another who has written with a degree of sympathy towards the way of *bhakti*; as noted, he is will-

---

112 For example: Rudolf Otto, *Christianity and the Indian Religion of Grace* (Madras, 1929); Prudent De Letter, *The Christian and Hindu Concept of Grace* (Calcutta, 1958); Mariasusai Dhavamony, *The Love of God According to Saiva Siddhanta* (Oxford, 1971); Joseph Neethilal, 'God's Response to Man's Bakti [sic] in Hinduism – Especially as Found in Tulsidas', *IES*, 12 (1973), 49-57; Stephen C Neill, *Bhakti: Hindu and Christian* (Madras, 1974); *Grace in Saiva Siddhanta, Vedanta, Islam and Christianity*, edited by Albrecht Frenz (Madurai, 1975); David C Scott, 'Hindu and Christian Bhakti: A Common Human Response to the Sacred', *IJT*, 29 (1980), 12-32; *Divine Grace and Human Response*, edited by CM Vadekkekara (Bangalore, 1981); T Dayanandan Francis, *Aspects of Christian and Hindu Bhakti* (Madras, 1987); Joseph Jaswant Raj, *Grace in the Saiva Siddhantam and in St Paul: a Contribution in Inter-Faith Cross-Cultural Understanding* (Madras: South India Salesian Society, 1989); A Frank Thompson, 'Christian Views of Hindu Bhakti', in *H-CD*, 176-90. Comparisons are also drawn between bhakti and some Christian devotion by Friedhelm Hardy, *Viraha Bhakti: the Early History of Krsna Devotion in South India* (Delhi, 1983), 569-75, and in Noel Sheth, 'Hindu forms of Devotion (Bhakti)', *TM*, 11 (1999), 70-90.

113 For example, AJ Appasamy, 'Christological Reconstruction and Ramanuja's Philosophy', *IRM*, 41 (1952), 170-76. On Ramanuja, see also JB Carman, *Theology of Ramanuja: An Essay in Interreligious Understanding* (New Haven and London, 1974).

114 The Cross and Indian Thought (Madras, 1932), 216-20.

115 Boyd, *An Introduction to* Indian *Christian Theology*, 213f. His two works translated into English are *Khristopanishad* (Bangalore, 1965) and *The Philosophy of Love* (Delhi, 1966). See also the relevant sections of *Manilal C Parekh. Dhanjibhai Fakirbhai*, edited by Robin Boyd (Madras, 1974).

ing to describe Christ as both *Isvara* and *avatara*.[116] And an evangelical has taken the fourfold understanding of salvation embraced by many adherents of *bhaktimarga* (*salokya*, co-existence with God; *samipya* or confrontation and encounter with God; *sarupya*, conformity to God; *sayujya*, communion) and argued for close parallels with the Christian understanding of moksa.[117] And Klostermaier also sees *bhaktimarga* as a means of enabling a Hindu-Christian conversation. One reason (made more interesting in the light of the discussion above of the Indian view of history) is that he sees much *bhaktimarga* as equivalent to the biblical understanding of 'salvation history'. This is partly because of the "insistence on the historicity of salvation" (centred on the various *avataras* in the *bhakti* tradition), and partly because of the way it treats history and biography (Klostermaier sees "striking parallels" between the Puranas, for example, and the Bible).[118] He sees close similarities between the devotion of various lovers of God in the Christian tradition and the *bhaktas* of Hinduism – all of whom know that the knowledge of God is made real and complete in love (100-02, 105). But perhaps the most far-reaching of Klostermaier's suggestions is his outline of a *Kristvidya* based on five traditional forms of *Isvara's* presence that Klostermaier attempts to show correspond with traditional Christian categories for the presence of Christ. These range from procession within the Trinity to incarnational and sacramental presence and "could help to point out the Unknown Christ of Hinduism" (104f). Not all Christians (and certainly not all Hindus) will be persuaded though the notion of various functions or 'presences' within the divine might be of some interest.

However, as also noted in the discussion of *avataras*, there are proponents of dialogue who argue that to portray Christianity as *bhaktimarga* is inevitably to devalue it in the estimation of some Hindus. This is especially true for the followers of *advaita vedanta*, for whom *bhaktimarga* is a preliminary and inferior stage in spiritual progress and understanding – one of what Vivekananda called the "little loves" that must be transcended on the way to the fullness of advaitic realisation.[119] Even without such an intentional portray-

---

116 See also his discussion of 'Personalism – Bhaktimarga', in *The Trinity and World Religions* (Madras, 1970), 18-24.

117 Paul Sudhakar, *The Fourfold Ideal* (Bombay, nd).

118 'Kristvidya', 100. The page references in the rest of this paragraph are to the same work.

119 From the discussion by Neufeldt in *H-CD*, 39. One interesting Christian response to this allegation is discussed in Arvind Sharma, 'Shankara's Bhakti and Swami Abhishiktananda's "Adult Faith"', *JD*, 15 (1990), 240-44;

al, to many Hindus Christianity appears as essentially a *bhakti* religion, not unlike the Krishna cult.[120] And, despite the assertions of Appasamy and others, there is still the question of whether most elaborations of *bhakti* understand salvation / *moksha* as a consequence of human devotion rather than the outcome of unmerited divine grace; if so, this is a continuing point of tension between the two traditions. Nonetheless, Christian commentators are well aware that the rise of theistic *bhakti* led to a new perception of *moksha* in personal categories over against notions of union with Brahman – or, as expressed by Ramakrishna in his elaboration of a devotion that maintained a distinction between the devotee and the Lord, the wish "to taste sugar, not become sugar".[121] And for that reason alone Christian proponents of dialogue will continue to appreciate the importance of *bhaktimarga* in the opening encounter.

F. *Advaita Vedanta*

As well as the theistic or personalist current of Hindu thought (exemplified in *bhaktimarga*), another category that might contribute to the search for an Indian christology is the philosophy of *vedanta* – especially in its *advaita* expression as expounded during the past one hundred years or so. What Stanley Samartha calls the influential, persuasive and tolerant spirit of neo-*vedanta* certainly appears to be "congenial to constructive dialogue between Hindus and Christians."[122] Nonetheless, it is still not clear whether a persuasive christology in advaitic terms will emerge in India or elsewhere, or whether, as has happened with fulfilment theories, its advocates will diminish in number. Until recently (and perhaps still) most of its proponents are Europeans and most of them Catholics; Protestants have preferred to emphasise human personality, the

---

Abhishiktananda describes faith in language very close to that used by Shankara and argues that adult faith consists in freeing oneself from everything in order to find God in one's innermost spirit. But for a mainly negative Christian appraisal of *bhakti* see: Sabapathy Kulandran, *Grace: a Comparative Study of the Doctrine in Christianity and Hinduism* (London, 1964). And for the view that the heart of *bhakti* is not worship but is mainly concerned with seeking favours from, and appeasing, various deities, see the controversial discussion in Chaudhuri, *Hinduism*, 90-95.

120 See, for example, Debjani Chatterjee, 'Living in a Multi-cultural Society', *ET*, 88 (1977), 177-80.

121 Cited in Thomas J Hopkins, *The Hindu Religious Tradition* (Belmont, CA: Dickenson, 1971), 118.

122 *The Hindu Response to the Unbound Christ* (Madras, 1974), 43.

importance of history and personal relationship with God. From the very considerable body of literature discussing the possible relationship between Christianity and *advaita vedanta* there is space only to consider those contributions that most directly relate to the quest for a christology in Indian categories.

Some aspects of *advaita* philosophy that are pertinent to the Hindu-Christian encounter have already been noted (chapter 1.F.1). There is, for example, the vedantic understanding of Christ as a *jivanmukta* (realised soul) or even as an advaitin,[123] a true *yogi*.[124] This understanding may, at least, constitute an "attempt to universalize Jesus Christ, to lift him out of his Jewish particularity and Western cultural involvement, in order to make him at home in the religious climate of India".[125] However, the suggestion that Christ thought or taught in or otherwise endorsed advaitin categories seems unacceptable to most Indian Christian – and especially Protestant – opinion.[126]

Nonetheless, there is a viewpoint that seeks to maintain both the distinctiveness and yet similarity of classical christology and advaitic experience. This view, susceptible of elaboration as a possible christological basis of dialogue, is advanced mainly by Catholic theologians – especially Abhishiktananda whose discussion merits

123 See, for example, Prajnananda, *Christ the Saviour* (Calcutta, 1961); Akhilananda, *Hindu View of Christ* (New York, 1949), 96 and *passim*. For a sympathetic appraisal of the christology of Swami Akhilananda (1894-1962) see Heinrich Barlage, *Christ – Saviour of Mankind. A Christian Appreciation of Swami Akhilananda* (St Augustin bei Bonn, 1977). Also interesting are: Prabhavananda, 'Lord's Prayer: A Vedantic Interpretation', *Prabuddha Bharata*, 82 (1972), 488-92; and Satprakashananda, *Hinduism and Christianity: Jesus Christ and His Teachings in the Light of Vedanta* (St Louis, 1975). Ronald Neufeldt quotes Vivekananda (appealing to the advaitin notion of identity) who claims "there is very little difference between the pure religion of Christ and that of Vedanta" ('Hindu Views of Christ', 170).

124 Akhilananda, *Hindu View of Christ*, 72.

125 Samartha, *The Hindu Response to the Unbound Christ*, 120.

126 See, for example, Samartha, *The Hindu Response to the Unbound Christ*, 162-200 and MM Thomas, *The Acknowledged Christ of the Indian Renaissance* (London, 1969), 161-90 (using Radhakrishnan as an example) and the works they cite. See also the rather acerbic review of Heinrich Barlage, *Christ – Saviour of Mankind:.A Christian Appreciation of Swami Akhilananda*. Veröffentlichungen des Missionspriesterseminars, 27 (St. Augustin, Switzerland, 1977) by Richard Fox Young, *IJT*, 30 (1981), 36-39.

particular attention,[127]despite some difficulties in determining the final shape of his thought.[128] For example, it has been argued that the religious consciousness of Jesus, especially as seen in his reported practice of prayer, implies a relationship with God in which there is consciousness both of distinction from and unity with God as Father; Jesus' address of God as "*Abba*" was the Jewish equivalent

---

127 Abhishiktananda offers the most thoroughgoing and profound of such proposals; see especially his *Saccidananda. A Christian Approach to Advaitic Experience*. Revised edition in English (Delhi, 1974). An excellent account of his life and thought is found in Marie-Madeleine Davy, *Henri Le Saux: Swami Abhishiktananda* (Paris, 1981). For further comments and analysis see also Emmanuel Vattakuzhy, *Indian Christian Sannyasa and Swami Abhishiktananda* (Bangalore, 1981); Wayne Teasdale, 'Abhishiktananda's Contemplative Theology', in *Monastic Studies*, 13 (1982), 179-99; Sara Grant, 'Time-bomb or Tomb-stone? Reflections on the Private Journal of Swami Abhishiktananda', *Vidyajyoti*, 52 (1988), 83-97; James E Royster, 'Dialogue in Depth: a Monastic Perspective', *Quarterly Review*, 9 (1989), 75-92; Arvind Sharma, 'Sankara's Bhakti and Swami Abhishiktananda's "Adult Faith"', *JD*, 15 (1990), 240-44; James A Wiseman, 'Enveloped by Mystery: the Spiritual Journey of Henri Le Saux/Abhishiktananda', *Eglise et Theologie*, 23 (1992), 241-260; Mathew N Schmalz, 'The Return from the Further Shore: Theological Implications of Christian Sannyasa', *Koinonia*, 5 (1993), 191-217; Michael Comans, 'Swami Abhishiktananda (Henri Le Saux, OSB) and Advaita: the Account of a Spiritual Journey', in *Religious Traditions in South Asia*, edited by G Oddie, 107-124; Antony Kalliath, *The Word in the Cave: The Experiential Journey of Swami Abhishiktananda to the Point of Hindu-Christian Meeting* (New Delhi: Intercultural Publications, 1996); Judson B Trapnell, 'Two Models of Christian Dialogue with Hindus: Bede Griffiths and Abhishiktananda', *VJTR*, 60 (1996), 101-10, 183-91, 243-54; George Gispert-Sauch, 'Christ and the Indian Mystical Tradition – Swami Abhishiktananda', *Jeevadhara*, 27 (1997), 193-206; Joseph Molleur, 'The Transformation of Dom Le Saux – Swami Abhishiktananda', *IJT*, 39 (1997), 35-42; J Glenn Friesen, 'Abhishiktananda: Hindu Advaitic Experience and Christian Beliefs', *HCSB*, 11 (1998), 31-38; Antony Kalliath, 'Swami Abhishiktananda: Theologian of Inculturation', *TM*, 1 (1998), 82-89. See also the study of Wayne R Teasdale, *Toward a Christian Vedanta* (Bangalore, 1987).

128 As a number of commentators note, towards the end of his life he expressed doubts about his theology and even wanted to disown what he has written because his written advocacy of a form of *advaita* did not correspond to his actual experiences; see, for example, Kalliath, *The Word in the Cave*, xi and James Stuart, *Swami Abhishiktananda: His Life Told Through His Letters* (Delhi: ISPCK, 1989), 341, 345, 349, 358. At the very least it must be said that for Abhishiktananda the tension between *advaita* and Christian faith is never fully resolved.

of the *advaitic* experience.[129] This religious consciousness might even be regarded as the central and normative religious experience within the Christian tradition, given the subsequent importance within Christian history of the experience and acknowledgement of God as Father by those who are 'in Christ'.[130] Mention must also be made of Sunder Rao's attempt to incorporate the experience and language of *advaita* into the experience and theology of what he calls *ananyatva*, a Christian 'non-duality': the experience of mutuality "which cancels the ultimate dualism of the divine and the human on the one hand, and on the other creates a oneness of the two".[131]

One aspect of *anubhava* as understood within *advaita* is the possibility of entry or assumption into the knowledge which Brahman has of itself and in which all duality vanishes – the experience to which the Upanishadic *mahavakyas* (great declarations) "*aham brahmasmi*" ("I am Brahman") and "*tattvamasi*" ("that you are")[132] bear witness.[133] Dupuis argues that the Upanishadic testimony of "*aham brahmasmi*" "finds in Jesus its truest application; in him the saying

---

129 See Abhishiktananda, 'Abba, Father', in his *Saccidananda*, 77-90 and *The Further Shore*, second edition (Delhi: ISPCK, 1984), 52; James Dupuis, 'Christ-Consciousness', in his *Jesus Christ and His Spirit* (Bangalore, 1977), 232-35 and 'Conscience du Christ et expérience d'advaita', *RTL*, 8 (1977), 448-60; Singh, *Preface to Personality*, 28-30, 76. The title of Jacob Kavunkal's *The "Abba" Experience of Jesus: Model and Motive for Mission in Asia* (Indore: Satprakasham Sanchar Kendra, 1995) is misleading, but chapter 2 does offer some reflections on the Kingdom of God as "the explication and realization of [Jesus'] 'Abba' experience" with the result that main task of Christians is not proclamation but growth in Abba-experience and its mediation to others; for a critique of Kavunkal's approach see Karotemprel, 'Asian Christological Trends and Christian Mission', 60-62. See also James DG Dunn, *Jesus and the Spirit* (London, 1975), ch 2, 'Jesus' Experience of God – Sonship'.

130 The experience that appears to be in mind in, for example, such New Testament passages as Romans 8.15 and Galatians 4.6. At this point Abhishiktananda's theology is universalistic: the experience of Jesus is not unique; he showed all humanity their divine 'sonship' and oneness with God. "All that the Christ said or thought about himself, is true of every man." (Stuart, *Swami Abhishiktananda*, 322).

131 *Ananyatva*, 25. It is because all life is held together in Christ that all 'otherness' is abolished (5). He sees such non-duality at the heart of Patristic discussions of the notions of the Trinity and Incarnation (*Ananyatva*, 21-26).

132 Brhadaranyaka Upanishad 1.4.10 and Chandogya Upanishad 6.8.7.

133 For a sympathetic elaboration, see: Abhishiktananda, *Initiation à la spiritualité des Upanishads: 'Vers l'autre rive'* (Sisteron, 1979). See also Dupuis, 'Christ-Consciousness', 236-38.

becomes literally true" – because of its correspondence both with the sayings of the Fourth Gospel and with the reported experience of Jesus of unity with the Father;[134] "it proclaims Jesus' personal awareness of belonging, along with the Father, to the sphere of divinity."[135] It implies that "between Yahweh-Father and Jesus-Son there is at once a distinction and a unity."[136] Abhishiktananda's christology underwent change[137] but in his later writings he repeatedly made the same point as Dupuis, though at greater length: that the *anubhava* of Jesus and of the Upanishadic sages is, despite necessary differences in terminology because of cultural context, essentially the same,[138] even if the 'advaitic' realisation of Jesus was only one component of his religious experience.[139] Both Dupuis and Abhishiktananda acknowledge the way in which Jesus persistently used personal and filial categories in expressing his own *anubhava* of God – categories which in *advaita* are inappropriate for any relationship with an Absolute that is *"ekam advitiyam"* ("one without a second"). If this is so, then the *anubhava* of Jesus (what Dupuis calls "his personal communion with the Father in the *advaita* of the divinity") fulfils the tireless Upanishadic quest for the experience of

---

134 'Christ-Consciousness', 239f. Lucien Legrand makes a similar point and explains that the "Gospels do not go into the metaphysics of that oneness of the Son with the Father, of that Christic *advaita*. They rather present a concrete description of what it meant concretely in terms of language and action, aims and options, life and death. The Gospel language is more existential than essential." ('Christic Advaita', in *Shabda, Shakti, Sangam*, [Christian section], 138 (article: 133-39). See also the comments of O Vercruysse, 'Christ as Brahman. Is the Experience of Christ as Brahman a Christian Experience?', *Sevartham*, 2 (1977), 97-103.

135 Dupuis, Toward a Christian Theology of Religious Pluralism, 273.

136 Dupuis, *Toward a Christian Theology of Religious Pluralism*, 270.

137 He began with the traditional Catholic understanding of Christ as the unique divine incarnation but his settled position seems to amount to the assertion that Jesus is fully human but a model for those who wish to understand the *advaitic* experience that he embraces.

138 See, for example, the chapter 'The Johannine Upanishads', in his *Hindu-Christian Meeting Point*, revised edition (Delhi, 1976), especially 84-93; see also *The Further Shore*, 52. A related point – that *Vedanta* and Christianity both begin with an attitude of unconditional response to a call – is made by Klostermaier, 'Kristvidya', 91f.

139 See his *Saccidananda*, 77-105. See also JDM Stuart, 'Abhishiktananda on Inner Awakening', *Vidyajyoti*, 46 (1982), 470-84; Vandana, *Jesus the Christ: Who Is He? What Is His Message?* (Anand: GS Prakash, 1987); Felix Wilfred, *Beyond Settled Foundations: the Journey of Indian Theology* (Madras: University of Madras, 1993), 192-94.

advaita and perhaps even

> resolves the insurmountable antinomy to which the experience of *advaita* leads – the antinomy between the values of absolute oneness, on the one hand and of personal communion, on the other. ... Jesus' awareness of his relationship with the Father is the supreme realisation of *advaita* in the human condition.[140]

On the other hand, *vedanta* also considers *viveka* (discrimination) to be indispensable for *Brahmavidya;* that is, the discrimination between Brahman and all that is not Brahman. And, as Klostermaier points out, there does seem to be "a parallel between the radicality with which Christ distinguishes Father and world and with which Vedanta distinguishes Brahman and non-Brahman".[141] Another potentially fruitful parallel is found in the distinction between *karma* as designating the 'normal' world of the non-eternal with its nexus of temporal cause and effect, and its opposite, *adhyatma,* meaning the realm of the Self, of Brahman. Klostermaier argues that the follower of *jnanamarga* (especially the advaitin) is disappointed at any portrayal of Christ in merely karmic terms – as in much of the synoptic Gospels – and so needs to be pointed to the *'adhyatmic* Christ'.

> It is the Fourth Gospel that succeeds in ... reporting parables and miracles in such a way as to make the Spirit and Absolute transparent. Paul constantly emphasises that the true Christ is a spiritual reality. ... The centre of the message is a spiritual reality. The Christian detachment from *karma* is as radical as that of Advaita.[142]

In Protestant circles there has been considerably less interest in *advaita* than among Catholics – perhaps because there is no comparable background to the kind of philosophical scholasticism that seems to have contributed to Catholic interest in Sankara for example. Nonetheless, in the opinion of Samartha, "no emerging theology and christology in India can afford to ignore the power and enduring influence of *advaita* on the Indian mind".[143] But perhaps the most thoroughgoing attempt to apply *advaita* to christology is to be found in KP Aleaz. In a series of books and articles he has

140 *Toward a Christian Theology of Religious Pluralism,* 273.

141 'Kristvidya', 95.

142 'Kristvidya', 109.

143 *One Christ – Many Religions,* 107; he also remarks that "for Christian thinkers in India to ignore *advaita* and its enduring influence on the life and thought of people is the easiest way to commit theological suicide" (108).

argued, for example, for *Jesus in Neo-Vedanta*[144] and *An Indian Jesus from Sankara's Thought*.[145] In his writings he employs a methodology that gives "complete authority to the authentic writings of Sankara in order to explain 'who Jesus is',"[146]- that is, to develop what he calls a dialogical Jesuology for the relational convergence of Hinduism and Christianity. One example of such a Sankara-inspired explanation is that the

> total dependence on the part of Jesus upon Brahman ... is expressed in the self-sacrifice of Jesus. The relevance of Jesus lies in his not claiming any significance for himself, in his total sacrifice of himself for others. ... The person of Jesus proclaims that if we identify any aspect of his person as Brahman we are in ignorance; but if we identify in every aspect of his person Brahman, and Brahman alone, we have come to the experience [of] who he truly is. ... But the Christian Church in its history has reversed this very often to affirm the reality of Jesus in the person of God and thus totally misinterpreted the meaning of Jesus. If that is so, it is India through Sankara's Advaita Vedanta who corrects the misinterpretation of the meaning of Jesus caused by the Christian Church through providing the ideological basis for the self-sacrifice of Jesus.[147]

This is certainly one of the more controversial aspects of Aleaz's approach: his repeated insistence that Western theology has misunderstood the death of Christ as an atonement for sin. However, it might be argued that Aleaz's distaste derives more from the criticism of atonement theory by representatives of neo-Hinduism than by flaws he is able to demonstrate in the traditional Christian understanding. Hence (as outlined above and following the theolo-

---

144 Subtitle: *A Meeting of Hinduism and Christianity* (Delhi: Kant Publications, 1995).

145 (Calcutta: Punthi Pustak, 1996); see also his *The Gospel of Indian Culture* (Calcutta: Punthi Pustak, 1994), especially the section 'The Gospel of God in Jesus Emerging from Indian Culture' (97-282); *Christian Thought Through Advaita Vedanta* (Delhi: ISPCK, 1996); 'An Understanding of Jesus from within the Advaita Vedanta – the Findings of Research', *NCCR*, 68 (1998), 168-82.

146 'An Indian Understanding of Jesus – Findings of a Research', *AJT*, 12 (1998), 119; he goes on to qualify this statement by writing that his findings are the result of a double experience "namely Jesus-experience and Advaita Vedanta experience" (119).

147 'An Indian Understanding of Jesus', 127. Several aspects of this assertion by Aleaz might be questioned: (i) the statement that Jesus claimed no significance for himself; (ii) the assertion that Sankara's Vedanta is needed to correct a (long and widely recognised) danger in christology.

gy of K Subba Rao) he explains the death of Jesus as a self-sacrifice that gives up the ignorance of duality caused by *maya* and expresses the unifying power of the Supreme Self..

Other Protestants have been less radical in their employment of *advaitic* categories. Dhanjibhai Fakirbhai is one of several Protestants who have found a qualified *advaita* (such as Ramanuja's) to be more amenable. Dhanjibhai outlines six different forms of *advaita* (that of Christ with his Father; Christ with the cosmos; Christ with his disciples; the disciples with one another; the mutual *advaita* of humanity; that of humanity with nature)[148]but only the first implies identity and the influence of *bhakti* is apparent as well. In turn, Robin Boyd's *Khristadvaita: A Theology for India* has been inspired by Dhanjibhai with its title a statement of the central Pauline theme of "faith-union with Christ which involves the Christian in God's great work of creation and new creation."[149] He is clear that "*Khristadvaita* is not to be understood in the sense of absolute monism or *advaita*. The formation of the term is more akin to the *visistadvaita* of Ramanuja."[150]

Even if the suggestion of a 'Christian *advaita*', based upon the experience of Jesus, were not wholly acceptable to Hindu proponents of *advaita*, its advocacy does point to the possibility of a dialogue in which each might learn from the other. The Christian might be reminded that the transcendent unity of God cannot be compromised (nor God's immanence dismissed as pantheism). While affirming the way in which Christ inserts humanity into God's irreducible "communion in nonduality", Dupuis believes that the unity that necessarily underlies this communion "can be strengthened by the experience of the nonduality (*advaita*) of Hindu mysticism."[151] The Christian might also be helped to realise (or to remember) that although God is the supreme *Atman*, and ultimately beyond all categories, God can also be sought and known in the *'guha'* ('cave') of the heart, as well as in the cosmos and in Christ. The virtues of interiority and contemplation as practised by advaitins, and the use of silence, might remind the Christian (especially the Protestant) of their benefits. The practice of detachment and renunciation (not without parallels in the example of Jesus) might also be noted.

---

148 *Manilal C Parekh; Dhanjibhai Fakirbhai: A Selection*, edited by Robin HS Boyd (Madras: Christian Literature Society, 1974), 211-13, 272, 280f.

149 (Madras: Christian Literature Society, 1977), viii.

150 *Khristadvaita*, 278; he adds that "it does not signify an ontological union with God, but rather that faith-union which none can put asunder" (278).

151 Dupuis, *Toward a Christian Theology of Religious Pluralism*, 278.

Even if the Christian were unable to abandon or even substantially to qualify the expression of a relationship with God in inter-personal categories, the advaitin witness might lead to the placing of the origin of that relationship at progressively 'deeper' levels within.[152] Given that the otherness of God means not merely that God is located outside the human being but that God is 'Utterly Other', the relationship with God "must be interiorized as it grows ... in the spirit of the human being" and the Hindu tradition of the *Atman* can help this deepening.[153] The seriousness of the Hindu quest for *advaita* might help clarify for Christians (and others) an understanding of Jesus' communion with his Father by offering a reminder that it is not reducible to the normal range of inter-personal relationships.[154] Christians might also learn from the holistic advaitin view of reality that integrates the various dualisms that have puzzled or troubled Christianity over the centuries.[155]

On the other hand, the Hindu advaitin partner in dialogue might, because of the testimony of Jesus, consider an understanding of the Absolute that includes, but is not confined to, personal categories (such as personal relationship and even confrontation) – a consideration facilitated by the possible acknowledgement that this relationship was 'realised' by one who was, at least in the limited sense described above, himself an advaitin. The divine-human relationship to which Christ witnesses might be called a way of reciprocal or mutual interiority – transcending or complementing what Cuttat

152 Chatterjee, for example, notes what she believes to have been, at least in some Christian reflection about knowledge of the divine, "a significant shift from metaphors of spatial height to those of depth" so that "the path seems open to a new dialogue between ... the Christian and the Hindu in terms of the 'within'" ('The Presuppositions of Inter-Religious Communication', *RSt*, 3 (1967), 400). The writings of Abhishiktananda, not least his *Prayer* (4th edition: Delhi, 1975), make the same point; on 'interiority' see also Cuttat, *The Encounter of Religions*, 67-83. The Christian theologian Paul Tillich is also said to have written: "God is only known by people who are prepared to plumb the depths of their own experience." (source unknown).

153 Dupuis, *Toward a Christian Theology of Religious Pluralism*, 277.

154 See Abhishiktananda, *Saccidananda*, 85f.

155 See the remarks of Amaladoss, 'Towards a Culture of Wholeness', *Vidyajyoti*, 47 (1983), 72f and, a greater length, Subhash Anand, 'Vedanta Hermeneutics: A Holistic Search for Wholeness', in *Interrelations and Interpretation: Philosophical Reflections on Science, Religion and Hermeneutics*, edited by Job Kozhamthadam (New Delhi: Intercultural Publications, 1997), 174-213.

calls the usual Hindu way of "solitary interiority".[156] It might also be asked whether the inward quest of *advaita vedanta* and its emphasis upon the ultimacy of Brahman over against the world (with its pressing needs) does not devalue the significance of those personal, socio-economic and socio-political issues that most Christians would see as falling under the critical but potentially redemptive scrutiny of Christ.[157] A Christian *advaita* might also draw attention to the unity of all in God; what Amaladoss calls "a communion of beings, not merely metaphysical but achieved in free participation ... – a communion that would respect pluralism and multiplicity".[158]

Nonetheless, an acceptance of such foundations for an *advaitic* christology depends on the clarification of several issues. There needs to be confidence that the originality of Jesus' self-awareness in unique filial categories and a sense of total dependence upon God can be determined and defined. Secondly there is the question of whether the *advaitic* realisation or awakening is, in fact, the same as Jesus' reported experience of a unique oneness in distinction with God (or, to put it in even more problematical Trinitarian terms, his awareness of the hypostatic union). It might, at best, be possible to argue for an analogous or parallel experiential base for identifying the "I am" of Jesus with the advaitic *"aham asmi"* – but that is all. Some assessment of the *advaitic* worldview is also required. Aleaz is critical of those who reject or reinterpret *advaita*; rather, "the coming together of Advaita Vedanta and Christian thought points to a possible future relational convergence of religions". Vedanta cannot be tied to any one religion; it represents "unity and universality in the midst of diversities."[159] He also believes that Sankara's thought rep-

156 See Jacques-Albert Cuttat, *Expérience chrétienne et spiritualité orientale* (Paris and Bruges, 1967).

157 As Mookenthottam writes of the theocentrism that he believes to predominate in Indian Catholic theology: while it "has the merit of developing a Christian advaitic spirituality, it has the disadvantage of overlooking the human, social and secular dimensions of life" (*Indian Theological Tendencies*, 175). See also the comments of MM Thomas, *Salvation and Humanisation* (Bangalore, 1971), 35. Sebastian Kappen also points out the way in which advaitic spirituality "can breed cosmic pessimism, escapism, and even absolute unconcern for the welfare of one's fellowmen." ('Jesus and Transculturation,' in *Asian Faces of Jesus*, 185.) Samartha, however, denies any implicit amorality: *One Christ – Many Religions*, 108f).

158 Michael Amaladoss in Lead Me to the Real: the Hindu-Christian Dialogue, 30.

159 *Christian Thought Through Advaita Vedanta*, xv, 1f.

resents the culmination of God's self-disclosure to Indians."[160] These assertions are hardly widespread in Indian Christian circles where, for example, Sankara's notion of *nirguna* [attributeless] Brahman is even more widely rejected for its apparent incoherence than it is among Hindus.

A further objection to an advaitin christology as outlined above is that it is hardly acceptable to those many Hindus who are not advaitins.[161] Discussion with Hindus suggests that Manickam is correct when he argues that the "contemporary Hindu tradition is firmly built on *bhaktyanubhava*" (the experiential component of a devotional approach to the divine) rather than what he calls the monistic intellectualism of those for whom the Hindu scriptures are normative.[162] If so, it might be possible to use the record of Christ's own reported life of *bhakti* as a component of the recognition of him as a *guru* – given the traditional Indian role assigned to the *guru* as the *pramana* (authoritative source) of *bhaktyanubhava*. (Any such portrayal would, of course, need to acknowledge the beliefs and sensitivities of other Indian traditions about *bhakti*; for example, the Vedantin conviction that the *Isvara* of theistic devotion is at a distinctly lower level than *nirguna* Brahman; and the disquiet of many secularised and other Indians at the multiple subjectivities of *bhakti* pietism.) Moreover, reflection on the encounter of *advaita* and Christianity has drawn attention to several significant points. (i) The central importance of Brahman – whose significance is often downplayed in Indian Christian circles because it is *nirguna* – is maintained. (ii) The role of the Spirit to whom little attention is given in Indian (as in most Western) theology outside of pietistic/*bhakti* circles is also affirmed.[163] (iii) The way in which an elaboration of the divine in Trinitarian categories might also help the discussion.[164]

---

160 'An Indian Understanding of Jesus', 119.

161 As Klostermaier notes "If we would content ourselves with a Christian Advaita it would cripple our *Kristvidya* and make it inaccessible for many" ('Kristvidya', 106).

162 Manickam, 'Anubhava as Pramana of an Indian Christology', 23.

163 See, for example, Abhishiktananda, *Saccidananda*, chapters 8 and 16; Sunder Rao, *Ananyatva*, 21f, 25-27.

164 A fine, lengthy example of such a discussion is found in von Brück, *The Unity of Reality: God, God-Experience, and Meditation in the Hindu-Christian Dialogue*; in it von Brück argues that the advaitic experience corresponds to and illuminates aspects of the experience of the Christian Trinity.

G. *Saccidananda* and Terms for Christ

One Vedantin description of Brahman is *Saccidananda*: the Absolute as *sat* (being), *cit* (consciousness / intelligence) and *ananda* (bliss). Although the compound term is not found as such in the Upanishads, it is derived from a number of late Upanishadic passages[165] and was then developed in the Vedanta tradition. Given that Brahman is both *nirguna* (attribute-less) and yet able to be described in this threefold way, and because the term seems closely to affirm attributes that the Christian scholastic tradition has assigned to God, a number of Indian Christians have sought to use the language of *Saccidananda* to elaborate the notion of God as Trinity. Keshub Chunder Sen,[166] Brahmabandhab Upadhyaya, Abhishiktananda and Monchanin are among those who have used the term to do precisely this.[167] The most thorough elaboration – though from a Christian trinitarian basis – is to be found in Abhishiktananda's volume *Saccidananda* in which he argues both that the fullest comprehension of Brahman is found in knowing Brahman as *Saccidananda* and that the Hindu ideal of union with Brahman is possible by means of union with Christ who, with the Spirit, is already in union with the Father. It is in terms of inter-personal experience that *Saccidananda*-Brahman is known in its triune fullness.[168] Bede Griffiths also argues that *Saccidananda* is complementary to the Trinitarian intuition of the Christian tradition[169] and

165 See the useful elaboration in: Ruth Reyna, *Introduction to Indian Philosophy* (New Delhi, 1971), 53f, where she argues that the term applies to *nirguna* (attributeless) Brahman only; it points to but does not define It.

166 According to David C Scott, Keshub was the first Indian Christian to elaborate the correspondence; see his anthology *Keshub Chunder Sen. A Selection*, edited with an Introduction by Scott (Madras, 1979), 40; for Keshub's own elaboration, see 228, 245.

167 See the discussion in Boyd, *Introduction to Indian Christian Theology, passim*, and his *Khristadvaita*, 413-17; he also defends the Christian use of *Saccidananda*: 415f. A translation of Brahmabandhab's impressive Sanskrit hymn on the Trinity, beginning, "I bow to *Saccidananda*", is found in *The Writings of Brahmabandhab Upadhyay*, volume 1, edited by Julius Lipner and George Gispert-Sauch (Bangalore: United Theological College, 1991), 125; for an analysis see George Gispert-Sauch, 'The Sanskrit Hymns of Brahmabandhav Upadhyay', *RS*, 19.4 (December 1972), 65. See too the discussion in Kurian Mathothu, *The Development of the Concept of Trimurti in Hinduism* (Palai, 1974), 39, 127-33.

168 See, for example, *Saccidananda*, Parts Two and Three (77-203).

169 Griffiths also believes that the Trinitarian experience is closer to the ultimate because of the added element of personal relationship, which has

Teasdale believes that *Saccidananda* and Trinity "share in a mystical continuum which makes an existential convergence possible".[170] Dupuis concludes, "the Hindu classical tradition probably offers in the *saccidananda* doctrine, the concept of God closest to the Christian Trinity that the history of religions has to offer."[171] And Gispert-Sauch – who writes of "that absolute moksha which is best defined as *Saccidananda*" – has proposed that an Indian christology be developed that is rooted in the awareness of the Spirit as the innermost bliss of God.[172]

In the *Saccidananda* analogy – Christ is seen as *Cit* – the divine act of knowing that conveniently approximates to the traditional Biblical categories of Wisdom and *Logos* that reveal the otherwise unknown God. This is a point taken up by Griffiths in his elaboration of the Son as *saguna* Brahman through whom the otherwise nameless Father – *nirguna* Brahman, the naked Godhead, the abyss of Being – receives a name.[173] It is perhaps significant that Keshub's interest in Christianity began in the Brahmo Samaj, with its firm belief in the Absolute, but developed in a christological direction (largely on experiential grounds) to give a central place in his life and beliefs to Christ as the *Cit* of the triune Brahman.[174] AJ Appasamy's personalist *bhakti* sympathies precluded an identification of *Logos* with *Cit*, but, he does appeal to Indian philosophical precedents (as well as to the *bhakti* tradition) for his emphasis upon the immanence of God in creation – an immanence which, in Christian theology, has often been linked with the role of the *Logos*.[175]

---

implications for the world of multiplicity including the implication that the created world is real; see Wayne Teasdale, 'Bede Griffiths and the Uniqueness of Christianity', *Communio*, 11 (1984), 177-86.

170 *Toward a Christian Vedanta*, 127.

171 Dupuis, *Toward a Christian Theology of Religious Pluralism*, 301; see his explanation for the claim 274-78.

172 George Gispert-Sauch, 'Notes for an Indian Christology', *VJTR*, 61 (1997), 764 (article 757-65).

173 Bede Griffiths, *Return to the Centre* (London, 1978), 12. Dupuis' explanation is that the transcendental perfection of knowledge is "put to use to express analogically the 'origin' of God the Son generated by the Father. ... Clearly, some new and deeper meaning is implied in the process, which goes beyond what the transcendental perfections imply by themselves in God." (*Toward a Christian Theology of Religious Pluralism*, 275).

174 See *Keshub Chunder Sen*, 225-34, 237-40 which includes discussion of Christ as "the *Chit*-Christ, pure and intelligent, the Word of God, mighty Logos" (238).

175 See his *Christianity as Bhakti Marga* (Madras, 1926), 34-49. He appeals both to Ramanuja and Sankara (41f).

The relationship between Brahman and the world is, of course, an important issue in Hinduism. Not unexpectedly, it is a debate into which Christians have entered – partly because of an opinion that "India needs a Christian concept of Logos. ... India needs the assurance of a steady, dependable relation between God the phenomenal world", including all nature and all history in which God acts with redemptive purpose and power.[176] Belief in the *Logos* as the effective agent of God in creation also has parallels with the notion of *sakti*.[177]Vineeth even elaborates the notion of "*Atman* as abiding *Logos*"[178] and a number of writers suggest *Om* as the most appropriate translation of the meaning and significance of *Logos*.[179] As subject matter for dialogue, the God-world relationship is important; the plausibility and relevance of the usual Hindu and Christian answers require continuing attention.

However, although *Cit* is used as an analogy of *Logos, sabda* (word) is perhaps a better Sanskrit equivalent and, given its importance in the Vedas, may be even more appropriate for expressing the christological category of the divine Word.[180] Although *sabda* literally means sound, it is in fact (according to the *karma marga*), the Vedic *mantra* – giving meaning and effective power to what is otherwise unintelligible sound. The Upanishads also link *sabda* with Brahman, speaking of Brahman in the form of Word[181] – all of which leads Klostermaier to assert that the *sabda* philosophy provides a basis on which to render intelligible the traditional Christian understanding

---

176 RM Clark, 'A Study of Christological Categories in the Indian Church', 258 (cited by Boyd, *An Introduction to Indian Christian Theology*, 239).

177 One of many examples is Aurobindo's linking of the evolutionary process with *cit* and *cit-sakti* ('Consciousness-Force'). See his *The Life Divine* (10th edition: Pondicherry, 1977), *passim*.

178 V Francis Vineeth in *Religions in Dialogue. East and West Meet*, edited by Zacharias Thundy and others (Lanham, MD, 1985), 211-27.

179 S Jesudason, *Unique Christ and Indigenous Christianity*, 4, 40; RD Ranade, *A Constructive Survey of Upanishadic Philosophy* (Bombay, 1968), 244f; Vivekananda, *Complete Works of Vivekananda* (Calcutta, 1969), vol. III, 57; Abhishiktananda, *Prayer*, 60; George Gillespie, '*Om* as Christian Syllable', *Foundations*, 17 (1974), 341f.

180 See Vivienne Mariau, 'Logos as Cit and Sabdabrahman: A Survey', *BTF*, 15 (1983), 39-57; Klostermaier, 'Kristvidya', 97-99, and the literature cited there; and XJ Puthenkalam ('Johannine "Logos" in the Indian Theological Context', *LW*, 88 (1982), 34- 48) who also uses *vac* ('speech' or 'word') as well as *sabda*.

181 According to Klostermaier, the ultimate *pramana* (authoritative standard for truth) is *sabda* alone, since *sabda* in its proper form is identical with Brahman ('Kristvidya', 95).

of *Logos* as the expression of the otherwise unknowable God. He also explores the Vedic images and practices associated with *yajna* (sacrifice) as suggestive of parallels with the Christian notion of the sacrifice of Christ – a notion made more intelligible to a Hindu when taken from the Indian world of discourse. Moreover, Klostermaier also believes that the concepts of *sabda* and *yajna* will actually enable Christians to gain new insights into their own christological beliefs and practices (for example, by the use of *japa* – the repetition of the name or names of God).[182]

Another Sanskrit term with possible christological implications is *purusa* (person) – a word used in the Upanishads and Gita to refer to the divine as active rather than passive or resting. Devanandan and Boyd, for example, suggest the use of *purusa* in place of the (Western) concepts of person and personal as they are used of God and Christ.[183] Yet another useful concept may be that of *prajnana* – (primeval intelligence; literally: 'pre-knowledge') as found in the earlier Upanishads (for example, Aitareya Up. 3.1.2-4). It receives a notable application by the Gujerati Christian writer Dhanjibhai Fakirbhai (1895-1967) who sees parallels with the use in the Fourth Gospel of the *Logos* terminology in elaborating the Christian notion of incarnation. He believes both that the notion of incarnation by Brahman is coherent and that the *prajnana* of the Upanishads is the same as the *Logos* of which the first generation of Christians spoke and for these reasons sees it as an appropriate means of explaining the incarnation in distinctly Hindu categories.[184]

In assessing the usefulness of the *Saccidananda* terminology, and other Indian words for Christ, the full weight of the two traditions' quite different perspectives must be felt. From the viewpoint of the *advaita*, the Christian appeal to the advantages of a tripersonal communion (both within the divine being and in the human-divine relationship) will seem like no advantage at all in the light of the Hindu belief that Brahman is transpersonal and that all personal determination of Brahman is therefore to be transcended in the quest to become one with it. However, if "the Christian mystery of communion surpasses, by completing it, the Hindu mysticism of identification",[185] then Christians will feel justified in their employment of

182 See 'Kristvidya', 105.

183 See Devanandan, *I Will Lift*, 60, 67f; Boyd, *Introduction to Indian Christian Theology*, 237.

184 See his *Adhyatma Darsana*, II. 1 (found in *Manilal C Parekh. Dhanjibhai Fakirbhai*, 278f). See also the discussion by Boyd, *Introduction to Indian Christian Theology*, 203-05 and 277f.

185 Dupuis, *Toward a Christian Theology of Religious Pluralism*, 277.

Saccidananda. But even if they do use the terminology they may also reflect on *advaitic* misgivings about the imperfections of all personal language cast in human categories about the divine. The Christian tradition has long known of the limitations of anthropomorphic language but the Hindu challenge will offer a reminder of the Mystery that is beyond all distinctions.

Within the Christian community, much may depend upon the importance attached the classical christological formulae (for example the Nicene and Chalcedonian formulae). If the central issues they attempt to address – the relationship between the divine and human in Jesus and the unity of Christ with both Father and Spirit – are considered normative for India, then the terminology we have examined will be useful indeed. If, however, those issues are regarded as insoluble, or relatively unimportant, then correspondingly less weight will be attached to the possible usefulness or the solutions supposedly offered by Indian terminology such as *Saccidananda*. As in the western church, so also in India opinions differ widely concerning the importance of the classical christological debates and credal formulae.

'*Saccidananda*' expresses for Hindus (or, at least, some Hindus) the highest point reached in the search for Brahman, and if at least some Christians believe that the fullness of *Saccidananda* is the fullness of the triune God made especially accessible in Christ, then the discussion may be important and fruitful; but both Hindu and Christian opinion are divided over these matters. Among Christians, for example, it has been pointed out that claims that reality itself is 'plural' in effect presuppose a supra-traditional vantagepoint. Milbank, in commenting on Panikkar's assertion that such plurality is 'the primordial myth' preserved in one form in the doctrines of Christianity and in other forms elsewhere, calls the assertion an ontological pluralism "at once neo-Vedantic and Trinitarian". Milbank goes on to argue that this is "an impossible union" because neo-Vedantic pluralism assumes a 'univocal' or 'indifferent' presence of transcendental power whereas Christian Trinitarianism remains irreducibly relational and communal in some way.[186]

Nonetheless, the very fact that a number of analogies are sought and employed from Hindu parallels points to the richness and depth of the meanings Christians have traditionally assigned to Christ, and acts as a reminder that Christians do not and cannot

186 John Milbank, 'The End of Dialogue', in *Christian Uniqueness Reconsidered*, 188f.

claim to possess all possible knowledge of *saguna* Christ: the one with many attributes.

H. Jesus as Social Liberator

Somewhat removed from the philosophical reflection that gave rise to the notion of *Saccidananda* is an emphasis that relates the life and death of Jesus to participation in the struggle for social justice in India. This links him with the quest for a liberational praxis in response to poverty, social injustice and exploitation that has gained prominence in Indian theology (both Catholic and Protestant) especially since the 1970s[187]- a theology critical of previous tendencies to contextualise the Christian message in upper caste and philosophical worldviews. The search for an appropriately contextualised Indian theology of liberation has coincided with the rise of organised movements within the 'Dalit' (formerly 'outcaste' or 'untouchable'), tribal and other marginalised and oppressed sections of Indian society and the perceived need for the Indian church to reflect critically from a starting point that takes contemporary experience as seriously as theological and other starting points. A Dalit perspective is especially important given that perhaps some 80% of Christians in India are of Dalit origins. It is said, for example, that there are "liberative, humanistic visions and values" in tribal and Dalit culture that have been overlooked in favour of a Western orientation in Indian theology.[188] Or theology has been expressed in a classical Indian philosophical framework – what Nirmal calls the "Brahmanic tradition" and about which "one wonders whether this kind of Indian Christian theology will ever have a mass appeal" by comparison with one that centres on the "God whom Jesus Christ

187 Indian theology at this point is clear indebted to wider Asian theology; see for example, Tissa Balasuriya, *Jesus Christ and Liberation* (Colombo: Centre for Society and Religion Publications, 1981); Aloysius Pieris, *An Asian Theology of Liberation* (Maryknoll, NY: Orbis, 1988); Michael Amaladoss, *Life in Freedom: Liberation Theologies of Asia* (Anand and Maryknoll, NY: Gujarat Sahitya Prakash and Orbis Books, 1997); *Liberation in Asia: Theological Perspectives*, edited by S Arokiasamy and George Gispert-Sauch (Anand: Gujarat Sahitya Prakash, 1997). For an interreligious perspective see *Religions and Liberation*, edited by Asghar Ali Engineer (Delhi: Ajanta Publications, 1989).

188 KC Abraham, 'Re-interpretation of Christian Tradition in Contemporary India', *AJT*, 9 (1995), 269.

revealed ... [who] is a Dalit God."[189] One advocate of dialogue has issued an appeal for 'Interreligious Dialogue from the Perspective of the Poor' – warning of the danger that Hindu-Christian (and other) dialogue might otherwise uphold the value system of India's elites.[190]

A christological response to Dalit concerns has begun to emerge in several ways. In general terms Christ is portrayed as inspiring those who resist oppression.[191] A Dalit theology is said to be slowly evolving "in and through our sufferings, the suffering God in Jesus Christ, and the Dalit Spirit."[192] The identity of Jesus can be construed in Dalit categories: "Jesus ... was himself a Dalit, despite his being a Jew." In fact, "both his humanity and his divinity are to be understood in terms of his dalitness."[193] The fact that Jesus has Gentile

---

189 AP Nirmal, 'Toward a Christian Dalit Theology', in *Indigenous People: Dalits. Dalit Issues in Today's Theological Debate,* edited by James Massey (Delhi: ISPCK, 1995), 215, 224. There is a large (and growing) literature on Dalit theology and a theology of Dalit concerns; see, for example, *Towards a Dalit Theology,* edited by ME Prabhakar (Delhi: ISPCK, 1988); *Emerging Dalit Theology,* edited by Xavier Irudayaraj (Madurai: Tamilnadu Theological Seminary, 1990); *Toward a Common Dalit Theology,* edited by Nirmal Minz (Madras: Gurukul Lutheran Theological College and Research Institute, 1990); *A Reader in Dalit Theology,* edited by AP Nirmal (Madras: Gurukul Lutheran Theological College and Research Institute, 1991); James Massey, *Roots of Dalit History, Christianity, Theology and Spirituality,* third edition (Delhi: ISPCK, 1996); Chandran, 'Confessing Jesus Christ as Liberator', in his *The Church in Mission,* 18-40; *Frontiers of Dalit Theology,* edited by V Devasahayam (Delhi: ISPCK, 1997); Sebastian CH Kim and KC Marak, *Good News for the Poor: the Challenge to the Church* (Delhi: ISPCK, 1997); Sathianathan Clarke, *Dalits and Christianity: Subaltern Religion and Liberation Theology in India* (New Delhi: Oxford University Press, 1998); *RS,* 45.4 (December 1998) is devoted to Dalit issues; Samuel Jayakumar, *Dalit Consciousness and Christian Conversion. Historical Resources for a Contemporary Debate* (Oxford and Delhi: Regnum International and ISPCK, 1999); L Stanislaus, *The Liberative Mission of the Church among Dalit Christians* (Delhi: ISPCK, 1999) with an excellent bibliography.

190 Walter Fernandes in *VJTR,* 59 (1995), 91-105; he goes on to call not only for dialogue based on liberation theology but also the liberation of theology from the dominant value systems.

191 For example, V Henry Davadas, *Christ Inspires Human Struggle for Freedom and Justice: A Freedom Fighter's Testimony* (Bangalore and Delhi: CISRS and ISPCK, 1993).

192 KP Aleaz, *The Gospel of Indian Culture* (Calcutta: Punti Pustak, 1994), 193.

193 Arvind P Nirmal, 'A Dialogue with Dalit Literature', in *Towards a Dalit Theology,* 65; also found as 'Towards a Christian Dalit Theology', in *A Reader in Dalit Theology,* 225. A Dalit writer comments that "Jesus Christ

ancestors, together with his Nazareth manifesto of liberation for the oppressed (Luke 4.18f), his compassion, healings and exorcisms, his table fellowship with 'sinners' and Samaritans, his forgiveness of sins, his confrontation of the powerful: all of these are said to show his intention to break the barriers of caste and untouchability.[194] A Dalit writer describes Christ as one who "started ... a peaceful social revolution against the exploitative system in order to establish a new social order"; he rejected oppression, affluence and poverty.[195] Such Dalit reflection on the significance of Christ continues a much longer tradition of Dalit responsiveness to him. A detailed historical study by Jayakumar shows that it was conversion to Christ that led Tamil Dalits to abandon the demeaning "Dalit mentality and begin a process of integration into the mainstream of Indian society."[196] In John Webster's history of Dalit Christians there is a narrative section (chapter 5) entitled 'Good News for Dalits'[197] whose first half contains a number of moving personal testimonies to the liberating role of Jesus.

Sometimes a christological focus is described over against the prevailing attitudes of the church; for example, a Seminar Statement noted that, "Quick to preach about Jesus' providential option for the poor, the church has failed to recognise that Jesus did not 'opt' for the poor – he identified himself totally with the poor. He was the hungry one, the thirsty, the naked, the imprisoned – he was the dalit."[198] And a discussion of 'Dalit Theology' contrasts the tendency of middle class Indian Christians to see Jesus Christ in individualistic, pietistic and otherworldly terms – as a "spiritual saviour" delivering from personal sin and guilt – whereas, for Dalits, Christ and salvation are said to be "integrally linked to their dehumanised social existence and their hope for a future in Christ, freed from all inhumanity and injustice."[199]

---

was born into a poor carpenter's family, considered in India to be a Dalit family" (Vijay Singh, 'The Dalit Self Respect Movement: Christian Contribution', in *Liberating Witness*, 429).

194 ME Prabhakar, 'Dalit Theology', in *Frontiers of Dalit Theology*, 414f and, in considerable detail, Stanislaus, *The Liberative Mission of the Church Among Dalit Christians*, 231-84.

195 Singh, 'The Dalit Self Respect Movement', 429).

196 *Dalit Consciousness and Christian Conversion*, xvi.

197 John CB Webster, *The Dalit Christians: A History* (Delhi: ISPCK, 1992).

198 *Toward a Common Dalit Theology*, 131. (The text quoted probably intended a reference to the liberation theology mantra about Jesus' *preferential* option for the poor.

199 Prabhakar, 'Dalit Theology', 405 (see also 409).

However, the extent and significance of the christological component of the emerging theology of liberation should not be overstated; there are some curious silences. When Aloysius Pieris describes 'A Theology of Liberation in Asian Churches', he makes virtually no mention of Christ (though he does have a section on 'The Messianic Role of the Masses').[200] TK John elaborates a 'Theology of Liberation and Gandhian Praxis' that seems to have no place for Christ.[201] In Webster's narrative of Dalit responses to Christ the subsequent theological reflection,[202] and Webster's own conclusions,[203] have no christological reference at all. Some of the reluctance to affirm (or affirm strongly) a christological focus may derive from Dalit (including Christian Dalit) misgivings about the relevance of any religiously inspired solution to Dalit oppression. One experienced observer considers that "Religious factors play a limited role in changing [Dalit] social consciousness" and that "Major religious traditions remain very much outside Dalits' history, culture, struggle and movements."[204] A further reason may be the belief that Dalit liberation will require an interreligious approach – and therefore one in which the apparent exclusiveness of a christocentric approach would seem to be inappropriate. At least some Christian Dalits, who once fought for justice simply as Christians while drawing almost exclusively on biblical resources, are now said to realise that there are resources for their struggle among other religious traditions as well; the 'Dalit Solidarity Programme', for example, has brought together Hindu, Buddhist, Christian, Muslim and Sikh Dalits.[205] One result is a call to include Dalit concerns in Hindu-Christian dialogue.[206] A further reason for the rather minimalist christological undergirding of Dalit theology might well be that, in both Protestant and Catholic circles, "Indian theology today

---

200 In *Liberation in Asia*, 17-38; the section on the Messianic role of the masses is 31-35.

201 In *Liberation in Asia*, 115-42.

202 The second half of chapter 5 of *The Dalit Christians: A History*.

203 *The Dalit Christians: A History*, 243-45.

204 AM Abraham Ayrookuzhiel, 'The Role of Religion in Dalit Social Liberation: Some Reflections', in *the Role of the Philosopher Today*, edited by Anand Amaladoss (Madras: TR Publications, 1994), 88f, 91.

205 See *Dalit Solidarity*, edited by Bhagavan Das and James Massey (Delhi: ISPCK, 1995); James Massey, 'Ingredients for a Dalit Theology', in *Towards a Dalit Theology*, 58f.

206 See, for example, AM Abraham Ayrookuzhiel, 'The Dalits, Religions and Interfaith Dialogue', *HCSB*, 7 (1994), 13-19.

proclaims an exceedingly modest Jesus"[207] and, as we have seen, is often reluctant to express itself in christocentric categories. This reluctance also reflects a degree of derivation from and dependence on (non-Indian) liberation theologies[208] whose christological content is usually as modest in scale as its suspicion of metaphysics is large.

Moreover, when christology is introduced, it is usually of the rather modest 'from below' species with Jesus described in those exemplarist and functional categories that are the least threatening in a pluralist context – with Jesus tending to be portrayed, in the words of Sathianathan Clarke, as "a co-sufferer and thus a model for human living. Thus it lifts up the selfless model of Jesus in order to invite others to follow his example of liberative praxis." Although Clarke acknowledges the worth of much of this model, he calls for the added balance of the "exalted and cosmic Jesus" as "able, trustworthy, and sufficient to liberate suffering communities. Because of this extra-mundane relatedness suffering is not hopeless and final."[209] But there is little indication that contemporary Indian liberation theologies will be inclined to strengthen the christological component in this way.

Another christological response has been a renewed interest in the notion of *satyagraha*. This 'insistence on truth' has come to mean that adherence to the truth of non-violence and appropriate passive resistance and non-co-operation (especially in the face of suffering and oppression) espoused by Gandhi and others. The well documented attention given by the leaders of the Hindu renaissance, from Ram Mohun Roy to Gandhi, to the life of Jesus in the face of suffering (including his own) has already been noted (see chapter 1.B and 1.F.1). According to MM Thomas, it is the example and teaching of Gandhi that "has made intelligible to India the idea of vicarious suffering",[210]with all its implications for understanding

---

207 Clarke, 'The Jesus of Nineteenth Century Indian Christian Theology', 42.

208 This dependence is well brought out in Jayakumar, *Dalit Consciousness and Christian Conversion*, chapter 1; his conclusion is that Dalit liberation theology is being "shaped by liberation theologies around the world and not by its own context" (30).

209 'The Jesus of Nineteenth Century Indian Christian Theology', 42. He later adds that "Indian Christian theology needs confidence to know and trust Jesus as the exalted and cosmic one; courage to discover and experience Jesus as the one in solidarity with the lowly and afflicted; and imagination to hold both these dimensions together in the God-man." (44).

210 *The Acknowledged Christ of the Indian Renaissance*, 235. See too the comments of Gnana Robinson, 'Jesus Christ, the Open Way and the Fellow-Struggler', *AJT*, 3 (1989), 411-13 (although he does not mention Gandhi).

the death of Christ and the value of suffering love in the social struggle. Elsewhere Thomas relates the life and death of Christ to the continuing struggle for liberation and justice in contemporary India.[211] The theme of the common suffering of both Jesus and Dalits is quite prominent in Dalit christology and it is linked with the participation of God in human pain as seen in the cross of Christ. So, "to know Jesus Christ is to know him as revealed in the struggles of Dalits for their liberation."[212] This is Jesus as *satyagrahi* – one who is firmly rooted in the truth and whose insistence on it leads to redemptive suffering. In this context Jesus might also be invoked as *jivanmukti*, the one who is truly liberated and so is able to liberate others.

According to Thomas, it is "the crucified Jesus as the pattern of a new humanness and the symbol of a cosmic ultimate reality of suffering love that has attracted religious reform-leaders and secular thinkers and the artistic world in India "[213](including individuals as varied as socialist leaders and Rabindranath Tagore). For such leaders reform and renewal meant searching the Hindu tradition "to bring out what was like Jesus and transforming that tradition in the light of Jesus." One consequence has been the recognition of human suffering "not only as metaphysical but also as a moral evil, and *ahimsa* reinterpreted and transformed by *agape* to create *satyagraha* in the struggle for justice."[214] If this is the case then Gandhi's emphasis upon such satya*graha* holds potential for unveiling a new insight into christology. Jesudasan is one Indian Christian who believes that it is possible to "see in Gandhi's *satyagraha* the incarnate presence and action of God".[215] Thomas makes the same point in writing

---

211 See, for example, his comments in 'A Christ-Centered Humanist Approach,' 52-55.

212 Prabhakar, 'Dalit Theology', 412 (see also 420-24).

213 Thomas, 'Christology and Pluralistic Consciousness', 106. See also the discussion of Thangaraj's *The Crucified Guru* in section 6.B above.

214 'A Christ-centered Humanist Approach to Other Religions', 53.

215 Ignatius Jesudasan, *A Gandhian Theology of Liberation* (Maryknoll, NY, 1984) 130; in similar vein: PD Devanandan, *Preparation for Dialogue* (Bangalore, 1964), 111. Of the many Christian discussions of Gandhi the most helpful at this point would include: D Thomas, 'What Jesus Meant to Gandhi', *RS*, 11.3 (September 1964), 13-28; Balwant AM Paradkar, 'Hindu Interpretation of Christ from Vivekananda to Radhakrishnan', *IJT*, 18 (1969), 70-73; Nirmal Minz, *Mahatma Gandhi and Hindu-Christian Dialogue* (Madras, 1970); 'Gandhiji's Approach to Religion and its Relevance to Indian Theology', *LW*, 87 (1981), 92-102; Samuel Rayan, 'The Truth that Sets Us Free', *Jeevadhara*, 14 (1984), 206-30; TK John, 'Truth's Appeal for Gandhi', *Jeevadhara*, 14 (1984), 231-43, and 'Theologie der Befreiung und gandhische

that wherever 'Love' identifies itself with the struggle of the oppressed for

> liberation toward a community of justice and love, and does not let the means betray the end, there is acknowledgement of the ultimacy of the Way of the Cross for the life of the world transcending all religious ... distinctions.[216]

Wilfred believes that the notion of *satyagrahi* is more easily comprehended in India than the liberator understood as prophet, a notion that he sees as located in the semitic religious traditions.[217]

It is true that the influence of Gandhi's ideals is considerably diminished in contemporary India (a kind of disappointment not unknown to Christians, in India and elsewhere) but that need not diminish the force of the appeal to *satyagraha* and related notions. However, the use of the *satyagraha* ideal might also require a lessened emphasis upon the cosmic christology and model of Christ as 'Lord' discussed in the previous chapter (with their temptations to triumphalism) and a correspondingly greater emphasis upon a theology of the cross with the model of Christ as the suffering servant, and Christian, as the followers of a crucified and not a conquering Messiah. At the same time, the theme of suffering is sometimes qualified lest suffering reinforces notions of powerlessness and victimhood – the acceptance of fate that constitutes an inner captivity. This may be heard in the plea that Dalit theology should project an image of Jesus that exemplifies "worth, dignity and freedom" and not a Jesus "who has a crown and who has attained glory, nor a Jesus who suffered to the end and was dead".[218]

One further feature of Dalit religious thought (and other forms of Indian liberation theology) is its strongly anti-Brahminical stance and its rejection of the Sanskrit language as a tool that legitimates and thus perpetuates Brahminical domination.[219] This is not surpris-

---

Praxis: eine soziale Spiritualität fur Indien', in *Verlass den Tempel*, edited by Felix Wilfred (Freiburg, 1988), 69-95.

216 Thomas, 'Christology and Pluralistic Consciousness', 108. For further discussion of MM Thomas' theology and its development on this topic see Hielke I Wolters, *Theology of Prophetic Participation: MM Thomas' Concept of Salvation and the Collective Struggle for Fuller Humanity in India* (Bangalore and Delhi: United Theological College and ISPCK, 1996).

217 Felix Wilfred, *Beyond Settled Foundations*, 195.

218 Franklyn J Balasundaram, 'The Contemporary Dalit Issues', in *Liberating Witness*, 419.

219 On the relationship of Dalit and traditional Hinduism see, for example, Ayrookuzhiel, 'The Dalits, Religions and Interfaith Dialogue'; SK Chatterji, 'Some Aspects of Dalit Ideology', in *Towards a Dalit Theology*, 6-9.

ing, given the association for Dalits of Brahminic ethnicity with oppression. However, a theology of *satyagraha* will be cautious about such rejection given that the *advaitic* tradition does contain important (if overlooked) elements of dissent and even anti-Brahminical sentiment that could well be used to help undergird a more popularist contextual theology.[220]

I. Further Towards an Indian Christological Basis for Dialogue

The intention of this chapter has been to outline a christology in distinctly Indian categories that might help sustain Christian-Hindu dialogue. Not every aspect of a possible Indian christology has been considered – only those most directly related to dialogue, or potential dialogue, and its justification (including some that have begun to emerge as part of the process of dialogue itself). Concerning the employment and further development of such a christology a number of comments might be made.

One assumption of the chapter is that the justification is best framed in christological categories. There are several reasons for this. (a) Christianity in India (and elsewhere) has always drawn attention to the unique and irreplaceable position occupied by Christ in Christian self-understanding. Comment has already been made about the advantages of a concrete christological focus over the more abstract notions of 'God' or 'Spirit' (see chapter 5.H above). (b) It might also be argued that it is the person of Jesus that, more effectively than any other aspect of Christianity, enables the Christian 'word' to be enculturated and understood. This is because "people cross the membranes between different cultures more effectively than ideas or concepts do"[221] and so to focus upon Christ is to help enable the determining measure of Christian belief (Christ) to take an appropriately central place in the discussion. If there are good reasons for a christological focus in Hindu-Christian dialogue, than there will be no quarrel with the attempt to elaborate this christology in distinctly Indian categories. As the writer of the Fourth Gospel and many others in the early church sought to invest the Stoic concept of *Logos,* for example, with the deeper and richer

220 See Timothy C Tennent, 'Ethnicity and the Sanskritic Tradition', *VJTR*, 61 (1997), 179-86; and 'Contextualizing the Sanskritic Tradition to Serve Dalit Theology', *Missiology*, 25 (1997), 343-49.

221 Heim, 'The Pilgrim Christ: Some Reflections on Theocentric Christology and Enculturation', in *Christian Faith and Multiform Culture in India*, edited by Somen Das (Bangalore, 1987), 119; see also 123.

meaning believed to have been made manifest in Christ,[222] so the Indian writers discussed have attempted to show that terminology derived from the Indian context is more meaningful and helpful for India, and perhaps for other places, than the received western theological terminology.[223]

For example, as Boyd pointed out in *India and the Latin Captivity of the Church,* western Christian theology has used Hebrew sacrificial and Roman juridical language to describe the death of Christ and its consequences but for many Indian theologians Christ saves by what he *is* rather than by what he does – which is one reason for considerable more Indian theological interest in the incarnation and life of Christ than in the cross and theories of the atonement. Moreover, even the apparent simplicity of the traditional Christian 'one Mediator' formula seems open to misunderstanding; as Gispert-Sauch points out, popular Christianity (especially Catholicism) offers a variety of 'mediators' or helps to salvation and he suggests that the upanishadic notion of 'union point' (*ekayanam*) better expresses the biblical understanding.[224] And there is, of course, no reason why a Christian should not be open to an elaboration or justification of dialogue in the categories in which a Hindu proponent of dialogue might seek to make it intelligible. Moreover, given the importance of what has been labelled 'secular' dialogue, a christological focus might be preferred on the grounds that the example of Christ provides a more compelling personal and practical focus in the quest for a just society than any basis grounded in

---

222 For an Indian comment, see Chrys Saldhanha, *Divine Pedagogy. A Patristic View of Non-Christian Religions* (Rome, 1984). Also helpful is Cheriyan Menacherry, 'Patriarchal Approaches towards "World Religions"', *Jeevadhara*, 14 (1984), 95-108.

223 In Chenchiah's words: "the negative plate of Jesus developed in a solution of Hinduism brings out hitherto unknown features of the portrait and these may prove exactly the 'Gospel' for our time" (in *Rethinking Christianity in India,* edited by DM Devasahayam and AN Sudarisanam (Madras, [c 1939]), 162). RS Sugirtharajah considers that recent attention to Jesus in theocentric and human terms has eliminated the possibility that 'Eastern' or Asian aspects of the worldview and lifestyle of Jesus might be added to the Jewish and Hellenistic categories in which he is usually considered; see his 'Jesus in Saffron Robes? The "Other" Jesus Whom Recent Biographers Forgot', *SWC*, 1 (1995), 103-10.

224 'Notes for an Indian Christology', 762f.

the more abstract notion of theocentrism[225] – as the example of Gandhi might inspire Hindus and be offered by them as an example for such dialogue.

1. *Christology as Contextual*

The attempt to devise an Indian christology also makes several assumptions. Firstly, that a contextualised theology continues to be needed. In a situation where pluralism is not only accepted but, in some circles increasingly welcomed as some kind of divine gift, there might well be a diminishing need for the kind of theology that might seem intended to *persuade* Hindus (and others) of the superiority of Christ or of any reason why he might become a preferred religious choice. It is understandable that Indian Christians might want to see Christ in Indian clothes as it were, but any implication that he fits the image of *guru* or *avatara* as well as or better than conventional Hindu options is likely to be rejected as imperialistic or arrogant – at least in progressive Protestant and perhaps most Catholic circles. Some conservative Hindu opinion would also deny Christians the use of such traditional categories. Secondly, there is the assumption that comparative reflection on related elements across the traditions is appropriate, provided that account is taken of the priority-status within each tradition of the topics being compared and that difference is noted as well as similarity.

Another problematical issue is the very quest for concepts in Hinduism with which to understand and elaborate christology. To study a topic in one religion in order to find its 'relevance' to another religious tradition is probably to introduce an inevitably distorting perspective. That is, criteria are introduced that are liable to be alien to the character of the religion under scrutiny. Simply to take terms such as *guru* or advaitin or *Cit* without due and careful realisation of their place within a coherent and structured system of belief is to risk considerable distortion of meaning.[226] Moreover, if the desirability of the inculturation of the Indian church is accepted (see chapter 3.H), and if inculturation is "creative assimilation and not mere borrowing", and if it "certainly implies entry into the total

225 According to Mookenthottam, christocentrism is "very relevant to the social and secular context of India" (*Indian Theological Tendencies*, 175) – by contrast with a theocentric approach.

226 For pertinent comment on this point by an ethnologist, see Meinhard Schuster, 'Religion und Mission in ethnologischer Sicht', *ZM*, 12 (1986), 241-49.

religiousness or ethos of the people" and "the shedding of what is foreign, colonial and alienative",[227] then the task is indeed enormous. The point has not yet been reached when it might be possible plausibly to declare all or most Indian or Christological titles or terms to be part of a joint or shared culture that is 'Indian' and not 'Hindu' or 'Christian'; but that time might come. The received christological titles (such as 'Christ', 'Lord', 'Saviour') do themselves carry considerable cultural weight from their original, but now distant, Jewish and Mediterranean contexts that Indian Christians can usually ignore. The difference with the Indian titles suggested earlier in the chapter is that Hinduism is a living context that cannot be ignored. One positive factor is the wide acceptance of the use and validity of analogy in Indian thought; this may, in fact, help predispose Indians, both Hindu and Christian, to the acceptance of terms and titles from the worldview of the other.[228]

Another christological dilemma is found in the discussion of salvation; the title 'saviour' is not unintelligible in a first century Jewish/Mediterranean setting but to use it in a Hindu context in which *karma* assumes considerable importance, is to raise problems for what, in western theology, at least, has been a central (even if at times, problematical) title for Christ.[229] On the other hand, the notion of *karma* may be somewhat less inflexible than Christians some-

227 [Indian Theological Association], 'Towards a Theology of Religions: An Indian Christian Perspective', *ITS*, 16 (1989), 80.

228 Discussions with both Hindus and Christians in India suggest that this is the case. It might also be one reason why Indian Christians are more sympathetic to the employment of Hindu terminology in christology than their (western) missionary colleagues; an analysis of the literature would probably confirm this.

229 The problem is much more real and profound than indicated by such comments of Sarvepalli Radhakrishnan as: "there is not much serious difference between Hinduism and Christianity on the question of the nature and means of salvation" (*Indian Religions* (Delhi, 1979), 144; this is because his notion of Christ's role as mediator is that of example – see 39, 118, 156); see also: KB Ramakrishna Rao, 'Salvation in Hinduism – a Religious Approach', *IMR*, 4 (1982), 323-31. Also helpful are the discussions by Whaling, *An Approach to Dialogue with Hinduism*, 58-61 and 85f; Chris Wigglesworth, 'Salvation/Liberation in Hinduism and Christianity', *TRACI/ETS Journal*, April 1978, 31-42, and *ITD*, 196-235.

times suppose.[230]

The major issue is probably how to achieve balance: balance between the continuing quest for clarity of understanding of what has been received about Christ (including clarity about the presuppositions of the western and Indian Christian theological traditions in which christology has been expressed) and the search for intelligibility in a quite different context, especially, as in India, a context with a complex religio-philosophical heritage of its own. The implication is that the user of christology in dialogue needs to be 'bilingual': fluent in the languages both of christological discourse and Hinduism.

A further issue is the question of how the appropriateness of the Indian christological titles might be evaluated and this, in turn, will depend in part on the theology of the religions that is employed. If some kind of fulfilment theory is embraced (see chapter 5.D above) then it could be argued that the place Hindus give to the notions of *guru, avatara, satyagrahi* and so on are part of the universal human search for God (perhaps even a divinely inspired search) that is fulfilled in Christ. For example, the notion of *avatara* could be seen as a Hindu 'stepping stone' to Christ

> inasmuch as it embodies the universal human aspiration to enter into contact with the Universal Reality of the Divine on a human plane – a desire, however, that must remain forever unfulfilled unless God takes the initiative of stooping down to us in becoming human.[231]

On the other hand, if Christ – or other aspects of divine self-revelation – is thought in some way to be present in Hinduism (see chapter 5.E above) then these notions might be regarded as more than human longing and might point to some form of active presence in which Hinduism and other religions "represent true interventions and authentic manifestations of God in the history of peoples; they form integral parts of one history of salvation that culminates in the Jesus Christ-event."[232]

The reminder that all theological discourse is unavoidably

---

230 Alongside the detailed discussion of AG Hogg in his *Karma and Redemption* (Madras, 1909; reprinted with an Introduction by Eric J Sharpe: Madras, 1970) needs to be placed the survey and conclusion of Arvind Sharma: "the fact that Hinduism provides for the transference of *karma* by a special person or a special act and for interference in *karma* by God or by sages suggests that the alleged inexorability of the law to a certain extent misrepresents the doctrine" ('Your Karma or Mine?', *Indian Cultures*, 37 (1982), 54).

231 Dupuis, *Toward a Christian Theology of Religious Pluralism*, 302f.

232 Dupuis, *Toward a Christian Theology of Religious Pluralism*, 303.

expressed in a contextualised framework illuminates one area of recent conflict between some Indian Catholic theologians and some Vatican-derived theological statements. Michael Amaladoss, for example, in reacting to the document 'Christianity and the World Religions' of the International Theological Commission[233] complains that, although Part 1 of the document emphasises the importance of context, contextual issues do not seem to affect the discourse in Part 2 where issues of salvation in Christ, and Scripture and tradition are discussed and where, he believes, the document simply reverts to an *a priori* theology 'from above' in asserting traditional Christian answers. He contrasts this methodology with what he says Indian and third world theologians have established: that doctrine must be in constant dialogue with the context in which it is to be expressed. The 'high' christology of western theological method (which is itself, he believes, derived from a particular context) "tends to be exclusive and does not leave much space for other manifestations of the Word in the world and in history." It also reinforces authoritarian ecclesiastical systems – and, on both counts, he feels that the contextual theologies of Asia can liberate the West.[234] However, the case for a comprehensive christology that is exclusively 'from below' is not yet fully made. As argued in chapter 5.I above, the advocates of high christology can also participate with sincerity in the Hindu-Christian dialogue; at the very least their christologies can and perhaps should be seen as complementary to those with other starting points.[235] Even as a number of different *sampradayas* (traditions) make up Hinduism, with no one combination acknowledged by all Hindus or free of all ambiguities, so there have always been a variety of christological emphases among Christians, Indian Christians included.

The reality of diversity and pluralism within christology raises the question of the extent to which this pluralism might be attributed to a functional consequence of belief in Christ; that is, to the wish for Christ to meet certain socio-culturally determined needs of a Christian community that is a minority in a pluralistic society (as it is in India, and as it was in the New Testament period as the first christologies were formulated). In fact, there seem to be several ten-

233 The ITC is a Commission of the Congregation for 'Doctrine of the Faith' of the Roman Curia.

234 'The Mystery of Christ and Other Religions', 327-38 (quote from 337).

235 For an example of an attempt to develop a christology that to balance these various starting points, and that is fully aware of the challenges of religious pluralism, see Jacques Dupuis, *Who Do You Say I Am? Introduction to Christology* (Maryknoll, NY: Orbis Books, 1994).

sions at this point. To what extent is or ought christology to be functional? To what extent ought it simply to derive from the reported experience(s) of Christ, both in New Testament times and in India (and elsewhere)? Or is it legitimate also to say that it 'should' or 'must' enable dialogue or assist in the Christian encounter with the fears and hopes of India?[236] – or the meeting of any number of other needs? This is one of the continuing issues in the quest for any contextualised christology. The tension between christology as received (in both biblical and western categories) and christology in functional terms may exist because of the need to adapt the understanding of Christ to new contexts. Christology simply as received from outside will – to a lesser or a greater extent – remain alien in form and substance in a new context.

On the other hand, a kind of *de facto* christology seems to have emerged simply because of the continuing appeal to Hindus of the person of Jesus. This appeal is seen in the frequency of his portrayal in *puja* rooms and temples, references to his life and teaching by *gurus* and other Hindus and in Indian literature, poetry, art and film. The same appeal seems to undergird the attention given to Christ in the Hindu renaissance – an attention whose purposes included that of portraying Christ as Asian or Oriental, in order, as Neufeldt puts it, "to claim Christ and the teachings of Christ ... as indigenous to India, and to attack eurocentric notions of Christ". In fact, Neufeldt considers that a common theme in Hindu depictions of Christ is that of "Christ as the quintessential Hindu, the one who lives Hindu ideals as they ought to be lived and teaches the essence of Hindu truth as it ought to be taught".[237] Reference has already been made to the phenomenon of double-belonging and unbaptised believers in Christ (see above, chapter 4.C.3). It could be concluded that the person of Jesus has entered the Hindu world where Christianity and its churches (and theologies) have failed.[238]

The development of this *de facto* christology may simply point to a Hindu assimilation of Jesus to the model of *guru*, or charismatic healer, or teacher of *advaita* along with an avoidance, unknowing or otherwise, of other possible implications and challenges of his life and teaching. But if these implications are couched in traditional christological terms (for example: incarnation of the only Son of God, revelation of and atonement by a unique saviour, vindication and victory through resurrection) then there is the problem of why Hindus should accept the implications of a religious worldview so

236 See, for example, Irudayaraj, 'An Attempt at Indian Christology', 14.
237 Ronald W Neufeldt, 'Hindu Views of Christ', 172f.

different from their own. Ariarajah goes so far as to assign the failure of the Christian missionary movement in Asia to its presentation of 'christology' rather than the person of Jesus. An appropriate Asian christology, he argues, should "be based on the conviction that all persons are free to respond to Christ in the way they choose".[239] Christ's Jewish followers (true to their needs and worldview) responded to him in one way; Hindus and other Asians will respond in quite different ways because their context is so different.

This argument raises significant questions; for example, about (a) the undoubted liberty of an individual or community in the formulating of a response to Christ; (b) the place of the supposedly normative Christian scripture (and tradition), since that scripture and tradition do make christological claims; and (c) the balance between (a) and the setting aside of (b) as a response is made, along with the possibility that the christology formulated in a given context might not only have been creatively transformed, but transformed in such a way as to distort its (original) content – assuming that content is known, or claimed to be known.[240] The freedom of (a) also raises the possibilities of 'domestication' (the co-option of Christ to endorse a variety of domestic causes – some contentious – in a given context) or even his being forced into the mould of any number of ideological and religious categories. Moreover, there is always the danger of reductionism – for example, of a pragmatic kind (in which the needs of Christian ministry are seen as more important than truth-claims about Christ)[241]or the meaning of Jesus is seen by a sympathetic

---

238 Kaj Baagø considers that even if Christianity were to disappear from India, the name of Christ, and his teaching, would still be honoured and cherished ('Rom Mohan Roy's Christology – an Early Attempt at Demythologization?', *BTF*, 1.1 (January 1967), 31.

239 Ariarajah, 'Christology in Asia', 33. But it must be asked whether it is possible ever to present the person of Jesus bereft of christology. Christological claims are always present, even in the Gospel accounts of the life of Jesus; for an Indian comment along these lines see: Moti Lal Pandit, 'Selected Readers' Responses to Wesley Ariarajah's Letter', *IRM*, 72 (1983), 93f.

240 As Raimundo Panikkar asks about the portrayals of Christ that emerged during the 19th century Bengali renaissance: "Where is the criterion to set the criteria to know whether they were deforming the image" of Christ? ('The Relation of the Gospels to Hindu Culture and Religion', in *Jesus and Man's Hope*, edited by Donald G Miller and Dikran Y Hadidian (Pittsburgh, 1971), volume II, 252f).

241 See, for example, the discussion in Jacob Kavunkal, 'Ministry-centred or Dogma-centred? Christo-centrism Re-examined', *Verbum SVD*, 34 (1993), 237-49.

Hindu simply as a variant of the eternal *Dharma*,[242] or by a Christian as one of a number of ways to the divine.[243] In a survey of Asian christological trends, Karotemprel concludes that, alongside positive features, a number of recent Asian christologies have relativised Christ who is "reduced to one among many saviours and indicators of the path of salvation." He expresses concern about the ahistorical nature of such christologies, their dislocation from the New Testament and apostolic witness, and a pragmatism that could mean that "every generation will be 'creating' an imaginary Jesus Christ to suit its philosophy, politics and culture and not the Jesus Christ of history".[244]

One means of minimising these shortcomings is to attempt to elaborate christology in dialogue with Hindus, with a mutual encouragement to learn from one another in the ways suggested in the discussion of christological terminology above, and also with reference to the Christian tradition, both historical, local and global (while acknowledging the temptation to domestication in those contexts as well). Perhaps this is the perennial challenge for Indian Christian theology: how to be faithful both to the *sruti* and to a cultural environment that includes responses to Christ from Hindu reformers, artists and many others; and how to allow the *sruti* (including its witness to Christ) to speak clearly and intelligibly in the Indian context, but without allowing that context or any other worldview to distort its content.

A further problem concerns the rather difficult and complex terminology sometimes employed in the quest for an Indian christology. The use of such terminology does imply an acquaintance with Indian philosophical categories and it may be the case that "for the modern educated [person] in India religion is philosophy or it is nothing."[245] However, Samartha argues forcefully that *advaita* is not elitist because it is a *darshana* (vision of reality) rather than a philos-

242 Chaturvedi Badrinath, *Finding Jesus in Dharma. Christianity in India* (Delhi: ISPCK, 2000) in which, although he clearly respects Jesus as an authoritative spiritual liberator (albeit disfigured by the church) he nonetheless concludes: "Faith, trust, love, and truth – these are the meaning of Jesus as they are of Dharma" (185).

243 Felix Wilfred, *Beyond Settled Foundations*, 190-97.

244 'Asian Christological Trends and Christian Mission', 69, 63. He attributes shortcomings to the way in which "most Asian Christologies tend to dissociate Christology from its historical and ontological roots" (67). He also find fault with what he calls "'Marga' Christology" in which Christian following of the 'way' of Christ replaces truth-claims about him (58-60).

245 Boyd, *Introduction to Indian Christian Theology*, 262.

ophy in the western sense; in Samartha's judgement *advaita* is a way of life for many and has an enduring and pervasive influence in holding together the enormous diversity of Indian cultural life.[246] Even if there is agreement with this point, the significance of advaitic or other philosophical terms when applied to christology is surely beyond the grasp of most of those – Hindu and Christian – who might be expected to benefit from it. But at the same time it must also be conceded that there are limits to understanding, and expressing simply, the mystery of Christ. The employment of appropriate but complex terminology (whether or not from philosophical categories) may simply be unavoidable if the complexities of the Christian understandings of Christ are to be communicated. In the same way Christians will not be surprised if the complexities of the Hindu understanding(s) of Krishna – for example – are found to require the employment of terminology from the world of Hindu philosophical discourse.

Another question that might be pursued is why earlier suggestions for an Indian christology have not been further developed, especially in the Protestant circles from which many of them came. For example, there are the christological reflections, already noted, of Chenchiah and Chakkarai in the 1930s and Appasamy over a much longer period. One impediment has been the way in which those who have been interested in the development of an Indian theology have usually been little inclined towards the conservative theology and priorities of the classical christological issues that Chenchiah, Chakkarai and Appasamy, for all their originality, assumed. It may also be true that a fully developed Indian christology will emerge only "from a Hindu Christian life which we are yet to live"[247] – or at least from a more fully inculturated Indian church. Perhaps the lack of development of the christologies of the first half of the twentieth century does point to a fundamental difficulty: a lack of coherence between the mainly western christologies of Indian Christians (or the worldviews that gave rise to them) and Hinduism. Despite some helpful and suggestive analogies and parallels with considerable potential for the elaboration and enhanced comprehension of christology in India, problems remain. Nonetheless, the quest for christological expression in distinctly Indian categories does as least strengthen one hermeneutical strategy. As Sugirtharajah points out, the defining of Jesus in Indian terms helped to provide an answer to those missionary and other critiques

246 Samartha, *One Christ – Many Religions*, 108f.

247 Irudayaraj, 'An Attempt at an Indian Christology', 14.

that appealed to Christ to justify opposition to religion as a whole (for example, Kraemerian and related critiques) or those directed against the supposed short-comings of Hinduism. In both cases Indian portrayals of Christ provided sustenance in the struggle against attitudes "that Indian Christians found offensive and degrading to their own rich and ancient traditions."[248]

And, there are a number of further possible ways in which Indian christology might yet develop.

2. *An Emphasis upon the Social Context*

The Indian context of a search for new forms of community and the struggle against injustice and all that dehumanises has already been elaborated as a vital aspect of the background for Hindu-Christian dialogue – and one that cannot be ignored; Both human need and the agenda of modernity will continue to press theology in that direction. A repeated theme of Devanandan was that "the determinative doctrine" of contemporary Hinduism is not derived from its classical expressions "but is built upon a new anthropology. ... The primary question that is of dominant concern to the modern Hindu thinker is the nature and destiny of man".[249] More recent trends may have slowed or even reversed that emphasis but, nonetheless, it might be argued that no christology (or any other aspect of theology) can be developed without reference to and participation in human community. Such a christology must be, in MM Thomas's view, "predominantly anthropological in its content"[250] – or, as he puts it elsewhere, it must centre on "the promise and power of Christ to humanize life."[251] It might also be described as a christology for *karma marga*.

It has already been argued above that the person of the historic Jesus has been able to enter the Hindu world in a way that christology (at least in most received western categories) has not and one reason is because such a person is seen as wholly identified with

---

248 RS Sugirtharajah, 'An Interpretive Foreword', in *Asian Faces of Jesus*, 4.

249 *Christian Concern in Hinduism* (Bangalore, 1961), 112. See also MM Thomas, *Man and the Universe of Faiths* (Madras, 1975), 63-80.

250 'Christology and Pluralistic Consciousness', *IBMR*, 10 (1986), 107. As Lipner puts it, "Christology from now on must be primarily praxo-centric, ... the stimulus to liberating experience and action should be a chief criterion of its validity" (review of Thangaraj, *The Crucified Guru* in *ER*, 49 (1997), 386).

251 'A Christ-centered Approach to Other Religions', 51.

humanity – including its suffering. There are several implications of such an anthropologically orientated christology.

(a) At the very least, this christology can function as the pattern and symbol of widely held ideals in the human community. Thomas goes so far as to see one level of 'koinonia' (fellowship) in Christ as that of "dialogue among people of different faiths inwardly being renewed by their acknowledgment of the ultimacy of the *pattern* of suffering servanthood as exemplified by the crucified Jesus"[252]- and the discussion above of Jesus as *Satyagrahi* has made this very point.

(b) It would move christology away from the less than satisfactory theocentric emphasis of Samartha and others, in part because such theocentrism takes insufficient account of the secular humanist ideologies that have contributed greatly to the creation of pluralistic consciousness (107).[253]

(c) Nonetheless, there are certain universal and even cosmic aspects of Thomas' christology that, he argues

> enable Christians to discern in every movement towards common humanity patterned after Jesus ... a faith-response to Jesus as the bearer of New Humanity, and to enter into dialogue with such a Christology as part of the Indian Churches' confession of faith (107).

In fact, he raises the question of a cosmic dimension in asking: whether, beyond differences of symbols, the person of Jesus in some sense has a "cosmic function in sharpening and in summing up in that person the suffering-servant streams of all religious and cultural traditions?" And he links this with the Pauline view of Jesus as the new Adam and with the new humanity in Christ – emphases that he notes as important to Devanandan also (106).[254]

Moreover, Thomas sees Gandhi as providing an Indian insight into such a cosmic or, at least, universal dimension when Gandhi writes that, in an image of the crucified Christ, "I saw there at once that nations like individuals could only be made through the agony

---

252 'Christology and Pluralistic Consciousness', 108 (original emphasis). The page numbers in the following two paragraphs of text refer to this article. See also his *Risking Christ for Christ's Sake. Towards an Ecumenical Theology of Pluralism* (Geneva, 1987), 114f.

253 These are discussed at some length in Thomas' *The Secular Ideologies of India and the Secular Meaning of Christ* (Madras, 1976).

254 See above, chapter 1.D.1 and his *Man and the Universe of Faiths*, 129-55. For a discussion that includes a comparative study of the topic in Chenchiah, Chakkarai and MM Thomas, see Frank Whaling, 'Indian Christian Theology: the Humanity of Christ and the New Humanity', *SJT*, 31 (1978), 319-35.

of the Cross and in no other way"; adding, on another occasion, about Jesus that

> the lives of all have, in some greater or lesser degree, been changed by [Jesus] presence, his actions and the words spoken by his divine voice. ... And because the life of Jesus has had the significance and the transcendence to which I have alluded, I believe that he belongs not solely to Christianity but to the entire world. (107f)

Thomas suggests that all such acknowledgements, both explicit and implicit, of Jesus as the mediator of newness, should meet with a positive response in the development of christology.

3. *Antiochene Christology*

It might also be asked whether the 'Antiochene' christological tradition might not be more coherent with Hinduism than the 'Alexandrian' tradition that has been dominant almost everywhere since the sixth century.[255] The christology of both traditions describes Christ as the *Logos*, so combining the notions of unity with and yet distinctiveness from God in the person of the Word-Son; but they also diverge significantly. Although the two christologies are complex and overlap at a number of points, the Antiochene differs from the Alexandrian (and hence from the main current of western christology as received in India) in several ways that may warrant consideration in an Indian context.

(a) Whereas the Alexandrian model predicates actions of the Son, in Antiochene christology actions are predicated of the fully human Jesus; that is, the Word is not perceived as subject and therefore as ontologically overwhelming the person. (The Chalcedonian defini-

---

255 The two christologies belong to two divergent schools of thought rather than to localised theologies. The Antiochene christology could more accurately be called a *Logos-anthropos* christology; the Alexandrian a *Logos-sarx* christology. Two comprehensive discussions are found in Aloys Grillmeier, *Christ in Christian Tradition*, volume 1, second revised edition (Et: London and Oxford, 1975), 167-439, and RV Sellers, *Two Ancient Christologies: A Study in the Christological Thought of the Schools of Alexandria and Antioch in the Early History of Christian Doctrine* (London, 1954). See also DF Wells, *The Person of Christ: A Biblical and Historical Analysis of the Incarnation* (Illinois: Crossway, 1984), 98-109; P Schaff, editor, *History of the Christian Church* (Grand Rapids: Eerdmans, 1910), 4.3; §135 – 140, JND Kelly, *Early Christian Doctrines*, 153-158; 301-302. Useful background material is also found in DS Wallace-Hadrill, *Christian Antioch: a Study of Early Christian Thought in the East* (Cambridge: Cambridge University Press, 1982).

tion affirms that, even after the resurrection, the risen humanity of Jesus continues to be human; the divine does not overcome it.) This emphasis, it should be noted, derives from two concerns: (i) to underline continuity and interpenetration between God and the world (as opposed to the discontinuity emphasised by the Alexandrians); and (ii) not to compromise the divine transcendence by ascribing suffering and change to the immutable God. Because the risen humanity of Jesus shares in the life both of God and of the world in a new way it is possible to develop this in the direction of a cosmic christology that can embrace Hindu concerns (and even the Hindu 'story' as well).

(b) The 'high' Alexandrine christology tends to be exclusive in its truth-claims and, as an Indian commentator and advocate of Hindu-Christian dialogue notes, "does not leave much space for other manifestations of the word in the world and in history."[256] Another Indian Catholic theologian explicitly contrasts the two christologies in describing what he sees as the dominance of Alexandrian christology (and a related hierarchical authoritarianism) before the Second Vatican Council followed by a shift to an Antiochene perspective after the Council. This latter christology centres on "Jesus the Human, who revealed a compassionate God whose Kingdom transcends the boundaries of the Church, and therefore makes dialogue with other religions … an imperative."[257]

(c) In Antiochene christology the uniqueness of Christ is not asserted as a conclusion derived from ontological presuppositions about the divine Word, but consists in his extraordinarily graced will. His union with God is one of reciprocal love; it is a uniqueness of perfection – a difference of degree, not kind, from the union others might (and do) experience. It is a christology of grace.

(d) This means that the redemption won by Christ is not the result of his being a divine redeemer who in some way divinises his followers; it is wrought by his graced and resurrected humanity as these are the recipients of the Word.[258]

Some of the advantages of this Antiochene christology, in an

---

256 Amaladoss, 'The Mystery of Christ and Other Religions', 337.

257 Jacob Parappally, 'One Jesus – Many Christologies', *VJTR*, 61 (1997), 711; a section entitled 'From Alexandrian to Antiochene Christology' is found from 710-12. Parappally sees the shift in christological emphasis as parallel to a shift from christocentrism to theocentrism (712-15).

258 Christ is he "in whom God the Word accomplishes the Redemption of mankind through the free activity of a perfectly obedient man" (RA Norris, *Manhood and Christ. A Study of the Christology of Theodore of Mopsuestia* (London, 1967), 237).

Indian context, are that it seems to bypass a number of difficulties for the Hindu dialogue partner:

- the description of God in primarily trinitarian terms;
- the suffering of God after God's entry into human history;
- Christian notions of unparalleled uniqueness for Christ.

Whether these advantages are purchased at too great a cost is open to question, of course. Some aspects of such a christology are, in fact, found in the writings of Sen and Chakkarai, each of whom seems to have embraced a kenotic view of Christ with his divinity described as an unparalleled selflessness leading to a dynamic moral unity with the Father.[259]

In western theology, Antiochene christology has been criticised for its apparent endorsement of a parallelism of natures within Christ, a less than complete unity between divine and human in Christ, and doubts about whether an adoptive or merit christology, focused upon one person in history, can claim the universal consequences usually ascribed to Christ.[260] Nonetheless, the Antiochene position is not without its more recent advocates; it is very much a christology 'from below' – to point to one parallel. Attention might also be drawn to DM Baillie's elaboration of the paradox of divine grace that enables both free and responsible human action and the outworking of the grace of God in an individual.[261] Also in line with the Antiochene position is a New Zealander's "christology of grace" with its conclusion that "Jesus' uniqueness consists in his being particularly claimed, designated, destined, invited, expected ... to bear and represent God's reality".[262]

4. *An Indian Ananda Spirit Christology?*

In western theology there is a longstanding tradition of a Biblically derived Spirit christology, often linked with an Antiochene approach. Such an 'inspiration christology' (which John Hick calls

---

259 For example, see Sen's lecture 'India Asks: Who is Christ?' (found in *Keshub Chunder Sen*), especially 203-10; the discussion by Neufeldt, 'Hindu Views of Christ', 163-66; and Chakkarai, *Jesus the Avatar*, 89.

260 For some suggestions concerning an answer to this last point, see: Joanne McW Dewart, 'Christological Particularity: Need It Be a Scandal?', *ATR*, 62 (1980), 72-74.

261 See his *God Was in Christ. An Essay on Incarnation and Atonement*, revised edition (London, 1961), 93, 114-18.

262 Frank Nichol, 'Towards a Christology of Grace', *Pacifica*, 3 (1990), 323-34 (quotation from 333).

"the simplest, least theoretical or speculative, and most directly experiential understanding of Jesus", especially in a pluralistic context[263]) became unpopular because of its association with a form of adoptionism in which Jesus 'qualified' for the incarnation by some merit of his own and not by virtue of his oneness with the Father. But one of the strengths of the position was (and is) its links with salvation history, especially its eschatological dimension: Jesus as the one on whom the Spirit came at the inauguration of the new age. And it is not difficult to see the way in which at least some of its principal deficiencies might begin to be overcome. As Rosato points out, one of the decisive mistakes by the earliest proponents of Spirit christology was an overemphasis upon the descent of the Spirit on Jesus at his baptism and an overlooking of the place of the Spirit in the (eschatologically) more decisive event of the resurrection. It is the latter event that enables a link not only between the Spirit and the human life and ministry of Jesus but with his eternal reality as Son of God – a reality revealed in the resurrection by the power of the Spirit in which Jesus is revealed as the very centre of salvation history.[264]

An elaboration of this Spirit christology in Indian categories

---

263 See his 'An Inspiration Christology for a Religiously Plural World', in *Encountering Jesus. A Debate on Christology,* edited by Stephen T Davis (Atlanta, 1988), 5-38 (quotation from 22); for further elaboration of Hick's inspiration christology see his *Disputed Questions in Theology and the Philosophy of Religion* (New Haven: Yale University Press, 1993). For a sturdy critique of Hick's inspiration christology and the functionalist platform on which it seems largely to be based see Paul J Griffiths, 'The Uniqueness of Christian Doctrine Defended', in *Christian Uniqueness Reconsidered,* 159-62.

264 Philip J Rosato, 'Spirit Christology: Ambiguity and Promise', *TS,* 38 (1977), 423-39. A similar emphasis is found in Ralph Del Colle, *Christ and Spirit: Spirit-Christology in Trinitarian Perspective* (New York and Oxford: Oxford University Press, 1994). Also useful is Paul W Newman, *A Spirit Christology. Recovering the Biblical Paradigm of Christian Faith* (Lanham, MD: University Press of America, 1987); For some further recent examples of Spirit christology, see: TG Weinandy, *The Father's Spirit of Sonship: Reconceiving the Trinity* (Edinburgh: T & T Clark, 1995), and 'The Case for Spirit Christology: Some Reflections,' *The Thomist* 59 (1995), 173-188; G Badcock, *Light of Truth and Fire of Love: A Theology of the Holy Spirit* (Grand Rapids, MI: Eerdmans, 1997); GWP McFarlane, *Why Do You Believe What You believe About The Holy Spirit?* (Carlisle: Paternoster, 1998); DM Coffey, 'The Theandric Nature of Christ,' *TS,* 60 (1999), 405-431. And, of course, there are may others in Christian history who have attempted to develop forms of Spirit christology – too many, in fact, to begin to list.

could build on the longstanding use of *ananda* (bliss or joy) to speak of the Holy Spirit (noting that the Vedantic tradition has often identified *ananda* with Brahman[265]). Although the fullness of the Spirit was always with Jesus, it could be argued, with Gispert-Sauch, that

> as a result of the bondage of human karma that *ananda* remains unmanifest until the moment of his [Jesus'] death and resurrection when it explodes to pervade all the layers of his being and indeed to spread to the whole Universe .... Here is the distinction between the person of Christ and the other human beings: he possesses in its fullness that substantial bliss, and he is able to share it with all human beings by participation, a bliss however that has passed through the sorrows of this world as he accepted suffering and death ... in solidarity and love with the human race. Therefore God has exalted him and from his bliss we all receive.[266]

In order to preserve the classical convention that is the Word, not the Spirit, that becomes incarnate, Gispert-Sauch goes on to argue that

> the Bliss which 'reposes' upon the *Logos* was not a participation but the fullness of the divine bliss that made the Logos present and active in Jesus. ... All human beings ... participate in that bliss because they share in the same pattern of God's self-communication – they share that *matra*, that 'measured participation', that makes them brothers and sisters of Jesus, 'the first born among all humans ...'[267]

Despite the appeal of such an Indian Spirit christology, it will have to answer a number of questions, especially about the *functional* form taken by a number of its formulations. In these the significance of Jesus is concluded from his function (for example, in mediating the presence or salvation of God) rather than from the ontological status of his person or from some kind of identity with the divine. Aleaz, for example, can write that "functionally in the way Jesus mediates God to us, he is God for us .... But analogously

265 Following the Brhadaranyaka Upanishad, 3.9.29.

266 'Notes for an Indian Christology', 761; he substantiates his argument at this point from John 1.16 ("Of his fullness we have all received, grace upon grace") and from the Brhadaranyaka Upanishad 4.3.32 ("all other beings live upon a mere portion of that *ananda* [Brahman]").

267 'Notes for an Indian Christology', 762 (he goes on to add that such a christology does not need the Greek categories of person and nature). Del Colle makes a similar point when, summarising Tillich, he writes that "the Spirit which was present in Jesus and made him Christ is the same Spirit that draws all our human concerns into the realm of salvation" (*Christ and the Spirit*, 200).

what happened to Jesus can happen to other persons."[268] Thangaraj calls for a "strictly" functionalist christology as an aid to moving away from substantialist categories; he believes that "the difference between Jesus and other gurus is not in kind or in degree but in pragmatic value".[269] But this kind of functionalist hermeneutic will not be acceptable to large sections of Indian Christian thought[270] especially if it insists on either a functionalist or substantialist interpretation of Christ – though it may be possible to see Christ in both categories rather than insisting on one at the expense of the other. As Dupuis points out, the New Testament itself suggests that it was subsequent reflection on the dynamics of eschatological faith that "compelled ... the necessary ascent from the functionality of the man Jesus to the ontology of the Son Incarnate".[271] In other words, it might well be possible to shape an Indian christology as both 'from above' and 'from below' – even as Radhakrishnan is able to able to comprehend Christ as both 'from above' (as a divine *avatara* / 'descent') and 'from below' (an example of the human realisation of divinity).[272]

5. *The Inevitability of Metaphysics*

At a number of points the advocacy of a functionalist christology has been noted and this particular species of christology often includes a hermeneutic of suspicion when it comes to metaphysical assertions. A number of advocates of dialogue are insistent that, in a world of pressing human need, Christian and Hindu identity should be expressed not so much in the quest for right knowledge about the nature of God or the person and place of Christ but in clarifying the means of liberative praxis in response to issues of justice, peace and the integrity of creation. However, a number of commentators have also pointed out the unavoidability of metaphysical questions in an Indian setting and in the discussion of christology. This need not be an alternative to right praxis (however much conservative or pietistic Christians or Hindus might seem to endorse this disjunction) but as an issue that cannot be avoided – even if sat-

268 KP Aleaz, 'Paul Knitter's Proposal for Relational Uniqueness of Jesus', *IJT*, 40 (1998), 54.

269 *The Crucified Guru*, 121, 125.

270 The objections are well summarised in Karotemprel, 'Asian Christological Trends'.

271 Jacques Dupuis, 'Jesus with an Asian Face', *TM*, 2 (1999), 15.

272 *The Heart of Hindusthan*, 101.

isfying answers remain elusive. As Julius Lipner points out about Thangaraj's eschewal of metaphysics,

> there is plenty of metaphysics in Saiva Siddhanta ... and Christians will continue to ask, indeed need to ask, what Christ is. For Christians Christ must remain a living reality, alive not only psychologically or in the collective memory, but really, here and now, in his saving graciousness. Thus necessarily metaphysics re-enters through the back door.[273]

It does seem as if much of the rejection of metaphysics centres on a functionalist view of religion – usually the view that the function of religion is to enable some kind of transformation; Thangaraj makes it clear that this is his view of religious beliefs. However, as critics have pointed out, those who profess religious doctrines usually believe they

> express truths about the way things are, truths which are what they are independently of the transformative effects professing them might have, and ... this indisputable historical fact raises certain difficulties for a purely functionalist reading of religious doctrines.[274]

MM Thomas also points out the ubiquitous place of metaphysics in Indian life and the necessity of discussion of issues such as God, nature and humanity "in order to defend the 'divine agenda in history' as of more than marginal interest in the endless cycles of cosmic coming into being and ceasing to be." Far from being of marginal (or even negative) importance in the quest for a liberative praxis, Indian christology is "a metaphysical struggle to affirm the spiritual significance of the creative and historical process and liberative human action." If the Christian contribution to transforming liberation is to be made "in any ultimately significant manner" it should continue to embrace not only secular history as the realm of unique divine disclosure in Christ, "but also learn to speak of this both in secular humanist and metaphysical categories."[275] For these reasons, then, it would seem unwise to attempt to formulate an Indian christology without a confident appeal to metaphysical undergirdings.

---

273 Review of *The Crucified Guru* in *ER*, 49 (1997), 386.

274 Paul J Griffiths, 'The Uniqueness of Christian Doctrine Defended', in *Christian Uniqueness Reconsidered*, 160; his critique has John Hick's inspiration christology mainly in mind.

275 'A Christ-centered Humanist Approach to Other Religions', 60. He goes on to add that he is persuaded "that Christocentrism is what relates God, church, and kingdom to one another and keeps that relation inviolate" (61).

6. The Utility of Narrative Form

There may also be advantages in including a substantial narrative element to the attempt to construct an Indian christology (or even attempting to construct the whole in a narrative genre). In the West it is largely the critique of postmodernism that has led theologians to turn to history and narrative to replace an earlier reliance on philosophy. This study has several times emphasised how the person of Jesus enables communication across the Hindu-Christian interface and it is communicating the *story* of Jesus perhaps best allows that to happen. The shortcomings demonstrated in the search for appropriate Indian titles for Christ may be offset by the use of narrative. Even as the New Testament understands and explains the Christ-event in the light of the history of Israel, so it might also be possible to attempt to do the same in the light of Indian history.[276] This would probably make unavoidable some modest form of fulfilment theorising but careful note would be taken of the shortcomings of previous formulations in these terms (for example, by the employment of a rigorous methodology in the making of appropriate comparisons; the avoidance of assumptions of superiority; the addition of an eschatological element that enables a critique of the Christian tradition).

The narrative dimension of the Christian message takes the themes of universally intended salvation history and election to elaborate the universal purpose of Yahweh that leads to the coming of the promised Messiah. The genre of narrative enables the elements of continuity and discontinuity to receive appropriate emphasis and it extends the story into the eschaton as well. As Fackre puts it – in calling this perspective that of "narrative particularity" – "an eschatological universality joins a christological particularity and a Noachic commonality."[277] Moreover, the narrative, both explicitly and implicitly, invites its hearers to assess and even to join the story. The narrative genre (as opposed to all abstract accounts of the Christian message) has some distinct strategic advantages in postmodern and pluralist India – advantages over

---

276 There are a few comments about this possibility in Michael Amaladoss, 'Who Do You Say That I Am? Speaking of Jesus in India Today', *VJTR*, 60 (1996), 782-94.

277 Gabriel Fackre, 'Christ and Religious Pluralism', 'Christ and Religious Pluralism: the Current Debate', *PE*, 7 (1998), 394f; this "narrative particularity" seems to be Fackre's own position among the many he outlines (see his conclusion (395)).

what might be called all merely propositional presentations of the Christian message.

It is true that the narrative will have some distinctive characteristics because of the need to portray an eschatological dimension. Because the risen humanity of Jesus is said to participate in the life both of God and of the world in a new way, it is possible to develop this in the direction of a cosmic christology that can embrace Hindu concerns (and even the Hindu 'story' as well). Something like a cosmic christology is needed to make this clear – and to help Protestants (especially) to realise that the salvation that Christ brings is no mere individual transaction but a cosmic process.[278] And it goes without saying that any Christian advocacy of the narrative genre will need to be open to a parallel presentation of any one of the Hindu stories that purports to include the Christian story as well; it has been an implicit feature of advaita vedanta that its apologists have long seen the *sanatana dharma* as embracing all the other 'lesser' understandings of reality.

However, the actual presentation of the story of Jesus would need careful presentation in any narrative account. One possible way is to note that the New Testament itself offers what Dupuis calls "a progressive contextual presentation of the mystery of Jesus Christ." This starts with the progressive discovery of the fully human Jesus before moving on "gradually to the elaboration of the mystery of his person ... in the light of the paschal experience of the disciples." Moreover, this is the same pedagogical principle used by Jesus "to make himself progressively understood by his followers" (and often by means of stories, as with most *gurus*) – and the whole process is best presented and elaborated in narrative terms. Dupuis also argues that most previous presentations of Jesus – whether by Hindus or by Christians – have too quickly moved on to doctrinal assertions or conclusions about him "with little foundation in the concrete historical reality of Jesus, the man from Nazareth". One remedy is to note that in Asia "to foster the discovery of the person of Jesus is more important than teaching doctrines about him".[279]Again, the narrative genre enables this process and those who use it might well note that the first Christian disciples only really 'saw' Jesus (and their own misunderstandings of him) with

278 See the remarks of Amaladoss, 'The Mystery of Christ and Other Religions', 332f, 336 where he refers to Ephesians 1.3-14; 1 Corinthians 15.28; Romans 8; John 17.

279 Jacques Dupuis, 'Jesus with an Asian Face', 7-9.

the benefit of hindsight as they realised that in him a new eschatological age had dawned. And Dupuis also notes how Jesus had intentionally kept away from traditional Jewish messianic titles but that the apostolic church later employed these. Other titles were found to be less problematical; some were found to be more suitable in some contexts than others. His suggestion is that a similar method be employed when narrating the story of Jesus: the cautious application of any titles even if, when eventually used, they have acquired new meaning because of new understanding of Jesus.[280]

Finally, it might also be noted that a narrative christology is amenable to a variety of means of communication beyond the merely verbal and written. Some of these (drama, film, and other visual presentations) will continue to be highly appropriate in an Indian setting.

J. Conclusions

The need for a distinctly Indian christology or christologies to undergird the Indian Christian community's response to the challenge of its pluralistic and changing context does not diminish. No one response will (or could) purport to represent all the possible Indian approaches and analogies. In both the Hindu and Christian traditions, a variety of christology can, then, be used to offer at least a partial justification of Hindu-Christian dialogue, and in three senses:

(a) A 'weak' justification (making fewest christological assumptions) would employ an exemplarist model of Christ. It would advocate dialogue on the grounds that Christ's openness to others, especially those outside his own community of faith, is both justification and incentive for dialogue. The theocentrism of the model would commend it both to Christian and to many Hindu pluralists. The analogy of the incarnation, despite its limitations, might also be used, as might the emphases on anthropology and the employment of an appropriate mix of both Antiochene and Alexandrine christological categories.

(b) A 'strong' christological justification would employ a much more substantial range of christological presuppositions. It would explain the Christ-event in cosmic immanent categories as the hidden or unknown Christ or *Logos* present among Hindus. Such a christological justification is dependent upon (i) the presentation of

280 Jacques Dupuis, 'Jesus with an Asian Face', 16.

a coherent and plausible version of a cosmic christology, and (ii) the defence of its christocentrism – perhaps in the qualified sense advanced above.

(c) An 'Indian' christological justification can also be offered, partly as a result of the Hindu-Christian encounter to date. Such a justification uses distinctly Indian categories and (i) renders christology, and other aspects of Christian belief and practice, more intelligible in an Indian context especially, perhaps, if embodied in a narrative framework; (ii) is enlarged by the dialogue itself; and (iii) offers some common ground and, as noted, the prospect of mutual enrichment. (And, of course, it is possible to combine either (a) or (b) with (c).)

However, despite the considerable potential of the christologies discussed, it might also be concluded that a *wholly* christocentric justification of Hindu-Christian dialogue is difficult to sustain. As suggested in the discussion of christocentrism (see above chapter 5.I) some aspects of the trinitarian and pneumatological dimensions of a theology of religious encounter and dialogue may be even more appropriate than christology.

CHAPTER 7

Conclusions

This work has attempted to do three things. It has described key aspects of the Hindu-Christian encounter in India and has described and defined the intentional meeting known as dialogue. Secondly, it has offered a critical analysis of the considerable volume of discussion about or generated by the dialogue. Finally, it has asked whether the dialogue can be justified and even enlarged in distinctly Indian and christological categories.

A. Description and Analysis

Hindu-Christian dialogue has been examined in its Indian setting in an attempt to understand why, especially for some Christians, it has displaced other models for interreligious relationships. A number of reasons are suggested and discussed and it is noted that, from about 1960, the word 'dialogue' began to be used with increasing frequency in both Protestant and Catholic circles – and even among Hindus – partly because of the impetus given by a number of events and publications in the first few years of the 1960s. In India, the late nineteenth and early twentieth centuries saw an increasing advocacy of a shift away from more traditional missionary and evangelistic emphases and towards a more accommodating and positive evaluation of Hinduism. Important antecedents to formal dialogue are found among Hindus and Christians, both national and missionary, Protestant and Catholic; these are elaborated in some detail.

Among Hindus, the most accommodating attitudes towards dialogue have usually been found among the proponents of Vedanta. The view of Christ held by these and other Hindus, especially those influenced by the Hindu renaissance, has been a fruitful point of discussion in the Hindu-Christian encounter. On the Christian side of the encounter considerable changes in attitude during the past century and a half are also described as some, but certainly not all, Christians in India have moved towards complementing or even replacing monologue with dialogue. Such dialogue – informal and formal – can be traced in the writings of individuals, groups and institutions. The role of western missionaries in this movement is also noted and discussed.

1. *The Meaning and Practice of Dialogue*

A comprehensive review of the considerable volume of discussion about the Hindu-Christian dialogue has revealed that although no precise or universally agreed definition has been agreed, a typology has begun to emerge. Although the categories do overlap, the term dialogue is usually found to mean an intentional meeting in one of the following categories:

- 'Discursive' dialogue: discourse as a (shared) quest for clarity of understanding.
- 'Secular' dialogue: discussion intended to facilitate a joint response to 'secular' problems, and the response itself.
- 'Interior' dialogue: the preparation of the Christian participant(s) prior to the actual meeting.
- 'Existential' dialogue: emphasising the direct and open acceptance of the other, and the other's spirituality.

One feature of the suggested typology is its ordering in terms of increasing complexity based upon an increasing range of presuppositions. However, the dialogue, even as defined in these fairly comprehensive categories, provides a less than full picture of the Hindu-Christian interface unless account is also taken of the means by which dialogue, both informal and formal, actually occurs. These means are elaborated in some detail.

The work has also examined the conditions, and inhibiting factors, that stand between the various means of dialogue and the production of its intended results. The supposed results of dialogue, as announced by its advocates, are also carefully noted.

2. *The Justification of Dialogue*

A number of reasons are given for the justification of Hindu-Christian dialogue. These too can be arranged in order of increasing complexity according to the range and plausibility of the presuppositions on which they are based.

The reasons are found to fall into two categories. Firstly, there are reasons shared by both Hindu and Christian participants in dialogue. These range from the need for understanding and the reduction of intercommunal tension through to an appeal to common or complementary religious experience. The second category is found to comprise a set of reasons that offer more distinctly Christian theological reasons for engagement in dialogue. These range from the perceived need to increase the 'inculturation' of the Indian Church through to dialogue as either implied or required by the Christian gospel, especially its motivation of love for the other.

Each of the proffered reasons for dialogue is found to have points of validity; however, they frequently seem to conceal a number of often unacknowledged presuppositions whose exposure raises a number of problems. Attention must be given to these issues if dialogue is to commend itself to the Hindu and Christian communities (both in and beyond India).

3. *Impediments to Dialogue*

Although the elaboration of Hindu-Christian dialogue in chapters 3 and 4 shows it to be a plausible exercise, able to be described and justified in considerable detail, several persistent difficulties are identified and discussed. Despite the force of these impediments to dialogue – both practical and theoretical – none seems to offer sufficient reason to abandon its advocacy in the face of the many reasons advanced for its justification. There may be no reasonable alternative to proceeding, even in the face of the ambiguities, tensions and lack of clarity and tensions that persist. In fact, solutions to the problems might not be found apart from persistence in dialogue itself.

B. Theological Analysis and Reflection

1. *Theology and Dialogue*

Although dialogue is what Sharma calls "a field reality... not a theoretical construct" this does not mean that its theoretical basis is unimportant. As Sharma goes on to add:

> Practice without underlying theory confuses the opportunistic with the providential. Practical action without theoretical context either contributes to alienation from both, or provides the scope for other ideologies, or methodologies ... to provide the context.[1]

Within the Christian tradition this theoretical basis is theology.

The full implications of Hindu-Christian dialogue for Christian theology, both in India and globally, are as yet uncertain but one consequence has been the increased attention given to the theology

1 Arvind Sharma, 'Towards a Theory of Dialogue,' 36. The same point – the need for a critical framework – is made by Felix Wilfred, 'Dialogue Gasping for Breath? Towards New Frontiers in Inter-Religious Dialogue,' *Vidyajoti*, 51 (1987), 449-66.

of inter-religious relationships. The pluralistic context of contemporary theological reflection cannot be ignored. In fact, it could be argued that any theology that calls itself 'ecumenical' – especially any that remains conscious of derivation from the former IMC (given that body's substantial role in the formation of the WCC) – ought not to remain isolated from the concerns of the whole *oikoumene* ['inhabited world'] including the existence and challenges of global religious pluralism. Theological reflection ought no longer to remain a domestic, self-sufficient (even narcissistic) Christian undertaking.[2]

The formation of a theology of religions that takes account of the openness and progress of recent decades may still require a new and appropriate theological method. Theologians from the 'third world' (especially) will increasingly challenge the agnosticism or attempted neutrality that has replaced the ecclesiocentrism or other exclusive opinions of many of their western colleagues. Duraisingh believes that common human experience in general (especially "dialogical experience") and the Christian tradition together form two essential sources for theology and missiology – with neither to be held above the other as a norm.[3] The Statement of the (ecumenical) Indian Theological Association links such a new theological method with inter-religious praxis. Praxis is regarded as an essential constituent of theological method, and it "generates and clarifies the vision and the way of life, another name for which is spirituality"[4]. One example of a radical inter-religious praxis is suggested by Panikkar who calls for a holistic '*dialogos*' that goes beyond the respective *logoi* of the two traditions to the *mythoi* that give them meaning and life.[5]

Such changes imply a radical shift in the starting point for the tra-

---

2 See, for example, John Britto Chethimattam, 'Towards a World Theology: an Interreligious Approach to Theological Issues,' in *Religions in Dialogue. East and West Meet*, edited by ZP Thundy and others (Lanham, MD, 1985), 295-314; the discussion by (the Indian theologian) J Paul Rajashekar, 'Dialogue with People of Other Faiths and Ecumenical Theology,' *ER*, 39 (1987), 455-61.

3 Christopher Duraisingh, 'Issues in Mission and Dialogue: Some Reflections,' *IRM*, 78 (1988), 404.

4 'Towards a Theology for Religions: An Indian Christian Perspective,' 82. The statement goes on to describe this "spirituality for inter-religious praxis" as "a habitual disposition in a Christian that is rooted in his/her faith and open to values in other faiths which enables him/her to relate in friendly and creative manner with the people of other faiths" (2).

5 'The Ongoing Dialogue,' xiv.

ditional Christian evaluation of Hinduism with its questions of revelation and salvation – and whether these might or might not be discerned in Hinduism. Such questions are derived from a western theological framework and remain centred on Christianity. This is a not indefensible starting point but, to the extent that it derives from the western "experience of long centuries of isolation of Christianity from the other religions" (as Wilfred alleges),[6] then the substantially different question of the appropriate place of Christianity in a religiously plural India might also be raised. That, in turn, implies a need for a fundamental revision of theology so that, for example, it employs an Asian epistemology or epistemologies[7] and makes extensive use of Asian mythology and symbolic language,[8] signs, images and artistic forms.[9] Lipner believes that theologians need to be 'bilingual' – bilingual not only linguistically, but culturally and theologically as well and explains that:

> Theology, in any religious tradition, must become increasingly bilingual. It is a methodological imperative of our time, characterised as it is by global communication and other networks of extraordinary interpenetration.[10]

It is also significant to note Raimundo Panikkar's rejection of any "universal theology of religion" (which is what Wilfred seems to want) on the grounds that (i) it is impossible to do theology from some neutral position that would be acceptable to the religions; (ii) the attempt to be universal is a longstanding example of western

---

6 'Dialogue Gasping for Breath?,' 450.

7 See, for example, the attempt in KP Aleaz, *The Role of Pramanas in Hindu-Christian Epistemology* (Calcutta, 1991); and *An Indian Jesus from Sankara's Thought* (Calcutta, 1997).

8 Wilfred argues for this in his 'Dialogue Gasping for Breath?,' 460-66.

9 See, as an example, the comments of the Indian Catholic artist Jyoti Sahi, 'Cosmos and Primal Permanence: An Artist's Perspective on Indian Symbol and Myth,' in *Re-visioning India's Religious Traditions,* edited by David C Scott and Israel Selvanayagam (Delhi, 1996), 155-71. It might also be noted that this is an area in which Catholic practice is considerably more creative than Protestant; for some of the reasons see Samartha, *One Christ – Many Religions,* 106. On the place of art as a kind of informal dialogue, see chapter 2.A.3.

10 Julius Lipner, review of Thangaraj, *The Crucified Guru,* in *ER,* 49 (1997), 386f. He also adds that "The "old school" – the over40s, say – may be excused, perhaps, for continuing to write monolingual theologies, theologies stuck in the myopia of a single lingual-cultural framework. This was the only kind of training open to them. The next generation should not be able to offer this excuse. But for this new approach, an informed methodology is requisite" (387).

colonialism or Christian imperialism; and (iii) such an attempt diminishes the importance of religious pluralism.[11] If such – or more modest – changes in theology are to be effected, one important requirement on the Christian side would be corresponding changes in the attitudes of clergy and other leaders. This will be influenced by their education and formation which, it is not frequently observed (by this and other writers), usually contributes little towards an understanding of the faiths of others.[12] It might also be helpful to remind conservative Christian critics of dialogue that all theology is unavoidably contextual; no expression of the faith is the same as expressions of past centuries because context and culture shape such expressions. If that context and culture include the presence of other faith traditions then (at least in Christian terms) the notion of the ubiquitous 'general revelation' of God might be seen as sufficient and even necessary reason for the content of theology to consider such data – with some form of dialogue as the means of its evaluation.

However, some cautionary and critical comments must also be made about the role of theology in the Hindu-Christian encounter. As we have repeatedly observed, the place of presuppositions – about the nature of the Absolute, the mutuality of faith, and many other matters – is often unacknowledged. This might well render doubtful, or much less certain, the often-confident conclusions and prescriptive comments of advocates of dialogue about the changes they believe must be made to traditionally central Christian doctrines. Eric Sharpe is one who believes that much of the theology of the recent Hindu-Christian encounter is unreasonably speculative. In commenting on the enormous diversity within both Hinduism and Christianity he observes that, until the enthusiast for dialogue

> learns to take seriously the possibility that there might be more than one explanation of temporarily acceptable forms of words,

11 The call is explicitly heard in *Toward a Universal Theology of Religion*, edited by Leonard Swidler (especially in Swidler's 'Interreligious and Interideological Dialogue: the Matrix for All Systematic Reflection Today' (5 – 50)); Panikkar's response is entitled 'The Invisible Harmony: A Universal Theory of Religion or a Cosmic Confidence in Reality?' (118-53).

12 Some factual information and recommendations are found in: *Ministerial Formation in a Multi-Faith Milieu. Implications of Interfaith Dialogue for Theological Education*, edited by Sam Amirtham and S Wesley Ariarajah (Geneva, 1986). Also relevant is some (but not all) of Thomas M Manickam, 'Indian Seminary Training and Ancient Indian Education Ideals' (*ITS*, (1982), 45-60).

> the actual encounters of actual Hindus and actual Christians ... may well remain subordinate to speculation about the ultimate meaning of those encounters.[13]

In other words, it is possible that one reason for the advocacy of dialogue is a diminished sense of theological conviction, or a revised and more modest sense of conviction, especially about those theological affirmations that would once have sustained a sense of Christian uniqueness and mission.[14] It is not without significance that the first WCC inter-faith study process, begun in 1956 was titled 'The Word of God and the Living Faiths of Men'; some three decades later (in 1984) the process was called 'My Neighbour's Faith and Mine'. The quest for a shared basis for dialogue in common humanity and a search for community at the very least moves what might be called a transcendent or 'spiritual' dimension into the background. The tendency to talk about culture rather than religion might be further evidence of such a trend.[15] Christian texts discussing Hinduism are now rarely critical (except when commenting on the exploitation or fostering of communal tensions) and generally positive in tone.

There seems to be a tendency (though one that would be time-consuming to document) towards an attenuated theology in which christological claims continue to be made but in an increasingly less central, less normative, and less confident manner. The not insubstantial reasons for this shift have already been discussed (in chapter 5.I) – especially the shift from a confident deductive to a more tentative inductive hermeneutic in which experience of the religions counted as much (or more) than traditional theological foundations. Nirmal,

---

13 Eric J Sharpe, 'Hindu-Christian Dialogue in Europe,' in *H-CD*, 112. An earlier observation of Sharpe's was that the reasons for the development of interest in dialogue are "to be seen far less in the progressive development of Christian theology ... than in the progressive disintegration of Christian theological thought" (*Faith Meets Faith*, 132).

14 For example, in his analysis of CISRS, Thompson claims that, since the early 1980s, there has been a decrease in explicitly theological analysis in the Institute's journal *Religion and Society* (A Frank Thompson, *The Christian Institute for the Study of Religion and Society: a Research Arm of Christian Churches in India* (Lewiston, NY, 1992), 149f).

15 See, for example, KP Aleaz, *The Gospel of Indian Culture* (Calcutta, 1994), a substantial work – a post-doctoral study sponsored by the World Council of Churches – in which the author seems almost embarrassed by the notion of religion, usually choosing to use the term 'culture' as a substitute. The same point is observable in his 'Gospel and Culture: Some Indian Reflections,' *IJT*, 37 (1994), 64-75.

for example, illustrates the shift in his complaint about the way in which conservative Christians are concerned, when entering dialogue, to safeguard the notion of the uniqueness of Christ, "rather than examining the adequacy of the doctrine ... in the light of actual dialogue experience."[16] Apart from some conservative Protestant and Catholic circles (and there by no means universally) it seems unlikely that cosmic christology will continue widely to be advocated as a basis for Hindu-Christian dialogue. In fact, christology itself may receive diminishing attention by comparison with an emphasis upon the Kingdom of God (perhaps especially in Catholic circles), upon the Spirit (perhaps especially in conciliar Protestant circles,[17] and in some Pentecostal circles[18]) and upon Trinitarian theology in both Catholic and Protestant reflection.[19]

---

16 Arvind Nirmal, 'Redefining the Economy of Salvation,' *IJT*, 30 (1981), 214; cf similar comments by Wesley Ariarajah in his *Hindus and Christians: a Century of Protestant Ecumenical Thought* (Amsterdam and Grand Rapids, MI, 1991), 195-213.

17 It might be noted that whereas the themes chosen for the first six WCC Assemblies were christological in content, that chosen for the seventh (February 1991) was pneumatological ('Come Holy Spirit – Renew the Whole Creation'), and for the eighth (December 1998) was 'Turn to God – Rejoice in Hope').

18 See, for example, the writings of Amos Yong: 'The Turn to Pneumatology in Christian Theology of Religions: Conduit or Detour?,' *JES*, 35 (1998), 437-454; '"Not Knowing Where the Wind Blows...": On Envisioning a Pentecostal-Charismatic Theology of Religions,' *Journal of Pentecostal Studies*, 14 (1999), 81-112; *Discerning the Spirit(s): A Pentecostal-Charismatic Contribution to Christian Theology of Religions*. Journal of Pentecostal Theology Supplement Series, 20 (Sheffield: Sheffield Academic Press, 2000).

19 For example, the Catholic *Theses on Interreligious Dialogue* claims that "the basis of dialogue ... is divine and trinitarian: the creative and salvific will of the Father, the cosmic outreach of the redemptive action of Jesus who is the Christ, and the recreative and fulfilling mystery of the Spirit" (9). For a constructive and original attempt to explore traditional Christian understandings of the Trinity in the light of the experience of *advaita* see von Brück, *The Unity of Reality: God, God-Experience, and Meditation in the Hindu-Christian Dialogue*; in it von Brück argues that the advaitic experience corresponds to and illuminates aspects of the experience of the Christian Trinity. A Protestant symposium that explores the issue in more general terms is *The Trinity in a Pluralistic Age: Theological Essays on Culture and Religion*, edited by Kevin J Vanhoozer (Grand Rapids, MI, 1997). See also the interesting comments of John Hick, 'Trinity and Incarnation in the Light of Religious Pluralism,' in *Three Faiths – One God*, edited by John Hick and Edmund S Meltzer (London, 1989), 197-210.

Much will depend upon the definition of theology itself. Theology may be defined as the attempt to understand and explain the Christian faith in terms of its own inner structure while using (and perhaps even transforming) the patterns of thought available from the immediate context. In an Indian context, this would mean that theology begins with the *sruti* (Christian scripture) with its subsequent *yukti* (inference and development) taken from one or more of the Indian worldviews. The issues, then, that must be addressed to the theology of Hindu-Christian dialogue, and to any undergirding of it by a distinctly Indian christology, are at least threefold. Firstly, whether the theology has been faithful both to the sruti and the Indian cultural context in which it needs to be both coherent and plausible. Secondly, there is the formulation of those critical principles by which the balance might be measured. A third consideration is the part, if any, to be played by other faiths in this process not only of relating the content of theology to a given context but also of understanding and reunderstanding the content in that context – in this case the Hindu tradition.[20]

Only a few theologians have attempted fully to allow the Hindu context to reshape Christian theology. Two examples (Abhishiktananda and Panikkar) have already been noted[21] and Dhavamony might also be mentioned.[22] One more recent work might also be commended as a model: *Theology after Vedanta: an Experiment in Comparative Theology* by Francis Clooney.[23] In it Clooney offers a critical reconsideration of his own Catholic tradition (using themes from the Summa of Aquinas and its commentarial tradition) after a close non-reductionist reading of and immersion in Advaita texts especially as understood in the light of the exegetical tradition centred on Sankara and Amalananda. The process is one that Clooney calls the "rereading and retrieval of one's prior theology after an appropriation of Vedanta."[24] He also acknowledges that this appropriation may not only bring out

---

20 The call for all Asian theology to be a 'dialogical theology' has already been noted: see above, chapter 3.H.

21 See above, chapter 1.E.1 and chapter 5.F.

22 See, for example, Mariasusai Dhavamony, 'Indian Perspectives in the New Paradigms of Theology,' in *Paradigm Change in Theology. A Symposium for the Future*, edited by Hans Küng and David Tracy (Edinburgh: T & T Clark, 1989), 424-36.

23 Albany, NY, 1993; among the many commendatory reviews see, for example, that by Harold Coward in *HCSB*, 6 (1993), 56-59.

24 *Theology after Vedanta*, 153.

aspects of theology not previously seen,[25] but also may change the means by which its truth is conceptualised. His methodology – the attempt to read and reflect on his own tradition from within the horizons of Vedanta – is one consequence of a recognition that theology is a dynamic interplay between content and context; or, as Clooney sees it, this is the

> distinctive tension between an adherence to the universal claim of one's own religion and an acknowledgement of the working of the truth of the Christian religion outside its boundaries.[26]

But whether it is possible to offer a critical restatement of Christian beliefs in the context of a non-reductionist reading of the Hindu traditions is not yet clear.

2. *The Christological Justification of Dialogue*

Because dialogue is, in many ways, a departure for Christian advocates from the traditional Christian theologies of mission and the evaluation of other faiths, its theological justification is especially important. Because christology has always been centrally important to the self-understanding of the Christian tradition,[27] the questions are asked: might christology be used to justify dialogue between Christians and Hindus? And, if so, what shape might that justification take? Two possible christological bases (the example of the Christ of the four Gospels, and the analogy of the incarnation) are examined and found to be of limited value. A more persuasive and comprehensive justification for dialogue is offered by cosmic christology (provided that coherent and plausible expressions of such a christology can be given). The implications for dialogue from such christological foundations include, for example:

(a) openness to others – because of the supposed presence of Christ who is in some way found in each partner in dialogue;

(b) a further basis for dialogue is found in the common humani-

25 For example, he writes that "new meanings will be constructed for the Bible and the theological systems composed from it, new meanings that can occur only due to the event of juxtaposition with these non-Christian texts" (*Theology after Vedanta*, 194).

26 *Theology after Vedanta*, 194f. Although Clooney is critical of the typology of exclusivism, inclusivism and pluralism, this last passage reveals his inclination to inclusivism – a position not without its weaknesses among which is the charge of a somewhat patronising co-option of Hinduism.

27 To give but one of many possible examples, see Allan Delotovo, 'Toward a Christ-centred Way of Doing Theology in Asia,' *AJT*, 3 (1989), 330-34.

ty said to be a consequence of the new Humanity/Kingdom inaugurated by Christ;

(c) it also seems that christology has a number of advantages over other possible – but more abstract and less concrete – shared starting points for Hindus and Christians such as 'God' or 'Spirit'.

(d) as Christianity faces the possibility of a Copernican-like displacement in its own remapping of the universe of religions, christology (at least as construed in traditional terms) might help make clear at least some universal implications of faith in Christ.

However, it is also acknowledged that traditional christology will need to be rehabilitated and the plausibility of the notion of some cosmic dimension to the person of Christ will also need to be established and defended and not merely reasserted. An attempt has been made to do this in the light of criticisms directed at any christocentric view of reality and a defence of a qualified christocentrism is offered. Such a Christocentrism will be seen in some Christian circles as not only desirable but also essential if the longstanding affirmation that 'Jesus is Lord' is to continue to be made. Such an affirmation sees Christ not only as a potential (and pragmatically convenient) link between the religious but also as the means of sounding the themes of crisis, judgement and redemption for every religious tradition – including Christianity itself.

3. *An Indian Christological Basis for Dialogue*

Chapter 6 has described the way in which a number of concepts taken from Indian worldviews might contribute to a view of Christ in distinctly Indian categories – and so facilitate dialogue. Moreover, it seems as if aspects of such a christology have begun to emerge from the Hindu-Christian encounter itself. There are a number of Indian concepts with considerable potential for this elaboration and from enhanced comprehension and restatement of christology in India. Such christology could well incorporate some or all of the following components:

- the shared ideal of the *guru*/master, especially as apprehended by a *sisya*/disciple;
- the *avatara* concept, with due care to avoid both the Hindu and conservative Christian tendencies towards docetism and the Christian apologetic inclination towards an imperialism of the historical;

- an emphasis upon the role of *anubhava*, as seen, for example, in the potential importance of *bhaktimarga* in any Indian *kristvidya*;
- the elaboration of a Christian advaita, based on the apparent religious consciousness of Jesus, as a kind of experiential *jnana-marga* (though not one claiming identity with the divine);
- the possible use of *Cit* and other Indian terminology to replace (or help explain) christological terms derived from Hebrew or Greek or Western contexts;
- all with due sensitivity to the problems raised by christocentrism in an Indian context, while noting the way in which a number of these Indian concepts might also serve to correct some potentially distorting western theological emphases.

However, one fundamental difficulty is also discerned: a lack of coherence between Hinduism – and its worldview(s) – and the mainly western christologies found in the Indian churches. The suggestion is made that christology, or some aspects of it, be cast into Antiochene categories, rather than those of the Alexandrian model that has been dominant in western christology. At a number of points Antiochene christology avoids emphases that are difficult for Hindus to understand or accept; and it has a number of christological emphases that seem more congruent with Hinduism than the Alexandrian model.

Nonetheless, several fundamental questions remain concerning the quest for such a christological basis for dialogue. For example:

- Ought christology to be formulated in a functional manner in order to justify or facilitate dialogue? – or is christology, at least as traditionally conceived (with its heavily metaphysical framework), irretrievably distorted by such a formulation?
- Must a distinctly Christian view of God (for example, as Trinitarian or comprehensively dualistic) be asserted alongside, or as a necessary part of, christology?
- Given the variety of the Christian and christological approaches, is it desirable and preferable simply to state that, as in Hinduism, a variety of *darsanas* are claimed?

It is concluded that a christological justification of Hindu-Christian dialogue can be offered in three senses:

(a) 'Weak' (making fewest christological assumptions) in which an exemplarist and theocentric christology is used.

(b) 'Strong' (dependent upon more substantial presuppositions) in which a cosmic christology is employed and its attendant christocentrism is defended in qualified terms.

(c) 'Indian' in an attempt to make both christology and a Christian advocacy of dialogue intelligible to Hindu participants.

However, it is also concluded that, for the Christian community, christology offers only a partial and suggestive, but not comprehensive, justification of dialogue with Hindus. In a number of significant ways the enterprise of dialogue is enhanced and even strengthened by christological underpinnings – but these are unlikely by themselves to be persuasive.

C. The Future Dialogue

1. A Variety of Responses

The study has attempted to show that there are adequate and, for some, compelling reasons for dialogue. It may be that yet more plausible reasons will be found to convince those Christians and Hindus who remain indifferent to or in some ways opposed the possibility of a fruitful encounter between the traditions. In the light of conclusions already drawn, what might be said about the future of Hindu-Christian dialogue?

There is nothing to suggest that the progress of Hindu-Christian dialogue in India is inexorable or assured in any way, or that more than some personal and intercommunal mutual understanding and harmony is necessarily delivered by it. Some recent commentators are pessimistic about its present and future prospects.[28] Various reasons are given; for example, dialogue is "suffocated and constricted by the narrowness of the theological ambit in which it is moving".[29] It is hindered because "a significant number" of Indian scholar-participants in dialogue, both Hindu and Christian, have moved to positions in the West.[30] To others the situation seems a little anaemic, with the largest misunderstandings overcome and a certain degree of tolerance established.[31] Stanley Samartha, one of the most experienced commentators (among Protestants, at least) is pessimistic. He considers the Protestant community as a whole to have made little

---

28 See, for example, the overview of Felix Machado, 'Hindu-Christian Encounter: General Problematic,' *Vidyajyoti*, 60 (1996), 825-42.

29 Felix Wilfred, 'Dialogue Gasping for Breath? Towards New Frontiers in Inter-Religious Dialogue,' *Vidyajyoti*, 51 (1987), 466.

30 Richard W Taylor, 'Current Hindu-Christian Dialogue in India,' in *H-CD*, 120.

31 Raimundo Panikkar, 'The Ongoing Dialogue,' in *H-CD*, xvii.

advance on its position in the 1960s; he sees Catholic initiatives at a stalemate with most participants repeating the same formulae and unwilling to move ahead. In fact, he thinks that the dialogue could degenerate into a kind of religious tourism if Christians remain unwilling, as he sees it, to purify their motives and take more seriously the responses of Hindu partners in dialogue.[32] Other observers are more optimistic, with one pair of commentators claiming that Hindu-Christian dialogue "has directly or indirectly created a ferment of change. Its achievements foreshadow a fruitful future of silent revolution in the religious life of the country".[33] Another advocate calls Hindu-Christian dialogue, "perhaps one of the greatest intellectual adventures of our time".[34]

As for the future of the encounter, it seems likely that a variety of attitudes will persist.[35] These attitudes may be described under four headings.

(a) Indifference to or Conservative Rejection of Dialogue

There are those who will continue to regard the gap between church and temple as too great to be bridged. They will continue to regard with indifference or to reject the intentional meeting that is called dialogue and will remain silently, as it were, within their own communities of faith – either because of inertia or conviction, and not without a degree of contentment as well. In itself, this silence need not necessarily be construed in negative terms. Moltmann points out that dialogue is only one possibility in the encounter of religions; "we also know, by way of contrast, of the amicable coexis-

---

32 Stanley J Samartha, *One Christ – Many Religions*, Faith Meets Faith Series (Maryknoll, NY, 1991), 78, 13.

33 Anand Nayak and Anne-Marie Abrard, 'Hindu-Christian Dialogue in India,' *PMVB*, no. 88 (January 1982), 21; see also the positive assessments of Anand Amaladass, 'Dialogue in India,' *HCSB*, 1 (1988), 7f, and Godwin R Singh, 'Is Dialogue at a Dead End?,' *NCCR*, 106 (1986), 130-36.

34 Klaus Klostermaier in *ITD*, 238.

35 The range of Hindu attitudes to dialogue is parallel to that surveyed in *Modern Indian Responses to Religious Pluralism*, Part 1 'Responses from With Hinduism' – though, it must also be added that the conservative suspicion of pluralism (and dialogue) has hardened in recent years. On the Christian side, but also with discernible parallels among Hindus, the attributes might helpfully be elaborated in terms of the continuum described by David Ford: repetition [of past formulations] – engagement [with the contemporary world] – correlation – integration (David F Ford, 'Introduction to Modern Christian Theology' in *The Modern Theologians: An Introduction to Christian Theology in the Twentieth Century*, edited by David F Ford, second edition (Oxford, 1997), 1-3).

tence of different religious communities without war, without conflict, without disputations and without dialogue"[36] – which is, of course, the situation for most Hindu-Christian neighbours in India who, without anxiety, live in no less harmony than with neighbours from their own religious communities.

This harmony is not, however, ubiquitous. Particular attention might well be given to the present and future impact upon dialogue of the conservative and sometimes militant forms of the two traditions. A number of observers have concluded that the chief obstacle to dialogue is 'fundamentalism'.[37] The formation of the ideological identity of the 'fundamentalist' species of Christianity and Hinduism is complex but seems often to include a negative reaction to modernity in general and to the ideologies of modernism and secularism in particular. Such fundamentalisms often include a negative and militant reaction to the other tradition or, at least, to the

---

36 Jurgen Moltmann, 'Is "Pluralistic Theology" Useful for the Dialogue of World Religions?' in *Christian Uniqueness Reconsidered*, 150f. While Moltmann draws most of his conclusions from west and east Europe, he also relates his thesis about the non-necessity of dialogue to Africa and Asia (151); he also concedes that another means of avoiding dialogue is by simultaneous multiple religious allegiances (152), a phenomenon not unknown in India (see chapter 4.C.3 above). See also Ainslie T Embree, *Utopias in Conflict: Religion and Nationalism in Modern India* (Los Angeles, 1990) in which he points out the proven ability of Indian culture in enabling many cultures to live side by side in a spirit that is neither toleration, nor absorption, nor synthesis (see 24f); and JV Ferreira, 'Religious Nationalism in India,' in *Dialogue in Action. Essays in Honour of Johannes Aagaard*, edited by edited by Thunberg, Pandit and Fogh-Hansen (New Delhi, 1988), 152-78.

37 See, for example, TN Madan, *Modern Myths, Locked Minds. Secularism and Fundamentalism in India* (Delhi: Oxford University Press, 1996); Robert E Frykenberg, 'Contesting the Limits of Tolerance/Intolerance and Toleration: Some Observations on Fundamentalism,' *South Asian Survey* 4 (1997) 13-23. Also useful is *Religious Fundamentalism – an Asian Perspective*, edited by John S Augustine (Bangalore: SATHRI, 1992). For discussion of fundamentalism in an Indian Christian context see Lionel Caplan, *Class and Culture in Urban India: Fundamentalism in a Christian Community* (Oxford, 1987), especially the Introduction and chapters 7 and 8; for some comments on some Hindu parallels see Israel Selvanayagam, 'The Roots of Hindu Fundamentalism: a Historical Overview,' *AJT*, 10 (1996), 440-50. See also the analyses of David C Scott, 'Religious Fundamentalism and Pluralism in India,' *HCSB*, 7 (1994), 45-47 (in which he especially draws attention to the role of communalism) and Gabriele Dietrich, 'The Size of Communalism and Fundamentalism in India,' in *Re-visioning India's Religious Traditions*, 205-12.

perceived threat of missionary-minded or aggressive forms of those traditions (against which all advocates of dialogue should combine according to Ariarajah[38]) and this reaction may well be related to the issue of communal and personal identities, especially when the formation of these identities has taken place in isolation from other communities.[39] The result is not conducive to dialogue. As Fornberg points out

> It belongs to the nature of fundamentalism that all criteria of truth must be found within the borders of one's own religion, and often even within one's own group, and the consequent conviction that all others are wrong. This stance discourages interreligious contact.[40]

In a discussion of religious identity in contemporary India, Diana Eck cites evidence for what she calls "the breakdown of a workable pluralism".[41] She considers there to have been a significant shift away from the mainly tolerant acceptance of religious diversity in the past to the present situation in which such diversity is increasingly seen or promoted as abnormal or even threatening. In other words, there has been, in India, a change to a society whose diversity is now "competitive" and "communalist". There is "a new kind of virulence in the public celebration of festivals" as Indian society's "old tolerance for ambiguity is beginning to weaken".[42] These are claims that warrant serious reflection, including critical sociological analysis.[43] Conversely, the social sciences might also be able to identify some of those psychological and group processes that con-

---

38 S Wesley Ariarajah, 'A World Council of Churches' Perspective on the Future of Hindu-Christian Dialogue,' in *H-CD*, 256. On the rise of militancy among Christians, Hindus and Muslims see Stanley Samartha, 'The Temper of Crusades and the Spirit of Dialogue,' *NCCR*, 104 (1984), 474-78 and Xavier Kochuparampil, 'Religious Tolerance – Intolerance in India,' *Exchange* 27(1998), 371-77.

39 See the study by Stanley J Samartha, 'Religious Identity in a Multi-Faith Society,' *CD*, no. 13 (December 1987), 4-10, 21. See also above, chapter 4.A.1(f), 4.C.1(b) and 4.C.2.a.

40 Tord Fornberg, *The Problem of Christianity in Multi-religious Societies of Today*, Toronto Studies in Theology, 70 (Lewiston, NY: Edwin Mellen Press, 1995), 259.

41 See Diana L Eck, 'Moderator's Report. Working Group on Dialogue,' *CD*, no. 14 (June 1988), 5f.

42 Eck, 'Moderator's Report,' 6.

43 For example, Sammy Smooha, 'Pluralism and Conflict: A Theoretical Exploration,' *Plural Societies*, 6.3 (Autumn 1975), 69-89.

tribute to social identity[44] and that help determine the receptivity of one (religious) community to another.[45]

A further factor in the rise of militancy and religious intolerance is the politicisation of religion as attempts are made to use or exploit religious sympathy, allegiance and fears or threats, for political ends. This kind of instrumentalistic strategy of stigmatisation and ethnoreligious mobilisation has been exacerbated in contemporary India by the way in which Hindu communalist and nationalist loyalties have been portrayed as necessarily synonymous.[46] Not only is this ethnonationalistic redefinition of democracy as majoritarianism disadvantageous to the Muslim, Sikh, Christian and other minority communities, it seems also to have contributed to the revival and spread of Hindu nationalism.[47] An example is the way in which the

---

44 Especially if in India the church, in fact, "in many places constitutes virtually an independent caste group" (Boyd, *Introduction to Indian Christian Theology*, 249f).

45 See, for example, the discussions of the relationship in *Social Identity and Intergroup Relations*, edited by Henri Tajfel (London, 1982); and Robert L Montgomery, 'Receptivity to an Outside Religion: Light from Interaction between Sociology and Missiology,' *Missiology*, 14 (1986), 287-99. Sudhir Kakar offers a psychoanalytical comment on aspects of interreligious conflict in his *The Colours of Violence* (New Delhi: Viking, 1995). Also helpful is the analysis of Vincent Gabriel Furtado, 'Philosophical Background of Interreligious Conflicts and Their Resolution,' *JD*, 23 (1998), 141-62. A challenging but potentially helpful sociological analysis is also provided by George Pattery's use of the theses of Rene Girard concerning the role in interreligious conflict of desire, envy, rivalry anger and a community's projection of the consequences of these emotions onto a sacrificial victim; see Pattery, 'Mimetic Desire and Sacred Violence: Understanding Rene Girard from the Indian Context,' *VJTR*, 58 (1994), 15-32.

46 Even the usually sympathetic Stanley Samartha, in commenting on pan-Indian Hindu assertiveness, complains of "a majority community with a minority complex" (*One Christ – Many Religions*, 23).

47 See, for example, Peter van der Veer, *Religious Nationalism: Hindus and Muslims in India* (Berkeley, CA: University of California Press, 1994); and 'The Ruined Centre: Religious and Mass Politics in India,' *Journal of International Affairs* 50(1996), 254-77; Gerald James Larson, *India's Agony over Religion*, SUNY Series in Religious Studies (Albany, NY: State University of New York Press, 1995); *Contesting the Nation: Religion, Community and the Politics of Democracy in India*, edited by David Ludden (Philadelphia, PA: University of Pennsylvania, 1995); Christophe Jaffrelot, *The Hindu Nationalist Movement in India*, (New York, NY: Columbia University Press, 1996); *Making India Hindu*, edited by David Ludden (Delhi: Oxford University Press, 1996); Lise McKean, *Divine Enterprise: Gurus and the Hindu Nationalist Movement* (Chicago, IL and London:

controversial attempts to (re)build a temple at the supposed birthplace of Ram in north India have been made the common cause (even if not entirely voluntarily[48]) of many other Hindus, regardless of sectarian differences.[49] More moderate Hindu opinion is often dismayed at such militancy and sees it as running counter to other strands of Hindu opinion.[50] Communalist-nationalist militancy does, nonetheless, provide an opportunity for a different and cooperative spirit of dialogue and neighbourliness to be offered, difficult though that might be to sustain.[51] However as Taylor points out, the

---

University of Chicago Press, 1996); Stanley Tambiah, *Levelling Crowds: Ethnonationalist Conflicts and Collective Violence in South Asia* (Berkeley, CA and London: University of California Press, 1996); Thomas Blom Hansen, *The Saffron Wave: Democracy and Hindu Nationalism in Modern India* (Princeton, NJ: Princeton University Press, 1999). Chapters V ('Religious Nationalism') and VII ('Missionary Fundamentalism and Ayodhya Episode') of Mathew, *The Saffron Mission* also contain useful analyses and detailed bibliographies.

48 "Even those Hindus who were not devotees of Ram found their Hindu identity in peril unless they lent their voice to favour the *mandir*." (Scott, 'Religious Fundamentalism,' 46f.)

49 An example is the way in which the temple campaign has made the worship of Ram a popular cause in those parts of India where his veneration has not hitherto been particular popular. This writer has noted the recent growth of devotion to Ram in Vishakapatnam in Andra Pradesh, in the east of India, and there are similar reports from elsewhere in the east and south of the country.

50 "It is evident that the... ideology of a Hindu state is diametrically opposite to the concept of 'composite culture' propounded by Rabindranath Vivekananda and others." (A K Mazumdar, 'Hindu Fundamentalism,' *Shabda, Shakti, Sangam,* [Hindu section], 187.

51 See, for example: Stanley Samartha, 'Dialogue and the Politicization of Religions in India,' *IBMR*, 8 (1984), 104-07; Samuel Rayan, 'The Kingdom of God, Religious Pluralism and Communalism. The Kingdom of Justice and Peace,' *SEDOS Bulletin*, 24 (1992), 261-67; Lancy Lobo, 'Communalism and Christian Response in India,' *Vidyajyoti*, 59 (1995), 365-74; Rudolf C Heredia, 'Pluralism, Tolerance and Dialogue,' *Vidyajyoti*, 60 (1996), 255-64; 'Working for Harmony in the Contemporary World,' *CD*, no. 29 (1996), 16-20; KN Mishra, A Pushparajan and I Puthiadam, 'Call to Harmony through Dialogue,' *Vidyajyoti*, 60 (1996), 275-81; Christopher S Raj, 'Communalism: Options and Responses,' in *The Church in India: its Mission Tomorrow*, edited by F Hrangkhuma and Sebastian CH Kim (Pune and Delhi, 1996), 12-35; for a more substantial discussion of communalism and some positive religious responses to it, see: *Responding to Communalism. The Task of Religions and Theology*, edited by S Arokiasamy (Anand, 1991).

attacks of the most conservative Hindus tend to restrain those Hindus who might otherwise be more interested in or more cooperative toward dialogue.[52]

The issue of conversion is another topic that can inflame conservative Hindu opinion.[53] As already observed (chapter 2.D.1 above) the acceptance or rejection of religious pluralism also raises a cluster of issues such as tolerance, the rights of witness and conversion and the rights of reasonable defence against proselytism – and poses questions for all those Hindus and Christians whose uncritical endorsement of the virtues of pluralism is liable to be ignorant of or indifferent to those issues of institutional oppression that constitute one reason for the desire to convert. Discussion of these issues continues.

(b) Cautious Acknowledgement

A second group comprises those who, also firmly established within their tradition and embracing its truth claims (and even mission),

---

52 'Current Hindu-Christian Dialogue in India,' 125.

53 See, for example, the field 'conversions' in the forum maintained by 'The Hindu Universe' http://www.hindunet.org/conversions/, September 2001, and the material on the same topic in the forum of the Society for Hindu-Christian Studies (threads accessible through the archives maintained at http://www.acusd.edu/theo/hcs-l/archive/, September 2001). Some analysis of the latter is promised in Francis Clooney, 'Conversions in India: an Interim Report on the Discussion on the Hindu-Christian Studies List, January-March 1999,' *HCSB*, 12 (1999). For fairly recent Christian comment see: Jacob Kuvankal, 'Dialogue and Conversion,' *Vidyajyoti*, 54 (1990), 177-87; James H Kroeger, 'Naming the Conversion We Seek,' *Vidyajyoti*, 59 (1995), 107-25; *Mission and Conversion: a Reappraisal*, edited by Joseph Mattam and Sebastian CH Kim (Mumbai, 1996); SM Michael, 'Religious Freedom and Conversion,' *Vidyajyoti*, 62 (1998), 172-80. See also: Marc Spindler, 'Conversion in Focus: Anthropological Views and Missiological Projections,' *ZMR*, 81 (1997), 275-88; Ishanand Vempeny, *Conversion National Debate or Dialogue*, second edition (Anand: Gujarat Sahitya Prakash, 1999); *TM*, 2.3 (July-September 1999) has as its theme 'Conversion and Alienation'. The complexities of the conversion issue are also brought out by Andrew Wingate, *The Church and Conversion. A Study of Recent Conversions to and from Christianity in the Tamil Area of South India* (Delhi: ISPCK, 1997) and much of the recent discussion is surveyed in the special issue of *Jnanadeepa: Pune Journal of Religious Studies*, 3.1 (January 2000); and Lalsangkima Pachuau, 'Ecumenical Church and Religious Conversion: A Historical-Theological Study with Special Reference to India,' *MS*, 18 (2001), 181-201.

acknowledge the reality of religious pluralism with courtesy and varying degrees of enthusiasm – usually more from Hindus than from Christians – and also the possibility of partnership towards certain ends.

Perhaps the majority of literate Hindus, Catholics, and evangelical Protestants are found within this group. They could hardly be called advocates of Hindu-Christian dialogue (in either its formal or informal senses) but they, unlike the fundamentalists, are usually found to acknowledge that each religious tradition is cumulative to a greater or lesser extent and does, perhaps even should, undergo some change in the face of religious pluralism – for example more careful self-expression to avoid unnecessary misunderstanding or giving of offence. It could well be asserted that the very large majority of 'lay' Hindus and Christians are in these categories (a) and (b). However, in the case of Christianity it remains true that the most wholehearted advocates of dialogue are from the liberal wings of the tradition. Because, as Sharpe points out, the 'great tradition' of Christianity is, like Hinduism, made up of innumerable 'little traditions' (using the terminology of Milton Singer in his *When a Great Tradition Modernizes*) "it is simply irresponsible to assume that a Christian dialogue with Hinduism, initiated by Christians belonging to only one branch of the Christian tree, must result in a single 're-evaluation of Christian faith'"[54] – as the more liberal proponents of dialogue have often assumed.

(c) Advocacy of Dialogue

This position is embraced by those who see dialogue as what one advocate calls "a transforming friendship where the two traditions would interpenetrate and transform each other"[55]. Most of those, both Hindu and Christian, cited in the preceding chapters are in this category and the strengths and weaknesses of their positions have been elaborated in some detail.

(d) Beyond Dialogue

This category – in number by far the smallest of the four – comprises those who, because of the experience of Hindu-Christian (and possibly other) dialogue or, more likely, for other reasons, find little reason to preserve the two dharmas, as received; they look for a new and as yet somewhat unknown way forward beyond the cur-

54 *Faith Meets Faith*, 111f.
55 Ariarajah, 'A World Council of Churches' Perspective,' 258.

rent paradigms for dialogue.[56] This seems to be the viewpoint of Panikkar in his more recent writings. In one, he characterises the latest (post-colonial) phase of the Hindu-Christian meeting as "a predominantly doctrinal dialogue"[57] and goes on to call for a further phase which "challenges the fixed identity of both parties";[58] in another he argues that "in Christ there is neither Hindu nor Christian".[59] In yet another work he writes of his pilgrimage that: "I 'left' as a Christian, I 'found' myself a Hindu and I 'return' a Buddhist, without having ceased to be a Christian."[60] Duraisingh describes Indian "hyphenated" Christians; that is, those whose identity is determined by both the wider Indian religious as well as the Christian traditions.[61] (However, it must also be noted that although those for whom dialogue has had the outcome mentioned are few, there are other forces that press the two communities towards one another – and so blur the boundaries between them.)

2. *Modernity and Postmodernity*

(a) Secularisation

It seems likely that one component of modernity – secularisation

---

56 For a parallel suggestion from the Christian-Buddhist encounter, see John B Cobb, *Beyond Dialogue: Toward a Mutual Transformation of Christianity and Buddhism* (Philadelphia, 1982).

57 Raimundo Panikkar, 'The Ongoing Dialogue,' in *H-CD*, xv-xviii (quotation from xvi).

58 'The Ongoing Dialogue,' xvii.

59 Partial title by Panikkar of chapter 20 of *Religious Issues and Inter-Religious Dialogues*, edited by C Weihsun Fu and GE Spiegler (New York 1989). Another advocate of Hindu-Christian dialogue, Klaus Klostermaier, regards the boundary between Hinduism and Christianity as "fairly artificial" ('Dialogue in the Modern West,' *HCSB*, 1 (1988), 8; see also 9). See, in similar vein, Wilfred Cantwell Smith's argument that the religions have never been discrete bodies but have always borrowed from and been changed by one another: 'Traditions in Contact and Change: Towards a History of Religion in the Singular,' in *Traditions in Contact and Change*, edited by Peter Slater and others (Waterloo, Canada, 1983), 1-23.

60 Raimundo Panikkar, *The Intrareligious Dialogue* (New York, 1978), 2.

61 Christopher Duraisingh, 'A New Expression of Identity,' *RS*, 26.4 (December 1979), 95-101 and 'Indian Hyphenated Christians and Theological Reflections. Part II: Alternate Modes of Theologising now Prevalent in India,' *RS*, 27.2 (June 1980), 81-101. Also helpful is chapter 6 of Margaret Chatterjee, *The Religious Spectrum*.

(and secularism, its ideological expression) – will continue to influence Indian society and its religious traditions[62]. Modernisation will continue to erode traditional religious authority and press religion into the margins of life for some, especially the urbanised and better educated. It might therefore tend to weaken the walls of traditional isolation between Hindu and Christian and may thus even facilitate some kind of dialogue[63]. At the very least, it might lead to the recognition that, in the words of the Indian lay theologian MM Thomas, "bringing religions ... to dialogue on their traditional spiritual terms unaffected by the pressure of modernity is now impossible."[64] Moreover, it may be possible that, because of secularisation "both religions are on the brink of a mutation, different as the two mutations may be"[65]. Or, more likely, the presence of modernity and techno-economic globalisation will keep both traditions self-conscious (because of considerable exposure to other religious traditions and to currents that are indifferent or even hostile to religion) and even somewhat dynamic (because of resistance to change in the face of modernisation). This could mean each will change in unforeseeable ways and perhaps become increasingly self-aware in the face of critical and negative comments from those who embrace a secular worldview – both within and outside the two traditions and from those somewhere between faith and unbelief. In the face of continuing religious conflict in India (usually not directly Hindu-Christian) it may be that some Indians turn to secular humanism because of its usually unequivocal stand for human dignity and human rights.

On the other hand, secularism could be seen as provoking conservative opinions within the two traditions towards a greater con-

62 See above, chapters 2.C.2 and 3.D and also the comments by AM Abraham Ayrookuzhiel on 'The Secular Option,' in his 'The State of Hinduism in 2000 AD – Some Emerging Trends,' *IJT*, 26 (1977), 88-91; and the more recent remarks of Michael Amaladoss, 'Secularization and India: Modernization and Religion in an Eastern Country,' *SEDOS Bulletin*, 24 (1992), 233-40. Also useful is CV Mathew and Charles Corwin, *Area of Light. The Indian Church and Modernization* (Delhi, 1994) and an excellent survey in sociological categories is found in Achin Vanaik, *The Furies of Indian Communalism. Religion, Modernity and Secularization* (London: Verso, 1997).

63 It should facilitate what we have called 'secular dialogue'; see chapter 2.C.2.above.

64 'A Christ-centred Humanist Approach to Other Religions in the Indian Pluralistic Context,' in Christian Uniqueness Reconsidered, 57.

65 Panikkar, 'The Ongoing Dialogue,' xv; Panikkar actually calls the process "secularity".

servatism[66] and moving progressive elements to become yet more progressive, creative and impatient. It can also be argued that nationalist appeal for Hindutva seeks to "redefine democracy as majoritarianism and secularism as tolerance, in order to present itself as more truly secular and democratic."[67] Klostermaier considers that "a massive shift has taken place in the understanding of key concepts of both traditional Christianity and Hinduism, much of it under the impact of modern science" – even if that shift is not yet fully recorded or understood.[68] The imposition of census taking may have made people choose one religious label – an example of consolidated Hindu (and Muslim and Christian) identity as a sign or consequence of modernity. But on the other hand Vishwanathan has offered a detailed and plausible justification of her claim that the process of imperial state formation in India emerged from liberal, secular and rights-based principles whose apparent purpose was the toleration of religious differences but whose outcome was the marginalisation of religious belief.[69] Others have also pointed out that secular institutions in India have experienced difficulty because they function in a society that is not itself secularised despite the introduction of secular discourse by a modernist elite;[70] and for yet others the issue of the continuing shadow of postcolonial influence is significant.[71]

However, despite the probability that a modern view of the world is certainly an increasingly shared context for both Hindu and Christian, it need not be assumed that modernity will have a

---

66 This is the argument of Mark Juergensmeyer, *Religious Nationalism Confronts the Secular State* (Delhi: Oxford University Press, 1993); see also MM Thomas, 'Religious Fundamentalism and Indian Secularism: The Present Crisis,' *JD*, 19 (1994), 26-35.

67 Vanaik, *The Furies of Indian Communalism*, 188.

68 Klaus Klostermaier, 'The Future of Hindu-Christian Dialogue,' in *H-CD*, 267. The impact of science on the two traditions is the subject of volume 10 (1997) of *HCSB*; see also the discussion by Sarojini Henry, 'The Encounter of Faith and Science in Interreligious Dialogue', *RS*, 46.1 & 2 (March-June 1999), 97-111.

69 Gauri Viswanathan, *Outside the Fold. Conversion, Modernity and Belief* (Princeton: Princeton University Press, 1998).

70 See, for example, Sudipta Kaviraj, 'Modernity and Politics in India,' *Daedulus* 129 (2000), 137-62; and the discussion in *Secularism and its Critics*, edited by Rajeer Bhargava (Delhi: Oxford University Press, 1998).

71 See, for example, Eaton, '(Re)imag(in)ing Other 2ness. In more general term, see the helpful discussion in *SWC* 5.2 (1999) in which the whole issue is given over to 'Postcolonialism and Religion.'

wholly negative impact upon the religions of India. One response is to assert the foundational presence of the Divine in the whole of life – however 'secular' that life is perceived to be.[72] Another response is to suggest, as did Samartha in 1984, that "the most marked characteristic of contemporary Indian life is not so much its secularity as its hunger for transcendence"[73]; if true, that hunger itself might provide a common incentive for dialogue. And yet another dimension is to note that, as in the West, at least some of the 'secular' features of modernity dissolve as all claims to privileged knowledge – including those of modernity – are rendered suspect. This postmodernising tendency might, in turn, permit a greater degree of liberty in suggesting an experiential reference point for the evaluation of life in general and religion in particular. It might also enhance the coexistence of traditional and modern worldviews as well as reinforcing India's traditional virtues of plurality and inclusiveness to the advantage of dialogue.

(b) Help from the Internet?

There is, however, one rather new source of help that modernity might provide for the Hindu-Christian dialogue: locations on the internet websites. Firstly, there is the multitude of sites that provide (or supposedly provide) information about the two traditions – usually from within the tradition itself – though the quality of the material varies greatly.[74] Given that one condition for dialogue is access to accurate information about religious tradition, these websites have potential value for a fruitful encounter. But there are two other categories of sites that are of potential help for Christian-Hindu dialogue.

Firstly, there are sites that give, or purport to give, information about and analysis of the other tradition; that is, sites that offer a Hindu or a Christian perspective on interreligious relations in gen-

---

72 See, for example, Subhash Anand, 'Consecrated Secularity: Theological Basis and Practical Implications,' *Vidyajyoti*, 59 (1995), 145-60.

73 'Dialogue and the Politicization of Religions in India,' 105; the same point is also made by Abraham Kuruvilla in a section entitled 'The Mood of Spiritual Searching,' 492f of his 'God's Gracious Turning: Spirituality and Repentance in India Today,' *IRM*, 87 (1998).

74 For example, in May 1999 the site http://www.zdnetcom/yil/content/mag/9804/godonandoff.html reported the Yahoo! search engine as identifying 9,459 sites offering information on Christianity and 154 sites offering information on Hinduism. Perhaps the most comprehensive and best organised site for Hinduism is 'The Hindu Universe' http://www.hindunet.org/home.html.

eral and the Hindu-Christian relationship in particular.[75] Secondly, there are those sites that actually enable a form of dialogue. For example, the site 'The Hindu Universe' has an interactive forum on 'Hindu and Christian Relations',[76] and The Society for Hindu-Christian Studies (see below) maintains a similar site.[77] However, at the time of writing, most of these internet sites are located in North America; that fact, together with the obvious limitations of access, limits the relevance of the internet for Hindu-Christian relations – at least for the time being, even if its potential benefit might grow in coming years. (And mention should also be made of websites whose intentions seem likely to worsen relations between the two traditions.[78])

(c) Hindu-Christian Studies

The academic study of the encounter (including Christians and Hindus studying each other's tradition) is also a relatively new endeavour. There are a number of promising beginnings to this enterprise and some of them have already been described.[79] The scholarly study of religion is an asset, as is the formation of The Society for Hindu-Christian Studies with its declared purpose of creating

> a forum for the presentation of historical research and studies of contemporary practice, for the fostering of dialogue and interreligious conversation, carried forward in a spirit of openness, respect and true inquiry.[80]

But, as with the use of the Internet, the suspicion remains that this is a rather privileged western perspective – or "necessary luxury in the context of today's pluralism,"[81] as Clooney puts it. Among the impediments to the dialogue, Christian advocates not infrequently mention a lack of interest among Hindus.

In the midst of today's flourishing pluralism, serious research

---

75 For example, 'The Hindu Universe' site has a category 'Interfaith Relations'.

76 Accessible at http://www.hindunet.org/forum/discus/messages/70/70.html, May 1999.

77 Accessible through the Society's homepage (http://www.acusd.edu/theo/hcs-l).

78 See, for example, http://www.hinduunity.org with its severely critical anti-Christian (and anti-Muslim and pro-Zionist) rhetoric.

79 See above, chapter 2.A.4.

80 The Society for Hindu-Christian Studies, 'Statement of Purpose,' http://www.acusd.edu/theo/hcs-l/society-info.html, May 1999, 1.

81 See Francis Clooney, 'Hindu-Christian Studies as a Necessary Luxury in the Context of Today's Pluralism,' *HCSB*, 7 (1994), 39-44.

> about the "other's religion" is still primarily, even if not exclusively, a Christian and western project. ... Are there deeper reasons that make it so rare that Hindu scholars study Christianity seriously? If it is really not of interest to Hindu scholars to study the Christian tradition in any depth, would this mean that there really are Christian and Western roots undergirding cross-religious study in general?[82]

Clooney does concede that there is an economic dimension to this perceived imbalance and calls for individual research to be accompanied by "larger cooperative ventures" in what he calls "Hindu-Christian study".[83]

3. *The Question of Common Ground*

There has been, during the decades under discussion, a growing trend towards the notion of shared humanity and community as the common ground on which participants in dialogue meet – rather than any metaphysical or 'religious' basis. Although there is certainly an ecumenical convergence in the theology of inter-religious relations, this quest for a basis for dialogue in the secular realm has tended to be a Protestant concern though it is not entirely absent from Catholic discussions.[84] Those who wish to maintain common humanity and shared community as the basis for dialogue could argue, as does MM Thomas, that the core of Christian spirituality is found not in its mystical and individual aspects, but in its incarnational, prophetic and social emphases.[85] This he contrasts with

---

82 Clooney, 'Hindu-Christian Studies as a Necessary Luxury,' 41, 43.

83 Clooney, 'Hindu-Christian Studies as a Necessary Luxury,' 42-44.

84 For a discussion see: Anton Houtepan, *Theology of the 'Saeculum' in the Documents of Vatican II and of the World Council of Churches, 1961-1972* (Kampen, n.d. [c 1975]).

85 See his 'The Pattern of Christian Spirituality,' *RS*, 16.2 (June 1969), 64-68. Julius Lipner makes the same point in commenting on Hindu recognition that "through the catalytic effect of Christian teaching with its stress on the freedom and worth of the human *person* – which is not the same as stressing the worth of the spirit or atman" – there is little use in emphasizing the greatness of the spirit while discrimination and deprivation continue ('Through a Prism Brightly. The Christian Message in the Hindu World,' *Vidyajyoti*, 44 (1980), 157 (original emphasis)). Also useful are the comments of SM Michael, 'Anthropological Basis for Dialogue – an Impulse for Missionary Activity in our Time,' *Verbum SVD*, 30 (1989), 115-27. See also the plea of D S Amalorpavadass that all theology "must start from, dwell in, and end in reality", as part of an team of natural and social sciences ('New Theological Approaches in Asia,' *Verbum SVD*, 21 (1989), 288).

Hinduism whose "rich heritage of spirituality has an axis and a goal very different" from the incarnational and social axis of Christianity.[86]

Those who regard spirituality or shared religious experience as difficult to sustain as bases for a fruitful Hindu-Christian encounter often offer the goals of common human and pan-communal responsibilities for the building of communal and national harmony, and the struggle for social justice, as alternative bases. When Ariarajah discusses the future goals of Hindu-Christian dialogue, he lays special emphasis upon the promotion of inclusive community and such meeting as will remove misunderstanding and "open the way for common action in the struggles against the evils that dehumanise people"[87]. Problems relating to caste, marriage and conversion "are the concerns of all religious communities. ... These are human questions in the life of the nation. ... Inter-religious dialogues may help as the beginning of a new process of mutual help"[88]. That is, shared humanity becomes the medium of communication with a shared future a common concern. For this reason MM Thomas also argues that "anthropology understood in its broadest sense is the right point of entry into historically relevant and challenging interfaith theological discourse"[89].

However, several questions need still to be raised about this (mainly Protestant) appeal to common humanity. Firstly, given the influence of the neo-orthodox suspicion of religion, it might also be asked whether an increased awareness of religious pluralism has led to a kind of reductionism in which the two faiths are seen not as revealing aspects of the Absolute, but as human searches for the divine. The substantial appeals to common humanity and community-building might be seen as evidence of or a tendency towards such reductionism – although not necessarily so.

Secondly, the appeal to common humanity assumes a shared Hindu-Christian acceptance of such ideals as justice and peace but the problematical dimension of the assumption is made clear by asking *whose justice?* And *what kind of peace is envisioned?* [90]Even as it is difficult to sustain the notion of a common core of religious expe-

86 'The Pattern of Christian Spirituality,' 68.

87 'A World Council of Churches' Perspective,' 253.

88 Stanley J Samartha, 'Interreligious Relationships in the Secular State,' *CD*, no. 11 (December 1986), 26 (original emphasis).

89 'Christology and Pluralistic Consciousness,' *IBMR*, 10 (1986), 106.

90 To allude to the point made by Alisdair MacIntyre in his *Whose Justice? Which Rationality?* (University of Notre Dame Press, 1988).

rience, so it is difficult to posit agreement over the notion of common humanity.

Thirdly, to suggest common humanity as the basis of dialogue is to come up against the impediments to dialogue caused by the necessary limitations of the human condition. Such limitations include those already discussed in connection with the quest for an appropriate Indian christology (see chapter 6.I); they are the necessary corollaries of the generally incompatible presuppositional starting points of the two traditions, with this difficulty deriving from and/or compounded by the clearly finite and fallible condition of all human discourse and assertion-making. All this makes claims by either tradition of a prescriptive uniqueness considerably less plausible. These limitations and the dynamics underlying them are apparent within both Christianity and Hinduism; there is no reason to suppose that they do not confuse interreligious meeting and discourse as well. Further reflection on such limitations might well explore their psychological components: those self-centred and inevitably distorting dynamics of reductionism for the purposes of self-projection.[91] The apparent limitations might further be tested by enquiries about the commitment of each tradition to the institutional democracy that the ideal of common humanity might seem to require in a post colonial setting. Democracy offers not only a degree of protection for minorities such as Christianity and Islam but also constitutes the concrete expression of the common humanity that (alone?) can ensure the climate of safety and hope in which dialogue can be beneficially pursued. Such pursuit seems to require that each tradition has reason to commit itself to the institutional democracy and social and gender equality that the appeal to common humanity requires for an Indian society in which a genuine pluralism protects both minority and majority traditions against the oppressive consequences of some forms of centralisation.

Also of importance for the future of Hindu-Christian dialogue, at least on the Christian side, is the question of the somewhat contrasting emphases of Protestant and Catholic advocates. Significant Protestant-Catholic differences are discernible, with the Protestant emphasis upon the 'secular' context and goals of dialogue probably the most significant of them. Catholic advocates have tended to emphasise common spirituality as the basis of dialogue. A not untypical example is an Asian Catholic commission arguing that, "If we consider other religions positive elements in God's plan of

---

91 In this regard, see the comments of Harold Coward, *Pluralism. Challenge to World Religions* (Maryknoll, NY, 1985), 103f.

salvation, then we can envisage common praying in areas where our beliefs converge" – areas that will be discerned through dialogue, and a common reading of scriptures.[92] And, as noted, the notion of the Kingdom of God is increasingly used as part of an inclusive view of the religions which, with all humanity, are on a journey towards the Kingdom. So, Jesus "presumed a whole variety of religions and cultures from East and West meeting on the last day" (citing Luke 13.29 and Old Testament verses).[93]

One reason for the Protestant-Catholic divergence – or, at least, a reason that exacerbates the differences – may be that ecumenical relations appear to be in a somewhat underdeveloped state among the Indian churches, though the differences between academic theologians seem to be lessening. It is also interesting that at several points such Protestant evangelical concern as there is for dialogue seems to have more in common with Catholic assumptions about the importance of the 'spiritual' than those of progressive Protestant thought. Saphir Athyal, for example, explicitly rejects Christian-Hindu dialogue whose goal is to create a community of peace, justice and unity; such an objective, he argues, "can hardly be reconciled with the heart of the Christian faith." [94]

Nonetheless, the notion of shared humanity does at least point to the common fabric of life in which Hindu and Christian meet. Moreover, it underlines the point that political, economic and social factors profoundly influence the dialogical process.[95] Attention has already been drawn to the wide range of informal dialogue, called "a process of osmosis" in one Statement – a process which it is probably correct to say, "has not been theologically evaluated and artic-

---

92 *Theses on Interreligious Dialogue. An Essay in Pastoral Theological Reflection* (Hong Kong, 1987), 13f; the 'Pastoral Recommendations' that follow the theses are quite specific about the desirability of prayer together and even of an annual week of prayer and fellowship with people of other religions (19).

93 SJ Emmanuel, 'Inter-Religious Dialogue in Asia at a Turning Point. Towards New Christologies and Ecclesiologies,' *ZMR*, 7 (1989), 237 (see also 236). See, too, the comments of AM Abraham Ayrookuzhiel on a correspondence between traditional village Hinduism and Catholicism in terms of the acceptance of a ritual division of time, space, people and objects, and the abolition of the division in Protestantism: 'The Living Hindu Popular Religious Consciousness and Some Reflections on it in the Context of Hindu-Christian Dialogue,' *RS*, 26.1 (March 1979), 24f.

94 'The Gospel and Hinduism,' 154f.

95 A point well made and elaborated by Samartha, *One Christ – Many Religions*, 29.

ulated creatively"[96] – and to which future discussion, and sociological analysis, might fruitfully return. Such analysis might prove to be complex. Larson, for example, in writing of "India's agony over religion" argues that there are deeply rooted reasons from the past for what he calls the 'hybrid discourse of modernity' now heard in India. Not only is contemporary Indian culture multilayered and multistranded, but the dense texture of its multivocal discourses derives from the complex interplay of past and present strands of a longstanding 'hybridisation' of ideas and lifestyles.[97] This observation, however, serves to confirm the reality that there is no *one* ready-made and universally accepted context in which dialogue might be understood and pursued. The choice of such a context reveals logically prior choices about the kind of future thought to be important for India. As Mark Heim observes concerning the Christian approaches to dialogue, "each concrete choice to focus theology on a particular context involves at least an implicit empirical vision...of the future"[98] – and the same applies to choices made by Hindu proponents of dialogue.

4. *A Way Forward*

The practice of Hindu-Christian dialogue remains a rather novel undertaking and, for this reason, there are few models available from the past. However, the meeting of Hindu and Christian will continue both formally (with all the limitations of formal dialogue) and informally, if for no other reason than the human tendency to reflect on and talk about religious experience – quite apart from any notions of obligation, either Hindu or Christian, that could be called mission. Nonetheless, four suggestions might be made about the way ahead.

(a) Admit the Impediments

Clearly there are hindrances to the plausible advocacy and fruitful practice of dialogue and these have been elaborated at some length (see chapter 4.A). The fact of continuing disagreement about the nature of reality and other centrally-important religious issues (as defined – differently – by Hindus and Christians) need not, howev-

96 [Indian Theological Association], 'Towards a Theology of Religions: an Indian Christian Perspective,' *ITS*, 16 (1989), 78, 80.

97 Larson, *India's Agony over Religion*.

98 Mark Heim, 'Choosing Roots: The Contexts for Christian Theology in India,' *This World*, no. 21 (Spring 1988), 89.

er, be numbered among these; prior agreement is not a necessary condition for openness and dialogue especially if reflection upon the differences has been made part of a process of internal dialogue that can helpfully precede the actual encounter. In fact, as Paul Griffiths points out, most of the central claims of the great religious traditions tend to absoluteness. The tendencies are certainly found in Christianity and

> are characteristic...of many of the most interesting claims made by religious virtuosi of non-Christian traditions...It is just this tendency to absoluteness that makes religious truth-claims of such interest and gives them such power; to ignore it is to eviscerate them, to do them the disservice of making them other than what they take themselves to be.[99]

The task of dialogue need not be defined as the creation of some kind of unity from diversity, but as the offer of a degree of hope in the face of temptations to despair or worse. Conservative Christians and Hindus may well continue to disagree on the value of dialogue. Less conservative advocates may need reminding that

> there is no conceivable reason to limit, on a priori grounds, Hindu-Christian dialogue only to that form of verbal (or other) communication that results in agreement or eliminates witness and affirmation, in either direction, on principle.[100]

Nonetheless, "the history of this [Hindu-Christian] encounter has a loaded karma."[101] The hindrances are many and must be named and confronted if further progress is to be made. As Barnes points out

> Our history is part of our present, as indeed are the interpretations which we put on that history and the history of the other. We bring all this and so much more to the dialogue and sooner or later it all has to be acknowledged.[102]

As well as concern about both the communalism and centralising nationalism that generate misunderstanding, tension and even violence at times, there is also a place for the reassurance that dialogue does not intend to threaten the right of religious communities to self-definition. Dialogue is rarely between equals. Greater understanding of religious identity – its meaning, formation and maintenance, both personal and communal – may well be central to such considerations. However, because identity seems at times to be

---

99 Griffiths, *An Apology for Apologetics*, 3.
100 Sharpe, *Faith Meets Faith*, 113.
101 Raimundo Panikkar, 'The Ongoing Dialogue,' in *H-CD*, ix.
102 *Religions in Conversation*, 164.

linked with the desire to dominate, consideration might also be given to acceptance, as a condition for dialogue, of what Cragg calls "the principle of reciprocal realism", by which he means realism about "the dimension of sin and perversity which attaches to all human beings, most of all to religion". Dialogue should not avoid contentious issues; "dialogue is not the evasion or the repudiation of the controversial, it is the positive context of its emergence and, as such, the hope of its redemption".[103] And Knitter draws attention to what he calls "the Protestant principle" that religion is always corruptible; without a reminder of this principle dialogue cannot be realistic and too easily becomes "a sugary irenicism".[104] Perhaps effective confrontation with the multiplicity of impediments to dialogue is actually part of the journey of dialogue, and not otherwise – in which case their removal might not come, if at all, except from the journey itself. It is also possible that some help for the journey might be found in contemporary communication theory.[105]

(b) Acknowledge a Complex and Profound Meeting

It is unlikely that progress could be rapid or easy in an encounter of participants from two complex religious traditions whose complexity derives in part from the struggle to be faithful to the Mystery of faith or from the cumulative detail of the two traditions, especially the Hindu tradition with its network of culture and its tendencies towards eclecticism.[106] Moreover, the dialogue described soon becomes a complex, living relationship when it becomes a meeting between what for centuries have been living faiths for their adherents. Fears and suspicions continue to be present; "the wounds inflicted by centuries of religious rivalries, social isolation and political antagonism cannot be healed overnight"[107] and there is little possibility of eliminating them before dialogue can begin.[108] Within

---

103 Kenneth Cragg, 'Dialogue with Other Faiths,' in *Lambeth Essays on Faith*, edited by [AM Ramsey] (London, 1969), 36; see also ZAM, 17.

104 Paul Knitter, *No Other Name?* 115.

105 For an example of the application of a general theory of communicative pragmatics as applied to interreligious discourse see David J Kreiger, 'Communication Theory and Interreligious Dialogue,' *JES*, 30 (1993), 331-53.

106 Regarding the latter see the recent discussion of Brian A Hatcher, *Eclecticism and Modern Hindu Discourse* (Oxford: Oxford University Press, 1999).

107 Alfred De Souza, 'Dialogue between Religions in India,' *IMA*, 3.3 (August 1972), 79.

108 See further in Pattery, 'Mimetic desire and Sacred Violence'.

both traditions a wide range of reactions from resistance to indifference to receptivity to change is found. For this reason, dialogue may not always and everywhere be the best or the only response – despite the reasons advanced for its advocacy and practice. Depending on what the Hindu or Christian actually encounters it may be not unreasonable to accept or even advocate a variety of other responses; for example: resistance (even to the point of conflict), disputation, confession, uncertain coexistence, uneasy or confident silence.[109] There is a hardening of attitudes among some and a spirit of self-criticism and openness among others; but since the fears and suspicions have accumulated over centuries it will certainly take time for the isolation to yield to confidence and trust.

(c) Accept Ambiguity

Some Christian proponents of the dialogue, especially non-Indian advocates, stress the need to define key terms – for example, words such as 'religion' and 'faith' or even names for the divine. But such attempts at definition may, in fact, be difficult (or even impossible) and may frustrate dialogue when attempted across linguistic and religiocultural divides. Perhaps greater clarity will emerge in actual dialogue, or from reflection upon the experience of dialogue – and not before. Perhaps there is need to acknowledge the ambiguity that surrounds almost every other aspect of the role of the two traditions in India and even to enter into dialogue on less than convincing grounds in the hope that something new will be found. As Diana Eck puts it, mainly from her own experience as a Christian meeting the Hindu tradition,

> The boundaries of our various traditions need not be the places where we meet and contend over our differences, but might well be places where we meet and catch a glimpse of glory as seen by another.[110]

Perhaps 'paradox' is another word that will receive greater attention in examining the incentive to continue with dialogue in the face of difficulties and ambiguities. Perhaps there is an inescapable and unresolvable paradox in simultaneous commitments to the religious truth of a given tradition and genuine openness to the tradi-

---

109 See, for example, remarks along these lines by MM Thomas, 'A Christ-Centred Humanist Approach to Other Religions,' 58f and Jürgen Moltmann, 'Is "Pluralistic Theology" Useful for the Dialogue of World Religions?,' in *Christian Uniqueness Reconsidered*, 150f.

110 *Encountering God: a Spiritual Journey from Bozeman to Banaras* (Boston, 1993), 186.

tions of others. Barnes is probably right in his observation that the problems surrounding serious dialogue ultimately reduce themselves to some version of the loyalty versus openness dilemma.[111] But the notion of paradox is familiar to Hindus and Christians. If "the dialectics of either/or do not apply so easily to an Asian mentality,"[112] the Indian context might help encourage an attempt to live with both commitment and openness. Or, as one notable practitioner of dialogue puts it, "the light which we glimpse, or obscurely sense, shining in the hearts of men and women of different faiths also sharply illumines the sometimes disconcerting differences" as well – which leads her to call for the "shared acceptance of this paradox, in faith and deep mutual respect."[113] Klostermaier argues that only a paradox prepares the mind for a new experience. "Only a paradox induces an existential knowledge ... beyond the conceptual level in which the paradox constitutes a contradiction." The paradox is well known to the teachers of Brahmavidya also.[114]

(d) Proceed Nonetheless

Participants in dialogue cannot, however, simply wait for the hindrances to dialogue to be reduced or removed. Clearly many issues require further consideration but most Christians and Hindus cannot wait either for such clarification; nor can they be expected to do more than react in a tradition-specific way. The actual encounters happen before they are theorised upon. The lived encounter precedes theoretical reflection. Perhaps for Christians there is a "pilgrimage in tension"[115] because of the unprecedented re-evaluation within Christianity of its relationship to Hinduism. If Christian theology and praxis are in the midst of a comprehensive paradigm shift then multiple uncertainties are not unexpected, especially in

111 Barnes, *Religions in Conversation*, 114.

112 Panikkar, 'The Ongoing Dialogue,' xi.

113 Sara Grant, 'Ashrams and Inter-religious Spirituality,' *TM*, 1(1998), 96.

114 *ITD*, 96, citing Isa Upanisad 12; Bhagavadgita 7.4-13; 9.4-24; 10. (The problems of discourse 'beyond the conceptual level' have already been noted.) A Statement by Indian theologians declares that 'Like all realities, dialogue too is a paradox: a paradox of rootedness and mobility, conviction and openness, commitment to one's own ideas and open appreciation of others' ('Towards a Theology of Religions,' 77f). Note, however, the cautionary remarks concerning paradox by Boyd, *An Introduction to Indian Christian Theology*, 231.

115 Albert Nambiaparambil, 'Inter-religious Dialogue – a Pilgrimage in Tension,' in *Religions in Dialogue. East and West Meet*, 229-38.

the dynamic tension between Christian mission and dialogue. On the other hand, the very act of dialogue between Hindus and Christians has significance in itself for the two traditions and has a continuing and even subtly cumulative effect upon the way some at least within the two traditions regard one another. Perhaps the notion of dialogue is needed as an interim measure; certainly there is continuing need for the two communities to meet in some way and dialogue offers a not unfruitful means, at least for the time being. Clarity concerning the justification of Hindu-Christian dialogue might, in fact, come only through the actual experience of further dialogue itself – even if that clarity only confirms the insolubility of some of the problems raised. As Terry Muck points out, the realities of incommensurability among the religions are all too apparent; a more important question is whether this incommensurability will lead to arrogance and triumphalism or to mutual respect and genuine dialogue.[116] Nonetheless, progress is likely to be slow and the history of the Hindu-Christian encounter seems to suggest the desirability of restricting 'official' encouragement of dialogue to small groups (and individuals) with an avoidance by the Christian community of highly structured meetings.[117] It is, perhaps, an excessive number of such meetings that has led to the dialogical 'fatigue' observed in some circles.

Despite uncertainties, lack of clarity, tensions and sometimes anguish, there are, nonetheless, sufficient and even compelling reasons for the adventure of Hindu-Christian dialogue to continue. Both religious traditions contain substantial internal diversity and adaptability – which is why neither need feel threatened by the prospect of continuing and even greater dialogue that will lead into further unknown territory. As Margaret Chatterjee concludes, "The nature of the further shore becomes clear only as the journey continues."[118]

---

116 Terry C Muck, 'The Fruit of Incommensurability,' *BCS*, 16 (1996), 52-54.

117 Stanley Samartha suggests the church give greater recognition to such 'listening posts' and that in selected congregations inter-religious groups be formed in order to discuss not questions of religious truth but issues of faith and common social concern. But Samartha also recognises that realistically " it has to be dialogue of the *few* on behalf of the *many*." ('Christian Concern for Dialogue in India,' *CD*, no. 9 (December 1985), 5 (original emphasis)).

118 'Reflections on Religious Pluralism in the Indian Context,' 12.

SELECT BIBLIOGRAPHY

Abhishiktananda [Henri Le Saux], 'The Christians Meditate on the Upanishads', *Logos*, 6 (1966), 93-115

______, *Guru and Disciple*, translated by Heather Sanderman (London, 1974)

______, *Saccidananda: A Christian Approach to Advaitic Experience*, revised edition in English (Delhi, 1974)

______, 'The Upanishads and the Advaitic Experience', *Clergy Monthly*, 38 (1974), 474-86

______, *Hindu-Christian Meeting Point: Within the Cave of the Heart*, translated by Sara Grant, revised edition (Delhi, 1976)

______, 'The Depth-Dimension of Religious Dialogue', *Vidyajyoti*, 45 (1981), 202-21

Abhishiktananda and Raimundo Panikkar, *The Mountain of the Lord: Pilgrims of the Way* (Bangalore, 1966)

Abhishiktananda, and others, *The Secret of Arunachala: A Christian Hermit on Shiva's Holy Mountain* (Delhi, 1997)

Acharulparambil, Daniel, 'Hinduism and Christianity', *Omnis Terra*, no. 140 (1983), 367-77

Adappur, A, 'The Theology of Inter-Faith Dialogue', *Vidyajyoti*, 46 (1982), 485-98

Aleaz, KP, *Christian Thought Through Advaita Vedanta* (Delhi, 1996)

______, *An Indian Jesus from Sankara's Thought* (Calcutta, 1997)

All India Seminar: Church in India Today. Bangalore 1969 (New Delhi, nd [1969])

Amaladass, Anand, 'Dialogue in India', *Hindu-Christian Studies Bulletin*, 1 (1988), 7f

______, 'The Scope of Dialogue', *Hindu-Christian Studies Bulletin*, 2 (1989), 2-4

Amaladoss, Michael, 'Faith Meets Faith', *East Asian Pastoral Review*, 21 (1984), 370-76

______, 'Culture and Dialogue', *East Asian Pastoral Review*, 22 (1985), 67-75

______, 'Dialogue and Mission: Conflict or Convergence?', *Vidyajyoti*, 50 (1986), 62-86

______, 'Dialogue as Conflict Resolution: Creative Praxis', *Vidyjyoti*, 62 (1998), 21-36

______, 'The Mystery of Christ and Other Religions: An Indian Perspective', *Vidyjyoti*, 63 (1999), 327-338

Amaldass, T, 'Fellowship for The Promotion of Inter-Community Living in a Pluralistic Society', *Religion and Society*, 26.1 (March 1979), 73-77

'An Example of Meeting and Dialogue Between Hindus and Christians', *Bulletin, Secretariatus Pro Non Christianis*, 6 (1971), 115-21

Ariarajah, S Wesley, 'Towards a Theology of Dialogue', *Ecumenical Review*, 29 (1977), 3-11

______, 'Hindu Spirituality: An Invitation to Dialogue?', *Ecumenical Review*, 38 (1986), 75-81

______, 'Christology in Asia: Perspectives from Hindu-Christian Dialogue',

CTC Bulletin, 7.3 (Dec 1987), 32-36

______, 'The Implications of Recent Ecumenical Thought for the Christian-Hindu Relationship', PhD Dissertation, University of London, 1987

______, *Hindus and Christians: A Century of Protestant Ecumenical Thought* (Amsterdam and Grand Rapids, MI, 1991)

Arles, S, 'Hindu Response to Pluralism', *Evangelical Review of Theology*, 12 (1988), 196-207

Ayrookuzhiel, AM Abraham, 'The Living Hindu Popular Religious Consciousness and some Reflections on it in the Context of Hindu- Christian Dialogue', *Religion and Society*, 26.1 (March 1979), 5-25

Badrinath, Chaturvedi, *Finding Jesus in Dharma: Christianity in India* (Delhi, 2000)

'The Basis and Content of a Christian-Hindu Dialogue', *Religion and Society*, 6.1 (February 1959), 78-81

Bhaktipada, *Christ and Krishna*, second edition (Moundsville, West Virginia, 1987)

'Biennial Council Discussions on the Christian Basis, Meaning and Scope of Inter-Faith Dialogue', *Religion and Society*, 12.1 (March 1965), 74-76

Boyd, Robin HS, 'Continuing Dialogue in Gujarat', *Religion and Society*, 12.1 (March 1965), 76-81

Brockington, John L, *Hinduism and Christianity* (London and New York, NY, 1992)

CBCI Dialogue Commission, *Bulletin on Dialogue*, no. 1, (nd, [c July 1980])

CBCI Dialogue Commission, *Bulletin on Dialogue*, no. 2, (nd [c March 1981])

Chandran, J Russell, 'Christian Contribution to Religious Dialogue', *Islam and the Modern Age*, 3.2 (May 1972), 65-75

Chatterjee, Margaret, 'The Prospect for Hindu-Christian Interaction', *Hindu-Christian Studies Bulletin*, 2 (1989), 2

Chethimattam, John Britto, 'The Scope and Conditions of a Hindu-Christian Dialogue', *Concilium*, 3.1 (March 1965), 83-93

______, *Dialogue in Indian Tradition*, Dharmaram Studies, 3 (Bangalore, 1969)

______, 'Man's Dialogical Nature and the Dialogue of Religions', *Journal of Dharma*, 1 (1975), 10-29

______, 'Theology and Evangelization, Theology for a Dialogue and Theology of a Dialogue', *Jeevadhara*, 7 (1977), 379-96

______, 'Meaning and Scope of Interreligious Dialogue', *Jeevadhara*, 11 (1981), 319-34

______, 'Hundred Years of Hindu-Christian Dialogue', *Prabuddha Bharata*, (January 1995), 393f

Chowgule, Ashok, *Christianity in India: The Hindutva Perspective* (Mumbai, 1999)

The Church in India: its Mission Tomorrow, edited by F Hrangkhuma and Sebastian CH Kim (Pune and Delhi, 1996)

Clooney, Francis, 'Hindu-Christian Studies as a Necessary Luxury in the Context of Today's Pluralism,' *Hindu-Christian Studies Bulletin*, 7 (1994), 39-44

'Communication of The Catholic Bishops' Conference of India to the Roman Synod 1974', in *Report of the General Meeting of The Catholic Bishops' Conference of India, Calcutta, 1974* (New Delhi, 1974), 124-40

'Conclusions of the National Seminar on Crisis of Faith Dialogue Commission of the CBCI, May 9-12, 1977, Bangalore', *Vidyajyoti*, 41 (1977), 329-34

'Consultation on the Theology of Hindu-Christian Dialogue: Bombay, January 4th to 8th, 1969', *Religion and Society*, 16.2 (June 1969), 69-88

'Consultation Working Group Reports', *Religion and Society*, 26.1 (March 1979), 106-11

Coward, Howard, 'Hindu-Christian Dialogue, its Current Status', *Ecumenical Trends*, 16 (1987), 19-24

______, 'Hindu-Christian Dialogue: a Review', *Hindu-Christian Studies Bulletin*, 1 (1988), 1-5

Cuttat, Jacques-Albert, *The Encounter of Religions: A Dialogue between the West and the Orient with an Essay on the Prayer of Jesus* (New York, 1960)

______, *Spiritual Dialogue Between East and West*, second edition (New Delhi, 1962)

______, 'Incarnation and *Avatara*', *Frontier*, 4 (1961-62), 267-70

Cyriac, MV, *Meeting of Religions: A Reappraisal of the Christian Vision*, Dialogue Series (Madras and Madurai, 1982)

Das, RC, 'Shree Shree Yeeshu Khristu', *Indian Journal of Theology*, 14 (1965), 150-61

Das, Somen, editor, *Swami: Vivekananda and Christianity – Towards Harmony with Justice* (Calcutta, 1994)

David, Pradduka, 'A Basis for Christian – Hindu Conversation', *Religion and Society*, 6.1 (February 1959), 63-67

______, 'Dialogue in Action', *Religion and Society*, 26.1 (March 1979), 91-105

'Declaration by Participants of the Hindu – Christian Dialogue, Shantivanam, 17, 18, 19, January 1974', *Bulletin, Secretariatus Pro Non Christianis*, 9 (1974), 69f

Dempsey, Corinne G, *Kerala Christian Sainthood: Collisions of Culture and Worldview in South India* (Oxford and New York, NY, 2000)

De Smet, Richard V, 'Suggestions for an Indian Dialogical Theology', *Bangalore Theological Forum*, 5.1 (January-June 1973), 74-80

______, 'Recent Developments in the Christian Approach to the Hindu', *Lumen Vitae*, 29 (1974), 515-20

Devanandan, Paul David, 'The Christian Message in Relation to the Cultural Heritage of India', *Ecumenical Review*, 2 (1950), 241-49

______, 'The Challenge of Hinduism', *National Christian Council Review*, 72 (1952), 176-84

______, 'The Christian Attitude and Approach to Non- Christian Religions', *International Review of Missions*, 41 (1952), 177- 84

______, 'Resurgent Hinduism', in *Christianity and the Asian Revolution*, edited by Rajah B Manikam (Madras, 1954), pp. 23-37

______, The Renaissance of Hinduism: A Survey of Hindu Religious History from 1800-1950', *Theology Today*, 12 (1955), 189-205

______, 'Christian and Non-Christian Faith', *Indian Journal of Theology*, 3 (1957), 74-79

______, 'The Renascence of Hinduism in India', *Ecumenical Review*, 11 (1958), 52-65

______, *The Gospel and Renascent Hinduism*, IMC Research Pamphlets (London, 1959)

______, *The Gospel and the Hindu Intellectual*, Pamphlets on Religion Series (Bangalore, 1959)

______, 'Renascent Religions and Religion', in *The Ecumenical Era in Church and Society: A Symposium in Honor of John A Mackay*, edited by Edward J Jurji (New York, 1959), 148-76

______, 'The Changing Content of Hindu Religious Terminology', *Indian Journal of Theology*, 7 (1961), 58-63

______, *Christian Concern in Hinduism* (Bangalore, 1961)

______, 'Religions in Modern India – Present Significance', *Church and Society*, 5 (September 1962), 15-21

______, *Christian Issues in Southern Asia* (New York, 1963)

______, *I Will Lift up Mine Eyes unto the Hills: Sermons and Bible Studies*, Devanandan Memorial Volume 1, edited by SJ Samartha and Nalini Devanandan (Bangalore, 1963)

______, *Preparation for Dialogue: A Collection of Essays on Hinduism and Christianity in New India*, Devanandan Memorial Volume 2, edited by Nalini Devanandan and MM Thomas (Bangalore, 1964)

Devaraja, Nand K, *Hinduism and Christianity* (Bombay, 1969)

______, 'Is the Meeting of Religions Possible?', *Journal of Dharma*, 1 (1975), 30-39

Devasenapathi, VA, 'Hinduism and Other Religions', in *Hinduism* (Patiala, 1969), 106-28

Dhavamony, Mariasusai, 'Christian Approaches to Hinduism: Points of Contact and Difficulties', *Gregorianum*, 53 (1972), 89-114

______, 'Dialogue hindou-chrétien', in *Dictionnaire des Religions*, Paul Poupard, Directeur de la Publication (Paris, 1984), 409-11

______, 'Indian Perspectives in the New Paradigms of Theology,' in *Paradigm Change in Theology. A Symposium for the Future*, edited by Hans Küng and David Tracy (Edinburgh, 1989), 424-36

Dialogue Between Men of Living Faiths: Papers Presented at a Consultation Held at Ajaltoun, Lebanon, March 1970, edited by Stanley J Samartha (Geneva, 1971)

Dialogue Commission of the Catholic Bishops' Conference of India, *Guidelines for Inter-Religious Dialogue (Revised Draft)* (Varanasi, 1977)

Dialogue in Action: Essays in Honour of Johannes Aagaard, edited by Lars Thunberg, Moti Lal Pandit and Carl Vihl Fogh (New Delhi, 1988)

Dialogue in Community. Essays in Honour of Stanley J Samartha, edited by Constantine D Jathanna (Balmatta, Mangalore, 1982)

'Dialogue Postponed: An Exchange Between Rev C Murray Rogers and Sivendra Prakash', *Asia Focus*, 5 (1970), 210-22

Dialogue with Asian Religions as Condition for Total Human Development (Colombo, 1978)

Divarkar, Parmananda R, 'Dialogue in India: Beyond "Cultural Adaptation"', *The Month*, 37, ns (1967), 273-78

______, 'Dialogue with Other Religions', in *A New Missionary Era*, edited by Padraig Flanagan (Maryknoll, NY, 1979), 69-74

Dockhorn, Kurt, 'Christ in Hinduism as Seen in Recent Indian Theology', *Religion and Society*, 21.4 (December 1974), 39-57

Dupuis, James/Jacques, 'The Presence of Christ in Hinduism', *Religion and Society*, 18.1 (March 1971), 33-45

______, 'Le Dialogue avec l'Hindouisme dans la Mission de l'Eglise en Inde', *Bulletin Pontificium Consilium pro Dialogo inter Religiones*, 24 (1989), 257-69

Dutt, K Guru, 'Is Inter-Religious Dialogue Possible?', *Religion and Society*, 23.3 (September 1976), 45-58

______, 'Is Inter-Religious Dialogue Possible?: A Clarification', *Religion and Society*, 24.1 (March 1977), 84-85

Ecumenism in India: Essays in Honour of the Rev MA Thomas, edited by Mathai Zachariah (Delhi, 1980)

'Editorial', *Religion and Society*, 12.1 (March 1965), 1-8

Faith in the Midst of Faiths: Reflections on Dialogue in Community, edited by Stanley J Samartha (Geneva, 1977)

Fallon, Pierre, 'A Critical Evaluation of the Hindu Interpretation of Christ', *Indian Journal of Theology*, 18 (1969), 81-87

______, 'Lettre de Calcutta', *Christus*, 22 (1975), 239-47

Fernandes, Angelo, 'Summons to Dialogue', in *The Summons to Dialogue: A National Seminar on Dialogue and Evangelization*. Federation of Asian Bishops' Conferences Papers, 34 (Hong Kong, 1987)

Findings of the National Consultation on the Mission of the Church in Contemporary India Held at Nasrapur, March 21-26, 1966 (Nagpur, nd [1966])

For the Sake of the Gospel, edited by Gnana Robinson (Madurai, 1980)

Francis, T Dayanandan, 'Dialog mit den Hindus im Alltag', *Zeitschrift für Mission*, 6 (1980), 16-24

Godwin, Clement, 'The First International Theological Conference on Evangelization and Dialogue in Asia, with Special Reference to the Indian Context', *Verbum SVD*, 13 (1972), 276-89

Goel, Sita Ram, *Pseudo-secularism, Christian Missions, and Hindu Resistance* (New Delhi, 1998)

The Gospel Among Our Hindu Neighbours, edited by Vinay Samuel and Chris Sugden (Bangalore and Madras, 1983)

Grant, Sara, 'Reflections on Hindu-Christian Dialogue in an Ashram Context', *Religion and Society*, 26.1 (March 1979), 42-58

______, *Towards An Alternative Theology: Confessions of a Non-dualist Christian* (Bangalore, 1991)

______, 'Ashrams and Inter-religious Spirituality,' *Third Millennium*, 1.3 (September 1998), 90-96

Gregorios, Paulose Mar, 'Dialogue with World Religions – Basic Approaches and Practical Experiences', *Indian Journal of Theology*, 29 (1980), 1-11

Griffiths, Bede, 'Meeting at Rajpur', *Clergy Monthly Supplement*, 6 (1962-1963), 137-55

______, 'The Dialogue with Hinduism', *Clergy Monthly Supplement*, 7 (1964-65), 144-49

______, 'Dialogue with Hinduism', *Catholic Mind*, June 1965, 36-42

______, *Christian Ashram: Essays Towards a Hindu-Christian Dialogue* (London, 1966). Reprinted as: *Christ in India, Essays Towards a Hindu-Christian Dialogue* (Bangalore, 1986)

______, 'Mission in Dialogue', *Indian Missiological Review*, 3 (1981), 43-53

______, *The Marriage of East and West* (London, 1982)

Heredia, Rudolf C, 'Pluralism, Tolerance and Dialogue,' *Vidyajyoti*, 60 (1996),

255-64

Hindu-Christian Dialogue: Perspectives and Encounters, edited by Harold Coward (Maryknoll, NY, 1989)

'Hindu-Christian Living Together', *Bulletin, Secretariatus Pro Non Christianis*, 8 (1973), 67-71

'Hindu-Christian Meeting Around the Bible and the Gita', *North India Churchman*, (June 1972), 2f

Hirudayam, Ignatius, 'Inter-Faith Dialogue in Madras', *Bulletin, Secretariatus Pro Non Christianis*, 5 (1970), 38-45

______, 'Dialogue in Tamilnadu', *Lumen Vitae*, 29 (1974), 418-28

______, 'Dialogue in Hinduism, I', *Sedos Bulletin*, 83, no. 8 (1983), 147f

Hooker, Roger H, 'Across The Threshold', *Religion and Society*, 18.1 (March 1971), 26-32

______, *Uncharted Journey* (London, 1973)

______, 'Three Steps Backwards', *Indian Journal of Theology*, 24 (1975), 1-8

______, 'Evangelism, Dialogue and Worship', *Vidyajyoti*, 40 (1976), 123-30

______, 'Some Hindu Impressions of Christ and Christianity', *New Fire*, 4 (1977), 273-76

______, *Journey into Varanasi* (London, 1978)

______, *Voices of Varanasi* (London, 1979)

______, *Themes in Hinduism and Christianity. A Comparative Study*. Studies in the Intercultural History of Christianity, 53 (Frankfurt am Main, 1989)

'India: Seminar on Dialogue with non Christians', *Omnis Terra*, no. 57 (January 1974), 98

Indian Voices in Today's Theological Debate, edited by Horst Bürkle and Wolfgang MW Roth, English translation (Lucknow, 1972)

Inter-Faith Dialogue and World Community, edited by Ch Sreenivasa Rao (Madras, 1991)

Irudayaraj, Xavier, 'An Attempt at an Indian Christology', *Indian Ecclesiastical Studies*, 9 (1970), 3-20

Ishpriya, 'Dialogue with Hindus, II', *Sedos Bulletin*, 83 no. 8 (1983), 149f

Jai Singh, Herbert, 'Inter-Faith Dialogue and the Search for Philosophical Truth', *Religion and Society*, 12.1 (March 1976), 45-50

Jathanna, OV, 'The Madras Rethinking Group and its Contributions to the Development of Indian Christian Theology', *Religion and Society*, 44.3 (September 1997), 74-97

Jones, E Stanley, *The Christ of the Indian Road* (London, 1926)

Kalapesi, Mary, 'Some Reflections on the Fourth Meeting on Hindu and Christian Spirituality at Jyotiniketan Ashram, April 1964', *Religion and Society*, 11.4 (December 1964), 71-76

Kalelkar, Kakasaheb, 'A Hindu Response', *Clergy Monthly Supplement*, 8 (1966-1967), 99-103

Kamaleson, Samuel T, 'The Use of Dialogue in Evangelism', unpublished paper, nd [c 1973]

Karokaran, Anto, *Evangelization and Diakonia: A Study in the Indian Perspective* (Bangalore, 1978)

Kattackal, Jacob, 'To Begin a Hindu Christian Dialogue', *Indian Ecclesiastical Studies*, 8 (1969), 133-38

______, 'Hinduism and Christianity', *Philippiniana Sacra*, 50 (1982), 74-82

Klostermaier, Klaus K, 'Einubung des inneren Zwiegesprächs', *Kairos*, 7 (1965), 54-61

______, 'Christians in Dialogue with Men of Other Faiths', *Clergy Monthly Supplement*, 8 (1966-1967), 240-46

______, 'Hindu-Christian Dialogue – its Religious and Cultural Implications', *Studies in Religion/Sciences Religieuses*, 1 (1967), 83-87

______, *Kristvidya: A Sketch of an Indian Christology*, Indian Christian Thought Series 8 (Bangalore, 1967)

______, 'Hindu-Christian Dialogue', *Journal of Ecumenical Studies*, 5 (1968), 21-44

______, 'Consultation on the Theology of Hindu- Christian Dialogue: Bombay, January 4th to 8th, 1969', *Bulletin, Secretariatus Pro Non Christianis*, 4 (1969), 126-29

______, *Hindu and Christian in Vrindaban*, translated by Antonia Fonseca (London, 1969)

______, 'A Hindu-Christian Dialogue on Truth', *Journal of Ecumenical Studies*, 12 (1975), 157-71

______, 'Interreligious Dialogue as a Method for the Study of Religion', *Journal of Ecumenical Studies*, 21 (1984), 755-59

______, *Indian Theology in Dialogue* (Madras, 1986)

Koothottil, Abraham, 'Christian Theology and Religious Dialogue', *Jeevadhara*, 11 (1981), 352-63

Kumar, Nirmal, 'An Overview of Dialogue in Madras Christian College', *Religion and Society*, 26.1 (March 1979), 88-90

Kuriedath, Jose, 'Dialogue in Indian Tradition', *Bulletin, Secretariatus Pro Non Christianis*, 9 (1974), 233-38

Kuttianimattathil, Jose, *Practice and Theology of Interreligious Dialogue A Critical Study of the Indian Christian Attempts Since Vatican II* (Bangalore, 1995)

Lead Me to the Real: The Hindu-Christian Dialogue, Federation of Asian Bishops' Conferences Papers, 36 (Hong Kong, 1984)

Lederle, Matthew R, 'Inter-Religious Meeting on Religious Experience (March 2-3, 1974)', *Bulletin, Secretariatus Pro Non Christianis*, 9 (1974), 223f

______, 'Discovery of Dialogue', *Religion and Society*, 26.1 (March 1979), 59-72

______, 'Ashrams and Dialogue', *Word and Worship*, 17 (1984), 108-13

______, 'Dialog mit dem Hinduismus', *Geist und Leben*, 59 (1986), 380-88

Light and Life We Seek to Share All India Consultation on Evangelization (Bangalore, 1973)

Living Faiths and the Ecumenical Movement, edited by Stanley J Samartha (Geneva, 1971)

Living Faiths and Ultimate Goals: A Continuing Dialogue, edited by Stanley J Samartha (Geneva, 1974)

Luke, PY and JB Carman, *Village Christians and Hindu Culture: Study of a Rural Church in Andhra Pradesh, South India*, World Studies of Churches in Mission (London, 1968)

Machado, Felix, 'Hindu-Christian Encounter: General Problematic,' *Vidyajyoti*, 60 (1996), 825-42

Madtha, William, 'Virasaivism and Christianity: An Ecumenical Dialogue on

Doctrine', *Journal of the Karnatak University (Humanities)*, 20 (1976), 30-41

Mampra, Thomas, 'Encounter between Hinduism and Christianity: A Historico Theological Appraisal', *Journal of Dharma*, 1 (1976), 246-66

'Man and Religion: A Dialogue with Panikkar', *Jeevadhara*, 11 (1981), 5-32

Mariau, Vivienne, 'Logos as Cit and Sabdabrahman. A Survey', *Bangalore Theological Forum*, 15.1 (January 1983), 39-57

Martin, Sandy, 'Jesus Darshun', *World Faiths Encounter*, 6 (Nov 1993), 18-22

Masson, Joseph, 'The Opinion of Various Hindus on Dialogue', *Bulletin, Secretariatus Pro Non Christianis*, 7 (1972), 37-44

Mataji, Vandana, *Living with Hindus, Hindu-Christian Dialogues: My Experiences and Reflections* (Bangalore and Delhi, 1999)

Mattam, Joseph, *Land of The Trinity. A Study of Modern Christian Approaches to Hinduism* (Bangalore, nd [1975])

Matthew, EV, 'Dialogue in the Context of Secular Events', *Religion and Society*, 12.1 (March 1965), 51-56

Maupilier, Maurice, *Les Mystiques Hindous-Chrétiens (1830-1967)* (Paris, 1985)

'Meeting of Religions', Editorial, *The Examiner*, 132 (1981), 753f

Meeting of Religions: New Orientations and Perspectives, edited by Thomas A Aykara (Bangalore, 1978)

Minz, Nirmal, *Mahatma Gandhi and Hindu-Christian Dialogue*, Inter-Religious Dialogue Series, 3 (Madras, 1970)

______, 'Theologies of Dialogue – a Critique', *Religion and Society*, 14.2 (June 1967), 7-20

'Mission is Dialogue: An Interview with Fr Bede Griffiths', *Verbum SVD*, 20 (1979), 363-71

Mishra, KN, A Pushparajan and I Puthiadam, 'Call to Harmony through Dialogue,' *Vidyajyoti*, 60 (1996), 275-81

Mitra, Kana, 'A Hindu Self-Reflection', *Journal of Ecumenical Studies*, 17 (1980), 121-24

______, 'Catholicism-Hinduism: A Vedantic Investigation of Raimundo Panikkar's Attempt at Bridgebuilding'. Dissertation, Temple University, 1980

Monchanin, Jules, *Mystique de L'Inde, Mystère Chrétien. Ecrits et Inédits*, edited by Suzanne Siauve, (Paris, 1974)

Monchanin, Jules and Henri Le Saux, *A Benedictine Ashram*, revised edition (Douglas, Isle of Man, 1964)

Moses, DG, *Religious Truth and the Relation between Religions*, Indian Research Series, 5 (Madras, 1950)

______, 'Some Reflections on Personal Dialogue', *Asia Focus*, 5 (1970), 249-51

Mukerji, Bithika, 'Christianity in the Reflection of Hinduism', *Concilium*, no. 183 (1986), 31-37

Mundadan, AM, 'Hindu-Christian Dialogue: Past Twenty-Five Years: A Survey of Indian Christian Literature', *Jeevadhara*, 11 (1981), 375-94

Mundadan, AM, *Indian Christians Search for Identity and Struggle for Autonomy* (Bangalore, 1984)

Muttumana, Mathew, *Christianity in Assam and Inter-Faith Dialogue: A Study on the Modern Religious Movements in North East India*, (Indore and Pune, 1984)

Nambiaparambil, Albert, 'Dialogue in India: an Examination and Evaluation',

Bulletin, Secretariatus Pro Non Christianis, 7 (1972), 64- 71

______, 'India-Kerala: Dialogue in India: an Examination and Evaluation', *Bulletin, Secretariatus Pro Non Christianis,* 7 (1972), 64-71

______, 'Inter-Religious Dialogue – Nature and Scope', *The Examiner,* 124 (1973), 549f

______, 'Dialogue in India: A Challenge to Redeem Hope', *Vidyajyoti,* 39 (1975), 111-26

______, 'Dialogue in India: An Analysis of the Situation, a Reflection on Experience', *Journal of Dharma,* 1 (1975), 267-83

______, 'India: Inter-Religious Fellowship of Satna', *Bulletin, Secretariatus Pro Non Christianis,* 11 (1976), 81-82

______, 'India-Bombay: Inter-Religious Sharing in Bombay', *Bulletin, Secretariatus Pro Non Christianis,* 11 (1976), 83-85

______, 'Some Personal Reflections on Inter-Religious Dialogue in India', *Bulletin, Secretariatus Pro Non Christianis,* 13 (1978), 237-39

______, 'The Meaning-Context of Inter-Religious Dialogue', *Vidyajyoti,* 43 (1979), 73-81

______, 'Identity and Openness after the Vatican Council – Tension of Dialogue', *Indian Journal of Theology,* 30 (1981), 204-10

______, 'India: a Testing Ground for Inter-religious Dialogue', *Bulletin, Secretariatus Pro Non Christianis,* 19 (1984), 346-50

Nayak, Anand and Anne-Marie Abrard, 'Hindu-Christian Dialogue in India', *Pro Mundi Vita Bulletin,* no. 88 (January 1982), 1-88

New Approaches to Inter-Faith Dialogue, edited by T Dayanandan Francis (Uppsala, 1980)

Nirmal, Arvind P, 'Some Theological Issues Connected with Inter-Faith Dialogue and Their Implication for Theological Education in India', *Bangalore Theological Forum,* 12 (1980), 107-29

Oddie, Geoffrey A, *Hindu and Christian in South – East Asia* (London, 1991)

Organ, Troy, 'Some Contributions of Hinduism to Christianity', *Religion in Life,* 47 (1978), 450-59

Panakal, Justin, 'Dialogue', *Living Word,* 95 (1989), 344-54

Panikkar, Raimundo, 'Letter to a Christian Student of Hinduism', *Logos* 3.2 (October 1962), 1-5

______, 'Sur l'Hermeneutique de la Tradition dans l'Hindouisme pour un Dialogue avec le Christianisme', *Archivio di Filosofia,* 32 (1963), 343-64

______, 'Hinduism and Christianity', *Cross Currents,* 13 (1963), 87-101

______, *The Unknown Christ of Hinduism* (London, 1964). Revised edition: *The Unknown Christ of Hinduism: Towards an Ecumenical Christophany* (London, 1981)

______, 'Confrontation Between Hinduism and Christ', *Logos,* 10.2 (June 1969), 43-51

______, 'Advaita and Bhakti: Love and Identity in a Hindu-Christian Dialogue', *Journal of Ecumenical Studies,* 7 (1970), 299-309

______, 'Rules of the Game in the Religious Encounter', *Asia Focus,* 5 (1970), 223-71

______, 'Inter-Religious Dialogue: Some Principles', *Journal of Ecumenical Studies,* 12 (1975), 407-09

Papali, Cyril B, 'Dialogue with Hinduism', *Euntes Docete*, 20 (1967), 231-40
______, 'Religious Dialogue with Hinduism', *Living Word* [Alwaye], 79 (1973), 243-60
Paradkar, Balwant AM, 'The Christian Encounter with Men of Other Faiths', *Religion and Society*, 14.2 (June 1967), 21-37
Pennington, Brian K, 'Renaissance or Retrenchment? Hindu-Christian Dialogue at a Crossroads', *Indian Journal of Theology*, 42 (2000), 74-87
Pereira, Aelred J, 'International Hindu-Christian Dialogue', *Examiner*, 132 (1981), 421f
Pieris, Aloysius, 'The Legitimacy and the Limitations of the Academic Approach to Inter-Faith Dialogue', *Dialogue*, ns, 1 (1974), 39-43
Pushparajan, A, 'Prospects of Christian Dialogue with Other Religions', *Journal of Dharma*, 8 (1983), 248-69
______, ed, *Pilgrims of Dialogue* (Munnar, 1991)
Puthenkalam, XJ, 'Christian Approaches to Other Religions: For an Inter-Faith Dialogue', *Living Word*, 87 (1981), 146-62
Puthiadam, Ignatius, 'Dialog im Zentrum des Hinduismus', *Die katholischen Missionen*, 102 (1983), 45-49
Pye-Smith, Charlie, *Rebels and Outcasts: A Journey through Christian India* (London, 1997)
Rajamoni, C, 'Dialogue in Kanyakumari District in the Context of Mission', *Religion and Society*, 26.1 (March 1979), 78-87
Rajan, R Sundara, 'Negations: An Article on Dialogue among Religions', *Religion and Society*, 21.4 (December 1974), 67-76
Rambachan, Anantanand, 'A Hindu Looks at Jesus', *Theology*, 88 (1985), 255-59
Rayan, Samuel, 'Dialogue with Hinduism', in *Modern Mission Dialogue: Theory and Practice*, edited by Jan Kerkhofs (Shannon, Ireland, 1969), 29-44
Redington, James D, 'The Hindu-Christian Dialogue and the Interior Dialogue', *Theological Studies*, 44 (1983), 587-603
'Religious Dialogue: Some Basic Considerations', *Dialogue*, ns, 6 (1979), 108-14
'Religious Resources for a Just Society'. A Hindu-Christian Dialogue (Geneva, 1981)
'Report of the Bombay Seminar on Dialogue with Non Christians (24-26 October 1973)', *Bulletin, Secretariatus Pro Non Christianis*, 9 (1974), 75-80
'Report on the Group for Asian Religions', *Bulletin, Secretariatus Pro Non Christianis*, 14 (1979), 191-94
Responding to Communalism: The Task of Religions and Theology, edited by S Arokiasamy (Anand, 1991)
Reyna, Ruth, 'Hinduism and Christianity', *Hinduism*, no. 70 (September-October, 1975), 8-10
Rogers, C Murray, 'The Content of a Christian-Hindu Dialogue', *Religion and Society*, 6.1 (February 1959), 68-71
______, 'Hindu and Christian – A Moment Breaks', *Religion and Society*, 12.1 (March 1965), 35-44
______, 'Hindu Ashram Heritage: God's Gift to the Church', *Concilium*, 9.1 (1965), 73-78
______, 'Inter-Faith Dialogue', *Asia Focus*, 5 (1970), 235-45
______, 'Swami the Friend', *Religion and Society*, 23.1 (March 1976), 76-87
Rossano, Pietro, 'From Rishikesh to Cape Comorin: Observations on

Interreligious Dialogue in India', *Bulletin, Secretariatus Pro Non Christianis*, 14 (1981), 75-78

Sadiq, John W, 'Inter-Faith Dialogue and Communication of the Gospel', *Religion and Society*, 12.1 (March 1965), 9-14

Samartha, Stanley J, *The Hindu Response to the Unbound Christ*, Inter-Religious Dialogue Series, 6 (English language version) (Madras, 1974)

______, 'Reflections on a Multilateral Dialogue: An Interpretation of a Meeting Held at Colombo, Sri Lanka, 17-26 April 1974', *Ecumenical Review*, 26 (1974), 637-46

______, 'Can Mount Sinai and River Ganga Meet?', *Ecumenical Institute for Advanced Theological Studies [Tantur, Jerusalem] Yearbook 1975-1976*, pp. 99-120

______, 'Partners in Community. Some Reflections on Hindu-Christian Relations Today', *Occasional Bulletin of Missionary Research*, 4 (1980), 78-82

______, 'Indian Realities and the Wholeness of Christ', *Missiology*, 10 (1982), 301-17

______, 'The Unknown Christ Made Better Known: A Review Article', *Religion and Society* 30.1 (March 1983), 52-61

______, 'The Other Side of the River', unpublished paper, 1983

______, 'Christian Concern for Dialogue in India', *Current Dialogue*, no. 9 (December 1985), 3-9

______, *One Christ – Many Religions*, Faith Meets Faith Series (Maryknoll, NY, 1991)

Sankaranarayanan, P, 'Hinduism and its Attitude to Christianity', *Religion and Society*, 6.1 (February 1959), 13-19

Saran, AK and Bede Griffiths, 'Further Towards a Hindu-Christian Dialogue', *Clergy Monthly*, 32 (1968), 213-20

Satprakashananda, *Hinduism and Christianity: Jesus Christ and His Teachings in the Light of Vedanta* (St Louis, 1974)

Schoonenberg, P., 'Christologie angesichts der Avatara Lehre', in *Epiphanie des Heils: Zur Heilsgegenwort in Indischer und christlicher Religion. Arbeitsdokumentation eines Symposium*, Publications of the De Nobili Research Library 9, edited by Gerhard Oberhammer (Vienna, 1982), 179-92

Scott, David C, 'A Christian Basis for Inter-Faith Dialogue', *Religion and Society*, 12.1 (March 1965), 15-29

Sebastian, J Jayakiran, 'Pressure on the Hyphen: Aspects of the Search for Identity Today in Indian Christian Theology', *Religion and Society*, 44.4 (Dec 1997), 27 – 41

Secretariatus Pro Non Christianis, *For a Dialogue with Hinduism* (Rome, nd)

Sen, PK, '"Jesus Christ – the Life of the World". A Hindu Response', *Indian Journal of Theology*, 31 (1982), 70-74

Service and Salvation: Nagpur Theological Conference on Evangelization, edited by Joseph Pathrapankal (Bangalore, 1973)

Seshagiri Rao, KL, *Mahatma Gandhi and CF Andrews: A Study in Hindu-Christian Dialogue* (Patiala, 1969)

______, 'Mahatma Gandhi's Experience in Interreligious Dialogue', *World Faiths Insight*, ns, no. 6 (January 1983), 2-10

______, 'Hindu-Christian Dialogue: A Hindu Perspective', *Hindu-Christian Studies Bulletin*, 14 (2001), 7-12

Sharma, Arvind, 'Some Misunderstandings of the Hindu Approach to Religious Plurality', *Religion*, 8 (1978), 133-54

______, 'All Religions Are – Equal? One? True? Same?: A Critical Examination of Some Formulations of the Neo-Hindu Position', *Philosophy East and West*, 29 (1979), 59-72

Sharpe, Eric J, 'Christ the Fulfiller', *Bangalore Theological Forum*, 3.1 (January-June 1969), 1-11

______, *Faith Meets Faith: Some Christian Attitudes to Hinduism in the Nineteenth and Twentieth Centuries* (London, 1977)

Shourie, Arun, *Harvesting Our Souls: Missionaries, Their Design, Their Claims* (New Delhi, 2000)

Singh, GR, 'Inter-Religious Dialogue and the Local Congregation', *South India Churchman*, January 1986, 11, 18

Singh, Herbert Jai, ed, *Inter-Religious Dialogue*, Devanandan Memorial Volume 3, (Bangalore, 1967)

Smet, Robert, *Le Problème d'une Théologie Hindoue-Chrétienne selon Raymond Panikkar*, Conferences et Travaux 5 (Louvain-la-Neuve, 1983)

Society and Religion: Essays in Honour of MM Thomas, edited by Richard W Taylor (Madras, 1976)

Staffner, Hans, *The Significance of Jesus Christ in Asia* (Anand, 1985)

'Statement of a Workshop on "The Issues in Hindu-Christian Relationship" Held in Madurai, 9-11 October 1995,' *Current Dialogue*, no. 29 (January 1996), 10-15.

'Statement of Hindu-Christian Dialogue, Varanasi, February 1992', *Hindu-Christian Studies Bulletin*, 5 (1992), 45f

Sudhakar, Paul, 'How to Prepare the Churches for Dialogue', *Religion and Society*, 26.1 (March 1979), 36-41

Sundararajan, KR, 'The Hindu Models of Interreligious Dialogue', *Journal of Ecumenical Studies*, 23 (1986), 239-50

Sunder Rao, Mark, 'Inter-Faith Dialogue and Spirituality', *Religion and Society*, 12.1 (March 1965), 30-34

Swami Abhishiktananda: The Man and His Teachings, edited by Vandana (New Delhi, 1986)

Teasdale, Wayne, 'Towards a Christian Vedanta: The Encounter of Hinduism and Christianity According to Bede Griffiths' (dissertation, Fordham University, New York, 1985)

Thakur Das, KN, 'Communal Tension. Is Interfaith Dialogue the Solution?', *Christian Conference of Asia News*, 22.9 (15 September 1987), 10-12

Thomas, MM, *The Acknowledged Christ of the Indian Renaissance*, second edition (Madras, 1976)

______, 'Christ-Centred Syncretism', *Religion and Society*, 26.1 (March 1979), 26-35

______, *Man and The Universe of Faiths*, Inter-Religious Dialogue Series, 7 (Madras, 1975)

______, 'The Absoluteness of Jesus Christ and Christ-centred Syncretism', *Ecumenical Review*, 37 (1985), 387-97

______, 'Religious Fundamentalism and Indian Secularism: The Present Crisis,' *Journal of Dharma*, 19 (1994), 26-35

Thomas, MM & Thomas, PT, *Towards an Indian Christian Theology: Life and Thoughts of Some Pioneers* (Turuvalla, 1998)

Thomas, TK, 'Dialogue as Presence: An Experiment in Interpretation', *Religion and Society*, 14.2 (June 1967), 38-47

______, 'Inter-Religious Dialogue', *South India Churchman*, February 1971, 9-10

______, 'Dialogue at a Dead-end?', *Christian Conference of Asia News*, 13.7 (15 July 1978), 1-2

Thompson, A Frank, *The Christian Institute for the Study of Religion and Society: a Research Arm of Christian Churches in India* (Lewiston, NY, 1992)

Towards World Community: The Colombo Papers, edited by Stanley J Samartha (Geneva, 1974)

Valles, Carlos G, 'Pastoral Approaches and Dialogue Methods – Towards a Hindu-Christian Theology', *Clergy Monthly*, 32 (1968), 116-20

Van Troy, J, 'Meeting Hindus in a University', *Clergy Monthly Supplement*, 8 (1966-1967), 253-64

Vattakuzhy, Emmanuel, *Indian Christian Sannyasa and Swami Abhishiktananda* (Bangalore, 1981)

Velamkunnel, Joseph, 'The Healing Mission and Interreligious Dialogue', *Vidyajyoti*, 63 (1999) 351-60

Venkatesananda, and Bede Griffiths, 'A Hindu Christian Dialogue', *Journal of Ecumenical Studies*, 5 (1968), 144-51

Vineeth, VF, 'The Concept of Dialogue and the Economy of Salvation', *Indian Journal of Theology*, 30 (1981), 152-57

______, 'Dialogue and Theology of Religious Pluralism: Theological Reflections', *Journal of Dharma*, 14 (1989), 376-96

______, 'Committed to Christ and Open to All Religions,' *Third Millennium*, 4 (2001), 22-32

Whaling, Frank, *An Approach to Dialogue with Hinduism* (Lucknow, 1966)

Wilfred, Felix, 'Dialogue Gasping for Breath? Towards New Frontiers in Inter-Religious Dialogue,' *Vidyajoti*, 51 (1987), 449-66

INDEX

Regnum Studies in Mission

Academic Monographs on Missiological Themes

(All titles paperback, 229 x 152mm)

Allan Anderson and Edmond Tang (eds.)
Asian and Pentecostal
The Charismatic Face of Christianity in Asia
(Published jointly with Asia Pacific Theological Seminary)

This book provides a thematic discussion and pioneering case studies on the history and development of Pentecostal and Charismatic churches in the countries of South Asia, South East Asia and East Asia.

***2005** / 1-870345-43-6 / approx. 600pp*

I. Mark Beaumont
Christology in Dialogue with Muslims
A Critical Analysis of Christian Presentations of Christ for Muslims from the Ninth and Twentieth Centuries

This book analyses Christian presentations of Christ for Muslims in the most creative periods of Christian-Muslim dialogue, the first half of the ninth century and the second half of the twentieth century. In these two periods, Christians made serious attempts to present their faith in Christ in terms that take into account Muslim perceptions of him, with a view to bridging the gap between Muslim and Christian convictions.

2005 / 1-870345-46-0 / xxvi + 228pp

Kwame Bediako
Theology and Identity
The Impact of Culture upon Christian Thought in the Second Century and in Modern Africa

The author examines the question of Christian identity in the context of the Graeco–Roman culture of the early Roman Empire. He then addresses the modern African predicament of quests for identity and integration.

1992 / 1-870345-10-X / xviii + 508pp

Gene Early

Leadership Expectations

How Executive Expectations are Created and Used in a Non-Profit Setting

The author creates an Expectation Enactment Analysis to study the role of the Chancellor of the University of the Nations-Kona, Hawaii, and is grounded in the field of managerial work, jobs, and behaviour, drawing on symbolic interactionism, role theory, role identity theory, and enactment theory. The result is a conceptual framework for further developing an understanding of managerial roles.

2005 / 1-870345-30-4 / xxiv + 276pp

Keith E. Eitel

Paradigm Wars

The Southern Baptist International Mission Board Faces the Third Millennium

The International Mission Board of the Southern Baptist Convention is the largest denominational mission agency in North America. This volume chronicles the historic and contemporary forces that led to the IMB's recent extensive reorganization, providing the most comprehensive case study to date of a historic mission agency restructuring to continue its mission purpose into the twenty-first century more effectively.

1999 / 1-870345-12-6 / x + 140pp

Tharcisse Gatwa

The Churches and Ethnic Ideology in the Rwandan Crises 1900-1994

Since the early years of the twentieth century Christianity has become a new factor in Rwandan society. This book investigates the role Christian churches played in the formulation and development of the racial ideology that culminated in the 1994 genocide.

***2005** / 1-870345-24-X / approx 300pp*

Gideon Githiga

The Church as the Bulwark against Authoritarianism

Development of Church and State Relations in Kenya, with Particular Reference to the Years after Political Independence 1963-1992

'All who care for love, peace and unity in Kenyan society will want to read this careful history by Bishop Githiga of how Kenyan Christians, drawing on the Bible, have sought to share the love of God, bring his peace and build up the unity of the nation, often in the face of great difficulties and opposition.' Canon Dr Chris Sugden, Oxford Centre for Mission Studies.

2002 / 1-870345-38-X / xviii + 218pp

July 2005

Samuel Jayakumar

Dalit Consciousness and Christian Conversion

Historical Resources for a Contemporary Debate

(Published jointly with ISPCK)

The main focus of this historical study is social change and transformation among the Dalit Christian communities in India. Historiography tests the evidence in the light of the conclusions of the modern Dalit liberation theologians.

1999 / 81-7214-497-0 / xxiv + 434pp

Samuel Jayakumar

Mission Reader

Historical Models for Wholistic Mission in the Indian Context

(Published jointly with ISPCK)

This book is written from an evangelical point of view revalidating and reaffirming the Christian commitment to wholistic mission. According to Jayakumar, the roots of the 'wholistic mission' combining 'evangelism and social concerns' are to be located in the history and tradition of Christian evangelism in the past; and the civilizing purpose of evangelism is compatible with modernity as an instrument in nation building.

2003 / 1-870345-42-8 / x + 250pp

Julie Ma

Mission Possible

Biblical Strategies for Reaching the Lost

Written as Julie Ma hiked the mountains to share God's news, this is a missiology book for the church which liberates missiology from the specialists for every believer. Nevertheless, it serves as a textbook that is simple and friendly, and yet solid in biblical interpretation. This book links the biblical teaching to the actual and contemporary missiological setting, thus serving two important purposes. Examples are clearly given which aid understanding, and the biblical development is brought in to our contemporary setting, thus making the Bible come alive.

2005 / 1-870345-37-1 / xvi + 142pp

Myung Sung-Hoon and Hong Young-Gi (eds.)

Charis and Charisma

David Yonggi Cho and the Growth of Yoido Full Gospel Church

This book discusses the factors responsible for the growth of the world's largest church. It expounds the role of the Holy Spirit, the leadership, prayer, preaching, cell groups and creativity in promoting church growth. It focuses on God's grace (charis) and inspiring leadership (charisma) as the two essential factors and the book's purpose is to present a model for church growth worldwide.

2003 / 1-870345-45-2 / xxii + 218pp

Bernhard Ott

Beyond Fragmentation: Integrating Mission and Theological Education

A Critical Assessment of some Recent Developments in Evangelical Theological Education

Beyond Fragmentation is an enquiry into the development of Mission Studies in evangelical theological education in Germany and German-speaking Switzerland between 1960 and 1995. This is carried out by a detailed examination of the paradigm shifts which have taken place in recent years in both the theology of mission and the understanding of theological education.

2001 / 1-870345-14-2 / xxviii + 382pp

Bob Robinson

Christians Meeting Hindus

An Analysis and Theological Critique of the Hindu-Christian Encounter in India

This book focuses on the Hindu-Christian encounter, especially the intentional meeting called dialogue, mainly during the last four decades of the twentieth century, and mainly in India itself.

2004 / 1-870345-39-8 / xviii + 392pp

Christopher Sugden

Seeking the Asian Face of Jesus

The Practice and Theology of Christian Social Witness in Indonesia and India 1974–1996

This study focuses on contemporary wholistic mission with the poor in India and Indonesia combined with the call to transformation of all life in Christ with micro-credit enterprise schemes. 'The literature on contextual theology now has a new standard to rise to' – Lamin Sanneh (Yale University, USA).

1997 / 1-870345-26-6 / xx + 496pp

Christopher Sugden

Gospel, Culture and Transformation

A Reprint, with a New Introduction, of Part Two of Seeking the Asian Face of Jesus

Gospel, Culture and Transformation explores the practice of mission especially in relation to transforming cultures and communities. Vinay Samuel has played a leading role in developing the understanding of mission as transformation, which he defines as follows: 'Transformation is to enable God's vision of society to be actualised in all relationships: social, economic and spiritual, so that God's will may be reflected in human society and his love experienced by all communities, especially the poor.'

2000 / 1-870345-32-0 / viii + 152pp

Hwa Yung

Mangoes or Bananas?

The Quest for an Authentic Asian Christian Theology

Asian Christian thought remains largely captive to Greek dualism and Enlightenment rationalism because of the overwhelming dominance of Western culture. Authentic contextual Christian theologies will emerge within Asian Christianity with a dual recovery of confidence in culture and the gospel.

1997 / 1-870345-25-8 / xii + 274pp

regnum

Regnum Books International
9 Holdom Avenue,
Bletchley,
Milton Keynes MK1 1QR,
United Kingdom
Web: www.authenticmedia.co.uk/paternoster

July 2005